Lecture Notes in Computer S

Commenced Publication in 1973
Founding and Former Series Editors:
Gerhard Goos, Juris Hartmanis, and Jan van Leeu

Editorial Board

Giovanni Di Crescenzo   Avi Rubin (Eds.)

Financial Cryptography and Data Security

10th International Conference, FC 2006
Anguilla, British West Indies, February 27-March 2, 2006
Revised Selected Papers

 Springer

Volume Editors

Giovanni Di Crescenzo
Telcordia Technologies
One Telcordia Drive 1K325, Piscataway, NJ, USA
E-mail: giovanni@research.telcordia.com

Avi Rubin
Johns Hopkins University (JHUISI)
3100 Wyman Park Drive, Baltimore, MD 21211 USA
E-mail: rubin@jhu.edu

Library of Congress Control Number: 2006933057

CR Subject Classification (1998): E.3, D.4.6, K.6.5, K.4.4, C.2, J.1, F.2.1-2

LNCS Sublibrary: SL 4 – Security and Cryptology

ISSN   0302-9743
ISBN-10   3-540-46255-4 Springer Berlin Heidelberg New York
ISBN-13   978-3-540-46255-2 Springer Berlin Heidelberg New York

Springer is a part of Springer Science+Business Media

springer.com

© Springer-Verlag Berlin Heidelberg 2006
Printed in Germany

Typesetting: Camera-ready by author, data conversion by Scientific Publishing Services, Chennai, India
Printed on acid-free paper   SPIN: 11889663   06/3142   5 4 3 2 1 0

Preface

The 10th International Conference on Financial Cryptography and Data Security (FC 2006) was held in Anguilla, British West Indies, from February 27 to March 2, 2006. This conference continues to be the premier international forum for research, advanced development, education, exploration, and debate regarding security in the context of finance and commerce.

As we were honoured to put together the program in this conference's 10th edition, we attempted to combine the naturally festive mood with its interdisciplinary nature. Kicking off the 10th-year festivities were a welcome speech by Victor Banks, the Minister of Finance of Anguilla, and our Keynote Address by the renowned cryptographer Ron Rivest. One of the most influential figures in cryptography, Ron reviewed some of his past predictions and lessons learned over the last 10 years, and prognosticated directions for the next decade. The conference also featured an invited talk by Michael Froomkin about the current legal landscape of financial cryptography, and two interesting panel sessions: one on identity management and a second one providing further reflections on the past 10 years of financial cryptography, featuring talks by Jacques Stern, and Nicko van Someren, representing reflections from the academic and industrial world, respectively. The technical program featured 19 regular papers and 6 short papers, selected out of 64 submissions, and as always, other conference attendees were invited to make short presentations during the rump session, which maintained its lively and colorful reputation.

Putting together such a strong program would not be possible without the hard work of the Program Committee and of a large number of external reviewers, whose names are listed on separate pages. Each submission was refereed by at least three experts, and often detailed technical discussions were necessary before decisions could be made. These were often challenging due to the high quality of the submitted papers, many of which could not be included in the program. Additional thanks go to all researchers who submitted papers, hoping that enough feedback was given to them for further developments of their work.

We also would like to thank this year's General Chair, Patrick McDaniel, for valuable assistance on several aspects of the conference organization, and the Local Arrangements Chair, Rafael Hirschfeld, for handling several logistics in Anguilla. Special thanks also go to Ted Lu for helping with setting up the Web-based submission and reviewing system, which was essential for handling such a large number of submissions and reviewers, and to William Enck for on-site logistic help. We hope to have fulfilled our goal of a successful conference. Like all its participants, we look forward to (at least) 10 more years of Financial Cryptography and Data Security!

June 2006

Giovanni Di Crescenzo
Avi Rubin

Organization

The Financial Cryptography and Data Security 2006 conference was organized by the International Financial Cryptography Association (IFCA).

Program Chairs

Giovanni Di Crescenzo	Telcordia Technologies
Avi Rubin	Johns Hopkins University

General Chair

Patrick Mc Daniel	Penn State University

Local Arrangements Chair

Rafael Hirschfeld	Unipay Technologies

Program Committee

Matt Blaze	University of Pennsylvania
Alfredo De Santis	Universitá di Salerno
Sven Dietrich	Carnegie Mellon University
Juan Garay	Bell Labs
Dan Geer	Verdasys
Ari Juels	RSA
Yoshi Kohno	University of California San Diego
Arjen Lenstra	Bell Labs and Technische Universiteit Eindhoven
Helger Lipmaa	Cybernetica AS and University of Tartu
Steve Myers	Indiana University
Andrew Odlyzko	University of Minnesota
Tatsuaki Okamoto	NTT
Carles Padro	Universitat Politecnica de Catalunya
Andrew Patrick	NRC Canada
Ahmad-Reza Sadeghi	Ruhr-University Bochum
Kazue Sako	NEC
Dawn Song	Carnegie Mellon University

Stuart Stubblebine	Univ. of California Davis and
	Stubblebine Labs
Adam Stubblefield	Independent Security Evaluators
Paul Syverson	Naval Research Lab
Mike Szydlo	RSA
Gene Tsudik	University of California Irvine
Doug Tygar	Berkeley University
Alma Whitten	Google
Yacov Yacobi	Microsoft Research
Yuliang Zheng	University of North Carolina
Moti Yung	RSA and Columbia University

Additional Referees

Michel Abdalla
Madhukar Anand
Asokan
Giuseppe Ateniese
Lujo Bauer
Don Beaver
John Bethencort
Ziad Bizri
Daniel Bleichenbacher
David Brumley
Dario Catalano
Liqun Chen
Yuqun Chen
Monica Chew
Paolo D'Arco
Breno de Medeiros
Yevgeniy Dodis

Edith Elkind
Umberto Ferraro
Jun Furukawa
Sabastian Gajek
Ulrich Huber
Markus Jakobsson
Mariusz Jakubowski
Mike Just
Manoj Kasichainula
Aggelos Kiayias
Larry Korba
Howard Lipson
Philip MacKenzie
Peter Montgomery
Kengo Mori
Jihye Kim
Lea Kissner

Vladimir Kolesnikov
Howard Lipson
Ferran Marques
Stephen Marsh
James Newsome
Lluis Padro
Bryan Parno
Nitesh Saxena
Kai Schramm
Micah Sherr
Ronggong Song
Isamu Teranishi
Ersin Uzun
Jason Waddle
Shouhuai Xu

Sponsors

EverBank (Silver sponsor)
Navio (Silver sponsor)
Offshore Information Services (Silver sponsor)
Google (Bronze sponsor)
NCipher (Bronze sponsor)
Bibit (Sponsor in kind)

Table of Contents

Authentication and Fraud Detection

Privacy

Reputation and Mix-Nets

Short Papers

Conditional Financial Cryptography

Payment Systems

Efficient Protocols

Phoolproof Phishing Prevention

Bryan Parno, Cynthia Kuo, and Adrian Perrig

Carnegie Mellon University

Abstract. Phishing, or web spoofing, is a growing problem: the Anti-Phishing Working Group (APWG) received almost 14,000 unique phishing reports in August 2005, a 56% jump over the number of reports in December 2004 [3]. For financial institutions, phishing is a particularly insidious problem, since trust forms the foundation for customer relationships, and phishing attacks undermine confidence in an institution.

Phishing attacks succeed by exploiting a user's inability to distinguish legitimate sites from spoofed sites. Most prior research focuses on assisting the user in making this distinction; however, users must make the right security decision every time. Unfortunately, humans are ill-suited for performing the security checks necessary for secure site identification, and a single mistake may result in a total compromise of the user's online account. Fundamentally, users should be authenticated using information that they cannot readily reveal to malicious parties. Placing less reliance on the user during the authentication process will enhance security and eliminate many forms of fraud.

We propose using a trusted device to perform mutual authentication that eliminates reliance on perfect user behavior, thwarts Man-in-the-Middle attacks after setup, and protects a user's account even in the presence of keyloggers and most forms of spyware. We demonstrate the practicality of our system with a prototype implementation.

Keywords: Identity Theft, Phishing and Social Engineering, Fraud Prevention, Secure Banking and Financial Web Services.

1 Introduction

In *phishing*, an automated form of social engineering, criminals use the Internet to fraudulently extract sensitive information from businesses and individuals, often by impersonating legitimate web sites. The potential for high rewards (e.g., through access to bank accounts and credit card numbers), the ease of sending forged email messages impersonating legitimate authorities, and the difficulty law enforcement has in pursuing the criminals has resulted in a surge of phishing attacks: estimates suggest that phishing affected 1.2 million U.S. citizens and cost businesses billions of dollars in 2004 alone [40]. Phishing also leads to additional business losses due to consumer fear. Anecdotal evidence suggests that an increasing number of people shy away from Internet commerce due to the threat of identity fraud, despite the tendency of US companies to assume the risk for fraud. Also, many users now default to distrusting any email they receive from financial institutions [16].

Current phishing attacks are still relatively modest in sophistication and have substantial room for improvement, as we discuss in Section 2.2. Thus, the research community and corporations need to make a concentrated effort to combat the increasingly

G. Di Crescenzo and A. Rubin (Eds.): FC 2006, LNCS 4107, pp. 1–19, 2006.
© IFCA/Springer-Verlag Berlin Heidelberg 2006

severe economic consequences of phishing. Unfortunately, as we discuss in Section 8, current anti-phishing techniques do not offer adequate safeguards for ordinary users.

We present three main contributions in this paper. First, we propose several design principles needed to counter phishing attacks: 1) sidestep the arms race, 2) provide mutual authentication, 3) reduce reliance on users, 4) avoid dependence on the browser's interface, and 5) forgo network monitoring. Anti-phishing solutions that fail to follow these principles will likely be overcome or circumvented by phishers.

Second, to fulfill our design principles, we propose a foolproof anti-phishing system that does not rely on users to *always* make the correct security decision. Our mutual authentication protocol uses a trusted device (e.g., a cellphone) both to manage a second authenticator for the user and to authenticate the server. Since a user cannot readily disclose the additional authenticator to a third party, attackers must obtain the user's password *and* compromise the trusted device to gain account access. By making the trusted device an active participant in the authentication process, our protocol protects the users against Man-in-the-Middle attacks.

Our approach also defends against keyloggers and other mechanisms designed to monitor user input. The user can easily employ our scheme across multiple platforms without relying on the information in the browser's display.

Finally, we demonstrate the practicality of our system with a prototype implementation. We use a cellphone as the trusted device, and we show that the system introduces minimal overhead. In addition, the server-side changes are minor, as well as backwards compatible.

2   Problem Definition

In this section, we consider various formulations of the phishing problem and survey phishing tactics, both those in use today and those likely to appear in the near future. We also consider the aspects of user behavior typically exploited by phishing attacks.

2.1   Goals and Assumptions

In this section, we enumerate the goals of an anti-phishing technique, arranged in decreasing order of protection and generality:

1. Ensure that a user's data only goes to the intended recipient.
2. Prevent a user's data from reaching an untrustworthy recipient.
3. Prevent an attacker from abusing a user's data.
4. Prevent an attacker from modifying a user's account.
5. Prevent an attacker from viewing a user's account.

Our scheme guarantees the last two goals via technical measures. Clearly, an ideal solution would also address the first goal. However, divining a user's intentions remains a difficult problem, particularly when even the user may find it difficult to quantify his or her precise intentions. The next two goals, while more constrained than the first, require complete control over the user's data. Although we present techniques to assist with the goal of preventing the user's data from reaching an untrustworthy recipient, ultimately, we cannot guarantee this result, since a determined user can always find some means of disclosing personal information to an adversary.

To realize our goals, we assume users can be trusted to correctly identify sites at which they wish to establish accounts. We justify this assumption on the basis of the following observations. First, phishing attacks generally target users with existing accounts. In other words, the phishers attempt to fool a victim with an online account into revealing information that the phishers can use to access that account. Second, users typically exercise greater caution when establishing an account than when using the account or when responding to an urgent notice concerning the account. This results in part from the natural analogue of the real world principle of caveat emptor, where consumers are accustomed to exercising caution when selecting the merchants they wish to patronize. However, consumers in the real world are unlikely to encounter a Man-in-the-Middle attack or an imitation store front, and so they have fewer natural defenses when online. Our solution addresses these new threats enabled by the digital marketplace. Our approach is largely orthogonal to existing anti-phishing solutions based on heuristics, and it can be combined with these earlier schemes, particularly to protect the user from a phishing attack during the initial account establishment.

2.2   Attacks

A typical phishing attack begins with an email to the victim, supposedly from a reputable institution, but actually from the phisher. The text of the message commonly warns the user that a problem exists with the user's account that must immediately be corrected. The victim is led to a spoofed website designed to resemble the institution's official website. At this point, the phishing site may launch a passive or an active attack. In a passive attack, the web page prompts the victim to enter account information (e.g., username and password) and may also request other personal details, such as the victim's Social Security number, bank account numbers, ATM PINs, etc. All of this information is relayed to the phisher, who can then use it to plunder the user's accounts. In an active attack, the phisher may act as a man-in-the-middle attacker, actively relaying information from the legitimate site to the user and back.

While early phishing emails typically employed plain text and grammatically incorrect English, current attacks demonstrate increased sophistication. Phishing emails and websites often employ the same visual elements as their legitimate counterparts. As a result, spoofed sites and legitimate sites are virtually indistinguishable to users. Phishers also exploit a number of DNS tricks to further obscure the nature of the attack. The spoofed site may use a domain name like www.ebay.com.kr, which very closely resembles eBay's actual domain, but instead points to a site in Korea. Some attacks use obscure URL conventions to craft domain names like www.ebay.com@192.168.0.5, while others exploit bugs in the browser's Unicode URL parsing and display code to conceal the site's true domain name [21].

Although most phishing attacks are initiated via email, there are many other potential means of initiation. The phisher could contact the victim via Instant Messenger, via a popup or other advertisement on another website, or even via fax [22]. Phishers can also exploit mistyped URLs by registering domain names like gooogle.com or goggle.com, or even employ techniques to artificially inflate their rankings in search engines. To make matters worse, researchers have discovered automated phishing kits circulating online that enable novice phishers to employ some of these techniques [36].

Attackers have also been quick to exploit attempts at user education. For instance, many users believe that a transaction is secure if they see the 'lock' icon displayed in the browser window. One possible attack uses JavaScript to display a spoofed lock image in the appropriate location [43]. Phishers may also acquire their own SSL certificate, relying on users' inability or unwillingness to verify the certificates they install. There have also been cases in which Certificate Authorities issued certificates to attackers posing as legitimate Microsoft employees [26]. Phishers can also try to confuse users by simultaneously loading a legitimate page and a spoofed page using HTML frames or popups. Unfortunately, even these techniques barely scratch the surface of potential phishing scams.

Despite the advances and innovations discussed above, phishing attacks are continuously evolving into increasingly sophisticated forms. For example, attackers have begun targeting specific individuals within an organization. These highly customized attacks, dubbed *spear-phishing*, often try to trick employees into installing malware or revealing their organizational passwords [31, 23]. As a more general form of advanced attack, Jakobsson introduces the notion of context-aware phishing in which an attacker exploits some knowledge about the victim in order to enhance the efficacy of the attack [19]. In a user study, Jakobsson found that context-aware phishing attacks dramatically enhanced the probability of a successful attack, from 3% percent for an ordinary attack to 48-96% for a specially-crafted context-aware attack. Another attack variant uses socially-aware phishing. In a socially-aware attack, the phisher uses publicly available information to craft an email that purports to come from someone the victim knows and trusts. To defend against phishing attacks, organizations are in a constant race to detect and take down phishing sites. In the future, this could become even more difficult with *distributed phishing attacks* [20], where each page a user visits is hosted at a different location and registered to a different owner.

2.3   User Issues

In this section, we consider user-related issues for phishing. Some of these observations were also made by Dhamija and Tygar [9].

First, users exhibit certain tendencies that inherently undermine security. Security is often a secondary concern; few users start a web browser with the objective of "doing security." Users want to make purchases, check their accounts and authorize payments online. Because of this, users will tend to ignore or, if they become too invasive, circumvent or disable security measures. Similarly, users have become habituated to ignoring strange warning boxes that appear when they access secure sites, and they blithely click through such warnings. Moreover, prior work shows that humans pick poor passwords with low entropy [42] and readily volunteer them to complete strangers [2]. Finally, users have become accustomed to computers and websites behaving erratically. They will often attribute the absence of security indicators to non-malicious errors [41]. In addition, most users cannot distinguish between actual hyperlinks and spoofed hyperlinks that display one URL but link to a different URL (i.e., URLs of the form: `<a href='http://phishing.org/'> <img src='ebay-url.jpg'> </a>`).

Furthermore, users are unable to reliably parse and understand domain names or PKI certificates.

Clearly, current technology makes it difficult for even a knowledgeable user to consistently make the right decision, particularly when security is not a primary goal. As a result, we argue that anti-phishing techniques must minimize the user's security responsibilities.

3 Design Principles

Based on the previous discussion, we advocate the following set of design principles for anti-phishing tools:

Sidestep the arms race. Many anti-phishing approaches face the same problem as anti-spam solutions: incremental solutions only provoke an ongoing arms race between researchers and adversaries. This typically gives the advantage to the attackers, since researchers are permanently stuck on the defensive. As soon as researchers introduce an improvement, attackers analyze it and develop a new twist on their current attacks that allows them to evade the new defenses. Instead, we need to research fundamental approaches for preventing phishing. As Clayton noted, we need a "Kilimanjaro effect," where the level of security overwhelms potential attackers, and only the most determined (and skilled) will succeed [7].

Provide mutual authentication. Most anti-phishing techniques strive to prevent phishing attacks by providing better authentication of the server. However, phishing actually exploits authentication failures on both the client and the server side. Initially, a phishing attack exploits the user's inability to properly authenticate a server before transmitting sensitive data. However, a second authentication failure occurs when the server allows the phisher to use the captured data to login as the victim. A complete anti-phishing solution must address both of these failures: clients should have strong guarantees that they are communicating with the intended recipient, and servers should have similarly strong guarantees that the client requesting service has a legitimate claim to the accounts it attempts to access.

Reduce reliance on users. The majority of current phishing countermeasures rely on users to assist in the detection of phishing sites and make decisions as to whether to continue when a potentially phishy site is found. Unfortunately, as discussed in Section 2.3, users are in many ways unsuited to authenticating others or themselves to others. As a result, we must move towards protocols that reduce human involvement or introduce additional information that cannot readily be revealed. These mechanisms add security without relying on perfectly correct user behavior, thus bringing security to a larger audience.

Avoid dependence on the browser's interface. The majority of current anti-phishing approaches propose modifications to the browser interface. Unfortunately, the browser interface is inherently insecure and can be easily circumvented by embedded JavaScript applications that mimic the "trusted" browser elements. In fact, researchers have shown mechanisms that imitate a secure SSL web page by forging security-related elements

---

The User Experience

Alice lives in New York and has an account at the National Bank of Anguilla. She often worries about the security of her online account. Recently, the bank began offering the Phoolproof cellphone authentication system to its customers. Alice is thrilled, but she cannot go to the bank in person to sign up. Alice contacts the bank. The bank mails a randomly chosen shared secret to the postal address on file.

When Alice receives the shared secret in the mail, she logs into the National Bank of Anguilla web page and navigates to the cellphone authentication signup page. The signup page prompts her to enter the shared secret into her cellphone (see Section 4.1 for technical details and alternatives). Alice confirms she wants to create a new account on her cellphone, and a bookmark for the National Bank of Anguilla then appears in her phone's list of secure sites.

From then on, whenever Alice wants to access her account, she navigates to the Anguilla bookmark on her cellphone, as shown in Figure 1. The phone directs her browser to the correct website, and Alice enters her username and password to login (see Section 4.2 for technical details). After login, the interaction with her bank remains unchanged.

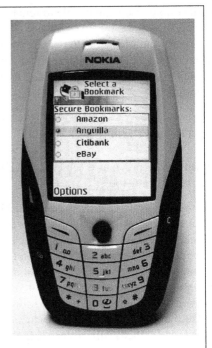

Fig. 1. Cellphone User Interface The cellphone displays the secure bookmarks for sites at which the user has established accounts

---

on the screen [43]. Even recent anti-phishing proposals that create trusted browser windows or input mechanisms are ultimately still vulnerable to JavaScript attacks [9, 33] Given the complexity of current web browsers and the multitude of attacks, we propose to avoid reliance on browser interfaces.

Forgo network monitoring. A naive approach to phishing prevention might involve monitoring a user's outgoing communication and intercepting sensitive data in transit. Unfortunately, this approach is unlikely to succeed. For example, suppose this approach is implemented to monitor information transmitted via HTML forms. An attacker could respond by using a Java applet or another form of dynamic scripting to transmit the user's response. Worse, client-side scripting could easily encrypt the outgoing data to prevent this type of monitoring entirely. In the end, this approach is unlikely to provide a satisfactory solution.

4   Our Phoolproof Anti-phishing System

While no automated procedure can provide complete protection, our protocol guards the secrecy and integrity of a user's existing online accounts so that attacks are no more

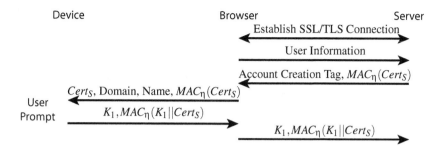

Fig. 2. Account Setup Protocol steps for establishing a new user account

effective than pre-Internet scams (e.g., an attacker may still be able to access a user's account by subverting a company insider). We base our system on the observation that users should be authenticated using an additional authenticator that they cannot readily reveal to malicious parties. Our scheme establishes the additional authenticator on a trusted device, such that an attacker must compromise the device *and* obtain the user's password to access the user's account.

The trusted device in our system can take the form of a cellphone, PDA or even a smart watch; in this paper, we assume the use of a cellphone. Users cannot readily disclose the authenticator on the cellphone to a third party, and servers will refuse to act on instructions received from someone purporting to be a particular user without presenting the proper authenticator. As discussed in Section 8, our technique is one of the first systems to prevent active Man-in-the-Middle attacks. In addition, the use of the cellphone allows us to minimize the effect of hijacked browser windows and facilitates user convenience, since it can be used at multiple machines. We assume that the user can establish a secure connection between their cellphone and their browser and that the cellphone itself has not been compromised. We discuss these assumptions further in Section 5.2.

Below, we explain how a user creates an account (or updates an existing account) using our protocol. We then define the protocol for account usage, as well as steps for recovering if the user's trusted device is lost or compromised.

4.1   Setup

To enable our system for an online account, the user must establish a shared secret with the server. This can be done using one of the out-of-band channels suggested below. These mechanisms for establishing a shared secret rely on institutions to implement measures that ensure 1) their new customers are who they say they are, and 2) the information in existing customers' files is accurate. Institutions have dealt with this problem since well before the existence of computers, and thus, they have well-established techniques for doing so.

The out-of-band channel used for establishing a shared secret can take many forms. For example, banks often utilize the postal service as a trusted side-channel. Alternatively, a telephone call may suffice. Banks could provide the shared secret at ATMs by displaying the shared secret in the form of a barcode that the user could photograph with the camera on a cellphone [25, 32]. As another possibility, initial account setup could be performed on the premises of the financial institution. That way, employees can be trained to assist users with setup; users' identification can be checked in person; and users can trust that they are associating with the correct institution. Trusted financial institutions could also provide setup services for organizations that lack brick-and-mortar infrastructure, such as online vendors.

Using one of the mechanisms discussed above, the institution sends a randomly chosen secret η to the user. The secret should be of sufficient length (e.g., 80-128 bits) to prevent brute-force attacks. The user navigates to the institution's website and initiates setup. The setup steps are summarized in Figure 2 and described below. The server responds with a specially crafted HTML tag (e.g., `<!-- SECURE-SETUP -->`), which signals the browser that account setup has been initiated. The server also authenticates its SSL/TLS certificate by including a MAC of the certificate, using the shared secret η as a key.

The browser contacts the cellphone via Bluetooth,[1] transmitting the server's SSL/TLS certificate, domain name, site name and MAC to the phone. The cellphone prompts the user to confirm the account creation (to avoid stealth installs by malicious sites) and enter the shared secret provided by the institution (if it has not already been entered, e.g., at the ATM or at the financial institution). It also verifies the MAC on the server's certificate and aborts the protocol if the verification fails. Assuming verification succeeds, the cellphone creates a public/private key pair $\{K_1, K_1^{-1}\}$ and saves a record associating the key pair with the server's certificate. It also creates a *secure bookmark* entry for the site, using the site's name and domain name. The cellphone sends the new public key authenticated with a MAC, using the shared secret as a key, to the server. The server associates the public key with the user's account, and henceforward, the client must use the protocol described in the next section to access the online account. All other online attempts to access the account will be denied.[2]

4.2 Secure Connection Establishment

Once the user's account has been enabled, the server will refuse access to the account unless the user is properly authenticated via the established public key pair *and* username/password combination. Thus, even if the user is tricked into revealing private information to a phisher or a social engineer, the attacker still cannot access the user's account.

A user who wishes to access the account must always initiate the connection using the secure bookmark on the cellphone. As an alternative, we could have the cellphone detect when a user navigates to a previously registered site. However, a cellphone is ill-equipped to detect if the user visits a phishing site and thus will be unable to prevent the user from disclosing private information to malicious parties. While a phisher would still be unable to access the user's account (without compromising the cellphone), we prefer to help prevent this unnecessary disclosure (see Section 5 for additional discussion).

---

[1] Our system is not exclusive to Bluetooth. Any mechanism that allows the user's trusted device to communicate with the browser (e.g., infrared, 802.11, USB cable, etc.) will suffice.

[2] Note that this does not preclude Alice from conducting business in person, for example.

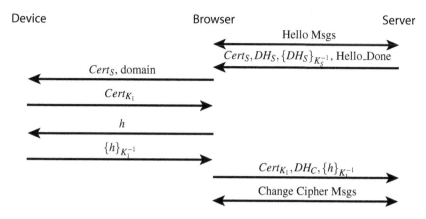

Fig. 3. Secure Connection Establishment The browser establishes an SSL/TLS connection to the server using client authentication, with help from the cellphone. DH_S and DH_C represent the Diffie-Hellman key material for the server and client respectively, and h is a secure MAC of the handshake messages. See Section 4.2 for additional details.

When the user selects a secure bookmark on the cellphone, the cellphone directs the browser to the associated URL. The use of secure bookmarks provides the user with a higher degree of server authentication and helps to protect the user from inadvertently arriving at a phishing site, either via a spoofed or a mistyped URL. When the remote server provides its SSL/TLS certificate, the browser forwards the certificate to the cellphone. If the certificate does not match the certificate previously provided, the cellphone closes the browser window and displays a warning message. If a server updates its certificate, then we need a protocol to update the server certificate stored on the cellphone; for example, the server could send the new certificate along with a signature using the previous private key, and upon successful verification, the cellphone can update the certificate it has stored.

If the certificate check is successful, the browser and the server then establish an SSL/TLS connection [11, 14]. The cellphone assists the browser in performing the client authentication portion of the SSL/TLS establishment, using the public key pair associated with this site (the SSL/TLS protocol includes a provision for user authentication, but this is rarely used today). Figure 3 summarizes the messages exchanged. Essentially, the browser initiates an SSL/TLS connection with Ephemeral Diffie-Hellman key agreement. After agreeing on the cryptographic parameters in the Hello messages, the server sends:

$$Cert_S, g, p, g^s mod\, p, \{g, p, g^s mod\, p\}_{K_S^{-1}} \qquad (1)$$

(i.e., its certificate, its ephemeral Diffie-Hellman key information and a signature on the key information) to the client. The browser retrieves the appropriate user certificate $Cert_{K_1}$ from the cellphone based on the server's certificate and domain. Then, the browser generates the necessary Diffie-Hellman key material and calculates a secure hash of the SSL/TLS master secret $\mathcal{K}$ (which is based on the derived Diffie-Hellman key) and all of the previous handshake messages (as well as the client's choice of Diffie-Hellman key material), HM, as follows:

$$h = MD5(\mathcal{K}||pad2||MD5(HM||\mathcal{K}||pad1))||SHA\text{-}1(\mathcal{K}||pad2||MD5(SHA\text{-}1||\mathcal{K}||pad1)) \quad (2)$$

(where $||$ represents concatenation) and sends the hash to the cellphone. The cellphone replies with a signature on h. Note that as long as the phone remains uncompromised, an attacker cannot produce this signature, and hence cannot successfully authenticate as the user. The browser forwards the signature to the server, along with the user's certificate and the client's Diffie-Hellman key material:

$$Cert_{K_1}, g^c \bmod p, \{h\}_{K_1^{-1}} \quad (3)$$

The browser and the server then exchange the final phase of an SSL/TLS negotiation. Once the user has been authenticated and the SSL/TLS connection has been established, the user can use the browser to conduct transactions and account inquiries as usual. Note that we do not change the SSL/TLS protocol; we merely use the cellphone to assist the browser establish a session key with the server.

4.3 Recovery

Inevitably, users will lose or break their cellphones, or replace them with newer models. When this happens, the user must revoke the old keys and establish a new key pair with a new cellphone. In the case of a lost cellphone, revocation prevents an attacker from accessing the user's accounts.

To revoke the old key pairs, we favor using a process that exists today: the user calls the institution via telephone. This is a well-established, familiar process. Today, customers already call credit card companies to report the loss of a card and to freeze any transactions on the account. With the loss of a cellphone, users would still call the institutions to revoke their keys. The institution would then send the information needed to establish a new key pair using the techniques described in Section 4.1.

We initially considered other methods, such as storing revocation information in the user's browser or on a USB key. However, telephone calls are superior for three reasons. First, users already know how to call customer service. The reuse of an existing business process reduces the costs – mental and monetary – for all parties. Second, cellphones are mobile devices that travel with their users, and users may lose them anywhere. A user whose cellphone is lost on a business trip should act immediately to minimize financial (or other) losses; waiting to access the revocation information stored at home is not acceptable. Finally, since revocation information is rarely used, it is easily lost. For example, if revocation information is stored on paper, CD's, or USB keys, it can be misplaced or damaged.

5 Security Analysis

In this section, we discuss the effectiveness of various attacks on our system.

5.1 Hijacking Account Setup or Re-establishment

The largest vulnerability in our system arises during account setup (or re-establishment), when the user must ensure that the account is created at a legitimate site. The server also faces an authentication problem, since it must ensure that the person creating the account is the person described by the user information submitted. However, as we discuss in Section 4.1, this threat can be mitigated by having users establish accounts in person, at trusted businesses.

A clever phisher may have a user's key pair revoked and hijack the account when the user tries to re-establish a new key pair. We do not consider this to be a grave threat, however. Phishing is so successful because the perpetrators target large numbers of people with a low success rate. It would be difficult for phishers to target a large number of people without attracting attention; a bank would surely notice if thousands of customers suddenly needed new key pairs. In addition, phishers typically have limited resources in the physical world. Sending information for key re-establishment through postal mail or requiring users to verify their identity in person would greatly reduce the effectiveness of a phishing attack.

5.2 Theft of the Trusted Device

Since the user's cellphone (or PDA) holds cryptographic keys for all of the user's accounts, device theft is a risk. After stealing the device, an attacker would still need the user's password(s) in order to compromise the accounts (a problem sufficient to deter casual attackers). The attacker must obtain the passwords before the user discovers the theft and revokes the stored keys. Nonetheless, additional layers of security may be desirable. For example, the cellphone could require the user to enter a PIN number or use biometrics to authorize use of the keys. A more security-conscious user could consider a tamper-resistant storage module for the cellphone to reduce the possibility of leaking the secret keys.

5.3 Malware on the Trusted Device

With the advent of more powerful cellphones and network-enabled PDAs, malware on mobile devices will become an increasingly serious problem. Attacks are inevitable – particularly if mobile devices are used to protect financial accounts.

Numerous vendors have released anti-malware software for mobile devices. More high-profile attacks may be required before the software becomes ubiquitous on mobile devices, as it is on computers.

For additional security, we could leverage a Trusted Platform Module (TPM) that will likely exist on future cellphone architectures. The keys would reside in the TPM's trusted storage facility. In the absence of additional security hardware, we could instead use recent advances in software attestation [35] to verify the integrity of both the trusted device and the user's computer. When the user's cellphone contacts the computer, each device attests to the security of its current state, and the SSL/TLS connection only proceeds if both parties are satisfied. As a result, a successful attack would require simultaneous compromise of both the user's cellphone and computer.

In addition, we can leverage the capture-resilient cryptographic mechanisms proposed by MacKenzie and Reiter [24]. In their approach, secrets and cryptographic operations are split up and performed on the mobile device and a server. Compromising either the mobile device or the server reveals no useful information. After loss of the mobile device, the user can revoke the information stored on the server.

5.4   Malware on the Computer

Our system protects the user against many forms of malware. For example, standard keyloggers would be ineffective, since they can only capture user input – and not the private key stored on the cellphone. However, without additional resources, we cannot protect users against certain classes of malicious code installed on users' computers. The two largest threats are malicious modifications to the browser and operating system kernel compromises. If the user's browser has been compromised, then the malicious code could use the cellphone to login to a legitimate site and subsequently redirect the connection to a phishing site. A kernel compromise would allow a similar attack. Both attacks require a significant and sophisticated compromise of the user's computer. As mentioned earlier, we can use new security hardware such as the TPM or software attestation techniques to mitigate these threats.

5.5   Attacks on the Network

Possible network-based attacks include Man-in-the-Middle attacks, pharming[3] attacks, and domain hijacking. None of these attacks will succeed against our system. By storing the user's public key, the server prevents a Man-in-the-Middle attack, since the attacker will not be able to attack the authenticated Diffie-Hellman values from the ephemeral Diffie-Hellman exchange. By checking the certificate provided by the server against the stored certificate, the cellphone even protects the user from DNS poisoning and domain hijacking. Thus, our scheme provides very strong guarantees of authenticity to both the client and the server and stops virtually all forms of phishing, DNS spoofing and pharming attacks.

5.6   Local Attacks on Bluetooth

Phishing attacks rely on the attacker's ability to target a large number of users and swindle them quickly without being caught. As a result, phishing attacks are typically conducted remotely. To provide an additional layer of protection, we can use existing research (e.g., from McCune et al. [25]) to establish a secure connection between the user's device and the computer they use, preventing attacks on the Bluetooth channel.

6   Discussion

6.1   Infrastructure

As described above, our protocol requires very minimal changes to existing infrastructure. In Section 7, we provide specific details of our prototype implementation to demonstrate the limited changes necessary to support our protocol.

For servers, the primary change is the addition of an extra record associated with a user's account to store the user's public key. Servers must also respond to account

---

[3] Pharming attacks exploit vulnerabilities in a DNS server to redirect users to another site. Such DNS attacks are powerful in conjunction with phishing, since the domain name appears to be correct.

creation requests by adding an extra HTML tag[4] to the page. The authentication of the user's public key uses existing options in the SSL/TLS protocol, so that the SSL/TLS protocol remains unchanged and client authentication code requires only minor tweaks.

From the client's perspective, the browser's portion of the protocol can be implemented as a simple browser extension, as we have done in our prototype, or it could eventually be incorporated into the browser itself.

As for the user's trusted device, cellphones today are one of the first examples of truly ubiquitous computing. According to a survey in 2003, over 49% of Americans and 90% of Europeans have cellphones [37]. However, as mentioned earlier, our protocol can work just as well with a user's PDA or other mobile-computing device (e.g., a smart watch). Using Bluetooth as a basis for communication between the trusted device and the computer is also increasing practical. According to the Bluetooth SIG, over five million units are shipped with Bluetooth every week, with an installed base of over 500 million units at the end of 2005 [4].

As we discuss in Section 7, the software for the user's trusted device can be developed in Java, simplifying portability between devices.

6.2 Deployment Incentives

Our system provides strong deployment incentives for both parties involved in online transactions. Consumers will be motivated to use the system, since it imparts very strong guarantees regarding the integrity of their online accounts and helps prevent them from inadvertently visiting a phishing website. Financial institutions and merchants will want to adopt a system that will help reduce losses due to phishing attacks. Our scheme can be deployed by individual organizations without the need for universal adoption and deployment. Each server that deploys the system benefits, regardless of whether or not it is adopted by other sites. In addition, the scheme can be deployed alongside legacy authentication so that legacy users will still be able to access their accounts.

6.3 Convenience

There are many other two-factor authentication schemes using stand-alone accessories, such as security tokens or smart cards [34]. However, each organization must currently issue its own accessory, and users are saddled with multiple accessories that may be confused or lost. Our system enables all this functionality to be consolidated onto one device the user already carries. Furthermore, our approach prevents Man-in-the-Middle attacks, which are still possible with many of the accessories since a one-time password entered into a browser window can be captured by a phishing site and exploited to hijack the user's account. Moreover, browser-based countermeasures can be inconvenient, since state kept on the browser may not be easily portable.

7 Prototype Implementation

To evaluate the usability and performance of our scheme, we developed a prototype on a cellphone, a web browser and a server. We discuss the details and performance results below.

---

[4] The tag is designed so that legacy clients will simply ignore it.

7.1 Implementation Details

Equipping a server with our system required very minimal changes, namely changes to two configuration options and the addition of two simple Perl scripts. From the server's perspective, our scheme requires no changes to the SSL/TLS protocol. Indeed, most major web servers, including Apache-SSL, Apache+mod_ssl and Microsoft's IIS already include an option for performing client authentication. In our case, we used Apache-SSL and enabled the SSLVerifyClient option that indicates that clients may present certificates, but the certificates need not be signed by a trusted Certificate Authority (since our client certificates are self-signed). We also enabled the SSLExportClient Certificates option that exports information about the client's certificate to CGI-accessible variables. Aside from these two minor configuration changes, we only needed two additional CGI scripts (written in Perl) to implement the server's side of the protocol. One script handles account creation and writes user information and public keys to a file. When the client attempts to use the account, it provides a self-signed certificate as part of the normal SSL/TLS authentication process. The server's existing SSL/TLS module verifies that the signature in the certificate corresponds to the public key enclosed and provides the information in the client's certificate to the authentication script. The authentication script checks the public key in the certificate against that associated with the user's account. If the keys match, then the authentication script permits the client to access the site. This approach has several benefits. First, the changes required are extremely minor and nonintrusive. Second, it still allows legacy clients to establish an SSL/TLS connection with the server. The authentication script can then detect whether the client has presented a legitimate certificate. If the script detects a legacy client, it can make a policy decision as to whether to allow the client access to the account, allow restricted access to the account, or redirect the client to the account creation page.

On the client side, we developed an extension to Firefox, an open-source web browser, to detect account creation. When the extension detects a page containing the account creation tag, it signals the cellphone with the appropriate information, and passes the cellphone's reply to the server. Similarly, when the user selects a secure bookmark on the cellphone, the cellphone sends the URL to the extension, which redirects the browser to the appropriate site. We also chose to apply a small patch to the Firefox code that handles the client authentication portion of the SSL/TLS exchange.[5] The patch passes the server's certificate to the cellphone, along with a hash of the SSL/TLS handshake messages and receives from the cellphone a certificate for the user's public key and a signature on the hash. The browser can then use these items to complete the SSL/TLS handshake. By involving the cellphone in the SSL/TLS computations, we guarantee that the private key for the account never leaves the phone, preventing even a compromised browser or OS from accessing it.

Our prototype runs on a Nokia 6630 cellphone. We developed a Java MIDlet (an application conforming to the Mobile Information Device Profile (MIDP) standard) that provides the functionality described in Section 4 with a user-friendly interface. A Java

---

[5] Instead of patching Firefox, we could also implement our scheme as an SSL/TLS proxy on the user's computer. This would enable our solution to work with proprietary browsers as well. However, the patch to Firefox was small and straightforward, so we chose that route for testing purposes.

Table 1. This table summarizes the performance overhead imposed by our scheme. The averages are calculated over 20 trials, and the keys created are 1024-bit RSA key pairs. Note that key creation happens offline and thus has little or no impact on the user's experience.

	Time (s)	[Min, Max] (s)
Key Creation	75.0	[29.8, 168.3]
Account Creation	0.4	[0.3, 0.5]
Site Navigation	0.2	[0.1, 0.2]
SSL/TLS Assistance	1.7	[1.6, 1.9]

implementation also simplifies porting the code to other devices. For the cryptographic operations, we used the light-weight cryptography library provided by Bouncy Castle [38]. Since key generation can require a minute or two, we precompute keys when the user first starts the application, rather than waiting until an account has been created. When the cellphone receives an account creation packet from the browser extension, it selects an unused key pair, assigns it to the server information provided by the browser extension, and then sends the key pair and the appropriate revocation messages to the browser extension. When the user selects a secure bookmark (see Figure 1), the cellphone sends the appropriate address to the browser extension. It also computes the appropriate signatures during the SSL/TLS exchange.

7.2 Performance

If our system is to provide a realistic defense against phishing attacks, it must impose minimal overhead, since a solution that significantly slows the web browsing experience will be unlikely to be adopted. Table 1 summarizes our performance measurements. These results represent the average over 20 trials, each run on a cold cellphone cache. Clearly, key creation takes the largest amount of time (which is understandable, given that the cellphone must create a 1024-bit RSA key pair), but since we precompute the keys, the user will not be affected by this overhead. We could also make use of the efficient key generation technique proposed by Modadugu et al. [27] to significantly decrease the delay. More importantly, account creation time is negligible, as is the delay for the cellphone to direct the browser to a given domain. The overhead for using the system during an SSL/TLS exchange requires less than two seconds on average, which is tolerable in most cases. Furthermore, newer phones already promise better performance, and an optimized implementation of the necessary cryptographic primitives in C would likely reduce the overhead by an order of magnitude (our current RSA implementation is written entirely in Java), though at the potential cost of additional overhead when porting the code to a new device. Together, these improvements would reduce the usage overhead to well under a second.

8   Related Work

The importance of the phishing problem has attracted much academic and industrial research. Many of the systems described below represent complementary approaches and could be used in conjunction with our system, particularly to help protect the user during account setup. We discuss related work in three categories: heuristic approaches, password modification, and origin authentication.

8.1 Heuristics

A popular initial approach for preventing phishing attempts is to find a pattern in phishing web sites and then alert the user if a given site matches the pattern. Several browser toolbars have been proposed to perform this function, for example SpoofGuard [5], TrustBar [18], eBay Toolbar [12], and SpoofStick [8]. Among other heuristics, these toolbars detect malicious URLs and inform the user about the true domain of the site visited. The Net Trust system incorporates information from users' social networks, as well as centralized authorities, to help users make decisions about a website's trustworthiness [15]. Unfortunately, heuristics are inherently imprecise and invite attackers to adapt to the defenses until they can bypass the heuristics. Such an approach can lead to an arms race as we describe in Section 3, with all of the problems it entails. In addition, Wu et al. found that 13-54% of users would still visit a phishing website, despite warnings from an anti-phishing toolbar [41].

8.2 Modified Passwords

Phishers often exploit the tendency of users to pick weak passwords and to re-use the same passwords at several websites. If a phisher obtains a password at a low-security site, they can use it to login to a high-security site as well.

One-time passwords are widely used in several contexts, including the S/Key system [17] and corporate uses such as Citibank [6]. The RSA SecurID system is a time-based one-time password, where the password is generated on a hardware token [34]. The user must enter the code in a web form and submit it to the server to show that she possesses the trusted device, but there is no server authentication on the user's part. In addition, the system is vulnerable to an active Man-in-the-Middle attack, since a phisher can intercept the value from the user and then use it to access the user's account. The PwdHash approach uses a cryptographic hash function computed on the user's password and the site name to derive a unique password for each site [33]. PwdHash is a promising system, but is ineffective against pharming or DNS spoofing attacks where a phisher presents the correct domain name to the browser but redirects the request to its server. In the case of DNS attacks, PwdHash will hand the correct password for the site to the phisher. Moreover, PwdHash does not prevent a phisher from breaking a weak master password using dictionary attacks.

Another approach is single-sign-on, where users sign in to a single site that will subsequently handle all authentications with other sites, but so far such systems have encountered consumer resistance, since they involve storing sensitive user data with a third party. If these services did grow in popularity, they would undoubtedly attract the same attention from phishers currently visited on individual sites. Another approach is "Verified by VISA," where merchants redirect clients to a special VISA site which requires a username and password to authenticate the transaction [1].

Unfortunately, none of these approaches provide sufficient protection against Man-in-the-Middle attacks, particularly if the phisher also uses DNS spoofing. As the user enters personal information into the phishing website, the phisher can forward the information to the legitimate banking site. Once authenticated, the adversary has full control over the hijacked connection. Banks have already reported such attacks against their one-time password systems [29]. Our approach precludes such Man-in-the-Middle attacks because the cell phone and server mutually authenticate each other and establish a session key end-to-end.

8.3 Origin Authentication

In this class of countermeasures, researchers propose user-based mechanisms to authenticate the server. Ideally, if the user arrives at a malicious website, he or she will detect that the phishing site is not the correct web site.

Jakobsson presents a theoretical framework for phishing attacks [19]. He also proposes better email authentication to prevent phishing email, in addition to better secrecy protection for user email addresses (such that phishers have a harder time harvesting email addresses from, for example, eBay).

The Petname project [39] associates a user-assigned nickname with each website visited. If the browser loads a page from a spoofed web site, the nickname will be missing or wrong – the approach relies on users to notice either case. In addition, users will likely choose predictable nicknames (e.g., nicknaming Amazon.com's website "Amazon"), making nicknames easy to spoof.

Dhamija and Tygar propose Dynamic Security Skins (DSS) to enable a user to authenticate the server [10, 9]. In their system, a server opens a user-customized popup window that displays an image only the correct server can produce. Similar to the Petname project, this approach relies on the user to perform the verification.

Myers proposes that servers display a series of images as users type their passwords [28]. It would be difficult for phishing sites to guess the correct sequence of images, and users know what images to expect. Again, this scheme relies on the user to perform the verification.

Similarly, PassMark stores a secure cookie on the client and sets up an image associated with the account that the user should remember [30]. Unfortunately, PassMark is a proprietary system – they do not disclose a detailed description of their approach.

All of these approaches require user diligence – even a single mistake on the user's part will result in a compromised account. Several of these approaches are also susceptible to Man-in-the-Middle attacks since a phisher can simply forward information between the browser and the legitimate site.

9 Conclusion

Phishing is a significant and growing problem which threatens to impose increasing monetary losses on businesses and to shatter consumer confidence in e-commerce. We observe that phishing attacks have the potential to become much more sophisticated, making user-based protection mechanisms fragile given the user population of non-experts. Instead of relying on users to protect themselves against phishing attacks (as previous work suggests), we propose mechanisms that do not rely on the user, but are based on cryptographic operations on a trusted mobile device that many users already possess. We anticipate that our approach would be deployed for websites requiring a high level of security, and that it would ultimately help in regaining consumer confidence in using web-based commerce. In conclusion, our system satisfies the guidelines published by the FDIC, which strongly urge financial institutions to adopt two-factor authentication for Internet-based financial services by the end of 2006 [13].

Acknowledgements

The authors would like to thank Jon McCune, Jason Rouse and Ai Qi Chua for their assistance in implementing the prototype. Ari Juels, Dawn Song, and Chris Karlof provided interesting discussions and insightful comments. We would also like to thank the anonymous reviewers for their helpful suggestions.

References

1. Verified by VISA. `http://usa.visa.com/personal/security/vbv/how_it_works.html`.
2. A. Adams and M. A. Sasse. Users are not the enemy. *Communications of the ACM*, 42(12):40–46, Dec. 1999.
3. Anti-Phishing Working Group. Phishing activity trends report. `http://antiphishing.org/apwg_phishing_activity_report_august_05.pdf`, Aug. 2005.
4. Bluetooth SIG. Bluetooth Technology Benefits. `http://www.bluetooth.com/Bluetooth/Learn/Benefits/`.
5. N. Chou, R. Ledesma, Y. Teraguchi, D. Boneh, and J. C. Mitchell. Client-side defense against web-based identity theft. In *NDSS*, Feb. 2004.
6. CitiBank. Virtual account numbers. `http://www.citibank.com/us/cards/tour/cb/shp_van.htm`.
7. R. Clayton. Who'd phish from the summit of kilimanjaro? In *Financial Cryptography*, pages 91–92, 2005.
8. Core Street. Spoofstick. `http://www.corestreet.com/spoofstick/`.
9. R. Dhamija and J. D. Tygar. The battle against phishing: Dynamic security skins. In *ACM Symposium on Usable Security and Privacy (SOUPS '05)*, July 2005.
10. R. Dhamija and J. D. Tygar. Phish and HIPs: Human interactive proofs to detect phishing attacks. In *Human Interactive Proofs: Second International Workshop (HIP 2005)*, May 2005.
11. T. Dierks and C. Allen. The TLS protocol version 1.0. Internet Request for Comment RFC 2246, Internet Engineering Task Force, Jan. 1999. Proposed Standard.
12. eBay. eBay toolbar. `http://pages.ebay.com/ebay_toolbar`.
13. FDIC. Authentication in an internet banking environment. Technical Report FIL-103-2005, Federal Deposit Insurance Corporation, Oct. 2005.
14. A. Freier, P. Kariton, and P. Kocher. The SSL protocol: Version 3.0. Internet draft, Netscape Communications, 1996.
15. A. Genkina, A. Friedman, and J. Camp. Net trust. Trustworthy Interfaces for Passwords and Personal Information (TIPPI) Workshop, June 2005.
16. G. Goth. Phishing attacks rising, but dollar losses down. *IEEE Security and Privacy*, 3(1):8, January–February 2005.
17. N. Haller. The S/Key one-time password system. In *Proceedings of the Symposium on Network and Distributed Systems Security*, pages 151–157, Feb. 1994.

18. A. Herzberg and A. Gbara. Trustbar: Protecting (even naive) web users from spoofing and phishing attacks. Cryptology ePrint Archive, Report 2004/155, 2004.

19. M. Jakobsson. Modeling and preventing phishing attacks. In *Financial Cryptography*, 2005.

20. M. Jakobsson and A. Young. Distributed phishing attacks. Workshop on Resilient Financial Information Systems, Mar. 2005.

21. E. Johanson. The state of homograph attacks. `http://www.shmoo.com/idn/homograph.txt`, Feb. 2005.

22. J. Leyden. Fax-back phishing scam targets paypal. `http://www.channelregister.co.uk/2005/08/11/fax-back_phishing_scam/`.

23. J. Leyden. Spear phishers launch targeted attacks. `http://www.theregister.co.uk/2005/08/02/ibm_malware_report/`, Aug. 2005.

24. P. MacKenzie and M. K. Reiter. Networked cryptographic devices resilient to capture. *International Journal of Information Security*, 2(1):1–20, Nov. 2003.

25. J. M. McCune, A. Perrig, and M. K. Reiter. Seeing is believing: Using camera phones for human-verifiable authentication. In *IEEE Symposium on Security and Privacy*, May 2005.

26. Microsoft. Erroneous VeriSign-issued digital certificates pose spoofing hazard. `http://www.microsoft.com/technet/security/bulletin/MS01-017.mspx`, 2001.

27. N. Modadugu, D. Boneh, and M. Kim. Generating RSA keys on a handheld using an untrusted server. In *RSA Conference 2000*, Jan. 2000.

28. S. Myers. Delayed password disclosure. Trustworthy Interfaces for Passwords and Personal Information (TIPPI) Workshop, June 2005.

29. Out-law.com. Phishing attack targets one-time passwords. `http://www.theregister.co.uk/2005/10/12/outlaw_phishing/`, Oct. 2005.

30. Passmark Security. Protecting your customers from phishing attacks: an introduction to passmarks. `http://www.passmarksecurity.com/`, 2005.

31. P. F. Roberts. Spear phishing attack targets credit unions. `http://www.eweek.com/article2/0,1895,1902896,00.asp`, Dec. 2005.

32. M. Rohs and B. Gfeller. Using camera-equipped mobile phones for interacting with real-world objects. In *Proceedings of Advances in Pervasive Computing*, pages 265–271, Apr. 2004.

33. B. Ross, C. Jackson, N. Miyake, D. Boneh, and J. C. Mitchell. Stronger password authentication using browser extensions. In *14th USENIX Security Symposium*, Aug. 2005.

34. RSA Security. Protecting against phishing by implementing strong two-factor authentication. `https://www.rsasecurity.com/products/securid/whitepapers/PHISH_WP_0904.pdf`, 2004.

35. A. Seshadri, M. Luk, E. Shi, A. Perrig, L. van Doorn, and P. Khosla. Pioneer: Verifying integrity and guaranteeing execution of code on legacy platforms. In *Proceedings of ACM Symposium on Operating Systems Principles (SOSP)*, pages 1–16, Oct. 2005.

36. Sophos. Do-it-yourself phishing kits found on the internet, reveals sophos. `http://www.sophos.com/spaminfo/articles/diyphishing.html`.

37. D. Standish. Telephonic youth. `http://www.techcentralstation.com/090903C.html`.

38. The Legion of the Bouncy Castle. Bouncy Castle crypto APIs. `http://www.bouncycastle.org`.

39. Waterken Inc. Petname tool. `http://www.waterken.com/user/PetnameTool/`, 2005.

40. Wikipedia. Phishing. `http://en.wikipedia.org/wiki/Phishing`.

41. M. Wu, S. Garfinkel, and R. Miller. Users are not dependable - how to make security indicators to better protect them. Talk presented at the Workshop for Trustworthy Interfaces for Passwords and Personal Information, June 2005.

42. J. Yan, A. Blackwell, R. Anderson, and A. Grant. Password memorability and security: Empirical results. *IEEE Security and Privacy*, 2(5):25–31, September–October 2004.

43. E. Ye and S. Smith. Trusted paths for browsers. In *Proceedings of the 11th USENIX Security Symposium*. USENIX, Aug. 2002.

A Protocol for Secure Public Instant Messaging*

Mohammad Mannan and Paul C. van Oorschot

School of Computer Science
Carleton University, Ottawa, Canada

Abstract. Although Instant Messaging (IM) services are now relatively long-standing and very popular as an instant way of communication over the Internet, they have received little attention from the security research community. Despite important differences distinguishing IM from other Internet applications, very few protocols have been designed to address the unique security issues of IM. In light of threats to existing IM networks, we present the Instant Messaging Key Exchange (IMKE) protocol as a step towards secure IM. A discussion of IM threat model assumptions and an analysis of IMKE relative to these using BAN-like logic is also provided. Based on our implementation of IMKE using the Jabber protocol, we provide insights on how IMKE may be integrated with popular IM protocols.

1 Introduction and Overview

Instant Messaging (IM) is a popular Internet based application enabling individuals to exchange text messages instantly and monitor the availability of a list of users in real-time. Starting as a casual application, mainly used by teenagers and college students, IM systems now connect Wall Street firms [9] and Navy warships [8]. The Gartner Group predicts that IM traffic will surpass email traffic by 2006 [31]. A survey report from the Radicati Group suggests that 85% of businesses use public IM services but only 12% use security-enhanced enterprise IM services and IM-specific policies [15].

Protocols currently used in popular public IM systems (e.g. AOL, Yahoo!, MSN and Google Instant Messenger) are open to many security threats [21]. Relying on SSL-based solutions – the most common security protocol of corporate IM systems – for security in public IM services has major limitations, e.g., messages may not be *private* when they go through the IM server [16]. Shortcomings of public and business IM protocols highlight the need of a secure IM protocol.

Contributions. We present a novel protocol called Instant Messaging Key Exchange (IMKE) for *strong* authentication and *secure* communications (see Table 1 for definitions) in IM systems. IMKE enables mutual strong authentication between users and an IM server, using a memorable password and a known server public key. IMKE provides security (authentication, confidentiality and integrity) for client-server and client-client IM connections *with* repudiation.

---

* Version: August 9, 2006. Contact author: `mmannan@scs.carleton.ca`.

Although pairs of users generally share no secret between themselves, IMKE enables secure and private communications among users through a trusted IM server, without revealing the contents of users' messages to the server.

An analysis of the protocol in terms of security using a BAN (Burrows-Abadi-Needham)-like logic [7] is provided.[1] The protocol has also been tested (with no flaws found) by the AVISPA (Automated Validation of Internet Security Protocols and Applications) formal analysis tool [1]. IMKE may be implemented using any well-known public key cryptosystem (e.g. RSA, ElGamal, elliptic curve) that supports encryption, without requiring any additional special constraints (unlike e.g. SNAPI [20]) for a safe protocol run.[2] In contrast, the majority of existing Password Authentication and Key Exchange (PAKE) protocols which require no known server public key are based on Diffie-Hellman (DH)-based key agreement; these must be carefully implemented to avoid many known attacks which exploit the structure of many choices of parameters in DH-based key agreement (e.g. [19]). Although IMKE has been designed as a secure IM protocol, it may also provide an alternative to other two- and three-party PAKE protocols (e.g. EKE [4]) beyond IM. IMKE may be used in server-mediated peer-to-peer (P2P) communications as well.

We have implemented a prototype of IMKE using the Jabber [30] open-source IM protocol (for details of the implementation and execution performance, see [23]). Although implementing IMKE requires changing both the IM server and client, our implementation provides evidence that IMKE may be integrated with existing public IM protocols without a large implementation effort, and keeping underlying messaging structures intact.

Organization. The sequel is organized as follows. §2 outlines motivation for IMKE and related work. In §3, we briefly discuss threats considered in IMKE, and list terminology, end user goals, and long- and short-term secrets of IMKE. The protocol messages are discussed in §4. §5 provides our IM threat model and a partial security analysis. §6 concludes.

2 Motivation and Related Work

We now discuss the motivation for IMKE, similarities and differences of IMKE with existing secure IM protocols and two- and three-party PAKE protocols.

Relationship of IMKE to Pluggable and Independent Secure IM Protocols. A *pluggable* security protocol – i.e. one that is implemented in a third-party client "add-on module" without requiring any changes to popular IM clients and servers – could easily be deployed at the client-end in addition to default IM clients. Therefore several initiatives, e.g., Off-the-record messaging [5], Gaim-e [25], have been taken to make IM secure using pluggable security protocols. Limitations of those proposed to date include: client-server messages remain

---

[1] We do not claim to give a full proof of the security of IMKE; and moreover, no such complete formal proof would be conclusive.

[2] However, general requirements for secure choice of public key parameters must of course be fulfilled.

plaintext, and the requirement of long-term client private keys, whose secrecy must be maintained.

Independent secure IM protocols developed in practice, e.g., Secure Internet Live Conferencing (SILC) [28], do not appear to have been peer-reviewed in an academic sense, nor designed to be integrated with popular IM protocols. A lightweight protocol which can easily be embedded into existing IM protocols (by IM service providers, changing both the IM client and server) seems practical to achieve security without limiting usability or requiring a large implementation effort. We propose IMKE to achieve such objectives. Although IMKE requires changes in both the client and server software, users do not need to maintain or *carry* any long-term public key. IMKE also secures client-server communications.

Relationship of IMKE to Two- and Three-Party Protocols. IM is essentially a three-party system. The IM server's main role is to enable trusted communications between users. In traditional models, a third-party is often considered a *disinterested* party [3]. In contrast, the IM server plays an active role in users' communications (e.g. forwarding users' messages). Therefore we take advantage of the presence of an active IM server in IMKE, e.g., by using the server as a trusted public key distribution center for clients.

Another major difference of IMKE with other three-party systems is that, although the IM server in IMKE helps establish a secure session between two clients, the server does not know the session key shared between the clients. This is a desirable property for consumer IM networks; users may want their conversations to be inaccessible to the IM server even though they must trust the server for login, sharing user profiles, etc.

In a typical three-party case, two users start a session[3] only when they need to communicate. The IM scenario is a bit different in the following way: users authenticate themselves only when they login to the IM server; then users initiate sessions with other online users whenever they wish to – i.e. logging in to the IM server does not necessarily precede IM sessions (e.g. text messaging, file transfer).

Two-party PAKE protocols that use a known server public key (e.g. [14]) have similarities with IMKE. These, as well as two-party password-only protocols (e.g. [4]) may be transformed into a three-party protocol in the following way: run two two-party protocols between the server and each of the users; then use the established secure channel to distribute communication primitives, e.g., public keys among users, thereby providing the communicating users a secure channel. The advantage of this approach is that several PAKE protocols are well-scrutinized, and some even come with *proofs* of security. However, we are interested in more efficient practical protocols, whereas these solutions may require up to three extra messages per protocol run – one for sending a client's public key to the server and two for verifying the public key. Also, even minor modifications to an existing protocol may invalidate its security attributes (not to mention any related security proofs).

---

[3] i.e. authenticating themselves to a trusted server, and each receiving a server-generated client-client session key.

An important idea behind IMKE is to avoid number theoretic relationships between a public key and a password. IMKE uses a known server public key to encrypt a random (session) key (e.g. 128 bits) and uses that key to encrypt the (weak) user-password and the user's dynamic public key. This enables IMKE to avoid partition attacks [4].

In summary, the design of IMKE is inspired by following considerations: (1) existing IM security solutions are inadequate to address IM threats; (2) existing PAKE protocols do not directly fit into the IM communications model; and (3) a lightweight security protocol, which can conveniently be embedded into popular IM protocols without breaking underlying messaging structures, is essential for a greater integration.

3   Setup for IMKE

In this section, we discuss threats considered in IMKE. We list the notation and terminology used, end user goals, and long- and short-term secrets for IMKE.

3.1   Threats Considered in IMKE

We summarize significant IM threats which are addressed by IMKE. We defer a more concrete discussion of the IM threat model to §5.1. IMKE provides no protocol level protection against general software and platform attacks. Further discussion of IM threats is provided elsewhere (e.g. [21]).

IM connections generally involve a client and a server, or two clients. Most IM threats arise from these connections being easily compromised. IMKE aims to provide security (confidentiality, authentication and integrity protection) for all IM connections. Impersonation attacks based on compromised connections are also prevented in IMKE, assuming no theft of users' passwords, including, e.g., through the use of keyloggers. The security related goal of availability is beyond the scope of our work – i.e. denial of service (DoS) attacks against IM clients or the server are not fully addressed by IMKE. However, IMKE helps the server and clients to limit the extent of these attacks. Replay of captured messages (from an ongoing session or older sessions) is also detected in IMKE. An attacker may spoof DNS entries in a user machine (the local DNS cache) to redirect all communications to a rogue IM server. IMKE prevents this attack from being successful by authenticating the IM server to users by using a password, and verifying the known server public key (online). IMKE helps complementary techniques to restrict the propagation of IM worms[4] to be more effective by securing IM connections.

3.2   Notation, Goals and Secrets

We specify IMKE notation and terminology in Table 1. A password is shared between an IM server and a user. This is the only long-term secret for users

---

[4] e.g., throttling file transfer and URL messages, challenging the sender of a file or URL message with an automated Turing test; see [22] for details.

and they choose their initial passwords during the IM account setup. A user may change the password whenever he/she wishes to do so. The server stores original passwords.[5] The other long-term secret is the IM server's private key (for decryption). A server public key generally remains valid for a long time (a year or more), and a key renewal is done by a client-update, i.e. by sending users the updated key when they attempt to log in. Clients' private keys (for decryption), session keys, and MAC keys are short-term secrets in IMKE. We assume that IM clients are installed with the digital certificate of the IM server.

Table 1. Notation and terminology used in IMKE

A, B, S	Two IM users (*Alice* and *Bob* respectively), and the IM server.
ID_A	User ID of A (unique within the IM service domain).
P_A	Password shared by A and S.
R_A	Random number generated by A.
$\{data\}_K$	Symmetric (secret-key) encryption of *data* using key K.
$\{data\}_{E_A}$	Asymmetric (public-key) encryption of *data* using A's public key KU_A.
X, Y	Concatenation of X and Y.
K_{AS}^s	Symmetric (s) session (encryption/decryption) key shared by A and S.
K_{AS}^m	Symmetric MAC key shared by A and S (m is short for MAC).
$[X]_{AS}$	MAC output of data X under key K_{AS}^m.
"Strong" password protocol	A passive or active attacker should be unable to gather enough information to launch an offline dictionary attack even if a relatively *weak* password is used [4].
Secure communications	Communications where authentication, integrity and confidentiality are achieved.
End-to-end security	Securing messages cryptographically across all points between an originating user and the intended recipient.
Repudiation	A way to ensure that the sender of a message *can* (later) deny having sent it. Some [5] believe this is important for casual IM conversations.
Forward secrecy	The property that the compromise of long-term keys does not compromise previously established session keys.

End-user Goals. The following are security-related goals (from end-users' perspectives) in IMKE. Terms denoted by asterisk (∗) are defined in Table 1. Fulfilling the end-user goals corresponds to the threats we consider in §3.1. We outline how IMKE achieves these goals in §5.

G1. Assurance of server's and clients' identities to the communicating parties without exposing clients' passwords to offline dictionary attacks.
G2. Secure communications∗ between a client and the IM server.
G3. Secure communications for messages directly sent between clients (cf. G5).
G4. Forward secrecy and repudiation.∗

---

[5] Alternatively, the server could store only an image or one-way hash of passwords to minimize the impact of the password (image) file exposure, although this typically still does not prevent brute force attacks on passwords.

G5. End-to-end security* for messages that are relayed through the IM server.
G6. Detection of replay attacks on clients and the IM server.

4   The IMKE Protocol

We now introduce the IMKE protocol, along with a discussion on protocol messages. We defer a more specific security analysis of IMKE messages to §5.2.

An IM session (e.g. text messaging) between two users is established in the following phases. A and B first authenticate to the server S, then S distributes A's public key to B and vice-versa, and then the users negotiate a session key to follow an IM session. Table 2 summarizes the protocol messages for these phases. Assume for now that f_i denotes a one-way cryptographic hash function (publicly known, see further discussion below). We describe the protocol messages in the following way: (1) the password authentication and key exchange, and client-server communications, and (2) client-client communications.

Table 2. Summary of IMKE messages (see Table 1 for notation)

Phases	Message Labels	Messages
Authentication and Key Exchange	a1	$A \rightarrow S : ID_A, \{K_{AS}\}_{E_S}, \{KU_A, f_1(P_A)\}_{K_{AS}}$
	a2	$A \leftarrow S : \{R_S\}_{E_A}, \{f_2(P_A)\}_{K_{AS}}$
	a3	$A \rightarrow S : f_3(R_S)$
Public Key Distribution	b1	$A \leftarrow S : \{KU_B, ID_B\}_{K_{AS}^s}, [KU_B, ID_B]_{AS}$
	b2	$B \leftarrow S : \{KU_A, ID_A\}_{K_{BS}^s}, [KU_A, ID_A]_{BS}$
Session Key Transport	c1	$A \rightarrow B : \{K_{AB}\}_{E_B}, \{R_A\}_{K_{AB}}$
	c2	$A \leftarrow B : \{R_B\}_{E_A}, \{f_6(R_A)\}_{K_{AB}}$
	c3	$A \rightarrow B : f_7(R_A, R_B)$

4.1   PAKE and Client-Server Communications

In the PAKE phase, A and S authenticate each other using P_A, establish a secret session key, and transport a verified dynamic public key from A to S. The server's public key KU_S is verified *online*, using e.g., the *public password* [14] method, whereby users verify the hash of the server public key represented in plain English words. Then the login process between A and S proceeds as follows:

1. A generates a dynamic public/private key pair (KU_A, KR_A), and a random symmetric key K_{AS}, and then encrypts K_{AS} with the server's public key. A sends message a1 (see Table 2 for message labels) to S.
2. S calculates $f_1(P_A)$ independently (S looks up P_A using ID_A), compares it with the corresponding value received in a1, and disconnects if they mismatch. Otherwise, S generates a random challenge R_S and responds with a2.

3. A calculates $f_2(P_A)$ independently and compares it with the corresponding value received in $a2$, and disconnects if they mismatch. Otherwise, A calculates the session key (encryption key) K_{AS}^s and MAC key K_{AS}^m as in (4.1), and responds with $a3$.

$$K_{AS}^s = f_4(K_{AS}, R_S), \ K_{AS}^m = f_5(R_S, K_{AS}) \tag{4.1}$$

4. S independently calculates $f_3(R_S)$ and compares it with the quantity received in message $a3$. If they mismatch, S disconnects; otherwise, S also calculates K_{AS}^s and K_{AS}^m as in (4.1). S now indicates A a successful IM client login using a message of the form (4.3).

After authentication, a client and server communications include, e.g., a server sends a user's contact list, a client requests to communicate with other users. To exchange data, A and S use:

$$A \rightarrow S : \{ClientData_A\}_{K_{AS}^s}, [ClientData_A]_{AS} \tag{4.2}$$

$$A \leftarrow S : \{ServerData\}_{K_{AS}^s}, [ServerData]_{AS} \tag{4.3}$$

Caveats. f_1 and f_2 must differ; otherwise, if an attacker can replace KU_S in A's system, he can deceive A without knowing P_A, i.e. the attacker can make A *readily* believe that she is communicating with the legitimate server. Nevertheless, even when f_1 and f_2 differ, replacing KU_S with the attacker's public key in a user's machine enables an offline dictionary attack on P_A. Having different f_1 and f_2 makes the attacker's active participation in the protocol harder.

R_S and K_{AS} must be large enough (e.g. 128-bit) to withstand an exhaustive search. A must encrypt KU_A in message $a1$. Otherwise the following attack may succeed. Suppose an adversary generates a new private-public key pair, and is able to replace KU_A with the fraudulent public key in message $a1$; this enables the adversary to decrypt R_S in $a2$ and send a correct reply to S in $a3$. Hence, IMKE requires the secrecy of A's public key in the PAKE phase. Examples of secret "public keys" exist in the literature (e.g. [13]). At the end of the PAKE phase, A and S zero out K_{AS} and R_S from the program memory to help in achieving forward secrecy (see §5.3).

The duration of the session key (K_{AS}^s) should be set carefully. This is important for clients in an *always-connected* mode, wherein clients stay logged in to S for a long period of time (e.g. days or weeks). A new session key should be negotiated after a certain period (e.g. a couple of hours) depending on the expected security level and size of the session key (e.g. a shorter period for 80-bit keys than 128-bit keys) to reduce consequences from cryptographic (e.g. brute-force) attacks on the key. To do so, A and S exchange two random values K_{AS1} and R_{S1} in the following way and generate the new session key and MAC key as before (cf. (4.1)). Either A or S can begin the key renewal process. The initiator must stop sending any messages before the new keys are established.

$$A \rightarrow S : \{\{K_{AS1}\}_{E_S}\}_{K_{AS}^s}, [\{K_{AS1}\}_{E_S}]_{AS} \tag{4.4}$$

$$A \leftarrow S : \{\{R_{S1}\}_{E_A}\}_{K_{AS}^s}, [\{R_{S1}\}_{E_A}]_{AS} \tag{4.5}$$

4.2   Client-Client Communications (Direct and Relayed)

Client to client communications include, e.g., server mediated/relayed messages, file transfer, audio/video chat. If A wants to send $ClientData_A$ to B (both must be logged in to S), she first sends her request to communicate with B to S (using message type (4.2)), and then the messages below follow:

1. A and B receive the other party's current dynamic public key from S through messages $b1$ and $b2$. Note that B and S authenticate each other and derive K_{BS}^s and K_{BS}^m in the analogous way described above for A.
2. Having each other's current public key, A and B exchange messages $c1$, $c2$ and $c3$. Then A and B derive the session key K_{AB}^s and MAC key K_{AB}^m:

$$K_{AB}^s = f_8(K_{AB}, R_B), \ K_{AB}^m = f_9(R_B, K_{AB}) \qquad (4.6)$$

3. Now, A sends $ClientData_A$ to B:

$$A \to B : \{ClientData_A\}_{K_{AB}^s}, [ClientData_A]_{AB} \qquad (4.7)$$

Caveats. Although client-to-client connection setup messages ($c1$, $c2$ and $c3$) can be exchanged directly between A and B, we suggest they be relayed through the server using messages (4.2, 4.3) – i.e. with the additional encryption and MAC – to reduce threats from DoS attacks on clients. However, while relaying the setup messages, a malicious IM server can launch a typical man-in-the-middle attack in the following way. When A notifies S that she wants to communicate with B, S generates a public key pair for B and distributes the rogue public key to A, and vice-versa. Now S can impersonate A to B and vice-versa, and thereby view or modify messages exchanged between the users. Apparently, if users exchange the connection setup messages directly, this attack could be avoided; but, if A and B get each other's network address for direct communication from S (which is the most usual case), then this attack is still possible. The attack is made possible – albeit detectable (see below) – by the facts that, (1) pairs of users do not share any long-term secret, and (2) they do not use any authenticated (long-term) public key. Note that, this is an *active attack* where the server needs to participate in a protocol run online.

In general, IM accounts are anonymous, i.e. users can get an IM account without giving explicit identification information to the server.[6] Therefore, the motivation to launch the aforementioned man-in-the-middle attack against random users appears less rewarding for the server. In a public IM service, if the server launches this attack against any pair of users, the attack could be exposed, e.g., if that pair attempts to verify their (per-login session) public keys through, e.g., a dynamically updated web site or another service. In contrast, if using SSL (see §1), the server has direct access to end-user content, and such an attack is not necessary. Complex methods, e.g., the *interlock* protocol [29], may

---

[6] From the IP address of a particular user, the server may be able to retrieve the user's location in many cases (e.g. [26]), and thereby associate an IM account to some (albeit indirect) identifying attributes of a real-world user.

also be considered to expose an intruding server. An area of future research is how to reduce the trust assumptions required on the server, and yet still have an efficient relaying protocol.

At the end of the session key transport (i.e. after $c3$), A and B also zero out ephemeral values R_A, R_B and K_{AB} from the program memory. Message (4.7) is used to send $ClientData_A$ directly from A to B. For relaying data through the server, the same message type can be used. If two clients communicate for a long time (in a session), they may re-negotiate a session key (and a MAC key) in a similar way as described for the client-server key renewal.

5   Security Analysis

In this section, we provide a partial BAN-like [7] analysis intended to provide a baseline of confidence in the security of IMKE. The setup for our analysis, and other security properties of IMKE are also discussed. While BAN analysis is somewhat informal in certain aspects and is well-known to have shortcomings (e.g. [6]), it is nonetheless helpful in explaining the reasonings behind security beliefs of protocol designers, and often leads to security flaws being uncovered. However, a more rigorous security analysis as well as a *proof* of security of IMKE using alternate (non-BAN) techniques would be preferable to provide supplementary confidence. (Note however, that such a proof does not necessarily guarantee security; see Koblitz and Menezes [17] for an interesting analysis of *provable security.*) We thus consider the BAN-like analysis to be a first step.

As an important additional confidence-building analysis step, we have had the protocol tested[7] using the AVISPA (Automated Validation of Internet Security Protocols and Applications) [1] formal analysis tool. The AVISPA tool claims to be a push-button, industrial-strength technology for the analysis of large-scale Internet security-sensitive protocols and applications. The tool did not to find any attack against IMKE.

5.1   Setup for the Analysis

Table 3 lists definitions used in the IMKE analysis (borrowed in part from Burrows et al. [7]). Table 4 lists the technical sub-goals of IMKE which are, although idealized, more concrete and specific than the end-user goals (recall §3.2), and are of the type which can be verified from a BAN analysis point of view. The analysis in §5.2 shows how IMKE achieves the technical sub-goals, and leading to the end-user goals. We also provide operational assumptions and an informal IM threat model for IMKE.

IM Threat Model and Operational Assumptions. A *threat model* identifies the threats a system is designed to counter, the nature of relevant classes of attackers (including their expected attack approaches and resources, e.g., techniques, tools, computational power, geographic access), as well as other environmental assumptions. This IM threat model is not what would typically be

---

[7] Test code is available at http://www.scs.carleton.ca/~mmannan/avispa-imke/

Table 3. BAN-like definitions used in the IMKE analysis

A *believes* X	User A behaves as if X is true.
A *once said* X	User A at some past time sent a message including X.
X is *fresh*	A message X is said to be *fresh* if (with very high probability) it has not been sent in a message at any time before the current protocol execution.
A *controls* X	User A is an authority on X (she has *jurisdiction* over X) and should be trusted on this matter.

Table 4. Technical sub-goals of IMKE

T1. A and S believe that they share a (secret) password P_A.*

T2. A believes that she is communicating (in real-time) with a other party that knows S's private key.

T3. S believes that it is communicating (in real-time) with a other party that knows A's private key.

T4. A believes that she is communicating (in real-time) with a other party that knows B's private key.

T5. B believes that he is communicating (in real-time) with a other party that knows A's private key.

T6. A and S believe that they share a (secret) session key and a MAC key.

T7. A and B believe that they share a (secret) session key and a MAC key.

---

* See assumption A1 below; this goal is fulfilled when both parties demonstrate knowledge of the pre-established password P_A.

expected of a *formalized* (academic) threat model, but it nonetheless provides a practically useful and clear definition of what types of attacks we intend that IMKE provides protection against. Now we list the IM threat model assumptions.

M1. The IM client software is *trusted*. By *trusted* we mean the IM client software has not been tampered with and the underlying operating system protects the IM client's memory space (RAM and virtual memory) from other programs (including malicious programs). This assumption is required as ephemeral secret keys are stored in the program memory.

M2. Communications between IM servers are secure using e.g., encryption and MAC. IMKE does not provide security for server-to-server messaging.

M3. Software and hardware keyloggers are not installed in a client system.

M4. Clients' keys stay only in program memory which are zeroed out while terminating the program.

M5. The server public key stored in client machines is verified at each login attempt (using e.g. the *public password* method [14]).

M6. Underlying communication channels need not be secure; attackers are assumed capable of viewing, altering, inserting and deleting any bitstream transfered from IM clients or servers.

M7. We consider *realistic attackers* [14] who can exhaustively search over a password dictionary (e.g. 2^{64} computational steps) but cannot defeat (in a reasonable amount of time) the cryptographic primitives (e.g. 2^{80} computational steps) used in the protocol.

We provide a few additional comments related to the above assumptions. Modern operating systems provide reasonable protection for process-memory spaces; yet, accessing a process's memory from the context of a compromised privileged (*root* or *administrator*) process is not difficult [2]. Zeroing out memory-resident secrets is not trivial [11] as well. An attacker can capture a user's password using a keylogger, i.e. a program or hardware device specialized in (secretly) recording keystrokes. Very few, if any, security guarantees can be provided in environments susceptible to keyloggers. However, threats from keyloggers are not insignificant. Also, attackers may collect passwords using social engineering techniques. Therefore, meeting the threat model assumptions in reality is not trivial. Nonetheless, these challenges are faced by many security protocols in practice. We now list operational assumptions of IMKE.

A1. Each IM user shares a user-chosen password only with the legitimate IM server (e.g. established *a priori* using out-of-band methods), and the password is not stored long-term on the user machine.

A2. The IM server's valid, authentic public key is known to all parties.

A3. Each party controls the private key for each public key pair they generate, i.e. the private key is not known or available to other parties.

A4. IMKE clients use fresh keys and challenge values where specified by the protocol, e.g., they do not intentionally reuse old values.

A5. The IM server relays clients' public keys correctly.

5.2   Analysis of IMKE Messages

We analyze IMKE messages and their possible implications in different phases of the protocol run. Refer to the earlier protocol description (§4) for the actions each party takes upon receiving a message. We start by analyzing message $a1$ (recall the message labels in Table 2). Upon successful verification of $f_1(P_A)$ by S, the locally calculated $f_1(P_A)$ by S is the same as the $f_1(P_A)$ retrieved from $a1$. Message $a1$ thus implies the following. (1) A believes that K_{AS} and KU_A are fresh, as they are freshly generated by herself. (2) Before the protocol run, S knows that it shares P_A with A. Here, S gains the evidence that the keys K_{AS} and KU_A which message $a1$ links to P_A, were generated by and associated with A. Hence, S believes the identity of A, which partially satisfies goal **T1**. (3) S believes that A once said that K_{AS} and KU_A are fresh. (4) S believes that A has a valid copy of its public key KU_S.

The successful verification of message $a2$ means that the locally calculated $f_2(P_A)$ by A is the same as the $f_2(P_A)$ decrypted from $a2$. This implies the following. (1) A believes that S knows P_A, thus satisfying goal **T1**. (2) Knowing the private key KR_S enables S to decrypt K_{AS} and KU_A in message $a1$. S encrypts $f_2(P_A)$ using K_{AS}; hence, the successful verification of $f_2(P_A)$ by A implies that A is communicating (in the current protocol run) with a party that knows S's private key, thus satisfying goal **T2**. (3) A believes that the current message $a2$ is fresh as KU_A is fresh; this provides assurance to A that the current protocol run is not a replay. (4) A believes that S once said that R_S is fresh.

The successful verification of message $a3$ by S means that the locally calculated $f_3(R_S)$ by S is the same as received in $a3$. This and the login success response from S to A imply the following. (1) S receives the evidence that A knows her private key KR_A, otherwise A could not decrypt R_S in message $a2$. Hence, goal **T3** is established. (2) The current message $a3$ is fresh as R_S is fresh; this guarantees S that the current protocol run is not a replay. (3) In message $a2$, A retrieves R_S using her dynamic private key for the current protocol run. At this point only S has a copy of A's public key. Therefore from the login success message, A believes that S possesses a valid copy of KU_A. (4) As both A and S derive the session key K^s_{AS} and MAC key K^m_{AS} from their ephemeral shared secrets (K_{AS} and R_S), goal **T6** is achieved.

From messages $b1$ and $b2$, A and B get each other's public keys from S securely. In $b1$, A receives the public key of B (KU_B) encrypted under the shared key K^s_{AS} providing confidentiality of KU_B. Also, the MAC in $b1$ provides integrity of KU_B. Message $b2$ provides similar guarantees to B for A's public key.

The successful verification of messages $c1$, $c2$ and $c3$ implies the following. (1) A believes that she shares K_{AB} with B, as only B could decrypt R_A in $c1$ and respond with a function of R_A in $c2$. (2) B believes that he shares K_{AB} with A, because only A knows KR_A which is necessary to recover R_B for use in message $c3$, and the chain of messages links R_B with R_A, and R_A back to K_{AB}. (3) A and B achieve some assurance of freshness through the random challenges R_A and R_B respectively. (4) A and B receive each other's public keys securely from a trusted source S (in messages $b1$ and $b2$). The successful verification of message $c2$ provides the evidence to A that B knows the private key corresponding to B's public key which A received earlier from S, thus satisfying goal **T4**. Message $c3$, when verified, provides the similar evidence to B, thus satisfying goal **T5**. (5) A and B derive the session key K^s_{AB} and the MAC key K^m_{AB} from their ephemeral shared secrets (K_{AB} and R_B), thus goal **T7** is achieved.

Satisfying End-user Goals. We now provide informal reasonings regarding how end-users' goals (recall §3.2) are satisfied. We argue that in the PAKE phase of IMKE, it is computationally infeasible to launch offline dictionary attacks on P_A (assuming our assumptions in §5.1 are not violated). To recover $f_1(P_A)$ from $a1$, an attacker apparently has to guess K_{AS}, which is computationally infeasible if K_{AS} is generated from a large key space (e.g. 128-bit). Another way to recover $f_1(P_A)$ is to learn K_{AS} by guessing the server's private key. Brute-force attacks on K_{AS} or KR_S appear to be computationally infeasible if the key length is chosen appropriately. To recover $f_2(P_A)$ from $a2$, an attacker must guess K_{AS}, which is infeasible. This apparently makes P_A resistant to offline dictionary attacks. As goal T1 is fulfilled in messages $a1$ and $a2$ without exposing P_A to offline dictionary attacks, IMKE achieves goal **G1**. Goal T6 establishes that A and S achieve confidentiality, and integrity (with authentication) using the secret session key K_{AS}^s and the MAC key K_{AS}^m respectively. Technical sub-goal T6, along with G1, now satisfies goal **G2**.

A and B do not authenticate each other directly. They trust the other party's identity as they receive each other's public key from S and trust S on the authenticity of those public keys. Thus fulfilling sub-goals T4, T5 and T7 provides A and B a way to communicate securely and satisfies goal **G3**.

Message authentication between A and B is achieved by MACs, instead of digital signatures. The same session and MAC keys are shared between A and B, which provide confidentiality and authentication of the messages exchanged. Any message created by A can also be created by B. Therefore the sender of a message can *repudiate* generating and sending the message. Clients' public keys are also temporary, hence binding an IM identity with a real user is technically impossible. The confidentiality of communications channels between users is protected by session keys generated from random nonces, instead of users' long-term secrets; so, the exposure of long-term secrets does not compromise past session keys. Thus repudiation and forward secrecy (goal **G4**) of users' messages are achieved (for more discussion on forward secrecy see §5.3). Direct or relayed messages (cf. message type (4.7)) between A and B are encrypted with K_{AB}^s, which is shared only between A and B (goal T7). Therefore S (or other malicious parties) cannot decrypt them, and thus goal **G5** is apparently satisfied.

If message $a1$ is replayed to a server by an attacker, the attacker cannot decrypt message $a2$ without knowing A's private key and K_{AS}. If message $a2$ is replayed to A by an attacker in a separate run of IMKE, A will refuse to reply with $a3$ as she will fail to decrypt $f_2(P_A)$ (A randomly generates K_{AS} in each run of the protocol). After A has successfully logged in to the server, A receives only messages of type (4.3) from S. Therefore, if message $a2$ is replayed to A after she logs in, A can readily detect the replay, and discard that message. If message $c1$ is replayed to B by an adversary, the adversary gains no useful information from B's reply in message $c2$. To detect replay attacks in data messages, $ClientData_A$ and $ServerData$ are appended/prepended with time-stamps or sequence numbers, with appropriate checks by the receiver (e.g. [24, p.417–418]). Freshly generated session keys and clients' public keys help in detecting replays from earlier protocol runs. Hence, goal **G6** is apparently satisfied.

Hence we have provided informal sketches of how end-user goals are satisfied.

5.3   Other Security Attributes of IMKE

Below we discuss a few more security attributes of IMKE. These properties make IMKE resistant to several recently devised attacks on security protocols.

Chaining of Messages. In the PAKE phase, messages $a1$ and $a2$ are cryptographically linked by KU_A, and messages $a2$ and $a3$ are cryptographically linked by R_S. Moreover, both KU_A and R_S are dynamically generated in each protocol run. According to Diffie et al. [12] this kind of the chaining of protocol messages may prevent *replay* and *interleaving* attacks.

Insider-Assisted Attacks. If either of A or B is a rogue user[8] participating in IMKE, we need to guard against the following attack: A or B learns the password of the other party, and the session keys that they share with other users. In IMKE, users never receive a protocol message containing any element related to other users' passwords or session keys; thus, IMKE avoids these insider-assisted attacks even when IMKE assumptions are violated by malicious users.

Exposure of Secrets. IMKE provides forward secrecy (see Table 1 for definition) as the disclosure of a client-server password (long-term secret keying material) does not compromise the secrecy of the exchanged session keys from protocol runs (using that password) before the exposure. Exposure of the IM server's long term private key allows an attacker to launch offline dictionary attacks on $f_1(P_A)$ although the attacker cannot compromise the session key or readily impersonate S. If the session key K_{AS}^s between A and S is exposed, an attacker cannot learn P_A. However, the disclosure of an ephemeral key K_{AS} (which is supposed to be zeroed out from the program memory after the PAKE phase) enables an offline dictionary attack on $f_1(P_A)$. Although the disclosure of A's dynamic private key (which exists in the program memory as long as A remains logged in[9]) enables an attacker to reply correctly in message $a3$, IMKE still provides forward secrecy.

When both the IM server's long term private key and a user's dynamic private key are exposed, an attacker can calculate the session key from the collected messages of a successful protocol run; in this case, the notion of forward secrecy breaks (for the targeted session).

In addition, IMKE is (apparently) also resistant to the *Denning-Sacco attack* [10], *many-to-many guessing attack* [18] etc. as discussed elsewhere [23].

6   Concluding Remarks

IMKE enables private and secure communications between two users who share no authentication tokens, mediated by a server on the Internet. The session key used for message encryption in IMKE is derived from short-lived *fresh* secrets, instead of any long-term secrets. This provides the confidence of forward secrecy to IMKE users. IMKE allows authentication of exchanged messages between two parties, and the sender is able to repudiate a message. Also, IMKE users require no hardware tokens or long-term user public keys to log in to the IM server.

Group-chat and chat-room [21] are heavily used features in IM. A future version of IMKE would ideally accommodate these features, as well as an online server public key verification method. Introducing methods to ensure human-in-the-loop during login, e.g., challenging with an automated Turing test, can stop

---

[8] For example, someone who, maliciously or naively, exposes his/her private key, password, or session/MAC keys.

[9] Private keys may easily be extracted from memory as Shamir and van Someren [32] outlined, if the operating system allows reading the entire memory space by any program. However, we assume that such an operation is not allowed; see assumption M1 in §5.1.

automated impersonation using compromised user name and password. However, deploying such a method for large IM networks may put an enormous load on IM servers; measures as outlined by Pinkas and Sander [27] can help minimize this.

The growing number of IM users in public and enterprise world provides evidence that IM is increasingly affecting instant user-communication over the Internet. We strongly advocate that security of IM systems should be taken seriously. IMKE is a step towards secure public IM systems. Note that typical end-users of IM systems are casual. A secure IM protocol, implemented in a restrictive user interface, might force such casual users to switch to a competing product that is less secure but more user-friendly. We emphasize that usability issues must be considered while designing a secure IM system.

Acknowledgements

We thank anonymous reviewers, as well as Liam Peyton, for their constructive comments which helped us improve the quality of this paper, and all members of Carleton's Digital Security Group for their enthusiastic discussions on this topic, especially Glenn Wurster, Anil Somayaji and Julie Thorpe. We thank Paul H. Drielsma of ETH, Zurich for carrying out a security analysis of IMKE using AVISPA [1]. The first author is partly supported by a Public Safety and Emergency Preparedness Canada (PSEPC) scholarship. The second author is Canada Research Chair in Network and Software Security, and is supported in part by an NSERC Discovery Grant, the Canada Research Chairs Program, and MITACS.

References

1. A. Armando et al. The AVISPA tool for the automated validation of Internet security protocols and applications. In *Computer Aided Verification - CAV 2005*, volume 3576 of *LNCS*, 2005. Project website, http://www.avispa-project.org.
2. R. Battistoni, E. Gabrielli, and L. V. Mancini. A host intrusion prevention system for Windows operating systems. In *ESORICS'04*, 2004.
3. M. Bellare and P. Rogaway. Provably secure session key distribution: the three party case. In *ACM Symposium on Theory of Computing (STOC '95)*, 1995.
4. S. Bellovin and M. Merritt. Encrypted Key Exchange: Password-based protocols secure against dictionary attacks. In *IEEE Symp. on Security and Privacy*, 1992.
5. N. Borisov, I. Goldberg, and E. Brewer. Off-the-record communication, or, why not to use PGP. In *ACM Workshop on Privacy in the Electronic Society*, 2004.
6. C. Boyd and W. Mao. On a limitation of BAN logic. In *Eurocrypt 1993*, volume 765 of *LNCS*, 1993.
7. M. Burrows, M. Abadi, and R. Needham. A logic of authentication. In *ACM Symposium on Operating Systems Principles*, 1989.
8. S. M. Cherry. IM means business. *IEEE Spectrum Online*, 39:28–32, Nov. 2002.
9. ComputerWorld staff. Instant Messaging takes 'financial' twist, Apr. 2002. News article, http://www.computerworld.com/.
10. D. E. Denning and G. M. Sacco. Timestamps in key distribution protocols. *Comm. ACM*, 24(8):533–536, 1981.

11. G. Di Crescenzo, N. Ferguson, R. Impagliazzo, and M. Jakobsson. How to forget a secret (extended abstract). In *STACS '99*, volume 1563 of *LNCS*, 1999.
12. W. Diffie, P. C. van Oorschot, and M. J. Wiener. Authentication and authenticated key exchanges. *Designs, Codes and Cryptography*, 2(2):107–125, 1992.
13. L. Gong, M. A. Lomas, R. M. Needham, and J. H. Saltzer. Protecting poorly chosen secrets from guessing attacks. *IEEE Selected Areas in Comm.*, 11(5), 1993.
14. S. Halevi and H. Krawczyk. Public-key cryptography and password protocols. *ACM Transactions on Information and Systems Security*, 2(3):230–268, 1999.
15. IT Strategy Center Staff. The coming IM threat, May 2005. News article, `http://www.itstrategycenter.com/itworld/Threat/viruses/coming_im_threat`.
16. H. Kikuchi, M. Tada, and S. Nakanishi. Secure Instant Messaging protocol preserving confidentiality against administrator. In *Advanced Information Networking and Applications (AINA'04)*, 2004.
17. N. Koblitz and A. Menezes. Another look at "provable security". *Journal of Cryptology (to appear, 2006)*.
18. T. Kwon. Practical authenticated key agreement using passwords. In *Information Security - ISC 2004*, volume 3225 of *LNCS*, 2004.
19. L. Law, A. Menezes, M. Qu, J. Solinas, and S. Vanstone. An efficient protocol for authenticated key agreement. *Designs, Codes and Cryptography*, 28(2), 2003.
20. P. D. MacKenzie, S. Patel, and R. Swaminathan. Password-authenticated key exchange based on RSA. In *Asiacrypt 2000*, volume 1976 of *LNCS*, 2000.
21. M. Mannan and P. C. van Oorschot. Secure public Instant Messaging: A survey. In *Privacy, Security and Trust (PST'04)*, 2004.
22. M. Mannan and P. C. van Oorschot. On Instant Messaging worms, analysis and countermeasures. In *ACM Workshop on Rapid Malcode (WORM'05)*, 2005.
23. M. Mannan and P. C. van Oorschot. A protocol for secure public Instant Messaging (extended version). Technical Report TR-06-01, Jan. 2006.
24. A. Menezes, P. C. van Oorschot, and S. Vanstone. *Handbook of Applied Cryptography*. CRC Press, 1996.
25. Open Source. Gaim-e. `http://gaim-e.sourceforge.net/`.
26. V. N. Padmanabhan and L. Subramanian. An investigation of geographic mapping techniques for Internet hosts. *ACM Computer Comm. Review*, 31(4), 2001.
27. B. Pinkas and T. Sander. Securing passwords against dictionary attacks. In *ACM Computer and Communications Security*, 2002.
28. P. Riikonen. Secure Internet Live Conferencing (SILC), protocol specification, Feb. 2004. Internet-Draft. `http://www.silcnet.org/docs/draft-riikonen-silc-spec-08.txt`.
29. R. L. Rivest and A. Shamir. How to expose an eavesdropper. *Comm. ACM*, 27(4):393–394, 1984.
30. P. Saint-Andre. Extensible messaging and presence protocol (XMPP): Core, Oct. 2004. RFC 3920, Status: Standards Track. `http://www.ietf.org/rfc/rfc3920.txt`.
31. SecurityPark.net Staff. Instant messaging: communications godsend or security back door?, July 2005. News article, `http//www.securitypark.co.uk/`.
32. A. Shamir and N. van Someren. Playing 'hide and seek' with stored keys. In *Financial Cryptography - FC '99*, volume 1648 of *LNCS*, 1999.

Using Automated Banking Certificates to Detect Unauthorised Financial Transactions

C. Corzo[1], F. Corzo S.[2], N. Zhang[1], and A. Carpenter[1]

[1] School of Computer Science, the University of Manchester,
Manchester M13 9PL, UK
{ccorzo, nzhang, acarpenter}@cs.man.ac.uk
[2] Universidad Escuela Colombiana de Ingeniería
fcorzos@escuelaing.edu.co

Abstract. New or emerging technologies such as e-services, e-/m-commerce, Cyber-payment, mobile banking and pay-as-you-go insurance services are opening up new avenues for criminals to commit computer-related financial fraud and online abuse. This serious situation has been evidenced by the UK Information Security Breach Survey 2004 and the UK National Hi-Tech Crime Unit's recent report, "Hi-Tech Crime: The Impact On UK Business[1]". It highlights that online financial fraud is one of the most serious e-crimes and takes the lion's share of over 60% of e-crime costs, and most of the financial fraud cases are committed by authorised insiders. Authorised insiders can more easily break the security barrier of a bank or a financial institution due to their operating privileges on the banking automated systems. Failure to detect such cases promptly can lead to (sometimes huge) financial loses and damage the reputation of financial institutions. This paper introduces a real-time fraud detection solution - the Transaction Authentication Service (TAS) - to tackle the problem of transaction manipulation by authorised insiders. The paper also introduces an important building block used in the design of TAS, Automated Banking Certificates (ABCs).

Keywords: Data integrity, financial fraud, Insider threats, Security architecture.

1 Introduction

With the increasing popularity of the Internet and Information Technology (IT), nearly all the sectors, such as the public, the retail and the banking and financial sectors, are adopting e-services and improving their Internet presence. Electronic financial services reduce costs, increase operational efficiency, and allow banking institutions to reach out to more customers. However, the e-service provisions are also opening up new avenues for criminals to commit computer-related financial fraud and online abuse. This serious situation has been evidenced by the UK Information Security Breach Survey 2004 and the UK National Hi-Tech Crime Unit's recent report, "Hi-Tech Crime: The Impact On UK Business[1]". It highlights that online financial fraud is one of the most serious e-crimes and takes the lion's share of over 60% of e-crime costs, and most of the financial fraud cases are committed by authorised insiders. This is because authorised users (e.g. banking employees) are assets and have the

---

[1] http://www.nhtcu.org/

G. Di Crescenzo and A. Rubin (Eds.): FC 2006, LNCS 4107, pp. 36–51, 2006.
© IFCA/Springer-Verlag Berlin Heidelberg 2006

privileges to access and operate on automated banking systems and to perform financial transactions using financial services provided by these systems. At the same time, they are also threats and in the position to more easily break any security barrier implemented in these systems and services [3]. In addition, the nature of e-services allows more fraudulent transactions to be performed within a given time period in comparison with manual ways of performing transactions. Each year, billions of pounds are lost in the banking sector due to fraud committed by authorised insiders through the exploitation of system vulnerabilities [2]. Therefore, more effective security measures are needed to detect promptly fraudulent or erroneous financial transactions performed by authorised users and to ensure transaction integrity.

In existing e-transaction systems, a transaction is said to be 'authentic' (1) if it is performed by an authorised entity (hardware, software or user), (2) if it has not been altered since it was generated, and (3) if it is not a replay of an earlier valid transaction. By this definition, an illegitimate transaction (e.g. an unauthorised transaction performed to launder dirty money) performed by an authorised user (e.g. a bank employee) will be regarded as authentic. In current banking systems, such transactions can only be identified by an audit that is usually executed after the transactions have already taken place. A more effective solution to fight against these fraudulent transactions performed by authorised insiders would be a real-time mechanism that can identify inconsistencies in transactions and detect them while they are taking place. This paper introduces such a solution, called Transaction Authentication Service (TAS). It makes use of Automated Banking Certificates (ABCs) – integrity protected transaction audit trails – and the workflow technology to ensure that any malicious or accidental alteration or manipulation of any of the transactions in a set entered by authorised users can be detected promptly.

In detail, the next section of this paper provides background on cryptographic primitives and security techniques which are used for the TAS design. In Section 3, notation and an example using the notation is presented. Section 4 provides identification of security breaches in banking transaction processes. In Section 5 the idea and the design requirements of an ABC are described. Section 6 gives the design of two types of ABC, intra-system and inter-system ABCs, and finally, the conclusion of the work is given in section 7.

2   Cryptographic Primitives and Security Techniques

This section gives an overview of the cryptographic primitives and security techniques that are used in the design of ABCs and TAS.

2.1   User Identification and Data Authentication

Traditionally, in order to prove that a transaction is authentic (i.e. the transaction is originated from an authorised entity, the data in the transaction has not been altered since it was created, and the transaction is not a replay of an earlier transaction), two authentication measures are required. One is the user identity authentication [16], and the other is data authentication [18].

User identity authentication is necessary to ensure that a transaction has come from a claimed source or performed by a claimed originator. This is typically done by having the user to demonstrate the possession/knowledge of a secret (e.g. a password or a private key) or possession of a smart token locked with a PIN (personal identification number) or some biometrics (e.g. fingerprint). This user identity authentication mechanism is used to help to prevent an *unauthorised* user from accessing a system/service and/or performing a transaction.

Data (or *message*) *authentication* is typically achieved by appending to the original message an authenticator, which is generated using a secret shared between the sender and the receiver, or a digital signature signed by the transaction originator. The authenticator is a function of the data in the transaction as well as the secret (or the signature key). When the authenticator and the message are received, the receiver calculates a fresh authenticator using the secret (or recovers the hash value in the signature) and the data received, and then compares this freshly computed authenticator (or the hash value) with the one received (or recovered). If both values are equal, then the data is said to be faithful to the one originated from the sender, and therefore the transaction is said to be authentic. The data authentication method is used to detect counterfeit or altered messages. If the transaction has been manipulated at source prior to being transmitted by the authorised sender, then this authentication method cannot detect the fraudulent manipulation.

The above discussions state that the user identity and message authentication methods can not detect fraudulent transactions manipulated at source by the authorised sender.

2.2 One Way Collision Free Hash Functions

The first person to prove the existence of collision free hash functions was Damgard [4]. A one-way collision free hash function is an algorithm that transforms data of any length into a fixed length data known as the hash value (or Message Digest). A hash value is like a checksum of a block of data. It should be one-way in that, given a hash value, it is nearly impossible to recover the data that produced the given hash value. In other words, it is computationally infeasible (i.e. it would take a very long time, e.g. hundreds of years, using a fast available computer) to invert the transformation. Moreover, an impostor should not be able to generate two sets of different data that would generate the same hash value [4, 17]. This property is called collision-free. A hash function possessing both one-way and collision-free properties is usually called a cryptographic (secure) hash function. However, it is important to highlight that some but not all hash functions have been broken by collision as shown in [20].

A cryptographic hash, with no current security function which can replace its functionality, has many uses in security arena. For instance, its one-way property can be used for password confidentiality preventing clear-text passwords having to be stored in a computer system [9]. Instead of storing a password in clear-text, the hash value of a password is stored instead. A user of an operating system where a password authentication method is implemented first enters a clear-text password. Then this clear-text password is used as the input of a one-way collision free hash function to generate the hash value of the password. The hash value is then compared to the authentic password hash value stored in the system. In this way, clear-text passwords are not exposed during transmission or in storage. This scheme provides password confidentiality allowing a user to prove the knowledge of a secret (i.e. the password) without exposing the secret. This method, however, does have one disadvantage, i.e. if an (authorised) entity, e.g. the system administrator, is able to add an entry for an unauthorised user, then the user, even if he/she is unauthorised, will still be able to access the system. In other words, without additional security control, this simple hashed password solution can prevent (to some extent) unauthorised accesses by external entities, but it can not protect the system against manipulation or threats imposed by authorised insiders (i.e. the system administrator).

In addition, a cryptographic hash function, jointly with the use of a symmetric key, can be used to generate a message authenticator, as mentioned in Section 2.1. For example, as initially proposed by Tsudik [16], a message (M) to be protected, and a secret key (K) shared by a group of authorised entities, are concatenated and then hashed to produce a key hashed value, HV, i.e. HV=hash(M∥K), where ∥ stands for concatenation. This scheme imposes some control in that only the entities with the knowledge of the secret key could generate an authentic hash value. However, due to the nature of the symmetric key cryptosystem, namely, more than one entities sharing the same key, the scheme does not protect against false denials that an event has actually taken place.

In systems dealing with e-transactions, the non-repudiation (i.e. protection against repudiation) security property is essential. A popular security service used to provide non-repudiation is a digital signature.

2.3 Digital Signatures

A digital signature is a signed digest typically used for entity identification and authentication. It can also be used for proof of message authenticity. In comparison with keyed hash values, this authentication method is slower, but can protect against non-repudiation. Digital signatures are implemented using an asymmetric cryptosystem [8]. In an asymmetrical cryptosystem, two matching keys are required per user; one of the key pair is privately held, and the other is made public (usually through the use of public key certificates). For example, if Ann is an entity then she is the only one that knows her private key, whereas all the communicating parties have access to her public key. The private key can be used by Ann to sign her signature on a message. The counterpart, say Bob, uses Ann's matching public key to verify if the message is indeed from the claimed sender, i.e. Ann, and that the message has not been changed during transit. This idea, first introduced by Diffie and Hellman [7], can be summarized as follows. If Ann needs to sign some data, M, she uses her private key Kr_{Ann} to generate a signed token, CT, on the hashed value of M with her private key, i.e. $CT=E_{KrAnn}(hash(M))$ (for the sake of simplicity, here we assume that some other essential information such as time stamps and the identity of the signer are also part of message M). Ann then sends the M together with token, CT, to Bob. Bob checks the message by using Ann's public key. If the authentication procedure is successful then Ann cannot easily repudiate that she is the author of the message because she is the only one who knows the private key.

Digitally signing the hash value of M, instead of signing the entire message M, has several advantages [5]. The major advantage is that the signing process is made more efficient because the hash value of some data is in most cases smaller in length than the original data, thus improving the response time of the digital signature signing process. With public key cryptosystems, a trusted third party is required in order to certify that the public key is the one that indeed belongs to Ann (i.e. it is a trustworthy public key and Ann has the matching private key). The first working asymmetric cryptosystem was proposed by Rivest, Shamir and Adleman [15], i.e. the so called RSA algorithm. Though a digital signature can provide message integrity, authenticity and non-repudiation protections, it along may not be sufficient where integrity is required for a group of inter-related messages as a whole. In other words, when a group of messages should be verified to determine if any of the messages in the group has been changed, deleted or omitted from the group, an additional mechanism is required. Interleaving data structures is such a mechanism that can be used for this purpose.

2.4 Interleaving Data Structures

Interleaving data structures [1] link two or more data in a group. It is important to define boundaries of this group. For example, the group can be defined as all data generated during one day by an automated financial system. An interleaving data structure provides integrity protection to a group of data so that any changes to the group can be detected.

Audit trail files frequently use interleaving data structures [1]. One strategy used to interleave data is to include bits from the previous created data so that a sequence is produced. For example, let us say that we have three data structures, named as data2, data3 and data4, and each data structure contains three fields. The first field contains a sequence number assigned to the data record of the data structure. The second field contains the data record of this data structure. Let us say, X, R, and U are the records of data2, data3, and data4, respectively. The third field contains the sequence number of the preceding data structure. Thus, we have, data2= {M, X, M-1}, data3= {M+1, R, M}, data4= {M+2, U, M+1}. In this way, if data3 is deleted from the audit log file then we can detect that there is a missing data record by observing the sequence on data4 and the sequence on data2. Equally, if a new unauthorised data record is inserted into the group, then this new record will not have the sequence number matching with the rest of the records, and the unauthorised data record can be detected. Therefore, we say that the interleaving data structure provides us with a means to protect the integrity of a set of data.

2.5 Digital Time Stamping

In our solution to be presented shortly, we use a time stamping scheme similar to that presented by Haber and Stornetta in [10]. The authors proposed to design an interleaving data structure for providing a digital time stamping service. In this system, a user makes a request to the time stamping service by sending its identification and the hash value of the document, M, that requires the timestamp. The timestamp system responds by creating a signed e-data record (C_{seq_num}) with a timestamp in the form of a digital certificate. The digital certificate contains a sequence number (seq_num), the date and time (date_time) when this timestamp is generated, the identification of the user (id_user) making the request, a hash value of the document (hash (M)), and some linking bits (link_bits) from a previous issued certificate. In detail, the signed certificate can be written as: C_{seq_num}(signed certificate)=(seq_num, date_time$_{seq\_num}$, id_user$_{seq\_num}$,   hash(M)$_{seq\_num}$,   link_bits$_{seq\_num}$),   where   link_bits$_{seq\_num}$ =   date_time$_{seq\_num-1}$, id_user$_{seq\_num-1}$, (hash(M))$_{seq\_num-1}$, (hash(link_bits))$_{seq\_num-1}$. A third party called the time stamping authority provides the time stamping service. A secure interleaving data structure and the provision of the time stamping service by a trusted entity prevents users from backdating or forward dating their documents. It also prevents users from denying that the document has been time stamped. This type of interleaving data structure can link a group of data one after the other (i.e. lineally).

2.6 Merkle's Hash trees

A Merkle Hash Tree (MHT) is a more elaborated interleaving data structure [12]. It is a binary tree with two types of nodes; one containing authenticators and the other containing the clear-text (e.g. Data 1 and Data 2) used for generating the authenticators in the MHT. Each parent in the tree contains the hash value of its two children (see Fig. 1). Leaves of the MHT are clear-text nodes, whereas the root contains the authenticator of all the data in the tree. In Merkle's proposal, the root of the tree is transmitted prior to the authentication procedure. An entity that needs to authenticate one data from a MHT requires only those hash values starting from the leaf and progressing to the root. This reduces the authentication data required for the authenticating procedure from n, where n is the number of data to be authenticated from a tree, to $\log_2 n$. One further advantage of this scheme is that in a MHT it is impossible to add new leaves once the root has been computed. This can help detect data that are added or deleted by authorised users.

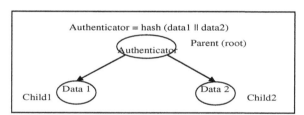

Fig. 1. An example of a Merkle hash tree

Merkle's hash trees have been used in several security solutions such as Certificate Revocation Lists [11], and Authenticated Dictionaries [13]. We use them in our design to provide an audit trail that enables prompt detection of unauthorised financial transactions performed by authorised users.

3 Notation

In the remaining part of this paper, the following notation is used:

$$CT_{ij}^{kl} \tag{1}$$

Notation shown on (1) stands for a transaction message generated by an authorised user i working for bank j using an automated service k for task l. In other words:
i: refers to an authorised user who generates the transaction.
j: refers to the bank for which the user *i* is working for.
k: refers to an automatic financial service. Five different financial services are used throughout this paper, as specified below:

k = 1; Financial Exchange (FE)
k = 2; Automated Clearing House (ACH)
k = 3; Central Security Depository (CSD)
k = 4; Automated Accounting System (AAS)
k = 5; MS for Mail Services (MS)

l: is a task identifier indexing the following tasks:

l =1 to buy a market instrument;
l =2 to sell a market instrument;
l =3 to pay a market instrument that has been reported as bought;
l =4 to transfer a market instrument that has been reported as sold;
l =5 to register a financial transaction; and
l =6 to report one of the previously described financial transactions.

3.1 An Illustrating Example

Fig. 2 illustrates the use of the notation. The values assigned to each index in CT depend on the tasks carried out within a banking workflow.

Suppose that Ann (i.e. i=1), Bob (i.e. i=2), Cat (i.e. i=3) and Dan (i.e. i=4) are authorised users (i.e. employees) working for bank A (j=1), and that bank A is a buyer. At bank A, the following transactions are performed:

- Ann buys a market instrument using FE ($CT_{1,1}^{1,1}$).

- Ann reports her financial transaction to Bob using MS ($CT_{1,1}^{5,6}$).

- Bob makes a payment transaction using ACH ($CT_{2,1}^{2,3}$).

- Bob reports his financial transaction to Dan using MS ($CT_{2,1}^{5,6}$).

- Dan registers the payment made by Bob using the AAS ($CT_{4,1}^{4,5}$) upon the transfer transaction made by Sue.

Similarly, the employees from bank B (i.e. the selling bank), Fraser (i.e. i=1), Steve (i.e. i=2), Sue (i.e. i=3) and Sam (i.e. i=4), will perform a set of corresponding tasks related to the selling tasks mentioned above. These corresponding tasks constitute another workflow in Bank B.

- Fraser sells a market instrument using FE ($CT_{1,2}^{1,2}$).

- Fraser reports his financial transaction to Sue ($CT_{1,2}^{5,6}$) using MS.

- Sue then transfers a market instrument ($CT_{2,2}^{3,4}$) using the CSD.

- Sue reports her financial transaction to Sam $CT_{2,2}^{5,6}$ using MS.

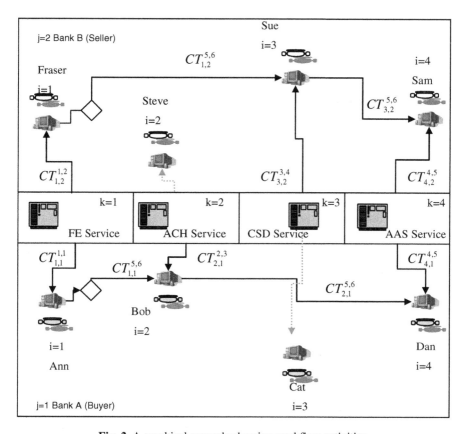

Fig. 2. A graphical example showing workflow activities

- Sam registers the transfer of a market instrument made by Sue using the AAS ($CT_{4,2}^{4,5}$) upon the payment transaction made by Bob.

The above example illustrates that a single stock dealing activity generates two separate workflows. One is at the buyer bank (i.e. bank A), and consists of tasks $CT_{1,1}^{1,1}$, $CT_{1,1}^{5,6}$, $CT_{2,1}^{2,3}$, $CT_{2,1}^{5,6}$, $CT_{4,1}^{4,5}$, and the other is by the seller bank (i.e. bank B), and consists of $CT_{1,2}^{1,2}$, $CT_{1,2}^{5,6}$, $CT_{2,2}^{3,4}$, $CT_{3,2}^{5,6}$, $CT_{4,2}^{4,5}$.

4   Identifying Security Breaches

In the above example, we can identify three security problems. The first problem is that Sue (from Bank B) may decide not to transfer a market instrument previously paid by bank A. In such circumstances, bank A will not be able to detect easily when the market instrument has not been transferred. In other words, one bank alone cannot easily audit the fulfilment of related tasks performed jointly by two or more counterpart banks.

Existing auditing procedures implemented for verifying the integrity of a flow of financial transactions is based merely on internal workflow tasks leaving out tasks performed by its counterpart bank, which may affect the outcome of financial activities (i.e. limited and static workflow definitions).

The second problem is that, currently, although external auditing services do generate audit trails for those financial transactions entered in each automated financial service, these audit trails are not sent to the financial institutions using these services (i.e. incomplete audit trails). In such circumstances, if Ann decides to manipulate the report that she sends to Bob (internally), either maliciously or accidentally by mistake, then bank A will probably not be able to detect such integrity drifts promptly.

The third problem is that Ann's report to Bob (of her financial transaction) depends totally on the information given by Ann. is the information received by Bob is not cross-checked with data on the financial service where Ann entered her financial transaction. In other words, Bob may not get a truthful report of Ann's activity because the verification procedure does not enable the involved parties (including the financial services) to crosscheck and verify the authenticity of financial transactions jointly performed.

In order to solve these problems we re-define the current audit workflow into one that includes an audit trail of e-tasks carried out by users from the same bank (e.g. Bank A), as well as the audit trail of related e-tasks performed by its counterpart (i.e. Bank B).This newly redefined audit workflow contains $CT_{1,1}^{1,1} \parallel CT_{1,1}^{5,6} \parallel CT_{2,1}^{2,3}$ $\parallel CT_{2,1}^{5,6} \parallel CT_{4,1}^{4,5} \parallel CT_{1,2}^{1,2} \parallel CT_{1,2}^{5,6} \parallel CT_{3,2}^{3,4} \parallel CT_{3,2}^{5,6} \parallel CT_{4,2}^{4,5}$.

Our strategy is to use a more complete data flow generated from a set of related tasks within this newly re-defined workflow in order to identify unauthorised financial transactions entered by authorised users. The new workflow is also dynamic, as shown in Fig. 3. For example, a financial transaction entered by Ann can trigger a financial transaction entered by Bob. By looking at the data flow generated from Ann's task, we can see that if Bob performs a payment, which has not triggered a corresponding transaction at Ann's side then there is a possibility that Bob may have performed either by mistake or on purpose an unauthorised financial transaction. In addition, Ann's financial transaction should have been triggered by a financial transaction entered at bank B (i.e. Fraser's financial transaction at bank B). We propose an audit trail, which is gathered and sent to both parties (i.e. bank A and Bank B) so that a crosscheck verification procedure (upon authentication) can take place. We call this authentication procedure the Transaction Authentication Service (TAS). We believe that TAS can detect integrity drifts within a workflow. We have not found in our literature review other systems aiming to detect unauthorised financial transaction entered by authorised users in this way.

TAS is a security service that consists of three main building blocks:

- An audit agent: responsible for gathering information and verifying the relationships between two or more audit trails, and linking them depending on their relationships.
- A mail service: responsible for dispatching the audit logs to another corresponding audit agent.

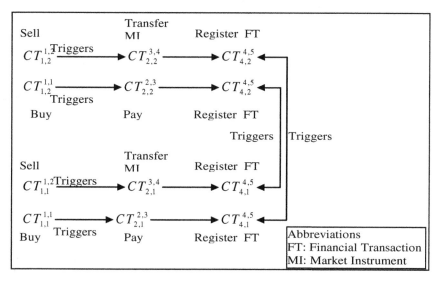

Fig. 3. A graphical example of a dynamic workflow cycle

- An Automated Banking Certificate (ABC): an integrity-protected audit trail, used to crosscheck and verify financial transactions generated from banking workflow activities.

We, in the following section, specify the security requirements of the ABC.

5 Requirement Specification

The main objective of designing ABCs is to enable cross transaction authentication within the newly re-defined workflow. For this purpose, we need to devise a systematic and structured means to generate, collect and maintain an integrity-protected audit trail related to a complete financial transaction workflow. This audit trail is done with an ABC.

The following requirements have been specified for the design of the ABCs.
1. *Authenticity*: to provide the means to enable a third party to verify that:

    a.   An ABC is generated by an authorised entity.
    b.   An ABC has not been altered after its creation.
    c.   An ABC is not a replay of an earlier valid financial transaction.

2. *Completeness*: to provide the means to enable a third party to verify that:

    a.   Two or more financial transactions are related and have been performed through the use of two or more automated financial systems.
    b.   There is no financial transaction that has been overlooked.

3. *Adaptability*: to provide flexible means to reflect the relationships among a set of related transactions within a workflow. These transactions can have the following relationships:

a. One-to-one: One financial transaction is entered into one automated financial service and subsequently one financial transaction is entered into a directly related automated financial service. For example, Ann makes a deal to buy a £5 bond in the FE automated financial service, Bob completes Ann's £5 deal by making a payment of £5 using the ACH automated financial service.

b. One-to-many: One financial transaction is entered into one automated financial service and subsequently more than one financial transaction is entered into a directly related automated financial service. For example, Ann makes a deal to buy a £5 bond in the FE automated financial service, Bob completes Ann's £5 deal by making two £2.50 payment financial transactions using the ACH automated financial service.

c. Many-to-one: More than one financial transaction is entered into one automated financial service and subsequently one financial transaction is entered into the subsequent automated financial service. For example, Ann makes two deals to buy one bond in each financial transaction by making use of the FE automated financial service. One deal is to buy a bond worth £3 and the other deal is to buy a bond worth £2, to the same bank. Bob completes Ann's deals by making one £5 payment using the ACH automated financial service.

d. Many-to-many: More than one financial transaction are entered into one automated financial service and more than one financial transactions are entered into the subsequent automated financial service. For example, Ann makes two deals to buy one bond in each financial transaction. One deal is to buy a bond worth £3 and the other deal is to buy a bond worth £2, to the same bank, by making use of the FE automated financial service. Bob completes Ann's deals by making two payments; one for £2.50 and the other one for £2.50, both are made using the ACH automated financial service.

6 Automated Banking Certificates (ABCs)

An ABC is a data structure that fulfils the requirements described in the previous section. It allows to the grouping of data records securely according to the way in which financial transactions take place. Each group, named transaction set from now on, contains a group of related financial transactions. For example, if Ann buys a market instrument worth £5, and Bob pays for this market instrument then these two financial transactions are grouped in the same transaction set.

A complete banking certificate (complete ABC) is a binary tree containing one transaction set, as shown in Fig. 4. The leaves in the complete ABC are called intra-system ABCs and the parents in the tree are called inter-system ABCs. Each intra-system ABC contains the audit data records of one financial transaction entered into one automated financial service. Each inter-system ABC contains the data that links the two related intra-system ABCs. Intra-system ABCs in one complete ABC can result from two or more related automated financial services increasing the depth of the tree. Intra-system ABCs and Inter-system ABCs are linked together depending on the workflow cycle formed from financial transactions generated by an activity.

An ABC provides the means to fulfil the requirements identified in section 5, i.e. 3a, 3b, 3c and 3d, as illustrated in Fig. 5.

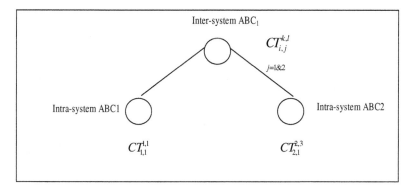

Fig. 4. A complete ABC

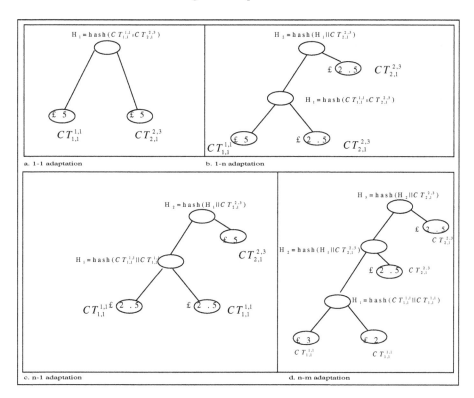

Fig. 5. Adaptation of a complete ABC

Each intra-system ABC (i.e. CT) contains several items of data, each with a specific purpose. It consists of a sequence number (seq_num), the identification (id_user), date and time (date_time), details of the financial transaction record (detail_ft), and certain linking information (link_bits), which come from the previously issued intra-system ABC. The form of an intra-system ABC is as follows:

$$CT_{i,j}^{k,l} = seq\_num, id\_user, date\_time, detail\_ft, link\_bit \parallel E_{KR(originator)} hash(seq\_num, id\_user, date\_time, detail\_ft, link\_bit)$$

where $link\_bit = detail\_ft_{seq\_num-1}, hash(link\_bit_{seq\_num-1})$

The seq_num field contains a sequence number which is assigned by a trusted third party to each financial transaction set (allocated when a buyer bank originated a complete transaction set). The data in seq_num and date_time fields enable the linkage of two intra-system ABCs. The detail_ft field provides details of one financial transaction, and link_bit (i.e. a concatenating sequence) links this intra-system ABC to the previous intra-system ABC that has triggered this current transaction. By looking at Fig. 3 we can see that $CT_{1,1}^{1,1}$ triggers $CT_{2,1}^{2,3}$ and $CT_{4,1}^{4,5}$ whereas in bank B $CT_{1,1}^{1,1}$ triggers $CT_{1,2}^{1,2}$, $CT_{2,2}^{3,4}$, $CT_{4,2}^{4,5}$.

A trusted party from the service provider's side signs each intra-system ABC. The signature on the intra-system ABC prevents the trusted party from denying the creation of an intra-system ABC. The data items of a data structure are given in Table 1. The signature is also appended to this data structure.

Table 1. Data structure definition of an intra-system ABC

Intra_system ABC SIGNATURE	seq_num	Id_user	date_time	detail_ft	link_bit		
					seq_num - 1	detail_ft- 1	hash(link_bit)
Int 256 bits	Int 32 bits	Char 256 bits	Long 64bits	Data Structure 1024 bits	int 32 bits	Data structure 1024 bits	Char (2) 256 bits

In this data structure, the design of detail_ft aims to provide minimum amount of required information needed to record a transaction. This field will be used to decide on what and how to construct the complete ABC of a workflow, which will in turn be used for cross checking and verifying the workflow tasks. The field detail_ft contains at least the following items: i (user identifier), j (bank identifier), k (automated financial service used), l (task performed), AM (Amount of money involved in the transaction), BIN (Buyers Identification Name), SIN (Sellers Identification Name), MI (Market Instrument identification) and NV (Nominal Value of a market instrument).

An inter-system ABC contains a hash value, and two data items that are used as input to generate this hash value. These data items vary depending on the context. It can be any of the three combinations. When the inter-system ABC is the parent of two leaves then these two data items are two intra-system ABCs. When the inter-system ABC is the parent of one sub-tree and a leaf then these two data items are an inter-system ABC and an intra-system ABC. When the inter-system ABC is the root of the tree, then these two data items are two inter-system ABCs. In other words, these two data items can be two intra-system ABCs, one intra-system ABC and one inter-system ABC, or two inter-system ABCs when the inter-system ABC is also the root of the tree. A trusted party located at the user's side that groups intra-system ABCs together through inter-system ABCs signs all inter-system ABCs. The root of a complete ABC is the authenticator of one complete transaction set.

An ABC has a three-dimensional audit trail. In a complete ABC contains an audit trail of the transactions within the same automated financial system of one bank, between two or more related automated financial systems of the same bank, and between the related transactions taken place in two or more different banks.

We have shown the design of one complete ABC, and shown how the records generated from related financial transactions are concatenated. This design provides integrity protection to the data set generated in each of the related automated financial services (intra-system ABCs), and to the data within one or more transaction sets. In other words, our approach allows the generation of audit trails of transactions that are performed with the automated financial services that are run by different banks but support a mutually involved financial activity.

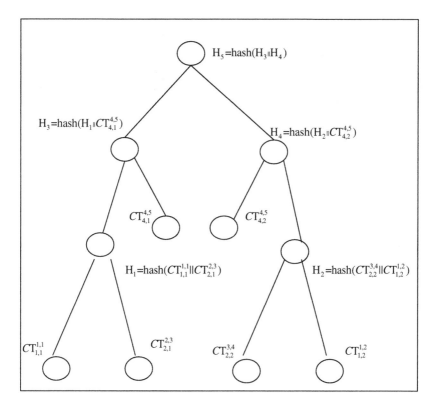

Fig. 6. The structure of audit trails in one complete ABC

By combining intra-system and inter-system ABCs, we can provide evidence of one transaction set in one complete ABC as shown in Fig. 6. Also, by detecting missing sequences within one transaction set we can detect irregularities. We can also detect unauthorised financial transactions entered by authorised users because we can crosscheck and verify the data contained in one complete ABC to track the entire workflow cycle.

7 Conclusions and Future Work

We have re-defined the concept of transactional workflow. The workflow should not be restricted to an institutional boundary, or an administrative domain. If necessary, such as in the case discussed in this paper, a workflow should encompass tasks performed in more than one institutions so long as the tasks are related. This concept is particularly important in today's world where large-scale and/or cross-institutional sharing of data, services, and CPU cycles is increasingly common. In this world of e-commerce, e-services, e-transactions, e-science, etc, a new way and framework is required to conduct auditing procedures.

Based upon our observations that an authorised transaction is either triggered by another transaction or triggering another transaction in a workflow, the paper has proposed a novel way of constructing audit trails for integrity drift detection in e-trading applications. We propose to use Automatic Banking Certificates (ABCs) to record transactional details of individual transactions and to use Merkle Hash Trees to record the relationships among transactions in a workflow. Any missing transaction(s) in the set indicates that there may be irregularities in the financial workflow (or activity). Cryptographic primitives, namely the digital signature techniques and one-way collision free hash function, and the idea of Merkle Hash Trees are used as building blocks of our solution.

We have shown that the detection of an unauthorised financial transaction made by an authorised user is achievable through the exploitation of inter-relationship of transactions generated by one financial activity. We are currently working on the generation and integration of intra-system and inter-system ABCs, a vital component in the design of the Transaction Authentication Service.

Acknowledgements

The first author gratefully acknowledges the financial supports given by the Bank of Columbia, and the School of Computer Science, University of Manchester, UK.

The authors wish to thank the anonymous referees for their constructive comments and valuable suggestions.

References

[1] Baldwin A. and Shiu S., 'Enabling shared audit data', Springer-Verlag-Heidelberg, ISC 2003, Lecture Notes in Computer Science, Volume 2851, Pages 14-28, 2003.

[2] Bank for International Settlements, 'Risk Management Priciples for electronic Banking', found at www.bs.org/publ/bcbs98.htm on January 2006.

[3] Corzo C. Zhang N, 'Towards a real-time solution to the security threats posed by authorised insiders', Proceedings of the ECIW 2004: The 3rd European conference on information warfare and security, Royal Holloway, University of London, UK, Page 51-60, 28-29 June 2004.

[4] Damgard I.,' Collision free hash functions and public key signatures', Springer-Verlag-Heidelberg, Advances in Cryptology, Eurocrypt 87, Lecture Notes in Computer Science, Volume 304, Pages 203-216, 1988.

[5] Damgard I.,' A design principle for hash functions', Springer-Verlag-Heidelberg, Advances in Cryptology, Crypto 89, Lecture Notes in Computer Science, Volume 435, Pages 416-427, 1990.

[6] Davies D. W. and Price W. L. , 'The application of digital signatures based on public-key cryptosystems' In Proc. Intl. Computer Communications Conference, Pages 525-530, October 1980.

[7] Diffie W. and Hellman M., 'New Directions in Cryptography', Information Theory, Transactions on IEEE, Volume 22, Issue 6, Pages 644-654, November 1976.

[8] Diffie W., 'Ten first years of public key cryptography', Proceedings of the IEEE, Volume 76, Issue 5, Pages 560-577, May 1988.

[9] Evans A., ' A user authentication scheme not requiring secrecy in the computer', Communications of the ACM, Volume 17, Number 8, Pages 437-442, August 1974.

[10] Haber S., Stornetta W., ' How to time-stamp a digital document', Springer-Verlag Berlin Heidelberg, Advances in Cryptology – Crypto 90, Lecture Notes in Computer Science, Volume 537, Pages 437-455, 1991.

[11] Kocher P., 'On certificate revocation and validation', Springer-Verlag-Heidelberg, FC'98, Lecture Notes in Computer Science, Volume 1465, Pages 172-177, 1998.

[12] Merkle R., ' A certified digital signature', Springer-Verlag Berlin Heidelberg, Advances in Cryptology – Crypto 89, Lecture Notes in Computer Science, Volume 435, Pages 218-238, 1990.

[13] Muñoz J., Forbe J, Oscar Esparza, ' Certificate revocation system implementation based on the Merkle hash tree', Springer-Verlag Berlin Heidelberg , Journal of Information Security, Volume 2, Number 2, 2004.

[14] Naor M., Nissim K., 'Certificate revocation and certificate update', IEEE Journal on selected areas in Communications, Volume 18, Issue 4, Pages 561-570, April 2000.

[15] Rivest R., Shamir A. and Adleman L., ' A method for obtaining digital signatures and public key cryptosystems', Communications of the ACM, Volume 21, Number 2, February 1978.

[16] Tsudik G.,'Message authentication with one-way hash functions', Eleventh Annual Joint Conference of the IEEE Computer and Communications Societies, IEEE, pages 2055-5059, Volume 3, May 1992.

[17] O'Gorman, ' Comparing passwords, tokens, and biometrics for user authentication', Proceedings of the IEEE, Volume 91, Issue 12, Pages 2021-2040, December 2003.

[18] Rivest R.,'The MD4 Message Digest Algorithm', Springer-Verlag Berlin Heidelberg, Advances in Cryptology – Crypto 90, Lecture Notes in Computer Science, Volume 537, Pages 303-311, 1991.

[19] Simmons G., ' The practice of authentication', Springer-Verlag Berlin Heidelberg, Advances in Cryptology – Eurocrypt 85, Lecture Notes in Computer Science, Volume 219, Pages 261-272, 1986.

[20] Wang X., Yu , 'How to Break MD5 and other Hash functions', Springer-Verlag Berlin Heidelberg, Advances in Cryptology – Eurocrypt 2005, Lecture Notes in Computer Science, LNCS 3494, Pages 19-35, 2005.

Privacy in Encrypted Content Distribution Using Private Broadcast Encryption

Adam Barth[1], Dan Boneh[1,*], and Brent Waters[2]

[1] Stanford University, Stanford, CA 94305
{abarth, dabo}@cs.stanford.edu
[2] SRI International, Menlo Park, CA 94025
bwaters@csl.sri.com

Abstract. In many content distribution systems it is important both to restrict access to content to authorized users and to protect the identities of these users. We discover that current systems for encrypting content to sets of users are subject to attacks on user privacy. We propose a new mechanism, private broadcast encryption, to protect the privacy of users of encrypted file systems and content delivery systems. We construct a private broadcast scheme, with a strong privacy guarantee against an active attacker, that achieves ciphertext length, encryption time, and decryption time comparable with the non-private schemes currently used in encrypted file systems.

1 Introduction

In both large and small scale content distribution systems it is often important to make certain data available to only a select set of users. In commercial content distribution, for example, a company may wish for its digital media to be available only to paying customers. On a smaller scale, suppose a department's faculty need to access the academic transcripts of graduate applicants. If electronic copies of the transcripts were stored on the department's file server, they should only be accessible by the faculty and students.

It is often equally important to protect the identities of the users who are able to access protected content. Students receiving an email from an instructor notifying all students failing a class would likely wish to keep their identities private. Commercial sites often not want to disclose identities of customers because competitors might use this information for targeted advertising. If an employee is up for promotion, a company might wish to hide who is on his promotion committee and therefore who is able to read his performance evaluation.

Employing a trusted server is the most commonly used method for protecting both electronic content and the privacy of users who can access it. Whenever a user wishes to access content stored on a trusted server, the user contacts the server, authenticates himself or herself, and is sent the content over a secure channel. As long as the server behaves correctly, only authorized users will be

---

* Supported by NSF.

able to access the content and which users are authorized to access which content will not be divulged, even to other authorized users. While this simple method of data protection is adequate for some applications, it has some significant drawbacks. First, both data content and user privacy are subject to attack if the server is compromised. Additionally, content providers often not distribute their data directly, but for economic reasons outsource distribution to third parties or use peer-to-peer networks. In this case, the content owners will no longer be directly in control of data distribution.

For these reasons, we examine the problem of efficiently distributing encrypted content in such a way that (1) only authorized users can read the content and (2) the identities of authorized users are hidden. We study this problem for the case of encrypted file systems. However, our results can be generalized to larger content distribution systems, including encrypted email.

Encrypted File Systems. Encrypted file systems implement read access control by encrypting the contents of files such that only users with read permission are able to perform decryption. Typical encrypted file systems, such as Windows EFS, encrypt each file under its own symmetric key, K_F, and then encrypt the symmetric key separately under the public keys of those users authorized to access the file, labeling these encryptions with user identities to speed decryption (Fig. 1(a)).

$$
\begin{array}{ll}
\text{(a)} \quad A : \{K_F\}_{\mathsf{pk}_A} & \text{(b)} \quad \{K_F\}_{\mathsf{pk}_B} \\
\qquad B : \{K_F\}_{\mathsf{pk}_B} & \qquad \{K_F\}_{\mathsf{pk}_C} \\
\qquad C : \{K_F\}_{\mathsf{pk}_C} & \qquad \{K_F\}_{\mathsf{pk}_A} \\
\qquad \{F\}_{K_F} & \qquad \{F\}_{K_F}
\end{array}
$$

Fig. 1. Simple constructions of broadcast encryption systems. File F is encrypted under the key K_F, which in turn is encrypted under the public keys of users A, B, and C. (a) The scheme typically used by encrypted file systems reveals the set of users authorized to access F. (b) Modifying this scheme by removing the labels, using a key-private cryptosystem, and randomly reordering the users yields a private broadcast scheme resistant to passive attacks on recipient privacy, but decryption time is increased because recipients must attempt to decrypt each unlabeled component. These simple schemes are both vulnerable to active attacks.

While these systems protect file contents from unauthorized users, they do little to protect the identities of users allowed to access the file. Who can access a file, however, is often more sensitive than the contents of the file itself. Suppose, for example, a university provides a document on its file server to students with low average grades. To maintain the privacy of the students, the set of authorized users should be kept private, not only from outsiders, but from the students in the group as well.

Current implementations expose the identities of authorized users in two ways. First, the individual public key encryptions of the symmetric key, K_F, are labeled with the identity of the user, as shown in Fig. 1(a). These labels direct authorized users to their encryptions of K_F, speeding decryption. Second, even without these labels, an adversary examining the actual ciphertexts can learn information about the user's identity. For example, suppose an attacker wants to determine whether Alice or Bob has access to a particular file. Further suppose Alice has a 1024-bit key and Bob has a 2048-bit key. An attacker can easily determine which of the two has access to the file by examining the encryption of K_F, specifically the ciphertext length. Thus, the encryptions of K_F leak some information about who has access to the file.

Private Broadcast Encryption. Our goal is to provide recipient privacy: an encrypted file should hide who can access its contents. We approach the problem of recipient privacy by introducing a notion we call *private broadcast encryption*. A private broadcast encryption scheme encrypts a message to several recipients while hiding the identities of the recipients, even from each other.

The most straightforward construction of a private broadcast encryption scheme is to modify the scheme currently used in encrypted file systems by removing the identifying labels and using a public key system that does not reveal the public key associated with a ciphertext, such as ElGamal or Cramer-Shoup [1] (Fig. 1(b)). While this scheme is secure against passive attacks on recipient privacy, it has two disadvantages. First, decryption time is increased as recipient must perform, on average, $n/2$ trial decryptions to obtain K_F, where n is the number of message recipients. Second, an active attacker can mount a chosen-ciphertext attack and learn whether a user can decrypt a message.

Returning to our example, consider an active attacker who is authorized to decrypt the document for students with low average grades, where the list of authorized users should be private. Now, suppose that the attacker wishes to determine whether Alice can read the document. Because the attacker is a legitimate recipient, he or she knows K_F and can maliciously prepare a different encrypted file by replacing the encrypted contents of the original file with content of the attacker's choice, encrypted under K_F. Alice is able to read this maliciously created file if, and only if, she can read the original file. For example, a malicious legitimate recipient of the document could copy the document header, but replace the document body with the message "please visit the following URL for free music," as illustrated in Fig. 2. Students with low average grades will expose themselves when they visit the given URL because they are the only ones who can read the message.

While one could avoid this attack by giving separate encryptions for each user of the bulk data, this would greatly increase the overall storage demands, as the contents of each file would need to be replicated for each authorized user. We solve this problem by building efficient *private broadcast encryption* systems that are secure under chosen-ciphertext attacks. Our construction achieves storage space, encryption time, and decryption time comparable to schemes currently employed in encrypted file systems.

The remainder of the paper is organized as follows. We define private broadcast encryption in Sect. 2, giving a game definition of recipient privacy under a

(a) $c_1; c_2; c_3; \{F\}_{K_F}$ (b) $c_1; c_2; c_3; \{F'\}_{K_F}$

Fig. 2. Active attack on recipient privacy. (a) The sensitive document, F, is encrypted for three recipients. If the attacker is a recipient, he or she learns K_F. (b) The malicious document created by an attacker contains F' of the attacker's choice and can be decrypted by the same users as the original document. Recipients of the original document can be discovered by tricking them into decrypting the malicious document.

chosen-ciphertext attack. In Sect. 3, we examine the PGP encryption system and demonstrate attacks against recipient privacy. We present our private broadcast encryption constructions in Sect. 4. Finally, we conclude in Sect. 5.

1.1   Related Work

The notion of key privacy in the public key setting was first formalized by Bellare et. al. [1]. A public key encryption system is key-private if ciphertexts do not leak information about the public keys for which they were encrypted. Specifically, an adversary viewing a chosen message encrypted under one of two public keys is unable to guess (with non-negligible advantage) which public key was used to produce the ciphertext. The authors formalize these definitions for key privacy under chosen-plaintext attack (IK-CPA) and chosen-ciphertext attacks (IK-CCA). They show that ElGamal and Cramer-Shoup are secure under these definitions, respectively, when public keys share a common prime modulus.

Our constructions use a key-private public key system as a component in building private broadcast encryption systems. One interesting observation is that the straightforward construction of a private broadcast encryption scheme using an IK-CCA secure encryption scheme does not result in a private broadcast encryption system resistant to chosen-ciphertext attacks.

Previous work on broadcast encryption has focused on increasing collusion resistance and reducing the length of the ciphertext [2, 3, 4]. We differ from these works in that we focus on maintaining the privacy of users, but do not attempt to achieve ciphertext overhead that is sub-linear in the number of users. Whether private broadcast encryption systems can be realized with sub-linear ciphertext overhead is currently an open problem.

2   Private Broadcast Encryption

In this section, we define private broadcast encryption in terms of its correctness and security properties. A private broadcast encryption system consists of four algorithms.

- $I \leftarrow \mathsf{Setup}(\lambda)$. Setup is a randomized algorithm that generates global parameters I for the system from a security parameter λ.

- $(\mathsf{pk}, \mathsf{sk}) \leftarrow \mathsf{Keygen}(I)$. Keygen is a randomized algorithm that generates public-private key pairs from the global parameters I.
- $C \leftarrow \mathsf{Encrypt}(S, M)$. Encrypt is a randomized algorithm that generates a ciphertext C for a message M using a set of public keys $S = \{\mathsf{pk}_1, \ldots, \mathsf{pk}_n\}$ generated by $\mathsf{Keygen}(I)$.
- $M \leftarrow \mathsf{Decrypt}(\mathsf{sk}, C)$. Decrypt extracts M from a ciphertext C using a private key sk if the corresponding public key $\mathsf{pk} \in S$, where S is the set used to generate C. Decrypt can also return $\perp$ if $\mathsf{pk} \notin S$ or if C is malformed.

For ElGamal-like systems, the global parameters I simply contain the prime p and generator $g \in \mathbb{Z}_p$. This definition enables each user to generate his or her own public-private key pair individually.

The definition above departs from the standard definition of broadcast encryption in that the standard definition explicitly provides S, the set of recipients, to the Decrypt algorithm. Here we omit this parameter in order to capture systems that hide S. There is no loss of generality, however, as S can be included in the ciphertext, C, directly.

2.1   Recipient Privacy

We define a notion of recipient privacy under a chosen-ciphertext attack for private broadcast encryption systems using a game between a challenger and an adversary. This game ensures that the adversary cannot distinguish a ciphertext intended for one recipient set from a ciphertext intended for another recipient set. To model a chosen-ciphertext attack we allow the adversary to issue decryption queries. More precisely, the game defining recipient privacy of a private broadcast encryption system with n users is as follows:

Init: The challenger runs $I \leftarrow \mathsf{Setup}(\lambda)$ and publishes the global parameters I. The adversary outputs $S_0, S_1 \subseteq \{1, \ldots, n\}$ such that $|S_0| = |S_1|$.
Setup: The challenger generates keys for each potential recipient, $(\mathsf{pk}_i, \mathsf{sk}_i) \leftarrow \mathsf{Keygen}(I)$, and sends to the adversary each pk_i for $i \in S_0 \cup S_1$ as well as each sk_i for $i \in S_0 \cap S_1$.
Phase 1: The adversary makes decryption queries of the form (u, C), where $u \in S_0 \cup S_1$, and the challenger returns the decryption $\mathsf{Decrypt}(\mathsf{sk}_u, C)$. The adversary may repeat this step as desired.
Challenge: The adversary gives the challenger a message M. The challenger picks a random $b \in \{0, 1\}$, runs $C^* \leftarrow \mathsf{Encrypt}(\{\mathsf{pk}_i \mid i \in S_b\}, M)$, and sends ciphertext C^* to the adversary.
Phase 2: The adversary makes more decryption queries, with the restriction that the query ciphertext $C \neq C^*$. The adversary may repeat this step as desired.
Guess: The adversary outputs its guess $b' \in \{0, 1\}$.

We say that the adversary wins the game if $b' = b$.

Definition 1. *A private broadcast encryption system is (t, q, n, ϵ) CCA recipient private if, for all t-time adversaries A, the probability A wins the above game using recipient sets of size at most n and making at most q decryption queries is at most $1/2 + \epsilon$.*

Definition 2. *A private broadcast encryption system is (t, n, ϵ) CPA recipient private if it is $(t, 0, n, \epsilon)$ CCA recipient private.*

In addition to recipient privacy, a secure broadcast encryption scheme must be semantically secure against CCA attacks under the standard definition of semantic security for broadcast encryption systems (see for example [5]).

A standard hybrid argument [6] shows that our definition also implies unlinkability among sets of ciphertexts. We also observe our definition of recipient privacy allows C to leak the number of recipients, just as semantic security allows a ciphertext to leak the length of the plaintext. The number of recipients can be hidden by padding the recipient set to a given size using dummy recipients.

Just as public key encryption is a special case of broadcast encryption, key privacy is a special case of recipient privacy. In key privacy [1], the adversary is restricted to $n = 1$, that is to recipient sets S_0 and S_1 of size 1, mirroring the restriction on the public key Encrypt algorithm to encrypt only for a single recipient. Therefore, the IK-CCA definition is equivalent to our recipient privacy definition with $n = 1$.

3   Broadcast Encryption in Practice

In this section, we make concrete our discussion of privacy problems in broadcast encryption systems by examining broadcast encryption systems used in practice. We study the widely used OpenPGP [7] encryption standard and the GNU Privacy Guard (GPG) [8] implementation as well as discuss the systems used by Windows EFS and by Microsoft Outlook.

3.1   The PGP Encryption System

While OpenPGP is commonly associated with encrypted email, it can be used as a general encryption system. When encrypting a message to multiple recipients, OpenPGP functions as a broadcast encryption system: it encrypts each message under a symmetric key K and then encrypts K to each user using his or her public key. Either ElGamal or RSA encryption can be used for the public key encryption.

Key IDs and Recipient Privacy. In standard operation, GPG completely exposes recipient identities (including blind-carbon-copy recipients). Figure 3 contains a transcript of an attempted GPG decryption of a ciphertext created with a PGP implementation. The ciphertext reveals the key IDs of two recipients. A key's ID

is essentially its hash. PGP uses key IDs for two purposes. First, public keys in
the Web of Trust are indexed by key ID. For example, the MIT PGP Public Key
Server [9], when queried for a specific name, returns the key IDs, names, and
email addresses of the principals with the specified name. A principal's public key
can then be retrieved by querying the server by key ID. Second, key IDs are used
in ciphertexts to label encryptions of the message key (Fig. 1(a)). These labels
speed decryption because the decryptor knows his or her key ID and can locate
the encryption of the message key he or she is able to decrypt. Unfortunately,
attackers also know key IDs. Moreover, after examining a ciphertext, an attacker
need only query a public key server to learn the full name and email address of
the owner of the associated public key.

```
C:\gpg>gpg --verbose -d message.txt
gpg: armor header: Version: GnuPG v1.2.2 (MingW32)
gpg: public key is 3CF61C7B
gpg: public key is 028EAE1C
```

Fig. 3. Transcript of an attempted GPG decryption of a file encrypted for two users.
The identities of the users are completely exposed by their key IDs. These key IDs can
be translated to real identities by a reverse look up on a public key directory.

Throwing Away Key IDs. The OpenPGP standard allows implementations to
omit key IDs from ciphertexts by replacing them with zeros (ostensibly to foil
traffic analysis [10]). This option is available in GPG using the `--throw-keyids`
command line option, but is disabled by default and thus will not be used if
the command is not given. Omitting key IDs increases the amount of work
required to decrypt a message. A message without key IDs, encrypted to n
recipients, contains n unidentified ciphertexts. To decrypt the message, every
recipient must attempt to decrypt each ciphertext, performing on average $n/2$
decryption operations.

Even when omitting key IDs, GPG does not achieve recipient privacy. When
GPG generates an ElGamal public key, it does so in the group of integers modulo
a random prime. Thus, different principals are very likely to have public keys
in different groups, making GPG encryptions vulnerable to passive key privacy
attacks. These attacks can be directly translated into attacks on CPA recipient
privacy. GPG could defend against these attacks by using the same prime for
every public key, for example one standardized by NIST [11].

Active Attack. While omitting key IDs and standardizing the group used for
public keys achieves CPA recipient privacy, it does not achieve CCA recipient
privacy. An active attacker could determine the recipients as follows. Suppose
Charlie, the attacker, received the encrypted message $\{K\}_{\mathsf{pk}_A} \| \{K\}_{\mathsf{pk}_C} \| \{M\}_K$
and wishes to determine whether Alice or Bob was the other recipient. As Char-
lie possesses his private key sk_C, he can recover K, the message key. He can
then encrypt a new message M' for the same recipient as the original message,

$\{K\}_{\mathsf{pk}_A}\|\{M'\}_K$, by copying the first portion of the header and encrypting M' under K. When Alice decrypts this message, she obtains M', whereas when Bob decrypts this message, he does not obtain M'.

This active attack is potentially more dangerous than the passive attack in practice. If an attacker wishes to determine a recipient from a large pool of recipients, the passive attack will likely only eliminate some fraction of the possible recipients. An active attack, however, could probe each of the potential recipients individually and learn exactly which ones were recipients of the original message.

3.2   Other Broadcast Systems

Windows EFS. An encrypted file system can be viewed as a broadcast encryption system: the file system itself is the broadcast channel, the files are the messages, and the users who can access a file are the broadcast recipients. The underlying broadcast encryption scheme used in the Windows Encrypted File System (EFS) is vulnerable to privacy attacks. A file in EFS is encrypted under a symmetric key, which in turn is encrypted under the public keys of the users authorized to read the file. These encryptions of the symmetric key are stored in the file header and are usually accessible only to the operating system kernel. An attacker who has physical access to the storage media, for example by duplicating a file server's hard drive or stealing a backup copy of the file system, can learn the list of users authorized to read a file by directly examining the ciphertext component labels.

Outlook. Microsoft Outlook, like many S/MIME clients, is vulnerable to attacks on recipient privacy. When Outlook sends an encrypted email message to multiple recipients, it prepares a single encrypted message and sends copies of that ciphertext to each recipient. Components of the ciphertext are labeled with the issuer and serial number of each recipient's public key certificate. Many certificate authorities, including VeriSign [12], provide a free directory service that translates certificate serial numbers into the certificates themselves. This reveals the identities of all recipients, compromising the privacy of blind-carbon-copy (BCC) recipients. Worse, if a BCC recipient uses a self-signed certificate, Outlook includes his or her full name and email address *in the clear* in the message ciphertext sent to all recipients.

In addition to these passive attacks, active attacks on recipient privacy are particularly easy to mount against encrypted email systems. Each legitimate message recipient can mount an active attack simply by sending a carefully constructed email message to a suspected recipient. Some S/MIME clients avoid these attacks by separately encrypting messages for each recipient. This prevents legitimate recipients both from learning the identities of other message recipients and from learning the number of other recipients. However, sending separate encryptions decreases mail server efficiency and uses more bandwidth.

4 Constructions

In this section, we present two constructions for private broadcast encryption that achieve CCA recipient privacy. The first is a generic construction from any public key encryption scheme that has key indistinguishability under chosen-ciphertext attacks (IK-CCA) [1]. The disadvantage of this first scheme is that decryption time is linear in the number of recipients because the decryption algorithm must try decrypting each ciphertext component until it decrypts successfully. The second construction is a specialized system in which the decryption algorithm performs one asymmetric key operation to locate the appropriate ciphertext component (if one exists). This construction is more efficient for decryptors than the first because no trial decryptions are required. We describe our two schemes and give intuition for their security.

Both constructions require the underlying public key scheme to be *strongly correct*. Essentially, a public key scheme is strongly correct if decrypting a ciphertext encrypted for one key with another key results in $\perp$, the reject symbol, with high probability. While this property is not ensured by the standard public key definitions, most CCA-secure cryptosystems, such as Cramer-Shoup, are strongly correct. Before giving a formal definition of strong correctness, we define a function that generates a random encryption of a given message and then returns the decryption of that ciphertext with a different random key.

$$\mathsf{Test}(M): \quad I \leftarrow \mathsf{Init}(\lambda); \; (\mathsf{pk}_0, \mathsf{sk}_0) \leftarrow \mathsf{Gen}(I); \; C \leftarrow \mathsf{Enc}_{\mathsf{pk}_0}(M);$$
$$(\mathsf{pk}_1, \mathsf{sk}_1) \leftarrow \mathsf{Gen}(I); \; \mathsf{Return} \; \mathsf{Dec}_{\mathsf{sk}_1}(C).$$

Definition 3. *A public key scheme* (Init, Gen, Enc, Dec) *is ϵ strongly correct if, for all M, the probability* $\mathsf{Test}(M) \neq \perp$ *is at most ϵ.*

4.1 Generic CCA Recipient Private Construction

We realize our first construction by modifying the simple CPA recipient private construction (Fig. 1(b)). Encrypt first generates a random signature and verification key for a one-time, strongly[1] unforgeable signature scheme [13, 14] such as RSA full-domain hash. Then, the encryption algorithm encrypts a ciphertext component containing the generated verification key using a public key encryption scheme that has key-indistinguishability under CCA attacks (IK-CCA). Finally, the algorithm signs the entire ciphertext with the signing key.

The decryption algorithm attempts to decrypt each ciphertext component. If the public key decryption is successful (i.e. returns non-$\perp$), Decrypt will decrypt the message only if the signature verifies under the extracted verification key. Intuitively, an adversary cannot reuse a ciphertext component from the challenge ciphertext in another ciphertext because he or she will be unable to sign the new ciphertext under the same verification key. We now give a formal description of our scheme.

---

[1] In a strongly unforgeable signature scheme, an adversary cannot output a new signature, even on a previously signed message.

Given a strongly correct, IK-CCA public key scheme (Init, Gen, Enc, Dec), a strongly existentially unforgeable signature scheme (Sig-Gen, Sig, Ver), and semantically secure symmetric key encryption and decryption algorithms (E, D), we construct a private broadcast encryption system as follows.

Setup(λ): Return Init(λ).
Keygen(I): Run (pk, sk) $\leftarrow$ Gen(I) and return (pk, sk).
Encrypt(S, M):
  1. (vk, sk) $\leftarrow$ Sig-Gen(λ).
  2. Choose a random symmetric key K.
  3. For each pk $\in S$, $c_{\mathsf{pk}} \leftarrow$ Enc$_{\mathsf{pk}}$(vk$||K$).
  4. Let C_1 be the concatenation of the c_{pk}, in random order.
  5. $C_2 \leftarrow E_K(M)$.
  6. $\sigma \leftarrow$ Sig$_{\mathsf{sk}}(C_1||C_2)$.
  7. Return the ciphertext $C = \sigma||C_1||C_2$.
Decrypt(sk, C): Parse C as $\sigma||C_1||C_2$ and $C_1 = c_1||\cdots||c_m$. For each $i \in \{1, \ldots, m\}$:
  1. $p \leftarrow$ Dec(sk, c_i).
  2. If p is $\perp$, then continue to the next i.
  3. Otherwise, parse p as vk$||K$.
  4. If Ver$_{\mathsf{vk}}(C_1||C_2, \sigma)$, return $M = D_K(C_2)$.
  If none of the c_i decrypts and verifies, return $\perp$.

Notice the time taken by Decrypt to execute could leak information. Recipient privacy relies on the attacker being unable to determine whether a decryption fails because $p = \perp$ or because the signature did not verify. Implementations must take care to prevent such timing attacks. We state our main theorem as follows. Due to space constraints, we give the proof in the full version of the paper [15].

Theorem 1. *If* (Init, Gen, Enc, Dec) *is both ϵ_1 strongly correct and (t, q, ϵ_2) CCA key private and* (Sig-Gen, Sig, Ver) *is $(t, 1, \epsilon_3)$ strongly existentially unforgeable, the above construction is $(t, q, n, n(\epsilon_1 + \epsilon_2 + \epsilon_3))$ CCA recipient private.*

The semantic security of our scheme follows in a straightforward manner. Because our scheme achieves broadcast encryption by concatenating public key encryptions, each user can generate his or her own public key and have an authority issue a certificate binding it to his or her identity.

4.2   CCA Recipient Privacy with Efficient Decryption

To decrypt a ciphertext in the CCA recipient private scheme above, a recipient must attempt to decrypt $n/2$ components of the ciphertext, on average, where n is the number of recipients. Non-private schemes improve performance by labeling ciphertext components with recipient identities, directing the attention of decryptors to appropriate ciphertext components. However, these labels reveal the identities of the recipients.

In this section, we construct a private broadcast encryption system that requires only a constant number of cryptographic operations in order to decrypt, regardless of the number of recipients. Our scheme is similar to the previous one with small modifications. Each private key is extended with a random exponent a and each public key is extended with the corresponding value g^a. The encryption algorithm first chooses a random exponent r and labels the ciphertext component for the public key (pk, g^a) with $H(g^{ra})$, where the hash function H is modeled as a random oracle. When decrypting, each user first calculates $H(g^{ra})$ and then uses the result to locate the ciphertext component encrypted for him or her. Users need only perform one public key decryption to recover the message.

The recipient privacy of this scheme relies on a group G in which the computational Diffie-Hellman problem is believed to be hard, but there exists an efficient algorithm for testing Diffie-Hellman tuples (i.e. CDH is hard, but DDH is easy). For example, groups with efficiently computable bilinear maps are widely believed to have this property [16]. The algorithm for deciding DDH is used in the simulation proof, but not in the construction itself. The requirement that DDH be easy can be relaxed, at the cost of a looser reduction.

Let G be a group, with generator g, where CDH is hard and DDH is easy and let $H : G \to \{0,1\}^\lambda$ be a hash function that is modeled as a random oracle (for some security parameter λ). Given a strongly correct, IK-CCA public key scheme $(\mathsf{Init}, \mathsf{Gen}, \mathsf{Enc}, \mathsf{Dec})$, a strongly existentially unforgeable signature scheme $(\mathsf{Sig\text{-}Gen}, \mathsf{Sig}, \mathsf{Ver})$, and semantically secure symmetric key encryption and decryption algorithms (E, D), we construct a private broadcast encryption system as follows.

Setup(λ): Return $\mathsf{Init}(\lambda)$.

Keygen(I): Run $(\mathsf{pk}, \mathsf{sk}) \leftarrow \mathsf{Gen}(I)$ and choose a random exponent a. Let $\mathsf{pk}' = (\mathsf{pk}, g^a)$ and $\mathsf{sk}' = (\mathsf{sk}, a)$. Return $(\mathsf{pk}', \mathsf{sk}')$.

Encrypt(S, M):
1. $(\mathsf{vk}, \mathsf{sk}) \leftarrow \mathsf{Sig\text{-}Gen}(\lambda)$.
2. Choose a random symmetric key K.
3. Choose a random exponent r and set $T = g^r$.
4. For each $(\mathsf{pk}, g^a) \in S$, $c_{\mathsf{pk}} \leftarrow H(g^{ar}) || \mathsf{Enc}_{\mathsf{pk}}(\mathsf{vk} || g^{ar} || K)$.
5. Let C_1 be the concatenation of the c_{pk}, ordered by their values of $H(g^{ar})$.
6. $C_2 \leftarrow E_K(M)$
7. $\sigma \leftarrow \mathsf{Sig}_{\mathsf{sk}}(T || C_1 || C_2)$.
8. Return the ciphertext $C = \sigma || T || C_1 || C_2$.

Decrypt$((\mathsf{sk}, a), C)$: Parse C as $\sigma || T || C_1 || C_2$ and $C_1 = c_1 || \cdots || c_m$.
1. Calculate $l = H(T^a) = H(g^{ar})$.
2. Find c_j such that $c_j = l || c$ for some c, if it exists, else return $\perp$ and stop.
3. Calculate $p \leftarrow \mathsf{Dec}(\mathsf{sk}, c)$.
4. If p is $\perp$, return $\perp$ and stop.
5. Otherwise, parse p as $\mathsf{vk} || x || K$.
6. If $x \neq T^a$, return $\perp$ and stop.
7. If $\mathsf{Ver}_{\mathsf{vk}}(T || C_1 || C_2, \sigma)$, return $M = D_K(C_2)$; otherwise, return $\perp$.

Notice decryption time is independent of the number of recipients. Also, the algorithm for deciding DDH tuples is not used in the construction. The DDH decisions algorithm is used by the simulator in the proof of the following theorem to recognize when the adversary has successfully computed a ciphertext component label (and thus can be used to defeat CDH). Due to space constraints, we give the proof in the full version of the paper [15].

Theorem 2. *If* (Init, Gen, Enc, Dec) *is* ϵ_1 *strongly correct,* (t, q, ϵ_2) *CCA semantically secure and* (t, q, ϵ_3) *CCA key private,* (Sig-Gen, Sig, Ver) *is* $(t, 1, \epsilon_4)$ *strongly existentially unforgeable, CDH is* (t, ϵ_5) *hard in* G*, and DDH is efficiently computable in* G*, then the above construction is* $(t, q, n, n(\epsilon_1 + 2\epsilon_2 + \epsilon_3 + \epsilon_4 + 2\epsilon_5))$ *CCA recipient private.*

4.3   Identity-Based Encryption Extensions

We can extend our constructions to use Identity-Based Encryption (IBE) [17, 18] by using an anonymous IBE [19, 20] scheme. An IBE scheme is called anonymous if a ciphertext does not reveal the identity under which it was encrypted. The Boneh-Franklin scheme [18] has this property, for example. Identity-based encryption is advantageous in our setting where the identities of the recipients should be kept private because an identity-based encryption algorithm need not retrieve a recipient's public key certificate in order to encrypt to him or her. Typical public key systems require encryptors to obtain the public keys of recipients over a network. An eavesdropper could potentially ascertain information about message recipients by monitoring the public keys requested by the encryptor. An IBE encryptor, however, need not make such network requests and avoids this potential vulnerability.

5   Conclusions

In many content distribution applications it is important to protect both the content being distributed and the identities of users allowed to access the content. Currently, encrypted file systems and encrypted email systems fail to protect the privacy of their users. User privacy is compromised because the underlying encryption schemes disclose the identities of a ciphertext's recipients. Many such systems simply give away the identities of the users in the form of labels attached to the ciphertext. Additionally, those systems that attempt to avoid disclosing the recipient's identity, such as GnuPG, are vulnerable to having their user's privacy compromised by a new chosen-ciphertext attack that we introduced.

Our proposed mechanism, private broadcast encryption, enables the efficient encryption of messages to multiple recipients without revealing the identities of message recipients, even to other recipients. We presented two constructions of private broadcast encryption systems. Both of these satisfy a strong definition of recipient privacy under active attacks. The second additionally achieves decryption in a constant number of cryptographic operations, performing comparably to current systems that do not provide user privacy.

References

1. Bellare, M., Boldyreva, A., Desai, A., Pointcheval, D.: Key-privacy in public-key encryption. In: ASIACRYPT '01: Proceedings of the 7th International Conference on the Theory and Application of Cryptology and Information Security. Volume 2238 of LNCS., Springer–Verlag (2001) 566–582
2. Fiat, A., Naor, M.: Broadcast encryption. In: CRYPTO '93: Proceedings of Advances in Cryptology. Volume 773 of LNCS., Springer–Verlag (1994) 480–491
3. Naor, M., Pinkas, B.: Efficient trace and revoke schemes. In: Financial cryptography 2000. Volume 1962 of LNCS., Springer–Verlag (2000) 1–20
4. Naor, D., Naor, M., Lotspiech, J.: Revocation and tracing schemes for stateless receivers. In: CRYPTO '01: Proceedings of Advances in Cryptology. Volume 2139 of LNCS., Springer–Verlag (2001) 41–62
5. Boneh, D., Gentry, C., Waters, B.: Collusion resistant broadcast encryption with short ciphertexts and private keys. In: CRYPTO '05: Proceedings of Advances in Cryptology. Volume 3621 of LNCS., Springer–Verlag (2005) 258–275
6. Bellare, M., Boldyreva, A., Micali, S.: Public-key encryption in a multi-user setting: Security proofs and improvements. In: EUROCRYPT '00: Proceedings of International Conference on the Theory and Application of Cryptographic Techniques. Volume 1807 of LNCS., Springer–Verlag (2000) 259–274
7. OpenPGP: The OpenPGP alliance home page (2005) http://www.openpgp.org/.
8. Werner Koch: The GNU privacy guard (2005) http://www.gnupg.org/.
9. MIT: MIT PGP public key server (2005) http://pgpkeys.mit.edu/.
10. Callas, J., Donnerhacke, L., Finney, H., Thayer, R.: RFC 2440: OpenPGP message format (1998) http://www.ietf.org/rfc/rfc2440.txt.
11. National Institute of Standards and Technology: Digital signature standard (DSS) (2000) http://www.csrc.nist.gov/publications/fips/.
12. VeriSign: Search for digital IDs (2005) https://digitalid.verisign.com/services/client/.
13. Lamport, L.: Constructing digital signatures from a one way function. Technical report, SRI International (1979)
14. Rompel, J.: One-way functions are necessary and sufficient for secure signatures. In: STOC '90: Proceedings of the Twenty-Second Annual ACM Symposium on Theory of Computing, ACM Press (1990) 387–394
15. Barth, A., Boneh, D., Waters, B.: Privacy in encrypted content distribution using private broadcast encryption (2006) http://www.adambarth.org/papers/barth-boneh-waters-2006-full.pdf.
16. Joux, A., Nguyen, K.: Separating Decision Diffie-Hellman from Diffie-Hellman in cryptographic groups. Technical Report eprint.iacr.org/2001/003 (2001)
17. Shamir, A.: Identity-based cryptosystems and signature schemes. In: CRYPTO '84: Advances in Cryptology. Volume 196 of LNCS., Springer–Verlag (1985) 47–53
18. Boneh, D., Franklin, M.K.: Identity-based encryption from the Weil pairing. In: CRYPTO '01: Proceedings of Advances in Cryptology. Volume 2139 of LNCS., Springer–Verlag (2001) 213–229
19. Boneh, D., Di Crescenzo, G., Ostrovsky, R., Persiano, G.: Public key encryption with keyword search. In: EUROCRYPT '04: Proceedings of International Conference on the Theory and Application of Cryptographic Techniques. Volume 3027 of LNCS., Springer–Verlag (2004) 506–522
20. Abdalla, M., Bellare, M., Catalano, D., Kiltz, E., Kohno, T., Lange, T., Malone-Lee, J., Neven, G., Paillier, P., Shi, H.: Searchable encryption revisited: Consistency properties, relation to anonymous IBE, and extensions. Technical Report eprint.iacr.org/2005/254 (2005)

A Private Stable Matching Algorithm

Philippe Golle

Palo Alto Research Center
3333 Coyote Hill Road, Palo Alto, CA 94304, USA
pgolle@parc.com

Abstract. Existing stable matching algorithms reveal the preferences of all participants, as well as the history of matches made and broken in the course of computing a stable match. This information leakage not only violates the privacy of participants, but also leaves matching algorithms vulnerable to manipulation [8, 10, 25].

To address these limitations, this paper proposes a *private* stable matching algorithm, based on the famous algorithm of Gale and Shapley [6]. Our private algorithm is run by a number of independent parties whom we call the Matching Authorities. As long as a majority of Matching Authorities are honest, our protocol correctly outputs a stable match, and reveals no other information than what can be learned from that match and from the preferences of participants controlled by the adversary. The security and privacy of our protocol are based on re-encryption mix networks and on an additively homomorphic semantically secure public-key encryption scheme such as Paillier.

1 Introduction

Stable matching algorithms are best explained with the terminology of marriage and are thus also known as stable marriage algorithms. Let us consider an equal number n of men and women. We assume that every man ranks the n women according to how desirable each is to him, without ties. Similarly, every woman ranks the n men according to how desirable each is to her, without ties.

A match is a bijection between men and women, or equivalently a set of n heterosexual monogamous marriages between the n men and the n women. Ideally, a perfect match would pair every man with the woman he likes best and vice versa. Clearly the preferences expressed by men and women rarely allow for a perfect match. For example, if two men rank the same woman first, one of them at least will have to settle for a less desirable partner.

A weaker requirement is to find a match that is, if not perfect, then at least *stable*. Consider a match in which a man A is married to a woman B and a man A' to a woman B'. If A prefers B' to his wife B, and B' prefers A to her husband A', A and B' both have an incentive to leave their partner and marry each other (the match is thus unstable). A *stable* match is a match such that there is no man and woman that both like each other better than their respective partners. When a match is stable, all couples are static: a man tempted to abandon his

G. Di Crescenzo and A. Rubin (Eds.): FC 2006, LNCS 4107, pp. 65–80, 2006.
© IFCA/Springer-Verlag Berlin Heidelberg 2006

wife for another woman he ranks higher will be rebuffed, since that woman ranks her partner higher than the new suitor.

A stable matching algorithm takes as inputs the preferences of men for women and of women for men, and outputs a stable matching between them. Efficient stable matching algorithms are well known [6] and have important real-world applications. They are used notably to assign graduating medical students to residency programs at hospitals in the US [15], Canada [3] and Scotland [23]: a stable match between students and hospitals is computed automatically based on the preferences of students for hospitals and of hospitals for students. In Norway and Singapore [25], stable matching algorithms are used to assign students to schools and universities. In fact, the use of stable matching algorithms is sufficiently widespread that there exist companies dedicated solely to administering matching programs. National Matching Services [14], for example, administers matching programs for psychology internships in the US and Canada [1], for articling positions with law firms in Alberta (Canada) and for many others. All told, stable matching algorithms impact the careers of tens of thousands of students and professionals annually.

Considering the stakes involved and the sensitive nature of the preferences expressed, stable matching algorithms should afford participants the maximum amount of privacy possible. Ideally, the algorithm should output a stable match without leaking any additional information. Unfortunately, existing stable matching algorithms fall far short of that ideal. They take as input the complete list of preferences of men and women (or students and hospitals), and reveal the complete history of engagements made and broken in the process of computing a stable match.

This information leakage violates the privacy of participants, and potentially exposes them to embarrassment or ridicule. Consider for example that no medical student would like it to be known that she was matched to her least favorite hospital. Worse still, the public disclosure of preferences leaves matching algorithms vulnerable to manipulation [8, 10, 25]: under certain circumstances, participants with knowledge of the preferences of other participants have incentives to alter their own true preference list (see Section 2 for detail).

In the absence of a better solution, these problems have up to now been weakly mitigated by the assumption that all participants trust a third party to receive their preference lists, run the algorithm and output a stable match without revealing any other information. This approach requires a considerable amount of trust in a single entity and runs counter to the security tenet that trust should be distributed. Reliance on a single trusted third party is particularly problematic when the third party must protect the interests of participants with unequal power and influence. The third party is at risk of corruption by the more powerful protocol participants (e.g. the hospitals) at the expense of the less powerful participants (e.g. the medical students). To afford equal privacy protection to all participants, we propose a private stable matching algorithm.

Our private stable matching algorithm is based on the famous algorithm of Gale and Shapley [6], which we review in Section 2. The private algorithm is run by a number of independent parties whom we call the Matching Authorities. As long as a majority of Matching Authorities are honest, our protocol correctly outputs a stable match, and reveals no other information than what can be learned from that match and from the preferences of participants controlled by the adversary. The security and privacy of our protocol are based on re-encryption mix networks and on an additively homomorphic semantically secure public-key encryption scheme such as Paillier.

1.1 Financial Applications of Stable Matching Algorithms

The stable matching problem describes a two-sided, one-to-one matching market. The most famous examples of such markets are college admissions and entry-level labor markets. But examples of two-sided markets go far beyond labor markets [20, 21]. Among others examples, two-sided markets have been used to model the matching of venture capitalists and companies in capital markets [24] and the matching of suppliers and consumers in supply chain networks [17]. Aside from matching markets, the use of stable matching algorithms has recently been proposed to determine stable winner allocations in certain types of multi-unit or combinatorial auctions [2].

2 Gale-Shapley Stable Matching Algorithm

There exist several formulations of the stable matching problem, all closely related. In this section and the rest of the paper, we consider a model of one-to-one matchings (i.e. no polygamy), with complete preference lists (i.e every man ranks all women and every woman ranks all men). The results of this paper can easily be adapted to other models. For example, the many-to-one model (in which one hospital has internship slots for multiple students) reduces to the one-to-one model by cloning an appropriate number of times the participants who accept multiple partners.

We review the famous stable matching algorithm of Gale and Shapley [6]. In this algorithm, men and women play different roles. Arbitrarily, we present a matching algorithm in which men propose to women (these roles can naturally be reversed). The algorithm takes as input the lists of preferences of men and women. Throughout the algorithm, men and women are divided into two groups: those that are *engaged*, and those that are *free* (i.e. not yet or no longer engaged). Initially, all men and all women are free.

As long as the group of free men is non-empty, the algorithm selects at random one man A from the group of free men. Man A proposes to the woman whom he ranks highest among the women to whom he has never proposed before (let's call this woman B). One of three things may happen:

- B is free. In this case, A and B are engaged to each other and both move to the engaged group.

- B is already engaged to A' and ranks A ahead of A'. In this case, B breaks her engagement to A' and instead gets engaged to A. A and B join the engaged group, whereas A' goes back to the group of free men.
- B is already engaged to A' and ranks A' ahead of A. In this case, B stays engaged to A' and A stays in the group of free men.

Properties and limitations. Let n denote the number of men and women. The algorithm terminates in at most n^2 steps and outputs a match that is stable (see [6] for more detail). This "men-propose" algorithm is men-optimal [19]: the optimal strategy for men is to reveal their true preference lists, as long as all other participants also reveal their true preferences. Women on the other hand have incentives to falsify their preferences [25] in men-propose algorithms, assuming they have full knowledge of the preference lists of all participants. This attack is of real practical concern. In fact, the Gale-Shapley algorithm gives women all the knowledge they need to manipulate the algorithm, since it exposes the complete preference lists of men and women, together with the entire history of engagements made and broken.

Private Gale-Shapley with Secure Multiparty Computation. Generic secure multiparty computation techniques [26, 9] allow n men and n women to compute privately the outcome of the Gale-Shapley algorithm. However, these generic techniques are ill-suited for this purpose:

- **Generic protocols incur high computation and communication costs.** It is hard to estimate precisely the number of gates required to build a circuit that implements the (randomized) Gale-Shapley algorithm. A lower bound is $O(n^2 \log(n))$ gates to perform n^2 comparisons between values of $\log(n)$ bits. With n players, this gives a lower bound on the computational and communication cost of the protocol of $O(n^3 \log(n))$ against passive adversaries. Against an active adversary corrupting less than $n/2$ of the players, the lower bound on the computational and communication cost is $O(n^4 \log(n))$ using the most efficient multiparty computation protocol [4]. In contrast, our protocol incurs a computational and communication cost of $O(n^3)$.
- **Generic protocols are impractical.** The process of building a circuit that implements Gale-Shapley is difficult and error-prone. In contrast, our protocol relies on standard cryptographic components (mix networks) with known efficient implementations.

Efficient private variant of Gale-Shapley. In this paper, we propose an efficient private variant of the Gale-Shapley matching algorithm that is based on mix networks rather than generic secure multiparty computations. A private variant of Gale-Shapley must address two main problems. The first problem is to redesign the algorithm so as to hide the history of engagements made and broken, the number of participants free or engaged at any given point, as well as any other information about the internal state of the algorithm. We propose a solution to this problem in Section 4. The second problem is that the preferences of participants must be encrypted. We solve this problem in Section 5 and 6. Finally, we present a complete private stable matching algorithm in Section 7 and analyze its properties in Section 8.

3   Model and Definitions

Our algorithm is run jointly by a number of independent parties whom we call matching authorities. The matching authorities collectively run a number of distributed cryptographic protocols, such as distributed key generation, re-encryption mix networks, oblivious tests of plaintext equalities, etc. These protocols serve as building blocks for our private stable matching algorithm and are described in Section 5.

The security and privacy of our stable matching algorithm reduces to the security and privacy of the underlying cryptographic building blocks. We can thus define our adversarial model loosely as the intersection of the adversarial models of the building blocks. For simplicity, we present our results assuming a "honest-but-curious" adversary. More precisely, we consider a static adversary who has passive control over up to all the participants (men and women), and passive control over up to all but one of the matching authorities, as is commonly assumed in the literature on mix networks. Our techniques can easily be extended to accommodate active adversaries, as discussed in Section 8.1.

Definition 1. (Private stable matching algorithm) *An algorithm for computing a stable match is private if it outputs a stable match and reveals no other information to the adversary than what the adversary can learn from that match and from the preferences of the participants it controls.*

4   Hiding the Internal State of the Algorithm

We propose a variant of the Gale-Shapley algorithm that hides its internal state variables, such as the number of men and women free and engaged at any given time, or the history of engagements made and broken. The algorithm described here will not become private until it is combined in Section 7 with the techniques of Sections 5 and 6. It is presented here in non-private form to simplify the understanding of later sections. As before, the algorithm takes as input the lists of preferences of n men and n women and outputs a stable match between them.

Rankings. Let $A_1, \ldots, A_n$ denote n men and $B_1, \ldots, B_n$ denote n women. Every man ranks the women from most to least desired. Thus, a man assigns rank 0 to the woman he likes best, rank 1 to his second place favorite, and so on all the way to rank $n-1$ to the woman he likes the least (rankings do not allow for ties). Similarly, every woman assigns ranks to men from 0 (most favorite man) to $n-1$ (least favorite man). Being ranked *ahead* of someone means being assigned a lower rank, and thus being preferred to that other person. Being ranked *behind* someone means being assigned a higher rank, and thus being less desired than that other person.

Notations. The preference of man A_i is a vector $\boldsymbol{a}_i = (r_{i,1}, \ldots, r_{i,n})$, where $r_{i,j} \in \{0, n-1\}$ is the rank of woman B_j for man A_i. Similarly, the preference of woman B_j is a vector $\boldsymbol{b}_j = (s_{j,1}, \ldots, s_{j,n})$, where $s_{j,i} \in \{0, \ldots, n-1\}$ is the rank of man A_i for woman B_j. The algorithm takes as inputs the vectors $\boldsymbol{a}_1, \ldots, \boldsymbol{a}_n$ and $\boldsymbol{b}_1, \ldots, \boldsymbol{b}_n$.

Preprocessing. The first step of the algorithm consists of introducing an additional n "fake" men, denoted $A_{n+1}, \ldots, A_{2n}$ (no fake women are defined). The preferences of fake men for women are unimportant to the algorithm. Arbitrarily, we let $\boldsymbol{a}_i = (0, 1, \ldots, n-1)$ for $i = n+1, \ldots, 2n$. The preferences $\boldsymbol{b}_j$ of women must be augmented to reflect the addition of the fake men. As long as women rank all fake men behind all real men, their preferences are unimportant to the algorithm. Arbitrarily, we let every woman B_j assign rank $s_{j,i} = i - 1$ to man A_i for $i = n+1, \ldots, 2n$. We keep the notation $\boldsymbol{b}_j$ for the vector of $2n$ elements that encodes the augmented preference of woman B_j. After this preprocessing step, the algorithm has $2n$ vectors $\boldsymbol{a}_1, \ldots, \boldsymbol{a}_{2n}$ (each vector contains n elements that express the rankings assigned by one man to the n women) and n vectors $\boldsymbol{b}_1, \ldots, \boldsymbol{b}_n$ (each vector contains $2n$ elements that express the rankings assigned by one woman to the $2n$ men). Note that the introduction of fake men, and the corresponding update of preferences is done entirely by the algorithm without any involvement from real men or real women.

Computing a stable match. The algorithm proceeds in n rounds. We let $\mathcal{E}_k$ denote the set of engaged men and $\mathcal{F}_k$ denote the set of free men at the beginning of round $k = 1, \ldots, n+1$ (there are only n rounds; with a slight abuse of notation, we let $\mathcal{F}_{n+1}$ and $\mathcal{E}_{n+1}$ denote the set of free and engaged men at the *end* of the last round). Initially, all real men are free $\mathcal{F}_1 = \{A_1, \ldots, A_n\}$, and all fake men are engaged $\mathcal{E}_1 = \{A_{n+1}, \ldots, A_{2n}\}$. Arbitrarily, we let fake man A_{n+i} be initially engaged to women B_i. The other sets are initially empty: $\mathcal{E}_k = \mathcal{F}_k = \emptyset$ for $k > 1$. The algorithm executes the following routine for $k = 1, \ldots, n$:

- While the set $\mathcal{F}_k$ is non-empty, select at random one man (denoted A_i) from $\mathcal{F}_k$. A_i proposes to the woman whom he ranks highest among the women to whom he has never proposed before (let's call this woman B_j). Note that women B_j is always already engaged to a man $A_{i'}$, for some $i' \neq i$. One of two things may happen:
  - If B_j ranks A_i ahead of $A_{i'}$, B_j breaks her engagement to $A_{i'}$ and becomes engaged to A_i. Man A_i is removed from the set $\mathcal{F}_k$ and added to $\mathcal{E}_k$, whereas man $A_{i'}$ is removed from $\mathcal{E}_k$ and added to $\mathcal{F}_{k+1}$.
  - If B_j ranks A_i behind $A_{i'}$, she stays engaged to $A_{i'}$. Man A_i is removed from set $\mathcal{F}_k$ and added to set $\mathcal{F}_{k+1}$.
- When $\mathcal{F}_k$ is empty, we define $\mathcal{E}_{k+1} = \mathcal{E}_k$.

The algorithm ends after n rounds and outputs the set $\mathcal{E}_{n+1}$ of engaged men and their current partners.

Invariants. Note that this algorithm preserves certain invariants. All n women are always engaged to some man. During round k, the number of engaged men is always exactly $|\mathcal{E}_k| = n$. Engaged men do not move progressively from set $\mathcal{E}_k$ to set $\mathcal{E}_{k+1}$ during round k, but rather they move all at once at the end of round k. Every time a new proposal is made, the cardinality of $\mathcal{F}_k$ decreases by one, the cardinality of $\mathcal{F}_{k+1}$ increases by one and the cardinality of $\mathcal{E}_k$ is unchanged, irrespective of whether a woman changes partner or not.

Proposition 1. *This algorithm outputs a stable match between the real men $A_1, \ldots, A_n$ and the n women $B_1, \ldots, B_n$.*

Proof. We must prove that the match is stable and involves only real men (no fake men). The proof that the final match is stable is exactly similar to that given for the original Gale-Shapley algorithm in [6].

The proof that the final match involves only real men is by contradiction. We observe first that once a woman is engaged to a real man, she will stay engaged to real men in subsequent rounds, since all women rank all real men ahead of all fake men. Now assume that a fake man A_i is engaged to a woman B_j when the algorithm ends after n rounds. This implies that B_j was never engaged to a real man. Since there are only n women, there must be at least one real man $A_{i'}$ who remains free at the end of the protocol. Now the free real man $A_{i'}$ must have proposed to all n women, B_j included, and must have been rejected by all. But B_j, who was always engaged to fake men, could not reject $A_{i'}$ without breaking the assumption that all women prefer real men to fake men.   □

5   Cryptographic Building Blocks

Our private stable matching algorithm uses cryptographic building blocks which we now describe briefly. These building blocks are all standard distributed cryptographic algorithms run jointly by the matching authorities.

Threshold Paillier encryption. The Paillier encryption scheme [18] allows for threshold encryption [5, 7]. In what follows, all ciphertexts are encrypted with a threshold version of Paillier. The matching authorities hold shares of the corresponding decryption key, such that a quorum consisting of all parties can decrypt.

Robust re-encryption mix network. A re-encryption mix network re-encrypts and permutes a number of input (Paillier) ciphertexts. In our application, the matching authorities play the role of mix servers. If we allow active adversaries (see Section 8.1), we must use robust re-encryption mixnets such as [11] or [16]. When we say the matching authorities "mix" a set of inputs according to a permutation π, we mean that they run the set of inputs through a mix network and we let π denote the global (secret) permutation (which is not known to the matching authorities).

Oblivious test of plaintext equality. Let $E(m_1)$ and $E(m_2)$ be two Paillier ciphertexts. An oblivious test of plaintext equality [12, 13] lets the joint holders of the decryption key determine whether $m_1 = m_2$ without revealing any other information (hence the name oblivious). We denote this protocol EQTEST$(E(m_1), E(m_2))$. The protocol outputs either $m_1 = m_2$ or $m_1 \neq m_2$.

Repeated test of plaintext equality. The protocol INDEX$(a, E(\rho))$ takes as input a vector $a = (E(a_1), \ldots, E(a_n))$ of n Paillier ciphertexts and an additional Paillier ciphertext $E(\rho)$ such that there exists one and only one value $i \in \{1, \ldots, n\}$ for which $\rho = a_i$. The protocol outputs the index i such that $a_i = \rho$. The protocol INDEX can be implemented with n instances of EQTEST.

Finding the larger of 2 plaintexts. Let $E(m_1)$ and $E(m_2)$ be two Paillier ciphertexts such that $m_1, m_2 \in \{0, \ldots, n-1\}$ and $m_1 \neq m_2$. We propose a protocol COMPARE$(E(m_1), E(m_2))$ that outputs true if $m_1 > m_2$ and false otherwise, without leaking any other information. The protocol proceeds as follows. For $i = 1, \ldots, n-1$, the matching authorities compute ciphertext $D_i = E(m_1 - m_2 - i)$ using Paillier's additive homomorphism. Note that $m_1 > m_2$ if and only if one of the ciphertexts D_i is an encryption of 0. The matching authorities mix (i.e. re-encrypt and permute) the set of ciphertexts $D_1, \ldots, D_{n-1}$. Let $D'_1, \ldots, D'_{n-1}$ denote the mixed set. The matching authorities then compute EQTEST$(D'_i, E(0))$ for $i = 1, \ldots, n-1$. If an equality is found, they output true, otherwise they output false.

6   Encrypting Preferences

Let E denote the encryption function for a threshold public-key encryption scheme with an additive homomorphism, such as for example a threshold version [5, 7] of the Paillier encryption scheme [18]. We assume that the matching authorities are the joint holders of the private decryption key.

Let $A_1, \ldots, A_m$ be m men and $B_1, \ldots, B_n$ be n women. As in Section 4, we let $r_{i,j} \in \{0, \ldots, n-1\}$ denote the rank of woman B_j for man A_i, and $s_{j,i} \in \{0, \ldots, m-1\}$ denote the rank of man A_i for woman B_j. We define $p_{i,j} = E(r_{i,j})$ and $a_i = (p_{i,1}, \ldots, p_{i,n})$. Similarly, we define $q_{j,i} = E(s_{j,i})$ and $b_j = (q_{j,1}, \ldots, q_{j,m})$.

6.1   Bid Creation

We define a "bid" as an encrypted representation of the preferences of one men for women, together with additional "book-keeping" information. For $i \in \{1, \ldots, m\}$, the bid W_i that represents the preferences of man A_i consists of $3n + 2$ Paillier ciphertexts defined as follows:

- An encryption $E(i)$ of the index i of man A_i.
- The vector $a_i = (p_{i,1}, \ldots, p_{i,n})$.
- A vector $v_i = (E(1), \ldots, E(n))$.
- The vector $q_i = (q_{1,i}, \ldots, q_{n,i})$.
- A ciphertext $E(\rho)$, where ρ is the number of times the bid has been rejected. Initially $\rho = 0$.

The role of the ciphertext $E(i)$ is to maintain the association between bid W_i and the man A_i whose preferences the bid expresses. The vector $\boldsymbol{a}_i$ encodes the preferences of man A_i for women $B_1, \ldots, B_n$. As we shall see, the elements of $\boldsymbol{a}_i$ are permuted at random in the course of the private stable matching algorithm. Thus the need for the vector $\boldsymbol{v}_i$, whose role is to maintain the association between the rankings contained in $\boldsymbol{a}_i$ and the women these rankings pertain to: the element in position j of $\boldsymbol{v}_i$ is always an encryption of the index of the woman whose rank is given by the element in position j of $\boldsymbol{a}_i$. The vector $\boldsymbol{q}_i$ encodes the initial rank given to man A_i by women $B_1, \ldots, B_n$. Finally, the ciphertext $E(\rho)$ records the number of times that the bid has been rejected: the value ρ is updated every time an engagement is broken.

Free and engaged bids. A bid by itself, as defined above, is called a free bid because it is not paired up with a woman. A bid paired up with a woman is called an engaged bid. More precisely, an engaged bid is a triplet $(W_i,\ E(j),\ q_{j,i})$, where:

- $W_i = [E(i),\ \boldsymbol{a}_i,\ \boldsymbol{v}_i,\ \boldsymbol{q}_i,\ E(\rho)]$ is the bid of man A_i
- $E(j)$ is an encryption of the index $j \in \{1, \ldots, n\}$ of a woman B_j
- $q_{j,i}$ is an encryption of the rank given to man A_i by woman B_j

Breaking an engagement. Let $(W_i,\ E(j),\ q_{j,i})$ be an engaged bid. If this bid loses woman B_j to another bid, we update it as follows. First, we strip the triplet of the values $E(j)$ and $q_{j,i}$, keeping only the free bid W_i. Next, we increment the counter ρ in W_i by one, using Paillier's additive homomorphism (i.e. we multiply $E(\rho)$ by $E(1)$ to obtain $E(\rho + 1)$).

6.2   Bid Mixing

The Paillier cryptosystem allows for semantically secure re-encryption of ciphertexts. Since bids (both free and engaged) are made up of Paillier ciphertexts, they can be re-encrypted, and in particular they can be mixed with a re-encryption mix network. We consider two types of mixing for bids: "external" mixing and "internal" mixing.

External bid mixing. External mixing takes as input a set of bids, either all free or all engaged, and mixes them in a way that hides the order of the bids but preserves the internal position of ciphertexts *within* a bid. External mixing considers bids as atomic elements and preserves their internal integrity. More precisely, let us consider an initial ordering of k free bids $W_1, \ldots, W_k$ and let σ be a permutation on k elements. The external mixing operation re-encrypts all the Paillier ciphertexts in all the bids (preserving the order of ciphertexts within each bid) and outputs $W_{\sigma(1)}, \ldots, W_{\sigma(k)}$. A set of engaged bids can be mixed externally in exactly the same way. In this paper, free and engaged bids are never mixed externally together (since free bids are made of $3n + 2$ ciphertexts and engaged bids of $3n + 4$, they would not blend together). Intuitively, external bid mixing hides which bid encodes the preferences of which man.

Internal bid mixing. Internal mixing takes as input a set of bids that may contain both free and engaged bids. These bids are mixed "internally" in a way that hides the order of a subset of the ciphertexts within the bids but preserves the order of the bids themselves. More precisely, let us consider a set of k bids and let π be a permutation on n elements. The bids in the set are processed one by one, and output in the same order as they were given as input. A free bid is processed as follows. Let $W_i = [E(i), \boldsymbol{a}_i, \boldsymbol{v}_i, \boldsymbol{q}_i, E(\rho)]$ be a free bid. We define the internally permuted bid as $\pi(W_i) = [E(i), \pi(\boldsymbol{a}_i), \pi(\boldsymbol{v}_i), \pi(\boldsymbol{q}_i), E(\rho)]$, where the permuted vectors $\pi(\boldsymbol{a}_i)$, $\pi(\boldsymbol{v}_i)$ and $\pi(\boldsymbol{q}_i)$ are defined as follows:

Let $\boldsymbol{a}_i = (p_{i,1}, \ldots, p_{i,n})$. Let $p'_{i,1}, \ldots, p'_{i,n}$ be re-encryptions of the ciphertexts $p_{i,1}, \ldots, p_{i,n}$. We let $\pi(\boldsymbol{a}_i) = (p'_{i,\pi(1)}, \ldots, p'_{i,\pi(n)})$. The vectors $\pi(\boldsymbol{v}_i)$ and $\pi(\boldsymbol{q}_i)$ are defined in exactly the same way.

Engaged bids are processed in the same way. Let $(W_i, E(j), q_{j,i})$ be an engaged bid. We define the corresponding internally permuted engaged bid as $(\pi(W_i), E(j), q_{j,i})$.

Note that the same internal permutation π is applied to all the bids in the set. Note also that, as always in mix networks, the global permutation π is in fact the combination of permutations chosen by all the matching authorities, so that the matching authorities themselves do not know π (unless they all collude). Intuitively, internal mixing hides which woman a particular ciphertext pertains to.

6.3   Conflicts Between Bids

Opening a free bid. Let $\pi(W_i) = [E(i), \pi(\boldsymbol{a}_i), \pi(\boldsymbol{v}_i), \pi(\boldsymbol{q}_i), E(\rho)]$ be a free bid that has been internally permuted by a permutation π on n elements. Since π is the result of one (or several) internal bid mixing operations, it is not known to the matching authorities. Let j be the index of the woman B_j assigned rank ρ by that bid. Opening W_i means determining $E(j)$ and $q_{j,i} = E(s_{j,i})$ without learning anything else about the bid. Note that opening a bid would be trivial if the permutation π were known. Without knowledge of π, the matching authorities open a bid as follows. The matching authorities jointly compute $\alpha = \mathsf{INDEX}(\pi(\boldsymbol{a}_i), E(\rho))$. Since the same permutation π is applied to $\boldsymbol{a}_i, \boldsymbol{v}_i$ and $\boldsymbol{q}_i$, the element in position α of $\pi(\boldsymbol{v}_i)$ is $E(j)$ and the element in position α of $\pi(\boldsymbol{q}_i)$ is $q_{j,i} = E(s_{j,i})$.

Detecting a conflict. Let $\pi(W_i)$ be a free bid, and let $\left(\pi(W_{i'}), E(j'), q_{j',i'} \right)$ be an engaged bid, both internally permuted according to the same permutation π on n elements (we assume again that π is not known to the matching authorities). Let $E(j)$ and $q_{j,i}$ be the ciphertexts obtained when the free bid $\pi(W_i)$ is opened. Detecting a conflict between these two bids means determining whether $j = j'$, without learning anything else about the bids. To do so, the matching authorities jointly compute $\mathsf{EQTEST}(E(j), E(j'))$. The bids conflict if and only if EQTEST returns an equality.

Resolving a conflict. Let $\pi(W_i)$ be a free bid that opens up to $E(j), q_{j,i}$ and conflicts with an engaged bid $\left(\pi(W_{i'}),\ E(j),\ q_{j,i'}\right)$ for woman B_j. Resolving the conflict means outputting a new free bid and a new engaged bid such that:

- if B_j ranks A_i ahead of $A_{i'}$, the free bid is a re-encryption of $W_{i'}$ and the engaged bid is a re-encryption of $(W_i,\ E(j),\ q_{j,i})$
- if B_j ranks A_i behind $A_{i'}$, the free bid is a re-encryption of W_i and the engaged bid is a re-encryption of $(W_{i'},\ E(j),\ q_{j,i'})$

without revealing anything else about the bids (in particular the protocol does not reveal which bid wins the contested woman). To resolve the conflict, the matching authorities first create an engaged bid $\left(\pi(W_i),\ E(j),\ q_{j,i}\right)$ out of the free bid $\pi(W_i)$. The two engaged bids are then mixed externally. Let $q'_{j,i'}$ and $q'_{j,i}$ denote the re-encrypted and permuted images of $q_{j,i'}$ and $q_{j,i}$. The matching authorities jointly compute COMPARE$(q'_{j,i'}, q'_{j,i})$. The result of this comparison determines (privately) which bid stays engaged, and which is stripped of B_j to make a free bid.

7   Private Stable Matching Algorithm

We describe a private algorithm for finding a stable matching in which men propose to women. The algorithm follows the general structure of the algorithm described in Section 4, but operates on encrypted bids to preserve privacy. The algorithm is run by a number of matching authorities. We use the notations defined in Section 6.

Setup. In a setup step, the matching authorities jointly generate the public/private key pair for a threshold public-key encryption scheme E with an additive homomorphism. For example, E may be a threshold version [5, 7] of the Paillier encryption scheme [18].

Input submission. As before, we let $r_{i,j} \in \{0, \ldots, n-1\}$ denote the rank of woman B_j for man A_i, and $s_{j,i} \in \{0, \ldots, n-1\}$ denote the rank of man A_i for woman B_j. Every man A_i submits a vector of n Paillier ciphertexts

$$a_i = (p_{i,1}, \ldots, p_{i,n}),$$

where $p_{i,j} = E(r_{i,j})$, and every woman B_i similarly submits a vector of n Paillier ciphertexts

$$b_j = (q_{j,1}, \ldots, q_{j,n}),$$

where $q_{j,i} = E(s_{j,i})$.

Addition of fake men. The matching authorities define an additional n fake men $A_{n+1}, \ldots, A_{2n}$ as described in Section 4. Specifically, the matching authorities define $r_{i,j} = j - i + n \mod (n-1)$ for $i \in \{n+1, \ldots, 2n\}$ and $j \in \{1, \ldots, n\}$

and compute the corresponding vectors $a_i = (p_{i,1}, \ldots, p_{i,n})$ for $i = n+1, \ldots, 2n$, where $p_{i,j} = E(r_{i,j})$. The matching authorities also define $s_{j,i} = i - 1$ for $j \in \{1, n\}$ and $i \in \{n + 1, 2n\}$ and augment the vectors b_j with these new values (we keep the notation b_j for the augmented vectors): $b_j = (q_{j,1}, \ldots, q_{j,2n})$. After this preprocessing step, the matching authorities have $2n$ vectors $a_1, \ldots, a_{2n}$ (each vector contains n ciphertexts that express the rankings assigned by one man to the n women) and n vectors $b_1, \ldots, b_n$ (each vector contains $2n$ ciphertexts that express the rankings assigned by one woman to the $2n$ men).

Bid creation. The matching authorities create $2n$ bids $W_1, \ldots, W_{2n}$, where W_i encodes the preferences of man A_i. Bid W_i is defined as follows (see Section 6.1):

$$W_i = [E(i),\ a_i,\ v_i,\ q_i,\ E(0)]$$

Throughout the algorithm, bids are divided into free bids and engaged bids. Initially, the n bids corresponding to real men are free: $\mathcal{F}_1 = (W_1, \ldots, W_n)$, whereas the n bids corresponding to the fake men are engaged: $\mathcal{E}_1 = (W_{n+1}, \ldots, W_{2n})$. More precisely, man W_{n+j} is paired with woman B_j. For $j = 1, \ldots, n$ the engaged bid of (fake) man A_{n+j} is thus defined as:

$$\left(W_{n+j},\ E(j),\ q_{j,n+j} \right)$$

Initial mixing. The sets $\mathcal{E}_1$ and $\mathcal{F}_1$ are each independently mixed externally by the matching authorities. Next, the matching authorities mix internally the set $\mathcal{E}_1 \cup \mathcal{F}_1$.

Computing a stable match. As in Section 4, the core of our private stable matching algorithm proceeds in n rounds. We let $\mathcal{E}_k$ denote the set of engaged bids and $\mathcal{F}_k$ denote the set of free bids at the beginning of round $k = 1, \ldots, n+1$. The algorithm executes the following routine for $k = 1, \ldots, n$:

While the set $\mathcal{F}_k$ is non-empty, select at random one free bid (denoted W_i) from $\mathcal{F}_k$. Then:

1. The matching authorities jointly open up bid W_i, and learn $E(j)$ and $q_{j,i} = E(s_{j,i})$.
2. There is always exactly one engaged bid in $\mathcal{E}_k$ that conflicts with W_i. The matching authorities jointly find that engaged bid using (at most $|\mathcal{E}_k| = n$ times) the conflict detection protocol described in Section 6.3. Let's call the conflicting engaged bid $(W_{i'}, E(j), q_{j,i'})$.
3. Using the conflict resolution protocol of Section 6.3, the matching authorities resolve the conflict. The conflict resolution protocol does not reveal which bid wins but it ensures that one bid (either W_i or $W_{i'}$) is added to $\mathcal{E}_k$ and the other to $\mathcal{F}_{k+1}$. For clarity, we explain what happens behind the scene:
   - If W_i wins, it becomes an engaged bid $(W_i, E(j), E(s_{j,i}))$ and is moved from the set $\mathcal{F}_k$ to the set $\mathcal{E}_k$. The engagement of bid $(W_{i'}, E(j), E(s_{j,i'}))$ is broken (see Section 6.1) and the newly free bid $W_{i'}$ moves from the set $\mathcal{E}_k$ to $\mathcal{F}_{k+1}$.

- If W_i loses, it remains free and moves from $\mathcal{F}_k$ to $\mathcal{F}_{k+1}$. The engaged bid $(W_{i'}, E(j), E(s_{j,i}))$ stays in the set $\mathcal{E}_k$.
4. The set $\mathcal{E}_k$ is mixed externally. All bids in the sets $\mathcal{E}_k \cup \mathcal{F}_k \cup \mathcal{F}_{k+1}$ are then mixed internally.

At the end of the round (when the set $\mathcal{F}_k$ is empty), we define $\mathcal{E}_{k+1} = \mathcal{E}_k$. The sets $\mathcal{E}_{k+1}$ and $\mathcal{F}_{k+1}$ are independently mixed externally. The set $\mathcal{E}_{k+1} \cup \mathcal{F}_{k+1}$ is then mixed internally.

Bid decryption and final output. After n rounds, the final set $\mathcal{E}_{n+1}$ consists of n engaged bids of the form $(W_i, E(j), E(s_{j,i}))$, where $W_i = [E(i), a_i, v_i, q_i, E(\rho)]$. At this point, the matching authorities retain only two ciphertexts from an engaged bid: $E(i)$ and $E(j)$. The matching authorities thus obtain n pairs of the form $(E(i); E(j))$. These pairs $(E(i); E(j))$ are (externally) mixed by the matching authorities, then jointly decrypted. The decryption of pair $(E(i); E(j))$ reveals than man A_i is paired with woman B_j.

8   Properties

Proposition 2. *The algorithm of Section 7 terminates after n rounds and outputs a stable matching between n real men and n real women. The computational cost of the algorithm is dominated by the cost of running $3n^2$ re-encryption mix networks on at most $2n$ Paillier ciphertexts. The corresponding communication cost is $O(n^3)$.*

Since we assume an honest-but-curious passive adversary, the proof of correctness follows directly from Proposition 1. The computational cost is dominated by the cost of re-encryption mix networks. For every element in $\mathcal{F}_k$ in every round k, the matching authorities must run 3 re-encryption mix networks: one to resolve the conflict between bids, one for external mixing and one for internal mixing. The overall computational cost is thus $O(n^3)$ modular exponentiations. This is a substantial cost, but not unreasonable considering that stable matching algorithms are typically run off-line and that low latency is not a requirement. In practice, stable matching algorithms involving up to a few thousands of participants could be run privately within a day on commodity hardware.

Proposition 3. *The algorithm of Section 7 is private according to Definition 1, assuming Paillier encryption is semantically secure and the underlying re-encryption mix network is private.*

Proof (Sketch). In the execution of the protocol, the matching authorities compute and output intermediate values (Paillier ciphertexts, modular integers and boolean values), then finally a stable match. We prove that a passive adversary cannot distinguish between the sequence of intermediate values produced by the protocol, and a random sequence of intermediate values drawn from an appropriate probability distribution. The proof is by contradiction. If an adversary $\mathcal{A}$ can distinguish with non-negligible advantage the output of the algorithm from random, then by a standard hybrid argument, there exists one intermediate value V that $\mathcal{A}$ can distinguish from random.

If V is a Paillier ciphertext, we can use $\mathcal{A}$ to break the semantic security of Paillier encryption, contradicting our assumption about Paillier's security.

If V is a modular integer or a boolean value, the value of V depends on the internal or external permutation applied by the matching authorities immediately before computing V. Thus if $\mathcal{A}$ can distinguish between different values of V, we can use $\mathcal{A}$ to distinguish between the outputs produced by a re-encryption mix-network using different permutations, breaking the assumption that the mix network is private.   □

8.1   Active Adversaries

We have assumed a passive adversary throughout, but our techniques can be extended to accommodate active adversaries at the cost of additional proofs of correct execution. We consider here an active adversary who has static control over up to all the participants (men and women), and static control over up to a strict minority of matching authorities. We must augment the private stable matching algorithms of Section 7 with proofs of correct protocol execution by participants and matching authorities. These proofs are verified by the matching authorities (a strict majority of whom is assumed honest).

The participants need only prove to the matching authorities that the preference vectors they submit ($\boldsymbol{a}_i$ for man A_i and $\boldsymbol{b}_j$ for woman B_j) follow the protocol specifications, i.e. are Paillier encryptions of a permutation of the set $\{0, \ldots, n-1\}$. We use non-interactive zero-knowledge (NIZK) proofs that the decryption $E^{-1}(C)$ of a Paillier ciphertext C lies within a given plaintext set $\{0, \ldots, n-1\}$. For Paillier encryption, these proofs reduce to proving knowledge of the root of the randomization factor [5]. These proofs can also be combined conjunctively and disjunctively using standard techniques [22]. We can thus prove that a vector $\boldsymbol{a}_i = (E(r_1), \ldots, E(r_n))$ is well-formed with the following NIZK proof: $\bigwedge_{j \in \{0, \ldots, n-1\}} \left(\bigvee_{i \in \{1, \ldots, n\}} (E^{-1}(E(r_i)) = j) \right).$

The correct behavior of matching authorities must itself be verified. The building blocks of Section 5 all accept variants that are secure against active adversaries. As usual, a matching authority caught not following the protocol is excluded from future computations and replaced by a new authority.

9   Conclusion

We have proposed a private stable matching algorithm based on a variant of the Gale-Shapley algorithm. Assuming a majority of honest matching authorities, our protocol correctly outputs a stable match, and reveals no other information than what can be learned from that match and from the preferences of participants controlled by the adversary. We have proved the security and privacy of our protocol based on assumptions about standard distributed cryptographic protocols. Our protocol is practical and we hope that it will be used to offer greater privacy to the tens of thousands of students and professionals whose careers are affected every year by matching algorithms.

References

1. Association of Psychology Postdoctoral and Internship Centers. http://www.appic.org/match/
2. C. Bandela, Y. Chen, A. Kahng, I. Mandoiu and A. Zelikovsky. Multiple-object XOR auctions with buyer preferences and seller priorities. In *Competitive Bidding and Auctions*, K.K. Lai and S. Wang, ed. Kluwer Academic Publishers.
3. Canadian Resident Matching Service (CaRMS). http://www.carms.ca/jsp/main.jsp
4. R. Cramer, I. Damgård, S. Dziembowski, M. Hirt and T. Rabin. Efficient multi-party computations secure against an adaptive adversary. In *Proc. of Eurocrypt'99*, pp. 311–326.
5. I. Damgård and M. Jurik. A generalisation, a simplification and some applications of Paillier's probabilistic public-key system. In *Proc. of Public Key Cryptography 2001*, pp. 119–136.
6. D. Gale and H. S. Shapley. College Admissions and the Stability of Marriage. American Mathematical Monthly, 1962.
7. P.-A. Fouque, G. Poupard, and J. Stern. Sharing decryption in the context of voting or lotteries. In *Proceedings of Financial Cryptography 2000*, pp. 90–104, 2000.
8. D. Gale and M. Sotomayor. Ms Machiavelli and the Stable Matching Problem. In *American Mathematical Monthly*, 92, pp. 261–268, 1985.
9. O. Goldreich, S. Micali and A. Widgerson. How to play any mental game. In *STOC'87*, pp. 218–229. ACM, 1987.
10. D. Gusfield and R. Irving. The Stable Marriage Problem: Structure and Algorithms. MIT Press.
11. M. Jakobsson, A. Juels, and R. Rivest. Making mix nets robust for electronic voting by randomized partial checking. In *Proc. of USENIX'02*, pp. 339–353.
12. M. Jakobsson and C. Schnorr. Efficient Oblivious Proofs of Correct Exponentiation. In *Proc. of CMS 99*.
13. H. Lipmaa. Verifiable homomorphic oblivious transfer and private equality test. In *Proc. of Asiacrypt 2003*, pp. 416–433. LNCS 2894.
14. National Matching Services Inc. http://www.natmatch.com/
15. National Resident Matching Program (NRMP). http://www.nrmp.org/
16. A. Neff. A verifiable secret shuffle and its application to e-voting. In *Proc. of ACM CCS '01*, pp. 116–125.
17. M. Ostrovsky. Stability in supply chain networks. Available on the web at economics.uchicago.edu/download/Supply%20Chains%20-%20December%2012012.pdf
18. P. Paillier. Public-Key Cryptosystems Based on Composite Degree Residuosity Classes. In *Proc. of Eurocrypt 1999*, pp. 223–238. LNCS 1592, Springer Verlag.
19. A. Roth. The Economics of Matching: Stability and Incentives. In *Mathematics of Operations Research*, 7, pp. 617–628, 1982.
20. A. Roth and M. Sotomayor. Two-sided matching: a study in game-theoretic modeling and analysis. Econometric Society Monograph Series (1990). New York: Cambridge University Press.

21. Al Roth's game theory, experimental economics, and market design page. Bibliography of two-sided matching. On the web at `http://kuznets.fas.harvard.edu/~aroth/bib.html#matchbib`

22. A. D. Santis, G. D. Crescenzo, G. Persiano, and M. Yung. On monotone formula closure of szk. In *Proc. of the IEEE FOCS 1994*, pages 454–465, 1994.

23. Scottish PRHO Allocation (SPA) scheme. `http://www.nes.scot.nhs.uk/spa/`

24. M. Soerensen. How smart is smart money? An empirical two-sided matching model of venture capital. Available on the web at `http://finance.wharton.upenn.edu/department/Seminar/2004SpringRecruiting/Micro/SorensenPaper-micro-012204.pdf`

25. C.-P. Teo, J. Sethuraman and W.-P. Tan. Gale-Shapley stable marriage problem revisited: strategic issues and applications. In *Proc. of IPCO '99: the 7th Conference on Integer Programming and Combinatorial Optimisation*, pp. 429–438. LNCS 1610.

26. A. C. Yao. Protocols for secure computations. In *FOCS'82*, pp. 160–164. IEEE Computer Society, 1982.

Private Policy Negotiation

Klaus Kursawe[1,2], Gregory Neven[1,3], and Pim Tuyls[2]

[1] Dept. of Electrical Engineering, Katholieke Universiteit Leuven
Kasteelpark Arenberg 10, B-3001 Heverlee, Belgium
{Klaus.Kursawe, Gregory.Neven}@esat.kuleuven.be
[2] Philips Research, Professor Holstlaan 4, 5656 AA Eindhoven, The Netherlands
Pim.Tuyls@philips.com
[3] Département d'Informatique, Ecole Normale Supérieure,
45 Rue d'Ulm, 75230 Paris Cedex 05, France

Abstract. With the increasing importance of correctly handling privacy-sensitive data, significant work has been put in expressing and enforcing privacy policies. Less work has been done however on *negotiating* a privacy policy, especially if the negotiation process itself is considered privacy-sensitive. In this paper, we present a formal definition of the *mutually privacy-preserving policy negotiation problem*, i.e. the problem of negotiating what data will be revealed under what conditions, while no party learns anything about the other parties' preferences other than the outcome of the negotiation.

We validate the definition by providing a reference solution using two-party computation techniques based on homomorphic encryption systems. Based on an evaluation of the efficiency of our protocol in terms of computation, bandwidth and communication rounds, we conclude that our solution is practically feasible for simple policies or high-bandwidth communication channels.

1 Introduction

With the increasing amount of electronic data produced by day-to-day interactions, as well as the ability to link or otherwise process this data, the handling of privacy-sensitive personal data has emerged as an important field in computer security. Many online services require the user to submit some information about himself (e.g. name, address, ...) in order to access the service. The type of information to be provided is described in a *policy*.

Substantial work has been done on defining privacy policies (e.g. P3P [23] and EPAL [3]), and their enforcement [19,5,7]. Less work however has been done on policy *negotiation*. Usually, it is assumed that both sides somehow agree on a common policy specifying what data will be transmitted and how sensitive data should be handled. In various settings, this negotiation is complicated by the effect that a person's privacy preferences may already give away information about that person. Since the vast majority of the population is still willing to reveal seemingly innocent data (e.g. their consumption of alcohol), a person that

G. Di Crescenzo and A. Rubin (Eds.): FC 2006, LNCS 4107, pp. 81–95, 2006.
© IFCA/Springer-Verlag Berlin Heidelberg 2006

considers this piece of data as sensitive might quickly raise suspicion and consequently be treated with a worst-case assumption (e.g. that he's an alcoholic).

Given that both parties' preferences themselves are to be considered as private data, can they still discover whether a matching policy exists, and if so, what this policy is? In this paper, we answer this question in a positive way.

Our contributions. We formally define the problem of negotiating a privacy policy from two sets of preferences, in such a way that no party learns any information about the other's preferences other than the policy agreed upon. We then develop a concrete protocol by implementing (a special case of) the definition as a boolean circuit, and using efficient two-party computation techniques based on threshold homomorphic cryptosystems of [20] to evaluate it. Based on a detailed analysis of the efficiency of our protocol in terms of bandwidth, rounds of communication and computational overhead, we conclude that while this protocol is efficient enough for reasonably small policies, its overhead becomes prohibitive for larger ones. Therefore, we see our protocol more as a proof-of-concept, and as a benchmark against which the performance of future special-purpose protocols can be measured.

Related work: policy frameworks. The most common framework for privacy policy negotiation today is the Platform for Privacy Preferences Project (P3P) [23]. A P3P policy consists of a number of attributes (e.g. the user's name, address,...), and the conditions tied to the user's willingness to reveal these attributes (e.g., it may not be forwarded to third parties, and has to be deleted once it is no longer needed). P3P was designed with two goals in mind. Firstly, it creates transparency about an organization's privacy policy. Secondly, it allows for automatic comparison of the policies. To reduce the initial complexity of the standard, the current version of P3P deliberately left out any negotiation. Rather, the server simply reveals its policy, and the client then proceeds with the interaction, or not. In some sense, this does protect the client's privacy, but the server's policy is fully exposed.

Our negotiation protocol can be used within the context of P3P, though some practical restrictions may be necessary for efficiency reasons. The design of P3P is hierarchical in the sense that attributes (e.g. first name, last name) can be contained in other attributes (e.g. name). In the non-private case, this is not a problem – a policy may group attributes and thus not need to individually specify the preferences for each and every attribute. Our protocol, however, cannot efficiently handle such groups, as it makes the number of attributes too large to be practical. Also, P3P allows a policy designer to freely define attributes. This poses a problem for automated systems such as ours, as a user may not have predefined his preference on an attribute that the server defined.

Another popular framework for the definition of privacy policies is the *Enterprise Privacy Authorization Language* (EPAL) [3]. EPAL is designed as a backend language to be used internally inside an enterprise, allowing to automatically enforce its privacy rules. As such, EPAL allows a fine-grained and flexible set of rules, which also represent the internal data flows within the corporation. While the possibility to express complex policies makes EPAL interesting for secret negotiations, its complexity makes it hard even to compare policies [3], let alone to negotiate them without revealing any information about the preferences.

The theoretical model for policy negotiations proposed by Yu et al. [25] focuses on allowing for a maximal independence in choice of strategy between the negotiating parties, without sacrificing efficient interoperability. They mainly consider a setting in which credential holders prove certified properties to a server, whereas we consider clients submitting unverified personal data, but their techniques can be applied to both types of negotiations. More importantly, they recognize the need to protect sensitive details of the parties' preferences [21, 25], and propose protocols achieving this goal through a gradual release of requirements. Thereby, the disclosure of sensitive requirements is postponed until a certain level of trust has been established. It is hard to quantify however how much privacy this approach actually gives for general policies. In contrast, we employ cryptographic techniques guaranteeing that the only information leaked about the other party's preferences is the policy that was agreed upon.

Related work: cryptographic protocols. The problem of private policy negotiation is a specific instance of secure two-party computation [24, 17], which is the problem where two parties want to jointly evaluate a function on private inputs, while leaking no other information about their inputs than what is implied by the result. An efficient approach to secure two-party computation in the multiparty setting is to model the function as a boolean circuit, and to use a threshold homomorphic encryption scheme to evaluate it on encrypted inputs [1, 13, 9, 20]. (See Section 2 for more details on this approach.) We build on these results by implementing policy negotiation as a boolean circuit and evaluating it using the multiplication gates of [20]. The recently proposed double-homomorphic encryption scheme of [6] cannot be applied to our setting because it can only handle circuits with a single level of multiplication gates. Though some attacks exist for the schemes underlying our (and in fact, most) zero knowledge circuits implementations with a dishonest majority [8], they can be resolved by applying a slightly weaker model than usuall and carefull implemenatation, as the cheating party would clearly be exposed before any damage is done.

Private policy negotiation is also related to the problems of private matching and set intersection [14], where two parties want to compute the intersection of their private datasets. Private set intersection could be used for a basic form of policy negotiation by letting the client's dataset contain the attributes that the client is willing to reveal, and letting the server's dataset contain the attributes that he wants to see. A matching policy exists if the intersection is equal to the server's dataset (which has to be determined using an extra zero knowledge comparison technique). Our protocol however supports more flexible preferences, allowing the client to express which attributes cannot be revealed *together*, and allowing the server to declare multiple combinations as sufficient for accessing the service. Moreover, to be useful in the model provided by existing privacy frameworks, we need to be able to model obligations. A user may well be willing to reveal data he otherwise would keep private if he is promised that it will be deleted within a week, or not forwarded to a third party.

Policy-based cryptography [4, 2] is a way of enforcing need-to-know policies on the distribution of data, by allowing to encrypt data such that only users with certain roles can decrypt it. A trusted authority has the responsibility of issuing role certificates to the appropriate users. This line of work is complementary to ours, as it considers policy *enforcement* rather than negotiation. Moreover, their solution is not fully privacy preserving, as the ciphertexts leak information on the policies of the parties involved.

Further use cases. While our protocol was originally designed to negotiate privacy preferences, the approach can be used in various other settings as well.

Assume two people want to find out whether they share common interests in order to decide if they should go on a date. To prevent humiliation, no interests are revealed unless shared by the other person, if any at all. In its simplest form, every party has a constant set of interests. A more complex setting is where each party has several sets of interests, corresponding to the different offers the party is willing to make. For example, a person may simultaneously seek quick affairs and more permanent relationships. Furthermore, he does not want a partner matching the "permanent relationship policy" to know that he was also looking for a quick affair, even if (or especially if) a match happens.

The protocol may further be used for classical negotiation deals, i.e., for buying goods or services. Classical private negotiation systems are one-dimensional, i.e., both parties define an amount of money they are willing to spend or want to get, respectively, and the system tells them if a deal can happen (and potentially, for how much). However, most negotiations today have more facets. The seller may offer some discount if paid in cash, or if several items are bought, and the buyer may pay more if home delivery is ensured, or the warranty is extended. Assuming the number of options is not exceedingly high, our protocol delivers a practical way to privately negotiate the proper conditions.

2   Secure Two-Party Computation

We have chosen to use the tools of [20] based on threshold homomorphic cryptosystems for various reasons. Firstly, threshold homomorphic cryptosystems allow for very efficient solutions of multi-party computation problems that are resistant against active adversaries [18, 10, 9]. There exist very efficient distributed key generation protocols for the discrete logarithm setting, making it attractive for ad-hoc contacts. Moreover, discrete-logarithm based protocols can be implemented using elliptic curves, resulting in smaller bandwidth requirements. Compared to the mix and match technique of [18] it offers the same round complexity of $O(d)$, where d is the depth of the circuit being evaluated, but it is much more efficient for multiplications. (More precisely, the techniques developed in [20] are about ten times more efficient.)

2.1   Cryptographic Tools

Homomorphic encryption. Given an encryption function E, a public key p with corresponding secret key s, and a message m, we denote by $E_p(m)$ the encryption of m with the public key p. An encryption function E is called additively *homomorphic* if for all messages m_1 and m_2, we have $E_p(m_1 + m_2) = E_p(m_1)E_p(m_2)$.

We describe briefly the homomorphic version of the El Gamal cryptosystem. Let $G = \langle g \rangle$ denote a finite cyclic (multiplicative) group of prime order q for which the Decision Diffie-Hellman (DDH) problem is assumed to be infeasible: given $g^x, g^y, g^z \in_R G$, it is infeasible to decide whether $xy \equiv z$ (mod q).

The public key of the El Gamal cryptosystem is an element $h \in G$ and the encryption of a message $m \in \mathbb{Z}_q$ is given by the pair $(a, b) = (g^r, h^r g^m)$ where $r \in_r \mathbb{Z}_q$. The secret key s is given by $s = \log_g h$.

Given the private key s, decryption of the ciphertext $(a, b) = (g^r, g^m h^r)$ is performed by first calculating $b/a^s = g^m$, and then solving for $m \in \mathbb{Z}_q$. This is done by restricting ourselves to messages m belonging to a sufficiently small domain $M \subseteq \mathbb{Z}_q$ which allows for exhaustive testing. Here, we take $M = \{0, 1\}$.

We define the multiplication of two ciphertexts (for the same public key) (a, b) and (a', b') by $(a, b)(a', b') = (aa', bb')$. It readily follows that this encryption scheme is additively homomorphic for this multiplication. It is well known that under the DDH assumption, this cryptosystem is semantically secure [20].

For ease of notation, we will use $[\![m]\!]$ to denote an encryption of the message m under some understood public key. In this notation we have $[\![x]\!][\![y]\!] = [\![x + y]\!]$ and $[\![x]\!]^y = [\![xy]\!]$.

Threshold decryption. In an (n, t) threshold cryptosystem [11], the private key is distributed over n parties such that only coalitions of size at least t parties can decrypt the message hidden inside a ciphertext. In this paper we use a $(2, 2)$ threshold cryptosystem where encryptions are computed with a common public key h but decryption is performed by running a protocol between the two involved parties. Every party holds a share $s_i \in \mathbb{Z}_q$ of the private key $s = s_1 + s_2 = \log_g h$, where the corresponding value $h_i = g^{s_i}$ is public. For decryption of the ciphertext (a, b), the players P_1 and P_2 produce a decryption share $d_i = a^{s_i}$ $(i = 1, 2)$ together with a proof that $\log_a d_i = \log_g h_i$. Assuming that both players produce correct decryption shares, the message is recovered from solving $g^m = b/a^s$ (where a^s is obtained as $d_1 d_2$) for m. Finally, it is checked whether $m \in \{0, 1\}$. If this does not hold decryption fails. In case both parties need to obtain the decrypted value, the protocol has to be run in a *fair* way. A protocol for this is given in [20].

Distributed key generation. In order to set up the key generation in a P2P situation, the users have to run a distributed key generation (DKG) protocol. We describe very briefly a practical protocol [15] here. In the first step, both parties broadcast a Pedersen commitment $c_i = g^{s_i} h'^{r_i}$, with $s_i, r_i \in_R \mathbb{Z}_q$ along with a proof of knowledge for s_i, r_i. In the second step, both parties broadcast r_i along with a proof of knowledge of $\log_g h_i$, where $h_i = c_i / h'^{r_i}$. The joint public key is $h = h_1 h_2$, with corresponding private key $s = s_1 + s_2$. In many practical cases, a more lightweight one-round protocol[4] can be used. Then, both players broadcast $h_i = g^{s_i}$ and a proof of knowledge of s_i.

2.2 Secure Two-Party Computation from Homomorphic Encryption

In order to be able to securely evaluate any circuit using an additive homomorphic encryption scheme, a protocol for secure multiplication is needed. We briefly remind the *private multiplier gate* and *the conditional gate* developed in [20]. Those protocols are simulatable even in the malicious case.

First consider the situation where the encryptions $[\![x]\!] = (a, b) = (g^r, g^x h^r)$ and $[\![y]\!] = (c, d)$ are given with player P_1 knowing x. Player P_1 computes on its own a randomized encryption $[\![xy]\!] = (e, f) = (g^s, h^s)[\![y]\!]^x$, with $s \in_R \mathbb{Z}_q$, using the homomorphic properties. Finally player P_1 broadcasts $[\![xy]\!]$ along with a proof showing that this is the correct output.

Next we consider the *conditional gate* which takes only encrypted inputs. Let $[\![x]\!], [\![y]\!]$ denote encryptions, with $x \in \{-1, 1\} \subseteq \mathbb{Z}_q$ and $y \in \mathbb{Z}_q$. The following protocol enables players P_1 and P_2, to compute an encryption $[\![xy]\!]$ securely.

1. Player P_1 broadcasts an encryption $[\![s_1]\!]$, with $s_1 \in_R \{-1, 1\}$. Then P_1 applies the private-multiplier multiplication protocol to multiplier s_1 and multiplicands $[\![x]\!]$ and $[\![y]\!]$, yielding random encryptions $[\![s_1 x]\!]$ and $[\![s_1 y]\!]$. Analogously, player P_2 broadcasts an encryption $[\![s_2]\!]$, with $s_2 \in_R \{-1, 1\}$. Then P_2 applies the private-multiplier multiplication protocol to multiplier s_2 and multiplicands $[\![s_1 x]\!]$ and $[\![s_1 y]\!]$, yielding random encryptions $[\![s_1 s_2 x]\!]$ and $[\![s_1 s_2 y]\!]$.
2. The players jointly decrypt $[\![s_1 s_2 x]\!]$ to obtain $s_1 s_2 x$. If decryption fails because $s_1 s_2 x \notin \{-1, 1\}$, the protocol is aborted.
3. Given $s_1 s_2 x$ and $[\![s_1 s_2 y]\!]$, an encryption $[\![(s_1)^2 (s_2)^2 (xy)]\!] = [\![xy]\!]$ is computed publicly.

2.3 Secure Evaluation of Some Basic Gates

In Section 3 we turn the private policy negotiation problem into a problem of the secure evaluation of a function that can be described as a circuit consisting of basic *gates*, in casu NOT, OR and AND gates. For bits $x, y \in \{0, 1\}$, we use the shorthand notation $\neg x$ to denote the negation of x, we use $x \wedge y$ to denote the logical conjunction (AND) of x and y, and we use $x \vee y$ to denote the logical disjunction (OR) of x and y. We present protocols for the secure evaluation of those gates within the model of secure two-party computation; i.e. we consider two parties who evaluate these gates without revealing anything about their input (except the information that leaks from the output of the function).

AND with Encrypted Inputs. Given two encrypted bits $[\![x]\!]$ and $[\![y]\!]$, the players run a conditional gate on those two inputs to compute $[\![x \wedge y]\!]$.

---

[4] Although the trivial protocol allows one of the parties to influence the distribution of the public key h slightly, this need not be a problem for the application in which the key is used; see [16] for more details.

AND Gate with one Encrypted and one Unencrypted Input. Let x denote the private input and $\llbracket y \rrbracket$ the encrypted input which is available to both. The players run the private multiplier gate on inputs x and $\llbracket y \rrbracket$.

OR Gate with Encrypted Inputs. Given two encrypted bits $\llbracket x \rrbracket$ and $\llbracket y \rrbracket$, $\llbracket x \vee y \rrbracket$ is securely computed by running a conditional gate on the inputs $\llbracket x \rrbracket$ and $\llbracket y \rrbracket$. Then, using the homomorphic properties of the cryptosystem, they compute $\llbracket x \vee y \rrbracket$ as $\llbracket x + y - xy \rrbracket$.

OR with an Encrypted and an Unencrypted Input. Given unencrypted input x and encrypted input $\llbracket y \rrbracket$, the players run the private multiplier gate, yielding $\llbracket xy \rrbracket$. Then, the players compute $\llbracket x \vee y \rrbracket = \llbracket x + y - xy \rrbracket$.

NOT Gate on Encrypted Inputs. Computing $\llbracket \neg x \rrbracket$ given $\llbracket x \rrbracket$ is done by computing $\llbracket 1 - x \rrbracket$ publicly.

3   Private Policy Matching: Definition and Approaches

Formal definition. By the *preferences* of a user we mean a strategy defining which attributes (e.g. credit card number, address, ...) he is willing to reveal in order to gain access to certain service. The preferences of a server define the attributes he requires from a user before granting access to the service. Policy negotiation refers to the process of finding out whether a match exists between the attributes that the user wants to reveal and the set of attributes that the server requires. We say that a combination of attributes is a *matching policy* if it is acceptable to both the client and the server. We define the problem of policy matching more formally as follows.

Definition 1. *Let $\mathcal{A}$ be a set of attributes, and let $\mathcal{S}$ be a totally ordered set of scores with least element 0. Preferences over the set of attributes $\mathcal{A}$ are described by functions $f, g : 2^{\mathcal{A}} \rightarrow \mathcal{S}$ that assign to each combination of attributes $A \subseteq \mathcal{A}$ a score $s \in \mathcal{S}$, indicating the client's willingness to reveal the combination of attributes A (in the case of client preferences f), or indicating the server's inclination to accept that combination of attributes as sufficient to access the service (in the case of server preferences g). A matching function $M : 2^{\mathcal{A}} \times \mathcal{S} \times \mathcal{S} \rightarrow \mathcal{S}$ assigns a matching score to a combination $A \subseteq \mathcal{A}$ based on A, the client's willingness $f(A)$ and the server's acceptance $g(A)$. A combination A is said to be a matching policy with respect to client preferences f, server preferences g and matching function M if $M(A, f(A), g(A)) > 0$. The best matching policy is the combination $A \subseteq \mathcal{A}$ for which $M(A, f(A), g(A))$ is maximal.*

We introduced the set $\mathcal{S}$ to allow the expression of fine-grained preferences by assigning weights to sets of attributes. Throughout this paper however, we limit ourselves to the case $\mathcal{S} = \{0, 1\}$ and $M(A, f(A), g(A)) = 1$ iff $f(A) = g(A) = 1$, which corresponds to a client being either willing or unwilling to reveal a combination of attributes, a server either accepting a combination of attributes or not, and a match occurring whenever both parties accept the policy.

By *private policy negotiation* we mean a protocol between the client and the server during which they learn nothing about each other's preferences except whether a matching policy exists, and possibly what that matching policy is. In our model, we consider an active but static adversary who can corrupt one of both players and hence get access to all data of the corrupted player. External measures should be taken to prevent the client from extracting the server's preferences through repeated negotiations with different input preferences, e.g. by limiting the number of negotiations per client within a certain time interval or requiring human interaction.

A straightforward approach. Let $\mathcal{A} = \{a_0, \ldots, a_{n-1}\}$ be the set of the client's attributes (e.g. $a_0 =$ "credit card number", $a_1 =$ "birth date", ...). If x is a bit string of length n, then we refer to the individual bits of x as $x_0 \ldots x_{n-1}$. To each $x \in \{0,1\}^n$, we associate a set of attributes $A(x) = \{a_i \in \mathcal{A} : x_i = 1, 0 \leq i \leq n-1\}$. The client's preferences can be modeled as a boolean function $f : \{0,1\}^n \to \{0,1\}$, where $f(x) = 1$ if the client is willing to reveal the combination of attributes $A(x)$, and is 0 if he'd rather not reveal this combination. Likewise, the server's preferences can be modeled as a boolean function $g : \{0,1\}^n \to \{0,1\}$. A matching policy is an assignment $x \in \{0,1\}^n$ such that $f(x) = g(x) = 1$.

The functions $f(x)$ and $g(x)$ are most naturally represented through their truth tables. Deciding whether a matching policy exists comes down to finding a row with a 1 in the output column of both truth tables. The most straightforward way to implement this approach as a boolean circuit is to let the client's and server's input be the output column of the truth tables of f and g, and to design a circuit that outputs an index $x \in \mathbb{Z}_{2^n}$ such that $f(x) = g(x) = 1$. The size of this circuit (in number of inputs and number of gates), however, is $O(2^n)$, making it unsuitable for evaluation through secure two-party protocols.

Generating subsets. A more compact yet quite natural description of the client's and server's policies can be obtained by observing that in most real-world cases, f is a monotonically decreasing boolean function, meaning that if $f(A) = 1$ and $B \subseteq A$, then also $f(B) = 1$. Indeed, if the client is willing to show the combination of attributes A, then it is natural to assume that he is willing to show any subset of these attributes as well. Likewise, it is easy to see that usually g is monotonically increasing, meaning that if $g(A) = 1$ and $B \supseteq A$, then $g(B) = 1$. Indeed, if showing attributes A is sufficient to access the service, then so should be any combination $B \supseteq A$.

Definition 2. *Let $h : 2^{\mathcal{A}} \to \{0,1\}$ be a monotonically increasing boolean function. We say that $\mathcal{H} = \{H_1, \ldots, H_a\} \subseteq 2^{\mathcal{A}}$ is a set of generating subsets for h iff for all $A \subseteq \mathcal{A}$*

$$h(A) = 1 \quad \Leftrightarrow \quad \exists i \in \{1, \ldots, a\} : H_i \subseteq A .$$

Note that since f is a monotonically decreasing function, $\neg f$ is a monotonically increasing function that is described through its set of generating subsets $\mathcal{F} = \{F_1, \ldots, F_a\}$. Essentially, the sets $F_1, \ldots, F_a$ are the *minimal* combinations of attributes that the client does *not* want to reveal together. Likewise, the function g is described through its set of generating subsets $\mathcal{G} = \{G_1, \ldots, G_b\}$, where the sets $G_1, \ldots, G_b$ are the *minimal* combinations of attributes that the server wants to see before delivering the service.

These generating subsets are not only a very compact representation of the client's and server's preferences, they are at the also a natural way of thinking about such preferences. The client for example may be reluctant to simultaneously show his credit card number and his mother's maiden name (the latter is sometimes used as a backup secret to reactivate lost cards), independent of other attributes he has to reveal in addition to that. Analogously, the server knows the minimal information that he needs from users (e.g. name and either email address or phone number), but he won't mind getting extra attributes

Using the notation of generating subsets, finding a match is equivalent to finding a set of attributes $A \subseteq \mathcal{A}$ such that $F_i \not\subseteq A$ for all $F_i \in \mathcal{F}$, and there exists $G_j \in \mathcal{G}$ such that $G_j \subseteq A$.Without loss of generality, we can assume that the matching policy is one of the server's generating subsets, if a match exists. (This is the match with the smallest number of shown attributes.) Therefore, we can write the condition for the matching policy A more compactly as the set of attributes $G_j \in \mathcal{G}$ such that $\forall F_i \in \mathcal{F} : F_i \not\subseteq G_j$.

4   A Boolean Circuit for Policy Matching

A boolean circuit implementing the generating subsets approach is given in Figure 1. The client's input consists of the generating subsets $F_1, \ldots, F_a$ encoded as n-bit strings, where the j-th bit of F_i is 1 iff attribute $a_j \in F_i$. The server's input consists of the subsets $G_1, \ldots, G_b$ in the same encoding. Since the values of a and b leak information about the complexity of the client's and server's preferences, the circuit needs to be designed for some fixed maximum values of a and b. Note that this leads to a worst-case scenario from the point of view of efficiency, but this is unavoidable as otherwise the run time would leak information about the preferences. The client and server assign arbitrary values to unused F_i and G_j entries, but distinguish "real" subsets from "dummy" subsets by setting the additional input bits f_i and g_j to 1 or 0, respectively. The output of the circuit is the encoding of a matching policy M, and a bit e indicating whether a matching policy exists ($e = 1$) or not ($e = 0$). We will see that when no matching policy is found, M takes the value $0 \ldots 0$.

Gates with multiple fan-in in Figure 1 can be implemented as a cascade of binary gates (e.g. $x_0 \vee x_1 \vee x_2 \vee x_3 = ((x_0 \vee x_1) \vee x_2) \vee x_3$, or as a balanced tree of binary gates (e.g. $x_0 \vee x_1 \vee x_2 \vee x_3 = (x_0 \vee x_1) \vee (x_2 \vee x_3)$). Both options are equivalent in the total number of gates, but the latter option gives a better efficiency in terms of communication rounds, as we will see later. The thick lines in Figure 1 represent buses, which are essentially collections of parallel wires to carry words, rather than individual bits. Thick gates represent bitwise operations on words, e.g. the bitwise AND of n-bit words $x, y \in \{0,1\}^n$ is the n-bit word $z = (x_0 \wedge y_0, \ldots, x_{n-1} \wedge y_{n-1})$.

The circuit consists of two layers. The first layer checks, for all $j = 1, \ldots, b$, whether G_j is a suitable candidate for a matching policy, meaning that G_j does

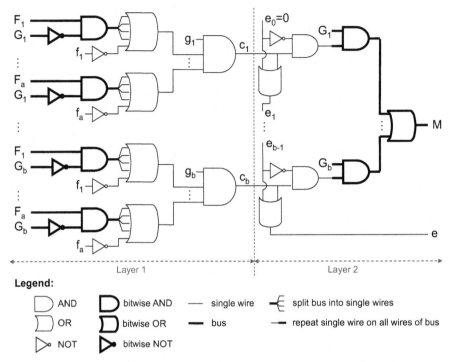

Fig. 1. An efficient circuit for policy negotiation The client's inputs are generating subsets $F_1, \ldots, F_a$, encoded as n-bit strings, and corresponding real-or-dummy bits $f_1, \ldots, f_a$. The server's inputs are generating subsets $G_1, \ldots, G_b$, strings, with corresponding real-or-dummy bits $g_1, \ldots, g_b$. The output e indicates whether a matching policy exists ($e = 1$) or not ($e = 0$). The output M is an encoding of a matching combination of attributes, or 0^n if no such policy exists.

not conflict with any of the client's sets F_i. The wire labeled c_j in Figure 1 carries a one if G_j is a candidate policy, and a zero if not. The second layer finds the candidate policy with the lowest index and outputs it as the matching policy. To select the match with the smallest index, the circuit uses intermediate variables e_j that are 1 iff a matching policy exists among $G_1, \ldots, G_j$, and the output bit $e = e_b$ is one iff a matching policy was found. AND-ing c_j with $\neg e_{j-1}$ ensures that the only non-zero bit coming out of any of the leftmost AND gates in Layer 2 is on the wire corresponding to the first match. The final gates of the circuit encode a matching policy onto the output bus M. If no matching policy was found, then M is set to 0^n, leaking no information about the server's preferences except the fact that no match exists with the given client preferences.

5   Policy Matching with Obligations

In this section, we extend the circuit to allow the client to express demands concerning certain attributes, such as that the data is deleted after a certain time, that it is not forwarded to third parties, or even to receive a discount in exchange for a certain attribute. The server expresses the promises he's willing to make for each attribute. A matching policy is then defined as a combination of attributes such that (1) they are deemed sufficient by the server to access the service, (2) the client is willing to reveal them, and (3) the server is willing to comply with the client's demands related to the revealed attributes. We extend Definition 1 with obligations as follows.

Definition 3. *Let $\mathcal{A}$ be a set of attributes, let $\mathcal{S}$ be a totally ordered set of scores with least element 0, let f, g be functions describing the client's and server's preferences, and let M be a matching function as in Definition 1. Let $\mathcal{O}$ be a set of obligations. The client's demand function $d : \mathcal{A} \to 2^{\mathcal{O}}$ associates to each attribute a set of obligations that the client demands from the server when revealing that attribute. The server's willingness function $w : \mathcal{A} \to 2^{\mathcal{O}}$ maps an attribute to the set of obligations that the server is willing to respect for that attribute. We say that $A \subseteq \mathcal{A}$ is a match with respect to preferences f, g, matching function M, demand function d and willingness function w if $M(A, f(A), g(A)) > 0$ and $\forall\, a \in A\; :\; d(a) \subseteq w(a)$. The best match is the subset $A \subseteq \mathcal{A}$ for which $M(A, f(A), g(A))$ is maximal.*

Again, we will only consider here the special case of Definition 3 where $\mathcal{S} = \{0, 1\}$, where f and g are monotonically decreasing, respectively increasing, boolean functions, and where the result of the matching function $M(A, f(A), g(A)) = 1$ iff $f(A) = g(A) = 1$. Let $\mathcal{O} = \{o_0, \ldots, o_{m-1}\}$ be the set of promises that the client can demand for each attribute (e.g. o_0 = "Delete after session", o_2 = "Delete after one year", o_3 = "Do not forward to third parties",…). The modi-

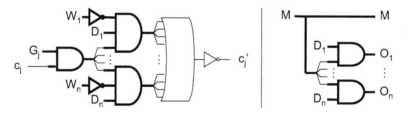

Fig. 2. Extensions to the circuit of Figure 1 to support promises. The circuit on the left computes whether the server is willing (as defined by additional server inputs $W_1, \ldots, W_n$) to meet the client's demands (as defined by additional client inputs $D_1, \ldots, D_n$) for all attributes in a candidate policy G_j. The circuit on the right encodes the agreed-upon promises as part of the output.

fications to the circuit of Figure 1 are depicted in Figure 2. The client's demand function and the server's willingness function are described by additional input sets $D_i = d(a_i)$ and $W_i = w(a_i)$ for $i = 0 \ldots m - 1$, respectively, encoded as m-bit strings. Apart from the matching policy M and a bit e indicating whether a match was found, the circuit now also outputs the obligations $O_0, \ldots, O_{n-1} \subseteq \mathcal{O}$ that the server has to adhere to for attributes $a_0, \ldots, a_{n-1}$.

The left circuit in Figure 2 is inserted b times between Layers 1 and 2 in Figure 1 on each wire c_j, $j = 1, \ldots, b$, replacing c_j with a bit c'_j before passing it to Layer 2. For each candidate policy G_j, this subcircuit computes a bit c'_j indicating whether the server is also willing to make all promises that the client requires for attributes in G_j. The right circuit in Figure 2 is to be appended to the right of the circuit in Figure 1. If attribute $a_i \in M$, then the bitwise AND gate encodes the client's demands D_i onto the output promises O_i, or it encodes the all-zeroes string if $a_i \notin M$.

6   The Private Policy Matching Protocol

Security. In Section 3, we transformed the policy negotiation problem into a function evaluation problem to which each of the two parties provides its own private inputs (policies). Let us denote the corresponding function by C. First, the function C is described as a circuit consisting of AND, OR and NOT gates in Section 3. It was shown that those gates can be evaluated if addition and multiplication can be performed on encrypted inputs. Addition on encrypted inputs follows immediately from the homomorphic property of the used cryptosystem and the multiplication is done with the *conditional gate* of [20]. The function C is then privately evaluated by the following protocol $\mathsf{Func}_C(F_1, \ldots, F_a; G_1, \ldots, G_a)$.

1. Both players encrypt their inputs; i.e. they encrypt (bit by bit) the strings describing their generating subsets. They broadcast zero-knowledge proofs that they know the content of their encryptions and that the values they encrypted are bits.
2. They carry out all the gates of the circuit that describes the function f by using the secure evaluation of the gates described in section 2.3. Gates that can be run in parallel will be securely evaluated in parallel, the others will be evaluated sequentially.
3. Finally, the output of the protocol is decrypted with a threshold decryption protocol.

Note that if the output should only be revealed to one of the players instead to both, then a threshold decryption with private outputs has to be used [20]. Finally, we mention that fairness can be achieved easily by using the fair decryption protocol developed in [20]. We have the following theorem.

Theorem 1. *On input of the generating subsets $F_1, \ldots, F_a$ and $G_1, \ldots, G_a$ of the client and the server respectively, the protocol Func_C evaluates the private policy negotiation without leaking any additional information about $F_1, \ldots, F_a$ and $G_1, \ldots, G_a$.*

Proof. Completeness of the Func_C protocol follows from the analysis in section 3 and of the construction of the gates in section 2.3. The fact that the Func_C protocol can be simulated follows from the following observation. The gates that are evaluated during the Func_C protocol consist on their turn of sequences of additions and multiplications. Hence it follows that the structure of the Func_C protocol follows exactly the structure of the function evaluation protocols in [9, 20]. This implies that the Func_C protocol can be simulated and hence leaks no additional information on its inputs $F_1, \ldots, F_a$ and $G_1, \ldots, G_a$.   □

From the description of the extensions to the circuit given in Section 5, it is straightforward to write down the full protocol for policy matching with obligations. Obviously, it consists entirely of AND, OR and NOT gates, and hence its security follows from a similar reasoning as made above.

Efficiency. In order to assess the practical feasibility of our protocol, we estimated the overhead incurred by evaluating the circuits given in Figures 1 and 2 using the techniques laid out in Section 2. (A constant factor on the number of gates can probably be saved by applying a design automation tool such as Xilinx.) A number of representative values are given in Table 1. For both the basic circuit and the extended circuit with obligations, we computed the total amount of data sent over the network, the number of communication rounds, and the number of exponentiations to be performed by each of the participants. The actual values were obtained by observing that the evaluation of an AND/OR gate on encrypted inputs involves 11 exponentiations from each participant and 26 group elements to be communicated over the network in 2 rounds; that the evaluation of an AND/OR gate with one known input involves 4 exponentiations by one of the participants and 10 group elements to be communicated in a single round; and that the evaluation of a NOT gate comes practically for free (using the homomorphic properties of the encryption scheme). We were able to save on the number of rounds by evaluating independent gates in parallel, and by implementing bitwise gates on n-bit vectors using binary gates organized in a tree of depth $\lceil \log_2 n \rceil$, rather than in a cascade.

Table 1. Efficiency estimates of our protocol for various parameter values when using the two-party computation protocol of [20] over 170-bit elliptic curves. We give the amount network traffic (bandwidth), the number of communication rounds and the number of exponentiations to be performed by each of the players for realistic values of the number of attributes n, the maximal number of client and server preferences a and b, and the maximal number of obligations per attribute m.

			without obligations			with obligations		
n	a,b	m	bandwidth	rounds	exponentiations	bandwidth	rounds	exponentiations
10	5	10	235 KB	16	$4.11 \cdot 10^3$	1.15 MB	36	$2.15 \cdot 10^4$
50	25	25	24.0 MB	24	$4.29 \cdot 10^5$	88.3 MB	52	$1.62 \cdot 10^6$
200	50	100	373 MB	30	$6.66 \cdot 10^6$	1.97 GB	66	$3.76 \cdot 10^7$

Asymptotically speaking, the basic circuit without obligations requires $O(abn)$ exponentiations to be computed and $O(abn)$ group elements to be communicated in $O(b + \log(bn))$ rounds. The circuit with obligations takes $O((a + m)bn)$ exponentiations and $O((a + m)bn)$ group elements in $O(b + \log(abmn))$ rounds.

From Table 1, one can see that our protocol is practically feasible only for relatively simple preferences and/or resourceful environments. For larger parameter values, the overhead may become prohibitive. This is due to both the use of generic cryptographic primitives and the severeness of our privacy requirements. We think that our implementation, however, can still serve as a benchmark for protocols that use specialized techniques or relaxed privacy requirements.

7   Conclusion

We consider this paper as a first step towards privacy preserving negotiation protocols, whereas the main goal is to cleanly define the problem and demonstrate its feasibility. Consequently, this work raises a number of new questions that need to be addressed for the system to become practical.

One issue is that our definitions of security are very strict. For many applications, this level of security is not required, while it prohibits possibly useful functionality such as user-defined or hierarchical attributes, or mixing data interpretation into the policy. It would be interesting to investigate whether a less strict privacy metric [22, 12] can be conceived under which more efficient protocols are possible.

Another issue is that our protocols use generic two-party computation. We expect that the cost of the protocols can be significantly brought down by designing special-purpose protocols that do not base on generic circuit evaluation.

Acknowledgements

The work of the first two authors was supported in part by the Concerted Research Action (GOA) Ambiorics 2005/11 of the Flemish Government and in part by the European Commission through the IST Programme under Contract IST-2002-507932 ECRYPT. Gregory Neven is a Postdoctoral Fellow of the Research Foundation – Flanders (FWO – Vlaanderen).

References

1. M. Abadi and J. Feigenbaum. Secure circuit evaluation. *J. Cryptology*, 2(1):1–12, 1990.
2. S. S. Al-Riyami, J. Malone-Lee, and N. P. Smart. Escrow-free encryption supporting cryptographic workflow. Cryptology ePrint Archive, Report 2004/258, 2004. Available from http://eprint.iacr.org/.
3. M. Backes, G. Karjoth, W. Bagga, and M. Schunter. Efficient comparison of enterprise privacy policies. In *ACM SAC 2004*, pages 375–382, New York, NY, USA, 2004. ACM Press.
4. W. Bagga and R. Molva. Policy-based cryptography and applications. In A. Patrick and M. Yung, editors, *Financial Cryptography 2005*, volume 3570 of *LNCS*, pages 72–87. Springer, 2005.
5. A. Barth and J. C. Mitchell. Enterprise privacy promises and enforcement. In *WITS '05: Proceedings of the 2005 workshop on Issues in the Theory of Security*, pages 58–66. ACM Press, 2005.
6. D. Boneh, E.-J. Goh, and K. Nissim. Evaluating 2-DNF formulas on ciphertexts. In J. Kilian, editor, *TCC 2005*, volume 3378 of *LNCS*, pages 325–341. Springer, 2005.

7. J. Camenisch and E. Van Herreweghen. Design and implementation of the idemix anonymous credential system. In *Proc. of the 9th CCS*, pages 21–30, New York, NY, USA, 2002. ACM Press.

8. R. Cleve. Limits on the security of coin flips when half the processors are faulty. In *Proc. of the 18th ACM STOC*, pages 364–369. ACM Press, 1986.

9. R. Cramer, I. Damgård, and J. B. Nielsen. Multiparty computation from threshold homomorphic encryption. In B. Pfitzmann, editor, *EUROCRYPT 2001*, volume 2045 of *LNCS*, pages 280–300. Springer, 2001.

10. I. Damgård and J. B. Nielsen. Universally composable efficient multiparty computation from threshold homomorphic encryption. In D. Boneh, editor, *CRYPTO 2003*, volume 2729 of *LNCS*, pages 565–582. Springer, 2003.

11. Y. Desmedt and Y. Frankel. Threshold cryptosystems. In G. Brassard, editor, *CRYPTO 1989*, volume 435 of *LNCS*, pages 307–315. Springer, 1990.

12. C. Díaz, S. Seys, J. Claessens, and B. Preneel. Towards measuring anonymity. In R. Dingledine and P. Syverson, editors, *PET 2002* , volume 2482 of *LNCS*. Springer, 2002.

13. M. K. Franklin and S. Haber. Joint encryption and message-efficient secure computation. *J. Cryptology*, 9(4):217–232, 1996.

14. M. J. Freedman, K. Nissim, and B. Pinkas. Efficient private matching and set intersection. In C. Cachin and J. Camenisch, editors, *EUROCRYPT 2004*, volume 3027 of *LNCS*, pages 1–19. Springer, 2004.

15. R. Gennaro, S. Jarecki, H. Krawczyk, and T. Rabin. Secure distributed key generation for discrete-log based cryptosystems. In J. Stern, editor, *EUROCRYPT 1999*, volume 1592 of *LNCS*, pages 295–310. Springer, 1999.

16. R. Gennaro, S. Jarecki, H. Krawczyk, and T. Rabin. Secure applications of Pedersen's distributed key generation protocol. In M. Joye, editor, *CT-RSA 2003*, volume 2964 of *LNCS*, pages 373–390. Springer, 2003.

17. O. Goldreich, S. Micali, and A. Wigderson. How to play any mental game or a completeness theorem for protocols with honest majority. In *Proc. of the 19th ACM STOC*, pages 218–229. ACM Press, 1987.

18. M. Jakobsson and A. Juels. Mix and match: Secure function evaluation via ciphertexts. In T. Okamoto, editor, *ASIACRYPT 2000*, volume 1976 of *LNCS*, pages 346–358. Springer, 2000.

19. M. C. Mont, S. Pearson, and P. Bramhall. Towards accountable management of identity and privacy: Sticky policies and enforceable tracing services. In *DEXA 2003* , pages 377–382. IEEE Computer Society, 2003.

20. B. Schoenmakers and P. Tuyls. Practical two-party computation based on the conditional gate. In P. J. Lee, editor, *ASIACRYPT 2004*, volume 3329 of *LNCS*, pages 119–136. Springer, 2004.

21. K. E. Seamons, M. Winslett, and T. Yu. Limiting the disclosure of access control policies during automated trust negotiation. In *NDSS 2001* . The Internet Society, 2001.

22. S. Steinbrecher and S. Köpsell. Modelling unlinkability. In R. Dingledine, editor, *PET 2003* , volume 2760 of *LNCS*. Springer, 2003.

23. W3C. The platform for privacy preferences 1.0 (P3P1.0) specification, 2002. http://www.w3.org/TR/P3P/.

24. A. C.-C. Yao. Protocols for secure computations. In IEEE, editor, *Proc. of the 23rd FOCS*, pages 160–164. IEEE Computer Society Press, 1982.

25. T. Yu, M. Winslett, and K. E. Seamons. Supporting structured credentials and sensitive policies through interoperable strategies for automated trust negotiation. *ACM Trans. Inf. Syst. Secur.*, 6:1–42, 2003.

Uncheatable Reputation for Distributed Computation Markets[*]

Bogdan Carbunar[1] and Radu Sion[2]

[1] Computer Science, Purdue University
(`carbunar@cs.purdue.edu`)
[2] Computer Science, Stony Brook University
(`sion@cs.stonybrook.edu`)

Abstract. Reputation systems aggregate mutual feedback of interacting peers into a "reputation" metric for each participant. This is then available to prospective service "requesters" (clients) for the purpose of evaluation and subsequent selection of potential service "providers" (servers). For a reputation framework to be effective, it is paramount for both the individual feedback and the reputation storage mechanisms to be trusted and able to deal with faulty behavior of participants such as "ballot stuffing" (un-earned positive feedback) and "bad-mouthing" (incorrect negative feedback). While, in human-driven (e.g. Ebay) environments, these issues are dealt with by hired personnel, on a case by case basis, in automated environments, this ad-hoc manner of handling is likely not acceptable. Stronger, secure mechanisms of trust are required.

In this paper we propose a solution for securing reputation mechanisms in computing markets and grids where servers offer and clients demand compute services. We introduce *threshold witnessing*, a mechanism in which a minimal set of "witnesses" provide service interaction feedback *and* sign associated ratings for the interacting parties. This endows traditional feedback rating with trust while handling both "ballot-stuffing" and "bad-mouthing" attacks. Witnessing relies on a challenge-response protocol in which servers provide verifiable computation execution proofs. An added benefit is ensuring computation result correctness.

Keywords: Trust, Reputation Systems, Electronic Commerce.

1 Introduction

In a reputation system, satisfaction feedback provided by interacting entities is aggregated and used in the construction of a "reputation" metric of each participant. This metric is then to be used by prospective service clients in evaluating and selecting among potential servers. One example of a reputation system is *eBay*. In a typical scenario, following a sale, the buyer provides a satisfaction rating which is then stored in a publicly available reputation profile of the seller which can be later consulted by prospective buyers.

---

[*] Find an extended version of this paper at http://www.cs.stonybrook.edu/~sion.

G. Di Crescenzo and A. Rubin (Eds.): FC 2006, LNCS 4107, pp. 96–110, 2006.
© IFCA/Springer-Verlag Berlin Heidelberg 2006

In the case of eBay, interacting entities are human. One could envision leveraging a paradigm of interaction feedback reputation in fully automated digital interactions, for example in distributed servicing systems. The promise of such reputation frameworks [3, 5, 6, 11, 12, 13, 20] is to offer a low cost, scalable method for assessing reliability (and possibly level of trust) of connected system entities. Now centralized trust becomes a costly, often un-realistic proposal. A distributed alternative for reputation management is required. In hostile settings, malicious behavior can interfere significantly with the ability to provide and manage interaction and service ratings (possibly with the purpose of inflicting reputation damage to the competition or the system itself). Nevertheless, these are the type of frameworks where a reputation paradigm would yield the most benefits, not only because of its scalability and virtually zero-cost, but mainly because of its potential to provide feedback to security and resource managers, essential in ad-hoc and faulty (possibly malicious) settings. This is why, for a reputation framework to be effective, it is paramount for both the individual feedback and the reputation storage mechanisms to be trusted and able to deal with faulty behavior of participants such as "ballot stuffing" (un-earned positive feedback) and "bad-mouthing" (incorrect negative feedback). While, in human-driven (e.g. Ebay) environments, these issues are handled by an army of hired individuals, in automated environments, this is likely not acceptable. Strong and secure automatic mechanisms of trust are required.

Here we introduce a solution for secure reputation management in a distributed computing environment. We believe this to be a first required step in the integration of reputation as a trusted automated assessment mechanism in distributed computing environments. Our solution is composed of two major elements: a proof of computation method (an extension of the "ringer" concept first introduced in [10]) and a "threshold witnessing" mechanism. In the witnessing protocol, a set of sufficient "witnesses" are gathered to witness service interactions and subsequently sign a document certifying a new associated rating. The witnessing is coupled with a mechanism of computation proofs which provides an (arbitrary high) confidence level that a particular set of computations was indeed performed by a given party. This is required in witnessing to make sure that ratings are in fact correlated to the quality of the result. The main contributions of this paper include: (i) the proposal and definition of the problem of securing rating correctness and their associated semantics (computational result correctness) in distributed computing markets, (ii) a solution proposing the use of *threshold witnessing* and *computation proofs* to produce securely signed ratings and (iii) the evaluation thereof, (iv) an extension to the *ringers* concept for arbitrary computations and an analysis of its applicability.

The paper is structured as follows. Section 2 introduces the main system and adversary models as well as some of the basic construction primitives. Section 3 overviews, details and analyzes our solution and its building blocks. Section 4 surveys related work and Section 5 concludes.

2 Model and Tools

2.1 Communication and System Model

Let n be the average total number of uniquely identified (e.g., through a numeric identifier Id(X))) processes or participants in the system at any given point in time. Due to the potentially dynamic nature of real systems (with participants joining and leaving continuously), defining n precisely is inherently hard.

The system's purpose is to provide a market for computations. Participants can export CPU cycles that others can use in exchange for payment. We assume that there exists a finite set of computation "services", $\{f_1, ..., f_s\}$ and each participant has the ability to perform them, albeit at different costs. Let Alice be a service provider and Bob a service requester. In such a computing market, as part of a service request, Bob specifies an amount he is willing to pay for it as well as additional quality of result constraints, e.g., time bounds. Bob's aim is to maximize the investment, for a set of computations it needs to perform.

For any interaction between Alice (Id(Alice) = A) and Bob (Id(Bob) = B), let there be a unique session identifier, e.g., a composition of the current time and the identities of the two parties, $sid(A, B, time) = H(A; B; time)$. We will use the notation sid when there is no ambiguity. Let f be a service provided, $f : \mathbb{D} \rightarrow \mathbb{I}$, and let $(x_i)_{i \in [1,a]} \in \mathbb{D}$ be the computation inputs.

As it is not central to our contribution, to model costs and execution times we are proposing the following intuitive model: (i) for a computation f and a given input data set $\{x_1, ..., x_a\}$ the amount of associated CPU instructions NI(f) required to compute it, can be determined easily (for simplicity we assume that for each x_i, this amount is the same); for every system participant X both (ii) the execution time per CPU instruction TPI(X) and (iii) the charged cost per time unit CPT(X) are publicly known and easily accessible to every other participant While this model can be made more complex, we believe it fits best the current scope. Thus, any entity can determine every other's entity associated cost and execution time. This is an important element in the process of matching a particular service request (including time and cost constraints) to the most appropriate service provider (see Section 3.1).

There exists a universal time authority that provides the current absolute time value (e.g., UTC) with a certain precision ϵ_t. There exists a PKI [14], that can distribute certified public keys to all participants. This enables them to sign and check signatures of others. We propose to use this same infrastructure to also provide verifiable threshold signatures [17]. More precisely, we use it to distribute to each participant a certified *master secret key share* and the *master public key*. The key shares are set up such that any c + 1 participants can sign an arbitrary message with the master secret key, and the correctness of any signature share can be verified by anyone in a non-interactive manner (c or less participants cannot perform the same operation, see Section 2.4).

We assume that the underlying distributed communication layer offers the following types of communication channels: (i) secure point to point between two entities (cost: ψ_{pp}), (ii) secure multicast within a group (cost per multicast:

ψ_{mcast}) and (iii) broadcast (cost per broadcast: ψ_{bcast}). The multicast channel allows group creation and message delivery to group members. Additionally, as the main focus of this paper is not on the communication layer we assume that there exist join/leave protocols for participating entities that enable them to both become aware of and communicate with the other entities in the system. The only extension that our solution proposes is to the join protocol, enabling new entities to gain knowledge of existing reputation values (see Section 3.1).

Let the ratings be numeric in our system. We say that a reputation is a *trustworthy enclosure* of a rating. More precisely, the reputation of participant X is $\mathtt{rep(X)} = S_{MK}(\mathtt{Id(X)}, \mathtt{rating(X)}, T)$, where $S_{MK}(M)$ denotes message M signed with the secret master key, $\mathtt{rating(X)} \in [0, 1]$ is X's rating (a higher value is a better rating), and T is the creation time of the reputation. Additionally, upon receiving the results r of an interaction of X performed in time ΔT, let $\rho()$ be any function that aggregates r and ΔT with the previous rating of X, to create the new rating of X; the new rating value of X becomes $\mathtt{rating_{new}(X)} = \rho(\mathtt{rating_{old}(X)}, r, \Delta T)$.

2.2 The Adversary

Let c be the upper bound on the number of active faulty participants at any point in time (e.g., no more than c participants can collude, crash or act dishonestly). The mechanisms proposed here are always secure but most efficient when the size of the input data sets a is truly large. More specifically, when on average, $a > (2c + 1)$ holds for (most of) the computation jobs in the system. To bring efficiency even for smaller input sets, one could envision a mechanism for gathering multiple inputs over a time period, until a critical mass is attained and only then submit them for execution.

The role of reputation ratings is then to allow service requesters to choose service providers with a good history. Of concern here are scenarios of *ballot stuffing* and *bad-mouthing* [7] in which participants collude in order to build fake pasts. In ballot stuffing un-earned good reputation ratings are provided to service providers by colluding clients. The main purpose of bad-mouthing is to provide incorrect negative ratings, possibly for the competition.

2.3 Ringers

Ringers were first introduced in [10]. The main idea is to (cheaply) provide computation proofs for the evaluation of a certain hypothesis over a large input set where only certain items will match (e.g., interesting patterns in [1]). Here we propose ringers in a distributed computing market context where a computation needs to be performed on *all* the data items in the input set.

In their initial version ringers work as follows. The first underlying assumption is that the computations in the system are non-invertible one-way. A service client wishes to get one of these computations h computed for a set of inputs, $\{x_1, ..., x_a\}$ by a service provider. To perform the computation it first computes a challenge ("ringer") to be submitted along with the inputs to the service provider. This challenge is exactly the result of applying h to one of the inputs

$h(x_t)$, where $t \in [1, a]$ is not known to the service provider. The implicit assumption here is that computing h for the entire input set is significantly more expensive than for a single item in the input (e.g, if a is large enough). The client then submits $\{x_1, ..., x_a\}$ *and* $h(x_t)$ to the service provider. In addition to the normal computation results $\{h(x_1), ..., h(x_a)\}$ the service provider is expected to return also (as a computation proof) the correct value for t. Due to the non-invertible nature of h, a correct return provides a confidence of actual computation over the set of inputs.

The main power of the ringers lies in the assumed non-invertibility of the performed computations. To directly fake a proof (and produce a "valid" t), the service provider would have to either: (i) act honest and perform a computations or (ii) cheat and perform only $0 \leq w < a$ computations hoping it finds the ringer in the process and, if not, guess. The probability to succeed in cheating is positively correlated to the amount of work performed; over the course of multiple interactions it can be forced to arbitrary small values. For more details see Section 3.3. The ringer construct (for arbitrary computations) in this paper is obtained by "wrapping" results in one-way, random crypto-hash functions. In other words, we lift the assumption of one-way non-invertibility for the computations in the system; h can be any function. The ringer challenge submitted to the service provider becomes now $H(h(x_t))$ where $H()$ is a one-way non-invertible cryptographic hash function. Thus, instead of the assumed one-wayness of computations, our extension puts the main power of ringers in the non-invertibility and randomness of the cryptographic hash deployed. Additionally, we extend the adversary model to also consider "guessing" (see Section 3.2).

2.4   Verifiable Threshold Signatures

The model of verifiable threshold signatures [17] consists of a set of n participants and a trusted dealer. Since we already assume the existence of a decentralized trusted infrastructure providing public key distribution, see Section 2.1, we can use it to play the part of the trusted dealer. Initially, the trusted infrastructure needs to generate a master public key PK, a verification key VK, n shares of a master secret key $SK_{i:1..n}$ and n verification keys $VK_{i:1..n}$. Each participant P_i receives PK, VK and its shares SK_i and VK_i, each certified by the trusted infrastructure. Additional secret and verification key shares can easily be generated later on, for the use of new participants that join the system. This is not generating a high overhead, requiring only the computation of a polynomial and an exponentiation [17]. The signature verification algorithm takes a message, its signature and the master key PK and determines if the signature is correct. The signature share verification algorithm takes a message, PK, VK, the signature share of process P_i, and VK_i and determines if the signature share is valid. The share combination algorithm takes as input a message, $c + 1$ valid signature shares for the message and PK and produces a valid signature of the message. Any c processes cannot collude and produce a valid signature of a message.

3   Solution

At an overview level our initial solution proceeds as follows (Figure 1 (a)). Bob wishes to get a given computation f executed over a set of input data items $\{x_1, ..., x_a\}$, in exchange for payment. Both the payment and the amount of time he is willing to wait for service completion are upper-bounded. In an initial *witness selection* phase (**step 1**, Section 3.1), Bob selects a set of $2c + 1$ computation "witnesses" W_i (this provides a threshold-secure way of avoiding illicit ratings). He then sends to all of them (via multicast) a service request including f, the inputs, the payment and target execution time upper bounds (**step 2**). The witnesses then perform a distributed *server selection* process

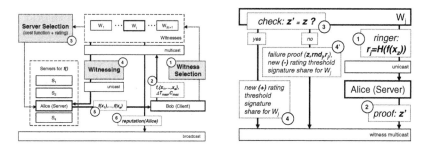

Fig. 1. (a) Solution Overview (b) Building Block: Witnessing Protocol

(**step 3**, Section 3.1), at the end of which the least-costly, best-reputation, available server is selected to perform f for Bob. As the adversary model in Section 2.2 guarantees a majority of the witnesses are honest and non-colluding, this process is to complete successfully. Let the selected server be "Alice". Note that the selection of Alice is not under the control of Bob. Alice is provided f and the input data set and the witnesses then initiate the process of *threshold witnessing* (**step 4**, Section 3.1) by sending (each in turn) a set of challenge ringers to Alice. Upon executing the computation Alice completes the witnessing process by returning the execution proofs associated with the challenge ringers to the witnesses, as well as the actual computation results back to Bob (**step 5**). Finally, depending on the proof correctness, the witnesses sign (using verifiable threshold signatures, Section 2.4) a new rating (a combination of the previous rating and "good" if correct proofs or "bad" otherwise) for Alice and distribute (broadcast) it (**step 6**, Section 3.1). If the rating does not change it is not distributed.

3.1   Building Blocks

Rating Storage Management. We start by first exploring the way the actual reputation information is stored. As the rating of each participant is ultimately a numeric value, in itself it can be easily altered. Our solution for introducing trust in reputation values is to allow their creation only if a certain number of participants agree on that reputation. For this, the reputation of participant X is stored signed with the secret master key, as $S_{MK}(Id(X), rating(X), T)$. Then, we use verifiable threshold signatures (see Section 2.4) to allow no less than $c + 1$ participants to sign a reputation with the secret master key. Thus, the reputation of a participant can be created or changed only if at least $c + 1$ participants agree on the participant's new rating.

Every participant stores the most recent reputation for every other participant together with: the time it takes the participant to execute an instruction, *time per instruction (TPI)*, and the amount charged by the participant per unit of its processor time, *cost per time (CPT)* (see Section 2.1). Both values are constant and signed with the participant's private key before distribution.

In order for participants to store consistent reputations, we need each joining participant to acquire the current view of the system, and a change in one's reputation to be advertised to all. It is thus straightforward to see that at most c participants may have an incorrect view of the system, since we assume that at most c participants are faulty. A joining participant has then to make its presence known through a broadcast message, followed by the transfer of reputations knowledge of at least $2c + 1$ participants, already part of the system. Specifically, when a participant X receives the broadcast message of a new participant, J, it stores J's identity under an initial, pre-agreed upon rating. X then retrieves the current time, T, and if the selection test is positive, that is, $H(Id(X), T) \bmod \lceil n/(2c + 1 + e) \rceil = 0$, X sends back to J its collection of reputations. J waits to receive $c + 1$ replies and then for each participant only stores the most recent reputation. Since we assume that the current time can be retrieved with error ϵ_t, each participant uses only the most significant bits of T in order to perform the selection test with the same value of T. e is a positive integer, used to ensure that at least $2c + 1$ of the participants will be selected.

Witness Selection. Before exporting a job, service client B first needs to select $2c + 1$ witnesses, ensuring that even if c participants are faulty, a majority, at least $c + 1$, will be honest and alive for the duration of the protocol. Since B already stores the reputations of all the participants, the witnesses can be elected randomly among them. This corresponds to **step 1** in Figure 1 (a). In **step 2**, B creates a multicast channel for the witnesses and sends the (signed) job description: f, the set of input values $(x_i)_{i \in [1, a]}$, the maximum time B is willing to wait for job completion, ΔT_{max}, and the maximum amount B is willing to pay for the computation, C_{max}, a signed digest $S_B(H(f, (x_i)_{i \in [1, a]}, \Delta T_{max}, C_{max}))$, along with a certificate containing B's public key, meant to prevent integrity attacks.

Server Selection. The $2c + 1$ witnesses need to first select the most suitable service provider (see **step 3** in Figure 1 (a)). This is performed subject to the following constraints. First, all participants X for which $TPI(X) \times NI(f) \times a$ is greater than ΔT_{max}, or $TPI(X) \times CPT(X) \times NI(f) \times a$ is greater than C_{max}, are not further considered. Secondly, the participant with the best reputation among the remaining ones is selected. Let that participant be Alice (A). Even with c faulty witnesses, no less than $c + 1$ witnesses will select A.

Next, A is added to the witness multicast group. The first witness in a certain order [4] ("the leader") multicasts the job description received from B. If the other witnesses receive this message, they know that A also received it, and stop; else, after waiting a small amount of time, the next witness in the ordering assumes leadership and sends this multicast. This continues until the witnesses hear the expected job description. In Section 3.1 we show that in fact the number of expected multicasts is exactly one.

Threshold Witnessing. The 4th step in Figure 1 (a), detailed in Figure 1 (b), depicts the service witnessing operation. This operation requires the $2c + 1$ witnesses to first export B's computation to A, then verify the accuracy of the computation performed by A, and based on the quality of the service performed, compute and sign the new rating of A. The essence of the service witnessing operation is the usage of ringers (see Section 2.3). We now show how the threshold witnessing operation is performed securely by $2c + 1$ external witnesses.

Ringer Generation. Each witness $W_{j:1..2c+1}$ selects one (or a small random number of values – we illustrate here the case with one single value for clarity) random value x_z from the input set $(x_i)_{i \in [1,a]}$ specified by B in the job description and computes a ringer $r_j = H(f(x_z))$. Based on the identities of A and B and the current time, W_j generates a unique session identifier, sid, (see Section 2.1). The purpose of sid is to prevent replay attacks by introducing a freshness element. Then W_j computes $S_{W_j}(H(Id(W_j), sid, r_j))$, and sends its identifier, $Id(W_j)$, sid, the ringer r_j, together with the signed digest and W_j's public key certificate to A (**step 1** in Figure 1 (b)). When A receives such a message, it verifies W_j's signature. Although A knows r_j and it may collude with a subset of the witnesses, none of them actually knows the x_z value generated by an honest witness. Also, since at most c witnesses can be malicious, at least $c + 1$ witnesses will be honest and generate good ones; these are enough to ensure A's cooperation.

A waits to receive $2c + 1$ valid messages for the same session identifier, sid. If, within a given time frame, starting with the receipt of the first ringer, A receives less than $c + 1$ such messages, it ignores the job received. Otherwise, A sends a multicast message to all the witnesses that participated. The message contains a concatenation of all the signed ringers received. The witnesses that receive this message, inquire the remaining witnesses for their ringers. If the remaining witnesses, less than $c + 1$ of them, show that they chose a different service provider, A should perform the job with only the initial ringers (necessarily from honest witnesses). If the remaining witnesses reply with ringers, A should perform the job using all ringers. This mechanism is required to avoid a case of malicious witnesses mounting a denial of service attack in which they don't send out ringers but claim Alice to be malicious. It also handles the case of a malicious Alice claiming to have not received all the ringers.

Revealing the Ringers. Next, A performs the computation and reveals the input values x_z hidden in the $2c + 1$ ringers. It creates a single message containing $S_{W_j}(H(Id(W_j), sid, r_j))$ and $S_A(H(Id(A), sid, z))$, for $j = 1..2c + 1$. The message also contains the results of the computation, $f(x_1), .., f(x_a)$, along with its signed digest. Note that the first signed digest was sent by W_j, and is used to prove the value of the ringer r_j. A then sends this message on the witness multicast channel (**step 2** in Figure 1 (b)). Each witness W_j verifies the correctness of only its own ringer, that is, $r_j = H(f(x_z))$. The multicast of A is meant to prevent a witness from falsely claiming that A did not send back a correct answer.

If any witness W_j discovers that A did not send back x_z or that $r_j \neq H(f(x_z))$, W_j sends a multicast message to all the other witnesses revealing this fact. The other witnesses are able to verify the claim by computing the correct answer to W_j's ringer and compare it with the answer sent back by Alice (received during A's previous multicast, **step 3** in Figure 1 (b)). This acts as the proof that A did not perform the entire computation. A negative rating is then issued.

Signature Generation. Based on A's current rating, $\texttt{rating}(A)$, the returned results of the current computation, r, and the time elapsed since A received the job description, ΔT, each witness W_j is able to compute A's new rating using the ρ function (see Section 2.1). In general, if A is caught cheating, either by not performing the entire computation or performing it slower than advertised, its rating will decrease, otherwise, it will increase. Each W_j then generates a verifiable signature share of A's new reputation, $S_{W_j}^{shr}(\texttt{Id}(A), \rho(\texttt{rating}(A), r, \Delta T), T)$, where T is the current time and $S_{W_j}^{shr}(M)$ denotes message M signed with W_j's share of the secret master key. Then W_j sends this value, along with its certified verification key VK_j (see Section 2.4) and A's new rating in clear, to all the other witnesses, using the group's multicast channel. Each witness waits to receive c correct signature shares for the same new reputation of A as the one generated by itself. As mentioned in Section 2.4, any participant can verify the validity of a signature share by using the master public key, master verification key and the verification key of the share, VK_j. Additionally, since no more than c witnesses are malicious, an honest witness will receive at least c such correct signature shares, ensuring progress. Since $c + 1$ different and correct signature shares are enough to generate a valid signature (see Section 2.4), each witness is able to generate the signed new rating of A locally.

Reputation Distribution. In the last stage of the protocol, depicted in **steps 5** and **6** in Figure 1 (a), the results of the computation are returned to B and the new reputation of A is distributed. Since we assume that A can only be lazy, if A performed the computation, it will send the correct results to B. The witnesses know each other's identities and a global ordering of the group members is assumed [4]. The first witness is in charge of sending the new reputation of A on the broadcast channel to all the participants in the system. If during this broadcast the remaining witnesses hear the expected reputation, they stop. However, if the next witness (in the given group order) does not hear the expected reputation in a given time frame, it will itself send A's new reputation on the broadcast channel. This process goes on until all the witnesses are satisfied with the distributed reputation. Note that a witness cannot simply send an incorrect reputation since it will be easily detected, as it would need a fresh timestamp and to be signed with the master key, that is, by at least $c + 1$ honest witnesses.

If *un-changing ratings are ignored*, the number of broadcasts is reduced to a fraction of $\frac{c}{n}$ (Section 3.3).

3.2   Attacks and Improvements

Cheating and Laziness.   Is *bad-mouthing* still possible? Due to the nature of the solution, issuing a bad rating requires a secured proof of non-compliance by Alice, that all witnesses agree with. This would only happen if at least one of them will show its ringer $H(f(x_z))$ for which Alice did not respond correctly with z. But, if Alice responded correctly, all messages are signed, ringers are non-invertible, and at most c of the witnesses are malicious, this is not possible.

Furthermore, a straight-forward ballot-stuffing attack, where clients create and duplicate simple compute jobs in order to artificially increase the ratings of preferred servers, is thwarted through the indirection introduced by the witnessing layer. For each job requested by a client, a server is chosen by $2c + 1$ witnesses, containing an honest majority.

Next, we ask what are the chances of malicious entities to succeed in cheating in the witnessing phase? In other words, is lazy behavior (resulting in *ballot-stuffing*) possible and how likely? An analysis on the power of ringers can be found in [10]. Without duplicating these results, here we are exploring a scenario not considered in [10]. Let us start by asking the question: For r ringers, what is the probability of "finding" (i.e., finding the rank of the corresponding input item in the item set) x of them by performing only $w < a$ work? In other words, what is the likelihood of cheating by simply finding the ringers after doing less work than required.

This can be modeled as a classical sampling experiment without replacement (retrieving x black balls out of w draws from a bowl of $(a - r)$ white and r black balls): $P_0(a, w, r, x) = \frac{\binom{r}{x} \times \binom{a-r}{w-x}}{\binom{a}{w}}$ where $x \in [\max(0, w + r - a), \min(r, w)]$. Additionally, we know the success probability of simple guessing of r ringers without performing any work is (choosing r out of a items): $P_1(a, r) = \frac{1}{\binom{a}{r}}$ A rational malicious Alice could deploy the following cheating strategy: do $w < a$ work (compute only w results) and, if not all the ringers are discovered (possible if also $r < w$), simply guess the remaining ones. It can be shown that the success probability of such a strategy is:

$$P(w, r) = \sum_{i=\max(0, w+r-a)}^{\min(r,w)} [P_0(a, w, r, i) \times P_1(a - w, r - i)] = \frac{1}{\binom{a}{r}} \sum_{i=\max(0, w+r-a)}^{\min(r,w)} \binom{w}{i}$$

To better understand what this means we depicted the behavior of $P(w, r)$ in Figure 2 for $b = 20$. It can be seen that (e.g., for $r = 5$) a significant amount of work (e.g., $w > \frac{3}{4}b$) needs to be performed to achieve even a 33% success probability. Figure 2 (b) illustrates the inverse dependency on the number of ringers r for specific values of performed work. The more challenges are presented to Alice, the less its probability of getting away with less work.

Maybe more importantly, Figure 2 (c) illustrates the inverse exponential dependency on the number of ringers r for specific values of performed work. The

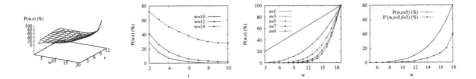

Fig. 2. The behavior of $P(w, r)$ ($a = 20$). (a) 3-dimensional view, (b) inverse dependency of r to w (2-dimensional cut through (a)). (c) The behavior of $P(w, r)$. A 2-dimensional cut through (a) showing the relationship between $P(w, r)$ and the amount of performed work w, plotted against the base case with one ringer ($r = 1$). (d) $P'(w, r, f)$ and $P(w, r)$ plotted for $r = 5$, $f = 3$.

more ringers are presented to Alice, the less its probability of getting away with less work. Over multiple interactions, lazy behavior is not sustainable as the probability of getting caught increases exponentially and the cheating success probability converges to 0: $\prod_{i=1}^{v}(P(w_i)) \to 0$, where $w_i < a$ is the work performed in each of the interactions.

Fake Ringers. There exists an important issue of concern with the above scheme. Because Alice knows the number of ringers, once she finds all of them she can simply stop working. One simple yet effective solution to this problem is to add "fake" ringers to the set of submitted ringers. In other words, instead of the witnesses computing and sending a total of $(r + f)$ *correct* ringers, they will compute just r correct ones and then simply generate $f > 0$ random ringer-like items and add them to the set. This has the additional benefit of reducing computation costs. Now Alice has to respond correctly only to the non-fake ones. Because she does not know which ones and how many of the challenges are fake, she is forced to execute all the queries to guarantee a correct answer (she cannot stop after it finds all the correct ones, as it doesn't know which ones and how many they are).

Introducing the fake ringers solves the issue of Alice being able to simply stop after discovering all the ringers. It also offers higher security assurances. Let us explore why by first assessing the impact of fake ringers on the success probability of Alice's malicious behavior $P'(w, r, f)$. To succeed, at each step, she needs to first guess *exactly* what the value of f is. If she is off even by one and replies with a value to a fake ringer (instead of stating it is fake), the witnesses know that Alice did not compute $f()$ over all the inputs. It can be shown that:

$$P'(w, r, f) = \frac{1}{\binom{a}{r}} \sum_{i=\max(0, w+r-a)}^{\min(r, w)} \left[\frac{\binom{w}{i}}{\min(a - w, \max(1, r + f - i))} \right]$$

where $\frac{1}{\min(a-w, \max(1, r+f-i))}$ is the probability of Alice guessing the value of r (and f) after performing w work and discovering i correct ringers. This is so because Alice knows that clearly $(r - i) \leq (a - w)$ (number of remaining ringers cannot exceed number of remaining un-considered inputs). Then, there are $(r - i) + f$ remaining possible values for f, only one of which is correct. The $\max()$ needs to be considered if $f = 0$ and Alice discovers all r ringers: it knows then that $f = 0$. In Figure 2 (d) the evolution of $P'(w, r, f)$ is plotted against $P(w, r)$ for $r = 5$, $f = 3$. Only 3 additional fake ringers (no additional cost) significantly decrease the cheating success probability of Alice (e.g., for $w = 17$ from 60% to 20%).

To function properly, deploying fake ringers requires the assumption that their number is random for every witnessing procedure and cannot be predicted by Alice. Now we are faced with solving the following problem: the witnesses have to make sure that, through-out time, both r and f are secret, randomly chosen and not correlated to each other or with their previous values.

But how can this be achieved in an environment where up to c of the witnesses could be malicious? If all the witnesses somehow agree upon values for r and f, nothing is stopping the malicious ones to leak these very values to Alice, thus defeating the advantages of fake ringers all-together. To solve this, we propose the following adjustment to the ringer generation mechanism. Instead of each witness generating exactly a single correct ringer, let it generate a random, secret number of correct and incorrect ringers. As a majority of witnesses are non-malicious, even if the rest of the witnesses are not cooperating, this mechanism will result in a random value for the (total) number of fake and real ringers, neither of which are known to, or under the control of any one party.

If c is large enough it may warrant the argument that, due to the law of large numbers, this will result, on average, in 50% true ringers and 50% false ones. This might make it easier for Alice to approximate the moment when it can simply stop and guess f. In that case, the following alternative can be deployed: each witness performs a separate witnessing round with Alice, (using its own random numbers of true and fake ringers). After initially performing all the computations (just once) for each such round, Alice will simply respond to the ringers challenges only. Let us also note that this alternative can be put into place at no additional cost, by having Alice not discard the computed results until all the witnesses have been satisfied. No extra computations will be required in each witnessing round.

3.3   Analysis

Communication Overhead.   Let us analyze the incurred communication costs. These are composed of: (i) the initial request multicast, in the witnessing stage, (ii) one multicast with the service request (witnesses to Alice), (iii) $2c + 1$ unicasts with ringers (each witness to Alice), (iv) one multicast with proofs (Alice to witnesses), (v) $2c + 1$ multicasts with threshold signature shares (within witnesses groups) and (vi) one final broadcast with the actual signed reputation:

$$\psi_{\text{comm}} = (1 + 1 + 1 + (2c + 1))\psi_{\text{mcast}} + (2c + 1)\psi_{\text{pp}} + \psi_{\text{bcast}}$$

If we normalize with respect to the cost of the point to point communication, (i.e., $\psi_{\text{pp}} = 1$):

$$\psi_{\text{comm}} = (2c + 4)\psi_{\text{mcast}} + \psi_{\text{bcast}} + (2c + 1)$$

To understand this better, let us assume a simple multicast mechanism that yields an average cost (number of messages) of $\psi_{mcast}(x) = \beta_{mcast}x$ (for a group of x members) where $\beta_{mcast} \in (0, 1)$:

$$\psi_{comm} = \beta_{mcast}(2c + 2)(2c + 4) + (2c + 1) + \psi_{bcast}$$

Now, if we consider that a traditional scenario deploying reputation ratings (without witnessing and computation proofs) would only pay the communication cost of distributing the ratings (ψ_{bcast}), the actual total incurred *overhead* for securing the rating mechanism is

$$\Delta\psi_{comm} = \beta_{mcast}(2c + 2)(2c + 4) + (2c + 1)$$

Thus, the communication overhead is of an $O(c^2)$ complexity order.

Let us now consider the optimization proposed in Section 3.1, namely, to not distribute un-changing ratings. Because we assume a maximum of c faulty parties, the ratio of negatively rated interactions is roughly $\frac{c}{n}$. Thus, intuitively, on average the ratio of interactions that result in "changing" ratings can also be considered roughly $\frac{c}{n}$. This results in an additional reduction of communication costs, as for $(1 - \frac{c}{n})$ of the interactions, stages (v) and (vi) are not necessary:

$$\Delta\psi_{comm} = \beta_{mcast}(2c + 2)(2c + 1)\frac{c}{n} + 2\beta_{mcast}(2c + 2) + (2c + 1)$$

Now the communication overhead is reduced to an order of $O(\frac{c^3}{n})$.

Computation Overhead. The computation overhead includes: (i) the generation of $2c + 1$ ringers by the witnesses, (ii) the computation of a hashes over each function output, by Alice and (iii) the generation of $(2c + 1)$ threshold signature shares for the new ratings by the witnesses. Let ω_f be the cost of computing f for one of the inputs. We have

$$\Delta\omega_{computation} = (2c + 1 + a)(\omega_{hash} + \omega_f) + (2c + 1)\omega_s$$

where ω_{hash} is the cost of hashing a function output (when generating a ringer) and ω_s is the cost of generating a threshold signature share.

Let us assess the complexity of computations as a function of a, the number of input items in the request data set. For this purpose $\omega_f = 1$. Also, because ratings are numeric and of small size, and the hashes are likely computed over finite amounts of data, in the current scope, to assess overhead dependency of a, we are considering both ω_s and ω_{hash} to be constants. The computation overheads are thus of an order of $O(c + a)$; because a > c, this becomes $O(a)$. If we apply the optimization proposed in Section 3.1 (i.e., not to distribute un-changing ratings) these costs are further reduced with $2c + 1$. This would still leave the computation complexity at $O(a)$, with smaller constants however.

4   Related Work

Due to the initial "social" dimension associated with reputation research, the essential issue of securing reputation mechanisms in automated environments has only recently [2, 6, 7, 8, 12, 15, 16] been identified. Resnick et al [15] provide an excellent overview of the problems of providing trust in such systems. Damiani et al. [6] extend Gnutella to include reputations not only for participants but also for individual resources. The paper describes several interesting attacks, such as pseudospoofing, ID stealth or shilling, and proposes a protocol that is secure against them. An extension of the security analysis for such attacks performed by multiple colluding participants would make for interesting future work.

Maybe closest to our research in terms of the actual strong security goals is the research by Dewan and Dasgupta [8]. There they propose a mechanism that allows each participant to store its own reputation, as a signed chain of past transactions. Drawbacks of such an approach include the inability to deal directly with attacks such as ballot stuffing or bad mouthing, nor with the issue of rating semantics and execution correctness. Their solution however is certainly elegant and space efficient when applicable. An additional difficulty however also resides in *securely* storing the record of the last transaction in a reputation chain.

In the area of verifiable distributed computations we already discussed work by Golle and Mironov [10]. Szada et al. [19] extend their solution to optimization functions, Monte Carlo simulations and sequential function applications. In the work of Du et al. [9], the service provider commits to the computed values using a Merkle tree. Then, the service provider is queried on the values computed for several sample inputs. The commitment prevents the service provider from changing the output of its computations.

For more related research please refer to the full version of this paper at http://www.cs.stonybrook.edu/~sion.

5 Conclusions

In this work we have studied the problem of providing a secure reputation infrastructure for distributed computations. Our solution uses ringers [10] to construct computation correctness proofs. We also constrain the generation and modification of reputations, by requiring at least one non-faulty external observer to agree with the new reputation. We achieve this by employing a novel threshold witnessing mechanism, coupled with threshold signatures. We analyze the communication and computation overheads, as well as the level of security achieved. We believe that in a significant number of scenarios the goal of achieving secure trust among participants is as important as the applicability of the system, and thus, well worth the overheads. In future work we plan on building a proof of concept of the proposed mechanisms and exploring their capability in bootstrapping and maintaining trust. We also plan to increase the level of security provided by our solution against actively malicious service providers.

References

1. SETI @ Home. Online at `http://setiathome.ssl.berkeley.edu`.
2. Karl Aberer and Zoran Despotovic. Managing trust in a peer-2-peer information system. In *Proceedings of the tenth international conference on Information and knowledge management*, pages 310–317. ACM Press, 2001.

3. Beulah Alunkal, Ivana Veljkovic, Gregor von Laszewski, and Kaizar Aminand. Reputation-based Grid Resource Selection. In *Proceedings of the Workshop on Adaptive Grid Middleware*, New Orleans, LA, September 2003.

4. Y. Amira, G. Ateniese, D. Hasse, Y. Kim, C. Nita-Rotaru, T. Schlossnagle andJ. Schultz, J. Stanton, and G. Tsudik. Secure group communication in asynchronous networks with failures: Integration and experiments. In *The 20th IEEE International Conference on Distributed Computing Systems*, pages 330–343, 2000.

5. Mao Chen and Jaswinder Pal Singh. Computing and using reputations for internet ratings. In *Proceedings of the 3rd ACM conference on Electronic Commerce*, pages 154–162. ACM Press, 2001.

6. Ernesto Damiani, De Capitani di Vimercati, Stefano Paraboschi, Pierangela Samarati, and Fabio Violante. A reputation-based approach for choosing reliable resources in peer-to-peer networks. In *Proceedings of the 9th ACM conference on Computer and communications security*, pages 207–216. ACM Press, 2002.

7. Chrysanthos Dellarocas. Immunizing online reputation reporting systems against unfair ratings and discriminatory behavior. In *Proceedings of the 2nd ACM conference on Electronic commerce*, pages 150–157. ACM Press, 2000.

8. Prashant Dewan and Partha Dasgupta. Securing reputation data in peer-to-peer networks. In *Proceedings of International Conference on Parallel and Distributed Computing and Systems PDCS*, 2004.

9. W. Du, J. Jia, M. Mangal, and M. Murugesan. Uncheatable grid computing. In *Proceedings of the 24th International Conference on Distributed Computing Systems (ICDCS'04)*, pages 4–11. IEEE Computer Society, 2004.

10. Philippe Golle and Ilya Mironov. Uncheatable distributed computations. In *Proceedings of the 2001 Conference on Topics in Cryptology*, Springer-Verlag, 2001.

11. Audun Josang and Roslan Ismail. The beta reputation system. In *Proceedings of the 15th Bled Electronic Commerce Conference*, 2002.

12. Sepandar D. Kamvar, Mario T. Schlosser, and Hector Garcia-Molina. The eigentrust algorithm for reputation management in p2p networks. In *WWW*, 2003.

13. T.G. Papaioannou and G.D. Stamoulis. Effective use of reputation in peer-to-peer environments. In *Proceedings of IEEE International Symposium on Cluster Computing and the Grid CCGrid*, pages 259–268, 2004.

14. Michael K. Reiter, Matthew K. Franklin, John B. Lacy, and Rebecca N. Wright. The Ω key management service. In *Proceedings of the 3rd ACM conference on Computer and communications security*, pages 38–47. ACM Press, 1996.

15. Paul Resnick, Richard Zeckhauser, Eric Friedman, and Ko Kuwabara. Reputation systems. *Communications of the ACM*, 2000.

16. A.A. Selcuk, E. Uzun, and M.R. Pariente. A reputation-based trust management system for p2p networks. In *Proceedings of the IEEE International Symposium on Cluster Computing and the Grid CCGrid*, pages 251–258, 2004.

17. Victor Shoup. Practical threshold signatures. In *Proceedings of Eurocrypt*, 2000.

18. Radu Sion. Query execution assurance for outsourced databases. In *Proceedings of the Very Large Databases Conference VLDB*, 2005.

19. D. Szajda, B. Lawson, and J. Owen. Hardening functions for large-scale distributed computations. In *Proceedings of IEEE Symposium on Security and Privacy*, pages 216–224, 2003.

20. Li Xiong and Ling Liu. A reputation-based trust model for peer-to-peer ecommerce communities [extended abstract]. In *Proceedings of the 4th ACM conference on Electronic commerce*, pages 228–229. ACM Press, 2003.

An Efficient Publicly Verifiable Mix-Net for Long Inputs

Jun Furukawa and Kazue Sako

NEC Corporation, 1753, Shimonumabe, Nakahara, Kawasaki 211-8666, Japan
j-furukawa@ay.jp.nec.com, k-sako@ab.jp.nec.com

Abstract. We propose here the first efficient publicly verifiable hybrid mix-net. Previous publicly verifiable mix-net was only efficient for short ciphertexts and was not suitable for mixing long messages. Previous hybrid mix-net can mix long messages but did not have public verifiability. The proposed scheme is efficient enough to treat large scale electronic questionnaires of long messages as well as voting with write-ins, and offers public verifiability of the correctness of the tally. The scheme is provably secure if we assume random oracles, semantic security of a one-time symmetric-key cryptosystem, and intractability of decision Diffie-Hellman problem.

Keywords: Hybrid-mix, public verifiability, multiple encryption, efficient.

1 Introduction

Mix-net[5] schemes are useful for applications which require anonymity, such as voting and anonymous questionnaires. The core technique in a mix-net scheme is to execute multiple rounds of shuffling and decryption by multiple, independent mixers, so that the output decryption can not be linked to any of the input encryptions. To ensure the correctness of output, it is desirable to have the property of public verifiability. A typical realization of a publicly verifiable mix-net scheme is that based on a zero-knowledge proof system for shuffling of ElGamal ciphertexts[1, 8, 9, 11, 12, 16, 20, 26].

However, these schemes only achieve their best efficiency when sets of ciphertexts are of a short length, one fixed to the length determined by the employed encryption algorithm. A typical length is, say 160 bits long. In order to verifiably shuffle texts of a fixed but a longer length, a straightforward approach, for example, is to divide each text into blocks of the predetermined short bits, re-encrypt each block, and concatenate them to form a string. Then, this block-wisely re-encrypted string is permuted. This approach requires public key operations and shuffle-proving operations for each block, thus the computational cost is linear in the length of the input. Another kind of mix-net scheme, referred to as "hybrid mixing,"[15, 21, 22, 25], is able to shuffle long ciphertexts efficiently, but the correctness of its shuffling is not publicly verifiable. It is only mutually verifiable among its component mixers.

G. Di Crescenzo and A. Rubin (Eds.): FC 2006, LNCS 4107, pp. 111–125, 2006.

Neither of these approaches would be applicable, when long messages, such as those which might form the replies to questionnaires or write-in votes, are to be tallied, and when the correctness of the tallying needs to be publicly verifiable. A scheme that is publicly verifiable and is capable of shuffling ciphertexts of long but common length efficiently is yet to be proposed.

Our Contributions: We propose here the first efficient hybrid-mixing scheme that provides public verifiability. In our scheme, the number of zero-knowledge arguments for proving a shuffle does not depend on the length of the input ciphertext. Although the resulting mix-net does not provide full public verifiability of the hybrid decryption in the case when a user and a mixer collude, the best adversary can do is to switch the input between a valid and an invalid one. Moreover, all the users whose input failed decrypted correctly are traced. We prove the security properties of the proposed scheme assuming the random oracle model, semantically secure one-time symmetric-key cryptosystem, and intractability of decision Diffie-Hellman problem.

In the course of constructing the verifiable hybrid-mix, we have developed (1) a new IND-ME-CCA secure [32] encryption scheme that multiply uses IND-CCA2 secure hybrid encryption and (2) a 3-move efficient perfect zero-knowledge argument for shuffle-and-decryption of ElGamal ciphertexts.

Construction of Our Mix-Net Scheme: A commonly adopted construction of publicly verifiable mix-net is a combination of IND-CCA2 secure encryption scheme that is suitable for shuffling, a secure group decryption scheme to be performed by mixers, and zero-knowledge arguments for shuffle and decryption. For example, a typical construction [1, 11] is a combination of IND-CCA2 secure ElGamal type cryptosystem, a threshold decryption scheme of ElGamal ciphertexts, and zero-knowledge arguments for shuffling and decrypting ElGamal ciphertexts. Such construction provides secure verifiable mix-net but suffers from the restriction that the input message should be within the domain of ElGamal encryption scheme.

Our construction follows the above approach, but we use a hybrid encryption instead of a plain ElGamal encryption so that we can handle long messages. In order to achieve the group decryption property, we designed a new multiple encryption scheme where hybrid encryptions are repeatedly applied each public key of the mixers. In order to achieve the secure threshold decryption property and IND-CCA2 secure property we devised our multiple encryption scheme to achieve the IND-ME-CCA secure [32] property with repetitive IND-CCA2 secure hybrid encryptions. For public verifiability, we add encryption of a hash of the plaintext in the ciphertext in each repetition to achieve the publicly verifiable hybrid decryption.

We also provide an zero-knowledge argument for shuffle of the proposed multiple encryption scheme. For this purpose, we use a perfect zero-knowledge argument for shuffle-and-decryption of ElGamal ciphertexts [17, 10]. We note that a cost we pay for public verifiability is that the length of the input ciphertext grows in linear in the number of mixers unlike the scheme in [25].

The rest of the paper is organized as follows. Section 2 proposes IND-ME-CCA secure multiple encryption scheme using IND-CCA2 secure hybrid encryption scheme with efficient verifiable decryption property. Section 3 illustrates our publicly verifiable mix-net scheme, Section 5 discusses with analysis on the efficiency of our mix-net scheme.

2 IND-ME-CCA Secure Multiple Encryption in Hybrid Setting

We present here our multiple encryption scheme that is suitable to be used in a verifiable mix net. We adopted the model from [32] with modifications to add auxiliary output of *Dec* algorithm to suit for use in mix-net. A multiple encryption scheme *ME* is a public key encryption scheme, which consists of a set of a key generation algorithm (*MKey-Gen*), an encryption algorithm (*MEnc*), and a decryption algorithm (*MDec*). Each of these algorithms invokes respective algorithms of a public key encryption scheme (*Key-Gen, Enc, Dec*) for multiple times. We also adopt the security notion of multiple encryption called IND-ME-CCA which is introduced in [32]. This notion differs from IND-CCA2 security in the sense that the adversaries are allowed to access key exposure oracle. We note that our multiple encryption scheme additionally offers public verifiability of decryption, which is a property not considered in [32].

We provide a formal model and the definitions in the following:

Definition 1. (Multiple Encryption) *Multiple encryption scheme ME is a set of following algorithms (Key-Gen, Enc, Dec, MKey-Gen, MEnc, MDec):*

Key-Gen: *A probabilistic key generation algorithm that, given a security parameter 1^k, outputs a pair of a public key and a secret key (pk, sk).*

Enc: *A probabilistic encryption algorithm that, given the public key pk and a message M, outputs a cipher-text C.*

Dec: *An probabilistic algorithm that, given a ciphertext C and the secret key sk, outputs a message M (or $\perp$) and auxiliary data.*

MKey-Gen: *An algorithm that, given a security parameter 1^k, invokes Key-Gen m times to output a public key $\{pk^{(j)}\}_{j=1,...,m}$ and a secret key $\{sk^{(j)}\}_{j=1,...,m}$. We assume that the message space is $\mathcal{M}$ and the ciphertext space is $\mathcal{C}$.*

MEnc: *An algorithm that, given $M \in \mathcal{M}$ and a public key $\{pk^{(j)}\}_{j=1,...,m}$, repeatedly invokes Enc m times, where in the first invocation Enc takes $pk^{(1)}$ and M as input, in the second invocation Enc takes $pk^{(2)}$ and the output of the previous invocation as input, and so on. The output is a ciphertext $C \in \mathcal{C}$, which is thus multiply encrypted M.*

MDec: *A probabilistic algorithm that, given $C \in \mathcal{C}$ and a secret key $\{sk^{(j)}\}_{j=1,...,m}$, repeatedly invokes Dec m times to output $M \in \mathcal{M}$ and auxiliary data generated by Dec's. In j-th invocation, MDec gives $sk^{(j)}$ to Dec.*

Definition 2. (IND-ME-CCA [32]) *Assume any polynomially bounded adversary $\mathcal{A}$ plays the following game with ME. First, key generation algorithm*

MKey-Gen is run. The public key $PK = \{pk^{(j)}\}_{j=1,...,m}$ is given to $\mathcal{A}$ and an challenging oracle $\mathcal{CO}$. The secret key $SK = \{sk^{(j)}\}_{j=1,...,m}$ is given to a decryption oracle $\mathcal{DO}$ and a key exposure oracle $\mathcal{KE}$. If two messages $M_0, M_1 \in \mathcal{M}$ and $b \in \{0,1\}$ are given to $\mathcal{CO}$, it outputs $C_* = \text{MEnc}(M_b) \in \mathcal{C}$. If index $j \in \{1,...,m\}$ is given to $\mathcal{KE}$, it returns $sk^{(j)}$. $\mathcal{A}$ is allowed to invoke $\mathcal{KE}$ only $(m-1)$ times. When $C \in \mathcal{C}$ such that $C \neq C_*$ is given, $\mathcal{DO}$ executes MDec to obtain decryption of C and auxiliary data. ϵ_{neg} is a negligible function of k. We call this ME IND-ME-CCA secure. if

$$\Pr\left[b = b' \,\middle|\, \begin{array}{l} (PK, SK) \leftarrow \text{MKey-Gen}(1^k), (M_0, M_1, state) \leftarrow \mathcal{A}(PK)^{\mathcal{DO},\mathcal{KE}} \\ b \leftarrow_R \{0,1\}, C_* \leftarrow \mathcal{CO}(M_0, M_1, b), b' \leftarrow \mathcal{A}(PK, state)^{\mathcal{DO},\mathcal{KE}} \end{array}\right]$$

$$< \frac{1}{2} + \epsilon_{neg}.$$

2.1   The Idea of the Proposed Multiple Encryption Scheme

In the proposed encryption scheme, the following three operations are repeated m times using m independent symmetric keys $\{K^{(j)}\}_{j=1,...,m}$ and m public keys $\{X^{(j)}\}_{j=1,...,m}$. (1) Symmetric-key encryption of the input ciphertext $\mu^{(j)}$ using a symmetric key $K^{(j)}$, and ElGamal encryption of this symmetric key $\{K^{(j)}\}$. (2) Hashing the input ciphertext $\mu^{(j)}$, and ElGamal encryption of this hashed value, and (3) generating a proof that the user himself was engaged in this repetition.

The first procedure is the main function of hybrid encryption scheme. The second procedure generates hashed value that will be used to verify decryptions. If we compare this value to the hash of a decrypted text using symmetric-key cryptosystem, we can efficiently verify that that the symmetric-key decryption has been operated correctly. The case of colluding user and one of the decryptor is discussed in Remark 1.

The third procedure comprises the core technique to make the total encryption scheme IND-ME-CCA secure. The main purpose of the procedure is to make sure that the user himself performed the encryption, and not an adversary who has eavesdropped some intermediate data. A simplified description for the third procedure is as follows: Let G be a generator of an elliptic curve E [1]. In $(m-j+1)$-th repetition of the third procedure, user generates $(E^{(j)}, J^{(j)}) = ([r^{(j)}]X^{(j)}, [r^{(j)}]G + J^{(j+1)})$, which is an encryption of $J^{(j+1)} = [r^{(m)} + \cdots + r^{(j+1)}]G$ and provides the knowledge of the random number $r^{(j)}$. After m-th repetition, the output is $([r^{(1)}]X^{(1)}, [r^{(m)} + \cdots + r^{(1)}]G)$. The user also provides the proof on the knowledge of $r^{(m)} + \cdots + r^{(1)}$.

The scheme is so designed to achieve malleability, that is, that even if a malicious adversary copied a j-th partially decrypted ciphertext and submitted a modified version of this copy to the mix-net, he will be detected. This is because the adversary will fail to prove the knowledge of at least one random number used for generating ciphertexts unless he can solve the discrete logarithm problem.

---

[1] Any DDH hard cyclic group suits for our purpose. But, we use the notation of scalar multiplication in elliptic curves since we need many superscripts and subscripts.

Therefore, by adding these operations, we can restrict the accepted ciphertexts to be those which the submitter himself engaged in very repetition himself.

2.2 Proposed Multiple Encryption with Verifiable Decryption

We define $k, q, E, G, \mathcal{O}, \mathcal{H}_E, \mathcal{H}_q$, and $\mathcal{H}_\sigma$ as follows: k is a security parameter, q is a prime such that $|q| = k$ and $q \bmod 3 = 2$, E is a set of points on an elliptic curve of an order q, G is a generator of E, $\mathcal{O}$ is the zero of E, $\mathcal{H}_E, \mathcal{H}_q$, and $\mathcal{H}_\sigma$ are cryptographic hash functions that map, respectively, arbitrary strings to points in E, arbitrary strings to elements of $\mathbb{Z}/q\mathbb{Z}$, and arbitrary points in E to $k/2$ bit strings. Let $(\mathrm{enc}_\kappa, \mathrm{dec}_\kappa)$ be an encryption algorithm and a decryption algorithm of a symmetric-key cryptosystem which is semantically secure under chosen plaintext attack, where κ is a symmetric-key of length $k/2$. The message space $\mathcal{M}$ is $\{0,1\}^\ell$ and the corresponding ciphertext space of MEnc is denoted by $\mathcal{C}$.

We first describe the key generation phase.

MKey-Gen: Given a security parameter 1^k, first chooses an arbitrary set of parameters
$(q, E, G, \ell, \mathcal{H}_E, \mathcal{H}_q, \mathcal{H}_\sigma, (\mathrm{enc}_\kappa, \mathrm{dec}_\kappa), \mathcal{M}, \mathcal{C})$, which we call $\mathcal{D}$, then MKey-Gen invokes Key-Gen m times with $\mathcal{D}$ to obtain public keys $\{X^{(j)}\}_{j=1,\dots,m}$ and secret keys $\{x^{(j)}\}_{j=1,\dots,m}$. Finally, MKey-Gen outputs $\mathcal{D}, \{X^{(j)}\}_{j=1,\dots,m}$, and $\{x^{(j)}\}_{j=1,\dots,m}$.

Key-Gen: Given $\mathcal{D}$ in j-th invocation, outputs a randomly chosen secret key $x^{(j)} \in_R \mathbb{Z}/q\mathbb{Z}$ and an ElGamal public key

$$X^{(j)} = [x^{(j)}]G. \tag{1}$$

We will now show how to multiply encrypt a message $M \in \mathcal{M}$. The first invocation of Enc is performed on the message M using a public key $X^{(m)}$. Then, its output, $\mu^{(m-1)}$, will be the input to the next invocation of Enc. The output $\mu^{(0)}$ of the last invocation together with the additional proof of knowledge will be the final output of our multiple encryption algorithm Enc. Let a message space and a ciphertext space of $(m - j + 1)$-th invocation of Enc be denoted as $\mathcal{M}^{(j)}$ and $\mathcal{C}^{(j)}$, where $\mathcal{C}^{(j)} = \mathcal{M}^{(j-1)}$.

As we will see below in Eq.(2), each element in $\mu^{(j-1)} \in \mathcal{C}^{(j)}$ can be represented as a structure of multiple data $\mu^{(m)} = (M, \mathcal{O})$.

Enc: The ElGamal public key $X^{(j)}$ and a message $\mu^{(j)} \in \mathcal{M}^{(j)}$ are given. Enc randomly chooses $K^{(j)} \in_R E$, a tuple $(r_K^{(j)}, r_H^{(j)}, r_J^{(j)}) \in_R (\mathbb{Z}/q\mathbb{Z})^3$, and a tuple $(s_K^{(j)}, s_H^{(j)}, s_J^{(j)}) \in_R (\mathbb{Z}/q\mathbb{Z})^3$. The message $\mu^{(j)}$ is encrypted in hybrid manner, that is, data $K^{(j)}$ is encrypted with ElGamal public key $X^{(j)}$, while $K^{(j)}$ transformed to a symmetric key $\kappa^{(j)}$ and used to encrypt $\mu^{(j)}$ with symmetric encryption $\mathrm{enc}_{\kappa^{(j)}}$

$$(E_K^{(j)}, D_K^{(j)}) = \left([r_K^{(j)}]X^{(j)}, [r_K^{(j)}]G + K^{(j)}\right), \kappa^{(j)} = \mathcal{H}_\sigma(K^{(j)}), \chi^{(j)} = \mathrm{enc}_{\kappa^{(j)}}(\mu^{(j)}).$$

The input message $\mu^{(j)}$ is hashed and then encrypted with ElGamal public key $X^{(j)}$ to be used in verification of the decryption.

$$H^{(j)} = \mathcal{H}_E(\mu^{(j)}) \;,\; (E_H^{(j)}, D_H^{(j)}) = \left([r_H^{(j)}]X^{(j)}, [r_H^{(j)}]G + H^{(j)}\right).$$

The element $J^{(j+1)}$ in $\mu^{(j)}$ is encrypted to be used to prove that the user himself was engaged in the computation, which operation makes total multiple encryption IND-ME-CCA secure.

$$(E_J^{(j)}, J^{(j)}) = \left([r_J^{(j)}]X^{(j)}, [r_J^{(j)}]G + J^{(j+1)}\right)$$

The rest of the data are introduced to make the procedure Enc IND-CCA2 secure [23] by using the technique presented in [29]. The data $P_K^{(j)}, P_H^{(j)}$, and $P_J^{(j)}$ are twin encryption parts of the above public-key encryptions and the data $(c^{(j)}, t_K^{(j)}, t_H^{(j)}, t_J^{(j)})$ is a non-interactive proof of these twin encryptions.

$$(F_K^{(j)}, F_H^{(j)}, F_J^{(j)}) = ([s_K^{(j)}]X^{(j)}, [s_H^{(j)}]X^{(j)}, [s_J^{(j)}]X^{(j)})$$
$$Y_K^{(j)} = \mathcal{H}_E(\mathcal{D}, \chi^{(j)}, X^{(j)}, E_K^{(j)}, D_K^{(j)}, E_H^{(j)}, D_H^{(j)}, E_J^{(j)}, J^{(j)}, F_K^{(j)}, F_H^{(j)}, F_J^{(j)}, \text{key})$$
$$Y_H^{(j)} = \mathcal{H}_E(\mathcal{D}, \chi^{(j)}, X^{(j)}, E_K^{(j)}, D_K^{(j)}, E_H^{(j)}, D_H^{(j)}, E_J^{(j)}, J^{(j)}, F_K^{(j)}, F_H^{(j)}, F_J^{(j)}, \text{hsh})$$
$$Y_J^{(j)} = \mathcal{H}_E(\mathcal{D}, \chi^{(j)}, X^{(j)}, E_K^{(j)}, D_K^{(j)}, E_H^{(j)}, D_H^{(j)}, E_J^{(j)}, J^{(j)}, F_K^{(j)}, F_H^{(j)}, F_J^{(j)}, \text{jnt})$$
$$(P_K^{(j)}, P_H^{(j)}, P_J^{(j)}) = ([r_K^{(j)}]Y_K^{(j)}, [r_H^{(j)}]Y_H^{(j)}, [r_J^{(j)}]Y_J^{(j)})$$
$$(Q_K^{(j)}, Q_H^{(j)}, Q_J^{(j)}) = ([s_K^{(j)}]Y_K^{(j)}, [s_H^{(j)}]Y_H^{(j)}, [s_J^{(j)}]Y_J^{(j)})$$
$$c^{(j)} = \mathcal{H}_q(\mathcal{D}, \chi^{(j)}, X^{(j)}, E_K^{(j)}, D_K^{(j)}, E_H^{(j)}, D_H^{(j)}, E_J^{(j)}, J^{(j)}, Y_K^{(j)}, Y_H^{(j)}, Y_J^{(j)},$$
$$P_K^{(j)}, P_H^{(j)}, P_J^{(j)}, F_K^{(j)}, Q_K^{(j)}, F_H^{(j)}, Q_H^{(j)}, F_J^{(j)}, Q_J^{(j)})$$
$$(t_K^{(j)}, t_H^{(j)}, t_J^{(j)}) = (s_K^{(j)} - c^{(j)}r_K^{(j)}, s_H^{(j)} - c^{(j)}r_H^{(j)}, s_J^{(j)} - c^{(j)}r_J^{(j)}) \bmod q$$

Here, key, hsh, and jnt are strings. Then Enc outputs a ciphertext

$$\mu^{(j-1)} = \{\chi^{(j)}, c^{(j)}, E_K^{(j)}, D_K^{(j)}, E_H^{(j)}, D_H^{(j)}, E_J^{(j)}, J^{(j)},$$
$$P_K^{(j)}, P_H^{(j)}, P_J^{(j)}, t_K^{(j)}, t_H^{(j)}, t_J^{(j)}) \in \mathcal{C}^{(j)}. \tag{2}$$

MEnc: A message $M \in \mathcal{M}$ and a public key $\{X^{(j)}\}_{j=1,\dots,m}$ are given. $MEnc$ first sets $J^{(m+1)} = \mathcal{O}$ and $\mu^{(m)} = (M, J^{(m+1)})$. Next, $MEnc$ repeatedly invokes Enc m times to generate

$$\mu^{(0)} = Enc(X^{(1)}, Enc(\cdots Enc(X^{(m-1)}, Enc(X^{(m)}, \mu^{(m)}))\cdots))$$

Next, $MEnc$ proves the knowledge of sum of the randomness $\sum_{j=1}^{m} r_J^{(j)}$ used in the all invocations. For that purpose, it randomly chooses $s_J^{(0)} \in_R \mathbb{Z}/q\mathbb{Z}$ and generates

$$R_J^{(0)} = [s_J^{(0)}]G \;,\; G_J = \mathcal{H}_E(\mathcal{D}, \mu^{(0)}, R_J^{(0)}) \;,\; R_J = [s_J^{(0)}]G_J \;,\; J = [\sum_{j=1}^{m} r_J^{(j)}]G_J$$

$$c^{(0)} = \mathcal{H}_q(\mathcal{D}, \mu^{(0)}, G_J, J, R_J^{(0)}, R_J, \mathcal{U}) \;,\; t_J^{(0)} = s_J^{(0)} - c^{(0)} \sum_{j=1}^{m} r_J^{(j)} \bmod q$$

where $\mathcal{U}$ is an identity of user. Finally, *MEnc* outputs a cipher-text

$$C = (\mu^{(0)}, J, c^{(0)}, t_J^{(0)}) \in \mathcal{C} \tag{3}$$

Dec: The secret key $x^{(j)}$ and cipher-text $\mu^{(j-1)} \in \mathcal{C}^{(j)}$ are given. We assume here $\{\mu^{(j)}\}_j$ are parsed as Eq.(2). *Dec* first computes

$$(F_K^{(j)}, F_H^{(j)}, F_J^{(j)}) = ([t_K^{(j)}]X^{(j)} + [c^{(j)}]E_K^{(j)}, [t_H^{(j)}]X^{(j)} + [c^{(j)}]E_H^{(j)}, [t_J^{(j)}]X^{(j)} + [c^{(j)}]E_J^{(j)})$$

$$Y_K^{(j)} = \mathcal{H}_E(\mathcal{D}, \chi^{(j)}, X^{(j)}, E_K^{(j)}, D_K^{(j)}, E_H^{(j)}, D_H^{(j)}, E_J^{(j)}, J^{(j)}, F_K^{(j)}, F_H^{(j)}, F_J^{(j)}, \text{key})$$

$$Y_H^{(j)} = \mathcal{H}_E(\mathcal{D}, \chi^{(j)}, X^{(j)}, E_K^{(j)}, D_K^{(j)}, E_H^{(j)}, D_H^{(j)}, E_J^{(j)}, J^{(j)}, F_K^{(j)}, F_H^{(j)}, F_J^{(j)}, \text{hsh})$$

$$Y_J^{(j)} = \mathcal{H}_E(\mathcal{D}, \chi^{(j)}, X^{(j)}, E_K^{(j)}, D_K^{(j)}, E_H^{(j)}, D_H^{(j)}, E_J^{(j)}, J^{(j)}, F_K^{(j)}, F_H^{(j)}, F_J^{(j)}, \text{jnt})$$

Next, *Dec* verifies if

$$\begin{aligned}
c^{(j)} = \ & \mathcal{H}_q(\mathcal{D}, \chi^{(j)}, X^{(j)}, E_K^{(j)}, D_K^{(j)}, E_H^{(j)}, D_H^{(j)}, E_J^{(j)}, J^{(j)}, \\
& Y_K^{(j)}, Y_H^{(j)}, Y_J^{(j)}, P_K^{(j)}, P_H^{(j)}, P_J^{(j)}, F_K^{(j)}, [t_K^{(j)}]Y_K^{(j)} + [c^{(j)}]P_K^{(j)}, F_H^{(j)}, \\
& [t_H^{(j)}]Y_H^{(j)} + [c^{(j)}]P_H^{(j)}, F_J^{(j)}, [t_J^{(j)}]Y_J^{(j)} + [c^{(j)}]P_J^{(j)})
\end{aligned} \tag{4}$$

hold. If not, *Dec* outputs $\perp_1^{(j)}$ and stops. Next, *Dec* computes

$$K^{(j)\dagger} = D_K^{(j)} - [1/x^{(j)}]E_K^{(j)} \tag{5}$$

$$H^{(j)\dagger} = D_H^{(j)} - [1/x^{(j)}]E_H^{(j)} \tag{6}$$

$$J^{(j+1)\dagger} = J^{(j)} - [1/x^{(j)}]E_J^{(j)} \tag{7}$$

$$\kappa^{(j)} = \mathcal{H}_\sigma(K^{(j)\dagger}) \tag{8}$$

$$\mu^{(j)} = \text{dec}_{\kappa^{(j)}}(\chi^{(j)}) \tag{9}$$

and outputs $H^{(j)\dagger}$ and $J^{(j+1)\dagger}$. Next, if either of the following equations does not hold,

$$H^{(j)\dagger} = \mathcal{H}_q(\mu^{(j)}) , \quad J^{(j+1)\dagger} = J^{(j+1)} \in \mu^{(j)} \tag{10}$$

Dec outputs $K^{(j)\dagger}$ and $\perp_2^{(j)}$ and stops. Finally, *Dec* outputs $\mu^{(j)} \in \mathcal{M}^{(j)}$.
MDec: A ciphertext $C \in \mathcal{C}$ and the secret key $\{x^{(j)}\}_{j=1,\dots,m}$ are given. *MDec* first computes

$$R_J^{(0)} = [t_J^{(0)}]G + [c^{(0)}]J^{(1)} , \quad G_J = \mathcal{H}_E(\mathcal{D}, \mu^{(0)}, R_J^{(0)})$$

and verifiers if

$$c^{(0)} = \mathcal{H}_q(\mathcal{D}, \mu^{(0)}, G_J, J, R_J^{(0)}, [t_J^{(0)}]G_J + [c^{(0)}]J, \mathcal{U}) \tag{11}$$

holds. If not *MDec* outputs $\perp$ and stops. Next, *MDec* recursively invokes *Dec* m-times to generate

$$\mu^{(m)} = (M, \mathcal{O}) = \text{Dec}(\text{Dec}(\cdots \text{Dec}(\text{Dec}(\mu^{(1)}))\cdots)).$$

If any of invocations of *Dec* stops, *MDec* also stops. *MDec* outputs the output of each invoked *Dec*. Finally, *MDec* outputs first elements M of $\mu^{(m)}$ and stops.

Theorem 1. *The proposed multiple encryption scheme is IND-ME-CCA secure and Encryption scheme* (Key-Gen, Enc, Dec) *is IND-CCA2 secure assuming random oracles, intractability of decision Diffie-Hellman problem, and semantic security of the one-time symmetric-key cryptosystem. (The proof is given in [10].)*

The possible output of *Dec* and *MDec* are either results of decryption or one of the set of symbols $\{\perp, \perp_1^{(j)}, \perp_2^{(j)}\}$. Each symbol represents that the input ciphertext was improperly generated. In order to prove the validity of the decryption result or these symbols, we introduce interactive protocols *Ver* and *MVer*. *Ver* is performed between a prover $\mathcal{P}$ and a verifier $\mathcal{V}$ to prove the validity of the output of *Dec*, and *MVer* is performed between a prover $\mathcal{MP}$ and a verifier $\mathcal{MV}$ to prove the validity of the output of *MDec*.

Ver: $\mathcal{P}$ and $\mathcal{V}$ are given $\mu^{(j-1)} \in \mathcal{C}^{(j)}$ and the output *Out* of *Dec*. $\mathcal{P}$ is also given $x^{(j)}$. Suppose *Out* $= \perp_1$. Then, $\mathcal{V}$ evaluates Eq.(4). If this holds, $\mathcal{V}$ rejects $\mathcal{P}$ and stops. Otherwise $\mathcal{V}$ accepts $\mathcal{P}$ and stops.

　　Suppose that *Out* $\neq \perp_1$. $\mathcal{V}$ first checks if Eq.(4) holds or not. If it does not hold, $\mathcal{V}$ rejects $\mathcal{P}$ and stops. Next, $\mathcal{P}$ proves to $\mathcal{V}$ in zero-knowledge the knowledge of $x^{(j)}$ satisfying Eqs, (1), (6), and (7). $\mathcal{V}$ rejects $\mathcal{P}$ and stops if this proof in unacceptable. Next, if the output of *Dec* was $\perp_2$, $\mathcal{P}$ additionally proves to $\mathcal{V}$ in zero-knowledge the knowledge of $x^{(j)}$ satisfying Eqs, (1) and (5). $\mathcal{V}$ rejects $\mathcal{P}$ and stops if this proof in unacceptable. Finally, $\mathcal{V}$ accepts $\mathcal{P}$ and stops if neither of the above proofs are unacceptable.

MVer $\mathcal{MP}$ and $\mathcal{MV}$ are given given a ciphertext $C \in \mathcal{C}$ and the output *Out* of *MDec*. $\mathcal{MP}$ is given secret keys $\{x^{(j)}\}_{j=1,\ldots,m}$. Suppose *Out* $= \perp$. Then, $\mathcal{MV}$ evaluates Eq. (11). If this holds, $\mathcal{MV}$ rejects $\mathcal{MP}$ and stops. Otherwise $\mathcal{MV}$ accepts $\mathcal{MP}$ and stops.

　　Suppose *Out* $\neq \perp$. $\mathcal{MV}$ first checks if Eq. (11) holds or not. If it does not, $\mathcal{MV}$ rejects $\mathcal{MP}$ and stops. Next, $\mathcal{MP}$ plays the role of $\mathcal{P}$ in all *Ver* with respect to all *Dec* invoked by *MDec*. If any of $\mathcal{V}$ rejects $\mathcal{P}$ in *Ver*, $\mathcal{MV}$ rejects $\mathcal{MP}$. Otherwise, $\mathcal{MV}$ accepts $\mathcal{MP}$.

From the construction, one can easily observe that the following theorems hold.

Theorem 2. *Suppose that $C \in \mathcal{C}$ is an encryption of $M \in \mathcal{M}$ generated by honestly following Algorithm MEnc. $\mathcal{MP}$ will be accepted by $\mathcal{MV}$ in MVer when M is input to $\mathcal{MP}$ and $\mathcal{MV}$ as the output of MDec. Here, we assume random oracles.* □

Theorem 3. *No polynomial time adversary is able to output $(C, M', M) \in \mathcal{C} \times (\mathcal{M})^2$ such that $M' \neq M$ and the adversary will be accepted by $\mathcal{MV}$ as $\mathcal{MP}$ in MVer with non negligible probability both when they are given M and when they are given M'. Here, we assume random oracles.* □

Remark 1. As Theorem 3 assures, no ciphertext can be decrypted in two valid messages, no matter how the ciphertext is generated. But our scheme can not

prevent an adversary to generate a ciphertext that can be treated in two ways
by a malicious decryptor: either it is decrypted to a 'correct' message, or claimed
invalid(i.e. malicious decryptor outputs $\perp_2$)

The strategy for the adversary and the corrupted j-th decrypter to generate
such ciphertext is as follows. The adversary executes multiple encryption up to
$m - j + 1$-th iteration and obtain $\chi^{(j)} \in \mu^{(j-1)}$. But then he starts the next
iteration starting with a different data, say $\chi^{(j)*}$, and process correctly then.
Thus generated ciphertext will be processed without any problem until the j-th
iteration of decryption. If j-th decryptor is honest, he will output $\perp_2$ and $K^{(j)}$
and show that the decryption of $\mathcal{H}_E(\text{dec}_{\mathcal{H}_\sigma(K^{(j)})}(\chi^{(j*)}))$ does not coincide with
$H^{(j)\dagger} = \mathcal{H}_E(\text{dec}_{\mathcal{H}_\sigma(K^{(j)})}(\chi^{(j)}))$. A malicious j-th decryptor has a choice, whether
to honestly claim the ciphertext is malicious, or to secretly replace $\chi^{(j)*}$ with $\chi^{(j)}$
obtained from the adversary and continue the procedure assuming nothing has
happened. The semantic advantage of this attack is the adversary can decide
his input to be either valid message or invalid, not at the submission of the
encrypted input but in the midst of decryption, when the colluding decryptor
proceeds.

3   Publicly Verifiable Mix-Net Under Hybrid Construction

Now we will present our publicly verifiable mix-net that can mix long messages.
The idea of the construction is as follows: The input to the mix-net will be a
list of ciphertext, where each ciphertext is generated by a user following the
multiple encryption scheme proposed in Section 2. Within a mix-net, each mixer
performs *Dec* to each ciphertext in the input list. He then permute the list
of the decrypted data which will be the input list to the next mixer. Thus
the mixers comprise *MDec* of the proposed multiple encryption scheme but the
correspondence between the input ciphertext and the output message is hidden
due to the permutation.

In Section 2, we have shown that the decryption can be done verifiably. In
this sectionwe present how to do so without revealing the permutation. The way
we achieved the verifiability of decryption is by adding an encryption of the hash
value of resulting decryption in the input ciphertext. If we compare the set of
encryptions of the hashed values in the input list and the set of values where
hash function is applied to the decrypted messages, the latter should be a set
of decryptions of the former set. Therefore, by performing the zero-knowledge
argument of shuffle-and-decrypt on these sets, we can prove that the output list
is a correct decryption of the input list.

We note that [17] provides 7-move zero-knowledge argument of shuffle-and-
decrypt. We provide in Section 4 an alternative scheme which provide 3-move
zero-knowledge argument but the detail is omitted for space limitations.

Our mix-net satisfies anonymity property defined in [3], whose definition is
presented in the following:

Definition 3. (Anonymity)[3]. *Let $\mathcal{A}$ be an adversary that plays the following game. At any moment of the game, $\mathcal{A}$ is allowed to corrupt up to t_u users and t_m servers. Once corrupted, the user or the server is thoroughly controlled by $\mathcal{A}$.*

1. *$(y, x) \leftarrow G_{mix}(1^k)$. Public-key y and each shared decryption key x_i is given to M_i.*
2. *$\mathcal{A}$ is given y and allowed to invoke M an arbitrary number of times for arbitrary chosen input ciphertexts (i.e., $\mathcal{A}$ can use M as a decryption oracle).*
3. *. $\mathcal{A}$ outputs $L_C = (\mu_1, \ldots, \mu_n)$ that is a list of messages chosen from $\mathcal{M}_y$.*
4. *Choose a permutation, $\pi \leftarrow \Pi_n$. Each U_i is given $\mu_{\pi(i)}$ privately and outputs ciphertext C_i. If U_i is corrupted and outputs nothing, let C_i be an empty string. Let $\mathbf{C} = \{C_1, \ldots, C_n\}$.*
5. *M performs mix processing on $\mathbf{C}$.*
6. *$\mathcal{A}$ is again allowed to invoke M an arbitrary number of times for arbitrarily chosen input ciphertexts except for the ones included in $\mathbf{C}$.*
7. *$\mathcal{A}$ outputs $(i^*, j^*) \in \{1, \ldots, n\}$. The restriction is that $U_{i^*} \notin U_{\mathcal{A}}$ (i.e., U_{i^*} has never been corrupted).*

$\mathcal{A}$ wins the game if $\pi(i^*) = j^*$. Mix-net is anonymous against (t_u, t_m)-limited adaptive and active adversary A if the probability that any polynomial-time (t_u, t_m)-limited adaptive and active adversary $\mathcal{A}$ wins the above game is at most $\frac{1}{n-t_u} + \epsilon$ where ϵ is negligible in k. Probability is taken over the coin flips of G_{mix}, U, M, A and the choice of π.

3.1 Proposed Mix-Net

Players of our mix-net are m mixers $\{\mathcal{S}^{(j)}\}_{j=1,\ldots,m}$, n users $\{\mathcal{U}_i\}_{i=1,\ldots,n}$, and a verifier $\mathcal{V}$. The scheme is composed of the following steps: (1) Setup, (2) Public-Key Generation, (3) Message Encryption, and (4) Shuffle and Prove. We assume that the input to a mixer $S^{(j)}$, which is an output of the previous mixers, has been publicly verified of its correctness. If this assumption is not appropriate, $S^{(j)}$ needs to verify previous Mixers $\{S^{(h)}\}_{h<j}$.

Setup: In Setup, domain parameters of the scheme are determined. They are a security parameter k, an elliptic curve E of prime order q, a randomly chosen generator G of the curve E, the length ℓ of the messages, a semantically secure one-time symmetric-key cryptosystem (enc_κ, dec_κ), and cryptographic hash functions $\mathcal{H}_E, \mathcal{H}_q$, and $\mathcal{H}_\sigma$.

Public-key Generation: Given the domain parameters, each server $\mathcal{S}^{(j)}$ generates its own secret key $x^{(j)}$ and the corresponding public-key $X^{(j)}$ as described in Section 2.

Message Encryption: Each user $\mathcal{U}_i$ encrypts the message M_i of length ℓ following the encryption scheme proposed in Section 2, and sends the ciphertext C_i to $\mathcal{S}^{(1)}$ with a signature of $\mathcal{U}_i$.

Shuffle and Prove: Suppose $\mathcal{S}^{(1)}$ is given $\{C_i\}_{i=1,\ldots,n}$. Mixers $\{\mathcal{S}^{(j)}\}$ collaboratively decrypts all multiply encrypted ciphertexts $\{C_i\}_{i=1,\ldots,n}$ as in the following. We assume every ciphertext in $\{C_i\}$ and $\{\mu_i^{(j)}\}$ are parsed as Eqs. (3) and (2).

1. $\mathcal{S}^{(1)}$ verifies the validity of each signature attached to $\{C_i\}_{i=1,\ldots,n}$. $\mathcal{S}^{(1)}$ also verifies that each $c_i^{(0)} \in C_i$ include correct $\mathcal{U}_i$. From the all elements μ_i in C_i that are accepted in the above verification, $\mathcal{S}^{(1)}$ generates the the set $\{\mu_i\}_{i=1,\ldots,n^{(1)}}$.
2. From $j = 1$ to $j = m$ do the following:
   (a) Each $\mathcal{S}^{(j)}$ receives a set $\{\mu_i^{(j)}\}_{i=1,\ldots,n^{(j)}}$.
   (b) $\mathcal{S}^{(j)}$ deletes μ_i which does not satisfy Eq.(4) from the set.
   (c) $\mathcal{S}^{(j)}$ continue decryption of each ciphertext in the set as Eqs. (5), (6), (7), (8), and (9).
   (d) For each ciphertext μ_i that does not satisfy Eqs. (10), $S^{(j)}$ reveals $H^{(j)\dagger}$, $J^{(j+1)\dagger}$, and $K^{(j)\dagger}$ as Dec does. Then $S^{(j)}$ proves to $\mathcal{V}$ in zero-knowledge the knowledge of $x^{(j)}$ satisfying (1), (5), (6), and (7) as in Ver does.
   (e) From ciphertexts μ_i's that satisfy Eqs. (10), $\mathcal{S}^{(j)}$ generates a set $\{\mu_i\}_{i=1,\ldots,n^{(j+1)}}$. Here indices are reallocated. $\mathcal{S}^{(j)}$ randomly permutes the order of the corresponding $\{\mu_i^{(j+1)}, H_i^{(j)\dagger}, J_i^{(j+1)\dagger}\}_{i=1,\ldots,n^{(j+1)}}$ and reallocates their indices. $\mathcal{S}^{(j)}$ proves to $\mathcal{V}$ in zero-knowledge, using the argument proposed in [17] or in [10], the knowledge of $x^{(j)}$ and an permutation of $\{1,\ldots,n^{(j+1)}\}$ that prove the validity of generating a set $\{H_i^{(j)\dagger}, J_i^{(j+1)\dagger}\}_{i=1,\ldots,n^{(j+1)}}$ from $\{\mu_i\}_{i=1,\ldots,n^{(j+1)}}$.
3. $\{M_i\}_{i=1,\ldots,n}$ output by $\mathcal{S}^{(m)}$ is the output of the mix-net.

Theorem 4. *The proposed mix-net is anonymous assuming random oracles, intractability of decision Diffie-Hellman problem, and semantic security of the one-time symmetric-key cryptosystem. (The proof is given in [10].)*

From the property of our hybrid encryption scheme described in Remark 1, our mix-net does not provide full public verifiability unlike the one proposed in [26, 1, 12, 20, 16, 9]. However, it satisfies a stronger notion of robustness than that proposed in [22] as follows: (1) Our scheme allows any verifier to verify the validity of the output to a certain extent whereas that in [22] only allows mixers to verify it. (2) The scheme in [22] allows colluding mixer and user to find two translations (renderings) for a ciphertext. Thus, such colluders are able to arbitrary switch messages during their mixing procedure without being detected. However, our scheme only allows them to switch messages between a valid message and an invalid message as described in Remark 1.

Definition 4. *We say a ciphertext $C \in \mathcal{C}$ is correct if MDec, given C, outputs a message in $m \in \mathcal{M}$. We call m as the correct decryption of C.*

Definition 5. *Let $MDec^f$ be the same as MDec except that it uses the pair (f, f^{-1}) of a permutation f of strings and its inverse instead of the pair (enc_κ, dec_κ). We say a message $m \in \mathcal{M}$ is the correct translation of a ciphertext $C \in \mathcal{C}$ if there exists some f such that $MDec^f$, given C, outputs m.*

Definition 6. *(Correctness) Let $\mathcal{I}$ be a set of all ciphertexts input to the mix-net and $\mathcal{O}$ be the set of all the output messages of mix-met. We say a $\mathcal{O}$ is correct with respect to $\mathcal{I}$ if the following hold:*

1. *Let $\mathcal{I}' \subset \mathcal{I}$ be the full set of correct ciphertexts. Then, there exists $\mathcal{O}' \subset \mathcal{O}$ that contains a unique correct decryption of every element in $\mathcal{I}'$.*
2. *There exists $\hat{\mathcal{I}} \subset \mathcal{I} \setminus \mathcal{I}'$ such that $\hat{\mathcal{O}} := \mathcal{O} \setminus \mathcal{O}'$ contains the full set of the correct translation of $\hat{\mathcal{I}}$.*

Definition 7. *(Robustness) We say a mix-net is* robust *if the following hold:*

1. *$\mathcal{V}$ accepts the protocol if all the mixers are honest.*
2. *The output $\mathcal{O}$ of the mix-net is correct with respect to its input $\mathcal{I}$ with overwhelming probability if $\mathcal{V}$ accepts the protocol.*
3. *It is computationally difficult to find two correct translations for any ciphertext $C \in \mathcal{C}$.*
4. *For ciphertexts that are not decrypted into a message in $\mathcal{M}$ but into $\perp, \perp_1$, or $\perp_2$, the mixers are able to find their corresponding users in publicly verifiable manner.*

In our mix-net, as noted in Remark 1, a malicious user colluding with a mixer can generate a ciphertext C which the mixer can decide to provide the unique correct translation of C or it claim it invalid. Any ciphertexts that is claimed invalid will be traced back in a publicly verifiable manner to the original user who submitted the ciphertext. It is indeed a weakness in our mix-net, that a collusion have advantage of delaying the decision of the input ciphertext, although the choice is between a valid message and an invalid message. It may be a problem if it is the last mixer who enjoys this advantage since he can decide his choice after seeing the other inputs. To make this advantage insignificant, one can make the output of the mix-net to be a ciphertext that additionally need to be decrypted in a threshold manner. The same strategy is also used in the hybrid mix-net of [22].

Theorem 5. *The protocol is robust assuming random oracles.*

Proof. The theorem follows from Theorems 2 and 3 and the construction of the scheme. Here, random oracles are used only within the IND-ME-CCA encryption scheme.

4   3-Move Zero-Knowledge Argument for Shuffle-and-Decrypt

In this section, we discuss an alternative way to prove here shuffle-and-decryption. Since using the 7-move scheme presented in [17] suffices to build our publicly verifiable hybrid mix-net, we will only provide the ideas to construct 3-move zero knowledge argument. Details appear in the full version of this paper [10].

Our 3-move scheme is based on the perfect zero knowledge argument for shuffle proposed in [9] combined with a decryption proof. [9] is perfect zero-knowledge version of [12]. As discussed in [11], a sequential composition of zero-knowledge arguments on shuffle and that on decryption does not provide zero-knowledge argument on shuffle-and-decrypt since the intermediate state is not simulatable. So the combination is not straight forward.

In [9], a prover is given an input ciphertexts set $(G'_i, M'_i)_{i=1,...,n}$ and its shuffled ciphertexts set $(G'_i, M'_i)_{i=1,...,n}$ such that

$$(G'_i, M'_i) = ([s_i]G_0 + G_{\pi^{-1}(i)}, [s_i]M_0 + M_{\pi^{-1}(i)}) \quad i = 1, \ldots, n$$

holds for witness set of a $\{s_i \in \mathbb{Z}/q\mathbb{Z}\}_{i=1,...,n}$ and a permutation π. Then the prover proves to the verifier the knowledge of the witness by exploiting the property of permutation matrices.

Now we consider constructing a zero-knowledge argument for shuffle-and-decryption by composing the above zero-knowledge argument for shuffle and a zero-knowledge proof for decryption. As previously stated, the intermediate state, that is, $(M'_i)_{i=1,...,n}$, is unsimulatable. The rest of the message that prover generates is simulatable.

We avoid this problem by using

$$\bar{M}_i = [s''_i]M_{-1} + [s_i]M_0 + M_{\pi^{-1}(i)} \quad i = 1, \ldots, n$$

instead of the above $(M'_i)_{i=1,...,n}$, where $\{s''_i \in_R \mathbb{Z}/q\mathbb{Z}\}_{i=1,...,n}$ is randomly chosen elements in $(\mathbb{Z}/p\mathbb{Z})^*$ and M_{-1} is a public parameter. Since $\bar{M}_i$ can be considered as a perfect hiding commitment of M'_i, a simulation of $\bar{M}_i$ will be possible.

We need some new methods to prove the knowledge of committed $\{s_i\}_{i=1,...,n}$ instead of knowledge of simple exponents, which can be obtained using similar tricks that appears in [9]. Applying these methods we are able to construct a perfect zero-knowledge argument for shuffle-and-decryption of Elements ciphertexts.

5   Efficiency of the Proposed Verifiable Mix-Net

Most costly computation in our scheme is scalar multiplications over the elliptic curve. But the amount of these computations does not depend on the length of input ciphertext ℓ. The only computations that depends on the length ℓ are hash function and symmetric-key operations, which is negligibly small compared to scalar multiplications. Therefore, we estimate the computational cost by the number of scalar multiplications required in our scheme. We also estimate the amount of data that each player need to communicate. These results of estimation are given in Table 1, where $|q|$ is 160, m is the number of mixers, and n is the number of users. Here, the cost for mixers does not include the cost for verifying other mixers.

We now give estimates in how fast our scheme can be implemented. Suppose that $n = 100,000$, $m = 3$, and that available computers are Pentium III

Table 1. Complexity

	user	j-th mixer	verifying j-th mixer
# of scalar multiplications	$15m + 3$	$32n$	$32n$
communication bits	$2080m + \ell + 480$	$(2080j + \ell + 960)n$	$(2080j + \ell + 960)n$

(700MHz) machines. Suppose that it takes 100μ sec to compute a single scalar multiplication in E by one computer. Such an implementation and experiment are reported in [4]. Suppose that each mixer has two machines, one machine for verifications of the previous mixers, and the other for shuffling and proving the correctness of its shuffle. We assume mixers generate Fiat-Shamir transformations of proofs so that any mixer is able to verify the proofs independently and in parallel without assuming trusted verifier. Such a operation makes the total time required for the proposed verifiable mix-net linear in the number of the mixers. Using variants of fixed-based comb method and simultaneous modular exponentiations in [19], we can estimate the total time required for mix-net, which tallies $100,000$ long ciphertexts and proves and verifies its correctness by 3 mixers, to be less than 10 minutes.

References

1. M. Abe: Mix-Networks on Permutation Networks. ASIACRYPT '99, pp. 258-273, Springer-Verlag, 1999.
2. Michael Ben-Or, Oded Goldreich, Shafi Goldwasser, Johan Håstad, Joe Kilian, Silvio Micali, and Phillip Rogaway: Everything Provable is Provable in Zero-Knowledge. CRYPTO 1988: 37-56.
3. Masayuki Abe and Hideki Imai: Flaws in Some Robust Optimistic Mix-Nets. ACISP 2003: 39-50.
4. Tetsutaro Kobayashi, Kazumaro Aoki, Fumitaka Hoshino, and Hiroaki Oguro: Software Implementation of Parallel Elliptic Curve Cryptosystem. The 2001 Symposium on Cryptography and Information Security, Oiso, Japan, Vol 1, pp.299-303, 2001.
5. D. Chaum: Untraceable Electronic Mail, Return Addresses, and Digital Pseudonyms. Communications of the ACM, Vol.24, No.2, pp. 84-88, (1981).
6. R.Cramer and V. Shoup: Design and analysis of practical public-key encryption scheme secure against adaptive chosen ciphertext attack. SIAM Journal on Computing, Vol. 33, No. 1, pp. 167-226, 2003.
7. Pierre-Alain Fouque and David Pointcheval: Threshold Cryptosystems Secure against Chosen-Ciphertext Attacks. ASIACRYPT 2001: 351-368.
8. J. Furukawa: Efficient, Verifiable Shuffle Decryption and Its Requirement of Unlinkability. Public Key Cryptography 2004, pp. 319-332.
9. J. Furukawa: Efficient and Verifiable Shuffling and Shuffle-Decryption. IEICE Trans. Fundamentals, Vol.E88-A, No.1, pp.172-188, 2005.
10. Efficient Publicly Verifiable Mix-net for Long Inputs. Full paper. Manuscript.
11. J. Furukawa, K. Mori, S. Obana, and K. Sako: An Implementation of a Universally Verifiable Electronic Voting Scheme based on Shuffling. Financial Cryptography 2002.

12. J. Furukawa and K. Sako: An Efficient scheme for Proving an Shuffle. CRYPTO 2001, pp. 368-387 (2001).
13. Rosario Gennaro and Victor Shoup: A Note on an Encryption Scheme of Kurosawa and Desmedt. Cryptology ePrint Archive, Report 2004/194
14. L. Goldenberg, L. Vaidman, and S. Wiesner: Quantum Gambling, Phys. Rev. Lett., 82, pp.3356-3359, 1999.
15. P. Golle, S. Zhong, D. Boneh, M. Jakobsson, and A. Juels, Optimistic mixing for exit-polls. ASIACRYPT 2002, pp. 451-465 (2002).
16. Jens Groth: A verifiable Secret Shuffle of Holomorphic Encryptions. Public Key Cryptography 2003 pp. 145-160 (2003).
17. Jens Groth: A Verifiable Secret Shuffle of Homomorphic Encryptions. Cryptology ePrint Archive, Report 2005/246
18. Kaoru Kurosawa and Yvo Desmedt: A New Paradigm of Hybrid Encryption Scheme. Crypto 2004, pp. 426-442.
19. A. Menezes, C. van Oorschot, and S. Vanstone, Handbook of Applied Cryptography. CRC Press, pp. 617-627, (1997).
20. C.A. Neff: A Verifiable Secret Shuffle and its Application to E-Voting. ACMCCS 01 pp. 116-125 (2001).
21. M. Jakobsson, A practical mix. Eurocrypt '98, pp. 448-461 (1998).
22. A. Juels and M. Jakobsson, An optimally robust hybrid mix network. Proc. of the 20th annual ACM Symposium on Principles of Distributed Computation, 2001.
23. Moni Naor and Moti Yung: Public-key Cryptosystems Provably Secure against Chosen Ciphertext Attacks. STOC 1990: 427-437.
24. Lan Nguyen, Reihaneh Safavi-Naini, and Kaoru Kurosawa: Verifiable Shuffles: A Formal Model and a Paillier-Based Efficient Construction with Provable Security. ACNS 2004: 61-75
25. M. Ohkubo and M .Abe: A length-invariant hybrid mix. ASIACRYPT 2000, pp. 178-191 (2000).
26. K. Sako and J. Kilian: Receipt-free mix-type voting scheme –A practical solution to the implementation of voting booth. Eurocrypt '95, pp. 393-403 (1995).
27. K. Sako, A Network Voting System Using a Mix-net in a Japanese Private Organization. DIMACS Workshop on Electronic Voting – Theory and Practice 2004.
28. Claus-Peter Schnorr and Markus Jakobsson: Security of Signed ElGamal Encryption. ASIACRYPT 2000: 73-89.
29. Victor Shoup and Rosario Gennaro, Securing Threshold Cryptosystems against Chosen Ciphertext Attack. EUROCRYPT 1998, pp.1-16
30. Y. Tsiounis and M. Yung, On the Security of ElGamal Based Encryption. Public Key Cryptography 1998: 117-134.
31. Douglas Wikström: A Universally Composable Mix-Net. TCC 2004: 317-335.
32. R. Zhang, G. Hanaoka, J. Shikata, and H. Imai, On the Security of Multiple Encryption or CCA-security+CCA-security=CCA-security?. Public Key Cryptography 2004, pp.360-374.

Auditable Privacy:
On Tamper-Evident Mix Networks

Jong Youl Choi[1], Philippe Golle[2], and Markus Jakobsson[3]

[1] Dept. of Computer Science, Indiana University at Bloomington, IN 47405, USA
jychoi@cs.indiana.edu
[2] Palo Alto Research Center, 3333 Coyote Hill Rd, Palo Alto, CA 94304, USA
Philippe.Golle@parc.com
[3] School of Informatics, Indiana University at Bloomington, IN 47406, USA
markus@indiana.edu

Abstract. We introduce the notion of tamper-evidence for mix networks in order to defend against attacks aimed at covertly leaking secret information held by corrupted mix servers. This is achieved by letting observers (which need not be trusted) verify the absence of covert channels by means of techniques we introduce herein. Our tamper-evident mix network is a type of re-encryption mixnet in which a server proves that the permutation and re-encryption factors that it uses are correctly derived from a random seed to which the server is committed.

Keywords. Mix network, covert channel, malware, observer, subliminal channel, tamper-evident.

1 Introduction

In several countries, experiments with electronic voting are taking place. While the primary political goal is to increase voter turnout by allowing for streamlined casting of votes, electronic voting also offers substantial benefits in terms of precision, speed of tallying and privacy guarantees. The flip-side is the difficulty to guarantee these properties, and maintain security when under attack. Electronic voting, not surprisingly, has been at the heart of intense debate.

In electronic voting, just as in manual voting, security properties related to concrete phenomena are easier to guarantee than those related to abstract phenomena. In particular, the desirable property of correctness (the accurate counting of votes) is easier to guarantee than privacy (retaining secrecy of who voted for whom). Tallying – while time consuming and subjective in its current incarnation – is by nature easily auditable. One can duplicate functionality, and count votes in multiple ways in order to ascertain that each vote was counted exactly once. However, no similar auditing process has been proposed to verify that privacy was maintained – neither for manual nor for electronic voting. The reason, informally stated, is that *a leak is a leak is a leak.*

Failure to guarantee privacy is particularly severe in the social context of vote buying, and the technical context of malicious code, and makes any transition

G. Di Crescenzo and A. Rubin (Eds.): FC 2006, LNCS 4107, pp. 126–141, 2006.

to electronic elections fraught with the risk of large-scale abuse. In particular, it was shown [24, 25] how covert channels can be employed to intentionally (and unnoticeably) leak secret information to collaborators. Covert channels allow tallying machines to leak either their secret keys, the state of their pseudo-random generators, or information about the votes they process. There is also real-life evidence [21] that malicious code (written to specification) has been used to spy on voters. While public code audits may address such concerns to some extent, they are hardly a panacea, especially given the difficulty of ascertaining that the audited code is in fact the code that gets loaded and deployed.

We study how to ensure public verifiability of privacy for synchronous mix networks, with direct applications to electronic elections (see, e.g., [2]). We consider an adversary that *fully controls* all servers in a mix network at all time, *except* during an initial setup phase. In the setup phase, the servers are free from adversarial control and can establish and exchange keys. The adversary only gains control over the servers after the completion of the setup phase. This models both typical malware attacks, and attacks in which the software developer writes software that "switches behavior" [28] to a malicious mode after some initial testing has established that the software is correct. We note that corruption during the setup phase can be detected using zero-knowledge proof techniques such as, for example, Juels and Guajardo's scheme [9].

Following [3], we assume the existence of *observers*, whose sole purpose is to monitor the input-output behavior of servers being observed, and determine if any of the generated transcripts could contain information that should not have been included. Observers are not provided with any secret information. Consequently, we do not have to trust observers – apart from having to trust that at least one of them is honest. There is no limit on the number of possible observers, and there is no way for the adversary to determine how many there are. Moreover, given that we employ *undercover* observers, i.e., observers that do not need to interact with any mix server in order to perform their duties (except for when they raise alerts), there is also no clear way to locate them.

While [3] is concerned with the potential leak of private key information from corrupted servers of a certification authority, we focus instead on *any* type of leak from mix servers. (In particular, we consider both leaks of the secret key and leaks that somehow reveal parts of the permutation applied by the mix network.) Although the main principles are closely related on a conceptual level, the technical approaches differ in more ways than they coincide.

The crux of our investigation is how to eliminate all covert channels [24] from communication channels in a mix network. For concreteness, imagine malware that leaks the permutation applied by a corrupted mix server by encoding this permutation in the publicly available random strings associated with mixing (whether in the ciphertexts or the proof of robustness.) Or, conversely, consider malware that applies to a set of inputs a permutation that looks random, but is known to and chosen by the attacker.

To prevent such attacks, we need to both ensure that no covert channels can be established[1], as well as ascertain that no "exterior randomness" is used in place of the intended "interior randomness". Technically, these two requirements translate to exactly the same issue: the ability to audit that all the randomness used by a server was correctly generated by the server's on-board pseudo-random generator. This must be done without exposing the actual state of the pseudo-random generator, since we do not wish to have to place any trust in observers – other than the assumption that at least one of them would truthfully alert the community if any irregularity is detected.

To protect the *observers* from attacks aimed at suppressing their activity, we use the notion of *undercover* observers (as introduced in [3]). Undercover observers are network participants that verify non-interactive proofs (or witnesses) of consistent generation and use of randomness, and which do not need to advertise their existence until they detect cheating and raise an alert.

The construction of witnesses of correct randomness is made difficult by the fact that these must not reveal what randomness is used, but must still eliminate covert channels with all but an exponentially small probability, and must not introduce covert channels themselves. In particular, this makes most of the recently developed techniques for efficient mixing unsuitable, since there is no apparent way to prove a disjunction in a way that (a) uses only pre-committed random strings, and (b) does not reveal what component of the proof the prover knows a witness to. (However, we will show that our proposed technique in fact can be used to implement such a proof, by ways of first implementing a mix network that has the property.)

Also, it is interesting to note that the traditional use of cut-and-choose techniques is not suitable either. It is clear that commitments *that are not opened* can trivially be made to leak a logarithmic amount of information (in the length of the commitment). In a situation with binary challenges, this allows an attacker to select one commitment in a $(2 \times k)$ matrix of commitments, and use the selected commitment to leak the information in question. Since this commitment will only be audited with a 50% probability, this corresponds to a success rate of an attacker of 50%. While it is easy to reduce this success rate, we note that a success rate that is polynomial in the length of the transcripts is not desirable. However, defying the intuition associated with this example, we show how to use vectors of homomorphic commitments to generate witnesses that defend against attacks with all but an exponential probability. This is applied both to re-encryption exponents and to permutations (as either could potentially be used to implement a covert channel.) More precisely, we introduce a method by which commitments are tied together in a pairwise manner, and where it is impossible to modify *either* of the two committed values without this being detected when *only one of them* is opened up.

While we base our design on a mix network construction that is not highly efficient [18], we note that the overhead caused by the addition of our security

---

[1] For practical reasons, we do not consider timing channels; we will discuss this later on.

measures is *minimal*. In spite of the difficulties to design protocols that implement tamper-evidence, we see no reason why more efficient designs could not be feasible. Thus, tamper-evidence is not a theoretical curiosity, but a practically achievable goal. It is our hope that tamper-evidence will become a mainstream design feature of any protocol that is potentially vulnerable to coercive attacks, particularly in the context of electronic elections.

Organization of the paper. We begin by outlining related work (section 2), followed by a description of our model and requirements (section 3), and a brief overview of re-encryption mix networks (section 4). In section 5, we present collapsed Merkle hash trees that will serve as a building block for our protocol. Finally, we present our tamper-evident mix network protocol in section 6, together with relevant proofs.

2   Related Work

The concept of covert channels in cryptographic protocols was introduced in 1983 in the seminal work of Simmons [24, 25]. Simmons specifically demonstrated the use of the Digital Signature Standard (DSS) signature scheme for covert communication. This showed that a secrete message could be hidden inside the authenticator. Young and Yung [29, 30] later showed the existence of covert channels in the key establishment algorithms of signature schemes.

Desmedt [4] presented a practical authentication scheme free of covert-channels, in which an observer (named "active warden") intercepts all the messages exchanged between two parties and verifies that they are free from covert information before passing them on. The observer defined by Desmedt is "active" in the sense that it interacts with the communicating parties. In contrast, [3] defines signature schemes which can be verified free of covert channels by *undercover* observers. Undercover observers verify signatures non-interactively, so that their stealthy existence can remain a secret at least up until the point when they detect an incorrect signature and raise an alarm. Undercover observers are preferable to active observers, because they are far less vulnerable to attacks aimed at suppressing their activity. This paper adopts the model of undercover observers of [3], but considers the far more complicated problem of ensuring the covert-free (or "tamper-evident") operation of a mix network.

To motivate our tamper-evident mixnet construction, we review briefly other mix networks in the literature and highlight the difficulties in making them tamper-evident. As a first example, consider the mix network recently proposed by Jakobsson, Juels and Rivest [10], and later used in the election scheme put forward by Chaum [2]. Therein, each mix server re-encrypts and permutes a list of n input ciphertexts *two times*, and commits to the ciphertext values in-between the two rounds. Then, a set of verifiers selects some n challenges[2] ; if the ith challenge is a zero (resp. one) then the computation resulting in (resp.

---

[2] As usual, this step can be replaced by a random oracle if the Fiat Shamir heuristic is employed for challenge selection.

starting from) the ith ciphertext value in-between the two rounds is revealed. Whereas this method does not result in the maximum anonymity set (namely n), it still provides reasonable anonymity for many applications, and at a very low cost. There is no straightforward way to design a tamper-evident variant of this scheme, since pairs of commitments (to the left and to the right) do not have the property that the modification of one of the values invalidates *both* commitments. This results in a success probability of 50% for an adversary. This can trivially be limited to $1/k$ if one were to employ k successive rounds of re-encryption and permutation. The cost of this, though, would be linear in k.

Turning now to a second (and rather common) class of mix network constructions, let us take a brief look at a scheme suggested by Abe [1]. Therein, the inputs are broken up in pairs, each one of which is mixed; the resulting list of ciphertexts are then (deterministically) shifted around and paired up, and the resulting pairs are mixed. This is repeated a logarithmic number of times in the number of input ciphertexts. In each mix-of-two, it is proven that either the identity permutation is used, or the "cross-over" permutation – along with corresponding proofs of correct re-encryption. This type of construction therefore employs disjunctive proofs. While we can construct tamper-evident disjunctive proofs using our proposed mix network scheme, we have not been able to find any simple (and inexpensive) construction for disjunctive proofs. Naturally, the same holds for disjunctive proofs involving larger number of inputs. Thus, this class of mix network schemes are not easily adopted to implement tamper-evidence.

Given that electronic elections is one of our motivating applications, it is meaningful to consider the impact of our approach in such settings. An interesting example of a situation in which our construction has an immediate impact is the coercive attack proposed by Michels and Horster [16] in which an attacker succeeds in verifying the value of a cast vote by corrupting both a voter and some random subset of mix servers. If an approach like ours is deployed (and the model changed correspondingly) then such an attack will be detected, and thus, will fail.

Some approaches, such as [17, 22], allow servers to verify each other's actions to avoid leaks of secret information (such as random permutations.) Our approach, in contrast, prevents the *replacement* of the state of the pseudo-random generator. Moreover, and in comparison to these efforts, our scheme reduces the threats associated with potential covert channels caused by use of interaction.

The strongest relation to previous work is found in the collusion-free protocols defined by Lepinksi, Micali, and Shelat [14], which allow for the detection of collusion by malicious participants during the execution of the protocol. Our proposed scheme can be considered as the first practical implementation of collusion-free protocol for mix-networks. While [14] presents a well-defined abstract structure for collusion-free protocols, its application to mix networks is not obvious, in particular given the need to retain privacy. From that point of view, our contribution is to present a practical implementation eliminating collusions, i.e., possibilities to build covert-channels while maintaining privacy guarantees.

3   Model

Participants. We consider the following entities: *users*, *servers*, and *observers*. In addition, we assume the existence of an *authority* and an *attacker*.

- The users generate ciphertexts and post these to a public bulletin board $\mathcal{BB}$.
- Sequentially, the servers read the contents of $\mathcal{BB}$ and process portions of its contents in batches, writing the results of the operation back to $\mathcal{BB}$. These results consist of a set of ciphertexts (that constitute the inputs to the next server in the sequence) and a witness of tamper-freeness. The witness of tamper-freeness constitutes evidence that the (pseudo) random source of the server was not tampered with, and that the operation of the server correctly proceeded according to that random source. As we shall see, the witness of tamper-freeness implies the correctness of the mixing operation, and thus our servers do not need to provide an additional proof of correct mixing.
- The *attacker* is allowed to corrupt all but two of the users all of the time; this is corruption in the standard cryptographic sense, involving full read and write access to the compromised machines. The servers are also able to corrupt *all* of the servers all the time except during the key generation phase; this corruption allows full write access to compromised machines, but requires any information to be read from the machine to be transmitted using the standard communication media (as opposed to a secret side-channel). Thus, it is assumed that an attacker can send messages to corrupted servers out of band, but that all communication in the opposite direction (from a corrupted server to the attacker) must utilize the $\mathcal{BB}$, to which all servers have constant read and (appendive) write access. The latter is not a standard cryptographic assumption, but corresponds to realistic attacks in which software is corrupted by a "remote" attacker able to inject or replace code, e.g., by means of malware. Finally, the attacker is assumed able to corrupt (in the standard sense) all but one observer all of the time.
- The *observers* access $\mathcal{BB}$ and verify the correctness of witnesses posted thereon; if any witness is invalid (or missing) then any uncorrupted observer will initiate an alert.
- When an alert occurs, the *authority* will verify the validity of the alert (that it was done in accordance with the protocol specifications) and then physically disconnect any server whose witness was found to be invalid or missing[3].

Note that our techniques do not protect against timing covert-channels. However, by imposing strict requirements on synchronization or introducing random delays, one can protect against timing attacks as well, at the cost of a somewhat reduced (but predictable) throughput.

---

[3] We are mainly concerned with *detection*. After such detection, one can act on that information using standard methods, such as emulation or replacement of the faulty servers.

Goals

- **Correctness/robustness.** The goal of the honest servers is to generate an output that consists of a set of ciphertexts, with a one-to-one correspondence to the batch of input ciphertexts given as input to the sequence of servers. Two ciphertexts must both decrypt to the same plaintext in order for us to say that they correspond to each other.
- **Privacy.** The goal of the attacker is to determine the mapping between input and output ciphertexts (for input ciphertexts not generated by users he has corrupted) with a probability of success that is significantly better than what could be achieved by a guess made uniformly at random from the possible mappings; or to extract information from a server that allows it to be impersonated with a probability of success that is significantly better that the probability of success that can be achieved without corruption of any servers[4].
- **Tamper-evidence.** The goal of the observers is to detect the use of any randomness inconsistent with the initial state of the corresponding server. This effectively corresponds to preventing covert communication and avoiding that the output of a corrupted server is a non-trivial function of information communicated to it by the attacker.

Trust. For the correctness property to hold, it is normally required that a majority of mix servers are honest. In our setting, though, it suffices that one observer and the authority are uncorrupted[5].

Similarly, for the privacy property to hold in our proposed scheme, no trust assumptions need to be made of either users or servers, but we have to assume that at least one observer and the authority are uncorrupted. If we recall that the main role of the observer is to detect inconsistent use of the randomness used for privacy, we can provide *correctness against privacy abuse* to build covert channel.

We do not need to trust any server with keeping any secret information of any other server. We assume that the authority will promptly disconnect any server failing to generate and output a valid witness for each transcript it writes to the bulletin board.

---

[4] We note that the second goal does not necessarily subsume the first. Consider, for example, a re-encryption mix network in which each server authenticates its output using its secret key. Knowledge of this key will not allow the attacker to determine the permutation, but knowledge of the state of pseudo-random generator does. In contrast, if we consider a decryption mix server based on padded RSA ciphertexts, it is clear that knowledge of the secret key will allow an adversary to infer the permutation.

[5] Alternatively, the correctness property can be seen to hold in a slightly different model in which there is no authority. Then, the requirement is instead that at least one observer is uncorrupted, and that all consumers of information pay attention to alerts.

Remark 1: Note that we make two simultaneous and different trust assumptions on servers. As far as tamper-evidence is concerned, we assume that the servers are honest (i.e., not corrupted) during the key generation phase. However, in terms of the protocol robustness, we do not make this assumption. This means that our protocol remains robust even if servers are corrupted during the key generation phase, whereas the same does not hold for tamper-evidence.

Remark 2: We note that in the following, we only address how to make re-encryption mixing tamper-evident. In most applications involving re-encryption mix networks, there is a phase involving decryption of output ciphertexts. We may assume that this functionality (which can be made tamper-evident following the techniques presented in [3]) can be blocked by the authority in the case of an alert. Practically speaking, this will be possible if a sufficient number of decryption servers can be disconnected immediately upon detection of an irregularity in the mix phase. In the following, we focus solely on the re-encryption mix process, and do not address the decryption process any further.

4   Preliminaries

We give a brief overview of re-encryption mix networks [18] based on the ElGamal cryptosystem (a more detailed description can be found, e.g., in [6]):

- **Key generation:** let p and q be primes such that $q \mid (p - 1)$ and let $g \in \mathbb{Z}_p^*$ be an element of order q, such that the ElGamal cryptosystem defined by g in $\mathbb{Z}_p^*$ is semantically secure against plaintext attacks [32] and also adaptive chosen plaintext attacks. Consider a (t, l)-threshold encryption scheme [7] where the secret key is shared among l mix-servers. For $i = 1, \cdots, l$, mix-server $\mathcal{S}_i$ has secret key $x_i \in \mathbb{Z}_q^*$ and publicizes the corresponding public key $y_i = g^{x_i} \mod p$. Let $y = \prod_{i=1}^{l} y_i \mod p$.

- **Batch generation:** Let m_j denote the plaintext input of user U_j for $j = 1, \cdots, n$. The ElGamal encryption of m_j is

$$\mathsf{Enc}(m_j, r_j) \triangleq (g^{r_j}, y^{r_j} m_j),$$

  where $r_j \in \mathbb{Z}_q^*$ is chosen uniformly at random. Let the ciphertext be $(a_j, b_j) = \mathsf{Enc}(m_j, r_j)$. Each user U_j submits the ciphertext (a_j, b_j) as well as a proof of knowledge for the corresponding plaintext m_j (See [8]).

- **Mixing phase:** Each mix-server $\mathcal{S}_i$ performs two operations: re-encryption and permutation. More precisely, server $\mathcal{S}_i$ takes as input a list of n ciphertexts $((a_1, b_1), \cdots, (a_n, b_n))$ from $\mathcal{BB}$. For $j = 1, \ldots, n$, server $\mathcal{S}_i$ re-encrypts input (a_j, b_j) as follows:

$$(a'_j, b'_j) = \mathsf{ReEnc}\left((a_j, b_j), \alpha_j\right) \triangleq \left(g^{\alpha_j} \cdot a_j, \; y^{\alpha_j} \cdot b_j\right),$$

where α_j is a re-encryption parameter chosen at random in $\mathbb{Z}_q^*$. Server $\mathcal{S}_i$ then chooses a random permutation π on $\{1, 2, \cdots, l\}$ and outputs to $\mathcal{BB}$ the permuted list $\left(\left(a'_{\pi(1)}, b'_{\pi(1)}\right), \cdots, \left(a'_{\pi(n)}, b'_{\pi(n)}\right)\right)$.

– **Decryption phase:** A quorum of mix servers can do a threshold decryption of the final set of outputs, which yields the set of inputs $(m_1, \cdots, m_n)$ permuted according to the successive permutations applied by the l mix servers.

5   Building Block – Merkle Hash Tree Verification

A Merkle tree [15] is a tree consisting of nodes whose values are a one-way hash function (for example, SHA-1 or MD5) of the values of their children nodes. Due to their simplicity, Merkle trees are used for a wide range of secure authentication schemes. A Merkle tree is generally a binary tree where the value at a node N in the tree is defined with respect to the values N_{left} and N_{right} of its children by

$$N \triangleq h(N_{left} \,\|\, N_{right})$$

where h denotes a one-way hash function and "$\|$" denotes concatenation.

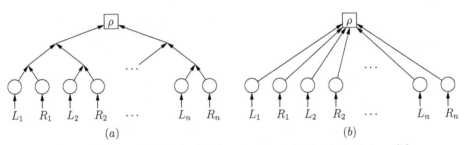

Fig. 1. A binary Merkle hash (a) and collapsed Merkle hash tree (b)

For better efficiency, our protocol does not use binary Merkle trees, but instead collapsed Merkle hash trees in which $2n$ leaves are connected to the root of the tree directly as shown in Fig. 1(b). In our protocol, the $2n$ leaves of the collapsed Merkle hash tree will be the elements of two sets $(L_1, \cdots, L_n)$ and $(R_1, \cdots, R_n)$ each of size n. We define a function MerTree that takes these sets as inputs and outputs the root ρ of the corresponding collapsed Merkle hash tree:

$$\mathsf{MerTree}((L_1, \cdots, L_n), (R_1, \cdots, R_n)) \triangleq h\Big(h(L_1) \,\|\, h(R_1) \,\|\, \cdots \,\|\, h(L_n) \,\|\, h(R_n)\Big)$$

The root ρ of the tree functions as a commitment to the sets $(L_1, \cdots, L_n)$ and $(R_1, \cdots, R_n)$. Note that this commitment can be verified given:

– either $(L_1, \cdots, L_n)$ and $(h(R_1), \cdots, h(R_n))$
– or $(h(L_1), \cdots, h(L_n))$ and $(R_1, \cdots, R_n)$.

6   Tamper-Evident Mix Network

We propose a tamper-evident mix network in which each mix server pre-generates a random permutation together with a sequence of random re-encryption parameters that will be used to re-encrypt and mix the input batch. As explained in section 3, we assume that the generation of these parameters occurs in a setup phase prior to mixing, during which the mix servers are uncorrupted. During the mixing phase, the mix server outputs a proof that it operates in accordance with pre-generated parameters. Any deviation from these parameters invalidates the corresponding proof with all but negligible probability. This mix-network protocol thus ensures that the operation of mix-servers is tamper-evident.

Key generation. As explained in section 4, the l mix servers jointly generate the secret and public parameters for a (t, l)-threshold ElGamal encryption scheme. The public parameters are two primes p and q such that $q|(p-1)$ and an element $g \in \mathbb{Z}_p^*$ of order q. For $i = 1, \ldots, l$, we let $x_i \in \mathbb{Z}_q^*$ denote the secret key of mix-server $\mathcal{S}_i$ and $y_i = g^{x_i} \mod p$ the corresponding public key. We let $y = \prod_{i=1}^l y_i \mod p$.

Let κ be a security parameter, such that $2^{-\kappa}$ constitutes an acceptable error probability (for example $\kappa = 80$). To prove tamper-evident mixing, each server $\mathcal{S}_i$ generates additional values as follows. For notational clarity, we omit the suffix i, but it should be clear that each server generates its own set of the following values:

- a random permutation π on n elements
- n random values $\alpha_j \in \mathbb{Z}_q^*$ ($j = 1, \cdots, n$) which are used as re-encryption parameters in the mixing phase
- κ pairs of permutations on n elements $\left(\sigma^{(1)}, \tau^{(1)}\right), \ldots, \left(\sigma^{(\kappa)}, \tau^{(\kappa)}\right)$ such that $\pi = \tau^{(k)} \circ \sigma^{(k)}$ for all $k = 1, \cdots, \kappa$. (As notational simplicity, we will continue to represent the index k in the superscripted braces.)
- κn pairs of integers $\left(\beta_j^{(k)}, \delta_j^{(k)}\right) \in \mathbb{Z}_q^* \times \mathbb{Z}_q^*$ such that $\alpha_j = \beta_j^{(k)} + \delta_j^{(k)}$ for all $j = 1, \ldots, n$ and $k = 1, \cdots, \kappa$.

The mix then computes commitments to the values $\sigma^{(k)}, \tau^{(k)}, \beta_j^{(k)}, \delta_j^{(k)}$ using collapsed Merkle hash trees. More precisely, the mix server constructs κ collapsed Merkle hash trees $T^{(1)}, \ldots, T^{(\kappa)}$. For $k = 1, \cdots, \kappa$, the leaves of $T^{(k)}$ consist of the following $2n + 2$ values in this order:

$$\sigma^{(k)}, \tau^{(k)}, \left(\beta_1^{(k)}, \ldots, \beta_n^{(k)}\right), \left(\delta_{\pi(1)}^{(k)}, \delta_{\pi(n)}^{(k)}\right).$$

We let $\rho^{(k)}$ denote the root of $T^{(k)}$. Each mix-server publicizes the root values $\rho^{(1)}, \ldots, \rho^{(\kappa)}$ of its Merkle trees.

Batch generation. Each user U_j ($j = 1, \cdots, n$) encrypts its plaintext message m_j by using group ElGamal encryption as described in Section 3 and posts the corresponding ciphertext to $\mathcal{BB}$.

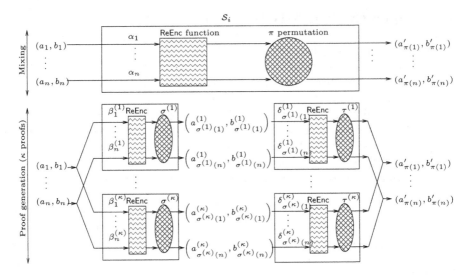

Fig. 2. Overview - A mix-server $\mathcal{S}_i$ re-encrypts the input (a_j, b_j) by $\mathsf{ReEnc}((a_j, b_j), \alpha_j)$ for $j = 1, \cdots, n$ and outputs $(a'_{\pi(j)}, b'_{\pi(j)})$ which is permuted according to the permutation π. In the meanwhile, the mix-server computes as proof κ sets of values; for $k = 1, \ldots, \kappa$, the prover $\mathcal{P}$ computes (for $j = 1, \ldots, n$) the values $\left(a_j^{(k)}, b_j^{(k)} \right) = \mathsf{ReEnc}\left((a_j, b_j), \beta_j^{(k)} \right)$ and outputs $\mathcal{W}^{(k)} = \left(a^{(k)}_{\sigma^{(k)}(1)}, b^{(k)}_{\sigma^{(k)}(1)} \right), \ldots, \left(a^{(k)}_{\sigma^{(k)}(n)}, b^{(k)}_{\sigma^{(k)}(n)} \right)$.

Mixing phase. For $i = 1, \cdots, l$, mix-server $\mathcal{S}_i$ reads from $\mathcal{BB}$ the list of n ciphertexts output by $\mathcal{S}_{i-1}$ (the first server $\mathcal{S}_1$ gets from $\mathcal{BB}$ the list of n inputs ciphertexts submitted by the n users). We denote this list of ciphertexts by $((a_1, b_1), \ldots, (a_n, b_n))$. For $j = 1, \ldots, n$, server $\mathcal{S}_i$ re-encrypts the input (a_j, b_j) as follows:

$$\left(a'_j, b'_j \right) = \mathsf{ReEnc}\left((a_j, b_j), \alpha_j \right),$$

where the α_j are the values generated by $\mathcal{S}_i$ in the key generation phase (again, we omit the index i for notational clarity). The mix server $\mathcal{S}_i$ then outputs these values permuted according to the permutation π, i.e.

$$\left(a'_{\pi(1)}, b'_{\pi(1)} \right), \cdots, \left(a'_{\pi(n)}, b'_{\pi(n)} \right).$$

Proof of tamper-evidence. The mixnet outputs a witness of tamper-freeness. This witness is computed non-interactively. However, the construction of the witness is easier to understand if we describe it in terms of an interaction between a prover $\mathcal{P}$ (the mix-server) and a verifier $\mathcal{V}$ (the observers). It will be immediately clear that this interactive protocol can be turned into a non-interactive witness using the Fiat-Shamir heuristic.

1. **(Commitments)** For $k = 1, \ldots, \kappa$, the prover $\mathcal{P}$ computes (for $j = 1, \ldots, n$) the values

$$\left(a_j^{(k)}, b_j^{(k)} \right) = \mathsf{ReEnc} \left((a_j, b_j), \ \beta_j^{(k)} \right) \tag{1}$$

and outputs

$$\mathcal{W}^{(k)} = \left(a_{\sigma^{(k)}(1)}^{(k)}, b_{\sigma^{(k)}(1)}^{(k)} \right), \ldots, \left(a_{\sigma^{(k)}(n)}^{(k)}, b_{\sigma^{(k)}(n)}^{(k)} \right) \tag{2}$$

2. **(Challenges)** The verifier $\mathcal{V}$ outputs κ random challenges $c^{(1)}, \ldots, c^{(\kappa)} \in \{0, 1\}$.

3. **(Response to challenges)** For $k = 1, \cdots, \kappa$:
   - If $c^{(k)} = 0$: $\mathcal{P}$ outputs $\sigma^{(k)}$, $h\left(\tau^{(k)}\right)$, $\beta_1^{(k)}, \ldots, \beta_n^{(k)}$ and
   $h\left(\delta_{\pi^{(k)}(1)}^{(k)}\right), \ldots, h\left(\delta_{\pi^{(k)}(n)}^{(k)}\right)$
   - If $c^{(k)} = 1$: $\mathcal{P}$ outputs $h\left(\sigma^{(k)}\right)$, $\tau^{(k)}$, $h\left(\beta_1^{(k)}\right), \ldots, h\left(\beta_n^{(k)}\right)$ and
   $\delta_{\pi^{(k)}(1)}^{(k)}, \cdots, \delta_{\pi^{(k)}(n)}^{(k)}$

4. **(Verification)** For $k = 1, \cdots, \kappa$, the verifier checks the following depending on the value of $c^{(k)}$:

   - If $c^{(k)} = 0$: $\mathcal{V}$ re-encrypts input (a_j, b_j) with re-encryption factors $\beta_j^{(k)}$, then permutes them according to permutation $\sigma^{(k)}$ and checks that the result matches the set $\mathcal{W}^{(k)}$ received from $\mathcal{P}$ in Step 1.

   - If $c^{(k)} = 1$: $\mathcal{V}$ re-encrypts output $\left(a'_{\pi(j)}, b'_{\pi(j)} \right)$ with re-encryption factors $-\delta_{\pi^{(k)}(j)}^{(k)}$, then permutes them according to the inverse of permutation $\tau^{(k)}$ and checks that the result matches the set $\mathcal{W}^{(k)}$ received from $\mathcal{P}$ in Step 1.

   Finally, $\mathcal{V}$ reconstructs the collapsed Merkle hash tree $T^{(k)}$ and verifies that the root of that tree is equal to the root $\rho^{(k)}$ output by server $\mathcal{S}_i$ in the key generation step. It should be clear that the values output at the end of step 3 enable $\mathcal{V}$ to reconstruct the Merkle hash tree $T^{(k)}$ regardless of whether $c^{(k)} = 0$ or $c^{(k)} = 1$.
   If any of the verification steps fails, the verifier $\mathcal{V}$ raises an alarm and the prover (i.e. mix-server $\mathcal{S}_i$) is discarded.

Non-interactive proof of tamper-evidence. The interactive protocol given above to verify the tamper-freeness of a mix server's operation can be transformed into a non-interactive protocol with the Fiat-Shamir heuristic (also known as the random oracle model): the κ challenges in Step 1 of the proof can be replaced by the κ left-most bits of the hash of $\left((a'_{\pi(1)}, b'_{\pi(1)}), \cdots, (a'_{\pi(n)}, b'_{\pi(n)}) \right)$. A non-interactive protocol allows proofs of tamper-freeness to be verified by *undercover* observers. Undercover observers need not reveal their existence until they detect an incorrect proof and raise an alarm.

Decryption phase The final outputs of the mix server is decrypted by a quorum of mix servers. Quorum ElGamal decryption can be made tamper-evident following the techniques of [3].

6.1   Properties

Proposition 1. *If the hash function h is second pre-image resistant, then a dishonest prover $\mathcal{P}$ can cheat the verifier $\mathcal{V}$ with probability at most $2^{-\kappa}$ in the proof of tamper-evidence.*

Proof. The proof is by contraposition. Let us assume the existence of a prover $\mathcal{P}$ who can cheat the verifier $\mathcal{V}$ in the proof of tamper-evidence with probability $2^{-\kappa} + \epsilon$. We show how to use $\mathcal{P}$ to find a second pre-image for the function h. We proceed as follows:

1. $\mathcal{V}$ executes one instance of the key generation step described in Section 6. In particular, $\mathcal{V}$ outputs the roots $\rho^{(1)}, \ldots, \rho^{(\kappa)}$ of κ collapsed Merkle hash trees $T^{(1)}, \ldots, T^{(\kappa)}$. $\mathcal{V}$ also outputs a batch of n input ciphertexts $((a_1, b_1), \ldots, (a_n, b_n))$.
2. $\mathcal{P}$ outputs a new batch of n ciphertexts $((a_1'', b_1''), \ldots, (a_n'', b_n''))$, such that there exists at least one index $j \in \{1, \ldots, n\}$ such that

$$(a_j'', b_j'') \neq \mathsf{ReEnc}\left(\left(a_{\pi(j)}, b_{\pi(j)}\right), \alpha_{\pi(j)}\right).$$

   This condition expresses the assumption that $\mathcal{P}$ is a dishonest prover.
3. $\mathcal{P}$ outputs commitments $\mathcal{W}^{(k)}$ for $k = 1, \ldots, \kappa$. We distinguish two cases:
   - If $\mathcal{W}^{(k)}$ is *not equal* to the re-encryption of the inputs (a_j, b_j) with re-encryption factors $\beta_j^{(k)}$ permuted according to permutation $\sigma^{(k)}$, then we say that the commitment $\mathcal{W}^{(k)}$ is "input-incorrect" and we define $\bar{c}^{(k)} = 1$.
   - Otherwise, the commitment $\mathcal{W}^{(k)}$ is *equal* to the re-encryption of the inputs (a_j, b_j) with re-encryption factors $\beta_j^{(k)}$ permuted according to permutation $\sigma^{(k)}$. But since $(a_j'', b_j'') \neq \mathsf{ReEnc}\left(\left(a_{\pi(j)}, b_{\pi(j)}\right), \alpha_{\pi(j)}\right)$, it must then be the case that $\mathcal{W}^{(k)}$ is *not equal* to the re-encryption of the outputs $(a_{\pi(j)}', b_{\pi(j)}')$ with re-encryption factors $-\delta_{\pi^{(k)}(j)}^{(k)}$ permuted according to the inverse of permutation $\tau^{(k)}$. We say then that the commitment $\mathcal{W}^{(k)}$ is "output-incorrect" and we define $\bar{c}^{(k)} = 0$.
4. The verifier $\mathcal{V}$ outputs κ random challenges $c^{(1)}, \ldots, c^{(\kappa)} \in \{0, 1\}$.
5. The prover responds to these challenges and the responses are verified by $\mathcal{V}$ as described in the protocol of section 6.

With probability $2^{-\kappa}$, we have $\bar{c}^{(k)} = c^{(k)}$ for all $k = 1, \ldots, \kappa$. The prover, however, succeeds in convincing the verifier with probability $2^{-\kappa} + \epsilon$. It follows that with probability ϵ, the prover succeeds in convincing the verifier when there exists an index k such that $\bar{c}^{(k)} \neq c^{(k)}$. In this case, we show how to compute a second pre-image for the function h.

Without loss of generality, let us assume that for some $k \in \{1, \ldots, \kappa\}$, we have $\bar{c}^{(k)} = 1$ and $c^{(k)} = 0$. In other words, the commitment $\mathcal{W}^{(k)}$ is "input-incorrect", and $\mathcal{V}$ verifies the relationship between the inputs and the commitment. The root $\rho^{(k)}$ of the Merkle tree $T^{(k)}$ commits $\mathcal{P}$ to the values $\sigma^{(k)}, \tau^{(k)}, \beta_1^{(k)}, \ldots, \beta_n^{(k)}$ and $\delta_1^{(k)}, \ldots, \delta_n^{(k)}$. Let us denote $\sigma'^{(k)}, \tau'^{(k)}, \beta_1'^{(k)}, \ldots, \beta_n'^{(k)}$ and $\delta_1'^{(k)}, \ldots, \delta_n'^{(k)}$ the values used by $\mathcal{P}$ to compute $\mathcal{W}^{(k)}$. Let us denote $T'^{(k)}$ the collapsed Merkle tree computed with these alternate values and let $\rho'^{(k)}$ be the root of that tree. We know two things:

- The commitment $\mathcal{W}^{(k)}$ is "input-incorrect". Thus $\left(\sigma'^{(k)}, \beta_1'^{(k)}, \ldots, \beta_n'^{(k)}\right) \neq \left(\sigma^{(k)}, \beta_1^{(k)}, \ldots, \beta_n^{(k)}\right)$.
- The proof succeeds. Thus $\rho^{(k)} = \rho'^{(k)}$.

Thus we have used $\mathcal{P}$ to compute a second pre-image for the function h.   □

Proposition 2. *Our mix network protocol is tamper-evident.*

Proof. This is an immediate corollary of Proposition 1. The proof of tamper-evidence ensures that the operation of every mix server is entirely deterministic based on the inputs committed to in the key generation step.   □

Proposition 3. *Our mix network protocol guarantees correctness.*

Proof. The correctness of the mixing follows immediately from tamper-freeness. Indeed, we assume that correct re-encryption factors and permutations are selected in the key-generation phase, since the mix server is assumed uncorrupted during that phase (see our model and its justification in Section 3).   □

7   Conclusion

Motivated by electronic elections, much research has been devoted to building mix networks that are secure against privacy threats, and whose operation can be verified correct. This paper introduces a new notion of security, which we call *tamper-evidence*. A mix server is tamper-evident if any variation from a prescribed deterministic mode of operation is detectable. The tamper-evident mix network scheme we propose extends the security requirements of mix networks to the run-time detection of covert channels (which constitute one kind of disallowed variation from the prescribed deterministic operation). The tamper-evidence of mix servers is verified by non-interactive observers, whom we call *undercover* observers. Undercover observers can operate stealthily (at least up to the point when they must raise an alarm) and are thus nearly impossible to detect and attack.

References

1. M. Abe. Mix-networks on permutation networks, In *ASIACRYPT '99*, LNCS 1716, Springer-Verlag, 1999. pp. 258–273.
2. D. Chaum. Secret Ballot Receipts: True Voter-Verifiable Elections. RSA Crypto-Bytes, Volume 7, No. 2, 2004.

3. J. Choi, P. Golle, and M. Jakobsson. Tamper-Evident Digital Signatures: Protecting Certification Authorities Against Malware. IACR ePrint report, No. 147, 2005.
4. Y. Desmedt. Subliminal-free authentication and signature. In *Advances in Cryptology – Eurocrypt '88*, LNCS 330. Springer-Verlag, 1988. pp. 23–33.
5. A. Fiat and A. Shamir. How to prove yourself: Practical Solution to Identification and Signature Problems. In *Advances in Cryptology – Crypto'86*, LNCS 26. Springer-Verlag, 1987. pp. 186–194.
6. P. Golle and M. Jakobsson. Reusable Anonymous Return Channels. In *Proc. of the Workshop on Privacy in the Electronic Society(WPES) '03*, ACM Press, 2003, pp. 94–100.
7. R. Gennaro, S. Jarecki, H. Krawczyk, and T. Rabin. Secure Distributed Key Generation for Discrete-Log Based Cryptosystems. In *Proc. of Eurocrypt '99*, LNCS 1592, Springer-Verlag, 1999. pp. 295–310.
8. M. Jakobsson. A practical mix. In *Proc. of Eurocrypt '98*, LNCS 1403, Springer-Verlag, 1998. pp. 448–461.
9. A. Juels and J. Guajardo. RSA Key Generation with Verifiable Randomness. In *Public Key Cryptography 2002*, LNCS 2274, Springer-Verlag, 2002. pp. 357–374.
10. M. Jakobsson, A. Juels, and R. Rivest. Making mix nets robust for electronic voting by randomized partial checking. In *Proc. of USENIX'02*, pp. 339–353.
11. M. Jakobsson, T. Leighton, S. Micali, and M. Szydlo. Fractal Merkle Tree Representation and Traversal. In *Proc. of RSA Cryptographers' Track 2003*, 2003.
12. M. Jakobsson and M. Yung. Distributed "Magic Ink" Signatures. In *Advances in Cryptology – Eurocrypt '97*, LNCS 1233, Springer-Verlag, 1997. pp. 450–464.
13. C. Karlof, N. Sastry, and D. Wagner, Cryptographic Voting Protocols: A Systems Perspective. In *USENIX Security '05*, August 2005. pp. 33–50.
14. M. Lepinksi, S. Micali, and A. Shelat. Collusion-Free Protocols. In *STOC '05*, ACM Press, 2005.
15. R. Merkle. Secrecy, authentication, and public key systems. Ph.D. dissertation, Dept. of Electrical Engineering, Stanford Univ., 1979.
16. M. Michels and P. Horster. Some remarks on a receipt-free and universally verifiable mix-type voting scheme. In K. Kim and T. Matsumoto, editors, *ASIACRYPT '96*, LNCS 1163, Springer-Verlag, 1996.
17. C. A. Neff. A verifiable secret shuffle and its application to e-voting. In *Proc. of CCS '01*. ACM Press, 2001. pp. 116–125
18. W. Ogata, K. Kurosawa, K. Sako, and K. Takatani. Fault tolerant anonymous channel. In *Proc. of ICICS '97*, LNCS 1334, Springer-Verlag, 1997. pp. 440–444.
19. C. Park, K. Itho, and K. Kurosawa. All/Nothing Election Scheme and Anonymous Channel. In *Proceeding of Eurocrypt '93*, 1993.
20. D. Pointcheval and J. Stern. Security proofs for signature schemes. In *Advances in Cryptology – Eurocrypt '96*, LNCS 1070. Springer-Verlag, 1996. pp. 387–398.
21. Pedro A.D. Rezende. Electronic Voting Systems – Is Brazil Ahead of its Time?. RSA CryptoBytes, Volume 7, No. 2, 2004.
22. M. K. Reiter and X. Wang. Fragile Mixing. In *Proc. of CCS '04*, 2004. pp. 227–235
23. C. P. Schnorr. Efficient Signature Generation for Smart Cards. In *Proc. of Crypto '89*, 1989. pp. 239–252.
24. G. J. Simmons. The prisoners' problem and the subliminal channel. In *Proc. of Crypto '83*, 1983. pp. 51–67.
25. G. J. Simmons. The subliminal channel and digital signature. In *Proc. of Eurocrypt '84*, LNCS 209, Springer-Verlag, 1996. pp. 364–378.

26. M. E. Smid and D. K. Branstad. Response to comments on the NIST proposed Digital Signature Standard. In *Proc. of Crypto '92*, LNCS 740. Springer-Verlag, 1992. pp. 76–87.

27. M. Stadler, Publicly Verifiable Secret Sharing, In *Advances in Cryptology – Eurocrypt '96*, LNCS 1070, Springer-Verlag, 1996. pp. 190–199.

28. A. Young and M. Yung. The Dark Side of "Black-Box" Cryptography, or: Should We Trust Capstone? In *Proc. of Crypto 1996*, 1996. pp. 89–103.

29. A. Young and M. Yung. The prevalence of Kleptographic attacks on discrete-log based cryptosystems. In *Proc. of Crypto '97*, 1997. pp. 264–276.

30. A. Young and M. Yung. Kleptography: using cryptography against cryptography. In *Proc. of Eurocrypt '97*, LNCS 1233, Springer-Verlag, 1997. pp. 62–74.

31. A. Young and M. Yung. Auto-Recoverable and Auto-Certifiable Cryptosystems. In *Advances in Cryptology – Eurocrypt '98*, LNCS 1403, Springer-Verlag, 1998. pp. 119–133.

32. Y. Tsiounis and M. Yung. On the Security of ElGamal Based Encryption. In *Proc. of PKC '98*, LNCS 1431, Springer-Verlag, Feb. 1998. pp. 117–134

A Practical Implementation of Secure Auctions Based on Multiparty Integer Computation[*]

Peter Bogetoft[1], Ivan Damgård[2], Thomas Jakobsen[2], Kurt Nielsen[1], Jakob Pagter[2], and Tomas Toft[2]

[1] Department of Economics, Agricultural University, Copenhagen
[2] Department of Computer Science, University of Aarhus

Abstract. In this paper we consider the problem of constructing secure auctions based on techniques from modern cryptography. We combine knowledge from economics, threshold cryptography and security engineering to implement secure auctions for practical real-world problems.

1 Introduction

The area of secure auctions combines three different areas of research: economics (mechanism design), cryptology, and security engineering.

From economy and game theory, we know that many forms of auctions and trading mechanisms rely on/can benefit from a trusted third party (TTP), also known as a mediator or social planner. However, in a real application, it will often be the case that such a TTP cannot be found, or is very expensive to establish (since one basically has to counter-bribe it). Multiparty computation can be used to "implement" such a TTP in such a way that we only need to trust some fraction, say a majority, of the parties. Our goal is to investigate if this can also work in practice, and our work indicates that the answer is yes.

In this paper we give an overview of practical cryptographic protocols which securely implements basic integer operations. Detail of these protocols can be found in [7] and [20]. We also give an overview of specific types of auctions which are practically realizable based upon these protocols. Detail of these auctions can be found in [2], but the details of the applications areas are held confidential due to commercial interests of the industry partners. Finally, we give a report on the empirical results from our prototype implementation.

2 Secure Auctions

Secure auctions are emerging as a field of research in its own right. In recent years a number of contributions have been made (e.g. [10, 17, 3, 4, 21, 15]).

---

[*] This work is sponsored by the Danish Research Agency.

G. Di Crescenzo and A. Rubin (Eds.): FC 2006, LNCS 4107, pp. 142–147, 2006.
© IFCA/Springer-Verlag Berlin Heidelberg 2006

In this paper, our primary motivating application is the case of double auctions with many sellers and buyers (hundreds or thousands), and where a single divisible commodity is traded. Bidding in such an auction ideally involves submitting full schemes or strategies to an auctioneer, i.e., bidders should specify the quantities they want to sell or buy as a function of the price per unit. Based on the bids, the auctioneer then computes the so called market clearing price, i.e., the price that best balance aggregated demand and supply. Knowledge of individual bids may be of great value to others, who may use this knowledge to better their own situation. It is important to note that this does not only apply to the current auction going on. A bid contains information about the bidder's general economic situation, and such information can be (mis)used in many other contexts. Hence, if bidders are not fully convinced that their bids are kept private—i.e., are used only for the purpose intented—they may deviate from playing the otherwise optimal strategy.

Assuming that the communication of bids is secure, the auctioneer is the primary target of attacks on both off- and on-line auctions. Hence much work has been done on how to ensure the trustworthiness of the auctioneer[1]. One approach to this is to replace him by a set of n Trusted Third Parties (TTPs), where it is assumed that at most some number t of TTPs are corrupt, so called threshold trust. With this assumption, one can emulate the auctioneer via multiparty computation (MPC) (see e.g. [19, 12, 8]).

3   Contributions and Relation to Previous Work

To our knowledge the only other secure double auction is that of [21]. They realise two types of double auctions, McAfee and Yokoo, both of which only auction a single item. Our auctions handle multiple items (in fact, one of our real-life auction handles multiple items of three different goods).

From the perspective of implementation this paper contributes the first—to our knowledge—practically feasible implementation of the multiple TTP trust model based on MPC, and our results give strong empirical evidence that our protocols are sufficiently efficient for real-world applications. To some extent this adresses an open challenge from Malkhi et al. [16].

We are currently only aware of similar work by Malkhi et al. [16] and Feigenbaum et al. [9]. Malkhi et al. use a two TTP trust model based on Yao encryption and constructs a full system called FairPlay including a special purpose language and compiler (this system is available on-line, see [16]). They implement several functions in this system and provide benchmarks on performance. The system of Feigenbaum et al. is dedicated to a particular problem, a salary survey. Their procotol supports a multiple TTP trust model, but their current implementation only use two TTPs. In fact, the implementation of Feigenbaum et al. uses parts of the FairPlay system.

---

[1] There are many other threats towards auctions. Most importantly, collusion among the participants also known as bidding rings. Though in auctions with many participants bidding rings are unlikely to be successful.

4   The Cryptographic Protocols

In our protocols we have (many) *Input Clients*, who supply inputs to the computation and a set of n TTPs, who are responsible for executing the computation, such as computing an auction result. We assume that input clients can communicate privately with the TTPs, and also that TTPs can broadcast information to all TTPs. We want the computation to be secure, even if up to t of the TTPs are corrupted by an adversary. Typical values of (n, t) might be (3,1) or (5,2).

Using Canetti's universal Composability Framework[5], we can specify what we want to achieve as an ideal functionality, which can be thought of as an incorruptible computer which can do the following:

- Confidentially receive as input a set of integers from each input client.
- Execute a built-in program. The program may use the standard integer arithmetic operations and comparisons.
  The program is public and part of the specification of the functionality.
- Send the outputs of the program to the players.

If we use a protocol securely realizing this functionality to play the role of an auctioneer, we obtain an auction with the desired security properties – assuming, of course, that the computation to done by the auctioneer can be specified using integer operations as specified above,

In [7][20], protocols realizing the above functionality are presented. The protocols are shown to be secure under standard cryptographic assumptions, namely existence of a secure public-key cryptosystem and a secure pseudorandom function. Under these assumptions, the protocols can tolerate any set of less than $n/2$ TTPs being *passively corrupt*, i.e. they may share all their information but they continue to follow the protocol. *Active* corruption, where corrupted parties may deviate from the protocol, can also be handled using standard methods, although this has not yet been implemented.

We essentially assume that the clients giving input always follow the protocol. This assumption could be removed at the expense of some efficiency, however, such participants in a typical application will be bidders in an auction, who take part because it is in their interest to do so. The chosen auction mechanisms make sure that they can expect no economic gain from providing inputs of incorrect form. Hence protecting against dishonest bidders is not our first priority, and is handled only by having the client software check that the inputs are contributed correctly.

Since our goal in this paper is to report on the implementation and its implications, we only give a short summary of the protocols here: We use Shamir secret sharing and input clients provide input by distributing shares of the inputs privately to the TTPs. We use the pseudorandom secret sharing technique from [6], this allows us to create sharings of random values without interaction, and also saves work in several other cases. This immediately allows addition, multiplication and multiplication by constants using standard techniques.

Comparison is more involved and seems to require that we look at individual bits of a shared number. For instance, if we know about shared numbers a, b that

$0 \leq a, b < 2^l$, we can easily compute shares in the number $2^l + a - b$, and we have $a \geq b$ if and only if the $l + 1$'st least significant bit of $2^l + a - b$ is set. Converting shares mod p of an unknown number to shares of individual bits is possible, but quite cumbersome (see [1]). In [7],[20] (using ideas from [13]), a different approach is taken by observing that it is much easier to compute a *random* shared number together with shares of its individual bits. This can be done in a preprocessing phase. Once the inputs are supplied, we can combine the preprocessed data with the shares of $2^l + a - b$ to get securely the bit we are after.

5   Double Auction Design

A relatively small fraction of the literature on auctions considers *multi-unit dou-ble auctions*, or exchanges, where sellers and buyers reallocate multiple units of a product or a service (Klemperer [14] provides a recent survey of the litera-ture in auctions). Important real world markets are double auctions, e.g. the typical stock exchanges. Consider a large number of both sellers and buyers that meet in a double auction to exchange multiple items of a good. The sell-ers have well-defined supply schemes represented by a set of quantity-price bids $(s_1, p_1), (s_2, p_2), \ldots, (s_L, p_L)$. Here, s_l is the quantity seller i offer for sale at p_l. In this general representation, the supply scheme consists of L bids, one for each of the L possible bid prices. Likewise the buyers have well-defined demand schemes represented by a set of quantity-price bids $(d_1, p_1), (d_2, p_2), \ldots, (d_L, p_L)$. The de-mand and supply schemes are assumed to be monotone in the price. That is for any two prices p_h and p_l where $p_h \leq p_l$, we have $s_h \leq s_l$, i.e. a seller will supply at least the same when the price increases, and $d_h \geq d_l$, i.e. a buyer will demand at least the same when the price falls. All trade is executed at the same market clearing price. Bids to buy above and sell below the market clearing price are accepted, the remaining bids are rejected. The market clearing price is computed as follows: Let I be the number of buyers, J the number of sellers, and i and j be the associated counters. For any price $p_l, l = 1, 2, \ldots, L$, the aggregated demand is given by $AD_l = \sum_{i=1}^{I} d_l^i$ and the aggregated supply is $AS_l = \sum_{j=1}^{J} s_l^j$. Also the excess demand is defined as $Z_l = AD_l - AS_l, \forall l = 1, 2, \ldots, L$. We then define the market clearing price to be p_l, where l is such that Z_l is closest to zero. With price-taking behavior the optimal bidding strategy is simply to sub-mit the true demand and/or supply schemes, see e.g. Nautz [18]. It is easy to see that this computation can be done using the protocols we described. The correct value of l can be found by binary search using $O(\log L)$ comparisons due to the monotonicity of AD_l, AS_l. Each comparison result can be made public: once the market clearing price is public, it is also known whether $AD_l > AS_l$ for each l.

6   Prototype

We have implemented the cryptographic protocols of [7] as well as the auctions of [2] on top of the protocols. Our main conclusion from implementing this prototype is that this approach is indeed feasible in practice. A demo of the implementation is found at http://www.sikkerhed.alexandra.dk/uk/projects/scet.htm.

Our setup ignores some practical and theoretical issues that should be handled by a commercial application. These include key management, integrity of the executed programs, etc. Further we introduce a coordinator component, facilitating, e.g., the required broadcast functionality. All code is written on the Microsoft .Net platform using C# , using the communication libraries etc. of this platform.

We present here measurements on multiplication and comparison of 32 bit integers. More details can be found in [11]. The coordinator and all but one TTP were run on seperate Win XP machines (3.1GHz dual core, 2GB ram) placed on the university LAN; the last TTP was run on another Win XP machine (1.7GHz, 512MB ram) accessing the coordinator via a ADSL internet connection (1024/256 bits/s) over a VPN connection. The first table show times (in milliseconds) for doing x multiplications. Parallel execution is faster since the same amount of data can be sent in fewer rounds of communication. This is reflected in the tables below, where our parallel measurements have been fitted into a linear approximation, $ax+b$, to estimate this constant (see [11] for further details).

(n,t)	(3,1)	(5,2)	(7,3)
sequential execution	$42x$	$47x$	$70x$
parallel execution	$3x + 41$	$7x + 43$	$29x + 44$

The next table shows times for doing x comparisons (time in milliseconds).

(n,t)	(3,1)	(5,2)	(7,3)
pre-processing (s)	$420x$	$680x$	$1780x$
pre-processing (p)	$320x + 90$	$580x + 90$	$1700x + 90$
evaluation	$354x$	$405x$	$617x$

Based on the benchmarks of comparisons the double auction certainly seem feasible for a wide range of parameters (say, a price grid of size $L = 2000$—leading to some 11 comparisons—corresponding to the actual numbers of real-world markets as described in [2]).

References

1. ALGESHEIMER, J., CAMENISCH, J., AND SHOUP, V. Efficient computation modulo a shared secret with application to the generation of shared safe-prime products. In *Advances in Cryptology - CRYPTO 2002* (Berlin, 2002), M. Yung, Ed., Springer-Verlag, pp. 417–432.
2. BOGETOFT, P., AND NIELSEN, K. Work in progress. 2005.
3. BRANDT, F. Cryptographic protocols for secure second-price auctions. *Lecture Notes in Computer Science 2182* (2001), 154–??.
4. BRANDT, F., AND SANDHOLM, T. Efficient privacy-preserving protocols for multi-unit auctions. In *Proceedings of the 9th International Conference on Financial Cryptography and Data Security (FC)* (2005), A. Patrick and M. Yung, Eds., Lecture Notes in Computer Science (LNCS), Springer.

5. CANETTI, R. Universally composable security: A new paradigm for cryptographic protocols. http://eprint.iacr.org/2000/067, 2005.

6. CRAMER, R., DAMGÅRD, I., AND ISHAI, Y. Share conversion, pseudorandom secret-sharing and applications to secure computation. In *Proceedings of the Second Theory of Cryptography Conference* (2005), pp. 342–362.

7. DAMGÅRD, I., AND TOFT, T. Work in progress. 2005.

8. DAMGÅRD, I. B., CRAMER, R., AND NIELSEN, J. B. Multiparty computation from threshold homomorphic encryption. In *Advances in Cryptology - EuroCrypt 2001 Proceedings* (2001), B. Pfitzmann, Ed., vol. 2045, pp. 280–300.

9. FEIGENBAUM, J., PINKAS, B., RYGER, R. S., AND JAIN, F. S. Secure Computation of Surveys. In *EU Workshop on Secure Multiparty Protocols* (2004).

10. FRANKLIN, M., AND REITER, M. The Design and Implementation of a Secure Auction Service. In *Proc. IEEE Symp. on Security and Privacy* (Oakland, Ca, 1995), IEEE Computer Society Press, pp. 2–14.

11. FROM, S. L., AND JAKOBSEN, T. Secure Multi-Party Computation on Integers. Master's thesis, Department of Computer Science, University of Aarhus, 2006. In preparation.

12. GOLDREICH, O., MICALI, S., AND WIGDERSON, A. How to play any mental gamer or a completeness theorem for protocols with honest majority. In *19th Symp. on Theory of Computing (STOC)* (1987), ACM, pp. 218–229.

13. I.DAMGÅRD, N.FITZI, J.NIELSEN, AND T.TOFT. How to split a shared secret into shared bits in constant-round. *The Eprint archive, nr. 2005/140 www.iacr.org* (2005).

14. KLEMPERER, P. Auction theory: A guide to the literature. *Journal of Economic Survey 13*, 3 (1999), 227–286.

15. LIPMAA, H., ASOKAN, N., AND NIEMI, V. Secure vickrey auctions without threshold trust. In *Financial Cryptography 2002* (2002), vol. 2357 of *Lecture Notes in Computer Science*.

16. MALKHI, D., NISAN, N., PINKAS, B., AND SELLA, Y. Fairplay - A Secure Two-Party Computation System. In *Proceedings of the 13th USENIX Security Symposium* (2004), pp. 287–302.

17. NAOR, M., PINKAS, B., AND SUMNER, R. Privacy preserving auctions and mechanism design. In *1st ACM Conf. on Electronic Commerce* (1999), ACM, pp. 129–139.

18. NAUTZ, D. Optimal bidding in multi-unit auctions with many bidders. *Economics Letters 48* (1995), 301–306.

19. SHAMIR, A. How to share a secret. *Communications of the ACM 22*, 11 (November 1979), 612–613.

20. T.TOFT. Secure integer computation with application in economics. *Progress Report, available from author, tomas@daimi.au.dk* (2005).

21. WANG, C., LEUNG, H., AND WANG, Y. Secure double auction protocols with full privacy protection. In *Information Security and Cryptography - ICISC 2003: 6th International Conference* (2003).

Defeating Malicious Servers in a Blind Signatures Based Voting System[*]

Sébastien Canard, Matthieu Gaud, and Jacques Traoré

France Telecom R&D
42, rue des Coutures, BP6243, 14066 Caen Cedex, France
{sebastien.canard, matthieu.gaud, jacques.traore}@francetelecom.com

Abstract. In this paper, we present two failures in the blind signatures based voting system Votopia [2] which was used at the 2002 World Soccer Cup. We then propose a fix which relies on *fair blind signatures*. The resulting scheme is practical, satisfies the fundamental needs of security in electronic voting, including *public verifiability*, and compares favorably with other like systems in terms of computational cost. As an illustration, our variant of Votopia was successfully trialed during the French referendum on the European Constitution in May 2005.

1 Introduction

A blind signature scheme is a protocol allowing to get a signature from a signer such that the signer's view of the protocol cannot be linked to the resulting message-signature pair.

Blind signatures can be used in applications where anonymity of a message is required such as untraceable electronic cash or electronic voting. One of the standard electronic voting scheme using blind signatures was proposed by Fujioka, Ohta and Okamoto (FOO for short) at Auscrypt'92. Unfortunately, their scheme suffers from several major drawbacks. The main one is that all voters have to participate to the ballot counting process. This means that each voter must stay until all other voters complete the casting stage, which makes the scheme unpractical for real life. In [3], Ohkubo et al. showed how to avoid this inconvenience by proposing a variant of FOO's voting scheme with a simple mix-net that allows voters to "vote and go": they need not to make any action after voting. Votopia [2] is a practical implementation of this system and was used at the 2002 FIFA World Cup to select the Most Valuable Players.

In this paper, we first focus on the security of Votopia. We describe two failures where the first *mix server* in the system can affect the result of the election in an unnoticeable way. We then show how to repair Votopia [2]. The resulting scheme remains practical for large scale elections, allows voters to "vote and go" and satisfies the fundamental needs of security in electronic voting, including public verifiability (that is, anyone can check the validity of the whole voting process).

---

[*] Work partially supported by the French Ministry of Research RNRT Project "CRYPTO++".

The key component that makes our voting protocol convenient for voters and publicly verifiable is a (threshold) fair blind signature scheme, a variant of a blind signature scheme introduced by Stadler et al. at *Eurocrypt'95*. In this variant, the signer can, with the help of a trusted authority (or a quorum of authorities), either identify from the transcript of a signing session the resulting signature (*signature tracing*) or link a message-signature pair to the corresponding signing session (*session tracing*).

2   Protocol Failures in Votopia

Five basic entities are involved in the Votopia voting system [2]: the voters ($\mathcal{V}_i$ will denote the voter i), an Admin Server $\mathcal{AS}$, the mix servers or *mix-net* $\mathcal{M}$ ($\mathcal{M}_i$ will denote the mix server i), the talliers $\mathcal{T}$ ($\mathcal{T}_j$ will denote the tallier j) and a bulletin board $\mathcal{BB}$ which, as usual, is publicly readable and which every participant can write to (into his own section) but nobody can delete from. The role of these different entities will be clarified in the sequel. The system makes use of the following cryptographic primitives: a threshold encryption scheme, a digital signature scheme, a blind signature scheme and a *simple* mix-net (i.e. not *universally verifiable*). Any secure implementation of these primitives suits this system. We will therefore use generic notation to describe such primitives: $E_{\mathcal{T}}$ and $D_{\mathcal{T}}$ will denote respectively $\mathcal{T}$'s threshold encryption and decryption schemes whereas $E_{\mathcal{M}}$ will denote $\mathcal{M}$'s "encryption scheme". B and UB will denote respectively the blinding and unblinding functions of the blind signature scheme. In the sequel, we will assume that each eligible voter has a pair of keys of an agreed signature scheme and that the corresponding public key was certified by $\mathcal{AS}$. S_i (respectively $S_{\mathcal{AS}}$) will denote $\mathcal{V}_i$'s signing function (respectively $\mathcal{AS}$'s signing function), C_i the certificate of the corresponding public key and $\mathcal{V}_i$'s identifier is denoted by Id_i.

Voting Stage

1. $\mathcal{V}_i$ selects the vote v_i of his choice and encrypts v_i with $\mathcal{T}$'s public key of the threshold encryption scheme as $x_i = E_{\mathcal{T}}(v_i)$. $\mathcal{V}_i$ blinds x_i as $e_i = B(x_i, r_i)$, where r_i is a randomly chosen blinding factor. $\mathcal{V}_i$ signs e_i as $s_i = S_i(e_i)$ and sends (Id_i, C_i, e_i, s_i) to $\mathcal{AS}$.
2. $\mathcal{AS}$ checks that the signature s_i is valid and that it comes from a registered voter who has not already submitted a blind ballot. If all these verifications are valid (the protocol is aborted otherwise), then $\mathcal{AS}$ signs e_i as $d_i = S_{\mathcal{AS}}(e_i)$ and sends d_i to $\mathcal{V}_i$. At the end of the voting phase, $\mathcal{AS}$ announces the number of voters receiving $\mathcal{AS}$'s signature, and publishes the final list $L_{\mathcal{AS}}$ of (Id_i, C_i, e_i, s_i).
3. $\mathcal{V}_i$ retrieves the desired signature y_i of ballot x_i by $y_i = UB(d_i, r_i)$. $\mathcal{V}_i$ encrypts (x_i, y_i) with the "encryption key" of the mix-net as $c_i = E_{\mathcal{M}}(x_i, y_i)$. $\mathcal{V}_i$ signs c_i as $\sigma_i = S_i(c_i)$ and sends $(Id_i, C_i, c_i, \sigma_i)$ to $\mathcal{BB}$.
4. $\mathcal{BB}$ checks the signature of the posted message and checks that Id_i appears in $L_{\mathcal{AS}}$. $\mathcal{BB}$ publishes the list $L_{\mathcal{BB}}$ of $(Id_i, C_i, c_i, \sigma_i)$.

Counting Stage

1. $\mathcal{M}$ decrypts the list of c_i and outputs the list L of (x_i, y_i) in random order.
2. $\mathcal{T}$ checks the signature y_i of x_i. If the verification fails, $\mathcal{T}$ claims that y_i is not a valid signature on x_i by publishing (x_i, y_i). If more than t (the threshold) talliers claim about the same (x_i, y_i), the mix servers have to reveal the corresponding c_i and prove in zero-knowledge that (x_i, y_i) is the correct result of decryption of c_i (we call *back-tracing* such procedure). Each tallier checks the proofs issued by each mix server. If the checks fail, the mix server that issued a wrong proof is disqualified. If all proofs are valid, it means that the voter cast an invalid vote. Thus, the vote is excluded from further steps of the counting stage. After excluding the invalid results of mix processing, $\mathcal{T}$ (cooperatively) decrypts ballots x_i and retrieves vote v_i as $v_i = D_{\mathcal{T}}(x_i)$. $\mathcal{T}$ then publishes the result of the election.

In [2], Kim et al. emphasize on the fact that their system satisfies the "vote and go" property. Here, we will show that if we really let the voters "vote and go" then their system doesn't satisfy the *accuracy* requirement (that is the impossibility to alter a cast ballot). More precisely, we will show that the first mix server (and only this mix) can modify the result of the election in an unnoticeable way. Indeed, since the ballots sent to $\mathcal{BB}$ are signed by the voters (see step 3 of the voting stage), this first mix can easily recognize or substitute the ballots that come from voters who are members of a political party different from its own. We distinguish two cases: the case where the number n of (encrypted) ballots sent to $\mathcal{BB}$ is smaller than the number N of voters who interacted with $\mathcal{AS}$ (which could correspond to the case where some voters obtained their ballots from $\mathcal{AS}$ and finally decided not to cast it) and the case where n is equal to N.

1) $n < N$. Suppose that the first mix server, denoted by $\mathcal{M}_1$, has $m \leqslant N - n$ accomplices. $\mathcal{M}_1$ can ask its m accomplices to execute step 1 and step 2 of the voting stage (and consequently to obtain valid signed ballots from $\mathcal{AS}$) but not the following steps (in other words, they will not send their ballots to $\mathcal{BB}$). $\mathcal{M}_1$ can then replace m valid ballots of targeted voters by the m ballots of its accomplices. As the latter ballots are valid (they contain $\mathcal{AS}$'s signature) there will be no anomaly in the list L. The back-tracing procedure will consequently not be executed and no one will detect the subterfuge. This fraud will thus allow $\mathcal{M}_1$ and its accomplices to affect the result of the election.

2) $n = N$. As in the previous case, we suppose that $\mathcal{M}_1$, has m ($m < N$) accomplices. $\mathcal{M}_1$ asks its accomplices to obtain valid signed ballots from $\mathcal{AS}$. But this time, the accomplices will not abstain from casting their ballots. Rather, they will send dummy ballots to $\mathcal{BB}$, while keeping the valid ballots provided by $\mathcal{AS}$ for future use. $\mathcal{M}_1$ can then replace m valid ballots of its choice by the m ballots of its accomplices. Obviously, the dummy ballots will be detected and discarded in the counting stage. (Note that the back-tracing procedure will not detect $\mathcal{M}_1$'s substitution). So $\mathcal{T}$ will decrypt the remaining ballots (after having discarded the invalid ones) and tallies the final result. Again, this subterfuge will allow $\mathcal{M}_1$ and its accomplices to modify the result of the election.

Another issue is what should be done in case of a "suicide attack" : suppose that the first mix server substitutes an invalid ballot for the valid one posted by a targeted voter. The substitution will be detected after the decryption of the full list of ballots in a provisional tally, and the cheating mix-server identified. But what should be done now? Either the excluded vote is added in the final tally, in which case it will be exposed as the difference between the provisional and final tally or else the vote cannot be counted!

3   Our Electronic Voting Scheme

Our aim in this section is to repair Votopia. Before describing our main proposal, we envision several approaches that seem possible.

Possible Approaches: to detect the frauds described above, we could require the active participation of the voters in the counting stage to verify that their votes were counted (i.e., that their pairs (x_i, y_i) appear in the list L). However, this would clearly contradict the "vote and go" property and it would be impractical for large scale elections to force all voters to check the result. Furthermore, although each voter can check that his or her vote was correctly counted, no voter can be assured that all ballots were tallied correctly. Such solution would only provide *individual verifiability* and not *public verifiability*. Moreover, it is not clear how a voter can complain to the scrutineers or officials of the election without taking the risk of compromising the privacy of his or her vote.

Another option is to have the first mix server provide a proof of correct mixing. But this doesn't solve the problem anymore. Indeed, if the first mix server colludes with the second one, as well as with malicious voters, they will still be able to change valid votes in an unnoticeable way (in a similar manner at what was done by the first mix server in section 2). This remark remains valid even if we assume that the first k mix servers (among the l servers) provide a proof of correct mixing (with $k \leqslant l - 2$). In this case a collusion of malicious voters and the $k + 1$ first servers will still be able to manipulate votes.

A radical solution to overcome such shortcomings is therefore to require that all mix servers prove that they have correctly mixed the set of encrypted ballots. In other words a solution would be to use a *universally verifiable mix-net*. But if verifiable mixes are used anyway, there is no need for blind signatures at all! So we cannot assume that the mixes are verifiable when considering the use of blind signatures for efficiency reasons. Still, the security must be ensured.

We try to solve this seemingly paradox in the next section by using a threshold fair blind signature scheme and two *simple* mix-nets (care must be taken however on the choice of these mix-nets), though *robust* against server failures (which means that when a server is unavailable, it is possible to replace it by another one). However, we would like to emphasize that in most cases, the mix servers will not have to prove that the mixing was done correctly. Our solution can then be seen as an *optimistic mix-type voting scheme* [1]. As we will see, a cheating mix server will always be detected. Therefore, if the penalties for cheating are severe this will preclude any attempt.

In the sequel, we will denote by $\mathcal{M}$ and $\mathcal{TM}$ the two sets of mix-net servers (where $\mathcal{TM}_j$ will denote the mix server j) and by $E_{\mathcal{M}}$ and $E_{\mathcal{TM}}$ their respective encryption scheme. The "private key" of $\mathcal{M}$ will be denoted by $SK_{\mathcal{M}}$ and the one of $\mathcal{TM}$ by $SK_{\mathcal{TM}}$. We will denote by $\mathcal{J}$ the revocation authorities of the threshold fair blind signature scheme ($FBSS$ for short) and by $REV_{\mathcal{J}}$ the corresponding signature tracing mechanism.

We saw that the problem of Votopia comes from the fact that some votes can easily be removed or substituted by other valid ballots (by valid we mean a correctly formed ballot that was signed by the Admin Server). We want to repair Votopia by making everybody sure that, before tallying the result of the election, the ballot box doesn't contain any fraudulent ballots. We consider that fraudulent votes can be deployed either by mix servers and/or voters and from various types of actions: adding, removing or replacing a valid ballot by another one. Owing to space limitations, we will only give a sketch of our fix.

Voting Stage. This stage is similar to the one of Votopia (see section 2). The main differences are that $x_i = E_{\mathcal{TM}}(v_i)$ instead of $x_i = E_{\mathcal{T}}(v_i)$ and that y_i is a (threshold) fair blind signature of x_i rather than a conventional blind signature. (We would also like to stress that, as usual, the voter should prove that he knows the plaintext of c_i in order to prevent *vote-duplication*). At closing time of the poll, the two lists $L_{\mathcal{BB}}$ and $L_{\mathcal{AS}}$ are compared. If Id_i appears in $L_{\mathcal{BB}}$ but not in $L_{\mathcal{AS}}$, which means that $\mathcal{V}_i$ didn't request a fair blind signature, then $(Id_i, C_i, c_i, \sigma_i)$ is removed from $L_{\mathcal{BB}}$. If a voter $\mathcal{V}_i$ requested a fair blind signature to $\mathcal{AS}$ but didn't submit (deliberately or owing to a network failure for example) a ballot to $\mathcal{BB}$ (which means that there is an entry (Id_i, C_i, e_i, s_i) in $L_{\mathcal{AS}}$ but not a corresponding one $(Id_i, C_i, c_i, \sigma_i)$ in $L_{\mathcal{BB}}$), then the anonymity of e_i is revoked. The value $f_i = REV_{\mathcal{J}}(e_i)$ is then put in a black list RL so that everybody can recognize the message-signature pair (x_i, y_i) later. Note that by using $REV_{\mathcal{J}}$, we do not compromise the privacy of the vote v_i of $\mathcal{V}_i$: depending on the fair blind signature scheme used, the revocation authorities can at most obtain y_i but not x_i!

Counting Stage. $\mathcal{M}$ decrypts the list of c_i and outputs the list L of (x_i, y_i) in random order.

Case 1: if all pairs (x_i, y_i) are found to be correct (i.e., no pair (x_i, y_i) contains an invalid signature y_i, "belongs" to RL or is duplicated) then $SK_{\mathcal{TM}}$ is revealed (which means that all the mix servers $\mathcal{TM}_i$ have to reveal their own private keys). The ballots x_i are decrypted (using $SK_{\mathcal{TM}}$). $\mathcal{TM}$ outputs the corresponding votes v_i and then publishes the result of the election.

Case 2: otherwise for each incorrect pair (x_i, y_i), the back tracing algorithm (see section 2, step 2 of the counting phase of Votopia) is used to determine whether this anomaly comes from a mix server or a voter.

Case 2.1: if a mix server cannot prove that it correctly decrypted and permuted such a suspicious pair (x_i, y_i), it is then disqualified. $SK_{\mathcal{M}}$ is revealed, which means that all the mix servers $\mathcal{M}_i$ have to reveal their own private keys (as we use a robust mix-net, it is then possible to retrieve the key of any malicious mix server even if the latter refuses to cooperate). The list of c_i is decrypted using $SK_\mathcal{M}$ and a new list L containing all the decrypted (x_i, y_i) is sent to $\mathcal{TM}$. $\mathcal{TM}$ decrypts and randomly permutes the list of x_i (but this time, the mix servers have to prove that they correctly decrypt and mix their inputs, which is costly), outputs the corresponding votes v_i in random order and publishes the result of the election (we thus solve the issue of *suicide attacks*).

Case 2.2: if no mix server cheats this means that the fraud comes from a voter. The misbehaving voter is identified (thanks to the back tracing algorithm) and the anonymity of the blind ballot e_i she submitted to $\mathcal{AS}$ is revoked. The pair (x_i, y_i) is removed from L and the revoked value $f_i = REV_\mathcal{J}(e_i)$ is put on the black list RL. We then redo the counting stage with the new lists L and RL.

At the end of the protocol, the lists $L_{\mathcal{AS}}$, $L_{\mathcal{BB}}$, RL, L_0, L and every step of the counting phase (as well as the intermediate lists outputted by the mix-servers and the back-tracing procedures) are made public. Therefore, anybody can check that only invalid ballots are discarded and that the outcome of the election is consistent with the valid cast ballots (public verifiability), provided however that all the voting entities will not collude. Indeed, if one mix-server and all the admin servers collude, they can produce as many valid ballots as they wish and substitute the ballots of legitimate voters with the fraudulent ones they produced.

4   Conclusion

In this paper, we have shown some weaknesses of Votopia [2] and proposed a heuristic method, relying on fair blind signatures, to defeat our attacks. Our solution, which can be seen as an optimistic mix-type voting system based on fair blind signatures, provides, almost for free, both individual and public verifiability so that everyone can be convinced of the correctness of the voting result. In terms of efficiency, it appears that our solution, when all goes well (which is a priori always the case), is better than existing mix-net based solutions. We therefore believe that fair blind signatures could represent a more promising alternative for secure on-line voting than ordinary blind signatures and an appealing direction for future work.

References

1. P. Golle, S. Zhong, D. Boneh, M. Jakobsson and A. Juels, Optimistic Mixing for Exit-Polls, *Asiacrypt'02*, volume 2501 of LNCS, pages 451-465, 2002.
2. K. Kim, J. Kim, B. Lee and G. Ahn, Experimental Design of Worldwide Internet Voting System using PKI, *SSGRR2001*, 2001.
3. M. Ohkubo, F. Miura, M. Abe, A. Fujioka and T. Okamoto, An Improvement on a Practical Secret Voting Scheme, *Information Security'99*, volume 1729 of LNCS, pages 225-234, 1999.

Pairing Based Threshold Cryptography Improving on Libert-Quisquater and Baek-Zheng
(Extended Abstract)

Yvo Desmedt[1,*] and Tanja Lange[2,**]

[1] Information Security, Department of Computer Science,
University College London, UK
y.desmedt@cs.ucl.ac.uk
[2] Technical University of Denmark, Matematiktorvet 303
2800 Kongens Lyngby, Denmark
t.lange@mat.dtu.dk

Abstract. In this paper we apply techniques from secret sharing and threshold decryption to show how to properly design an ID-based threshold system in which one assumes no trust in any party.

In our scheme:

- We avoid that any single machine ever knew the master secret s of the trusted authority (TA). Instead only *shares* of it will be known by parties of the distributed TA and it can be seen as a *virtual key*.
- The threshold t_{TA} and the number of shareholders n_{TA} used by the distributed TA do not need to be identical to the ones used by user ID. Moreover, each user ID can use its own values for the threshold t_i and the number of parties n_i that will acquire shares.
- No single machine will ever know the secret key of the user – this means no single machine in the distributed TA and no shareholder of the user ID and not ID itself.

Like Baek and Zheng suggest, such a scheme can be turned into a mediated system.

Keywords: Threshold cryptography, Mediated system, Redistribution schemes, Secret sharing, ID-based cryptography, Pairings, Distributed keys.

1 Introduction

To deal with the loss of privacy involved with accepting an ID-based system where one (trusted) entity knows the secret keys of all users, one should apply

* Part of this research was done while visiting the ITSC Bochum, work supported in parts by NSF ANI-0087641.
** The work described in this paper has been supported in part by the European Commission through the IST Programme under Contract IST-2002-507932 ECRYPT. The information in this document reflects only the authors' views, is provided as is and no guarantee or warranty is given that the information is fit for any particular purpose. The user thereof uses the information at its sole risk and liability.

G. Di Crescenzo and A. Rubin (Eds.): FC 2006, LNCS 4107, pp. 154–159, 2006.

schemes to share the master key among a system of mutually untrusted servers. For the users it is also desirable to share their private keys in order to prevent loss or theft. Secret sharing schemes allow one to distribute critical data among n servers such that any t out of these n servers can jointly recover the secret but any lower number of players is not able to learn any information about the secret. The problem of transforming an t_1-out-of-n_1 scheme into an t_2-out-of-n_2 scheme is usually referred to as *key redistribution* [8,11]. Typical applications can be found e. g. in the area of key escrow [7] and in dynamic systems where users leave or join a group and the shares need to be adjusted.

In their seminal paper on ID-based encryption, Boneh and Franklin [5] made a brief remark on distributed private key generation. Generalizing the ID-based mediated schemes built on RSA [2,9], Libert and Quisquater [13] at PODC 2003 proposed an ID-based mediated scheme based on pairings. This scheme is derived from a threshold pairing based protocol. The trusted authority (TA) shares its secret and issues shares of the user's private key. In their mediated version the TA uses a 2-out-of-2 sharing and sends only one part of the private key. Therefore, an interaction with the TA is needed for the execution of each protocol which implies that the TA can also act as a security mediator (SEM) and can easily stop helping in case of revocation. For ID-based cryptography as proposed in [17] the TA is supposed to issue the key once and then drop out of any interaction. In the scheme of [13] the second share of the user's private key is not computed and, hence, it must be the TA to play the role of the SEM, too.

To overcome this difficulty [1] share the private key of the user. Because now the decryption is performed by non-trusted shareholders, the mechanism to check the validity of the contributed parts of the decrypted message is more complicated as any certificate would be issued just by the very same untrusted parties. Furthermore, in [1] the private key is received by a single entity who then issues shares. The typical scenario being a head of unit going on leave and allowing people to act on his behalf provided that they have enough shares of the secret.

In this paper we look at the *whole* process and describe how one should handle a "distributed" TA sharing a *virtual key* not known to any entity and how to issue keys to participants. The proposals issued so far for secret sharing in ID-based cryptography are each missing some important points and since pairing based cryptography is now entering the world of standards and is available in commercial products we see the need for such a detailed case study. (Note that the techniques used are much simpler than those that have been used in the context of generating shares of the decryption exponent of RSA (see e.g. [3,16]).)

Our protocols scale well allowing the master key to be shared in an t_{TA}-out-of-n_{TA} manner and the secret key of user ID in an t_{ID}-out-of-n_{ID} manner, the numbers chosen by the user. To this aim we apply a key-redistribution scheme as proposed in [8]. These schemes work particularly efficient as soon as one deals with a homomorphic encryption which is satisfied for the main ingredient of ID-based cryptosystems.

2   Background on Pairings and ID-Based Cryptography

The ID-based system proposed by Boneh and Franklin [4,5] uses the discrete logarithm problem in two groups. To ease notation we assume that the first group is additive while the second one is written multiplicatively.

Definition 1. *Let G_1 and G_2 be two cyclic groups of prime order ℓ. A map $\hat{e} : G_1 \times G_1 \rightarrow G_2$ is called a* bilinear map *or* pairing *if for any integers a, b it satisfies*

$$\hat{e}(aP, bQ) = (\hat{e}(P, Q))^{ab}.$$

Throughout this paper we assume the pairing to be non-degenerate, i. e. there is at least a pair $P, Q \in G_1$ such that $\hat{e}(P, Q) \neq 1$. Since we are dealing with a prime order group this implies that $\hat{e}(P, Q)$ generates G_2.

For applications we assume that the discrete logarithm problem is hard in both groups G_1 and G_2.

To build an ID-based system on such a bilinear map $\hat{e}$ one needs a hash function H mapping identity strings to elements of G_1 and a key derivation function K. In the scheme by Boneh and Franklin [5] the TA starts by secretly selecting the master key $s < \ell$. He then publishes $P_{TA} = sP$ as the public master key together with the base point P. The public key of user ID_2 is given by $H(ID_2) \in G_1$. He obtains his private key $sH(ID_2)$ from the TA. Note that this operation is done only once.

If user ID_1 wants to send a message m to user ID_2 he chooses a random nonce r and computes rP and $k = \hat{e}(P_{TA}, H(ID_2))^r$. He then encrypts m to c under the key derived from k using some key derivation function and a symmetric encryption. The ciphertext consists of rP and c. To recover the message, ID_2 needs his private key $sH(ID_2)$ and computes $\hat{e}(rP, sH(ID_2)) = \hat{e}(P, H(ID_2))^{rs} = k$. He obtains m as decryption of c under the key derived from k. In the sequel we consider how the master key s and user's private keys $sH(ID)$ can be shared in a threshold manner ensuring that no entity ever has access to the full secret.

3   ID-Based Threshold Cryptography

This section shows that it is not necessary that one party ever possessed the master key s or the user's secret key $sH(ID)$ and that threshold systems can be applied on the TA's side as well as on the user's side so that there is no need to ever combine a secret key to issue the shares for the user ID or – on the user's side – to decrypt a given ciphertext. We refer to the full version of the paper for a complete presentation of the protocols and background.

Part 1 In the set-up phase the master secret key is *generated in a distributed manner* such that no single party ever knew it. For this part we suggest verifiable secret sharing schemes as [12,6] building on [10,14,15].

Part 2 To compute the secret key $sH(ID)$ of a user ID at least t_{TA} out of the n_{TA} shareholders of TA issue shares of $sH(ID)$ to the shareholders

U_i of ID in a t_{ID}-out-of-n_{ID} manner. It is important to notice that at no time during this process the user's secret key was known to any entity (assuming $1 < t_{TA}$ and $1 < t_{ID}$) and that we do not need any dependence between the number of shareholders and thresholds of ID and TA. This step is considered in more detail further on.

Part 3 To decrypt a ciphertext, t_{ID} out of the n_{ID} shareholders of ID compute partial decryptions of the ciphertext which are then combined by the user. This part works as in [1].

For all these steps the user's secret key and the plaintext message are hidden from the shareholders and the protocols can deal with dishonest shareholders by checking the shares.

Part 2 is the missing link in the previous proposals. This made it necessary for them to either have a shared master secret *or* a shared user secret. The idea is to apply resharing of secret according to Desmedt and Jajodia [8] in the setting of pairings. Note that the shares of the master secret are integers modulo ℓ (a prime) while the shares of ID's secret key are elements of G_1. We also make use of the pairing for verifying the contributed values to deal with dishonest parties.

Protocol 1 (Shared computation of shares of $sH(ID)$ (sketch))

In: Set $\{V_1, \ldots, V_{n_{TA}}\}$ of n_{TA} mutually untrusted authorities with their shares s_i of a joint secret s shared in an t_{TA}-out-of-n_{TA} manner, system parameters G_1, G_2, $P \in G_1$, pairing $\hat{e}$, user ID.
Out: Per shareholder $U_j \in \{U_1, \ldots, U_{n_{ID}}\}$ of user ID a valid share Q_j of $sH(ID)$ according to t_{ID}-out-of-n_{ID} distribution.

Step 1 *Each party V_i, $i = 1, \ldots, n_{TA}$ views his own share s_i as a secret and computes for each participant U_j, $j = 1, \ldots, n_{ID}$ a temporary share s_{ij} using an t_{ID}-out-of-n_{ID} scheme. Then he sends $Q_{ij} = s_{ij}H(ID)$ to U_j and publishes $R_{ij} = s_{ij}P$.*

Step 2 *Each participant U_j, $j = 1, \ldots, n_{ID}$, after having received Q_{ij} from each V_i, $i = 1, \ldots, n_{TA}$ checks whether $\hat{e}(Q_{ij}, P) = \hat{e}(H(ID), R_{ij})$. Then he computes his share as*

$$Q_j = \sum_{i=1}^{t_{TA}} c_{ij}Q_{ij},$$

where the c_{ij} are the Lagrange coefficients corresponding to the t_{TA}-out-of-n_{TA} threshold scheme.

Step 3 *Each user erases all $s_i, s_{ij},$ and Q_{ij} and keeps Q_j.*

4   Conclusions

One could observe that the techniques we used to enable threshold decryption together with a distributed generation of the user's secret key without the need for any party to ever know any secret key, are quite standard. However, the works by Libert-Quisquater (PODC 2003) and later by Baek-Zheng (PKC 2004) demonstrate that it is apparently not straightforward to find how to apply them for pairings.

Note that our solution generalizes trivially to other access structures. We used threshold schemes to make the text easier to read.

Our proposal could be applied in mediated schemes using a 2-out-of-2 sharing on the user's side where the mediator would be given one of the two shares. This example shows the importance that shares of $sH(ID)$ can be computed without ever having to know the value itself and also that $k = \hat{e}(rP, sH(ID))$ can be computed from shares such that at no time the secret $sH(ID)$ needs to be combined. This might be particularly interesting in view of key escrow.

References

1. J. Baek and Y. Zheng. Identity-based threshold decryption. In *Public Key Cryptography – PKC 2004*, number 2947 in Lecture Notes in Comput. Sci., pages 262–276. Springer-Verlag, 2004.
2. D. Boneh, X. Ding, and G. Tsudik. Identity based encryption using mediated RSA. In *3rd Workshop on Information Security Application, Proceedings*, 2002.
3. D. Boneh and M. Franklin. Efficient generation of shared RSA keys. In *Advances in Cryptology – Crypto 1997*, volume 1294 of *Lecture Notes in Comput. Sci.*, pages 425–439, Berlin, 1997. Springer-Verlag.
4. D. Boneh and M. Franklin. Identity based encryption from the Weil pairing. In *Advances in Cryptology – Crypto 2001*, volume 2139 of *Lecture Notes in Comput. Sci.*, pages 213–229. Springer-Verlag, Berlin, 2001.
5. D. Boneh and M. Franklin. Identity based encryption from the Weil pairing. *SIAM J. Comput.*, 32(3):586–615, 2003.
6. R. Canetti, R. Gennaro, S. Jarecki, H. Krawczyk, and T. Rabin. Adaptive Security for Threshold Cryptosystems. In *Advances in Cryptology – Crypto 1999*, volume 1666 of *Lecture Notes in Comput. Sci.*, pages 98–115. IACR and Springer-Verlag, 1999.
7. L. Chen, D. Gollmann, and C. Mitchell. Key escrow in mutually mistrusting domains. In *Security Protocols Workshop*, volume 1189 of *Lecture Notes in Computer Science*, pages 139–153. Springer, 1997.
8. Y. Desmedt and S. Jajodia. Redistributing secret shares to new access structures and its applications. Tech. Report ISSE-TR-97-01, George Mason University, July 1997. ftp://isse.gmu.edu/pub/techrep/97_01_jajodia.ps.gz.
9. X. Ding and G. Tsudik. Simple Identity-Based Cryptography with Mediated RSA. In *Topics in Cryptology – CT-RSA 2003*, volume 2612 of *Lecture Notes in Comput. Sci.*, pages 193–210, Berlin, 2003. Springer-Verlag.
10. P. Feldman. A practical scheme for non-interactive verifiable secret sharing. In *28th Annual Symp. on Foundations of Computer Science (FOCS)*, pages 427–437. IEEE Computer Society Press, 1987.
11. Y. Frankel, P. Gemmell, P. D. MacKenzie, and M. Yung. Optimal resilience proactive public key cryptosystems. In *38th Annual Symp. on Foundations of Computer Science (FOCS)*, pages 384–393. IEEE Computer Society Press, 1997.
12. R. Gennaro, S. Jarecki, H. Krawczyk, and T. Rabin. The (in)security of distributed key generation in dlog-based cryptosystems. In *Advances in Cryptology – Eurocrypt 1999*, volume 1592 of *Lecture Notes in Comput. Sci.*, pages 295–310. Springer-Verlag, 1999.

13. B. Libert and J.-J. Quisquater. Efficient revocation and threshold pairing based cryptosystems. In *Principles of Distributed Computing – PODC 2003*, pages 163–171. ACM, 2003.
14. T. Pedersen. A threshold cryptosystem without a trusted party. In *Advances in Cryptology – Eurocrypt 1991*, volume 547 of *Lecture Notes in Comput. Sci.*, pages 522–526, Berlin, 1991. Springer-Verlag.
15. T. Pedersen. Non-interactive and information-theoretic secure verifiable secret sharing. In *Advances in Cryptology – Crypto 1991*, volume 576 of *Lecture Notes in Comput. Sci.*, pages 129–140. Springer-Verlag, 1992.
16. G. Poupard and J. Stern. Generation of shared RSA keys by two parties. In *Advances in Cryptology – Asiacrypt 1998*, volume 1514 of *Lecture Notes in Comput. Sci.*, pages 11–24. Springer-Verlag, 1999.
17. A. Shamir. Identity-based cryptosystems and signature schemes. In *Advances in Cryptology – Crypto 1984*, number 196 in Lecture Notes in Comput. Sci. 196, pages 47–53. Springer-Verlag, 1984.

Credit Transfer for Market-Based Infrastructure

Tyler Close

HP Labs, Palo Alto
tyler.close@hp.com

Abstract. The lingua franca of a market-based resource allocation infrastructure is the credit transfer protocol. The protocol design determines the expressible access-control policies and the supported trading patterns. This paper presents a protocol supporting fine grained manipulation of ownership authorities for enhanced expressiveness.

1 Introduction

A rich body of research explores the use of market-based mechanisms for resource allocation within computing infrastructure. Aiming to reproduce the scalability and efficiency of market-based allocation within the general economy, this research proposes analogous institutions for allocating CPU cycles, memory, bandwidth, etc. within a computer, a data center, an intranet, or even the Internet. Participants in these infrastructures interact through the exchange of ownership claims, varyingly referred to as: money, tokens, tickets, claims, rights and here referred to as credits. Some designs propose a new credit transfer protocol, whereas others point to an existing ecash protocol. In each case, the choice of protocol influences the features of the resource allocation infrastructure.

This paper studies the impact of existing credit transfer protocols on the design and resulting features of market-based infrastructures, and proposes a new protocol. A list of crucial features provides the basis for analysis.

Strategyproof. From seminal works [1] to current ones [2, 3, 6, 8], the vision is of managing an ecosystem of self-interested parties who will seek advantage, even to the detriment of others. The challenge is therefore to design strategyproof [5] protocols that enable cooperation without vulnerability.

Universal. Just as in the general economy, different kinds of goods in a computational economy are more efficiently allocated by different kinds of auctions. An open infrastructure [1, 5] supports the composition [7] of varied, and even unforeseen, services via a universal credit transfer protocol.

Transparent. Simulation of market-based resource allocation has revealed that widespread access to comprehensive price information is key to market efficiency [2], much as it is in the general economy. A credit transfer protocol that ensures collection of price information helps create market transparency.

Liquid. Market participants react to changing requirements or market conditions by trading. Timely trading requires market liquidity. Creating market liquidity requires fungible assets [5] and support for arbitrageurs [7].

G. Di Crescenzo and A. Rubin (Eds.): FC 2006, LNCS 4107, pp. 160–165, 2006.

Segregated. As network resource allocation infrastructures, such has Planet-Lab [9], have grown, demand has evolved for segregation within the network. Without the autonomy to choose which participants they will transact with, and which not, some providers will choose not to participate at all, or even be compelled so. Providing a protocol that preserves the autonomy of resource providers is crucial to securing their participation [5].

Asymmetric. Some resource marketplaces, such as data center resource allocation infrastructures [4], are designed with defined consumer versus merchant roles that underlie the business plan. The credit transfer protocol must enable expression of asymmetric ownership roles.

Simple. Simplicity is a subjective requirement compared to the previously listed ones; however, its importance cannot be overlooked. Reducing coordination costs is crucial to creating a broadly inclusive infrastructure [5].

The preceding feature list is an amalgam of requirements set forth in a number of papers [1, 2, 3, 4, 5, 6, 7, 8], including all those presented in [5]. The review of existing credit transfer protocols does not yield one that satisfies all these requirements. To this end, the second half of this paper proposes the IOU protocol.

2   Prior Work

The full-length version of this paper [10] examines four different credit transfer protocols, each based on a different implementation mechanism: cryptographic ecash, certificate chains, signed messages, and distributed object capabilities. Despite disparate techniques, the protocols share common flaws that result from granting too much authority. Though working with different tools, each designer faced a similar task of choosing authority divisions, and patterns for exchanging these authorities, to represent credit transfer. Similar divisions of authority resulted in similar flaws, embodied in different mechanisms.

This short paper repeats the analysis of SHARP [3], one of the four credit transfer protocols examined in the original paper. SHARP is a framework for secure distributed resource management in an Internet-scale computing infrastructure. A SHARP prototype manages access to virtual machines in PlanetLab [9], a federation of servers across the Internet.

The medium of exchange in SHARP is the ticket. A ticket is a certificate chain, where each certificate in the chain is referred to as a claim. A claim is a signed assertion that a principal, identified by a public key, may be granted access to a resource set during a specified time interval. A resource set is a number of units of a specified type; for example, a number of virtual machines.

The principal identified by a claim may delegate access to another principal by producing a new ticket containing an additional claim asserting this delegation. Double spending, or generating multiple tickets delegating the same access claim, is explicitly allowed. This policy, called oversubscription, improves resource utilization.

SHARP principals interact by requesting and trading claims for resource sets. In theory, a principal, Bob, with access to a virtual server during a futur timeslice could trade this asset with another principal, Carol, with access to a virtual server during a present timeslice. Unfortunately, the details of the SHARP protocol complicate this exchange.

Appraisal complexity. In judging the value of the trade, Bob must consider not only the value of the two timeslices, but also the degree to which Carol is oversubscribing her timeslice. This information is not available to Bob at the time of the exchange and so must be a guess based on information provided by Carol, and Carol's reputation, as seen by Bob. The requirement to dynamically track the reputation of potential trading partners is an impediment to trade, reducing market liquidity.

Loss of fungibility. Since Carol may oversubscribe her claim, the timeslice offered by Carol is not interchangeable with one offered by David. The value of Carol's timeslice incorporates Carol's reputation and the value of David's timeslice incorporates David's reputation. Essentially, each claim is a new brand of currency with its own value proposition. Under the SHARP protocol, claims are not fungible. Fungible assets are crucial to market liquidity.

Value dilution. Completing the Bob and Carol trade results in the creation of two new tickets: one delegating Carol's claim to Bob and one delegating Bob's claim to Carol. These new claims again represent two new nonfungible brands of currency, but with more complicated value propositions. Since Bob may oversubscribe the claim delegated to him by Carol, its value to a prospective buyer is now a function of the value of the underlying timeslice, Carol's reputation and Bob's reputation. By taking possession of the asset, Bob has devalued it. Each trade of the asset further devalues it, as prospective buyers must take into account the possibility of oversubscription by an ever larger pool of principals. Devaluation of traded assets discourages participants from trading in response to changing market conditions.

Reputational burden. A new participant without an established reputation faces the daunting reality that the value of any acquired asset will immediately drop to zero, since prospective buyers have no means by which to appraise the trustworthiness of the claim. As a result, a new participant is unable to trade in response to changing requirements or market conditions.

Not segregated. Since the holder of a claim may delegate it to any other principal, the resource provider has no control over the pool of principals that may redeem the claim. The SHARP paper claims this shortcoming is mitigated by the nature of the asset, a virtual machine isolated from other virtual machines. However, if the legal responsibility for a denial of service attack falls to the site authority, this design deficiency may be a showstopper. For some asset classes, counter-party restriction is an absolute requirement.

Opaque markets. Using the SHARP protocol, two participants could agree on a trade and complete it as a purely bilateral operation. In this scenario, the pricing information generated by the trade is known only to the two participants. Other participants are unable to react to the lost price signal and so cannot adjust their trading activity to changing market conditions. This loss of transparency results in market inefficiency.

3   IOU Protocol

IOU is the object capability protocol shown in Figure 1. Notice the major authority divisions represented by the four interfaces. The authority to transfer credits between owners is distinct from the authority to be an owner and both are separate from the authority to approve new owners.

```
interface Account {                    interface Hold {
  GUID getBrand();                       GUID getBrand();
  int getBalance();                    }
  Hold accept();
  Hold offer(int amount);
  int reclaim(Hold child);
}
interface Terms {                      interface Restrictions {
  GUID getBrand();                       GUID getBrand();
  int transfer(Hold src, Hold dst);      Account approve();
}                                      }
```

Fig. 1. The IOU protocol

Account versus Hold. An Account embodies the authority to play a consumer role using a particular brand of credit. An Account maintains a count of credits of a specified brand. A brand of credit is represented by a GUID. An Account holder can spend credits by invoking offer() and passing the returned Hold to the payee. If the purchase does not complete, the credits in the Hold can be reclaimed by using it as an argument to a reclaim() invocation. Once this invocation completes, the argument Hold is destroyed and is no longer eligible to contain credits. Only a Hold produced by either this Account's offer() or accept() method is a valid argument to this Account's reclaim() method. The accept() method produces an empty Hold, into which a holder of a Terms object can transfer credits.

Terms. A Terms embodies the authority to transfer credits between participants. A Terms, together with an Account, provides the authority to play a merchant role for a particular brand of credit. The transfer() method transfers all credits in a source Hold to a destination Hold, returning the number of credits removed from the source Hold.

Restrictions. A Restrictions embodies the authority to play a conformance officer role for a particular brand of credit. The approve() method produces a new Account. The holder of the Restrictions can require that participants meet certain requirements before invoking approve() on their behalf.

The above authority divisions are crucial to satisfying the specified requirements.

Strategyproof. Effective property rights are the key to enabling strategyproof market mechanisms. In the IOU protocol, a participant can gain exclusive ownership of credits and has autonomy in the choice to redeem or sell them.

Universal. Similar to the reviewed protocols, the unit of account in the IOU protocol is a unit of a specified brand. A common protocol provides for the exclusive transfer of these credits from one owner to another. More specialized kinds of transfer are implemented through the creation of a derivative currency and an associated smart contract [6] for redeeming the derivative brand credits for the base brand credits. A smart contract is simply a software agent that performs credit transfers according to predetermined rules. An example is described in a later discussion of oversubscription in SHARP.

Transparent. The authority to transfer credits between distinct owners is reified in the Terms object. The creator of a brand of credit can ensure market transparency by only granting the Terms capability to market mechanisms that publish price information. In this case, owners of these credits are unable to trade with each other, except through authorized market mechanisms.

Liquid. In an exclusive transfer, credit ownership changes without accruing any encumbrances from past owners. This style of transfer ensures that all credits of a particular brand remain fungible.

Segregated. A resource provider can restrict its pool of counter-parties by keeping the Restrictions capability private and only granting an Account to an approved participant. Exclusive ownership of credits is only achievable by a participant with an Account, thus preserving the binding between credit owner and approved counter-party.

Asymmetric. A resource provider can also restrict the pool of authorized merchants, by restricting access to the Terms capability; without which, a participant is unable to take exclusive possession of offered credits.

Simple. The IOU protocol is highly configurable; however, this configuration is expressed through the composition of a small set of primitives. The entire protocol consists of four interfaces and a total of six methods (ignoring the brand property of each interface which is provided for optional type checking). Restriction of a participant's possible actions is expressed by the absence of a capability. In other words, access-control policy is expressed through the reduction of coordination costs. Further, fundamental features, such as double spending prevention, are not expressed through additional checks, but through the innate workings of the protocol, such as determining the amount of a received payment. In the IOU protocol, security is a side-effect of the way in which credit transfers are expressed.

4   Custom Transfer Via Derivatives

To improve resource utilization, a SHARP [3] participant may oversubscribe held resources. Using the IOU protocol, this non-exclusive ownership transfer is expressed through the creation of a derivative currency. A smart contract [6] allows holders of the oversubscribed, derivative currency to redeem it for units of the base currency. Creation of new currencies is now an explicit operation, instead of an implicit part of every transfer; thus preserving fungibility.

5   Conclusion

This paper summarizes requirements, drawn from the research literature on market-based resource allocation, for a credit transfer protocol. An analysis of existing protocols reveals which requirements have yet to be satisfied. The IOU protocol is described and found to satisfy all requirements set forth.

The IOU protocol disaggregates ownership authority into the authority to: hold, offer and transfer. This decomposition enables a wide range of access-control policies through the selective granting, or withholding, of capabilities.

The IOU protocol is used in DonutLab [8], a decentralized PlanetLab [9]. The DonutLab designers found the IOU protocol provided the flexibility required to meet their security goals, while being simple and productive to work with.

Acknowledgments

Bill Frantz, Norm Hardy, Alan Karp, Mark Miller, Chip Morningstar, Marc Stiegler and John Wilkes provided valuable feedback on early drafts of this paper.

References

1. Mark S. Miller and K. Eric Drexler; "Markets and computation: Agoric Open systems"; *The Ecology of Computation*; pp. 133-176; North-Holland; 1988.
2. Carl A. Waldspurger, Tad Hogg, Bernardo A. Huberman, Jeffrey O. Kephart and W. Scott Stornetta; "Spawn: A Distributed Computational Economy"; *IEEE Transactions on Software Engineering*, 18(2):103-117; 1992.
3. Yun Fu, Jeffrey Chase, Brent Chun, Stephen Schwab and Amin Vahdat; "SHARP: An Architecture for Secure Resource Peering"; *ACM Symposium on Operating Systems Principles (SOSP)*; October 2003.
4. Kevin Lai, Lars Rasmusson, Eytan Adar, Stephen Sorkin, Li Zhang, Bernardo A. Huberman; "Tycoon: an Implementation of a Distributed, Market-based Resource Allocation System"; *HP Tech. Rep.*; arXiv; 2005.
5. Chaki Ng, David C. Parkes and Margo Seltzer; "Strategyproof Computing: Systems Infrastructures for Self-Interested Parties"; *Workshop on Economics of Peer-to-Peer Systems*; June 2003.
6. Mark S. Miller, Chip Morningstar, Bill Frantz; "Capability-based Financial Instruments"; *Proceedings of Financial Cryptography 2000*
7. Michael P. Wellman; "Market-Oriented Programming: Some Early Lessons"; *Market-Based Control: A Paradigm for Distributed Resource Allocation*; World Scientific; River Edge, New Jersy; 1996.
8. Marc Stiegler, Mark S. Miller, Terry Stanley; "72 Hours to DonutLab: A PlanetLab with No Center"; Tech Report; Hewlett-Packard Labs; 2004.
9. Larry Peterson, Tom Anderson, David Culler, Timothy Roscoe; "A Blueprint for Introducing Disruptive Technology into the Internet"; *Proceedings of the ACM HotNets-1 Workshop*; Princeton, New Jersey, USA; October 2002.
10. Tyler Close; "Credit transfer within market-based resource allocation infrastructure"; *HPL-2006-5*; HP Tech. Rep.; 2006.

A Note on Chosen-Basis Decisional Diffie-Hellman Assumptions

Michael Szydlo

RSA Laboratories, Bedford, MA 01730
mszydlo@rsasecurity.com

Abstract. This note discusses two Decisional Diffie-Hellman assumption variants introduced by Abdalla and Pointcheval at Financial Cryptography' 05. Those authors introduce two new problems and associated assumptions called the *Chosen-Basis Decisional Diffie-Hellman assumption #1* (CDDH1), and the *Chosen-Basis Decisional Diffie-Hellman assumption #2* (CDDH2), and suggest that these assumptions warrant further analysis. The problems are each defined in terms of a formal experiment, and advantage function, and the assumption is that an adversary should have negligible advantage. However, in this note, we exhibit a simple adversary for each problem, such that the advantage is significant. These new assumptions were motivated by the requirements of a proof of security for a three-party password authentication scheme described by the same authors. We conclude that the level of security assurance provided by this scheme is an open question.

Keywords: Chosen basis, Decisional Diffie-Hellman, Interactive assumptions.

1 Introduction

The Decisional Diffie-Hellman assumption is a well-known cryptographic assumption. It is a simply stated, non-interactive assumption, and is often used as the basis of asymptotic and concrete security proofs. This note provides an analysis of two somewhat related assumptions introduced by Abdalla and Pointcheval at Financial Cryptography' 05[1]. The two new assumptions are more complex, and are defined with an interactive adversarial experiment, and corresponding advantage function. The authors conjectured that the new assumptions may be stronger than the usual Diffie-Hellman assumptions, and suggested that the new assumptions be studied further.

Our brief contribution is to provide an adversary for each such experiment which does have significant advantage. This shows that the assumptions themselves are not a sound basis for a security proof. These observations do not translate to a direct attack on the scheme, but only imply that the existence of a proof of security is an open issue.

G. Di Crescenzo and A. Rubin (Eds.): FC 2006, LNCS 4107, pp. 166–170, 2006.
© IFCA/Springer-Verlag Berlin Heidelberg 2006

2   The CDDH1 Problem

The first new assumption is called the *Chosen-Basis Decisional Diffie-Hellman Assumption #1*. The new supposedly hard problem makes use of a cyclic group G of prime order p, generated by a fixed public element g. This problem consists of an adversary running in two stages interacting in one of two games, specified by parameter $b = 0$ or $b = 1$. The adversary's goal is to distinguish between the two games, i.e., the goal is determine whether b is 0 or 1. In the first stage the adversary is presented with three random elements of G, $U = g^u$, $V = g^v$, and $X = g^x$, where u, v, x are random elements in Z_p. The adversary can use these elements to generate an element Y. Next, a random bit b_0 is generated, and b_1 is set to $b \oplus b_0$. Based on b_0 and b_1, and two random numbers r_0 and r_1, two pairs of group elements $(X_0, K_0); (X_1, K_1)$ and one group element Y_0 are calculated as in Definition 1, below and presented to the adversary. The adversary must then output its best guess at b .

The authors provide intuition suggesting that it would be difficult for an adversary to succeed with probability greater than $1/2$. This proceeds by evaluating two specific adversarial strategies. The first considers setting $Y = g^y$ in the first stage, so that Y has known discrete log. The second considers setting $Y = X/U$. Indeed, it does appear that if the adversary follows these approaches, it would likely be difficult to improve on the strategy of randomly guessing b in the last stage. However, there are other adversaries.

We first recap the formal definition of the experiment, which for consistency this definition is taken directly from [1]. Let us clarify some of the notation used in this definition. The expression $\overset{R}{\leftarrow}$ is used to denote an algorithm which is randomized, and in particular, $\overset{R}{\leftarrow} \{0,1\}$ denotes a uniformly random bit selection. The function CDH is defined in terms of the basis element g, so that $CDH(g^a, g^b)$ means g^{ab}. The two-stage adversary A is presented as having a variable number of arguments depending on whether the first argument is *find* or *guess*.

Definition 1. *Let G be a cyclic group of prime order p, generated by element g, and let A be an adversary. For any group elements U, V, and X in G, modular integers r_0 and r_1 in Z_p, and $b \in \{0, 1\}$ an experiment is defined by:*

Experiment $\mathbf{Exp}_{G,b}^{cddh1}(A, U, V, X, r_0, r_1)$

$$(Y, s) \overset{R}{\leftarrow} A(find, U, V, X)$$
$$b_0 \overset{R}{\leftarrow} \{0, 1\}; \; b_1 = b \oplus b_0$$
$$X_0 \leftarrow (X/U)^{r_{b_0}}; \; K_0 \leftarrow CDH(X/U, Y)^{r_{b_0}}$$
$$X_1 \leftarrow (X/V)^{r_{b_1}}; \; K_1 \leftarrow CDH(X/V, Y)^{r_{b_1}}$$
$$Y' \leftarrow Y^{r_0}$$
$$d \leftarrow A(guess, s, X_0, K_0, X_1, K_1, Y')$$
$$return \; d$$

The advantage of A with respect to (U, V, X, r_0, r_1) is defined to be

$$2Pr[\mathbf{Exp}_{G,b}^{cddh1}(A, U, V, X, r_0, r_1) = b] - 1.$$

The advantage function $\mathbf{Adv}_{G,b}^{cddh1}(A)$ of the entire experiment is defined to be the expected advantage when U, V, X, r_0, r_1 are chosen at random.

The CDDH1 assumption is that for a time bounded adversary A, the advantage $\mathbf{Adv}_{G,b}^{cddh1}(A)$ should be very small. However, we now exhibit an adversary which has advantage of approximately $1/2$. In the first stage, the adversary will select $Y = V/U$. Upon reception of X_0, X_1, and Y', the adversary will test whether $X_0/X_1 = Y'$. If this is true, the adversary will output 0, otherwise it will output 1.

We now analyze this adversary. The intuition is that the adversary will most likely be correct unless $b_0 = b_1 = 1$. To analyze the exact success probabilities, we use the fact that the condition $X_0/X_1 = Y'$ holds exactly when $(X/U)^{r_{b_0}}/(X/V)^{r_{b_1}} = (V/U)^{r_0}$. Then we consider four separate cases depending on the values of b_0 and b_1. Case 1: Suppose that $b_0 = b_1 = 0$ (so $b = 0$). Then the condition $X_0/X_1 = Y'$ hold with probability 1, so the adversary succeeds with probability 1. Case 2: Assume that $b_0 = 0$ and $b_1 = 1$ (so $b = 1$). Then, equality occurs when $(V/X)^{r_1} = (V/X)^{r_0}$, which happens exactly when $V = X$ or $r_0 = r_1$, an event of probability $1 - (1 - 1/p)^2$. Thus our adversary is correct with probability $1 - 2/p + p^2$. Case 3: A similar situation occurs when $b_0 = 1$ and $b_1 = 0$ (so $b = 1$), since equality holds when $(X/U)^{r_1} = (X/U)^{r_0}$. Case 4: Assume that $b_0 = b_1 = 1$ (so $b = 0$). Then equality holds when $(V/U)^{r_1} = (V/U)^{r_0}$, which happens exactly when $V = U$ or $r_0 = r_1$, an event of probability $1 - (1 - 1/p)^2$. In this case our adversary is correct with probability $2/p - p^2$. Collecting these results, our adversary is correct with probability $1 + (1 - 2/p + p^2) + (1 - 2/p + p^2) + 2/p - p^2$ divided by 4, or $3/4 - 1/2p + p^2/4$.

Since the probability of success is greater that $3/4 - 1/2p$, the advantage is about $2(3/4 - 1/2p) - 1 = 1/2 - 1/p$.

$$\mathbf{Adv}_{G,b}^{cddh1}(A) \approx 1/2.$$

Thus, this adversary effectively breaks the CDDH1 assumption. We could not find a way to improve this advantage further since we do not have an adversary which is effective in case $b_0 = b_1 = 1$.

3   The CDDH2 Problem

The second new assumption is called the *Chosen-Basis Decisional Diffie-Hellman Assumption #2*. This new assumption is somewhat simpler, and is also interactive. The problem resembles the previous one except that the adversary chooses X, and no values of K are computed. Before exhibiting our adversary, we recap the definition of the CDDH2 Experiment.

Definition 2. *Let G be a cyclic group of prime order p, generated by element g, and let A be an adversary. For any group elements U and V in G, modular integers r_0 and r_1 in Z_p, and $b \in \{0, 1\}$ an experiment is defined by:*

Experiment $\text{Exp}_{G,b}^{cddh2}(A, U, V, r_0, r_1)$

$(X, Y, s) \stackrel{R}{\leftarrow} A(find, U, V)$
$b_0 \stackrel{R}{\leftarrow} \{0, 1\}; b_1 = b \oplus b_0$
$X_0 \leftarrow (X/U)^{r_{b_0}}; X_1 \leftarrow (X/V)^{r_{b_1}}; Y' \leftarrow Y^{r_0}$
$d \leftarrow A(guess, s, X_0, X_1, Y')$
$return\ d$

The advantage of A with respect to (U, V, r_0, r_1) is defined to be

$$2Pr[\text{Exp}_{G,b}^{cddh2}(A, U, V, r_0, r_1) = b] - 1.$$

The advantage function $\text{Adv}_{G,b}^{cddh2}(A)$ of the entire experiment is defined to be the expected advantage when U, V, r_0, r_1 are chosen at random.

The CDDH2 assumption is that for a time bounded adversary A, the advantage $\text{Adv}_{G,b}^{cddh2}(A)$ should be very small. However, we now exhibit an adversary which has advantage of approximately 1! In the first stage, the adversary will select $X = \sqrt{(UV)}$. This requires the extraction of a square root in G, which can be efficiently found by raising to the power $(p+1)/2$. Y is selected arbitrarily. Upon reception of X_0 and X_1, the adversary will test whether $X_0 X_1 = 1$. If this is true, the adversary will output 0, otherwise it will output 1.

We now analyze this adversary. Notice that condition $X_0 X_1 = 1$ holds exactly when $(U/V)^{r_{b_0}/2} = (U/V)^{r_{b_1}/2}$. When $b_0 = b_1$, (so $b = 0$) this always holds, and the adversary is correct. Otherwise equality can hold only upon a coincidence $U = V$, or $r_0 = r_1$. Such a coincidence will happen with probability $1 - (1 - 1/p)^2 = 2/p - 1/p^2 < 2/p$, so the adversary will succeed in this case with probability greater than $1 - 2/p$. Averaging these cases, we see that our adversary is successful with probability greater than $1 - 1/p$, and the corresponding advantage is about $2(1 - 1/p) - 1 = 1 - 2/p$, just short of 1.

$$\text{Adv}_{G,b}^{cddh2}(A) \approx 1.$$

Thus, this adversary effectively breaks the CDDH2 assumption.

4   Conclusions

Due to the existence of the two adversaries we exhibit, the two new assumptions introduced in [1] appear not to useful variants of the classic Diffie-Hellman assumptions as they stand. The application of these assumptions to the proof of security of a three party password protocol in [1], thus appears to automatically render that security proof flawed. It is still possible that their protocol has desirable security properties, but the search for a reduction proof with respect to reasonable assumptions is an open research issue.

As a final note on the exposition of the first new hard problems, we notice the experiment only deals with ratios X/U and X/V, rather than X, U, and V, individually. This indicates that a simpler, equivalent formulation of the problem would have been possible. This might have made the existence of the type of adversary we exhibit more transparent.

In general, proofs based on non-interactive assumptions do appear to be more compelling, although finding appropriate non-interactive assumptions (with one-stage adversaries) on which to base the security proof might be a significant challenge. Finally, due to the difficulty of producing security proofs *post-facto*, it may be more practical to design cryptographic schemes with security proofs in mind.

Acknowledgments

The author wishes to thank the anonymous reviewers for suggestions to help clarify the presentation.

References

1. M. Abdalla, and D. Pointcheval *Interactive Diffie-Hellman Assumptions With Applications to Password-Based Authentication*. In A. Patrick and M. Yung. editors, Financial Cryptology'05, LNCS volume 3570, pp341-356, Springer-Verlag, 2005.

Cryptanalysis of a Partially Blind Signature Scheme
or *How to Make $100 Bills with $1 and $2 Ones*

Gwenaëlle Martinet, Guillaume Poupard, and Philippe Sola

DCSSI Crypto Lab, 51 boulevard de La Tour-Maubourg
F-75700 Paris 07 SP, France
{Gwenaelle.Martinet, Guillaume.Poupard}@sgdn.pm.gouv.fr
psola78@hotmail.com

Abstract. Partially blind signature scheme is a cryptographic primitive mainly used to design efficient and anonymous electronic cash systems. Due to this attractive application, some researchers have focused their interest on it. Cao, Lin and Xue recently proposed such a protocol based on RSA. In this paper we first show that this protocol does not meet the anonymous property since the bank is able to link a signature with a user. We then present a cryptanalysis of this scheme. In practical applications, a consequence would be the possibility for an attacker to forge, for example, valid $100 bills after the withdrawal of only two bank notes of $1 and $2.

Keywords: Cryptanalysis, partially blind signature, electronic cash.

1 Introduction

Blind signatures are variants of digital signature schemes for which the signer does not learn the message he actually signs. At first sight, such a primitive is surprising but it enables the design of electronic cash or voting system which protect the anonymity of users. This idea was initially introduced by Chaum [4] but many work has been done on this topic since then [5, 6].

In a very simple approach, an e-cash system can be described in the following way: first, a user withdraws a bill from the bank. This means that the bank digitally signs a message and decreases the balance of the user's account. Then, the user gives the electronic bill to the merchant when he wants to pay. Finally, the merchant gives the bill back to the bank to be refunded. Since the bill is electronically signed by the bank, the merchant and the bank itself can check its validity. However the double-spending of a bill can be avoided only in an online setting. Otherwise, the only solution is to trace dishonest users.

In order to make the money anonymous, a nice solution is to use blind signatures during withdrawal; in such a way, the bank is not able to link a withdrawn bill and an electronic banknote given by a merchant for refunding. We refer to [8] for an exhaustive bibliography on this topic. An elegant solution to cope with the necessity of checking the correctness of messages during blind signature is

G. Di Crescenzo and A. Rubin (Eds.): FC 2006, LNCS 4107, pp. 171–176, 2006.
© IFCA/Springer-Verlag Berlin Heidelberg 2006

to use so-called *partially* blind signatures. They have been introduced by Abe and Fujisaki [1] and further formalized by Abe and Okamoto [2]. In the e-cash scenario, the bank signs messages made of two parts; some information such as the value of the bill and the expiration date are visible by the signer but other data such as serial numbers are still invisible and blindly signed.

Recently, Cao, Lin and Xue [3] proposed such a partially blind signature protocol. We describe this scheme in section 2. Then, we show that the scheme does not fulfill the requirement on the anonymity of the user. We also show that this scheme is not secure since an attacker can generate valid signatures under the realistic assumption that concurrent signatures are allowed. In the e-cash scenario, the consequences could be dramatic; for example, it is possible to withdraw two small bills of, let's say, $1 and $2 and then to generate, without any communication with the bank and consequently without any modification of the account balance, a $100 bank note which has apparently been correctly signed by the bank. Furthermore, this cheating cannot be detected by the bank if the small bills are never spent.

2   The Cao-Lin-Xue Partially Blind Signature Scheme

Let us now remind the partially blind signature scheme proposed by Cao, Lin and Xue [3]. We consider two parties, a user and a signer; at the end of the protocol, the user obtains a valid signature issued by the signer for a message m of its choice and for a string a agreed by both the user and the signer.

The protocol uses a one-way hash function H that generates k-bit hash values. We also need a variant τ of H defined by $\tau(a) = 2^k + H(a)$.

The signer has a standard RSA signature key pair with large public exponent. More precisely, let p and q be two primes such that the factorization of $n = p \times q$ is intractable. The public exponent e is an integer larger than 2^{k+1} and relatively prime with $(p-1) \times (q-1)$. The private exponent d is the inverse of e modulo $(p-1) \times (q-1)$. The signer's public key is (e, n) and the private key is (d, n).

Let a be a string agreed by both the user and the signer. For example it may encode the value of a bill and an expiration date. This information is known by the signer and should not help to further reveal the anonymity of the user. We also consider a message m chosen by the user and not revealed to the signer; this message is blindly signed by the signer who must not learn information about m. The partially blind signature of the pair (a, m) is performed as described in figure 1. The following notations are used:

- $x \in_U X$ means that x is randomly chosen in the set X using a uniform distribution,
- $\mathbb{Z}_n$ denotes the set of integers modulo n,
- $\mathbb{Z}_n{}^*$ denotes the multiplicative group of invertible elements of $\mathbb{Z}_n$,
- all the computations are performed modulo the RSA modulus n,
- $H(x\|y)$ means that the hash value of the concatenation of the binary strings representing data x and y is computed using the hash function H.

User	Signer
Private input : a message m	
Choose a string a $\xrightarrow{\quad a \quad}$	check the validity of a $x \in_U \mathbb{Z}_n{}^*$
$\xleftarrow{\quad y \quad}$	$y = x^e \bmod n$
$r \in_U \mathbb{Z}_n{}^*, u \in_U \mathbb{Z}_n{}^*$	
$\alpha = r^e u H(m\|\|u^e y \bmod n) \bmod n$ $\xrightarrow{\quad \alpha \quad}$	
$\xleftarrow{\quad t, x \quad}$	$t = (\alpha x)^{-d\tau(a)} \bmod n$
$c = ux \bmod n$	
$s = r^{\tau(a)} t \bmod n$	
(s, c, a) is a signature of the message m	

Fig. 1. The Cao, Lin and Xue protocol from [3]

A signature (s, c, a) for a message m is valid if

$$s^e (H(m\|\|c^e)c)^{\tau(a)} = 1 \bmod n \tag{1}$$

The correctness of the protocol can be easily checked since, if both the user and the signer are honest and follow the protocol:

$$
\begin{aligned}
s^e (H(m\|\|c^e)c)^{\tau(a)} &= \left(r^{e\tau(a)} t^e \right) H(m\|\|u^e x^e)^{\tau(a)} u^{\tau(a)} x^{\tau(a)} \\
&= r^{e\tau(a)} \left(\alpha^{-ed\tau(a)} x^{-ed\tau(a)} \right) H(m\|\|u^e x^e)^{\tau(a)} u^{\tau(a)} x^{\tau(a)} \\
&= r^{e\tau(a)} r^{-e\tau(a)} u^{-\tau(a)} H(m\|\|u^e y)^{-\tau(a)} H(m\|\|u^e x^e)^{\tau(a)} u^{\tau(a)} \\
&= 1 \bmod n
\end{aligned}
$$

3 Anonymity in the Cao-Lin-Xue Scheme

The anonymity property ensures that a user and a valid signature cannot be linked, even by the signer. This property, also known as blindness property, has been formalized in [5]. Informally, it guarantees that an attacker cannot deduce from a target signature the transcript from which it is issued. Even the signer should not be able to trace a signature, *i.e.* the knowledge of the private signing key should not help to break this property.

Let us now consider the Cao-Lin-Xue scheme. In [3] the blindness property is considered. However the proof given is clearly wrong since the signer is able to link a signature with one of his transcript.

Using the notations of figure 1, let $\{(a, y_i, \alpha_i, t_i, x_i)\}$ be the set of transcripts between a signer and all the users. Let (s, c, a) a target signature for a message m, computed during the k-th transcript, $(a, y_k, \alpha_k, t_k, x_k)$. The signer's goal is to link this signature with one of the users. We suppose the value a is the same for all of the users, otherwise the signer trivially associates the signature with the corresponding transcript. For all the values i, since the signer knows the private signature key, he can compute the following values:

$$u = \frac{c}{x_i} \mod n \quad \text{and} \quad r = \left(\frac{\alpha_i}{u \times H(m||u^e y_i)}\right)^d \mod n$$

If $i = k$, then the values u and r computed are those used during the signature generation, i.e. $u = u_k$ and $r = r_k$. Otherwise, these values are random ones, linked neither with u_i and r_i nor with u_k and r_k. The signer then computes the value $s = r^{\tau(a)}t_i$ and checks if $s = s_i$. If the equality holds, then $k = i$ and the signer can link the target signature with a user. Otherwise, the transcript is not the one used to generate the target signature and the signer tries another one.

4   Cryptanalysis of Cao-Lin-Xue Scheme

4.1   Some Basic Ideas

A strong goal for an attacker may be to forge signatures, i.e. to generate valid signatures that has not been actually produced by the signer. Let us assume that we know two signatures (s_1, c_1, a_1) and (s_2, c_2, a_2) of the same message m for two different strings a_1 and a_2. In order to give the intuition of the attack, we analyze the consequences of the equality of c_1 and c_2. Let $c = c_1 = c_2$. Using the verification equation (1), we have:

$$s_1^e(H(m||c^e)c)^{\tau(a_1)} = 1 \mod n \quad \text{and} \quad s_2^e(H(m||c^e)c)^{\tau(a_2)} = 1 \mod n$$

We further consider what happens if $\tau(a_1)$ and $\tau(a_2)$ are relatively prime; as explained in details below, such an assumption is realistic. Using the Bezout theorem and the extended Euclid's algorithm, we can efficiently compute integers k and ℓ such that

$$k \times \tau(a_1) + \ell \times \tau(a_2) = 1 \tag{2}$$

Then, we can use the so-called Shamir's trick [7] and combine the two signatures:

$$\left(s_1^e(H(m||c^e)c)^{\tau(a_1)}\right)^k \times \left(s_2^e(H(m||c^e)c)^{\tau(a_2)}\right)^\ell = 1^k \times 1^\ell = 1 \mod n$$

This equation can be rearranged in the following way:

$$\left(s_1^k \times s_2^\ell\right)^e \times (H(m||c^e)c)^{k\tau(a_1)+\ell\tau(a_2)} = 1 \mod n$$

and finally, using the Bezout equation (2) and the notation $s = s_1^k \times s_2^\ell$,

$$s^e(H(m||c^e)c) = 1 \mod n \tag{3}$$

The *pseudo*-signature (s, c) can be interpreted as a signature of message m for a string $\bar{a}$ such that $\tau(\bar{a}) = 1$ even if, of course, we are not able to exhibit such a value $\bar{a}$. However, *pseudo*-signatures are very useful for an attacker since they can be immediately converted into valid signature $(\tilde{s}, \tilde{c}, \tilde{a})$ for **any string** $\tilde{a}$ by selecting $\tilde{s} = s^{\tau(\tilde{a})} \bmod n$ and $\tilde{c} = c$. Indeed, from equation (3), we have:

$$\tilde{s}^e \left((H(m||\tilde{c}^e)\tilde{c})^{\tau(\tilde{a})} \right) = s^{\tau(\tilde{a}) \times e} \left((H(m||c^e)c)^{\tau(\tilde{a})} \right.$$
$$= \left(s^e (H(m||c^e)c) \right)^{\tau(\tilde{a})}$$
$$= 1 \bmod n$$

Consequently, in the e-cash scenario, if the attacker can withdraw two banknotes of value \$1 and \$2 with the same secret message m, and then compute the *pseudo*-signature (s, c), he can choose a string $\tilde{a}$ that he would have used to withdraw a \$100 bill and derive from the *pseudo*-signature a valid signature for a \$100 banknote that has never been really withdrawn !

Those observations show that the goal of an attacker is reduced to obtaining two valid signatures (s_1, c, a_1) and (s_2, c, a_2) sharing the same c element and for the same message m. We now describe how this can be done in a concurrent scenario where two users can simultaneously interact with the signer.

4.2   Description of the Attack

Let us assume that two users can simultaneously request a partially blind signature, for two different strings a_1 and a_2 respectively, from the same signer. For example, the first user withdraws a \$1 banknote and a second one asks the bank for a \$2 bill. In practice, such a scenario seems realistic if the bank wants to be able to issue e-cash efficiently. Furthermore, the formal security model of Abe and Okamoto [2] explicitly allows *concurrent and interleaving* executions of signature protocols. In the sequel we consider those to users as a single attacker that performs simultaneously two blind signature protocols with the bank.

We further assume that the strings a_1 and a_2 are such that $\gcd(\tau(a_1), \tau(a_2)) = 1$. We think that in practice the attacker can easily choose a_1 and a_2 which fulfill this property. However, even if the attacker cannot choose the strings, we know from a well-known theorem of Dirichlet that the probability for two k-bit integers to be relatively prime tends towards $6/\pi^2 \approx 0.6$ for large enough values of k. Consequently, the probability of success of an attacker is larger than one half in any case. Furthermore, this condition may be relaxed since the attack can be easily modified to apply even if $\gcd(a_1, a_2) = \delta$. In that case, a pseudo-signature can be converted into a valid signature for any string $\tilde{a}$ such that δ divides $\tau(\tilde{a})$. Since the attacker chooses $\tilde{a}$, he can for example select an expiration date such that this property is verified.

As explained in section 4.1, since $\tau(a_1)$ and $\tau(a_2)$ are assumed to be relatively prime, we can apply the Bezout theorem and efficiently compute, using the extended Euclid's algorithm, two integer k and ℓ such that equation 2 is verified.

Then, the attack proceeds as described in figure 2; the attacker asks simultaneously for two blind signatures of the same (blinded) message m for the two different public strings a_1 and a_2. For each communication, represented by an arrow, we note with an index on the right which protocol it is part of.

Attacker		Signer
Choose a string a_1 and a_2		
s.t. $\gcd(\tau(a_1), \tau(a_2)) = 1$	$\xrightarrow{\quad a_1 \quad}_1$	check the validity of a_1
	$\xrightarrow{\quad a_2 \quad}_2$	check the validity of a_2
		$x_1 \in_U \mathbb{Z}_n^*$
	$\xleftarrow{\quad y_1 \quad}_1$	$y_1 = x_1^e \bmod n$
		$x_2 \in_U \mathbb{Z}_n^*$
	$\xleftarrow{\quad y_2 \quad}_2$	$y_2 = x_2^e \bmod n$
$r_1 \in_U \mathbb{Z}_n^*, r_2 \in_U \mathbb{Z}_n^*, u \in_U \mathbb{Z}_n^*$		
Compute k and ℓ s.t.		
$k\tau(a_1) + \ell\tau(a_2) = 1$		
$\xi = u^e y_1^{k\tau(a_1)} y_2^{\ell\tau(a_2)} \bmod n$		
$\alpha_1 = r_1^e u H(m\|\xi) \bmod n$	$\xrightarrow{\quad \alpha_1 \quad}_1$	
$\alpha_2 = r_2^e u H(m\|\xi) \bmod n$	$\xrightarrow{\quad \alpha_2 \quad}_2$	
	$\xleftarrow{\quad t_1, x_1 \quad}_1$	$t_1 = (\alpha_1 x_1)^{-d\tau(a_1)} \bmod n$
$c = u x_1^{k\tau(a_1)} x_2^{\ell\tau(a_2)} \bmod n$	$\xleftarrow{\quad t_2, x_2 \quad}_2$	$t_2 = (\alpha_2 x_2)^{-d\tau(a_2)} \bmod n$
$s = \left(r_1^{\tau(a_1)} t_1 \right)^k \left(r_2^{\tau(a_2)} t_2 \right)^{\ell} \bmod n$		
(s, c) is a *pseudo*-signature of the message m		

Fig. 2. Concurrent attack of the Cao, Lin and Xue protocol [3]

The attacker uses the bezout coefficients to combine y_1 and y_2 into ξ. At the end of the two interleaved protocol's executions he obtains a *pseudo*-signature (s, c) for the chosen message m. Indeed, $s^e(H(m\|c^e)c) = 1 \bmod n$. As explained in section 4.1, it enables to compute valid signatures for **any** string $\tilde{a}$.

References

1. M. Abe and E. Fujisaki. How to Date Blind Signatures. In *Asiacrypt '96*, LNCS 1163, pages 244–251. Springer-Verlag, 1996.
2. M. Abe and T. Okamoto. Provably Secure Partially Blind Signatures. In *Crypto 2000*, LNCS 1880, pages 271–286. Springer-Verlag, 2000.
3. T. Cao, D. Lin, and R. Xue. A randomized RSA-based partially blind signature scheme for electronic cash. *Computers and Security*, 24(1):44–49, february 2005.
4. D. Chaum. Blind Signatures for Untraceable Payments. In *Crypto '82*, pages 199–203. Plenum, NY, 1983.
5. A. Juels, M. Luby, and R. Ostrovsky. Security of Blind Digital Signatures. In *Crypto '97*, LNCS. Springer-Verlag, 1997.
6. D. Pointcheval and J. Stern. Security Arguments for Digital Signatures and Blind Signatures. *Journal of Cryptology*, 13(3):361–396, 2000.
7. A. Shamir. On the Generation of Cryptographically Strong Pseudo-Random Sequences. *ACM Transaction on Computer Systems*, 1(1):38–44, February 1983.
8. Y. Tsiounis. *Efficient Electronic Cash: New Notions and Techniques.* PhD thesis, Northeastern University, june 1997.

A Generic Construction for Token-Controlled Public Key Encryption

David Galindo[1] and Javier Herranz[2,*]

[1] Institute for Computing and Information Sciences, Radboud University Nijmegen,
P.O.Box 9010, 6500 GL, Nijmegen, The Netherlands
d.galindo@cs.ru.nl
[2] INRIA Futurs- Laboratoire d'Informatique (LIX) École Polytechnique, 91128
Palaiseau Cedex, France
herranz@lix.polytechnique.fr

Abstract. Token-controlled public key encryption (TCPKE) schemes,
introduced in [1], offer many possibilities of application in financial or
legal scenarios. Roughly speaking, in a TCPKE scheme messages are encrypted by using a public key together with a secret token, in such a way
that the receiver is not able to decrypt this ciphertext until the token
is published or released. The communication overhead for releasing the
token is small in comparison with the ciphertext size.

However, the fact that the same ciphertext could decrypt to different messages under different tokens was not addressed in the original
work. In our opinion this is an essential security property that limits the
use of this primitive in practice. In this work, we formalize this natural
security goal and show that the schemes in [1] are insecure under this notion. In the second place, we propose a very simple and efficient generic
construction of TCPKE schemes, starting from any trapdoor partial one-
way function. This construction is obtained from a slight but powerful
modification of the celebrated Fujisaki-Okamoto transformation [7]. We
prove that the resulting schemes satisfy all the required security properties, in the random oracle model. Previous to this work, only particular
instantiations of TCPKE schemes were proposed.

Keywords: Public key encryption, provable security, timed-release cryptography, random oracle model.

1 Introduction

Baek, Safavi-Naini and Susilo [1] have recently introduced a cryptographic primitive called *token-controlled public key encryption* (TCPKE). The intuitive idea
is that the sender encrypts messages by using the public key of the receiver together with a secret token, in such a way that the receiver is able to decrypt
the ciphertext only when the token is delivered. The communication overhead
needed for releasing the token is small. This provides a solution to situations

---

* The work of the second author was carried out during the tenure of an ERCIM
fellowship.

G. Di Crescenzo and A. Rubin (Eds.): FC 2006, LNCS 4107, pp. 177–190, 2006.

where someone wants a receiver to obtain some confidential information only when some condition is fulfilled, but he is afraid he could not encrypt the message when this condition (a date, an event) is already satisfied. The sender can encrypt the message in advance and give the employed secret token to some external party (a lawyer, for example) under the requirement that this party will deliver the token to the intended receivers when the stated condition holds. Note that this notion is related to other previously considered primitives in the context of *timed-release* cryptography [11,13,6,10], where the receiver can decrypt a ciphertext only when some specific date arrives; a trusted entity is also needed in most of the proposals, which must perform some costly cryptographic operations. In token-controlled cryptography, the only cost for the external entity is to store and deliver a token when some condition (not necessarily related to time) is satisfied. Some desirable properties are that storing this token requires much less space than storing the ciphertext, and that the same token can control the decryption of multiple receivers without compromising security.

As a motivating example of application of token-controlled encryption, let us consider the will scenario explained in [1]: a millionaire writes his will m to his sons but he wants to keep it secret until his death. He can encrypt the will with a token-controlled scheme, provide his sons with the corresponding ciphertexts, and then give the used token τ to a lawyer. The lawyer should sign a document where he commits himself to give the token to the sons when the millionaire passes away. At that moment, each son could use his secret key and the obtained token to decrypt his ciphertext and recover the original will.

Other financial situations can be imagined where this notion is useful. Suppose that some person wants to keep some important documents (or money) in a safe-deposit box of a bank. He can encrypt the secret key which opens the box to his wife and his sons, by using a token-controlled scheme, and secretly deliver the token to the bank, along with the conditions in which the bank should provide his wife or his sons with the token, in order to allow them to open the box: death, illness, legal problems, etc.

Of course, it is important to properly define the security requirements for this cryptographic primitive. In [1] the authors define in essence two security properties. The first property intuitively ensures that a person who obtains a token cannot obtain any information about a message which has been encrypted to a different person with the same token. In the case of the will, for example, if the millionaire encrypts to each son only the part of the will which concerns that son, then each son should not be able to know the part of the will of the other sons, even after obtaining the employed (common) token.

The second property ensures that a receiver does not obtain any information about the encrypted message if he does not know the employed token. This is the most natural property for this kind of schemes.

1.1   Our Contributions

We introduce a new security property for TCPKE , which is named as *strong existential token unforgeability*; it is related to the possible misbehavior of the entity who is in charge of keeping and releasing the token. Roughly speaking, both the person who encrypts the message and the intended receivers want to be sure that this party will later provide the correct token. If this party tries to boycott the process and give a false token to the receivers, they should be able to detect this misbehavior. This property, which we believe is not only quite natural but essential, is not considered in [1]. In fact, the two TCPKE specific schemes proposed in [1] are insecure under this notion: a malicious 'trusted' party can deliver a false token τ' different from the valid token τ, without being detected for this, in such a way that the receiver will obtain a decrypted message m' different from the original message m. Obviously, this fact is unacceptable for any practical usage of TCPKE we can think of. This new security requirement follows the usual cryptographic practice of removing as much trust assumptions as possible on third parties.

After that, we present a simple, efficient and generic construction of token-controlled public key encryption schemes, starting from any trapdoor partial one-way function, which satisfies all the required security properties. The new construction is obtained from a slight modification of the Fujisaki-Okamoto (FO) transformation [7], and adds no computational overhead. The formal proofs hold in the random oracle model [4]. When implemented with El Gamal [8] or RSA [12] primitives, our conversion yields more efficient schemes than the ones previously proposed.

1.2   Further Applications

Encrypting into the future. Due to the fact that the same token τ can control the decryption of multiple ciphertexts/receivers, TCPKE provides a very efficient solution for sending messages into the future [13,6]: the sender encrypts multiple messages to multiple receivers by means of a TCPKE scheme, using the corresponding public keys but the same token. The sender provides to a third party the token and the date on which the receivers are able to read the confidential information. At the appointed time, the third party *publicly* announces the token, so every receiver is able to read the message. The confidentiality of the messages is not compromised, and every communication is off-line. This proposal favorably compares with the solution given in [5] using identity-based encryption, since the latter requires major band-with, private channels between the receivers and the third party as well as on-line communications.

'Private-opening' commitment scheme. A TCPKE scheme with strong existential token unforgeability can be seen as some sort of commitment scheme. A sender commits to a string m to a receiver by encrypting m using the public key of the receiver and a certain token τ, and sends the ciphertext to the receiver as the commitment. In the revealing phase, the sender releases τ to the receiver, who accepts m as the committed string if and only if decryption is successful. We notice that the opening algorithm can only be executed by the receiver, since he/she is the only entity in possession of his/her secret key.

1.3 Organization of this Paper

The rest of this work is organized as follows. In Section 2 we briefly explain some primitives and notation that will be used throughout the paper. In Section 3 we recall the definition of token-controlled public key encryption, and the security properties that these schemes should satisfy (including the new notion of *strong existential token unforgeability*). Later, we show that the previous schemes by Baek et al. are forgeable. In Section 4, we propose our construction of a general family of such schemes and provide the formal proofs that the resulting schemes satisfy the required security properties. We conclude in Section 5 by summing up our contributions and suggesting future research on to this topic.

2 Preliminaries

Notation. A probabilistic polynomial time algorithm will be named in short as PPT algorithm, while PT refers to polynomial time algorithms. 1^ℓ refers to the security parameter ℓ. If A is a non-empty set, then $x \leftarrow A$ denotes that x has been uniformly chosen in A. Finally, if $\mathcal{A}$ is an (probabilistic) algorithm, $x \leftarrow \mathcal{A}$ means that $\mathcal{A}$ has been executed on some specified input and its (random) output has been assigned to the variable x. We denote by $\mathsf{negl}(\ell)$ the class of negligible functions in the parameter ℓ.

2.1 Trapdoor Partial One-Way Functions

The material in this section is adapted from [9]. A trapdoor partial one-way (TPOW) function is a family of injective maps $f : X \times Y \to Z$, where X, Y and Z are polynomial size set families, with the following properties:

1. There exists a PPT algorithm TPOW.Gen that on input a security parameter 1^ℓ returns a pair (pk, sk) of public and secret keys, as well as a description of sets X_{pk}, Y_{pk}, Z_{pk}.
2. There exists a PPT algorithm TPOW.Eval that on input pk, $x \in X_{pk}$ and $y \in Y_{pk}$ outputs $f_{pk}(x, y)$.
3. There exists a PPT algorithm TPOW.Inv that on input sk, $f_{pk}(x, y)$, where $x \in X_{pk}$ and $y \in Y_{pk}$, outputs x.
4. for any PPT algorithm $\mathcal{A}^{\mathsf{POW}}$,

$$\mathsf{Adv}^f_{\mathcal{A}^{\mathsf{POW}}}(1^\ell) = \Pr\left[\mathcal{A}^{\mathsf{POW}}(pk, f_{pk}(x, y)) = x \mid x \leftarrow X_{pk}; \, y \leftarrow Y_{pk}\right] \in \mathsf{negl}(\ell)$$

X_{pk} is assumed to be a recognizable set for any valid pk. A set X_{pk} is *recognizable* if there exist a PT algorithm that on input a string s, with size polynomial in ℓ, outputs 1 if and only if $s \in X_{pk}$.

2.2 Public Key Encryption

In this section we recall the definition of a public key encryption (PKE) scheme. A PKE scheme consists of three probabilistic polynomial time (PPT) algorithms:

Key Generation, PKE.Gen: it takes as input a security parameter 1^ℓ and returns a pair (pk, sk) of public and secret keys, as well as a description of plaintext and ciphertext spaces, denoted as $\mathcal{M}_{pk}$ and $\mathcal{C}_{pk}$, respectively. It is assumed there exists a PPT algorithm that on input pk outputs the security parameter 1^ℓ.

Encryption, PKE.Enc: takes as inputs $m \in \mathcal{M}_{pk}$, and pk of the intended receiver; the output is a ciphertext $c \in \mathcal{C}_{pk}$.

Decryption, PKE.Dec: takes as inputs a ciphertext $c \in \mathcal{C}_{pk}$ and a secret key sk, returns either a message $m \in \mathcal{M}_{pk}$ or the special reject symbol $\perp$.

The standard security notion for PKE schemes is *indistinguishability against chosen-ciphertext attacks*, named in short as IND-CCA [3]. Let us denote as $\mathsf{Adv}_{\mathcal{B}_{\mathsf{PKE}}}^{\mathsf{IND-CCA}}(1^\ell)$ the advantage of an adversary $\mathcal{B}_{\mathsf{PKE}}$ in the IND-CCA game.

2.3 Fujisaki-Okamoto Transformation

Let f be a TPOW function family over the sets X, Y and Z. The asymmetric scheme $\mathsf{PKE}^f = (\mathsf{PKE.Gen}^f, \mathsf{PKE.Enc}^f, \mathsf{PKE.Dec}^f)$, proposed by Fujisaki and Okamoto [7], works as follows [1].

$\mathsf{PKE.Gen}^f$. First, run $(pk, sk) \leftarrow \mathsf{TPOW.Gen}^f(1^\ell)$ and let $\mathcal{M}_\ell = \{0,1\}^{p(\ell)}$. Let $G : X_{pk} \to \mathcal{M}_\ell$ and $H : X_{pk} \times \mathcal{M}_\ell \to Y_{pk}$ be hash functions to be modelled as random oracles [4]. Then $\mathcal{C}_{pk} = Z_{pk} \times \mathcal{M}_\ell$. Finally, the public key is pk together with the description of the hash functions and plaintext-ciphertext spaces.

$\mathsf{PKE.Enc}^f$. The ciphertext for a message $m \in \mathcal{M}_\ell$ is

$$c = (f_{pk}(x, y), G(x) \oplus m),$$

where $y = H(x, m)$ and x is uniformly chosen in X_{pk}.

$\mathsf{PKE.Dec}^f$. To decrypt a ciphertext $c = (c_1, c_2)$, firstly compute $x = \mathsf{TPOW.Inv}^f(c_1)$. Then, compute $m = G(x) \oplus c_2$ and return m if $c_1 = f_{pk}(x, H(x, m))$. Otherwise, return the reject symbol $\perp$. If it is not possible to compute either $\mathsf{TPOW.Inv}^f(c_1)$ or $G(x) \oplus c_2$, return $\perp$.

Let $\mathcal{B}_{\mathsf{PKE}^f}^{\mathsf{IND-CCA}}[t, \epsilon, q_G, q_H, q_D]$ denote an adversary against the IND-CCA security of the above cryptosystem that runs in time t with advantage ϵ, doing no more than q_G, q_H and q_D queries respectively to the random oracles G, H and to the decryption oracle. Then,

Theorem 1 ([7,9]). *If there exists an adversary* $\mathcal{B}_{\mathsf{PKE}^f}^{\mathsf{IND-CCA}}[t, \epsilon, q_G, q_H, q_D]$, *then there exists an adversary* $\mathcal{A}^{\mathsf{POW}}$ *for* f *in time* t' *with advantage* ϵ' *such that*

$$\epsilon \leq (2(q_G + q_H)\epsilon' + 1)\left(1 - \frac{1}{|Y_{pk}|} - \frac{1}{|\mathcal{M}_\ell|}\right)^{-q_D} - 1$$

---

[1] For the sake of simplicity, we only present here the case in which the symmetric scheme is the one-time pad.

and

$$t = t' - O((q_G + q_H) \log(|X_{pk}||M_\ell|)),$$

where $\log$ *is the logarithm in base 2.*

3 Token-Controlled Public Key Encryption

In this section we recall the definition of TCPKE given in [1], together with the necessary security properties that such a scheme should satisfy; the two first properties are taken from [1], whereas the last requirement is considered for the first time in this work. A TCPKE scheme consists of four probabilistic polynomial time (PPT) algorithms:

Key Generation, TCPKE.Gen: it takes as input a security parameter 1^ℓ and returns a pair (pk, sk) of secret and public keys, as well as a description of the plaintexts (or messages), ciphertexts and tokens spaces, denoted as $\mathcal{M}_{pk}$, $\mathcal{C}_{pk}$ and $\mathcal{T}_\ell$, respectively. It is assumed there exists a PPT algorithm that on input pk outputs the security parameter 1^ℓ.

Token Generation, TCPKE.Tok: it takes as input the security parameter 1^ℓ and returns a token $\tau \in \mathcal{T}_\ell$ chosen according to some probability distribution in $\mathcal{T}_\ell$.

Encryption, TCPKE.Enc: the encryption algorithm takes as inputs a message $m \in \mathcal{M}_{pk}$, a public key pk for the receiver and a token τ; the output is a ciphertext $c \in \mathcal{C}_{pk}$ of the message.

Decryption, TCPKE.Dec: this algorithm, taking as inputs a ciphertext $c \in \mathcal{C}_{pk}$, a secret key sk and a token τ, returns either a message $m \in \mathcal{M}_{pk}$ or the special reject symbol $\perp$.

3.1 Security Requirements

Next we present three requirements for a TCPKE scheme. In the original work [1], the authors define three properties; however, the two first properties are related to the same sort of attacks, one of them being stronger than the other. For this reason, we only consider here one of those two definitions.

TCPKE.1 **Security against Outsider Attacks.** In this first attack scenario, we want to protect the situation where the same token is used to encrypt messages to many different receivers; later, maybe some of these receivers obtain the correct token and aims at obtaining information about a message encrypted to some different receiver(s) with the same token. We want this to be infeasible. This security notion also captures the situation where the external entity (which knows the token) wants to obtain information about the messages encrypted with this token. Formally, we define security against this kind of attacks by considering an adversary $\mathcal{A}_1$ which tries to win the following game:

1. The algorithm $\tau \leftarrow$ TCPKE.Tok(1^ℓ) is executed one time, whereas the algorithm TCPKE.Gen is independently executed n times, namely $(pk_i, sk_i) \leftarrow$ TCPKE.Gen(1^ℓ) for $i = 1, \ldots, n$. The same security parameter 1^ℓ is taken as input for all these executions. The adversary $\mathcal{A}_1$ receives the public keys $pk_1, \ldots, pk_n$ and the token τ, but not the secret keys $sk_1, \ldots, sk_n$.
2. The adversary can make queries to a decryption oracle TCPKE.Dec(sk_i, τ, c), for secret keys sk_i (where $i \in \{1, \ldots, n\}$) and ciphertexts c that it adaptively chooses.
3. The adversary $\mathcal{A}_1$ outputs two messages $m_0, m_1 \in \bigcap_{1 \leq i \leq n} \mathcal{M}_{pk_i}$ of the same length. A random bit $b \in \{0, 1\}$ is chosen, and the encryption algorithm is executed for every $i = 1, \ldots, n$, giving $c_i^\star =$ TCPKE.Enc(pk_i, τ, m_b). The challenge ciphertexts $c_1^\star, \ldots, c_n^\star$ are given to $\mathcal{A}_1$.
4. The adversary can proceed as in step 2, with the restriction that it cannot ask for the decryption of a ciphertext $c_i^\star$ under secret key sk_i, for any $i = 1, \ldots, n$.
5. The adversary $\mathcal{A}_1$ outputs a guess $b' \in \{0, 1\}$.

The advantage of such an adversary against the TCPKE .1 property is defined as

$$\mathsf{Adv}_{\mathcal{A}_1}^{\mathsf{TCPKE}.1}(1^\ell) = |\, 2\Pr[b' = b] - 1|.$$

Definition 1. *A* TCPKE *scheme is* secure against outsider attacks *if, for any polynomially bounded n and for any PPT adversary $\mathcal{A}_1$ playing the game defined above, the function $\mathsf{Adv}_{\mathcal{A}_1}^{\mathsf{TCPKE}.1}(1^\ell)$ is negligible as a function of 1^ℓ.*

TCPKE.2 **Security against Insider Attacks.** In the second attack scenario, we consider a malicious user to whom the token has not been yet released. This user should be unable to obtain any information about the message encrypted in the received ciphertexts. Formally, this security notion is defined by the following game played against a challenger by some adversary $\mathcal{A}_2$:

1. The challenger chooses a security parameter 1^ℓ and executes $\tau \leftarrow$ TCPKE.Tok(1^ℓ). The obtained token is kept secret, whereas the security parameter 1^ℓ is given to $\mathcal{A}_2$.
2. The adversary runs $(pk, sk) \leftarrow$ TCPKE.Gen(1^ℓ) and can make queries to an *embedded-token encryption* oracle TCPKE.Enc(pk, τ, m), for messages m that it adaptively chooses.
3. The adversary $\mathcal{A}_2$ outputs two messages $m_0, m_1 \in \mathcal{M}_{pk}$ of the same length. The challenger chooses a random bit $b \in \{0, 1\}$, and executes the encryption algorithm to obtain $c^\star =$ TCPKE.Enc(pk, τ, m_b). The resulting challenge ciphertext $c^\star$ is given to $\mathcal{A}_2$.
4. The adversary can again proceed as in step 2, with no restrictions on its queries.
5. The adversary $\mathcal{A}_2$ outputs a bit $b' \in \{0, 1\}$.

The advantage of such an adversary against the TCPKE .2 property is defined as

$$\mathsf{Adv}_{\mathcal{A}_2}^{\mathsf{TCPKE}.2}(1^\ell) = |\, 2\Pr[b' = b] - 1|.$$

Definition 2. *A* TCPKE *scheme is* secure against insider attacks *if, for any PPT adversary* $\mathcal{A}_2$ *playing the game defined above, the function* $\mathsf{Adv}_{\mathcal{A}_2}^{\mathsf{TCPKE}.2}(1^\ell)$ *is negligible as a function of* 1^ℓ.

TCPKE.3 **Strong Existential Token Unforgeability.** Finally, we introduce a new security notion for TCPKE schemes which was not considered in [1]. In fact, the two schemes that are proposed in [1] do not satisfy this property (see below). Roughly speaking, the new notion ensures it is infeasible to obtain a valid ciphertext c such that correctly decrypts under two different tokens $\tau \neq \tau'$, giving as outputs two different valid messages $m \neq m'$. This is a strong security requirement, since we do not only ask that it is difficult to make up a fake token after a challenge ciphertext is received, but that this is infeasible even if we let the adversary choosing the challenge ciphertext.

We denote this desirable property for TCPKE schemes as *strong existential token unforgeability*, and is formally defined by considering an adversary A_3 who plays the following game against a challenger:

1. The challenger chooses a security parameter 1^ℓ and executes the algorithms $(pk, sk) \leftarrow$ TCPKE.Gen(1^ℓ). The challenged public key pk is given to $\mathcal{A}_3$, while the secret key sk is kept by the challenger.
2. The adversary can also make queries to a decryption oracle TCPKE.Dec (sk, τ, c), for pairs (τ, c) of ciphertexts and tokens that it adaptively chooses.
3. The adversary $\mathcal{A}_3$ outputs two different tokens τ and τ', and a ciphertext c.

The advantage of such an adversary against the unforgeability property of a TCPKE scheme is defined as

$$\mathsf{Adv}_{\mathcal{A}_3}^{\mathsf{TCPKE}.3}(1^\ell) \;=\; \Pr\left[\begin{array}{c} \mathsf{TCPKE.Dec}(sk, \tau, c) = m \neq m' = \mathsf{TCPKE.Dec}(sk, \tau', c) \\ \text{and } m \neq \perp \text{ and } m' \neq \perp \end{array}\right]$$

Definition 3. *A* TCPKE *scheme is* strong existentially token unforgeable *if, for any PPT adversary* $\mathcal{A}_3$ *playing the game defined above, the function* $\mathsf{Adv}_{\mathcal{A}_3}^{\mathsf{TCPKE},3}(1^\ell)$ *is negligible as a function of* 1^ℓ.

3.2   Previous TCPKE Schemes Are Forgeable

In this section we show that the two specific TCPKE schemes proposed in [1] do not satisfy the strong existential token unforgeability property. We will consider only their second specific scheme, based on ElGamal encryption + Schnorr signatures. The same analysis applies to their first scheme, which uses bilinear pairings techniques. Let us first recall the protocols of this scheme, called TCPKE^{ES}:

TCPKE.Gen^{ES}: the input is a security parameter 1^ℓ. A finite cyclic subgroup $\mathcal{G} = \langle g \rangle$ of the multiplicative group $\mathbb{Z}_p^*$ is chosen, where p is a prime and the order of $\mathcal{G}$ is a prime $q \geq 2^\ell$. The message and token spaces are defined as $\mathcal{M}_{pk} = \{0,1\}^{\ell_M}$ and $\mathcal{T}_\ell = \{0,1\}^{\ell_T}$, for some integer parameters ℓ_M and ℓ_T which infer from the security parameter 1^ℓ. Two hash functions $H_1 : \mathcal{G} \times \mathcal{G} \times \mathcal{T}_\ell \to \mathcal{M}_{pk}$ and $H_2 : \mathcal{M}_{pk} \times \mathcal{G} \to \mathbb{Z}_q^*$ are chosen. All these parameters are made public.

The user then chooses a random integer $sk \in \mathbb{Z}_q^*$ as his secret key, and defines the public key to be $pk = g^{sk}$ (formally, the public key will also contain all the previously defined parameters).

TCPKE.Tok^{ES}: it takes as input the security parameter 1^ℓ, infers the parameter ℓ_T, and chooses uniformly at random a token $\tau \in \mathcal{T}_\ell = \{0,1\}^{\ell_T}$.

TCPKE.Enc^{ES}: given a public key pk, a token τ and a message $m \in \{0,1\}^{\ell_M}$, this algorithm first chooses at random $r \in \mathbb{Z}_q^*$ and computes the values $u = g^r$, $\kappa = pk^r$, $K = H_1(u, \kappa, \tau)$ and $v = K \oplus m$. Later, a different integer $z \in \mathbb{Z}_q^*$ is chosen at random, and the values $\omega = g^z$, $h = H_2(v, \omega)$ and $s = z - hr$ are computed. The final ciphertext is defined as $c = (u, v, h, s)$.

TCPKE.Dec^{ES}: this algorithm takes as inputs a ciphertext $c = (u, v, h, s)$, a secret key sk and a token τ, and proceeds as follows:

- If $h = H_2(v, g^s u^h)$, then compute $\kappa = u^{sk}$ and $K = H_1(u, \kappa, \tau)$, and return $m = K \oplus v$.
- Otherwise, return $\perp$.

Now assume that a millionaire encrypts his will m by using a token τ and the public key pk of his son, obtaining as a result a ciphertext $c = (u, v, h, s)$. The ciphertext is made public, whereas the token τ is given to a lawyer.

The day when the millionaire dies, the lawyer is assumed to deliver the token τ to the son of the millionaire. However, if the lawyer is malicious, he can deliver a different token $\tau' \neq \tau$. The son of the millionaire will compute $\kappa = u^{sk}$ and $K' = H_1(u, \kappa, \tau')$, which with overwhelming probability will be different from the correct value $K = H_1(u, \kappa, \tau)$. Therefore, the son of the millionaire would obtain a final will $m' = K \oplus v \neq K' \oplus v = m$, different from the original will m encrypted by his father, and without being able to detect that he has been cheated by the lawyer.

4   TCPKE Schemes from Any TPOW Function

Let f be a TPOW function family over the sets X, Y and Z. The generic construction of TCPKE asymmetric schemes

$$\mathsf{TCPKE}^f = (\mathsf{TCPKE.Gen}^f, \mathsf{TCPKE.Tok}^f, \mathsf{TCPKE.Enc}^f, \mathsf{TCPKE.Dec}^f),$$

works as follows.

TCPKE.Gen^f. First, run $(pk, sk) \leftarrow$ TPOW.Gen$^f(1^\ell)$ and let $\mathcal{M}_\ell = \{0,1\}^{p(\ell)}$, $\mathcal{T}_\ell = \{0,1\}^{t(\ell)}$. Let $\widetilde{G} : X_{pk} \times \mathcal{T}_\ell \to \mathcal{M}_\ell$ and $\widetilde{H} : X_{pk} \times \mathcal{M}_\ell \to Y_{pk}$ be hash functions to be modelled as random oracles [4]. Then $\mathcal{C}_{pk} = Z_{pk} \times \mathcal{M}_\ell$. Finally, the public key is pk together with the description of the hash functions and plaintext-ciphertext spaces. The secret key is sk.

TCPKE.Tok^f. Output $\tau \leftarrow \mathcal{T}_\ell$.

TCPKE.Enc^f. The ciphertext for a message $m \in \mathcal{M}_\ell$ with token τ is

$$c = (f_{pk}(x, y), \widetilde{G}(x, \tau) \oplus m),$$

where $y = \widetilde{H}(x, m)$ and x is uniformly chosen in X_{pk}.

TCPKE.Dec^f. To decrypt a ciphertext $c = (c_1, c_2)$ using token τ, firstly compute $x = $ TPOW.Inv$^f(c_1)$. Then, compute $m = \widetilde{G}(x, \tau) \oplus c_2$ and return m if $c_1 = f_{pk}(x, \widetilde{H}(x, m))$. Otherwise, return the reject symbol $\perp$. If it is not possible to compute either TPOW.Inv$^f(c_1)$ or $\widetilde{G}(x, \tau) \oplus c_2$, return $\perp$.

4.1 Security Against TCPKE.1 Attacks

Let $\mathcal{A}^{\mathsf{TCPKE.1}}[n, t, \epsilon, q_G, q_H, q_D]$ denote an adversary against the TCPKE .1 security of the TCPKE^f scheme that runs, against n different public keys, in time t with advantage ϵ, doing no more than q_G, q_H, and q_D queries to the random oracles $\widetilde{G}$, $\widetilde{H}$ and to the decryption oracle respectively.

Theorem 2. *If there exists an adversary* $\mathcal{A}^{\mathsf{TCPKE.1}}[n, t, \epsilon, q_G, q_H, q_D]$ *against* TCPKE^f, *then there exists an adversary* $\mathcal{B}_{\mathsf{PKE}^f}^{\mathsf{IND-CCA}}[t + \mathcal{O}(q_G + q_H + n), \epsilon/n, q_G, q_H, q_D]$ *against* PKE^f.

Proof: We show that any adversary $\mathcal{A}^{\mathsf{TCPKE.1}}[n, t, \epsilon, q_G, q_H, q_D]$ against TCPKE^f can be used to construct an adversary $\mathcal{B}_{\mathsf{PKE}^f}^{\mathsf{IND-CCA}}[t, \epsilon, q_G, q_H, q_D]$ against PKE^f.

To do this, we proceed in two steps. In the first one, an adversary $\mathcal{A}$ against the TCPKE.1 security of TCPKE^f is converted into an adversary $\mathcal{F}$ against PKE^f in the multi-user setting considered by Bellare, Boldyreva and Micali in [2]. The adversary $\mathcal{F}$ simulates the environment of the TCPKE.1 game for $\mathcal{A}^{\mathsf{TCPKE.1}}$. The PKE^f challenger in the multi-user setting starts by giving n public keys $pk_1, \ldots, pk_n$ to $\mathcal{F}$ corresponding to the scheme PKE^f. After that, $\mathcal{F}$ chooses a polynomial p and sets $\mathcal{T}_\ell = \{0,1\}^{p(\ell)}$. $\mathcal{F}$ sends $pk'_i := (pk_i, \mathcal{T}_\ell)$ to $\mathcal{A}$, for $i = 1, \ldots, n$ as the public keys of n users of the TCPKE scheme. Next, $\mathcal{F}$ chooses a token $\tau \leftarrow \mathcal{T}_\ell$ and gives it to $\mathcal{A}$. The random oracles $\widetilde{H}_i, \widetilde{G}_i$, for $i = 1, \ldots, n$ are simulated by $\mathcal{F}$ by querying its random oracles H_i, G_i in the IND-CCA game in the multi-user setting (remember that H_i, G_i are part of the public key pk_i). In particular,

- $\widetilde{H}_i(\sigma) := H_i(\sigma)$ for any $\sigma \in \{0,1\}^\star$.
- $\widetilde{G}_i(x,\tau) := G_i(x)$ and $\widetilde{G}_i(x,\tau') := G_i(x,\tau')$ for any $x \in X_{pk}$, and $\tau' \neq \tau \in T_\ell$. Finally, $\widetilde{G}_i(\sigma) := G_i(\sigma)$ for any $\sigma \in \{0,1\}^\star$, s.t. $\sigma \notin X_{pk} \times T_\ell$.

The decryption queries made by $\mathcal{A}$ with respect to any sk_i are answered by $\mathcal{F}$ as

$$\mathsf{TCPKE.Dec}(c_1, c_2, sk_i') := \mathsf{PKE.Dec}(c_1, c_2, sk_i),$$

by querying its own decryption oracles in the multi-user IND-CCA game. It is easy to see that $\widetilde{H}_i$ and $\widetilde{G}_i$ behave as random oracles and that the simulation of $\mathcal{A}$ decryption queries is sound.

Once $\mathcal{A}$ starts the challenge phase, $\mathcal{F}$ sends to its IND-CCA multi-user challenger the messages m_0, m_1 chosen by $\mathcal{A}$, and obtains from its challenger ciphertexts $c_i^\star = \mathsf{PKE.Enc}(pk_i, m_b)$ for $i = 1, \ldots, n$. This list of n challenge ciphertexts is sent to $\mathcal{A}$, which outputs a guess b'. The same bit b' is output by $\mathcal{B}$ as its final guess.

The advantage of $\mathcal{F}$ in its IND-CCA game against PKE^f, in the multi-user setting, is exactly the same as the advantage of $\mathcal{A}$, that is, ϵ. The running time of $\mathcal{F}$ is the running time t of $\mathcal{A}$ plus $\mathcal{O}(q_G + q_H)$ to simulate the random oracle queries. Note that we are assuming that deciding if an element belongs to a set is a one unit time operation.

After that, the second reduction transforms an adversary $\mathcal{F}$ against PKE^f in the multi-user setting into an adversary $\mathcal{B}$ against PKE^f in the single-user setting. This reduction can be found in Theorem 1 of [2]. In this case, the advantage of $\mathcal{B}$ in its game is the advantage of $\mathcal{F}$ divided by n, and the running time of $\mathcal{B}$ is the running time of $\mathcal{A}$ plus $\mathcal{O}(\log n)$.

Putting together the two reductions, we obtain the result stated in this theorem: the advantage of $\mathcal{B}$ is ϵ/n, and its running time is $t + \mathcal{O}(q_G + q_H + n)$.   □

Corollary 1. *If f is a TPOW function, then the scheme TCPKE^f is TCPKE.1 secure.*

Proof: It follows immediately from Theorems 1 and 2.   □

4.2   Security Against TCPKE.2 Attacks

Let $\mathcal{A}^{\mathsf{TCPKE.2}}[t, \epsilon, q_G, q_H, q_E]$ denote an adversary against the TCPKE.2 security of the TCPKE^f scheme that runs in time t with advantage ϵ, doing no more than q_G, q_H, and q_E queries to the random oracles $\widetilde{G}$, $\widetilde{H}$ and to the embedded-token encryption oracle respectively.

Theorem 3. *Any adversary $\mathcal{A}^{\mathsf{TCPKE.2}}[t, \epsilon, q_G, q_H, q_E]$ satisfies $\epsilon \leq \dfrac{q_G + q_E}{2^{p(\ell)}}$, where $T_\ell = \{0,1\}^{p(\ell)}$ (in the random oracle model).*

Proof: Let us consider the challenge ciphertext $c^\star$ that $\mathcal{A}$ gets from the TCPKE.2 challenger. We denote by $x^\star, \tau^\star, y^\star$ the values

$$c^\star = (f_{pk}(x^\star, y^\star), G(x^\star, \tau^\star) \oplus m_b),$$

where $y^\star = H(x^\star, m_b)$. Let us denote by AskG the event that $\mathcal{A}$ queries G at the point $(x^\star, \tau^\star)$. Since G is modelled as a random oracle, the value b is independent from $\mathcal{A}$'s view as long as AskG does not hold. Therefore,

$$\Pr[b' = b] = \Pr[b' = b \ \wedge \ \mathsf{AskG}] + \Pr[b' = b \ \wedge \ \neg\mathsf{AskG}] =$$

$$= \Pr[b' = b \mid \mathsf{AskG}] \Pr[\mathsf{AskG}] + \frac{1}{2} \Pr[\wedge\mathsf{AskG}]$$

Due to the fact that $\mathcal{A}$ is in possession of the secret key sk, it can recover the randomness $x^\star$ from $c^\star$. If AskG holds, $\mathcal{A}$ can compute m_b from $c^\star$ and it can check if $c^\star = (f_{pk}(x^\star, y^\star), G(x^\star, \tau^\star) \oplus m_b)$. Therefore $\Pr[b' = b | \mathsf{AskG}] = 1$ and

$$\Pr[b' = b] = \frac{1}{2} + \frac{1}{2} \Pr[\mathsf{AskG}].$$

Finally, it lacks to compute an upper bound for $\Pr[\mathsf{AskG}]$. To do this, notice that $\mathcal{A}$ has two ways of evaluating G at $(x, \tau^\star)$ for $x \in X_{pk}$:

- By directly querying G at $(x, \tau^\star)$.
- By querying the embedded-encryption oracle $c = (c_1, c_2) = \mathsf{TCPKE.Enc}(pk, \tau^\star, m)$ on $m \in \mathcal{M}_\ell$. Let $x \in X_{pk}$ the randomness used by the encryption oracle. Then, $\mathcal{A}$ can recover x by using the secret key sk and it computes $G(x, \tau^\star) := c_2 \oplus H(x, m)$.

It follows that $\Pr[\mathsf{AskG}] \leq \dfrac{q_G + q_E}{2^{p(\ell)}}$, where $\mathcal{T}_\ell = \{0, 1\}^{p(\ell)}$. Finally,

$$\epsilon = \mid 2 \Pr[b' = b] - 1 \mid \ \leq \ \frac{q_G + q_E}{2^{p(\ell)}}.$$

$\square$

4.3   Security Against TCPKE.3 Attacks

Let $\mathcal{A}^{\mathsf{TCPKE.3}}[t, \epsilon, q_G, q_H, q_D]$ denote an adversary against the TCPKE.3 security of the TCPKE^f scheme that runs in time t with advantage ϵ, doing no more than q_G, q_H, and q_D queries to the random oracles $\widetilde{G}$, $\widetilde{H}$ and to the decryption oracle respectively.

Theorem 4. *Any adversary* $\mathcal{A}^{\mathsf{TCPKE.3}}[t, \epsilon, q_G, q_H, q_D]$ *satisfies* $\epsilon \leq \dfrac{1}{|Y_{pk}|}$ *(in the random oracle model).*

Proof. The goal of $\mathcal{A}$ is to find $m \neq m' \in \mathcal{M}_\ell$, $c \in \mathcal{C}_{pk}$ and $\tau \neq \tau' \in \mathcal{T}_\ell$ such that

$$c = (f_{pk}(x, \widetilde{H}(x, m)), \widetilde{G}(x, \tau) \oplus m) = (f_{pk}(x', \widetilde{H}(x', m')), \widetilde{G}(x', \tau') \oplus m) \quad (1)$$

From the definition of a TPOW function, we know that f_{pk} is injective. Therefore, (1) implies that $x = x'$ and $\widetilde{H}(x, m) = \widetilde{H}(x, m')$. The fact that $\widetilde{H}$ is modelled as a random oracle implies that $\Pr[\widetilde{H}(x, m) = \widetilde{H}(x, m')] = 1/|Y_{pk}|$ for $m \neq m'$ and then it immediately follows $\mathsf{Adv}_{\mathcal{A}_3}^{\mathsf{TCPKE.3}}(1^\ell) \leq 1/|Y_{pk}|$. $\square$

4.4   Instantiation with RSA

For example, it is possible to instantiate our general construction by using RSA as the TPOW function. Note in particular that any injective trapdoor one-way function $\tilde{f}(x)$ such as RSA can be easily converted into a TPOW by using $f(x,y) = (\tilde{f}(x), y)$.

The TCPKE^{RSA} scheme resulting from this instantiation is almost as efficient as the RSA primitive. Moreover, in this case the concrete security result stated in Theorem 1 can be made tight, since the RSA TPOW function is easy verifiable, that is, given z it is easy to verify if there exists y such that $f(x,y) = z$. It is shown in [9] that easy verifiable functions provide a tight security reduction for the Fujisaki-Okamoto transformation, which in our case implies that that a TCPKE.1 adversary with advantage ϵ can be converted into an algorithm breaking RSA with advantage $n\epsilon$. On the contrary, the schemes in [1] present a less tighter security reduction under TCPKE.1 adversaries to the Computational Diffie-Hellman assumption.

5   Conclusion

In this paper we have revisited the work [1] where Baek, Safavi-Naini and Susilo introduced a new cryptographic primitive called token-controlled public key encryption. We have added a new security property which is naturally desirable for these schemes, and which is not satisfied by the specific schemes proposed in [1]. We believe that the essential security model for this primitive is now complete, although additional properties might be added in the future.

In the second part of our work, we propose and analyze a general construction of TCPKE schemes from trapdoor partial one-way functions. The resulting schemes are simple and efficient, and satisfy the three required security properties in the random oracle model. Previously, only particular instantiations of TCPKE were known, and they were less efficient than the schemes obtained with our construction when instantiated with El Gamal or RSA trapdoor functions. The natural problem which remains open is to design a secure token-controlled public key encryption scheme in the standard model.

References

1. J. Baek, R. Safavi-Naini and W. Susilo. Token-controlled public key encryption. *Proceedings of ISPEC'05*, Springer-Verlag, LNCS **3439**, pp. 386–397 (2005).
2. M. Bellare, A. Boldyreva and S. Micali. Public-key encryption in a multi-user setting: security proofs and improvements. *Advances in Cryptology - Proceedings of Eurocrypt'00*, Springer-Verlag, LNCS **1807**, pp. 259–274 (2000).
3. M. Bellare, A. Desai, D. Pointcheval and P. Rogaway. Relations among notions of security for public-key encryption schemes. *Advances in Cryptology - Proceedings of Crypto'98*, Springer-Verlag, LNCS **1462**, pp. 26–45 (1998).
4. M. Bellare and P. Rogaway. Random oracles are practical: a paradigm for designing efficient protocols. *Proceedings of CCS'93*, ACM, pp. 62–73 (1993).

5. D. Boneh and M. Franklin. Identity-Based encryption from the Weil pairing. *SIAM Journal of Computing*, **32** (3), pp. 586–615 (2003). An extended abstract of the same title appeared at Crypto'01.
6. G. Di Crescenzo, R. Ostrovsky and S. Rajagopalan. Conditional oblivious transfer and timed-release encryption. *Advances in Cryptology - Proceedings of Eurocrypt'99*, Springer-Verlag, LNCS **1592**, pp. 74–89 (1999).
7. E. Fujisaki and T. Okamoto. Secure integration of asymmetric and symmetric encryption schemes. *Advances in Cryptology - Proceedings of Crypto'99*, Springer-Verlag, LNCS **1666**, pp. 537–554 (1999).
8. T. ElGamal. A public key cryptosystem and a signature scheme based on discrete logarithms. *IEEE Transactions on Information Theory* **31** (4), pp. 469–472 (1985).
9. D. Galindo, S. Martín, P. Morillo and J.L. Villar. Fujisaki-Okamoto hybrid encryption revisited. *International Journal of Information Security*, **4** (4) pp. 228–241 (2005).
10. J. Garay and C. Pomerance. Timed fair exchange of standard signatures. *Proceedings of Financial Cryptography'03*, Springer-Verlag, LNCS **2742**, pp. 190–207 (2003).
11. T. May. Timed-release crypto. Manuscript available at `http://www.cyphernet.org/cyphernomicon/chapter14/14.5.html` (1993).
12. R. L. Rivest, A. Shamir and L. M. Adleman. A method for obtaining digital signatures and public-key cryptosystems. *Communications of the ACM* **21** (2), pp. 120–126 (1978).
13. R. Rivest, A. Shamir and D. Wagner. Timed-lock puzzles and timed-release crypto. Technical report, MIT/LCS/TR-684 (1996).

Timed-Release and Key-Insulated Public Key Encryption

Jung Hee Cheon[1], Nicholas Hopper[2], Yongdae Kim[2], and Ivan Osipkov[2,*]

[1] Seoul National University, Korea
jhcheon@math.snu.ac.kr
[2] University of Minnesota - Twin Cities
{hopper, kyd, osipkov}@cs.umn.edu

Abstract. In this paper we consider two security notions related to Identity Based Encryption: Key-insulated public key encryption, introduced by Dodis, Katz, Xu and Yung; and Timed-Release Public Key cryptography, introduced independently by May and Rivest, Shamir and Wagner. We first formalize the notion of secure timed-release public key encryption, and show that, despite several differences in its formulation, it is equivalent to strongly key-insulated public key encryption (with optimal threshold and random access key updates). Next, we introduce the concept of an authenticated timed-release cryptosystem, briefly consider generic constructions, and then give a construction based on a single primitive which is efficient and provably secure.

Keywords: timed-release, authenticated encryption, key-insulated encryption.

1 Introduction

Timed-Release cryptography. The goal of timed-release cryptography is to "send a message into the future." One way to do this is to encrypt a message such that the receiver cannot decrypt the ciphertext until a specific time in the future. Such a primitive would have many practical applications, a few examples include preventing a dishonest auctioneer from prior opening of bids in a sealed-bid auction [26], preventing early opening of votes in e-voting schemes, and delayed verification of a signed document, such as electronic lotteries [28] and check cashing. The problem of timed-release cryptography was first mentioned by May [21] and then discussed in detail by Rivest *et. al.* [26]. Let us assume that Alice wants to send a message to Bob such that Bob will not be able to open it until a certain time. The possible solutions fall into two categories:

– Time-lock puzzle approach. Alice encrypts her message and Bob needs to perform non-parallelizable computation without stopping for the required time to decrypt it.

---

* The third and the fourth authors were supported, in part, by NSF Career Grant CNS-0448423 and by the Intelligent Storage Consortium at the Digital Technology Center (DTC), University of Minnesota. The first author was supported by Korea Telecom. *: Contact author.

– Agent-based approach. Alice encrypts a message such that Bob needs some secret value, published by a trusted agent on the required date, in order to decrypt the message.

The first approach puts immense computational overhead on the message receiver, which makes it impractical for real-life scenarios. In addition, knowing the computational complexity of decryption, while giving us a lower bound on the time Bob may need to decrypt the message, does not guarantee that the plaintext will be available at a certain date. Still, this approach is widely used for specific applications [9, 4, 28, 19, 18]. The agent-based approach, on the other hand, relieves Bob from performing non-stop computation, sets the date of decryption precisely and does not require Alice to have information on Bob's capabilities. This comes at a price, though: the agents have to be trusted and they have to be available at the designated time.

In this paper we concentrate on the agent-based approach. Several agent-based constructions were suggested by Rivest *et. al.* [26]. For example, the agent could encrypt messages on request with a secret key which will be published on a designated date by the agent. It also could precompute pairs of public/private keys, publish all public keys and release the private keys on the required days. A different scheme was proposed in [13], in which non-malleable encryption was used and receiver would engage in a conditional oblivious transfer protocol with the agent to decrypt the message. In [11], the authors proposed to use Boneh and Franklin's IBE scheme [8] for timed-release encryption: for that, one can replace the identity in an IBE scheme with the time of decryption. Similar proposals appear in [20, 7]. While some of these proposals contain informal proofs of security, none of them consider and/or give a formal treatment of the security properties of timed-release public key encryption (or TR-PKE).

Since all known efficient constructions rely on the Boneh-Franklin IBE construction, a natural question to ask is if the existence of IBE is necessary for an efficient timed-release public key encryption. In this paper, we formalize the security requirements of TR-PKE and show that indeed this is the case: the existence of secure TR-PKE is equivalent to the existence of strongly key-insulated encryption with optimal threshold and random access key updates; existence of which in turn is known to be equivalent to the existence of IBE [5, 14].

SKIE-OTRU: Strongly key-insulated encryption with Optimal Threshold and Random Access Key Updates. Strongly key-insulated encryption addresses the problem of computer intrusion by breaking up the lifetime of a public key into periods, and splitting the decryption key between the user (say, a mobile device) and a trusted "helper" (say, a desktop server) so that:

– (*Sequential Key Updates*) At the beginning of each time period, the helper securely transmits a "helper secret key" hsk_i to the user, which he combines with his previous key, usk_{i-1}, to obtain a secret key usk_i that will decrypt messages encrypted during time period i.

– (*Random Access Key Updates*) Given any usk_i and hsk_j, the user can compute usk_j. This is useful for error recovery and it also allows the user to decrypt old messages.

- (*User Compromise*) An adversary who is given access to (usk_i, hsk_i) for several time periods i cannot break the encryption for a new time period.
- (*Helper Compromise*) An adversary given only the hsk cannot break the encryption scheme.

Combining results of Bellare/Palacio [5] and Dodis/Katz [14] [1], it follows that *existence of SKIE-OTRU is equivalent to IBE.*

Authentication for Timed-Release Encryption. Many of the applications of timed-release cryptography mentioned above require some form of authentication as well. For example, if there is no authentication of bids in a sealed auction, any bidder may be able to forge bids for others, or force the auction to fail by submitting an unreasonably high bid. In this paper, we consider the security properties required by these applications and develop formal security conditions for a Timed-Release Public Key Authenticated Encryption (TR-PKAE) scheme.

One avenue for developing a TR-PKAE scheme would be composing an unauthenticated TR-PKE scheme with either a signature scheme or a (non-timed-release) PKAE scheme. Although such constructions are possible, we note that the details of this composition are not trivial; examples from [2, 14] illustrate that naive constructions can fail to provide the expected security properties. Additionally, we note that such schemes are likely to suffer a performance penalty relative to a scheme based on a single primitive. Thus we also introduce a provably secure construction of a TR-PKAE scheme that is essentially as efficient as previous constructions of *non-authenticated* TR-PKE schemes [11, 20, 7].

Our Contribution. This paper proposes a new primitive that provides timed-release public key authenticated encryption (in short, TR-PKAE). The contribution of this paper is four fold:

- We give the first formal analysis of the security requirements for timed-release public key encryption (TR-PKE) and show that this notion is equivalent to SKIE-OTRU.
- We introduce the notion of TR-PKAE, as satisfying four notions: IND-KC-CCA2, security against adaptive chosen ciphertext attacks under compromise of the timed-release agent and sender's private key; TUF-CTXT, or third-party unforgeability of ciphertexts; IND-RTR-KC-CCA2, or receiver undecryptability before release time under compromise of sender's private key; and RUF-TR-CTXT, or receiver unforgeability before release time.
- We introduce a protocol that provides authenticated timed-release public key encryption using a single primitive. The proposed protocol is essentially as efficient as Boneh and Franklin's chosen-ciphertext secure IBE scheme [8] (FullIdent, which will be referred to as BF-IBE in the rest of the paper) and is provably secure in the random oracle model. The proposed protocol requires minimal infrastructure (a single trusted agent) that can be shared among many applications and can be naturally converted to a threshold version,

---

[1] Bellare/Palacio showed that KIE-OTRU is equivalent to IBE, while Dodis/Katz showed equivalence of SKIE-OTRU and KIE-OTRU.

which provides robustness as well as stronger security by allowing outputs of multiple agents to be used.

Overview of our construction. Consider a public agent (similar to NTP server [23]), called TiPuS (<u>Ti</u>med-release <u>Pu</u>blic <u>S</u>erver), which at discrete time-intervals publishes new *self-authenticating* information $I_T = f(P_T, s)$ for current time T, where f and P_T are public, and s is secret. Alice can encrypt a message for Bob at time T using P_T, her private key and Bob's public key. *Only when* I_T *is published on day* T, will Bob be able to decrypt the message using I_T, his private key and Alice's public key.

We implement the above setting using an admissible bilinear map e (see Section 4.1), which along with the choice of groups and generator P is chosen independently of TiPuS. Each TiPuS chooses a secret $s \in \mathbb{Z}_q$ and publishes $P_{pub} = sP$. At time T, the TiPuS publishes $I_T = sP_T = sH(T)$ [2] (*i.e.* the private key for identity T in BF-IBE [8]), where H is a cryptographic hash function.

Let $(sk_a, pk_a) = (a, aP)$ and $(sk_b, pk_b) = (b, bP)$ be Alice's and Bob's authenticated private/public key pairs respectively. To *encrypt* message m for Bob, 1) Alice computes bilinear map $d = e(sP + r_1 \cdot bP, (r_2 + a)P_T)$ for random r_1, r_2, and applies hash function H_2 to obtain $K = H_2(d)$, 2) she then encrypts message m as $E_K(m)$, where E_K is a symmetric encryption using key K. Bob also receives $r_1 P_T$ and $r_2 P$. To *decrypt* the ciphertext, 1) Bob, having sP_T, computes d as $e(r_2 P + aP, sP_T + b \cdot r_1 P_T)$ [3], 2) applying hash function H_2, Bob computes K and uses it to decrypt $E_K(m)$.[4] The full detailed protocol and all required definitions/discussions are presented in later sections.

Note the following practical aspects exhibited by the scheme: 1) (*User Secret vs TiPuS Secret*) the secret value of TiPuS, system parameters and users' private keys are completely independent. It will be shown later that compromise of TiPuS does not jeopardize confidentiality and unforgeability of user ciphertexts; 2) (*Sharing*) the published value sP_T can be shared among multiple applications; 3) (*Scalability*) the protocol can take full advantage of a) several independent TiPuS's, [5] b) threshold generation of sP_T [24]. The increase in computational complexity is minimal when such schemes are applied to the protocol.

2   Timed-Release Public Key Encryption (TR-PKE)

In this section we formalize the functionality and security requirements for a timed-release public key encryption system. These requirements are meant

---

[2] The authenticity of I_T can be verified by checking equality $e(P_{pub}, P_T)$, since by bilinearity $e(sP, H(T)) = e(P, sH(T)) = e(P, H(T))^s$.

[3] Note that according to properties of bilinear map, $e(r_2 P + aP, sP_T + b \cdot r_1 P_T) = e((r_2 + a)P, (s + b \cdot r_1)P_T) = e((s + r_1 \cdot b)P, (r_2 + a)P_T) = d$.

[4] Without authentication, this scheme is similar to Bellare and Palacio's construction of an SKIE-OTRU scheme, in which $d = e(sP + bP, r_2 P_T)$. However note that it cannot be used for timed-release: the receiver can publish as public key $bP = \tau P - sP$ for any chosen τ allowing him to decrypt any ciphertext before designated time.

[5] If $s_i P$ is P_{pub} of the i-th token generator, then combined P_{pub} is $\sum s_i P$ and combined sP_T is $\sum s_i P_T$.

to capture the required security requirements not addressed in previous work [21, 26, 11, 20, 7]; in particular they do not address the authentication requirements, which we add in section 3.

2.1 Functional Requirements

Formally, we define a timed-release public-key encryption system Γ to be a tuple of five randomized algorithms:

- Setup, which given input 1^k (the security parameter), produces public parameters π_g, which include hash functions, message and ciphertext spaces among others.
- TRSetup, which on input π_g, produces a pair (δ, π_{tr}) where δ is a *master secret* and π_{tr} the corresponding timed-release public parameters. This setup is carried out by TiPuS which keeps the master secret key confidential, while all other parameters are public. *We denote the combined public parameters of π_g and π_{tr} by π.*
- KeyGen, given public parameters π_g, outputs a pair of secret key and public key (sk, pk).
- TG(π, δ, T) computes the token tkn_T corresponding to time T using (δ, π). This functionality is performed by TiPuS which publishes tkn_T at time T.
- Encrypt(π, pk, m, T) computes the timed-release ciphertext c denoting the encryption with public key pk of message m with public parameters π and time encoding T.
- Decrypt$(\pi, sk, \widehat{c}, tkn_T)$ outputs the plaintext corresponding to $\widehat{c}$ if decryption is successful or the special symbol `fail` otherwise.

For consistency, we require that Decrypt$(\pi, sk, $ Encrypt$(\pi, pk, m, T), $ TG$(\pi, \delta, T))=$ m, for all valid (pk, sk), (π, δ), T, and m,

2.2 Security

It is standard to require that the PKE cryptosystem be secure against adaptive chosen-ciphertext (IND-CCA2) adversaries [25, 3, 2]. Ideally, in TR-PKE, one should separate the timed-release security from security of PKE. Namely, TR-PKE should maintain receiver confidentiality properties even if the timed-release master secret is compromised. To that effect, we require that IND-CCA2 security against a third party is provided even when master secret is given to the adversary. We model this attack by a slightly modified IND-CCA2 game, shown in Figure 1. Here, in addition to adaptively choosing two "challenge plaintexts" that the adversary will need to distinguish between, he also adaptively chooses a "challenge time" for which his challenge ciphertext will be decrypted; he wins when he can tell whether his challenge ciphertext is an encryption of his first or second plaintext for the challenge time, given access to a decryption oracle and the master secret key of the TiPuS.

The timed-release functionality is provided by the token-generating infrastructure (i.e. TiPuS). Not knowing the corresponding token is what keeps the receiver from decrypting ciphertext until a designated time. To effect secure

Algorithm 2.1: $\mathsf{Exp}_{A,\Gamma}^{\mathsf{IND-CCA2}}(k)$

$\pi_g \leftarrow \mathsf{Setup}(1^k)$
$(\delta, \pi_{tr}) \leftarrow \mathsf{TRSetup}(1^k)$
$(pk, sk) \leftarrow \mathsf{KeyGen}(\pi_g)$
$(m_0, m_1, T^*) \leftarrow A^{\mathsf{Decrypt}(\pi, sk, \cdot, \cdot)}(\pi, \delta, pk)$
$\beta \leftarrow_R \{0, 1\}$
$c^* \leftarrow \mathsf{Encrypt}(\pi, pk, m_\beta, T^*)$
$\beta' \leftarrow A^{\mathsf{Decrypt}(\pi, sk, \cdot, \cdot)}(\pi, \delta, pk, c^*)$
if (A queried $\mathsf{Decrypt}(\pi, sk, c^*, tkn_{T^*})$)
   then return (false)
   else return ($\beta' = \beta$)

Algorithm 2.2: $\mathsf{Exp}_{A,\Gamma}^{\mathsf{IND-RTR-CCA2}}(k)$

$\pi_g \leftarrow \mathsf{Setup}(1^k)$
$(\delta, \pi_{tr}) \leftarrow \mathsf{TRSetup}(1^k)$
(m_0, m_1, pk^*, T^*)
   $\leftarrow A^{\mathsf{TG}(\pi, \delta, \cdot), \mathsf{Decrypt}^*(\pi, \delta, \cdot, \cdot, \cdot)}(\pi)$
$\beta \leftarrow_R \{0, 1\}$
$c^* \leftarrow \mathsf{Encrypt}(\pi, pk^*, m_\beta, T^*)$
$\beta' \leftarrow A^{\mathsf{TG}(\pi, \delta, \cdot), \mathsf{Decrypt}^*(\pi, \delta, \cdot, \cdot, \cdot)}(\pi, c^*)$
if (A queried $\mathsf{Decrypt}^*(\pi, sk^*, c^*, T^*)$,
   where sk^* corresponds to pk^*,
   or A queried $\mathsf{TG}(\pi, \delta, T^*)$)
   then return (false)
   else return ($\beta' = \beta$)

$$\mathsf{Adv}_{A,\Gamma}^{\mathsf{IND-CCA2}}(k) = \Pr[\mathsf{Exp}_{A,\Gamma}^{\mathsf{IND-CCA2}}(k) = \mathsf{true}] - \tfrac{1}{2}$$
$$\mathsf{Adv}_{A,\Gamma}^{\mathsf{IND-RTR-CCA2}}(k) = \Pr[\mathsf{Exp}_{A,\Gamma}^{\mathsf{IND-RTR-CCA2}}(k) = \mathsf{true}] - \tfrac{1}{2}$$

Fig. 1. TR-PKE security experiments for the IND-CCA2 and IND-RTR-CCA2 games

timed-release, any TR-PKE cryptosystem must provide confidentiality against the receiver itself until the corresponding token is made available. We model this property by the IND-RTR-CCA2 game, shown in Figure 1; in this game, we modify the basic IND-CCA2 game by allowing the adversary to adaptively choose receiver public key pk^* and time T^* for the challenge. Instead of access to the timed-release secret, the adversary is given access to arbitrary tokens tkn_T, where $T \neq T^*$, and a decryption oracle $\mathsf{Decrypt}^*(\pi, \delta, \cdot, \cdot, \cdot)$ which computes $\mathsf{Decrypt}(\pi, \cdot, \cdot, \mathsf{TG}(\pi, \delta, \cdot))$. The adversary may thus compute the decryption of any ciphertext for any time, *except* the challenge ciphertext in the challenge time T^* with chosen public key pk^*. We say a timed-release public-key cryptosystem Γ is secure if every polynomial time adversary A has negligible advantages $\mathsf{Adv}_{A,\Gamma}^{\mathsf{IND-CCA2}}(k)$ and $\mathsf{Adv}_{A,\Gamma}^{\mathsf{IND-RTR-CCA2}}(k)$.

2.3 Strongly Key-Insulated Public Encryption and Timed-Release

The notion of key-insulated public key encryption has been discussed in [15, 16, 5]. As mentioned previously, combining Bellare/Palacio [5] and Dodis/Katz [14] one obtains that the existence of secure SKIE-OTRU is a necessary and sufficient condition for the existence of secure IBE. Briefly, a SKIE-OTRU consists of following algorithms: KG, which generates a triple (pk, usk_0, hsk) of public key, initial user secret key, and master helper key; HKU which computes a *stage i helper secret key* hsk_i given (pk, hsk, i); UKU, which computes the *stage i user secret key* usk_i given i, pk, hsk_i, usk_{i-1}; RUKU, which computes the *stage i user secret key* usk_i given $i, j, pk, hsk_i, usk_j, \forall i \geq 1, j \geq 0$; Enc, which produces a ciphertext corresponding to m to be decrypted in stage i, given (pk, m, i); and Dec, which, given (i, pk, usk_i, c) attempts to decrypt a ciphertext for stage i. Intuitively, hsk is given to a "helper", who will securely transmit, at the beginning of each stage i, the secret hsk_i to the user. The user can then compute usk_i, delete any old usk's in his possession, and use usk_i to decrypt messages sent to him during stage i. Existence of RUKU facilitates error recovery and allows for decryption of old ciphertexts.

A SKIE (and SKIE-OTRU) scheme is considered CCA-secure with optimal threshold if two conditions hold: (1) given access to pk, a decryption oracle, and pairs (hsk_i, usk_i) of his choosing, an adversary cannot break the encryption scheme for a stage j for which he has not been given hsk_j; and (2) given pk, hsk, and a decryption oracle, an adversary cannot break the encryption scheme for any stage [15, 16, 5]. The idea of separation of the timed-release master and user secrets in a TR-PKE very closely parallels the notions of helper and user secrets in a key-insulated cryptosystem; and both involve a "time period" parameter for encryption and decryption. Furthermore, the two security conditions for a SKIE scheme, in which either user keys or helper keys are assumed to be compromised, closely resemble the conditions IND-CCA2 and IND-RTR-CCA2 developed here.

However, there is a key difference between the SKIE-OTRU and TR-PKE notions. In the SKIE-OTRU setting, a helper is associated with at most one user, and cooperates exclusively with that user, whereas in the TR-PKE setting, it is assumed that many users may use the services of the TiPuS server, but the interaction between each user and the server will be minimal. This results in several operational differences: 1) *User and Master Key Generation* – in a TR-PKE scheme, they are generated independently, whereas in a SKIE-OTRU they are generated jointly; 2) *Dissemination of secrets per time period* – a SKIE scheme must use a secure channel to send the hsk_i to only one user, whereas the tokens generated by a TiPuS are assumed to be publicly disseminated; 3) *Security notion of "user compromise"* – a SKIE scheme's notion of "user compromise" is limited to chosen time periods and the keys are generated by the victim, whereas in TR-PKE's notion the attacker is the user itself and can generate its public key adaptively (perhaps without necessarily knowing the corresponding secret key) in order to break timed-release confidentiality. The following theorem shows that despite these differences, these notions are essentially equivalent.

Theorem 1. *There exists a (chosen-ciphertext) secure timed-release public key cryptosystem if and only if there exists a secure strongly key-insulated public-key encryption scheme with optimal threshold that allows random-access key updates.*

Proof. (Sketch) Suppose we have a secure TR-PKE scheme $\Gamma = ($Setup, TRSetup, TG, Encrypt, Decrypt$)$. We construct a SKIE-OTRU scheme from Γ as follows. Set $\mathsf{KG}(1^k) = ((\pi, pk), sk, \delta)$, where $(\pi, \delta) \leftarrow \mathsf{TRSetup}(1^k)$ and $(pk, sk) \leftarrow \mathsf{KeyGen}(\pi)$; $\mathsf{HKU}((\pi, pk), \delta, i) = tkn_i$, where $tkn_i \leftarrow \mathsf{TG}(\pi, \delta, i)$; $\mathsf{UKU}(i, (\pi, pk), tkn_i, (sk, tkn_{i-1})) = (sk, tkn_i)$; $\mathsf{RUKU}(i, j, (\pi, pk), tkn_i, (sk, tkn_j)) = (sk, tkn_i)$; $\mathsf{Enc}((\pi, pk), m, i) = c$, where $c \leftarrow \mathsf{Encrypt}(\pi, pk, m, i)$; and set $\mathsf{Dec}(i, (\pi, pk), (sk, tkn_i), c) = \mathsf{Decrypt}(\pi, sk, c, tkn_i)$. This scheme essentially makes the TiPuS server in TR-PKE scheme Γ into a helper for an SKIE-OTRU scheme.

It is easy to see that this scheme must be a secure SKIE-OTRU scheme. Suppose an attacker given access to $spk = (\pi, pk)$, $hsk = \delta$ and a decryption oracle can break the scheme; then it is easy to see that such an adversary can also be used to mount an IND-CCA2 attack on Γ, since these are exactly the resources given to an adversary in the IND-CCA2 game. Likewise, an adversary who can break the scheme given access to $spk = (\pi, pk)$, selected $(usk_i, hsk_i) = (sk, tkn_i)$ pairs, and a decryption oracle can easily be used to mount an IND-RTR-CCA2 attack on Γ: when the SKIE adversary makes a corruption request for stage i, the corresponding RTR-CCA2 adversary queries its TG oracle for tkn_i and can forward (sk, tkn_i) to the SKIE adversary since the RTR-CCA2 adversary gets sk as an input; all other queries made by the SKIE adversary can be passed directly to the corresponding oracles of the RTR-CCA2 adversary.

Now suppose we have a secure SKIE-OTRU scheme Σ. If Σ has the additional property that KG can be implemented as two independent keying algorithms that generate (pk_h, hsk) and (pk_u, usk), then it is straightforward to transform Σ into a TR-PKE scheme. Since we would not expect this property to hold in general, we work around this problem as follows. We know that by the existence of Σ there also exists an ordinary chosen-ciphertext secure PKC $\Pi = (\mathsf{PKGen}, \mathsf{PKEnc}, \mathsf{PKDec})$. The idea behind our construction is that TRSetup will sample $(spk, hsk, usk_0) \leftarrow \Sigma.\mathsf{KG}(1^k)$ and set $\pi = spk$ and $\delta = (hsk, usk_0)$; KeyGen will sample $(pk, sk) \leftarrow \Pi.\mathsf{PKGen}(1^k)$ and output (pk, sk). $\mathsf{TG}(\pi, \delta, \mathsf{i})$ will first compute $hsk_i = \mathsf{HKU}(spk, hsk, i)$ and then use usk_0 and hsk_i to compute $tkn_i = usk_i = \mathsf{RUKU}(i, 0, spk, usk_0, hsk_i)$. Encryption and Decryption will use the multiple-encryption technique of Dodis and Katz [14].[6] Applying the results of [14], an IND-CCA2 attack on this scheme reduces to a chosen-ciphertext attack on Π, while an IND-RTR-CCA2 attack (even when receiver chooses its public key adaptively) on this scheme reduces to an SKIE chosen-ciphertext attack on Σ.

3   Authenticated TR-PKE (TR-PKAE)

The notion of authenticated encryption has been explored in depth in [2, 1]. In this section we adapt these definitions to give formal security and functionality requirements for a TR-PKAE scheme.

3.1   Basic Cryptosystem

The syntactic definition of a TR-PKAE is essentially the same as that of a TR-PKE with the addition of the sender's public and secret key. Namely, the types of Setup, TRSetup, KeyGen and TG stay the same, but Encrypt and Decrypt are modified to take into account sender's keys:

- Encrypt(π, sk_A, pk_B, m, T) returns an authenticated timed-release ciphertext c denoting the encryption from sender A to receiver B of m for time T.

---

[6] Specifically, to encrypt message m for time T, we: (1) pick $s_1 \leftarrow U_{|m|}$, and set $s_2 = m \oplus s_1$, (2) pick signing and verification keys (SK, VK) for a one-time signature scheme, (3) let $c_1 = \Sigma.\mathsf{Enc}^{VK}(spk, s_1, T)$, $c_2 = \Pi.\mathsf{PKEnc}^{VK}(pk, s_2)$, and (4) output $(VK, c_1, c_2, \mathsf{Sig}(VK, (T, c_1, c_2)))$. Decryption follows the scheme of [14], except that c_1 is decrypted using $tkn_T = usk_T$.

Algorithm 3.1: $\mathsf{Exp}_{A,\Gamma}^{\mathsf{IND-KC-CCA2}}(k)$

$\pi_g \leftarrow \mathsf{Setup}(1^k)$
$(\delta, \pi_{tr}) \leftarrow \mathsf{TRSetup}(1^k)$
$(pk_a, sk_a) \leftarrow \mathsf{KeyGen}(\pi_g)$
$(pk_b, sk_b) \leftarrow \mathsf{KeyGen}(\pi_g)$
$\kappa \leftarrow (\pi, \delta, pk_a, sk_a, pk_b)$
(m_0, m_1, T^*)
$\quad \leftarrow A^{\mathsf{Decrypt}(\pi, pk_a, sk_b, \cdot, \cdot)}(\kappa)$
$\beta \leftarrow_R \{0,1\}$
$c^* \leftarrow \mathsf{Encrypt}(\pi, sk_a, pk_b, m_\beta, T^*)$
$\beta' \leftarrow A^{\mathsf{Decrypt}(\pi, pk_a, sk_b, \cdot, \cdot)}(\kappa, c^*)$
if (A queried
$\quad \mathsf{Decrypt}(\pi, pk_a, sk_b, c^*, tkn_{T^*}))$
then return (false)
else return ($\beta' = \beta$)

Algorithm 3.2: $\mathsf{Exp}_{A,\Gamma}^{\mathsf{IND-RTR-KC-CCA2}}(k)$

$\pi_g \leftarrow \mathsf{Setup}(1^k)$
$(\delta, \pi_{tr}) \leftarrow \mathsf{TRSetup}(1^k)$
$(pk_a, sk_a) \leftarrow \mathsf{KeyGen}(\pi_g)$
$\kappa \leftarrow (\pi, pk_a, sk_a)$
(m_0, m_1, pk_b^*, T^*)
$\quad \leftarrow A^{\mathsf{TG}(\pi, \delta, \cdot), \mathsf{Decrypt}^*(\pi, \delta, pk_a, \cdot, \cdot, \cdot)}(\kappa)$
$\beta \leftarrow_R \{0,1\}$
$c^* \leftarrow \mathsf{Encrypt}(\pi, sk_a, pk_b^*, m_\beta, T^*)$
$\beta' \leftarrow A^{\mathsf{TG}(\pi, \delta, \cdot), \mathsf{Decrypt}^*(\pi, \delta, pk_a, \cdot, \cdot, \cdot)}(\kappa, c^*)$
if (A queried $\mathsf{Decrypt}^*(\pi, pk_a, sk_b^*, c^*, T^*)$
or $\mathsf{TG}(\pi, \delta, T^*))$
then return (false)
else return ($\beta' = \beta$)

$$\mathsf{Adv}_{A,\Gamma}^{\mathsf{IND-KC-CCA2}}(k) = \Pr[\mathsf{Exp}_{A,\Gamma}^{\mathsf{IND-KC-CCA2}}(k) = \mathsf{true}] - \tfrac{1}{2}$$
$$\mathsf{Adv}_{A,\Gamma}^{\mathsf{KC-RTR-KC-CCA2}}(k) = \Pr[\mathsf{Exp}_{A,\Gamma}^{\mathsf{IND-RTR-KC-CCA2}}(k) = \mathsf{true}] - \tfrac{1}{2}$$

Fig. 2. TR-PKAE experiments for the IND-KC-CCA2 and IND-RTR-KC-CCA2 games

- $\mathsf{Decrypt}(\pi, pk_A, sk_B, \widehat{c}, tkn_T)$ outputs plaintext $\widehat{m}$ if both decryption and authentication are successful and the special symbol `fail` otherwise.

The consistency requirement is modified to require that, for all valid (pk_A, sk_A), (pk_B, sk_B), (π, δ), T, and m, $\mathsf{Decrypt}(\pi, pk_A, sk_B, \mathsf{Encrypt}(\pi, sk_A, pk_B, m, T), \mathsf{TG}(\pi, \delta, T)) = m$.

3.2 Security

Confidentiality. The confidentiality requirements of a TR-PKAE are essentially the same as the confidentiality requirements of a TR-PKE; *except* that we make the conservative assumption that the third party (in the case of IND-CCA2) or the receiver (in the case of IND-RTR-CCA2) has compromised the sender's secret key. This results in two new notions, IND-KC-CCA2 and IND-RTR-KC-CCA2, which we define formally in Figure 2. As before, we say that a TR-PKAE scheme provides confidentiality if every polynomial time adversary has negligible advantage, as defined in Figure 2.

As in the case of TR-PKE, the difference between IND-KC-CCA2 and IND-RTR-KC-CCA2 is in reversal of adversary roles. In IND-RTR-KC-CCA2, the goal is to ensure security against the receiver itself prior to the designated time.

Ciphertext (Plaintext) Forgery. For authentication properties of TR-PKAE, we concentrate on ciphertext forgery (plaintext forgery is defined analogously). We consider two types of ciphertext forgery: *third-party forgery* (TUF-CTXT), by an adversary that does not know the sender's and receiver's private keys but knows the master secret; and *forgery by the ciphertext receiver* (RUF-CTXT) [2]. If the TR-PKAE is not secure against TUF-CTXT then the scheme cannot claim authentication properties since a third party may be able to forge new (perhaps decrypting to junk) ciphertexts between two users. If a TR-PKAE is not secure against RUF-CTXT, then the scheme does not provide non-repudiation [7] and furthermore, if the receiver's private key is compromised, the attacker can impersonate any sender to this receiver. We introduce the following games to model unforgeability (see Figure 3).

Timed-Release RUF-CTXT (RUF-TR-CTXT). We introduce a slightly weaker timed-release notion of RUF-CTXT [8], which requires that the receiver should not be able to forge ciphertext to himself for a future date. This notion has two important implications: (1) the receiver should discard any ciphertexts received past decryption dates if his private key may be compromised; and (2) the receiver may be able to prove to a third party that a ciphertext was generated by the alleged sender if he can produce a proof of ciphertext existence prior to the decryption date. The game in Figure 3 is an enhancement of the RUF-CTXT condition proposed by An [2] to allow adaptive adversarial behavior: the receiver is not given access to the token for a single, adaptively-chosen *challenge* time period; in addition, the adversary can choose any receiver public key in the encryption queries. We say that a TR-PKAE encryption is secure against RUF-TR-CTXT, if every polynomial-time adversary A has negligible advantage, $\mathsf{Adv}_{A,\Gamma}^{\mathsf{RUF-TR-CTXT}}(k)$, against the challenger in the RUF-TR-CTXT game.

TUF-CTXT. In addition to timed-release receiver unforgeability, we also require a time-independent third-party unforgeability (TUF-CTXT) condition, which allows to separate timed-release functionality from PKAE. Thus, in the TUF-CTXT game defined in Figure 3, the master key is given to the adversary. We say that a TR-PKAE scheme Γ is secure against TUF-CTXT if every polynomial time adversary A has negligible advantage, $\mathsf{Adv}_{A,\Gamma}^{\mathsf{TUF-CTXT}}(k)$, in k.

4 The Proposed TR-PKAE [9]

Following the proof of Theorem 1, one approach to achieve TR-PKAE would be to combine a key-insulated encryption scheme with a PKAE scheme in a modular fashion using techniques such as given in [14]. However, it is desirable for modern authenticated encryption to have one primitive that achieves the desired security

---

[7] Since the receiver can generate the ciphertext allegedly coming from another user to himself, the receiver will not be able to prove to anybody that ciphertext was generated by the alleged sender even if all secret information is disclosed.

[8] This allows us to avoid use of digital signature mechanisms.

[9] We can easily adapt the proposed TR-PKAE to SKIE-OTRU. However, receiver unforgeability will be lost although third-party unforgeability remains, resulting in a weaker form of authenticated SKIE-OTRU. This is expected since the proposed TR-PKAE does not use digital signature mechanisms, which can be added if receiver unforgeability is needed. Still, note that attacker which compromises "helper" of user A, still will not be able to forge ciphertexts to A from another user, and if user A's decryption keys are compromised for some time-periods attacker will not be able to forge ciphertexts to A for a new time-period.

Algorithm 3.3: $\mathsf{Exp}_{\mathcal{A},\Gamma}^{\mathsf{TUF-CTXT}}(k)$

$\pi_g \leftarrow \mathsf{Setup}(1^k)$
$(\delta, \pi_{tr}) \leftarrow \mathsf{TRSetup}(1^k)$
$(pk_a, sk_a) \leftarrow \mathsf{KeyGen}(\pi_g)$
$(pk_b, sk_b) \leftarrow \mathsf{KeyGen}(\pi_g)$
(c^*, T^*)
$\quad \leftarrow \mathcal{A}^{\mathsf{Encrypt}^*(\pi, sk_a, pk_b, \cdot, \cdot)}(\pi, \delta, pk_a, pk_b)$
if $(\mathsf{Decrypt}^*(\pi, \delta, pk_a, sk_b, c^*, T^*) = \mathtt{fail}$
or
$\mathsf{Encrypt}^*(\pi, sk_a, pk_b, \cdot, T^*)$ returned $c^*)$
  then return (false)
  else return (true)

Algorithm 3.4: $\mathsf{Exp}_{\mathcal{A},\Gamma}^{\mathsf{RUF-TR-CTXT}}(k)$

$\pi_g \leftarrow \mathsf{Setup}(1^k)$
$(\delta, \pi_{tr}) \leftarrow \mathsf{TRSetup}(1^k)$
$(pk_a, sk_a) \leftarrow \mathsf{KeyGen}(\pi_g)$
$(c^*, T^*, pk_b^*, sk_b^*)$
$\quad \leftarrow \mathcal{A}^{\mathsf{TG}(\pi, \delta, \cdot), \mathsf{Encrypt}^*(\pi, sk_a, \cdot, \cdot, \cdot)}(\pi, pk_a)$
if $(\mathsf{Decrypt}^*(\pi, \delta, pk_a, sk_b^*, c^*, T^*) = \mathtt{fail}$
or $\mathsf{Encrypt}^*(\pi, sk_a, pk_b^*, \cdot, T^*)$ returned c^*
or $(pk_b^*, sk_b^*) \notin [\mathsf{KeyGen}(1^k)]$
or $\mathcal{A}$ queried $\mathsf{TG}(T^*))$
  then return (false)
  else return (true)

$$\mathsf{Adv}_{\mathcal{A},\Gamma}^{\mathsf{TUF-CTXT}}(k) = \Pr[\mathsf{Exp}_{\mathcal{A},\Gamma}^{\mathsf{TUF-CTXT}}(k) = \mathsf{true}] \ .$$
$$\mathsf{Adv}_{\mathcal{A},\Gamma}^{\mathsf{RUF-TR-CTXT}}(k) = \Pr[\mathsf{Exp}_{\mathcal{A},\Gamma}^{\mathsf{RUF-TR-CTXT}}(k) = \mathsf{true} \ .$$

Fig. 3. TR-PKAE security experiments for the TUF-CTXT and RUF-TR-CTXT games

properties [10]: such solutions generally allow for a more efficient scheme, tighter
security bounds and more stringent security. Below we construct an example of
such a scheme that satisfies all of the above security requirements and is nearly as
efficient as BF-IBE scheme [8]. We start with a review of Bilinear Diffie-Hellman
Problem.

4.1 Bilinear Diffie-Hellman Problem

Let $\mathbb{G}_1$ and $\mathbb{G}_2$ be two abelian groups of prime order q. We will use additive
notation for group operation in $\mathbb{G}_1$ (where aP denotes P added a times for
$P \in \mathbb{G}_1, a \in \mathbb{Z}_q$) and multiplicative notation for $\mathbb{G}_2$ (g^a denotes the g multiplied
a times for element g of $\mathbb{G}_2$). Let $e : \mathbb{G}_1 \times \mathbb{G}_1 \to \mathbb{G}_2$ be an admissible bilinear
map [8]. The properties of the groups and constructions of e are explained in
detail in [8]. We assume that the *Decisional Diffie-Hellman Problem* (DDHP)
is hard in $\mathbb{G}_2$. Note that as a trivial consequence of DDHP assumption, the
Discrete Logarithm Problem (DLP) is also hard in $\mathbb{G}_2$. As a consequence of the
above assumptions, it follows that DLP is hard in $\mathbb{G}_1$ [22].

Let $\mathcal{G}$ be a *Bilinear Diffie-Hellman* (BDH) *Parameter Generator* [8], *i.e.* a
randomized algorithm that takes positive integer input k, runs in polynomial
time in k and outputs prime q, descriptions of $\mathbb{G}_1$, $\mathbb{G}_2$ of order q, description of
admissible bilinear map $e : \mathbb{G}_1 \times \mathbb{G}_1 \to \mathbb{G}_2$ along with polynomial deterministic
algorithms for group operations and e and generators $P \in \mathbb{G}_1, Q \in \mathbb{G}_2$. We say
that algorithm $\mathcal{A}$ has advantage $\epsilon(k)$ in solving the *computational* BDH Problem
(BDHP) for $\mathcal{G}$ if there exists k_0 such that:

$$\mathsf{Adv}_{\mathcal{A},\mathcal{G}}^{\mathsf{cbdh}}(k) = \Pr[\langle q, \mathbb{G}_1, \mathbb{G}_2, e \rangle \leftarrow \mathcal{G}(1^k), P \leftarrow \mathbb{G}_1^*, a, b, c \leftarrow \mathbb{Z}_q^* :$$
$$\mathcal{A}(q, \mathbb{G}_1, \mathbb{G}_2, e, P, aP, bP, cP) = e(P, P)^{abc}] \geq \epsilon(k), \forall k > k_0 \quad (1)$$

We say that $\mathcal{G}$ satisfies the *computational* BDH Assumption if for any randomized polynomial-time algorithm $\mathcal{A}$ and any polynomial $f \in \mathbb{Z}[x]$ we have $\mathsf{Adv}^{\mathsf{cbdh}}_{\mathcal{A},\mathcal{G}}(k) < 1/f(k)$ for sufficiently large k

4.2   Description of the Scheme

Let $\mathcal{G}$ be a *BDH Parameter Generator*. Figure 4 gives a complete description of our construction[10]. The symmetric encryption scheme used is a straightforward adaptation of the Fujisaki-Okamoto scheme [17]. We briefly demonstrate the consistency of the scheme before moving on to security considerations. Given ciphertext $c = \langle Q_1, Q_2, \sigma \oplus K, m \oplus H_4(\sigma) \rangle$ computed using sk_A, pk_B and T, we note that in the corresponding Decrypt computations we have 1) $\widehat{K} = K$ since $e(Q_2 + pk_a, sP_T + sk_b \cdot Q_1) = e(r_2 P + sk_a P, sP_T + sk_b \cdot r_1 P_T) = e([r_2 + sk_a]P, [s + r_1 \cdot sk_b]P_T) = e([s + r_1 \cdot sk_b]P, [r_2 + sk_a]P_T) = e(P_{pub} + r_1 \cdot pk_b, [r_2 + sk_a]P_T)$, 3) as in Fujisaki-Okamoto, it follows that $\widehat{\sigma} = \sigma$, $\widehat{m} = m$ and 4) $Q_1 = H_3(\widehat{\sigma}, \widehat{m})P$ and $Q_2 = H_4(\widehat{\sigma}, \widehat{m})P$. Thus the original plaintext is retrieved.

4.3   Security of the Scheme

The following security results apply to TR-PKAE. The hash functions are modeled as random oracles [6]. Due to space considerations, the detailed proofs of these results are omitted from this extended abstract and are available online [12]. First, we note the confidentiality properties of the proposed scheme.

Theorem 2 (IND-KC-CCA2). *Let $\mathcal{A}$ be a IND-KC-CCA2 adversary that makes q_2 queries to H_2. Assume that $\mathsf{Adv}^{\mathsf{IND-KC-CCA2}}_{\mathcal{A},TR\text{-}PKAE}(k) \geq \epsilon$. Then there exists an algorithm $\mathcal{B}$ that solves computational BDHP with advantage $\mathsf{Adv}^{\mathsf{cbdh}}_{\mathcal{B},\mathcal{G}}(k) \geq \frac{2\epsilon}{q_2}$ and running time $O(time(\mathcal{A}))$.*

Theorem 3 (IND-RTR-KC-CCA2). *Let $\mathcal{A}$ be a IND-RTR-KC-CCA2 adversary that makes q_d decryption queries, q_2 queries to H_2 and q_{tok} queries to TG. Assume that $\mathsf{Adv}^{\mathsf{IND-RTR-KC-CCA2}}_{\mathcal{A},TR\text{-}PKAE}(k) \geq \epsilon$. Then there exists an algorithm $\mathcal{B}$ that solves computational BDHP with advantage $\mathsf{Adv}^{\mathsf{cbdh}}_{\mathcal{B},\mathcal{G}}(k) \geq \frac{1}{4q_2 \cdot \max(q_2,q_d)} \left[\frac{\epsilon}{e \cdot (1+q_{tok})} \right]^3$ and running time $O(time(\mathcal{A}))$, where $e = 2.71828....$*

The proposed protocol also satisfies the authentication properties specified in the previous section, i.e., TUF-CTXT and RUF-TR-CTXT.

Theorem 4 (TUF-CTXT). *Let $\mathcal{A}$ be a TUF-CTXT adversary that makes q_e encryption queries and q_2 queries to H_2, and let $\mathsf{Adv}^{\mathsf{TUF-CTXT}}_{\mathcal{A},TR\text{-}PKAE}(k) \geq \epsilon$. Then there exists an algorithm $\mathcal{B}$ with computational BDHP advantage $\mathsf{Adv}^{\mathsf{cbdh}}_{\mathcal{B},\mathcal{G}}(k) \geq \frac{\epsilon}{2 \cdot q_e \cdot q_2}$ and running time $O(time(\mathcal{A}))$.*

---

[10] As in [8], we can weaken surjectivity assumption on hash function H_1. The security proofs and results will hold true with minor modifications. We skip the details and refer reader to [8].

Setup: Given security parameter $k \in \mathbb{Z}^+$, the following steps are followed

1: $\mathcal{G}$ takes k and generates a prime q, two groups $\mathbb{G}_1, \mathbb{G}_2$ of order q, an admissible bilinear map $e : \mathbb{G}_1 \times \mathbb{G}_1 \to \mathbb{G}_2$ and arbitrary generator $P \in \mathbb{G}_1$.

2: The following cryptographic hash functions are chosen: 1) $H_1 : \{0,1\}^* \to \mathbb{G}_1^*$, 2) $H_2 : \mathbb{G}_2 \to \{0,1\}^n$ for some n, 3) $H_3, H_4 : \{0,1\}^n \times \{0,1\}^n \to \mathbb{Z}_q^*$ and 4) $H_5 : \{0,1\}^n \to \{0,1\}^n$. These functions will be treated as random oracles in security considerations.

3: The message space is chosen to be $\mathcal{M} = \{0,1\}^n$ and the ciphertext space is $\mathcal{C} = \mathbb{G}_1^* \times \{0,1\}^n \times \{0,1\}^n$. The general system parameters are $\pi_g = \langle q, \mathbb{G}_1, \mathbb{G}_2, e, n, P, H_i, i = 1...5 \rangle$

TRSetup :

1: Choose $s \in_R \mathbb{Z}_q^*$ and set $P_{pub} = sP$.

2: The timed-release public system parameter is $\pi_{tr} = P_{pub}$ and the *master key* δ is $s \in \mathbb{Z}_q^*$. The combined public parameters are $\pi = \pi_g || \pi_{tr} = \langle q, \mathbb{G}_1, \mathbb{G}_2, e, n, P, P_{pub}, H_i, i = 1...5 \rangle$

KeyGen: Uniformly choose private key $sk = a \in \mathbb{Z}_q^*$, and compute the corresponding public key pk as $0 \neq aP \in \mathbb{G}_1^*$.

TG: On input the time encoding $T \in \{0,1\}^n$, output sP_T where $P_T = H_1(T)$

Encrypt: Given the private key sk_a of the sender, public key pk_b of receiver, plaintext $m \in \mathcal{M}$ and time encoding T, encryption is done as follows: 1) sample $\sigma \in_R \{0,1\}^n$, compute $r_1 = H_3(\sigma, m)$ and $r_2 = H_4(\sigma, m)$; set $Q_1 = r_1 P_T$ and $Q_2 = r_2 P$; 2) compute $\mathcal{L} = e(P_{pub} + r_1 \cdot pk_b, (r_2 + sk_a)P_T)$ and symmetric key $K = H_2(\mathcal{L})$ and 3) the ciphertext c is set to be $c = \langle Q_1, Q_2, \sigma \oplus K, m \oplus H_5(\sigma) \rangle$

Decrypt: Given ciphertext $c = \langle Q_1, Q_2, c_1, c_2 \rangle$ encrypted using sk_a, pk_b and time T, one decrypts it as follows: (1) obtain $tkn_T = sP_T$; (2) $\widehat{K} = H_2(e(Q_2 + pk_a, sP_T + sk_b \cdot Q_1))$; 3) retrieve $\widehat{\sigma} = c_1 \oplus \widehat{K}$ and compute $\widehat{m} = c_2 \oplus H_5(\widehat{\sigma})$ and 4) verify that $Q_1 = H_3(\widehat{\sigma}, \widehat{m})P$ and $Q_2 = H_4(\widehat{\sigma}, \widehat{m})P$; if so, output $\widehat{m}$, otherwise output `fail`.

Fig. 4. The proposed TR-PKAE scheme

Theorem 5 (RUF-TR-CTXT). *Let $\mathcal{A}$ be a* RUF-TR-CTXT *adversary that makes q_e encryption queries, q_2 queries to H_2, and q_{tok} queries to* TG, *and let* $\mathsf{Adv}_{\mathcal{A}, TR\text{-}PKAE}^{\mathsf{RUF\text{-}TR\text{-}CTXT}}(k) \geq \epsilon$. *Then there exists an algorithm $\mathcal{B}$ with computational BDHP advantage* $\mathsf{Adv}_{\mathcal{B}, \mathcal{G}}^{\mathsf{cbdh}}(k) \geq \frac{\epsilon}{2 \cdot q_2 \cdot q_e \cdot e \cdot (1 + q_{tok})}$ *and running time $O(time(\mathcal{A}))$, where $e = 2.71828....$*

5   Efficiency of TR-PKAE

To compare the proposed scheme to BF-IBE [8], note that, in terms of significant operations – *bilinear pairings, MapToPoint, exponentiations* – TR-PKAE adds 3 additional exponentiations in $\mathbb{G}_1$ for encryption and 2 for decryption. More precisely, encryption in TR-PKAE involves 1 bilinear map, 4 exponentiations in $\mathbb{G}_1$ and 1 MapToPoint (to compute P_T). The decryption involves 1 bilinear map and 3 exponentiations in $\mathbb{G}_1$ (assuming P_T is pre-computed). Second, the proposed scheme adds additional point in $\mathbb{G}_1$ to the ciphertext. Taking into account functionality of TR-PKAE and the fact that naive combinations yielding hybrid protocols generally fail to provide required security, we expect hybrid constructions of TR-PKAE to be at least as expensive as our scheme.

We implemented the proposed primitives using Miracl library v.4.8.3 [27] with Tate pairing for the bilinear map. The group $\mathbb{G}_1$ was chosen to be a subgroup of order q in a supersingular elliptic curve E over $\mathbb{F}_p$, where p is a 512 bit and q is a 160 bit primes. Group $\mathbb{G}_2$ was a subgroup of a finite field of order 1024 bits. We used a P4-3.2 GHz "Northwood" (800MHz FSB) with 2GB of 400 MHz RAM desktop. The performance measurements are summarized in Table 1 and are all averaged over 10000 runs, except that the RSA results were obtained by running OpenSSL v.0.9.8 *speed* command. As expected, the proposed TR-PKAE is somewhat more expensive than BF-IBE in encryption/decryption, but when BF-IBE is extended to provide comparable functionality to TR-PKAE we expect the resulting scheme to be at least as expensive as the proposed protocol.

Table 1. Cost of basic operations

Function	modulus (bits)	exponent (bits)	performance (msec)
RSA(Sig/Dec)	1024	1024	2.96
RSA(Ver/Enc)	1024	16 ($e = 2^{16} + 1$)	0.14
Scalar Mul in EC over $\mathbb{F}_p$	160	160	2.23
MapToPoint	512	-	1.52
Pairing	512	160	18.15
TR-PKAE Enc	512	160	29
TR-PKAE Dec	512	160	25
BF-IBE Enc	512	160	24
BF-IBE Dec	512	160	21

Acknowledgements

The authors thank Moti Yung for the excellent suggestion to bridge the link between timed-release and key-insulated encryption and many other invaluable comments, and the anonymous reviewers for helpful feedback.

References

1. M. Abdalla, M. Bellare, and P. Rogaway. The Oracle Diffie-Hellman Assumptions and an Analysis of DHIES. In *CT-RSA*, 2001.
2. J. H. An. Authenticated Encryption in the Public-Key Setting: Security Notions and Analyses. http://eprint.iacr.org/2001/079/, 2001.
3. M. Bellare, A. Desai, D. Pointcheval, and P. Rogaway. Relations Among Notions of Security for Public-Key Encryption Schemes. In *CRYPTO*, 1998.
4. M. Bellare and S. Goldwasser. Encapsulated Key Kscrow. Technical report, MIT/LCS/TR-688, 1996.

5. M. Bellare and A. Palacio. Protecting against Key Exposure: Strongly Key-Insulated Encryption with Optimal Threshold. http://eprint.iacr.org/2002/064/, 2002.

6. M. Bellare and P. Rogaway. Random Oracles are Practical: A Paradigm for Designing Efficient Protocols. In *ACM CCS*, 1995.

7. I. F. Blake and A. C.-F. Chan. Scalable, Server-Passive, User-Anonymous Timed Release Public Key Encryption from Bilinear Pairing. In *ICDCS*, 2005.

8. D. Boneh and M. Franklin. Identity Based Encryption from the Weil Pairing. In *CRYPTO*, 2003.

9. D. Boneh and M. Naor. Timed Commitments. In *CRYPTO*, 2000.

10. X. Boyen. Multipurpose Identity Based Signcryption: A Swiss Army Knife for Identity Based Cryptography. In *CRYPTO*, 2003.

11. L. Chen, K. Harrison, D. Soldera, and N. Smart. Applications of multiple trust authorities in pairing based cryptosystems. In *InfraSec*, 2002.

12. J. H. Cheon, N. Hopper, Y. Kim, and I. Osipkov. Timed-Release and Key-Insulated Public Key Encryption. Available from http://eprint.iacr.org/2004/231, 2004.

13. G. D. Crescenzo, R. Ostrovsky, and S. Rajagopalan. Conditional Oblivious Transfer and Timed-Release Encryption. In *EUROCRYPT*, 1999.

14. Y. Dodis and J. Katz. Chosen-Ciphertext Security of Multiple Encryption. In *Theory of Cryptography Conference*, 2005.

15. Y. Dodis, J. Katz, S. Xu, and M. Yung. Key-Insulated Public Key Cryptosystems. In *EUROCRYPT*, 2002.

16. Y. Dodis, J. Katz, S. Xu, and M. Yung. Strong Key-Insulated Signature Schemes. In *PKC*, 2003.

17. E. Fujisaki and T. Okamoto. Secure Integration of Asymmetric and Symmetric Encryption Schemes. In *CRYPTO*, 1999.

18. J. Garay and C. Pomerance. Timed Fair Exchange of Arbitrary Signatures. In *Financial Cryptography*, 2003.

19. J. A. Garay and C. Pomerance. Timed Fair Exchange of Standard Signatures. In *Financial Cryptography*, 2002.

20. K. H. Marco Casassa Mont and M. Sadler. The HP Time Vault Service: Exploiting IBE for Timed Release of Confidential Information . In *WWW*, 2003.

21. T. May. Timed-Release Crypto. http://www.cyphernet.org/cyphernomicon/chapter14/14.5.html-.

22. A. Menezes, T. Okamoto, and S. Vanstone. Reducing elliptic curve logarithms to logarithms in a finite field. In *IEEE Transactions on Information Theory IT-39*, 5, 1993.

23. D. Mills. Network Time Protocol (Version 3) Specification, Implementation. Technical Report 1305, RFC, 1992.

24. T. P. Pederson. A Threshold Cryptosystem Without a Trusted Party. In *EUROCRYPT*, 1991.

25. C. Rackoff and D. R. Simon. Non-Interactive Zero-Knowledge Proof of Knowledge and Chosen Ciphertext Attack. In *CRYPTO*, 1991.

26. R. L. Rivest, A. Shamir, and D. A. Wagner. Time-lock Puzzles and Time-released Crypto. Technical report, MIT/LCS/TR-684, 1996.

27. Shamus Software Ltd. MIRACL: Multiprecision Integer and Rational Arithmetic C/C++ Library. http://indigo.ie/~mscott/.

28. P. F. Syverson. Weakly Secret Bit Commitment: Applications to Lotteries and Fair Exchange. In *Computer Security Foundations Workshop*, 1998.

Conditional Encrypted Mapping and Comparing Encrypted Numbers

Ian F. Blake[1] and Vladimir Kolesnikov[2]

[1] Dept. ECE, University of Toronto, Canada
ifblake@comm.utoronto.ca
[2] Dept. Comp. Sci., University of Toronto, Canada
vlad@cs.utoronto.ca

Abstract. We consider the problem of comparing two encrypted numbers and its extension – transferring one of the two secrets, depending on the result of comparison. We show how to efficiently apply our solutions to practical settings, such as auctions with the semi-honest auctioneer, proxy selling, etc. We propose a new primitive, *Conditional Encrypted Mapping*, which captures common security properties of one round protocols in a variety of settings, which may be of independent interest.

Keywords: Two Millionaires with encrypted inputs, auctions, private selective payments, conditional encrypted mapping.

1   Introduction

In this paper we study secure evaluation of the Greater Than (GT) predicate. It is one of the most basic and widely used functionalities. It plays an especially important role in secure financial transactions and database mining applications.

Auctions and Bargaining. With the expansion of the Internet, electronic commerce and especially online auctions continue to grow at an impressive pace. Many sellers also discover the appeal of flexible pricing. For example, sites such as priceline.com ask a buyer for a price he is willing to pay for a product, and the deal is committed to if that price is greater than a certain (secret) threshold.

In many such situations, it is vital to maintain the privacy of bids of the players. Indeed, revealing an item's worth can result in artificially high prices or low bids, specifically targeted for a particular buyer or seller. While a winning bid or a committed deal may necessarily reveal the cost of the transaction, it is highly desirable to keep all other information (e.g. unsuccessful bids) secret.

There has been a large stream of work dedicated to ensuring privacy and security of online auctions and haggling (e.g.,[3,5,6,14]). Our work complements, extends, and builds on it. We discuss the Private Selective Payments protocols of Di Crescenzo [5] and show how our improvements benefit this application.

The need for comparing encrypted numbers. It is often beneficial to both sellers and buyers to employ a mutually semi-trusted server S to assist them in their transaction. The use of such a server simplifies secure protocol design, allowing for more efficient protocols. It allows the seller to be offline most of the

G. Di Crescenzo and A. Rubin (Eds.): FC 2006, LNCS 4107, pp. 206–220, 2006.
© IFCA/Springer-Verlag Berlin Heidelberg 2006

time, allowing S to act on behalf of the seller in handling bid requests. Further, a reputable S (such as eBay) may provide additional assurance of security to the potential buyer. However, since sellers and buyers wish to hide their inputs from S, the latter must work with, e.g. compare, *encrypted* numbers. We propose a formalization of this setting, as well as new, more efficient GT protocols for it.

Other applications. We mention other interesting applications that benefit from efficient secure evaluation of GT. These applications might need to employ a proxy server S, as above; if so, our work improves their performance as well.

In Distributed Database Mining, several parties, each having a private database, wish to determine some properties of, or perform computations on, their *joint* database. Many interesting properties and computations, such as transaction classification or rule mining, involve evaluating a very large number of instances of GT [10,13]. Our improvements also apply to solving interval membership problems (reduced to GT in [2]). The immediate uses lie in appointment scheduling, flexible timestamp verification, biometrics, etc. Certain kinds of set intersection problems, as studied in [7,9], can be represented succinctly as GT instances, resulting in more efficient solutions using our constructions.

1.1   Our Contributions, Setting and Outline of the Work

We approach several practical problems (auctions, proxy selling, GT) in a variety of settings, concentrating on a setting with a semi-honest helping server.

We are interested in one-round protocols, where clients send their encrypted inputs to a "cypto computer" S, who produces an output that can be decoded by the clients. Such scenarios arise in a variety of practical settings. To enable formal discussion of crucial parts of our protocols in a number of settings simultaneously, we extract what these settings have in common – the following requirements on the output of S: it allows the reconstruction of the value of the function, and does not contain any other information. This allows to postpone the (easy but tedious) discussion of setting-specific clients' privacy requirements. We formalize (Def. 1) a special case of this notion, which we call *Conditional Encrypted Mapping* (CEM). Here, S has two secrets s_0, s_1, is given encryptions of two values x, y, and outputs something that allows (only) reconstruction of $s_{Q(x,y)}$, where Q is a fixed public predicate. We note that our statistical privacy requirement on the output of S is very strong, e.g., precluding Yao's garbled circuit-based solutions.

We propose two new, more efficient CEM protocols for the GT predicate (Sect. 4). We use ideas of the recent protocol of Blake and Kolesnikov [2]. Their protocol requires S to know one of the compared numbers, and thus cannot be naturally cast as a CEM. We overcome this with a new tool – a randomized way to represent secrets to be transferred by S (presented in Sect. 4.3). The cost of our solution is comparable to that of [2]. We believe this method may be used to improve efficiency of other constructions relying on homomorphic encryptions.

In Sect. 5, we show how our constructions result in new, more efficient, protocols for the examples of private selective payments of Di Crescenzo [5] and proxy selling. We discuss methods of protection against malicious behavior of parties. We mention that efficient CEM schemes exist for any NC^1 predicate (Sect. 4.7).

In Sect. 6 we summarize and compare resource requirements of schemes based on the work of Di Crescenzo [5], Fischlin [6], Laur and Lipmaa [12] and ours.

2   Related Work

We discuss related work in both directions of our contributions – definition of CEM and concrete protocols for auction-like functionalities.

Variants of CEM. Several notions similar to CEM were previously proposed.

The notion of Conditional Oblivious Transfer (COT) was introduced by Di Crescenzo, Ostrovsky and Rajagopalan [4] in the context of timed-release encryption. It is a variant of Oblivious Transfer (OT) [16]. Intuitively, in COT, the two participants, a receiver R and a sender S, have private inputs x and y respectively, and share a public predicate $Q(\cdot, \cdot)$. S has a secret s he wishes (obliviously to himself) to transfer to R iff $Q(x, y) = 1$. If $Q(x, y) = 0$, no information about s is transferred to R. R's private input and the value of the predicate remain computationally hidden from S.

A similar notion to COT, Conditional Disclosure of Secrets (CDS), was introduced by Gertner, Ishai, Kushilevitz and Malkin [8] in the context of multi-server Symmetrically Private Information Retrieval (SPIR). In their work, the receiver of the secret apriori knows the inputs of the (many) senders. The secret is unknown to the receiver and sent to him only if a predicate holds on the inputs.

Aiello, Ishai and Reingold [1] adapt CDS into the single server setting, where the (single) sender holds *encryptions* of parts (i.e. bits) of input. The receiver knows both the input and the decryption key. Again, the receiver does not know the secret; it is sent to him only if a predicate holds on the input.

Laur and Lipmaa [12] extend the study of CDS for the case of additive homomorphic encryptions, give generic constructions and specific protocols (GT).

The lack of requirement of privacy of the value of $Q(x, y)$ and the sender's input often prevents the use of COT or CDS as a building block of other protocols. Di Crescenzo [5] described a stronger concept, Symmetrically-private COT, by additionally requiring that both parties' inputs x, y remain private. Later, Blake and Kolesnikov [2], independently proposed and formalized essentially the same notion, which they call Strong COT. Of the above, CEM is most similar to this notion. We note that CEM is a stronger notion, explicitly allowing reuse of generated encryption keys in multiple executions. We also have the feature of not specifying the precise security properties of the used encryptions, allowing for more flexibility and applicability (see Sect. 1.1 and 3 for more discussion).

Auctions and Private Selective Payments Protocols (PSPP). PSPP, introduced by Di Crescenzo [5], solve the following practical problem. A server has a private message representing, say, a signed authorization, and wants to give it to one among several clients, according to some public criteria, evaluated on the server's and clients' private inputs. Client's inputs may represent their auction bids, and a server's input may be a lowest acceptable price or a required signature. Di Crescenzo considers a natural instance of PSPP, where the highest bidding client obtains the authorization. He considers a setting with a helping semi-honest server and malicious clients.

Di Crescenzo designs his protocols in several phases. During *registration*, executed between each client and the server, the client's public/private key pair is established, and the server obtains the public key. Then the *selection* protocol is executed between all registered clients and the server, during which the selected client obtains the server's secret. Finally, in the *verification* phase, the selected client presents his claim – the obtained secret – and convinces the server that he indeed is the selected client. The registration and verification phases are designed using standard cryptographic tools; it is the selection phase that is the challenging computationally expensive area. The main contribution of [5] is the novel maximum bidder selection protocols.

Our main contribution, GT-CEM constructions, can be used to replace the core – the selection protocols – of the PSPP of [5] (with corresponding natural modifications of the other two phases). Appropriately modified protocols of Fischlin [6] and Laur and Lipmaa [12] can be similarly used. We discuss more details and the resulting efficiency improvements of our protocols in Sect. 5 and 6.

We mention, but do not discuss in detail the auction protocols for use in the settings, significantly different from ours. Naor, Pinkas and Sumner [14] use Yao's garbled circuit approach in the setting with a semi-honest mostly offline server, whose role is to ensure that the auctioneer does not cheat. Cachin [3] suggested a protocol for private bidding with the semi-honest server in the setting where the bidders additionally exchange messages between each other.

2.1   Notation, Definitions and Preliminaries

A function $\mu : N \mapsto R$ is *negligible* if for every positive polynomial $p(\cdot)$ there exists an N, such that for all $n > N, \mu(n) < 1/p(n)$. A probability is *overwhelming* if it is negligibly different from 1. Statistical distance between distributions X and Y is defined as $Dist(X, Y) = 1/2 \sum_\alpha |Pr(X = \alpha) - Pr(Y = \alpha)|$.

Informally, an encryption scheme $E = (Gen, Enc, Dec)$ is *additively homomorphic*, if it is possible to compute an encryption of $x + y$ from encryptions of x and y. E is *probabilistic* if its encryption function randomly encrypts plaintext as one of many possible ciphertexts. Many such schemes (e.g. Paillier [15]) exist.

We denote a uniform sampling of an element r of domain D by $r \in_R D$.

3   Conditional Encrypted Mapping

We consider the setting where one of the players is a facilitator of the computation of the multiparty functionality f. This player – the Server S – is given the encrypted inputs to f; he produces some representation of the value of f. The value of f can later be decoded from this representation using the private key of the employed encryption scheme. This scenario is appealing for its round efficiency and is widely applicable in practice. For example, it applies to auctions with semi-honest servers. There, the server S is given encryptions of parties' bids, and he wants to commit to a deal (e.g. by sending a secret) with the winner.

The first step in designing secure protocols is making explicit the setting in which they are run and the necessary security requirements. This is a difficult task, especially since we would like our constructions to be applicable to a variety of settings. For example, the server S may obtain encrypted inputs from parties A and B and let either A or B or a third party C decode the output. Protocols can use encryption schemes, which may or may not be re-initialized for each execution of the protocol. Players A, B or C may have different levels of trust.

Encompassing all these situations in one definition is difficult. We propose to extract and formalize what these definitions would have in common – requirements of correctness and privacy of the output of the semi-honest Server S. This modularity is very convenient, since we can now model S as a non-interactive algorithm. A variety of setting-specific requirements for hiding the input from the server can be later defined and satisfied with appropriate use of encryption.

Encrypted Mapping. We model the Server S as a polytime randomized mapping algorithm *Rmap*. *Rmap* takes as input the public key of the encryption scheme E, the (encrypted with E) input(s), and outputs some representation of the value of f. Of course, this output should be interpreted. We require existence of the polytime recovery procedure *Rec*, which takes the representation of the value of f and the private key of E and computes the intended output (this is the correctness condition). Further, we require that the randomized representation statistically hides all other information, ensuring privacy of arbitrary compositions of outputs of *Rmap* even against computationally unlimited attackers. We call the pair (*Rmap*, *Rec*) an Encrypted Mapping (EM). We formalize a variant of this notion in Def. 1 below.

We choose not to specify the requirements of security of encryption in the definition. This allows a protocol designer to concentrate on the high-level combinatorial properties of EM and defer discussion of detailed setting-specific concerns. Such low-level concerns include considering whether some inputs to S contain decryption keys (which would allow S to learn more than he should) and considering malicious behaviour, such as providing invalid or substituted inputs. A protocol designer can now first describe the combinatorial *Rmap* and *Rec*, which would imply solutions to a variety of settings in the semi-honest model, assuming the semantic security of the employed encryption scheme. Afterwards, the protocols can be adapted to a variety of specific settings and modified to withstand certain malicious behaviours (e.g. using the conditional disclosure techniques of [1,12]. See more in Sect. 5.1).

We wish to give a very strong definition, so that the constructions can be used in a variety of settings. In particular, we want our construction to work with all instantiations of used encryption schemes. In many popular encryption schemes (e.g. Paillier [15]) the plaintext domain D_P varies with different instantiations. Many interesting functions f are defined on fixed domains, independent of D_P. We handle this detail by ensuring that D_P includes the domain of inputs to f by appropriately modifying the family of encryptions to only include members with sufficiently large D_P. We note that a sufficiently large D_P is usually implied by the semantic security requirement of the scheme.

We remark that we achieve a very strong definition by quantifying over all valid inputs and randomness used by encryptions – i.e. over everything but the randomness used by $Rmap$. This, for example, ensures that adversary does not benefit from knowing the randomness used for encrypting inputs to $Rmap$.

Conditional Encrypted Mapping. In this work, we are mainly interested in constructing the protocols for transferring a secret (e.g. a sale commitment or a rejection) depending on whether a certain predicate on two inputs (e.g. the bid is greater than the asking price) holds. We call the corresponding EM a Conditional Encrypted Mapping (CEM). We give a formal definition for this special case and note that a more general EM definition can be naturally constructed.

We define CEM with respect to an encryption scheme $E = (Gen, Enc, Dec)$. Denote by (sk, pk) a public/private key pair for E, and by E_{pk} denote the initialized encryption scheme E. Let $D_{P_{pk}}$ denote the plaintext domain of E_{pk} and $D_{R_{pk}}$ denote the domain of randomness used by Enc_{pk}. Denote by $Enc_{pk,\alpha}(x)$ the encryption of x under pk using randomness α. Let $Q : D_Q \times D_Q \mapsto \{0,1\}$ be a deterministic predicate defined on a fixed domain. Recall, we only consider families of E_{pk} where $D_Q \subset D_{P_{pk}}$. Let ν be the security parameter[1]. Let D_S be the (fixed) domain of secrets[2].

Definition 1. *(Q-Conditional Encrypted Mapping) A Q-Conditional Encrypted Mapping (Q-CEM) is a pair of polytime algorithms $(Rmap, Rec)$ (with implicitly defined domain of mappings $D_{M_{pk}}$), such that the following holds.*

The probabilistic randomized mapping algorithm $Rmap$ takes as input (s_0, s_1, e_0, e_1, pk), where e_0, e_1 are encryptions under E_{pk}, and $s_0, s_1 \in D_S$. $Rmap$ outputs an element from $D_{M_{pk}}$. The deterministic recovery algorithm Rec takes as input secret key sk and an element from $D_{M_{pk}}$ and outputs an element from the domain of secrets D_S or a failure symbol $\perp$.

$Rmap$ and Rec satisfy the following conditions:

- *(correctness) $\forall (sk, pk) \leftarrow Gen(\nu), \forall s_0, s_1 \in D_S, \forall \alpha, \beta \in D_{R_{pk}}, \forall x, y \in D_Q$: with overwhelming probability in ν, taken over random inputs of $Rmap$: $Rec(Rmap(s_0, s_1, Enc_{pk,\alpha}(x), Enc_{pk,\beta}(y), pk), sk) = s_{Q(x,y)}$.*
- *(statistical privacy) $\exists Sim$, s.t. $\forall (sk, pk) \leftarrow Gen(\nu), \forall s_0, s_1 \in D_S, \forall x, y \in D_Q, \forall \alpha, \beta \in D_{R_{pk}}$: the statistical distance $Dist(Sim(s_{Q(x,y)}, pk), Rmap(s_0, s_1, Enc_{pk,\alpha}(x), Enc_{pk,\beta}(y), pk))$ is negligible in ν.*

Note, Def. 1 does not require E to have any security properties. Thus, formally, inputs e_0, e_1 to $Rmap$ are simply *encodings* of elements in D_Q (and Q-CEM can be constructed unconditionally). In practice, however, we envision using a semantically secure E; thus we call e_0, e_1 encryptions. Jumping ahead, we

---

[1] In practice, we are also interested in the correctness parameter λ. Security and correctness properties of Def. 1 are formulated with the notion of statistical closeness. Since ν and λ are polynomially related, we, for simplicity, use only the parameter ν.

[2] Even though for simplicity of presentation the domains D_Q and D_S are fixed, their elements representation is polynomially related to all other parameters. Further, in practice (and in our constructions), D_Q and D_S can grow with ν at no extra cost.

note that in our GT constructions 4.4, the inputs e_0, e_1 to *Rmap* are bitwise encryptions of the clients' bids. Note that Def. 1 allows this interpretation, since encrypting x bit-by-bit can be viewed as an encryption scheme itself.

Further, Def. 1 does not guarantee either correctness or privacy if e_0 or e_1 are not proper encryptions of elements of D_Q. This is sufficient in the semi-honest model; we discuss methods of handling malicious behaviour in Sect. 5.1.

4   The GT-CEM Construction and Protocols

Our construction builds on the ideas of the GT protocol of Blake and Kolesnikov [2]. Their protocol can be cast as a variant of GT-CEM, where one of the inputs is given in plaintext. We present their main idea and observe that a part of their protocol – the randomization procedure – requires S to know his input. In Sect. 4.2, we discuss the necessary properties of our new randomization, which works with encryptions only. In Sect. 4.3, we present such a randomization procedure and in Sect. 4.4 we give a GT-CEM construction. We give an alternative randomization procedure in Sect. 4.5, which can be incorporated into our GT-CEM.

4.1   The GT Protocol of [2]

We give a brief overview of the protocol and direct the reader to [2] for more details. Recall, there are two players, a receiver R with input x and a sender S with input y, s_0, s_1. S needs to send R the secret $s_{GT(x,y)}$.

The protocol operates on (homomorphically encrypted) bits of the inputs. The idea is to isolate the "important" position – the one where input bit strings first differ – by mapping it to a predetermined value and simultaneously randomizing values in all other positions. The rest is easily accomplished by applications of linear functions. In this work, we pay special attention to and improve the isolating randomization procedure.

In [2], the Receiver R sends bitwise additively homomorphic encryption of his input $x = \langle x_1, ..., x_n \rangle$ to the Sender S. For each bit position i, S computes (an encryption of) $f_i = x_i \oplus y_i$, i.e. whether $x_i = y_i$ (this requires the knowledge of y_i; knowing $Enc(y_i)$ is not sufficient). It is easy to see that $GT(x,y) = x_j$, where $j = min_{f_i \neq 0} i$. S's randomization procedure crucially relies on the fact that $f_j = 1$. Our randomization relies on the (encrypted) difference vector $d_i = x_i - y_i$, the "important element" of which may be (an encryption of) one of $\{-1, 1\}$.

4.2   The Intuition of GT-CEM and the Formalization of the Randomization Requirements

Recall, we are given secrets s_0, s_1 and bitwise encryptions of inputs x and y. We can compute an encryption of the bit difference vector d, where $d_i = x_i - y_i$. Elements of the difference vector d assume one of $\{-1, 0, 1\}$. Let $j = min_{d_i \neq 0} i$ be the index of the "important" position. Our goal is to isolate the value d_j by computing an encryption of vector μ, such that $\forall i \neq j, \mu_i \in_R D_{P_{pk}}$ and $\mu_j = d_j$. As in [2], we can obtain such μ_i for $i \geq j$ by computing for $i = 1..n$: $\mu_0 = 0; \mu_i = r_i\mu_{i-1} + d_i$, where $r_i \in_R D_{P_{pk}}$. Now vector μ is a vector of encryptions of (in order): one or more 0, either a 1 or a -1, one or more random elements of $D_{P_{pk}}$. We need to map the zeros of μ to random elements in $D_{P_{pk}}$, while preserving the properties of $\mu_i, i \geq j$. Our randomization maps $-1 \to s_0, 1 \to s_1$ (under encryption). At the same time, it maps 0 and random elements from $D_{P_{pk}}$ to random elements from $D_{P_{pk}}$. It is not hard to see (and we explicitly show it in Sect. 4.4) that such randomization naturally leads to a GT-CEM.

We believe that such randomization may be useful in other applications as well. Therefore, we formalize its requirements. We present the definition in a slightly more general way, by allowing arbitrary constants instead of $-1, 1$. Further natural extensions of this definition are possible.

Let $v_0, v_1 \in \mathbb{Z} \setminus \{0\}$ be fixed, and $v_0 \neq v_1$. Let $E, \nu, sk, pk, E_{pk}, D_{P_{pk}}, D_{R_{pk}}, D_S$ be as in Def. 1. Let $i \in \{0, 1\}$. We view v_i as an element of $D_{P_{pk}}$ in the natural manner (i.e. as $v_i \mod |D_{P_{pk}}|$). We note that even though this representation may vary with the choice of pk, v_i is a constant. Further, we require $v_i \neq 0 \mod |D_{P_{pk}}|$ and $v_0 \neq v_1 \mod |D_{P_{pk}}|$.

Definition 2. $((v_0, v_1)$-Randomizing Mapping) A (v_0, v_1) - Randomizing Mapping (RM) is a pair of polytime algorithms (Rmap, Rec) (with implicitly defined domain of mappings $D_{M_{pk}}$), such that the following holds.

The probabilistic randomized mapping algorithm Rmap takes as input (s_0, s_1, e, pk), where e is an encryption under E_{pk}, and $s_0, s_1 \in D_S$. Rmap outputs an element from $D_{M_{pk}}$. The deterministic recovery algorithm Rec takes as input secret key sk and an element from $D_{M_{pk}}$ and outputs an element from the domain of secrets D_S or a failure symbol $\perp$.

Rmap and Rec satisfy the following conditions:

- *(correctness)* $\forall (sk, pk) \leftarrow Gen(\nu), \forall i \in \{0, 1\}, \forall s_0, s_1 \in D_S, \forall \alpha \in D_{R_{pk}}$, for $x \in_R D_{P_{pk}}$, with overwhelming probability in ν:
  $Rec(Rmap(s_0, s_1, Enc_{pk,\alpha}(v_i), pk), sk) = s_i$
  $Rec(Rmap(s_0, s_1, Enc_{pk,\alpha}(x), pk), sk) = \perp$,
  where the probability is taken over choices of x and random inputs of Rmap.
- *(statistical privacy at v_0, v_1)* $\exists Sim$, s.t. $\forall (sk, pk) \leftarrow Gen(\nu), \forall s_0, s_1 \in D_S$, $\forall i \in \{0, 1\}, \forall \alpha \in D_{R_{pk}}$: the statistical distance $Dist(Sim(s_i, pk), Rmap(s_0, s_1, Enc_{pk,\alpha}(v_i), pk))$ is negligible in ν.
- *(statistical privacy at 0 and at random elements of $D_{P_{pk}}$)* $\exists Sim_0$, such that $\forall (sk, pk) \leftarrow Gen(\nu), \forall s_0, s_1 \in D_S, \forall \alpha \in D_{R_{pk}}$: the statistical distances $Dist(Sim_0(pk), Rmap(s_0, s_1, Enc_{pk,\alpha}(0), pk))$ and $Dist(Sim_0(pk), Rmap$ $(s_0, s_1, Enc_{pk,\alpha}(R), pk))$ are negligible in ν, where R is uniform on $D_{P_{pk}}$.

4.3   A Space-Efficient $(-1, 1)$-RM

We present a construction for $(-1, 1)$-RM, based on the Paillier encryption scheme [15], which we use to construct GT-CEM. Let E be the Paillier scheme initialized as described in Def. 2. Let Rmap be given an encryption under E_{pk}. Our $(-1, 1)$-RM is space optimal – Rmap outputs a single encryption under E_{pk}.

At first glance, the requirements on Rmap are conflicting: we must satisfy three data points $((v_0, s_0), (v_1, s_1), (0, random))$ with a linear function (only linear functions can be applied under the homomorphic encryption). Our idea is for

Rmap to produce not encryptions of secrets s_i, but of their *randomized encodings* S_i. We carefully randomize the encodings S_i, such that their linear combination of interest (i.e. the value that 0 is mapped to) is a random element in $D_{P_{pk}}$.

Let $f = ax + b$ be a linear mapping, such that $f(-1) = -a + b = S_0$ and $f(1) = a + b = S_1$. Then $b = (S_0 + S_1)/2$ and $a = S_1 - (S_0 + S_1)/2 = (S_1 - S_0)/2$. We want to ensure that $f(0) = b = (S_0 + S_1)/2$ is random, while, for $i \in \{0, 1\}$, S_i encodes s_i and contains no other information.

Construction 1 *($(-1, 1)$-RM)*
Let λ and ν be the correctness and security parameters. Let the plaintext group of E_{pk} be $D_{P_{pk}} = \mathbb{Z}_N$, where $N = pq$ is of bit size $n > \nu$. Let $k = \lfloor (n-1)/2 \rfloor$. Define the domain of secrets to be $D_S = D_{S_{pk}} = \{0, 1\}^{k-\lambda}$, and the domain of mappings $D_{M_{pk}}$ to be the domain of encryptions under E_{pk}.

Rmap on input (s_0, s_1, e, pk) proceeds as follows. Set $s_i' = s_i 0^\lambda$ (to help distinguish secrets from random strings). View s_0', s_1' as elements of $\mathbb{Z}_N$. Choose $R \in_R \mathbb{Z}_N$ and a bit $c \in_R \{0, 1\}$. Let r_1 (resp. r_0) be the integer represented by k lower (resp. remaining) bits of R, i.e. $R = r_0 2^k + r_1$.

Set S_0, S_1 as follows. If $c = 0$, then set $S_0 = r_0 2^k + s_0'$ and $S_1 = s_1' 2^k + r_1$. If $c = 1$, then set $S_0 = s_0' 2^k + r_1$ and $S_1 = r_0 2^k + s_1'$.

Compute $a = (S_1 - S_0)/2 \bmod N$ and $b = (S_0 + S_1)/2 \bmod N$.

Finally, apply $f = ax + b$ to e under the encryption and re-randomize the result, that is, choose $r' \in_R \mathbb{Z}_N^*$ and output $e^a g^b r'^N \bmod N^2$.

Rec on input (e', sk) proceeds as follows. Rec computes $d = Dec_{sk}(e')$. Let $d_n, ..., d_1$ be the bit representation of d. Let $D_1 = d_{2k}, ..., d_k$ and $D_0 = d_k, ..., d_1$. For $i \in \{0, 1\}$, if $D_i = s 0^\lambda$, output s and halt. Otherwise output $\bot$.

Theorem 1. *(Rmap, Rec) described in Construction 1 is a $(-1, 1)$-RM.*

Proof. (Sketch): We first show that the two correctness properties hold. It is easy to follow the construction of S_i and observe that either its lower k bits or the remaining bits contain the intended secret s_i. Further, the part of S_i that does not represent the secret is random. Therefore the secret is easily distinguishable thanks to the added trailing zeros. Thus, the first correctness condition holds with overwhelming probability in λ. Further, f applied by *Rmap* is a linear function, which is a permutation on $\mathbb{Z}_N$ with overwhelming probability in ν. (Indeed $f = ax + b$ is not a permutation only if $a = (S_1 - S_0)/2$ is not invertible.) Therefore, *Rmap*, evaluated on an encryption of a random element of $\mathbb{Z}_N$, produces a random encryption of a random element of $\mathbb{Z}_N$. It is easy to see that *Rec* outputs $\bot$ on an encryption of a random element with overwhelming probability in λ.

The privacy at v_0, v_1 condition also holds. Indeed, given a secret $s \in D_S$, and pk, the required $Sim(s, pk)$ simulates the output of $Rmap(s_0, s_1, Enc_{pk,\alpha}(v_i), pk)$ as follows. Choose a random bit $c' \in_R \{0, 1\}$ and a random $S' \in \mathbb{Z}_N$. If $c' = 0$ set the lower k bits of S' to be $s 0^\lambda$. If $c' = 1$ set the the higher $n - k$ bits of S' to be $s 0^\lambda$. Return a random encryption of S' under pk. It is easy to see that Sim satisfies the necessary conditions.

The privacy at 0 and at random elements of $\mathbb{Z}_N$ holds for the following reasons. Firstly, as shown in the proof of correctness, *Rmap*, evaluated on encryptions of random elements of $\mathbb{Z}_N$, produces random encryptions of random elements of $\mathbb{Z}_N$. This is easy to simulate with only knowing pk. It remains to show that $Rmap$ evaluated on an encryption of 0 does the same. Recall, $Rmap$ applies f to the input encryption. There are two cases.

If $c = 0$ then $f(0) = 1/2(S_0 + S_1) = 1/2(r_0 2^k + s_0 + s_1 2^k + r_1) = 1/2(r_0 2^k + r_1 + s_0 + s_1 2^k) = 1/2(R + s_0 + s_1 2^k)$.

If $c = 1$ then $f(0) = 1/2(S_0 + S_1) = 1/2(s_0 2^k + r_1 + r_0 2^k + s_1) = 1/2(r_0 2^k + r_1 + s_1 + s_0 2^k) = 1/2(R + s_1 + s_0 2^k)$.

In any case, $f(0)$ is random on $\mathbb{Z}_N$ due to the additive random term $R/2$. □

4.4 GT-CEM Based on Bitwise Paillier Encryption of Inputs

Let n be the length of the compared numbers. We will use the Paillier encryption scheme E to encrypt inputs to $Rmap$ in the bitwise manner. That is, $Gen(\nu)$ is run, fixing (sk, pk) and the instance E_{pk}. The inputs to $Rmap$ are (s_0, s_1, e_0, e_1, pk), where $e_0 = \langle Enc_{pk}(x_1), ..., Enc_{pk}(x_n) \rangle, e_1 = \langle Enc_{pk}(y_1), ..., Enc_{pk}(y_n) \rangle$, where x_1 and y_1 are the most significant bits. The sender additionally has the secrets $s_0, s_1 \in D_S$ as inputs. Let $(Rmap_1, Rec_1)$ be a $(-1, 1)$-RM based on the Paillier encryption scheme (e.g. Constr. 1), instantiated with E_{pk}. Let $D_{M_{pk1}}, D_{S_1}$ be the domains of mappings and secrets of $(Rmap_1, Rec_1)$.

Construction 2 *(GT-CEM)*
Let λ and ν be the correctness and security parameters. Let the plaintext group of E_{pk} be $D_{P_{pk}} = \mathbb{Z}_N$, where $N = pq$ is of bit size $n > \nu$. Define the domain of secrets $D_S = D_{S_1}$ and the domain of mappings $D_{M_{pk}} = D^n_{M_{pk1}}$.

$Rmap$ on input (s_0, s_1, e_0, e_1, pk) computes, for each $i = 1..n$:

1. *an encryption of the difference vector d, where $d_i = x_i - y_i$.*
2. *an encryption of vector γ, s.t. $\gamma_0 = 0$ and $\gamma_i = r_i \gamma_{i-1} + d_i$, where $r_i \in_R \mathbb{Z}_N$.*
3. *a randomized mapping vector μ, where $\mu_i = Rmap_1(s_0, s_1, Enc_{pk}(\gamma_i))$.*

$Rmap$ outputs a random permutation $\pi(\mu)$.
   Rec on input $(\mu'_1..\mu'_n, sk)$ proceeds as follows. For $i = 1..n$, let $z_i = Rec_1(\mu'_i, sk)$. If $z_i \neq \bot$, output z_i and halt. Otherwise, if $\forall i = 1..n, z_i = \bot$, output $\bot$.

Theorem 2. *Construction 2 is a GT-CEM.*

Proof. (Sketch) We will first show that Construction 2 satisfies the correctness requirement. It is easy to see that the homomorphic properties of the encryption scheme allow $Rmap$ and Rec to perform all necessary operations.

Let j be the position where x and y first differ; thus d_j determines $GT(x, y)$. With overwhelming probability, γ is a vector with the following structure: it starts with zero or more zeros, then, in position j, a one or a minus one, then a sequence of random elements in $\mathbb{Z}_N$. It is not hard to see that, by the correctness and privacy properties of $(-1, 1)$-RM, Rec, using Rec_1, will recover $s_{GT(x,y)}$.

We now show that the privacy condition holds as well. We construct simulator $\text{Sim}_{GT}(s, pk)$, where pk is the public key established in the setup phase and $s = s_{Q(x,y)}$. $\text{Sim}_{GT}(s, pk)$ has to generate a distribution statistically close to the output of $Rmap$. $\text{Sim}_{GT}(pk, s)$ proceeds as follows, using the simulators Sim_0 and Sim, required by $(-1, 1)$-RM. It runs $\text{Sim}_0(pk)$ $n - 1$ times and $\text{Sim}(s, pk)$ once, obtaining a vector z' of n simulated mappings. $\text{Sim}_R(s, pk)$ outputs a random permutation $\pi'(z')$. It is easy to see that $\text{Sim}_{GT}(pk, s)$ statistically simulates the output of $Rmap$, due to properties of Sim_0 and Sim. $\square$

4.5   A General (v_0, v_1)-RM Construction

We informally present the construction for any two constants v_0, v_1. We note that it can be naturally generalized for any number of constants $v_1, ..., v_n$.

$Rmap$ proceeds as follows. First, as in Construction 1, add trailing zeros to s_0, s_1 to distinguish them from random elements in $D_{P_{pk}}$. For $i = 1..2$ do the following. Choose random linear functions $f_i = a_i x + b_i$ on the plaintext domain $D_{P_{pk}}$ of the underlying (Paillier) encryption, such that $f_i(v_i) = s_i$. Apply f_i to the encrypted input, obtaining $Enc_{pk}(s_i)$ if $x = v_i$, or an encryption of a random value otherwise. Re-randomize and randomly permute the two obtained encryptions. It is easy to see that this sequence encodes at most a single secret s_i and contains no other information. Rec decrypts the vector, recognizes the secret and outputs it with overwhelming probability.

This (v_0, v_1)-RM can be used with Construction 2, producing GT-CEM with slightly different performance properties. Because this (v_0, v_1)-RM uses larger domains of mappings $D_{M_{pk}}$ than Construction 1, the resulting GT-CEM is less efficient for transferring smaller secrets. When the transferred secrets are large, this (v_0, v_1)-RM performs better due to slightly smaller loss in bandwidth due to redundancy in secrets. See Table in Sect. 6 for detailed comparisons.

4.6   Resource Analysis

We evaluate the message and modular multiplication efficiency of Construction 2, used with $(-1, 1)$-RM of Sect. 4.3 (which we refer to as CEM1) and of Sect. 4.5 (CEM2). The generated encryption key is reused for a polynomial number of executions of our protocols, thus we do not count the relatively small computational cost of key generation. Let n be the length of inputs x and y in base 2, and N be the size of the plaintext domain of the Paillier scheme. Then the message complexity (the size of the output of $Rmap$) of CEM1 is $l_1 = n \log(N^2) = 2n \log N$ bits, and that of CEM2 is $l_2 = 2n \log(N^2) = 4n \log N$. We do not count the encrypted inputs x, y for message complexity, since their length is usually small, and, in many settings, they are not sent to S, but computed by S.

To encrypt the $2n$ input bits, $2n \log N$ multiplications are required. Step 1 of Construction 2 requires n multiplications, and step 2 requires $(\log N + 1)n$ multiplications. Step 3 of CEM1 requires $(3 \log N + 2)n$ multiplications ($2 \log N + 1$ multiplications for application of the linear function f, and $\log N$ to re-randomize the encryption). Similarly, step 3 of CEM2 requires $(6 \log N + 4)n$ multiplications.

Rec of CEM1 (resp. CEM2) costs $2n \log N$ (resp. $4n \log N$) multiplications (We expect to perform half of them before Rec recovers the secret and halts).

In total, CEM1 (resp. CEM2) requires no more than $\approx 8n \log N$ (resp. $\approx 13n \log N$) modular multiplications. Of   those, $4n \log N$ (resp. $7n \log N$) are performed by $Rmap$, and $4n \log N$ (resp. $6n \log N$) are spent for encrypting inputs and reconstructing the output. Note that the encryption and re-encryption multiplications can be precomputed once the encryption scheme is initialized.

Our modular multiplications are four times slower than those of [5,6], since they are performed   mod N^2, while the Goldwasser-Micali (GM) multiplications (used in [5,6]) are   mod N.

One execution of CEM1 (resp. CEM2) allows transfers of secrets of size up to $(\log N)/2 - \lambda$ (resp. $\log N - \lambda$) for the same cost.

Care must be taken in choosing appropriate parameters for comparisons of our results with the performance of other schemes, in particular those based on the potentially weaker quadratic residuosity assumption ([5,6]). Note that in practice no known attack on the Paillier system is better than factoring the modulus N. Clearly, factoring based attacks would also be effective against the GM scheme with the same modulus size. Thus we assume that the security of Paillier and GM schemes with the same size moduli is approximately the same.

The performance comparisons are summarized in the Table in Sect. 6.

4.7   CEM for any $\mathbf{NC^1}$ Predicate From Homomorphic Encryption

We note that it is possible to construct CEM for any NC^1 predicate Q, using, for example, an information-theoretic abstraction of Yao's garbled circuit [11]. The idea is to assign two specially constructed secrets to each input wire of the (polysize) formula representation of the NC^1 circuit. Here each secret corresponds to one of the two possible wire values. The secrets satisfy the following property: a set of secrets, one for each wire of the circuit, allows us to compute the value of the circuit on the corresponding input, and carries no other information.

It is easy to use the homomorphic encryption properties to allow Rec to reconstruct only one appropriate secret for each wire. Combined with the tools discussed in the previous paragraph, this implies CEM for any NC^1 predicate.

5   Protocol Constructions from GT-CEM

As mentioned in the discussion of CEM in Sect. 3, natural protocol constructions immediately arise from CEM in the semi-honest model. We demonstrate this on a special case of PSPP of [5], where the server S runs the auction with two bidders C_0, C_1. (Our solution can naturally accomodate more bidders, using, e.g., technique of Sect. 5.2 of [5].) As discussed in Sect. 2 and [5], in the initialization phase, each of the clients generates and publishes his public key pk_i with S.

The main *selection* phase proceeds as follows. Each client C_i sends to S two encryptions of his input, with his own and with the other client's public keys (i.e. S obtains $Enc_{pk_i}(x_i), Enc_{pk_{1-i}}(x_i)$ from C_i). S applies GT-CEM twice (once under each key) and sends the outputs of $Rmap$ to the corresponding C_i for reconstruction. That is, S sends $m_i = Rmap(s_0, s_1, Enc_{pk_i}(x_i), Enc_{pk_i}(x_{1-i}), pk_i)$ to each C_i, who then applies $Rec(sk_i, m_i)$ and obtains s_1 if his bid is greater and s_0 otherwise. (We note that the receipt of the non-winning s_0 is crucial to hide the rank of the bid of C_i in auctions with more than two parties [5].)

It is easy to see that this protocol is secure in the semi-honest model. Indeed, by the definition of CEM, each m_i contains only the intended secret and no other information. Further, it is not hard to see that computationally-bounded S does not learn anything from seeing semantically secure encryptions of clients' bids (under a natural assumption that the secrets s_0, s_1 are a polytime computable function of the transcript of S's view of execution of the auction and arbitrary information available prior to the key generation phase).

5.1   Handling Malicious Behaviours

One of the main reasons for the introduction of the semi-honest facilitator is the simplification and efficiency improvement of protocols. In this discussion, we assume the presence of such semi-honest S running $Rmap$ and discuss methods of protection against malicious behaviour of other participants. We note that the CEM model is well suited for this task, since the malicious actions of parties are limited to improper input submission and reporting of the decoded output.

First, we observe that the free choice of secrets is a powerful tool. For example, when secrets are randomly chosen, they may serve as a proof of the value of Q in the evaluated Q-CEM. Indeed, the recipient of s_i is not able to claim $Q(x, y) = 1 - i$, since he cannot obtain s_{1-i}. Further, for example, secrets can contain S's signatures, proving the correctness of reconstruction to anyone.

A harder task is ensuring that malicious players do not gain from submitting contrived inputs to S. Firstly, zero-knowledge (ZK) techniques could be used to ensure players' compliance with the prescribed protocol. This is often computationally expensive and requires either a common random string or an extra round of interaction. There exist light-weight alternatives to ZK, such as conditional disclosures of Aiello, Ishai and Reingold [1] and Laur and Lipmaa [12]. Their idea, well suited for our setting, is to ensure that an improperly formed input will render useless the obtained output of $Rmap$. For example, suppose $Rmap$ requires input encryption e to be a Paillier encryption of a bit (i.e. that $Dec(e) \in \{0, 1\}$). We ensure that non-compliant inputs result in garbled output as follows. Let $s_0, s_1 \in D_S$ be inputs to $Rmap$. We choose a random $r \in_R D_S$ and run $Rmap$ with secrets $s_0 \oplus r, s_1 \oplus r$. We now only need a CEM procedure that would transfer r iff $Dec(e) \in \{0, 1\}$, which can be easily constructed.

5.2   Proxy Selling with a Secret Reserve Price

We sketch how to apply GT-CEM to an interesting variant of a proxy selling task, mentioned in the Introduction. Here, the seller wishes to be offline and delegate selling to the semi-trusted S. The seller initializes E_{pk}, publishes pk and sends an encryption $Enc_{pk}(x)$ of his lowest acceptable price (i.e. reserve) to S, who later interacts with buyers as follows. On an encrypted offer $Enc_{pk}(y)$, S replies with $Rmap(s_0, s_1, Enc_{pk}(y), Enc_{pk}(x), pk)$, where s_1 serves as S's certification of the successful buyer (e.g. in a form of a signature), and s_0 is a non-winning (e.g. empty) secret. Thus, successful buyers obtain (an encryption of) the contract, which they later present to the seller.

Combining GT-CEM with the general CEM techniques based on secret representations, described in sect. 4.7, allows us to obtain very efficient CEM depending on several GT evaluations. This allows us to proxy sell not only based on a reserve price, but on a price range, delivery date ranges, etc.

6   Comparison with Previous Work

We continue the resource analysis of Sect. 4.6. Note that the protocols of [5,6,12] can be appropriately modified to be cast as GT-CEM. We summarize the cost of comparable modular multiplications and communication of evaluating GT-CEM based on [5,6,12] and our constructions CEM1 and CEM2 (i.e. Construction 4.4 instantiated with $(-1,1)$-RM of Sect. 4.3 and 4.5 respectively).

Here c-bit secrets are transferred based on comparison of n-bit numbers. λ and ν are the correctness and security parameters, and $N > 2^\nu$ is the modulus of the employed encryption scheme (GM for [5,6] and Paillier for [12] and our work). We do not include the one-time cost of key generation. We measure communication as the size of the output of $Rmap$.

Solutions of [5,6] transfer one-bit secrets per execution, therefore c-bit secrets can be transferred at a factor c cost increase. Our CEM1 (resp. CEM2) protocols transfer secrets of size $c < \nu/2 - \lambda$ (resp. $c < \nu - \lambda$) per execution. Today's common parameters $\nu \approx 1000, \lambda \approx 40..80$ imply transfers of approximately 450 (resp. 950)-bit secrets per execution of CEM1 (resp. CEM2). For CEM of longer secrets, multiple execution is needed. Note the significant advantage of CEM1 for the most frequent case where the transfer of medium-size secrets is required.

Costs and Comparisons. GT-COT of [12] can be modified to obtain GT-CEM similar in cost to CEM2. Solution of [2] (in a more restricted setting, where one of the compared numbers is given in plaintext) carries approximately half of the cost of CEM2. Other costs and comparisons are summarized below. (The cost of (client-run) GM decryption, used in [6,5], is not less than $\log N$ modular multiplications. For simplicity, we assume that it is $\log N$.)

Protocol	Comparable Modular Multiplications			Communication	Comment
	client	server	total		
of [6]	$4nc\lambda \log N$	$24nc\lambda$	$32nc\lambda + 4nc\lambda \log N$	$4nc\lambda \log N$	
of [5]	$8n^2c \log N$	$12n^2c$	$12n^2c + 8n^2c \log N$	$8n^2c \log N$	
CEM1	$16n \log N$	$16n \log N$	$32n \log N$	$2n \log N$	$c < \nu/2 - \lambda$
CEM2	$24n \log N$	$28n \log N$	$52n \log N$	$4n \log N$	$c < \nu - \lambda$

Acknowledgements. The authors are very grateful to Charles Rackoff for many technical comments and suggestions on this paper. We also thank Sven Laur and Helger Lipmaa for discussions of CDS and their related work [12], Marc Fischlin for clarifications of the costs associated with his scheme [6], and the anonymous reviewers of FC 2006 for helpful comments and suggestions.

References

1. William Aiello, Yuval Ishai, and Omer Reingold. Priced oblivious transfer: How to sell digital goods. In *Proc. EUROCRYPT 2001*, pages 119–135, 2001.
2. Ian F. Blake and Vladimir Kolesnikov. Strong conditional oblivious transfer and computing on intervals. In *Advances in Cryptology - ASIACRYPT 2004*, volume 3329 of *Lecture Notes in Computer Science*, pages 515–529. Springer, 2004.
3. Christian Cachin. Efficient private bidding and auctions with an oblivious third party. In *Proceedings of the 6th ACM Conference on Computer and Communications Security*, pages 120–127. ACM Press, 1999.
4. G. Di Crescenzo, R. Ostrovsky, and S. Rajagopalan. Conditional oblivious transfer and time-released encryption. In *Proc. CRYPTO 99*, pages 74–89. Springer-Verlag, 1999. Lecture Notes in Computer Science, vol. 1592.
5. Giovanni Di Crescenzo. Private selective payment protocols. In *Financial Cryptography*, pages 72–89, 2000.
6. Marc Fischlin. A cost-effective pay-per-multiplication comparison method for millionaires. In *RSA Security 2001 Cryptographer's Track*, pages 457–471. Springer-Verlag, 2001. Lecture Notes in Computer Science, vol. 2020.
7. Michael J. Freedman, Kobbi Nissim, and Benny Pinkas. Efficient private matching and set intersection. In *Proc. EUROCRYPT 2004*, pages 1–19. Springer-Verlag, 2004. Lecture Notes in Computer Science, vol. 3027.
8. Yael Gertner, Yuval Ishai, Eyal Kushilevitz, and Tal Malkin. Protecting data privacy in private information retrieval schemes. In *STOC '98: Proceedings of the thirtieth annual ACM symposium on Theory of computing*, pages 151–160, New York, NY, USA, 1998. ACM Press.
9. Bart Goethals, Sven Laur, Helger Lipmaa, and Taneli Mielikäinen. On Private Scalar Product Computation for Privacy-Preserving Data Mining. In Choonsik Park and Seongtaek Chee, editors, *The 7th Annual International Conference in Information Security and Cryptology (ICISC 2004)*, volume 3506, pages 104–120, December 2–3, 2004.
10. M. Kantarcioglu and C. Clifton. Privacy-preserving distributed mining of association rules on horizontally partitioned data. In *ACM SIGMOD Workshop on Research Issues on Data Mining and Knowledge Discovery (DMKD'02)*, 2002.
11. Vladimir Kolesnikov. Gate evaluation secret sharing and secure one-round two-party computation. In *Advances in Cryptology - ASIACRYPT 2005*, volume 3788 of *Lecture Notes in Computer Science*, pages 136–155. Springer, 2005.
12. Sven Laur and Helger Lipmaa. Additive conditional disclosure of secrets and applications. Cryptology ePrint Archive, Report 2005/378, 2005. http://eprint.iacr.org/.
13. Yehuda Lindell and Benny Pinkas. Privacy preserving data mining. In *Proc. CRYPTO 00*, pages 20–24. Springer-Verlag, 2000. Lecture Notes in Computer Science, vol. 1880.
14. Moni Naor, Benny Pinkas, and Reuben Sumner. Privacy preserving auctions and mechanism design. In *1st ACM Conf. on Electronic Commerce*, pages 129–139, 1999.
15. Pascal Paillier. Public-key cryptosystems based on composite degree residuosity classes. In *Proc. EUROCRYPT 99*, pages 223–238. Springer-Verlag, 1999. Lecture Notes in Computer Science, vol. 1592.
16. M. Rabin. How to exchange secrets by oblivious transfer. Technical Report TR-81, Harvard Aiken Computation Laboratory, 1981.

Revisiting Oblivious Signature-Based Envelopes

Samad Nasserian[1] and Gene Tsudik[2]

[1] Computer Science Department, RWTH Aachen University,
52056 Aachen, Germany
samad.nasserian@rwth-aachen.de
[2] Computer Science Department, University of California, Irvine
Irvine, CA, 902697, USA
gts@ics.uci.edu

Abstract. In this paper, we investigate an interesting and practical cryptographic construct - Oblivious Signature-Based Envelopes (OSBEs) - recently introduced in [15]. OSBEs allow a sender to communicate information to a receiver such that the latter's rights (or roles) are unknown to the former. At the same time, a receiver can obtain the information only if it is authorized to access it. This makes OSBEs a natural fit for anonymity-oriented and privacy-preserving applications. Previous results yielded three OSBE constructs: one based on RSA and two based on Identity-Based Encryption (IBE). Our work focuses on the ElGamal signature family: we succeed in constructing practical and secure OSBE schemes for several well-known signature schemes, including: Schnorr, Nyberg-Rueppel, ElGamal and DSA. As illustrated by experiments with a prototype implementation, our schemes are more efficient than previous techniques. Furthermore, we show that some OSBE schemes, despite offering affiliation privacy for the receiver, result in no additional cost over schemes that do not offer this feature.

1 Introduction

The recent surge in popularity of electronic communication and electronic transaction prompts many natural concerns about anonymity and, more generally, privacy of communicating entities. In the last decade, there has been a lot interest in privacy-enhancing tools and techniques. Prominent topics include advanced cryptographic constructs, such as: blind signatures [10], group signatures (e.g., [4]), identity escrow (e.g., [14]), secret handshakes [2] and privacy-preserving trust negotiation [7].

In a recent paper [15], Li, et al. introduced a simple and interesting cryptographic concept termed OSBE: Oblivious Signature-Based Envelopes. One motivating scenario for OSBE is as follows: suppose that Bob is a Secret Service agent and has a digitally signed certificate asserting his membership. The rules of the trade stipulate that an agent must only reveal his certificate to another party if that party is also an agent. Thus, if Bob and Alice (who is also a secret agent) want to communicate securely, they are seemingly at an impasse since someone must reveal their certificate first. A simpler, and perhaps more appealing, scenario occurs if Alice is a regular entity without any specific affiliation.

G. Di Crescenzo and A. Rubin (Eds.): FC 2006, LNCS 4107, pp. 221–235, 2006.
© IFCA/Springer-Verlag Berlin Heidelberg 2006

However, she has some information that she is only willing to reveal to another party (who claims the name Bob) if that party has certain credentials, for example, Alice might be a potential informant and Bob might be an FBI agent. At the same time, Bob is unwilling – or not allowed – to reveal his credentials. In this case, Alice and Bob are also stuck since neither wants to be the first to reveal information. Note that, in both examples, Bob has a signed credential which he cannot reveal; specifically, Bob needs to keep the signature secret, whereas, the message covered by the signature is not secret at all.

An OSBE scheme can help in the aforementioned situations since it allows Alice to communicate information to Bob in such a way that: (1) Bob only obtains the information if he possesses appropriate credentials, (2) Alice does not determine whether Bob possesses such credentials, and (3) no other party learns anything about Alice's information and Bob's possession, or lack of, the credentials. A more detailed discussion about OSBE applications can be found in the extended version of this paper [19].

Besides introducing the OSBE concept, [15] presented three concrete OSBE schemes: RSA-OSBE, BLS-OSBE and Rabin-OSBE. The last two use Identity-Based Encryption (Boneh-Franklin [5] and Cocks [11] schemes, respectively) and do not require interaction, while RSA-OSBE is a 2-round protocol[1] with some very interesting properties. (A discussion of these properties is in Section 8). Notably, no OSBE schemes for any of the ElGamal family [13] of signature schemes have been developed. In fact, OSBE for DSA is explicitly mentioned as an open problem in [15]. In this paper, we begin where the work of [15] left off.

Contributions: Our main result is the development of a series of OSBE schemes for the ElGamal family of signature schemes, including Schnorr, Nyberg-Rueppel and DSA. We prove the security of Schnorr-OSBE and discuss the security of the other schemes. We analyze and compare their respective costs and present the results of our prototype implementation. Our schemes are very efficient and, in fact, demonstrate that, in some cases, added privacy introduces **no additional costs**.

Organization: This paper is organized as follows: the next section contains the necessary OSBE definitions. Section 3 shows the construction of OSBE for Schnorr signatures, followed by Section 4 which does the same for Nyberg/Rueppel signatures. Section 5 presents OSBE schemes for other ElGamal family signatures, including an OSBE scheme for the Digital Signature Algorithm (DSA). Costs of all OSBE schemes and the results of the implementation of the OSBE schemes are analyzed in Sections 6 and 7. Finally, we discuss certain other security features in Section 8

Remark: Due to length restrictions, certain relevant material is not included in this paper. An extended version [19] of this paper contains more detailed discussions of: related work, potential OSBE applications, secret handshake extensions as well as semantic security of OSBE schemes.

---

[1] See [19] for a re-cap of RSA-OSBE.

2 Preliminaries

This section presents some background material, including definitions of OSBE components and OSBE security properties. (Since much of the material in this section is adapted from [15], those familiar with [15] may wish to skip this section with no lack of continuity.)

An OSBE scheme enables a sender to encrypt a message and send it to a receiver who can decrypt the message **if and only if** the receiver has the right third party's signature (e.g., a signature from a certification authority) on a previously agreed upon message. However, the sender is not allowed to know – not even at the end – if the receiver has the right third party's signature. The sender is assured only that the encrypted message will only be decrypted if the receiver has the right signature. The components of an OSBE scheme are (1) a setup algorithm and (2) three parties S, R_1 and R_2 or sender, authorized receiver and unauthorized receiver (adversary), respectively. In other words, S is the party who wants to send message P to the authorized receiver who has the right signature on some authorization string M, e.g., M can be thought of as a certificate. R_1 is the receiver who has the right signature σ on message M and R_2 is the receiver who does not have σ and who might try to impersonate R_1.

An OSBE scheme consists of two phases: *Setup* and *Interaction*. (Note that [15] defines an additional *Open* phase. We merged it with *Interaction*.)

Setup: This algorithm generates two messages M and P and a public/private key-pair for a given signature scheme. It uses the secret key to generate a signature σ on an input message M. The values M and the public parameters/keys for the signature scheme are known to all parties. Whereas, P is known only to S and σ is known only to R_1. Since the setup algorithm generates the signature, we assume that it also takes the role of a certification authority (CA). (However, this is not a requirement.)

Interaction: In this phase, S communicates with the receiver R, which is either R_1 or R_2. However, in the process, S cannot distinguish between R_1 or R_2. At the end of this phase, if $R = R_1$, R_1 outputs message P.

An OSBE scheme must satisfy three properties: *soundness*, *obliviousness* and *semantic security against the receiver*, which are informally defined as (formal treatment of these properties can be found in [15]):

Soundness: An OSBE scheme is sound if the authorized receiver R_1 (who has the signature σ on message M) can output P with non-negligible probability at the end of the *Interaction* phase.

Obliviousness: An OSBE scheme is oblivious if, at the end of the interaction phase, S does not know whether it is communicating with R_1 or R_2. In other words, if one of: R_1 or R_2 is randomly picked to take part in the Interaction with S, the probability of S correctly guessing the other party is, at best, negligibly over $1/2$.

Semantic Security Against the Receiver: An OSBE scheme is semantically secure against the receiver if R_2 learns nothing about P. Even if P can be only one of two possible messages (selected by R_2), at the end of the Interaction phase,

R_2 cannot determine – with probability non-negligibly greater than $1/2$ – which message was actually sent.

In the remainder of this paper we use the term *negligible* to refer to functions with a certain property: a function $f(x)$ is said to be *negligible* if, for each polynomial $p(k)$, there exists a k_0 with

$$f(x) \leq \frac{1}{|p(k)|} \text{ for all } x \geq k_0 \qquad (1)$$

As discussed in Section 8 below, there are other features that could be desired from OSBE schemes.

3   OSBE with Schnorr Signatures

Recall that Schnorr's signature scheme works as follows [22]:

> Let p be a large prime and q be a large prime factor of $p-1$. Let g be an element of order q in $\mathbb{Z}_p^*$, $\mathcal{M}$ be the message space and $H : \mathcal{M} \to \mathbb{Z}_q^*$ be a suitable cryptographic hash function. The signer's secret key is: $a \in_R \mathbb{Z}_q^*$ and the corresponding public key is: $y = g^a \bmod p$. The values: p, q and y are public, while a is only known to the signer. A signature $\sigma = (e, s)$ on input message M is computed as follows:
>
> 1. select a random value $k \in_R \mathbb{Z}_q^*$
> 2. compute $e = H(M, g^k \bmod p)$
> 3. compute $s = ae + k \bmod q$
>
> A Schnorr signature is verified by checking that $H(M, g^s y^{-e} \bmod p)$ matches e.

Similar to RSA-OSBE [15] and all other non-IBE-based OSBE schemes, the interaction in Schnorr-OSBE is essentially a Diffie-Hellman style key agreement protocol. It is run between S and either R_1 or R_2 where the former is a legitimate certificate holder and the latter is an adversarial party. If S and R_1 take part in the protocol, then – at the end – both parties agree on the same shared secret key. Whereas, if S and R_2 run the protocol, then they compute distinct values and R_2 is unable to derive the key computed by S. Since the very nature of OSBE prohibits R_1 (or R_2) from authenticating to S, no key confirmation flows in either direction.

Once S computes the Diffie-Hellman secret K_S, it sends its message (P) to the other party (either R_1 or R_2) encrypted under a key derived from K_S.

R_1 starts the protocol by sending to S one part of its signature: $X = g^s y^{-e} \bmod p = g^k \bmod p$. S then generates a random $z \in_R \mathbb{Z}_q^*$ and computes its version of the secret as:

$$K_s = [y^{H(M,X)} X]^z = g^{(ae+k)z} \qquad (2)$$

and sends $Z = g^z \bmod p$ to R_1. R_1 knows the other half of the signature: $s = ae + k \bmod q$. It can thus easily compute $K_r = Z^s = g^{z(ae+k)}$. Both S

and R_1 employ a function $H'()$ for deriving from the Diffie-Hellman secret, the actual key to be used for the symmetric encryption of message P.

R_2 starts the protocol by sending to S a value $X' = g^{k'} \bmod p$ to S.[2] S then generates a random $z \in_R Z_q^*$ and computes its version of the secret as:

$$K_s = [y^{H(M,X')}X']^z \qquad (3)$$

and sends $Z = g^z \bmod p$ to R_2. As we will show in the proof of security of Schnorr-OSBE, R_2 cannot compute the Diffie-Hellman secret, since he does not have the necessary signature.

In more detail, Schnorr-OSBE is as follows:

Setup: On input of a security parameter t, this algorithm creates a Schnorr key: (p, q, g, a, y), selects a suitable cryptographic hash function H, a function H' for key derivation and two security parameters t_1 and t_2, which are linear in t. It also chooses a semantically secure symmetric encryption scheme $\mathcal{E}$, two messages M and P. It computes a Schnorr signature $\sigma = (e, s)$ on message M. Finally, it gives M, σ and (p, q, g, y) to R_1, M and (p, q, g, y) to R_2 and M, P and (p, q, g, y) to S.

Interaction

> Step 1a: $R_1 \longrightarrow S:$ $X = g^s \cdot y^{-e} \bmod p = g^k \bmod p$
> – OR
> Step 1b: $R_2 \longrightarrow S:$ $X = g^{k'} \bmod p$ for some $k' \in \mathbb{Z}_q^*$
> Step 2: S receives X, checks that: $(X)^{(p-1)/q} \bmod p \notin \{0, 1\}$, picks a random $z \in \{1..2^{t_1}q\}$ with $z \bmod q \neq 0$, computes $K_s = [y^{H(M,X)}X]^z$, $k_s = H'(K_s)$ and:
> Step 3: $S \longrightarrow R_1$ or $R_2:$ $Z = g^z \bmod p$, $C = \mathcal{E}_{k_s}[P]$
> Step 4: R_1 receives (Z, C), computes $K_r = Z^s \bmod p$, derives $k_r = H'(K_r)$ and finally decrypts C with k_r.

We now prove that Schnorr-OSBE is sound, oblivious and semantically secure against the receiver.

Soundness: To see that Schnorr-OSBE is sound, at the end of *Interaction*, $K_r = K_s$ has to hold. This is easily established, since:

$$K_s = [y^{H(M,X)}X]^z = [g^{ae}g^s y^{-e}]^z = [g^{ae+ae+k}g^{-ae}]^z = g^{sz} = Z^s = K_r \qquad (4)$$

Showing that Schnorr-OSBE is oblivious is similar to the proof of obliviousness for RSA-OSBE in [15]. We first re-state the notion of statistical indistinguishability. Two distribution families $D^1(t_1)$ and $D^2(t_1)$ are said to be **statistically indistinguishable** if:

$$\Sigma_y |Pr_{x \in D^1(t_1)}[x = y] - Pr_{x \in D^2(t_1)}[x = y]| \qquad (5)$$

---

[2] Note that R_2 has to send a value X' with $X'^{\frac{p-1}{q}} \bmod p \notin \{0, 1\}$ to S, i.e. there exists a $k' \in \{1, ..., q-1\}$ with $X' = g^{k'} \bmod p$. Otherwise, X' will be immediately rejected by S.

is negligible in t.

If two distribution families are statistically indistinguishable, then there exists no algorithm that can distinguish between the two with non-negligible advantage by sampling from them. We use this to prove the following theorem.

Theorem 1. Schnorr-OSBE is oblivious.

Proof (sketch): Two distribution families:

$$D^1(t_1) = \{g^s y^{-e} \bmod p = g^k \bmod p \mid k \in \{1..2^{t_1}q\}\} \tag{6}$$

and

$$D^2(t_1) = \{g^{k'} \bmod p \mid k' \in \{1..2^{t_1}q\}\} \tag{7}$$

range over the same values and, during each run of *Interaction*, a random value from one of these distribution families is sent by a communicating partner (either R_1 or R_2). Since these values are chosen at random and the two distribution families range over the same values, S cannot decide whether the other party is R_1 or R_2. Consequently, Schnorr-OSBE is oblivious.

In more detail, since q is the order of g, $D^1(t_1)$ and $D^2(t_1)$ (for a fixed t_1) each have q points. The probability difference on any point is at most $\frac{1}{2^{t_1}q}$, therefore, the total difference is at most $\frac{q}{2^{t_1}q} = \frac{1}{2^{t_1}}$. Since this quantity is negligible in t_1 and t_1 is linear in t, the total difference is also negligible in t. Thus, the two distribution sets are statistically indistinguishable.

Theorem 2. Assuming the non-existence of a polynomial time algorithm for solving the CDH Problem and that H and H' are modelled as random oracles, Schnorr-OSBE is secure against the receiver.

Proof. Schnorr-OSBE uses a semantically secure symmetric encryption algorithm and H' is modelled as a random oracle. Therefore, Schnorr-OSBE is semantically secure against the receiver if no polynomially bounded adversary, who does not possess the signature $\sigma = (e, s)$ on M, can compute with non-negligible probability the OSBE key $K_s = g^{z(ae+k)} \bmod p$. More precisely, Schnorr-OSBE is semantically secure against the receiver if there is no polynomially bounded adversary who can win with non-negligible probability the following game:

1. $\mathcal{A}$ is given a message M and the public key (p, q, g, y) with $y = g^a \bmod p$.
2. $\mathcal{A}$ chooses a value $X = g^k \bmod p$.[3]
3. $\mathcal{A}$ is given the value $Z = g^z \bmod p$.
4. $\mathcal{A}$ outputs a value K.

A wins the game if and only if $K = g^{z(ea+k)} \bmod p$ with $e = H(M, g^k)$. We prove our claim by contradiction. We show that if there is a polynomial adversary who wins the above game with non-negligible probability, then such an adversary

---

[3] Note that we do not make any assumptions about $\mathcal{A}$'s knowledge about k. $\mathcal{A}$ might know the value of k, it might have partial knowledge of k or k might even be completely unknown to $\mathcal{A}$.

can also solve every instance (g^a, g^z) of the CDH Problem in polynomial time. Assume there is an adversary $\mathcal{A}$ who does not have a signature $\sigma = (e, s)$ but who nevertheless wins the above game (i.e. computes the value $g^{z(ae+k)} \bmod p$) with non-negligible probability ϵ. Using the forking lemma [21], we know that then, $\mathcal{A}$ can be executed twice in a row with the same value $X = g^k \bmod p$ and different random oracles H and H' (such that $e = H(M, g^k) \neq H'(M, g^k) = e'$) and $\mathcal{A}$ wins both games with non-negligible probability of at least $\frac{\epsilon^2}{q_H}$, where q_H is the number of queries $\mathcal{A}$ makes to the hash function. This means, $\mathcal{A}$ can compute with non-negligible probability the values $K = g^{z(ea+k)} \bmod p$ and $K' = g^{z(e'a+k)} \bmod p$ with $e \neq e'$. Consequently, $\mathcal{A}$ can also efficiently compute g^{az}:

$$\left(\frac{K}{K'}\right)^{(e-e')^{-1}} = \left(g^{zea-ze'a}\right)^{(e-e')^{-1}} = \left(g^{za(e-e')}\right)^{(e-e')^{-1}} = g^{az} \bmod p. \quad (8)$$

However, this means that $\mathcal{A}$ can solve the CDH Problem in polynomial time, which is a contradiction to our assumption.

Note that the Schnorr signature scheme is existentially unforgeable assuming there is no polynomial time algorithm which can solve the Discrete Logarithm (DL) Problem [21]. Since we assume that there is no polynomial time algorithm for solving the CDH Problem, this also implies that there is no polynomial time algorithm which can solve the DL Problem. Therefore, assuming there is no polynomial time algorithm which can solve the DL Problem, a polynomial time adversary $\mathcal{A}$ cannot forge a signature on M in order to be able to compute the OSBE key.

4   Nyberg/Rueppel OSBE

We now turn to the Nyberg/Rueppel signature scheme. Recall that the Nyberg/Rueppel signature scheme [18] is as follows:

Let p be a large prime and q be a large prime factor of $p - 1$. Let g be an element of order q in $\mathbb{Z}_p^*$, $\mathcal{M}$ be the message space and $H : \mathcal{M} \to \mathbb{Z}_p$ be a suitable cryptographic hash function. (Note that the *textbook* description of Nyberg-Rueppel scheme does not require a hash function, since the scheme provides the *message recovery* feature.) The signer's secret key is: $a \in_R \mathbb{Z}_q^*$ and the corresponding public key is: $y = g^a \bmod p$. The values: p, q and y are public, while a is only known to the signer. A signature $\sigma = (e, s)$ on input message M is computed as follows:

1. select a random value $k \in_R \mathbb{Z}_q^*$ and set $h = H(M)$
2. compute $e = hg^{-k} \bmod p$
3. compute $s = ae + k \bmod q$

A Nyberg-Rueppel signature is verified by checking that: (1) $0 < e < p$, $0 < s < q$, and (2) $h' = g^s y^{-e} e \bmod p$ matches $h' = H(M)$.

NR-OSBE is very similar to Schnorr-OSBE presented above:

Setup: This algorithm takes as input a security parameter t and creates a Nyberg-Rueppel key: (p, q, g, a, y), selects a suitable cryptographic hash function H, a function H' for key derivation and two security parameters t_1 and t_2, which are linear in t. It also chooses a semantically secure symmetric encryption scheme $\mathcal{E}$, two messages M and P and computes $\sigma = (e, s)$ where:[4]

$$e = hg^{-k} \bmod p \text{ where } k \in_R \mathbb{Z}_q^*, \tag{9}$$

$$e \bmod q \neq 0 \text{ and } s = ae + k \bmod q \tag{10}$$

It then gives M, σ and (p, q, g, y) to R_1, M and (p, q, g, y) to R_2 and M, P and (p, q, g, y) to S.

Interaction: Although in the following, we describe actions for S, R_1 and R_2, it is understood that only one of $[R_1, R_2]$ actually participates in the protocol. (The term *participates* means: **sends a message in Step 1a/b below**.)

Step 1a: $R_1 \longrightarrow S$: $e = hg^{-k} \bmod p$
– OR
Step 1b: $R_2 \longrightarrow S$: $e = hg^{-k'} \bmod p$ for some $k' \in \mathbb{Z}_q^*$
Step 2: S receives e, checks that: $(e/h)^{(p-1)/q} \bmod q \notin \{0,1\}$, picks a random $z \in \{1..2^{t_1}q\}$, computes $K_s = [y^e(e/h)^{-1}]^z$ derives $k_s = H'(K_s)$ and:
Step 3: $S \longrightarrow R_1$ or R_2 : $Z = g^z \bmod p$, $C = \mathcal{E}_{k_s}[P]$
Step 4: R_1 receives (Z, C), computes $K_r = Z^s = g^{z(ae+k)}$, derives $k_r = H'(K_r)$ and finally decrypts C with k_r.
Note that, in Step 1b, the value e sent by R_2 must be such that: $(e/h)^{(p-1)/q} \bmod p \notin \{0,1\}$. In other words, e/h has to be in the unique group of order q, which is generated by g. If this is not the case, e is immediately rejected by S. Therefore, there must be $k' \in \{1..2^{t_1}q\}$ such that: $e = hg^{-k'} \bmod p$.

Soundness: To show that NR-OSBE is sound, S and R_1 must share the same symmetric key when the protocol completes successfully, i.e., $K_r = K_s$. It is easy to see that:

$$K_s = [y^e(e/h)^{-1}]^z = g^{(ae+k)z} = g^{zs} = Z^s = K_r \tag{11}$$

Theorem 3. NR-OSBE is oblivious.

Proof (sketch): Two distribution families:

$$D^1(t_1) = \{e = hg^{-k} \bmod p | k \in \{1..2^{t_1}q\}\} \tag{12}$$

and

$$D^2(t_1) = \{e = h \cdot g^{-k'} \bmod p | k \in \{1..2^{t_1}q\}\} \tag{13}$$

---

[4] We need the property $e \bmod q \neq 0$ for the proof of security of our scheme. Note that this is only a restriction on the signer and in particular no restriction on S or $R_{1/2}$.

range over the same values and, during each execution of the Diffie-Hellman key exchange protocol, a random value from one of the two families is sent by each party. Since these values are chosen at random and, since the two distribution families have the same values, S does not know if the other party is R_1 or R_2. Consequently NR-OSBE is oblivious. More concretely, since q is the order of g, both $D^1(t_1)$ and $D^2(t_1)$ (for a fixed t_1) have q points. The probability difference on any point is at most $\frac{1}{2^{t_1}q}$ and, therefore, the total difference is at most $\frac{q}{2^{t_1}q} = \frac{1}{2^{t_1}}$. Since the total difference is negligible in t_1 and t_1 is linear in t, the total difference is also negligible in t. Thus, two distribution sets are statistically indistinguishable.

Semantic security against the receiver: While proving the semantic security of Schnorr-OSBE is straightforward, the proof of the semantic security of Nyberg/Rueppel-OSBE and also that of ElGamal-OSBE and DSA-OSBE is far from easy, if standard cryptographic assumptions are to be made. Further discussion of semantic security for Nyberg/Rueppel-OSBE, ElGamal-OSBE and DSA-OSBE can be found in the extended version of this paper [19].

5   ElGamal and DSA OSBE

A number of ElGamal variants are known in the literature. The following 6 are taken from [16] (note that none of them corresponds to either Schnorr or Nyberg-Rueppel schemes):

(1) $s = (h - ag^k)k^{-1}$ (2) $s = (h - kg^k)a^{-1}$ (3) $s = ag^k + kh$
(4) $s = ah + kg^k$ (5) $s = (g^k - kh)a^{-1}$ (6) $s = (g^k - ah)k^{-1}$

All computations are done mod $(p - 1)$ and a smaller prime q is not required, although $(p - 1)$ cannot be a product of small factors (to prevent the so-called Pohlig-Hellman attack [20]). In each case, the second part of the signature is: $e = g^k \bmod p$.

It is easy to construct OSBE schemes for variants 3. and 4. above. In each case, the interaction component is as follows (the Setup component is trivial):

Step 1: $R_1 \longrightarrow S: \quad e = g^k \bmod p$
Step 2: S receives e, generates $z \in_R \{1..2^{t_1}q\}$, computes:

$$K_s = [y^e \cdot e^h]^z = g^{z(ag^k + kh)} \quad \text{for variant 3.} \tag{14}$$

$$K_s = [y^h \cdot e^e]^z = g^{z(ah + kg^k)} \quad \text{for variant 4.} \tag{15}$$

and derives $k_s = H'(K_s)$
Step 3: $S \longrightarrow R_1;: \quad Z = g^z \bmod p, \quad C = \mathcal{E}_{k_s}[P]$
Step 4: R_1 receives (Z, C), computes $K_r = Z^s$, derives $k_r = H'(K_r)$ and decrypts C with k_r.

To avoid repetition, we omit proofs of obliviousness and semantic security against the receiver for the above OSBE variants. Suffice it to say that the proofs are almost identical to those for Schnorr-OSBE and NR-OSBE.

OSBE constructs for variants 1., 2. , 5. and 6. are less trivial since the signing equation (computation of s) involves either a^{-1} or k^{-1}. We now focus on variant 1. since it represents the original ElGamal signature scheme [13] and also naturally leads to an OSBE scheme for DSA.

The Interaction Component in EG-OSBE is as follows:

Interaction:

Step 1: $R_1 \longrightarrow S: \quad e = g^k \bmod p$
Step 2: S receives e, generates $z \in_R \{1..2^{t_1}p\}$ with $e \bmod (p-1) \neq 0$, computes $K_s = y^{ez} \cdot g^{-hz} \bmod p$ and derives $k_s = H'(K_s)$
Step 3: $S \longrightarrow R_1;: \quad Z = e^z \bmod p, \quad C = \mathcal{E}_{k_s}[P]$
Step 4: R_1 receives (Z, C), computes $K_r = Z^{-s}$, derives $k_r = H'(K_r)$ and decrypts C with k_r.

Soundness. It is easy to see that:

$$K_s = y^{ez}g^{-hz} = g^{(ae-h)z} = g^{k(ae-h)k^{-1}z} = e^{-sz} = e^{-zs} = Z^{-s} = K_r \qquad (16)$$

Theorem 4. EG-OSBE is oblivious.

Proof. Almost identical to that for Schnorr-OSBE.

The Digital Signature Algorithm (DSA) [17] was developed by NIST as a more efficient alternative to ElGamal. The DSA signature scheme works as follows [17]:

Let p be a prime such that $p-1$ has a large prime divisor q, let g be an element of order q in $\mathbb{Z}_p^*$, $\mathcal{M}$ be the message space and $H : \mathcal{M} \to \mathbb{Z}_q^*$ be a cryptographic hash function. Furthermore, let $a \in_R \mathbb{Z}_q^*$ and $y = g^a \bmod p$ be signer secret and public keys, respectively. A DSA signature $\sigma = (e, s)$ on input message M is computed as follows:

1. generate $k \in_R \mathbb{Z}_q^*$ and set $h = H(M)$.
2. compute $e = (g^k \bmod p) \bmod q$ and $s = k^{-1}(h + ea) \bmod q$.
A DSA signature is verified by checking that: $(g^{s^{-1}h}y^{es^{-1}} \bmod p) \bmod q$ matches e.

To avoid unnecessary repetition, due to similarities between ElGamal and DSA, we omit the full description of DSA-OSBE. The only details worth mentioning involve the arithmetic of computing the secret:

1. $K_s = (y^e g^h)^z = g^{(ae+h)z}$
2. $K_r = Z^s = e^{zs} = g^{k(ae+h)k^{-1}z} = g^{(ae+h)z}$

Semantic security against the receiver: as mentioned in Section 4, proving the semantic security of Nyberg/Rueppel-OSBE, ElGamal-OSBE and DSA-OSBE is far from straightforward, if standard cryptographic assumptions are to be used. A discussion of the semantic security of these schemes can be found in [19].

6   Cost Analysis and Comparison

We now consider the communication and computation costs of the five schemes discussed in this paper, including RSA-OSBE. Table 1 below summarizes the results. (We do not include IBE-based OSBE schemes since they are non-interactive and, also, because BLS-IBE involves cryptographic operations in a very different setting, while Rabin-OSBE is very space-inefficient.) We collapse EG-OSBE and DSA-OSBE since they are substantially similar. However, we keep in mind that exponentiations and other modular arithmetic in DSA are appreciably cheaper than in ElGamal.

The number of rounds and the number of messages exchanged between the parties are the same (two rounds and two messages of constant length) for all OSBE schemes.

Schnorr-OSBE involves the most total exponentiations, while NR and EG/DSA have the fewest. Interestingly, all schemes require S to perform 3 exponentiations, whereas, R_1 performs between 1 and 3 exponentiations. Although we show the number of exponentiations for R_1 in RSA-OSBE as 2, this can be reduced to 1 by observing that R_1 does not need to generate a new blinding factor for each OSBE run. (Re-using blinding factors sacrifices the impostor obliviousness property – as discussed in Section 8 – but does not affect other security properties.) Other cost factors, such as inverses and multiplications, are relatively minor and we do not elaborate on them further.

Table 1. Cost Factors for Various OSBE Schemes

Costs:	NR	Schnorr	EG/DSA	RSA
protocol rounds	2	2	2	2
protocol messages	2	2	2	2
mod exps. for S	3	3	3	3
mod exps. for R_1	1	3	1	2
inverses for S	2	0	0	1
inverses for R_1	0	0	0	0
mod mults. for S	2	1	1	1
mod mults. for R_1	0	1	0	2

To put the costs of OSBE schemes into perspective, we consider the hypothetical scenario whereby S and R_1 communicate securely without OSBEs (i.e., without the obliviousness factor). If R_1's affiliation privacy were not an issue, S would expect R_1 to first supply a valid signed certificate. Verifying a certificate would involve a cryptographic operation (e.g., one exponentiation for RSA and two for DSA). This would be in addition to cryptographic operations necessary to compute a Diffie-Hellman session key: two for S and at least one for R_1. (Here we are assuming that S always computes a new Diffie-Hellman exponent, whereas R_1 does not; to mimic their respective actions in all of the above OSBE schemes.) It becomes clear that the total costs (three exponentiations for S and one for R_1) would be the same as these for $NR - OSBE$, $EG/DSA - OSBE$ and $RSA - OSBE$. This is an interesting observation demonstrating that, for some OSBE schemes, there is **no extra cost for added privacy**.

7   Implementation

Section 6 presented a comparison of the cost factors for different OSBE schemes. However, this only gives us a rough overview of the efficiency of OSBE schemes since arithmetic operations are performed in different algebraic structures. Consequently, a comparison of the number of multiplications alone does not provide a fair overall cost comparison. For instance, modular operations in ElGamal-OSBE are performed in $\mathbb{Z}_p^*$ while modular operations in DSA-OSBE are performed in a subgroup of $\mathbb{Z}_p^*$ (of order q) and are appreciably cheaper. Apart from that, arithmetic operations in BLS-IBE-OSBE scheme [6] – which were not considered in Section 6 – are performed in a different algebraic setting and thus a fair comparison becomes more difficult.

To provide a more accurate comparison, we implemented all OSBE schemes (including BLS-IBE-OSBE) in 'C'. We used the popular OpenSSL[5] cryptographic library for modular arithmetic with long integers and Miracl[6] library for the implementation of BLS-OSBE. We modified some functions in the Miracl IBE package and introduced some new data structures. The following modifications were made:

- The original IBE implementation uses AES to encrypt the message (using a randomly chosen session key) while all other our OSBE implementations use RC4. For the sake of consistency we replaced AES with RC4.
- Miracle saves the parameters of the IBE scheme, the extracted key corresponding to an ID string (which, in our case, is the signature), the ciphertext and the decrypted cleartext in separate files and loads them every time they are needed. Whereas, other OSBE schemes use user-defined data structures kept in memory. Once again, for consistency's sake, we modified Miracl to work with user-defined data structures.

We also consider two implementation flavors of RSA-OSBE: plain and optimized. Recall that in RSA-OSBE, R_1 sends to S a blinded RSA signature h^{x+d} using the blinding factor h^x. Since it is chosen anew for each interaction, RSA-OSBE provides two extra properties (discussed in Section 8): Perfect Forward Secrecy (PFS) and Impostor Obliviousness. However, it also requires one extra modular exponentiation and one extra modular multiplication for each interaction. This slows down the scheme. Since neither property is, strictly-speaking, required and since none of the other OSBE schemes provide them[7] we can improve the

---

[5] http://www.openssl.org/

[6] http://indigo.ie/ mscott/.

[7] Note, however, that PFS can be provided in all of these schemes using a blinding factor as described in Section 8.

performance of RSA-OSBE by re-using the same blinding factor. The optimized version is referred to as "RSA(optimized)" in Table 2 below.

We measured the schemes' performance with the following settings:

- For all ElGamal-family schemes we set $|p| = 1024$ and $q = 160$
- For RSA schemes we set $|n| = 1024$
- For BLS-IBE scheme we set $|p| = 512$ and $q = 160$

Our results (in milliseconds) are illustrated in Table 2. All of them were obtained on an IBM Thinkpad R40 with Pentium M processor running at 1.3Ghz with 256MB of RAM. The experimental OS platform was Debian Linux (Kernel Version 2.4.27). Timings for each scheme represent average values taken over $1,000$ executions. The results illustrate that the most efficient scheme is Schnorr-OSBE while BLS-IBE-OSBE is the least efficient one. We also observe that three El-Gamal family schemes (DSA-, NR- and Schnorr-OSBE) are more efficient than even the optimized RSA scheme.

Table 2. Average running time for different OSBE Schemes

# Runs:	RSA	RSA(optimized)	BLS-IBE(Miracl)	EG	DSA	NR	Schnorr
1,000	60.29	45.21	181.53	57.68	22.71	23.37	27.27

8   Additional Features

In addition to the two security properties specified in [15] and in Section 2 (sender obliviousness and semantic security against the receiver), another interesting and useful feature is Perfect Forward Secrecy (PFS). PFS is a well-known property particularly desirable in key distribution and key agreement protocols. Informally, PFS means that compromise of a long-term secret (or secrets) does not result in compromise of short-term (session or ephemeral) secrets. In [15], this feature is considered but neither recognized nor referred to as PFS. Instead, it is called *inability to recover a shared secret even if the adversary knows the signature* and is treated as a useful but not mandatory feature.

Another way to motivate PFS in OSBE is to re-state it as: security against the original signer (TTP or CA), i.e., the party who originally issued σ to R_1. Since the signer is assumed to know all such signatures, it can successfully eavesdrop on all communication between S and R_1, unless, of course, PFS is provided.

RSA-OSBE offers PFS, as proven in [15]. In contrast, none of the OSBE schemes presented in this paper offer PFS. This can be easily seen by observing that, in all variants, Interaction involves R_1 computing, in Step 4, $K_r = Z^s$ or $K_r = Z^{-s}$. An adversary – who at some point discovers $\sigma = (e, s)$ – can thus trivially compute $K_r = K_s$.

While we recognize and acknowledge lack of PFS as a shortcoming, a small change to each of our OSBE schemes would enable PFS. The change involves adding a new quantity: $g^b \bmod p$ (where R_1 picks b at random from $\mathbb{Z}_p^*$) to Step 1 of the Interaction. Then, S computes K_s' as $K_s \cdot g^{bz}$ where K_s is the secret as computed by S in each protocol as presented above. Similarly, R_1 computes K_r' as $K_r \cdot g^{bz}$. This change does not influence any OSBE security properties for our schemes but would introduce some additional computation costs.

Showing that PFS is attained entails proving that the adversary (who knows σ and can compute $K_r = K_s$) cannot compute K_s' or K_r', or equivalently, cannot compute g^{bz}. But, computing g^{bz} from g^z and g^b represents a solution to the CDH problem which is assumed to be intractable.

Another closely related feature is what we refer to as: **impostor obliviousness**. This, incidentally, is a new feature, not considered either in prior work. Suppose that S runs two different instances of OSBE Interaction, each time with someone who claims to be R_1 and claims to possess the necessary credentials (i.e., σ). We call an OSBE scheme *impostor-oblivious* if, after running both Interaction instances, S is unable to determine (with probability non-negligibly greater than $1/2$) whether one of the counter-parties was an impostor. This definition can be trivially extended to cover more than two Interaction instances.

Clearly, since our goal is to maximize anonymity, impostor-obliviousness is a very useful feature. Its main advantage is that, over multiple OSBE Interactions, the sender remains totally unaware of the genuineness of the population of receivers. It is easy to see that RSA-OSBE is impostor-oblivious, owing to the very same feature that provides PFS: randomized encryption of the RSA signature in Step 1 of RSA-OSBE Interaction. (Recall that in RSA-OSBE, for each Interaction, R_1 chooses a new random x and encrypts its RSA signature as $h^{x+d} \bmod n$.)

None of the OSBE schemes presented in this paper are impostor-oblivious. To see this, consider what happens if S engages in two instances of OSBE Interaction (using any of our proposed OSBE schemes): once with R_2 (the impostor) and once with R_1. Since each of our schemes involves revealing g^k in Step 1 of the Interaction component and this value is constant for a given signature σ, only R_1 reveals the correct g^k. Whereas, R_2 reveals some other value – $g^{k'}$. At that point, S would determine, with certainty, that one of the parties is an impostor. One of the items for our future work is the further investigation of impostor obliviousness for the proposed OSBE schemes.

References

1. N. Asokan, V. Shoup and M. Waidner, *Optimistic Fair Exchange of Digital Signatures* IEEE Journal on Selected Areas in Communications, Vol. 18, No. 4, April 2000.
2. D. Balfanz, G. Durfee, N. Shankar, D. Smetters, J. Staddon, and H. Wong, *Secret Handshakes from Pairing-Based Key Agreements*, In Proceedings of *IEEE Symposium on Research in Security and Privacy*, May 2003.

3. F. Bao, R. Deng and W. Mao, *Efficient and Practical Fair Exchange Protocols with Off-line TTP*, In Proceedings of 1998 IEEE Symposium on Security and Privacy, May 1998.

4. M. Bellare, D. Micciancio, and B. Warinschi, *Foundations of Group Signatures: Formal Definitions, Simplified Requirements and a Construction Based on General Assumptions*, In Proceedings of *EUROCRYPT 2003*.

5. D. Boneh and M. Franklin, *Identity-Based Encryption from the Weil Pairing*, SIAM Journal of Computing, Vol. 32, No. 3, pp. 586-615, 2003.

6. D. Boneh, B. Lynn, and H. Shacham, *Short Signatures from the Weil Pairing*, In Proceedings of Asiacrypt 2001, volume 2248 of LNCS, pages 51432. Springer-Verlag, 2001.

7. R. Bradshaw, J. Holt, and K. Seamons, *Concealing Complex Policies with Hidden Credentials*, In Proceedings of *ACM CCS 2004*.

8. S. Brands, *Rethinking Public Key Infrastructures and Digital Certificates: Building in Privacy*, MIT Press, August 2000.

9. C. Castelluccia, S. Jarecki, and G. Tsudik, *Secret handshakes from ca-oblivious encryption*, In Proceedings of *ASIACRYPT 2004*.

10. D. Chaum, *Blind Signatures for Untraceable Payments*, In Proceedings of CRYPTO 1982.

11. C. Cocks, *An Identity Based Encryption Scheme Based on Quadratic Residues*, In Proceedings of Cryptography and Coding: 8th IMA International Conference, Springer-Verlag, LNCS Vol. 2260/2001, December 2001.

12. W. Diffie and M. E. Hellman, *New Directions in Cryptography*, IEEE ToIT, Vol. 22 pp. 644–654, November 1976.

13. T. ElGamal, *A Public Key Cryptosystem and a Signature Scheme Based on Discrete Logarithms*, IEEE Transactions on Information Theory, Vol. 31, No. 4, 1985.

14. J. Kilian and E. Petrank, *Identity Escrow* In Proceedings of CRYPTO 1998.

15. N. Li, W. Du and D. Boneh, *Oblivious Signature-Based Envelopes*, In Proceedings of ACM Symposium on Principles of Distributed Computing (PODC'2003), 2003. Extended version to appear in of Distributed Computing, 2005.

16. A. Menezes, P. Van Oorschot and S. Vanstone, *Handbook of Applied Cryptography*, Chapter 11, CRC press, 2nd Edition, 2001.

17. National Institute of Standards and Technology, *Digital Signature Standard, NIST FIPS PUB 186*, U.S. Department of Commerce, 1994.

18. K. Nyberg and R. Rueppel, *A New Signature Scheme Based on DSA Giving Message Recovery*, In Proceedings of ACM Conference on Computer and Communications Security, November 1993.

19. S. Nasserian and G. Tsudik, *Revisiting Oblivious Signature-Based Envelopes*, Cryptology ePrint Archive Report 2005/283. Avaiable at *http://eprint.iacr.org/2005/283*.

20. S. Pohlig and M. Hellman, *An Improved Algorithm for Computing Logarithms over GF(p) and its Cryptographic Significance*, IEEE Transactions on Information Theory, Vol. 24 pp. 106-110, January 1978.

21. D. Pointcheval and J. Stern, *Security Proofs for Signature Schemes*, In Eurocrypt'96, pp. 387 - 398, 1996.

22. C. Schnorr, *Efficient Signature Generation by Smart Cards*, Journal of Cryptology, Vol. 4, pp. 161-174, 1991.

23. S. Xu and M. Yung. *k-Anonymous Secret Handshakes with Reusable Credentials*, In Proceedings of *ACM CCS 2004*.

Provably Secure Electronic Cash Based on Blind Multisignature Schemes

Yoshikazu Hanatani[1], Yuichi Komano[2], Kazuo Ohta[1],
and Noboru Kunihiro[1]

[1] The University of Electro-Communications,Chofugaoka 1-5-1,
Chofu-shi, Tokyo, Japan
{hana, ota, kunihiro}@ice.uec.ac.jp
[2] TOSHIBA Corporation, Komukai Toshiba-cho 1, Saiwai-ku,
Kawasaki-shi, Kanagawa, Japan
yuichi1.komano@toshiba.co.jp

Abstract. Though various blind multisignature schemes have been proposed for secure electronic cash, the formal model of security was not discussed. This paper first formalizes the security notions for e-cash schemes based on the blind multisignature scheme. We then construct a blind multisignature scheme and propose a new untraceable e-cash scheme which is provably secure under the DDH assumption in the random oracle model applying the blind multisignature scheme. The proposed scheme can ensure the framing attack by banks where they collude to simulate the double-spending of an honest user.

Keywords: Blind multisignature, electronic cash, provable security, random oracle model.

1 Introduction

1.1 Background

The on-line businesses including electronic commerce widely spread and many applications are researched. Especially, since the electronic cash (e-cash) scheme is basic primitive, many researches have been done on this topic. The security requirements for e-cash schemes are the untraceability for honest users, the traceability against dishonest users, and the unforgeability of e-cash. In order to realize the untraceability, Chaum proposed a blind signature scheme [7].

The blind signature scheme consists of three entities: a signer, a user and a verifier. The signer issues a signature for a message concealed by the user. The verifier checks whether the signature is valid or invalid with a public key of the signer. Recently, many provably secure blind signature schemes are proposed[14, 15, 3].

There are various untraceable e-cash schemes[8, 6, 10, 1] in which shops can verify the validity of the e-cash off-line. In these schemes, the user to whom the bank issues the e-cash can be indistinguishable. The user's privacy is protected by using the blind signature scheme, but the user's personal information is leaked

G. Di Crescenzo and A. Rubin (Eds.): FC 2006, LNCS 4107, pp. 236–250, 2006.

by spending the same e-cash twice (*double-spending*, hereafter). Because of this traceability against dishonest users, the double-spending is prevented by this deterrent.

In [1], Abe proposed a blind signature scheme which is provably secure with polynomially many signatures, by improving the partially blind signature scheme of [2]. This scheme allows the user to blind the tag public key so that the resulting signature can be verified with the real public key by the signer and the blinded tag key provided by the user. An untraceable e-cash scheme with the blind signature was also proposed in [1].

An untraceable e-cash scheme suffers from the framing by a bank where the bank could compute a private key of the user who had (erroneously) spent an e-cash of a small amount twice. In previous schemes [8, 6, 10, 1], since the e-cash is issued by only one bank, the bank can maliciously simulate the withdrawal and payment protocols with user's private key. We say this a *framing* attack. If the issuing function by a blind multisignature scheme is split among several banks and at least one of the banks is trusted, then this drawback can be avoided. The untraceable e-cash scheme in which the e-cash is issued by plural banks will be able to provide higher degree of robustness than that is issued by only one bank. Not only does it distribute burden among banks, but also it provides the security improvement: the damage caused by the secret leakage of only few banks will not affect the system, while in a system with one bank, the secret leakage of the bank will bring the security of total break of the system.

Horster et al. [11] introduced a notion of a blind multisignature scheme by applying a notion of the blind signature scheme to multisignature schemes, and gave a concrete blind multisignature scheme based on Meta-blind signature scheme. The blind multisignature scheme is utilized for constructing secure e-cash and e-voting systems without the framing attack. Afterwards, Chen et al. [9] gave another concrete scheme from a bilinear map. Unfortunately, the above two concrete blind multisignature schemes are not proven to be secure, and therefore, the security of the e-cash or e-voting system is questionable.

In the blind multisignature scheme, there are three entities; a group of signers, a user and a verifier. A signature is issued to the user who has hidden a message of signing target from the group of signers. The signers in the group must cooperate with each other, in order to produce a blind signature. The verifier can check the validity of the blind multisignature by using the public keys of corresponding signers.

1.2   Our Contribution

In this paper, we will construct a blind multisignature scheme based on [1] and propose a new untraceable e-cash scheme which is provably secure in the random oracle model [4] by applying it. To the best of our knowledge, this paper is the first one which discusses the formal security of the untraceable e-cash schemes based on the blind multisignature schemes. This paper is organized as follows. Section 2 reviews the definitions of intractable problems on which our proposed scheme is based, the concept of a blind multisignature scheme, and its security requirements. In sections 3 and 4, we will describe the proposed e-cash scheme and prove the security of proposed scheme, respectively.

1.3   Related Work

The notion of the multisignatures is introduced by Itakura and Nakamura[12]. In the multisignature scheme, multiple signers cooperate with each other to generate one signature for some message; the aim of the multisignature scheme is to reduce the length of the signature compared to that of concatenation of individual signatures. Micali et al. [13] provided a formal model for multisignature schemes, and proposed a provably secure multisignature scheme based on the discrete logarithm problem.

2   Security Definitions

Let us review the definitions of the discrete logarithm problem(DLP) and the decision Diffie-Hellman problem(DDHP)[5], and discuss the concept of a blind multisignature scheme and the security requirement of untraceable e-cash based on the blind multisignatures.

Definition 1 *(Negligible). We say that a function $\nu(\cdot)$ is negligible (for n) if for all constant c, there exists N such that for all $n > N$, $\nu(n) < 1/n^c$. We write such the negligible function $\nu(\cdot)$ as **negl**, hereafter.*

Definition 2 *(Discrete Logarithm Problem and Decision Diffie-Hellman Problem). Let $\mathbb{G}$ be a group of order p, where p is prime.*

- *A DL algorithm $\mathcal{A}$ for $\mathbb{G}$ is a probabilistic polynomial time (in $|p|$) algorithm with a success probability $\Pr[\mathcal{A}(p, g, g^a) = a]$ where g is a generator of $\mathbb{G}$. The group $\mathbb{G}$ satisfies the DLP assumption if there is no DL algorithm $\mathcal{A}$ for $\mathbb{G}$ with non-negligible success probability.*
- *A DDH algorithm $\mathcal{A}$ for $\mathbb{G}$ is a probabilistic polynomial time algorithm satisfying with an advantage $|\Pr[\mathcal{A}(p, g, g^a, g^b, g^{ab}) = "true"] - \Pr[\mathcal{A}(p, g, g^a, g^b, g^c) = "true"]|$ where g is a generator of $\mathbb{G}$. The group $\mathbb{G}$ satisfies the DDH assumption if there is no DDH algorithm $\mathcal{A}$ for $\mathbb{G}$ with non-negligible advantage.*

Definition 3 *(Blind Multisignature Scheme)*
A blind multisignature scheme is a quadruple $(\mathcal{G}, \{\mathcal{S}_i\}_i, \mathcal{U}, \mathcal{V})$, where $\{\mathcal{S}_i\}_i$ be a group of signers.
  $\mathcal{G}$ is a probabilistic polynomial-time algorithm which takes a security parameter k and outputs a pair of public and secret keys (pk, sk). After generating the key pair, the signer registers her public key to the PKI using zero-knowledge interactive proof(ZKIP) for the knowledge of her secret key.
  $\{\mathcal{S}_i\}_i$ and $\mathcal{U}$ are probabilistic polynomial-time interactive Turing machines (PPITM). Each $\mathcal{S}_i$ is given a key pair pk_i, sk_i which is produced by $\mathcal{G}(1^k)$, and

$\mathcal{U}$ is given a public key $\{pk\}$ and a message m. $\{\mathcal{S}_i\}_i$ and $\mathcal{U}$ engage in the interactive protocol with some polynomial number of rounds. At the end of this issuing protocol, $\{\mathcal{S}_i\}_i$ outputs either success or fail, and $\mathcal{U}$ outputs either $\sigma(m)$ or fail.

$\mathcal{V}$ is a deterministic polynomial-time algorithm which takes $(\{pk_i\}_i, m, \sigma(m)$, S-list) as an input to output accept or reject. Here S-list denotes a ID-list of signers $\{S_i\}_i$ who are concerned in signing.

In an untraceable e-cash scheme based on the blind multisignature scheme, there are three entities; a group of banks, a user and a shop. The e-cash is issued to the user who hides a user-ID (which corresponds the message m) from the resulting e-cash (which corresponds the blind multisignature). The banks in the group must cooperate with each other, in order to issue the e-cash. The verifier can check the validity of the e-cash by using the public keys of corresponding banks. We will describe the security requirements for untraceable e-cash as follows.

Definition 4 *(Completeness). Let (pk, sk) be a key pair generated by the key generation algorithm $\mathcal{G}$ properly. The untraceable e-cash schemes is complete if, (i) following the issuing protocol, $\{B_i\}_i$ and U always output success and e-cash, respectively, and (ii) following the payment protocol, the user U and the shop S always output success and accept, with $(\{pk_i\}_i,$ e-cash, B-list) issued by $\{B_i\}_i$ and U correctly.*

Definition 5 *(Untraceability for Honest Users). Let $\mathcal{D}^*$, $\{B_i\}_i$, and S be a distinguisher, a group of banks, and a shop, respectively. Let $\mathcal{U}_0, \mathcal{U}_1$ be honest users who follow the protocols. Let $view_{0B}$ and $view_{1B}$ be views of $\{B_i\}_i$ during the issuing protocol where $\mathcal{U}_b$ and $\mathcal{U}_{1-b}$ obtain e-cash respectively. Let $view_{bS}$ and $view_{(1-b)S}$ be views of S during the payment protocol where $\mathcal{U}_0$ and $\mathcal{U}_1$ spend e-cash respectively. $\mathcal{D}^*$, given $(view_{0B}, view_{1B}, view_{bS})$ for $b \in_R \{0, 1\}$, outputs $b' \in \{0, 1\}$. The e-cash scheme is untraceable for honest users if for all polynomial-time machines $\mathcal{D}^*$, $\{B_i\}_i$ and $\mathcal{S}$, $b' = b$ happens with probability $1/2 +$ **negl**.*

Definition 6 *(Traceability against Dishonest Users). Let $\mathcal{D}$, $\{B_i\}_i$, and S be a distinguisher, a group of honest banks, and an honest shop, respectively. $\{B_i\}_i$, and S follow the protocols. Let $\mathcal{U}^*$ be a dishonest user who used the same e-cash twice (double-spending). Let $view_B$ be views of $\{B_i\}_i$ during the issuing protocol where $\mathcal{U}^*$ obtains e-cash. Let $view_{0S}$ and $view_{1S}$ be views of S during the payment protocol where $\mathcal{U}^*$ spends the same e-cash respectively. $\mathcal{D}$, given $(view_B, view_{0S}, view_{1S})$, outputs an U^*'s ID. The e-cash scheme is traceable against dishonest users if, for all polynomial-time machines $\mathcal{U}^*$, there exists $\mathcal{D}$, $\mathcal{D}$ can detect the dishonest user $\mathcal{U}^*$ with probability $1 -$ **negl**.*

Definition 7 *(Attack Model to E-cash Scheme)*

> **Adaptive Chosen Message Attack(ACMA):** *A forger $\mathcal{F}_M$ can request an arbitrary group of banks to issue an e-cash. The forger $\mathcal{F}_M$ can also inquire the hash value for an arbitrary input of a hash function.*

Restricted Adaptive Insider Attack(restricted AIA): *The forger $\mathcal{F}_M$ can corrupt arbitrary banks and shops except a bank to be attacked. The corrupted banks leak their private keys to $\mathcal{F}_M$ but they follow a scheme. (They do not answer the queries from $\mathcal{F}_M$. So we call this attack a restricted AIA. Not that $\mathcal{F}_M$ is allowed to act as corruptted banks using their leaked private keys within $\mathcal{F}_M$.)*

Adaptive Insider Attack(AIA): *The forger $\mathcal{F}_M$ can corrupt arbitrary banks and shops except a bank to be attacked. The corrupted banks leak their secret information, and also answer the queries from the forger $\mathcal{F}_M$.*

The forger $\mathcal{F}_M$ generates an arbitrary keys (pk^*, sk^*), and registers pk^* as a public key of the corrupted bank B^* at the PKI. Note that from the property of ZKIP, the forger $\mathcal{F}_M$ cannot register pk^* to the PKI without knowing sk^*.

Definition 8 (*One-more Unforgeability of e-cash*). *The untraceable e-cash scheme based on the blind multisignature is $(l, l+1)$ unforgeable, if for all probabilistic polynomial-time algorithm $\mathcal{F}^*$, $\mathcal{F}^*$ uses $(l+1)$ number of e-cash at a shop with negligible success probability after $\mathcal{F}^*$ interacts with legitimate banks $\{B_i\}_i$ at most l times in the attack model.*

3   Proposed Scheme

We propose a new untraceable e-cash scheme based on a blind multisignature scheme. The blind multisignature scheme used here is based on the blind signature scheme proposed by Abe [1] .

Assumption. Assume that there is a trusted third party PKI which sets up a system parameter and authorizes a public key generated by each bank.

The PKI runs a probabilistic polynomial-time algorithm with security parameter k to generate the system parameter (p, q, g) where p and q are large primes which satisfy $q|p-1$, and g is a generator of the group $\langle g \rangle \subseteq \mathbb{Z}_p^*$ whose order is q, and randomly selects $h \in \langle g \rangle$. The PKI also publishes the following four hash functions :$\mathcal{H}_1 : \{0,1\}^* \to \langle g \rangle$, $\mathcal{H}_2 : \{0,1\}^* \to \langle g \rangle$, $\mathcal{H}_3 : \{0,1\}^* \to \mathbb{Z}_q$, and $\mathcal{H}_4 : \{0,1\}^* \to \mathbb{Z}_q$.

Let $\{B_0, B_1, \ldots, B_n\}$ be a group of banks which cooperate to issue e-cash. Each bank has three kinds of keys an issuing key, a guaranteeing key, and a tag key. The banks use these keys following the rules below. When a bank issues e-cash, the bank uses his issuing key and tag key. The issuing key certifies that the e-cash is issued by the issuing bank, and the tag key enables the issuing bank to trace a dishonest user who has spent the same e-cash twice. When the bank guarantees the e-cash which is issued by the other bank, the bank utilizes the guaranteeing key.

Let U be a user who has a savings account at the issuing bank[1] B_0. When the user asks B_0 to issued e-cash, the user selects one issuing bank B_0 and several

---

[1] Without loss of the generality, we denote 0 as the index of the bank where the user has a savings account.

guaranteeing banks. Let $\mathcal{B} \subseteq \{0, 1, \ldots, n\}$ be a list of bank's IDs which are chosen by the user.

We two untraceable e-cash schemes. One is the scheme in which only B_0 generates a tag. Though the length of e-cash is constant (independent of the number of banks), the unforgeability can be ensured against only ACMA & *restricted* AIA. The other is the scheme in which all banks sequentially generate tags, respectively. Though the length of e-cash is proportional to the number of banks, the unforgeability can be proven against ACMA & AIA. Here we call this scheme *full tag* scheme.

For simplicity, this paper will discusses only the former case. Figure 1 shows a model of the issuing protocol.

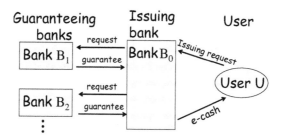

Fig. 1. Model of Issuing Protocol

3.1 Key Generation Protocol

Each bank $B_i (i = 1, 2, \ldots, n)$ selects a private key $x_{1,i}, x_{2,i} \in_R \mathbb{Z}_q$ and computes an issuing public key $y_{1,i} = g^{x_{1,i}} \bmod p$ and a guaranteeing public key $y_{2,i} = g^{x_{2,i}} \bmod p$. B_i also fixes a tag key $z_i = \mathcal{H}_1(p||q||g||h||y_{1,i}||y_{2,i})$. If $z_i = 1$, then B_i throws away the keys and tries to set new keys again. If $z_i \neq 1$, then B_i proves the possession of knowledge of his private keys $x_{1,i} = \log_g y_{1,i}$ and $x_{2,i} = \log_g y_{2,i}$ to the PKI with ZKIP[2] [16]. If the PKI is convinced, the public key is registered to the PKI. Here we assume sequential registrations.

The public and private keys of B_i are $(p, q, g, h, y_{1,i}, y_{2,i}, z_i)$ and $(x_{1,i}, x_{2,i})$ respectively.

3.2 Issuing Protocol

Let $\mathcal{B} = \{0; j, \ldots, k\}$ be a list of banks' IDs in participate issuing e-cash. 0 is an ID of the issuing bank, and $\{j, \ldots, k\}$ are IDs of the guaranteeing banks. Hereafter, all arithmetic operations are processed in $\mathbb{Z}_p$ unless otherwise noted. Figure 2 shows flows of issuing protocol.

---

[2] Without ZKIP, a malicious bank can forge a multisignature by registering a malicious public key. See [13] for details.

guarantee banks $\{B_j\}_{j\in\mathcal{B}\setminus\{0\}}$	issuing bank B_0	user $\mathcal{U}$
	$\xleftarrow{\text{requests}}$	$\xleftarrow{\mathcal{B}}$
$u_j \in_R \mathbb{Z}_q$ $a_j := g^{u_j}$	$\text{rnd} \in_R \{0,1\}^*$ $z_{1,0} := \mathcal{H}_2(\text{rnd})$	
	$\xleftarrow{\{a_j\}_{j\in\mathcal{B}\setminus\{0\}}}$ $z_{2,0} = \frac{z}{z_{1,0}}$ $u_0, s_1, s_2, d \in_R \mathbb{Z}_q$ $a_0 := g^{u_0}$ $a := \prod_{i\in\mathcal{B}} a_i$ $b_1 := g^{s_1} z_{1,0}^d$	
	$b_2 := h^{s_2} z_{2,0}^d$ · Record user ID and $z_{1,0}$ on database.	$\xrightarrow{\text{rnd},a,b_1,b_2}$ $b_1, b_2 \overset{?}{\in} \langle g\rangle$ $z_{1,0} := \mathcal{H}_2(\text{rnd})$ $\gamma \in_R \mathbb{Z}_q^*$ $\zeta := z_0^\gamma$ $\zeta_1 := z_{1,0}^\gamma$ $\zeta_2 := \frac{\zeta}{\zeta_1}$ $t_1, t_2, t_3, t_4, t_5 \in_R \mathbb{Z}_q^*$ $\alpha := a g^{t_1} \left(y_{1,0}\prod_{i\in\mathcal{B}\setminus\{0\}} y_{2,i}\right)^{t_2}$ $\beta_1 := b_1^\gamma g^{t_3}\zeta_1^{t_4}$ $\beta_2 := b_2^\gamma h^{t_5}\zeta_2^{t_4}$ $\tau \in_R \mathbb{Z}_q$ $\epsilon := \mathcal{H}_3(\zeta||\zeta_1||\alpha||\beta_1||\beta_2||z_0^\tau||\mathcal{B})$ $e := \epsilon - t_2 - t_4 \bmod q$
		$\xleftarrow{e}$
$r_j := u_j - cx_{2,j}$ $\bmod q$	$\xleftarrow{c}$ $c := e - d \bmod q$ $r_0 := u_0 - cx_{1,0}$	
	$\xrightarrow{\{r_j\}_{j\in\mathcal{B}\setminus\{0\}}}$ $\bmod q$	
	$r := \sum_{i\in\mathcal{B}} r_i$ $\bmod q$	$\xrightarrow{r,c,s_1,s_2,d}$ $a \overset{?}{=} g^r \left(y_{1,0}\prod_{i\in\mathcal{B}\setminus\{0\}} y_{2,i}\right)^c$ $b_1 \overset{?}{=} g^{s_1} z_1^d$ $b_2 \overset{?}{=} g^{s_2} z_2^d$ $\rho := r + t_1 \bmod q$ $\omega := c + t_2 \bmod q$ $\sigma_1 := \gamma s_1 + t_3 \bmod q$ $\sigma_2 := \gamma s_2 + t_5 \bmod q$ $\delta := d + t_4 \bmod q$ $(\zeta, \zeta_1, \rho, \omega, \sigma_1, \sigma_2, \delta, \mathcal{B}):e\text{-}cash$

Fig. 2. Proposed e-cash scheme (issuing protocol)

Step 1. The user U sends the issuing bank B_0 a list $\mathcal{B}$ which consist of an ID of issuing bank B_0 and IDs of guaranteeing banks $\{B_j\}_j$.

Step 2. B_0 requests the guarantees of the e-cash from banks $\{B_j\}_j$ in $\mathcal{B}$.

Step 3. Each B_j randomly selects $u_j \in \mathbb{Z}_q$, computes a commitment $a_j = g^{u_j}$ and send it to B_0.

Step 4. B_0 randomly chooses $u_0 \in \mathbb{Z}_q$, and computes a commitment $a_0 = g^{u_0}$. When B_0 receives the commitments $\{a_j\}$ from all guaranteeing banks, B_0 computes $a = \prod_{i\in\mathcal{B}} a_i$. B_0 then chooses a random string $\text{rnd} \in \{0,1\}^*$, and computes tag keys $z_{1,0} = \mathcal{H}_2(\text{rnd})$ and $z_{2,0} = z_0/z_{1,0}$. With these tag keys, B_0 computes commitments $b_1 = g^{s_1} z_{1,0}^d$ and $b_2 = h^{s_2} z_{2,0}^d$ with randomly chosen $s_1, s_2, d \in \mathbb{Z}_q$. These commitments (a, b_1, b_2) and rnd are sent to $\mathcal{U}$, and the tag key $z_{1,0}$ is recorded on a database of B_0 with ID of the user $\mathcal{U}$.

Step 5. $\mathcal{U}$ checks if $b_1, b_2 \in \langle g\rangle$ holds. If it does not hold, $\mathcal{U}$ outputs fail. Otherwise, $\mathcal{U}$ computes $z_{1,0} = \mathcal{H}_2(\text{rnd})$. $\mathcal{U}$ selects $\gamma \in \mathbb{Z}_q^*$ at random, and uses it to compute blind tag keys $\zeta := z_0^\gamma$, $\zeta_1 := z_{1,0}^\gamma$, and $\zeta_2 := \frac{\zeta}{\zeta_1}$. $\mathcal{U}$ then converts the commitments a, b_1 and b_2 into $\alpha := a g^{t_1} \left(y_{1,0} \prod_{j \in \mathcal{B} \setminus \{0\}} y_{2,j} \right)^{t_2}$,

$\beta_1 := b_1^\gamma g^{t_3} \zeta_1^{t_4}$, and $\beta_2 := b_2^\gamma h^{t_5} \zeta_2^{t_4}$ by using $t_1, t_2, t_3, t_4, t_5 \in_R \mathbb{Z}_q^*$. $\mathcal{U}$ randomly chooses $\tau \in \mathbb{Z}_q^*$, and computes $\epsilon := \mathcal{H}_3 \left(\zeta || \zeta_1 || \alpha || \beta_1 || \beta_2 || z_0^\tau || \mathcal{B} \right)$ and a challenge $e = \epsilon - t_2 - t_4 \bmod q$. $\mathcal{U}$ finally sends e to B_0.

Step 6. B_0 computes an answer $r_0 = u_0 - c x_{1,0} \bmod q$ where $c = e - d \bmod q$, and sends c to the guaranteeing banks $\{B_j\}_j$.

Step 7. Each B_j answers $r_j = u_j - c x_{2,j} \bmod q$.

Step 8. B_0 computes $r = \sum_{i \in \mathcal{B}} r_i \bmod q$ and sends the answers (r, c, s_1, s_2, d) to $\mathcal{U}$.

Step 9. $\mathcal{U}$ verifies whether the received answers satisfy the following equations;

$$a \overset{?}{=} g^r \left(y_{1,0} \prod_{i \in \mathcal{B} \setminus \{0\}} y_{2,i} \right)^c \;,\; b_1 \overset{?}{=} g^{s_1} z_{1,0}^d, \; b_2 \overset{?}{=} g^{s_2} z_{2,0}^d. \tag{1}$$

If the above equations hold, $\mathcal{U}$ converts the answers to $\rho := r + t_1 \bmod q$, $\omega := c + t_2 \bmod q$, $\sigma_1 := \gamma s_1 + t_3 \bmod q$, $\sigma_2 := \gamma s_2 + t_5 \bmod q$, and $\delta := d + t_4 \bmod q$, and checks whether $(\rho, \omega, \sigma_1, \sigma_2, \delta)$ satisfies Eq.(2).

$$\omega + \delta = \mathcal{H}_3 \left(\zeta || \zeta_1 || g^\rho \left(y_{1,0} \prod_{i \in \mathcal{B} \setminus \{0\}} y_{2,i} \right)^\omega || g^{\sigma_1} \zeta_1^\delta || h^{\sigma_2} \left(\frac{\zeta}{\zeta_1} \right)^\delta || z_0^\tau || \mathcal{B} \right) \bmod q \tag{2}$$

If Eq.(2) holds, $\mathcal{U}$ sets $e\text{-}cash = (\zeta, \zeta_1, \rho, \omega, \sigma_1, \sigma_2, \delta)$ and records $(e\text{-}cash, \tau, \gamma)$ on his database.

Note: To prevent issuing e-cash without $\mathcal{U}$'s agreement, $\mathcal{U}$ sends her signature and $\mathcal{B}$ to B_0 in the first step of issuing protocol. Then, the honest bank is able to notice that $\mathcal{U}$ agrees this issuing or not. Our scheme improved a resistance to the framing attack, because the honest bank dose not cooperate to the issuing protocol without the user's agreement.

3.3 Payment Protocol

The $\mathcal{U}$ uses the e-cash $(\zeta, \zeta_1, \rho, \omega, \sigma_1, \sigma_2, \delta, \mathcal{B})$ at a shop $\mathcal{S}$ as follows.

Step 1. $\mathcal{U}$ sends the e-cash to the shop $\mathcal{S}$.

Step 2. $\mathcal{S}$ selects a challenge $cha \in \{0,1\}^*$, and sends cha to $\mathcal{U}$.

Step 3. $\mathcal{U}$ computes $\epsilon_p = \mathcal{H}_4(z_0^\tau || e\text{-}cash || cha)$ and $\mu_p = \tau + \epsilon_p \gamma \bmod q$, and sends (μ_p, ϵ_p) to $\mathcal{S}$.

Step 4. $\mathcal{S}$ checks whether both Eq.(3) and Eq.(4) hold or not:

$$\omega + \delta \overset{?}{=} \mathcal{H}_3 \left(\zeta || \zeta_1 || g^\rho \left(y_{1,0} \prod_{i \in \mathcal{B} \setminus \{0\}} y_{2,i} \right)^\omega || g^{\sigma_1} \zeta_1^\delta || h^{\sigma_2} \left(\frac{\zeta}{\zeta_1} \right)^\delta || z^{\mu_p} \zeta^{\epsilon_p} || \mathcal{B} \right) \bmod q \tag{3}$$

$$\epsilon_p \overset{?}{=} \mathcal{H}_4(z^{\mu_p}\zeta^{\epsilon_p}||e\text{-}cash||cha) \tag{4}$$

If both equations hold, then $\mathcal{S}$ sends a service or goods to $\mathcal{U}$. Afterward, $\mathcal{S}$ sends the used e-cash and its transaction histories to the issuing bank B_0. If the e-cash isn't used twice, $\mathcal{S}$ exchanges the e-cash to a money and B_0 records the used e-cash and its transaction histories on its database; otherwise, B_0 traces the user who uses the same e-cash twice.

4   Security Considerations

In this section, we will prove that our scheme satisfies correctness, untraceability for honest users, traceability against dishonest users who double-spent the same money, and unforgeability.

4.1   Completeness

If all participants follow the protocols, the proposed scheme works properly.

Theorem 1. *If the banks* $\{B_i\}_i$*, the user* $\mathcal{U}$ *and the shop* $\mathcal{S}$ *follow the protocols;* $\{B_i\}$ *and* $\mathcal{U}$ *output success and e-cash in the issuing protocol, respectively,* $\mathcal{S}$ *accepts the resulting e-cash with probability 1 and in the payment protocol.*

Proof. We show that the resulting e-cash satisfies the following equations with probability 1 if $\mathcal{U}$, $\{B_i\}_{i \in \mathcal{B}}$ and $\mathcal{S}$ follow the issuing and payment protocols.

We first show that (r, c, s_1, s_2, d) satisfies Eq.(1) if $\{B_i\}_i$ and $\mathcal{U}$ follow the issuing protocol. Since we have

$$r = \sum_{i \in \mathcal{B}} u_i - c\left(x_{1,0} + \sum_{i \in \mathcal{B}\backslash\{0\}} x_{2,i}\right) \bmod q \quad \text{and} \tag{5}$$

$$\log_g\left(y_{1,0} \prod_{i \in \mathcal{B}\backslash\{0\}} y_{2,i}\right)^c = c\left(x_{1,0} + \sum_{i \in \mathcal{B}\backslash\{0\}} x_{2,i}\right) \bmod q, \tag{6}$$

Eq.(1) holds.

Next, we show the resulting $e\text{-}cash = (\omega, \rho, \sigma_1, \sigma_2, \delta, \mathcal{B}), \tau$ and γ satisfy Eq.(2). If $\{B_i\}_i$ and $\mathcal{U}$ follow the issuing protocol,

$$\omega + \delta = (c + t_2) + (d + t_4) = e + t_2 + t_4 = \epsilon \bmod q$$

holds. Therefore, in order to confirm that Eq.(2) holds, we have to see that $g^\rho(y_{1,0} \prod_{j \in \mathcal{B}\backslash\{0\}} y_{2,j})^\omega = \alpha$, $g^{\sigma_1}\zeta_1^\delta = \beta_1$, and $h^{\sigma_2}\zeta_2^\delta = \beta_2$ hold. In fact, with the first equation of Eq.(1),

$$g^\rho \left(y_{1,i} \prod_{j \in \mathcal{B} \setminus \{0\}} y_{2,j} \right)^\omega = g^r \left(y_{1,0} \prod_{i \in \mathcal{B} \setminus \{0\}} y_{2,i} \right)^c g^{t_1} \left(y_{1,0} \prod_{i \in \mathcal{B} \setminus \{0\}} y_{2,i} \right)^{t_2}$$

$$= ag^{t_1} \left(y_{1,0} \prod_{i \in \mathcal{B} \setminus \{0\}} y_{2,i} \right)^{t_2} = \alpha$$

holds. Moreover, from Eq(1), $g^{s_1} = b_1 z_1^{-d}$ holds, which implies

$$g^{\sigma_1} \zeta_1^\delta = g^{\gamma s_1 + t_3} \zeta_1^{d+t_4} = \left(b_1 z_1^{-d} \right)^\gamma g^{t_3} \zeta_1^{d+t_4} = b_1^\gamma g^{t_3} \zeta_1^{t_4} = \beta_1.$$

Similarly, from Eq(1), $h^{s_2} = b_2 z_2^{-d}$ holds, which implies

$$h^{\sigma_2} \left(\zeta / \zeta_1 \right)^\delta = h^{\gamma s_2 + t_5} \zeta_2^{d+t_4} = \left(b_2 z_2^{-d} \right)^\gamma h^{t_5} \zeta_2^{d+t_4} = b_2^\gamma h^{t_5} \zeta_2^{t_4} = \beta_2.$$

From the above equations, Eq.(2) holds.

Finally, we show that (μ_p, τ_p) satisfies Eq.(3) and Eq.(4) if $\mathcal{U}$ and $\mathcal{S}$ follow the payment protocol.

$\mu_p = \tau - \epsilon_p \gamma \mod q$ holds because of the step 3 of the payment protocol, so $z_0^{\mu_p} \zeta^{\epsilon_p} = z_0^{\tau - \epsilon_p \gamma} \zeta^{\epsilon_p} = z_0^\tau$ holds. Therefore, Eq.(3) and Eq.(4) hold, too ∎

4.2 Untraceability for Honest Users

We show that as long as a user spends the e-cash only once, no one can trace the user if the decision Diffie-Hellman problem is intractable.

Theorem 2. *If a user spends e-cash only once, no one can trace the user even if all banks and shops collude with each other, under the decision Diffie-Hellman assumption in the random oracle model.*

Proof. Suppose that there exist PPITMs $(\{B_i^*\}, S^*, D^*)$ which can trace the honest user with probability $1/2 + \epsilon$ where ϵ is non-negligible. Then we will construct an algorithm I which can solve the DDH problem by using $(\{B^*\}, S^*, D^*)$ as oracles. The aim of I to distinguish whether a quadruplet (A, B, C, D) is DDH tuplet or not, namely, whether $\log_A C = \log_B D$ holds or not. A construction of I is as follows.

Step 1. With an input (A, B, C, D), I selects $b \in_R \{0, 1\}$. I simulates two users U_0 and U_1 to run the issuing and payment protocols with $\{B_i^*\}_i$, S^*, and D^*. Without loss of generality, we denote the issuing bank[3] as B_0^*.

Step 2. If B_0^* asks $(p, q, g, h, y_{1,i}, y_{2,i})$ to $\mathcal{H}_1$, I simulates $z_0 = \mathcal{H}_1(p \| q \| g \| h \| y_{1,i} \| y_{2,i}) = A$. For the other queries from B_0^* to $\mathcal{H}_1$, I simulates z_i at random.

---

[3] In the proposed e-cash scheme, the issuing and guaranteeing banks are publicly verifiable. With regard to the untraceability for honest users, note that the users who spend e-cash issued and guaranteed by the same banks cannot be distinguishable.

Step 3. U_0 sends her ID and $\mathcal{B}$ to B_0^* to execute the issuing protocol. We call the execution run0. If B_0^* asks a random string rnd to $\mathcal{H}_2$ and if $b = 0$, then I simulates $z_{1,0} = \mathcal{H}_2(rnd) = B$. If B_0^* asks rnd to $\mathcal{H}_2$ and if $b = 1$, I answers $z_{1,0} \in \langle g \rangle$ at random. Let $View_{0B}$ be a view of $\{B_i^*\}_i$ in the run0.

Step 4. U_1 sends her ID and $\mathcal{B}$, which is the same list utilized in the run0, to B_0^* to execute the issuing protocol. We call the execution run1. If B_0^* asks rnd' to $\mathcal{H}_2$ and if $b = 1$, then I simulates $z_{1,0}' = \mathcal{H}_2(rnd') = B$. If B_0^* asks rnd' to $\mathcal{H}_2$ and if $b = 0$, I answers $z_{1,0}' \in \langle g \rangle$ at random. Let $View_{1B}$ be a view of $\{B_i^*\}_i$ in the run1.

Step 5. I sets $(\zeta, \zeta_1) = (C, D)$ and randomly chooses $\rho, \omega, \sigma_1, \sigma_2, \delta, \epsilon_p, \mu_p \in \mathbb{Z}_q^*$. The output of $\mathcal{H}_3$ is simulated by $\omega + \delta = \mathcal{H}_3(\zeta || \zeta_1 || g^\rho (y_{1,i} \cdot \prod_{j \in \mathcal{B} \setminus \{i\}} y_{2,j})^\omega || g^{\sigma_1} \zeta_1^\delta || h^{\sigma_2} \zeta_2^\delta || z^{\mu_p} \zeta^{\epsilon_p} || \mathcal{B})$. Let $(\zeta, \zeta_1, \rho, \omega, \sigma_1, \sigma_2, \delta)$ be e-cash.

Step 6. I uses the e-cash at a shop S in the payment protocol. If I receives the random string cha from S, then I simulates $\epsilon_p = \mathcal{H}_4(z^{\mu_p} \zeta^{\epsilon_p} || e\text{-}cash || cha)$ and sends (ϵ_p, μ_p) to S. Let $View_S$ be a view of S in the payment protocol.

Step 7. I inputs $(View_{0B}, View_{1B}, View_S)$ into D^* to receive b'.

Step 8. If $b = b'$ then I outputs $true$, otherwise outputs $false$.

The random oracles reply at random and record the query and answer on their lists, if there is no especially description.

In the above strategy, I can solve the DDH problem with non-negligible advantage. This is because if (A, B, C, D) is a DDH tuplet, $\log_z z_1 = \log_A B = \log_C D = \log_\zeta \zeta_1$ holds, and the e-cash can be produced only in run_b. In fact, the blinding factors t_1, t_2, t_3, t_4, and t_5 which can convert the $View_{bB}$ into the e-cash produced in step5. In run_{1-b}, however, the e-cash cannot be produced because $\log_z z_1 \neq \log_\zeta \zeta_1$ holds with overwhelming probability. Therefore, D^* which can break the untraceability for the honest user with $(View_{0B}, View_{1B}, View_S)$ can output correct b with probability $1/2 + \epsilon$.

On the other hand, if (A, B, C, D) is not a DDH tuplet, $\log_z z_1 = \log_A B \neq \log_C D = \log_\zeta \zeta_1$ holds in both runs. Thus the e-cash which is generated in Step5 cannot have the blinding factors t_1, t_2, t_3, t_4, and t_5 which convert either $View_{0B}$ or $View_{1B}$ into e-cash with overwhelming probability. Hence, b is independent from the runs, and $b' = b$ holds with probability $1/2$.

In the DDH problem, if (A, B, C, D) is chosen from DH tuplet or non-DH tuplet with probability $\frac{1}{2}$[4], the advantage of I is $1/2(1/2 + \epsilon) + 1/2(1/2) = 1/2 + \epsilon/2$, which contradicts the DDH assumption when ϵ is not negligible. ∎

4.3   Traceability Against Dishonest Users

As we will discuss later, we can assume that the proposed scheme is $(l, l+1)$-unforgeable, so the user cannot generate another e-cash from the issued one. Therefore, $\{B_i\}_i$ are not paid more than the issued e-cash if no one can use the same e-cash twice.

---

[4] The proof for the general case will be described in the final version.

Theorem 3. *Assume that $\mathcal{H}_4$ is a collision resistant hash function. In the proposed scheme, if a user U^* uses the same e-cash twice maliciously, the bank B_0 can trace U^* with overwhelming probability.*

Proof. Suppose that $\mathcal{U}^*$ uses the same e-cash $= (\zeta, \zeta_1, \rho, \omega, \sigma_1, \sigma_2, \delta, \mathcal{B})$ twice as $(e\text{-}cash, \epsilon_p, \mu_p)$ and $(e\text{-}cash, \epsilon'_p, \mu'_p)$. Since $\mathcal{H}_4$ is collision resistant and the input of $\mathcal{H}_4$ contains the random challenge cha of a shop $\mathcal{S}$, $\epsilon_p \neq \epsilon'_p$ holds with overwhelming probability. Moreover, since $\epsilon_p \neq \epsilon'_p$ and $z^{\mu_p} \zeta^{\epsilon_p} = z_0^\tau = z^{\mu'_p} \zeta^{\epsilon'_p}$, $\mu_p \neq \mu'_p$ also holds with overwhelming probability. With (ϵ_p, μ_p) and (ϵ'_p, μ'_p), B_0 is able to compute $\gamma = \frac{\mu'_p - \mu_p}{\epsilon_p - \epsilon'_p} \bmod q$ and $z_1 = \zeta_1^{\frac{1}{\gamma}}$.

B_0 keeps $(\mathrm{ID}_{U^*}, z_{1,0})$ in its database, therefore, B_0 can detect the user U^* by searching the database by $z_{1,0}$.

On the other hands, if $\epsilon_p = \mathcal{H}_4(z_0^\tau || e\text{-}cash || cha) = \epsilon'_p = \mathcal{H}_4(z_0^\tau || e\text{-}cash || cha')$ holds, the bank B_0 cannot specify U^*. This happens with probability $\frac{1}{q}$, and hence, B_0 can trace the dishonest user $\mathcal{U}^*$ with probability $1 - \frac{1}{q}$.   ∎

4.4   Unforgeability

Theorem 4. *The proposed scheme with simplified tag is $(l, l+1)$-unforgeable against ACMA & restricted AIA for polynomially bound l if the discrete logarithm problem is intractable in the random oracle model.*

Proof. The proof is done by reducing the forging problem of the blind signature scheme[1] of the *single* signer to that of the proposed e-cash scheme. Namely, given a public key (p, q, g, h, y, z) for a signer of the blind signature scheme [1] and corresponding signing oracle Σ, our aim is to construct the forging algorithm $\mathcal{F}$ against the blind signature scheme [1] with the forger $\mathcal{F}_M$ against the proposed e-cash scheme.

Note that, since the blind signature scheme [1] is proven to be unforgeable under the DLP assumption in the random oracle model, the reduction shows that the proposed scheme is also unforgeable.

There are two kinds of forgery against the proposed e-cash scheme; forging the e-cash issued by the issuing bank B_0, and forging a guaranteeing bank B_i. Note that, if $\mathcal{F}_M$ can $(l, l+1)$-forge the e-cash with non-negligible success probability, then $\mathcal{F}$ can $(l, l+1)$-forge the blind signature of [1] with non-negligible probability.

This proof deals with the forger who uses $l + 1$ forgeries of e-cash after the forger $(l, l+1)$-forges e-cash.

Firstly, we prove the unforgeability with respect to a issuing bank. Suppose that $\mathcal{F}_M$ forges the e-cash issued by B_0. For simplicity, assume that all banks except B_0 are corrupted by $\mathcal{F}_M$. Let ϵ_0 be the success probability of $\mathcal{F}_M$ to $(l, l+1)$-forge e-cash issued by B_0 and to use them.

Initializing: With the public key (p, q, g, h, y, z), $\mathcal{F}$ initializes the e-cash scheme.

Step 1. $\mathcal{F}$ sets the public key of B_0 as $y_{1,0} = y$, $y_{2,0} = g^{x_{2,0}}$ with a private key $x_{2,0} \in_R \mathbb{Z}_q$, and simulates $z_0 = \mathcal{H}_1(p||q||g||h||y_{1,0}||y_{2,0}) = z$.

Step 2. $\mathcal{F}$ sets the public keys $\{(y_{1,j} = g^{x_{1,j}}, y_{2,j} = g^{x_{2,j}}, z_j)\}_{j \in \mathcal{B} \setminus \{0\}}$ with private keys $x_{1,j}, x_{2,j} \in_R \mathbb{Z}_q$ of the other banks with the key generation protocol. Note that, $\mathcal{F}_M$ can issue the public keys for corrupted banks; however, $\mathcal{F}_M$ has to register the public keys to the PKI with ZKIP.

Forging e-cash: Corrupted banks leak their private keys to $\mathcal{F}_M$, but they calculates according to the protocol. For the queries of issuing the e-cash from $\mathcal{F}_M$, therefore, we simulate the answers of B_0 as follows. Here, $\mathcal{H}_3$ is regarded as the hash function $\mathcal{H}_3^*$ (the random oracle) utilized in the blind signature scheme [1], and note that $\mathcal{F}$ (or B_0) simulates the answer of $\mathcal{H}_3$ through $\mathcal{H}_3^*$.

- Simulation of B_0:
    Step 1. If B_0 is given a list of banks $\mathcal{B}$ by $\mathcal{F}_M$, B_0 asks a signature for message $m = \mathcal{B}$ to the signing oracle Σ and receives a commitment $(a, b_1, b_2, \text{rnd})$.
    Step 2. B_0 asks the guaranteeing banks in $\mathcal{B}$ for guarantees and receives $\{a_j\}_{j \in \mathcal{B} \setminus \{i\}}$ from them.
    Step 3. B_0 sends $(a, b_1, b_2, \text{rnd})$ to $\mathcal{F}_M$ and receives e from $\mathcal{F}_M$.
    Step 4. B_0 sends e to Σ and receives a signature (r, c, s_1, s_2, d). B_0 sends c to the guaranteeing banks.
    Step 5. B_0 receives $\{r_j\}_{j \in \mathcal{B} \setminus \{i\}}$ from each B_j.
    Step 6. B_0 computes r following the issuing protocol, and sends the blinded e-cash (r, c, s_1, s_2, d) to $\mathcal{F}_M$.

If $\mathcal{F}$ succeeds the simulation of B_0, $\mathcal{F}_M$ $(l, l+1)$-forges the e-cash with non-negligible probability and uses the e-cash $\{(\zeta_k, \zeta_{1,k}, \rho_k, \omega_k, \sigma_{1,k}, \sigma_{2,k}, \delta_k, \mathcal{B}_k)\}_{k=1}^{l+1}$.

Payment forged e-cash: To extract the elements of the blind signature scheme [1] from the forged e-cash, $\mathcal{F}$ executes this phase twice by resetting $\mathcal{F}_M$ with different random tapes.

- Simulation of a shop S:
    Step 1. If S receives e-cash from $\mathcal{F}_M$, then S sends a challenge cha to $\mathcal{F}_M$.
    Step 2. If S receives an answer (ϵ_p, μ_p), then S verifies the answer with Eq.(3) and Eq.(2). If the answer (ϵ_p, μ_p) is valid, then S records the e-cash and the answer on database of S.

In the first run, $\mathcal{F}_M$ uses $(l+1)$ e-cash at S^5. Therefore $\{(\epsilon_{p,k}, \mu_{p,k})\}_{k=1}^{l+1}$ is recorded on the database of B_0. This phase completes with probability ϵ_0.

In the second run, $\mathcal{F}$ resets $\mathcal{F}_M$ and restarts the payment phase by using different random tape. Note that, the challenges chosen by S are different from those used in the first run with overwhelming probability.

After ending these simulations, $\mathcal{F}$ has following values.

$$\{(\zeta_k, \zeta_{1,k}, \rho_k, \omega_k, \sigma_{1,k}, \sigma_{2,k}, \delta_k, \mathcal{B}_k), (\epsilon_{p,k}, \mu_{p,k}, cha), (\epsilon'_{p,k}, \mu'_{p,k}, cha')\}_{k=1}^{l+1}$$

---

[5] $\mathcal{F}_M$ can use each e-cash at different shop (simulated by $\mathcal{F}$).

We can extract $(l, l+1)$-forgery for Abe's blind signatures[1] from utilizing the $(l, l+1)$-forged e-cash is as follows. For $k = 1, 2, \ldots, l+1$, $\mathcal{F}$ can compute $\tilde{\rho}$ from (ρ_k, ω_k) and other banks' secret keys $\{x_{2,j}\}_{j \in \mathcal{B} \setminus \{i\}}$,

$$\tilde{\rho}_k := \rho_k + \omega_k \sum_{k \in \mathcal{B} \setminus \{0\}} x_{2,k} \bmod q. \tag{7}$$

From the step 3 of payment protocol, $(\epsilon_{p,k}, \mu_{p,k})$ and $(\epsilon'_{p,k}, \mu'_{p,k})$ hold $\mu_{p,k} = \tau_k + \gamma_k \epsilon_{p,k} \bmod q$ and $\mu'_{p,k} = \tau_k + \gamma_k \epsilon'_{p,k} \bmod q$. With these equations, $\mathcal{F}$ can also compute (τ_k, γ_k). Thus $\tilde{\mu}_k = \tau_k + \gamma_k \tilde{\delta}_k \bmod q$ is obtained. Therefore, $\mathcal{F}$ succeeds to $(l, l+1)$-forge the signature of Σ $\{(\zeta_k, \zeta_{1,k}, \tilde{\rho}_k, \omega_j, \sigma_{1,j}, \sigma_{2,j}, \delta_j, \tilde{\mu}_j, \mathcal{B})\}_{k=1}^{l+1}$.

The success probability of $\mathcal{F}$ is evaluated as follows. The probability with which $\mathcal{F}$ hits the prediction in initialization phase is $1/L$. The probability that $\mathcal{F}$ succeeds two simulations of "payment forged e-cash" is ϵ_0^2. $\mathcal{F}$ can compute all $\{\mu_{p,k}\}_{k=1}^{l+1}$, if the challenge of *first* and *second runs* are completely different such that $\{\epsilon_{p,k} \neq \epsilon'_{p,k}\}_{k=1}^{l+1}$: It happens with probability $(1 - \frac{1}{q})^{l+1}$. For sufficiently large q,

$$\left(1 - \frac{1}{q}\right)^{l+1} \geq \left(1 - \frac{1}{q}\right)^q \geq \frac{1}{4}.$$

So, the probability ϵ_1 that $\mathcal{F}$ succeeds to the output $(l, l+1)$-forgeries is

$$\epsilon_1 \geq \frac{\epsilon_0^2}{4L}.$$

Secondly, we prove the unforgeability with respect to a guaranteeing bank. The procedure is almost the same as the previous one. In the initialization phase, $\mathcal{F}$ guesses a bank B_j which is attacked, and sets its guaranteeing public key $y_{2,j} = y$. $\mathcal{F}$ guesses another bank B_k which may behaves the issuing bank sets its fixed tag key $z_k = z$ by simulating $\mathcal{H}_1$. Other keys are decided following the protocol. The other procedure is almost the same as the previous one. $\mathcal{F}$ succeeds to $(l, l+1)$-forge if the guesses are correct. Note that, in the case that the issuing bank is corrupted, $\mathcal{F}$ cannot answer all queries of $\mathcal{F}_M$. ∎

For example, if $\mathcal{F}_M$ asks the corrupted issuing bank B_0^* that "please open your commitments a, b_1, b_2", $\mathcal{F}$ cannot answer this question, because B_0^* receives a, b_1, b_2 directly from Σ, and $\mathcal{F}$ has no information about them.

Theorem 5. *The proposed full tag scheme is $(l, l+1)$-unforgeable against ACMA & AIA for polynomially bounded l if the discrete logarithm problem is intractable in the random oracle model.*

Proof. In this situation, $\mathcal{F}$ always sets public keys of Σ to the attacked bank. Thus the problem which occurs the above proof is avoided. ∎

5 Conclusion

We discussed the formal notions of the untraceable e-cash schemes based on the blind multisignature schemes, and presented the provably secure e-cash scheme under assumption of DDH problem in the random oracle model. To the best of our knowledge, this paper is the first one which discusses the formal security notions of the untraceable e-cash schemes based on blind multisignature schemes. We will describe the formal security of the blind multisignature and concrete provably secure scheme in a full paper. We will directly prove the unforgeability without depending the proof of [1].

References

[1] Masayuki Abe. A secure three-move blind signature scheme for polynomially many signatures. In *EUROCRYPT 2001*, pages 136–151, 2001.

[2] Masayuki Abe and Tatsuaki Okamoto. Provably secure partially blind signatures. In *CRYPTO 2000*, pages 271–286, 2000.

[3] Mihir Bellare, Chanathip Namprempre, David Pointcheval, and Michael Semanko. One-more-RSA-inversion problems and the security of chaum's blind signature scheme. In *J. Cryptology 16(3)*, pages 185–215, 2003.

[4] Mihir Bellare and Phillip Rogaway. Random oracles are practical: A paradigm for designing efficient protocols. In *ACM Conference on Computer and Communications Security 1993*, pages 62–73, 1993.

[5] Dan Boneh. The decision diffie-hellman problem. In *ANTS 1998*, pages 48–63, 1998.

[6] Stefan Brands. Untraceable off-line cash in wallet with observers (extended abstract). In *Advances in Cryptology – CRYPTO '93*, pages 302–318, 1993.

[7] David Chaum. Blind signatures for untraceable payments. In *Advances in Cryptology - CRYPTO'82*, pages 199–203, 1982.

[8] David Chaum, Amos Fiat, and Moni Naor. Untraceable electronic cash. In *Advances in Cryptology - CRYPTO'88*, pages 319–327, 1988.

[9] Xiaofeng Chen, Fangguo Zhang, and Kwangjo Kim. Id-based multi-proxy signature and blind multisignature from bilinear pairings. In *KIISC conference 2003*, pages 11–19, 2003.

[10] Matthew Franklin and Moti Yung. Secure and efficient off-line digital money. In *ICALP 1993*, pages 265–276, 1993.

[11] Patrick Horster, Markus Michels, and Holger Petersen. Blind multisignature scheme based on the discrete logarithm problem. In *Proc. of 11th Annual Computer Security Applications Conference*, pages 149–155, 1995.

[12] Kazuharu Itakura and Katsuhiro Nakamura. A public key cryptosystem suitable for digital multisignatures. In *NEC Research & Development, 71*, pages 1–8, 1983.

[13] Silvio Micali, Kazuo Ohta, and Leonid Reyzin. Accountable-subgroup multisignatures. In *ACM Conference on Computer and Communications Security 2001*, pages 245–254, 2001.

[14] David Pointcheval and Jacques Stern. Provably secure blind signature schemes. In *ASIACRYPT '96*, pages 252–265, 1996.

[15] David Pointcheval and Jacques Stern. Security arguments for digital signatures and blind signatures. In *J. Cryptology 13(3)*, pages 361–396, 2000.

[16] Claus Peter Schnorr. Efficient identification and signatures for smart cards. In *Advances in Cryptology - CRYPTO '89*, pages 239–252, 1989.

Efficient Provably Secure Restrictive Partially Blind Signatures from Bilinear Pairings*

Xiaofeng Chen[1], Fangguo Zhang[2], Yi Mu[3], and Willy Susilo[3]

[1] Department of Computer Science,
Sun Yat-sen University, Guangzhou 510275, P.R. China
isschxf@mail.sysu.edu.cn
[2] Department of Electronics and Communication Engineering,
Sun Yat-sen University, Guangzhou 510275, P.R. China
isszhfg@mail.sysu.edu.cn
[3] School of Information Technology and Computer Science,
University of Wollongong, Australia
{ymu, wsusilo}@uow.edu.au

Abstract. Restrictive blind signatures allow a recipient to receive a blind signature on a message unknown to the signer but the choice of the message is restricted and must conform to certain rules. Partially blind signatures allow a signer to explicitly include necessary information (expiration date, collateral conditions, or whatever) in the resulting signatures under some agreement with the receiver. Restrictive partially blind signatures incorporate the advantages of these two blind signatures. In this paper we first propose a new restrictive partially blind signature scheme from bilinear pairings. Since the proposed scheme does not use Chaum-Pedersen's knowledge proof protocol, it is much more efficient than the original restrictive partially blind signature scheme. We then present a formal proof of security in the random oracle model. Moreover, we use the proposed signature scheme to build an untraceable off-line electronic cash system followed Brand's construction.

Keywords: Restrictive partially blind signatures, Bilinear pairings, Electronic cash.

1 Introduction

Blind signatures, introduced by Chaum [10], allow a recipient to obtain a signature on message m without revealing anything about the message to the signer. Blind signatures play an important role in a plenty of applications such as electronic voting, electronic cash where anonymity is of great concern.

A serious problem in electronic cash schemes is double-spending. On-line electronic cash scheme provides a possible solution against double-spending. However, it requires that the shop must contact the bank during each transaction.

---

* Supported by National Natural Science Foundation of China (No. 60503006 and 60403007) and ARC Discovery Grant DP0557493.

G. Di Crescenzo and A. Rubin (Eds.): FC 2006, LNCS 4107, pp. 251–265, 2006.

So the bank will soon become the bottleneck of the systems. Chaum [11] also proposed an off-line electronic cash scheme, which ensures the bank to trace the double-spenders after the fact. However, such a system is very inefficient due to the cut-and-choose protocol.

Restrictive blind signatures were first introduced by Brands [7,8], which allow a recipient to receive a blind signature on a message unknown to the signer but the choice of the message is restricted and must conform to certain rules. Furthermore, he proposed a highly efficient electronic cash system, where the bank ensures that the user is restricted to embed his identity in the resulting blind signature. Brand's electronic cash system has received wide attention for its distinguished characters. However, Brand's original restrictive blind signature scheme is mainly based on Chaum-Pedersen's interactive zero-knowledge proof of common exponent [12]. The communication cost is a little high and the length of the signature is a little too long.

Partially blind signatures, first introduced by Abe and Fujisaki [1], allow a signer to produce a blind signature on a message for a recipient and the signature explicitly includes common agreed information which remains clearly visible despite the blinding process. This notion overcomes some disadvantages of fully blind signatures such as the signer has no control over the attributes except for those bound by the public key. Partial blind signatures play an important role in designing the efficient electronic cash system. For example, the bank does not require different public keys for different coin values. On the other hand, the size of the database that stored the previously spent coins to detect double-spending would not increase infinitely over time.

Maitland and Boyd [15] first incorporated these two blind signatures and proposed a provably secure restrictive partially blind signature scheme, which satisfies the partial blindness and restrictive blindness. Their scheme followed the construction proposed by Abe and Okamoto [2] and used Brand's restrictive blind signature scheme. Therefore, the scheme still uses Chaum-Pedersen's zero-knowledge proof of common exponent and this increases the communication cost and the length of the signature.

Our Contribution. In this paper we first propose a new restrictive blind signature scheme and a restrictive partially blind signature scheme from bilinear pairings, and the former can be regarded as a special case of the latter. Our blind signature schemes use the so-called gap Diffile-Hellman group [5,9,13], where Decisional Diffie-Hellman Problem (DDHP) can be solved in polynomial time but there is no polynomial time algorithm to solve Computational Diffie-Hellman Problem (CDHP) with non-negligible probability. So it is not required to use the inefficient zero-knowledge proof of common exponent to ensure the validity of a Diffie-Helllman tuple in our schemes. Compared to the original schemes, the advantages of our scheme are shorter length of the signature and lower communication complexity. Furthermore, we give a formal security proof for the proposed schemes in the random oracle model.

The rest of the paper is organized as follows: The definitions associated with restrictive partially blind signatures are introduced in Section 2. The proposed restrictive blind signature scheme is given in Section 3. The proposed restrictive partially blind signature scheme is given in Section 4. Finally, conclusions will be made in Section 5.

2   Definitions

Juels, Luby and Ostrovsky [14] gave a formal definition of blind signatures. They proved the existence of secure blind signatures assuming the one-way trapdoor permutation family. Pointcheval and Stern [17] showed the security of a certain type of efficient blind signature in the random oracle model. Later, they [16,18] developed a generic approach that converts logarithmically secure schemes into polynomially secure ones at the cost of two more data transmissions between the signer and the receiver.

Abe and Okamoto first presented the formal definition of partially blind signatures. Restrictive partially blind signatures can be regarded as partially blind signatures which also satisfies the property of restrictiveness. In the context of partially blind signatures, the signer and user are assumed to agree on a piece of information, denoted by *info*. In real applications, *info* may be decided by the negotiation between the signer and user. For the sake of simplicity, we omit the negotiation throughout this paper. In the following, we follow the definitions of [2,14,7] to give a formal definition of restrictive partially blind signatures.

Definition 1. *(Restrictive Partially Blind Signatures) A restrictive partially blind signature scheme is a four-tuple* $(\mathcal{PG}, \mathcal{KG}, \mathcal{SG}, \mathcal{SV})$.

- **System Parameters Generation** $\mathcal{PG}$**:** *On input a security parameter k, outputs the common system parameters* Params.
- **Key Generation** $\mathcal{KG}$**:** *On input* Params, *outputs a public and private key pair* (pk, sk).
- **Signature Generation** $\mathcal{SG}$**:** *Let U and S be two probabilistic interactive Turing machines and each of them has a public input tape, a private random tape, a private work tape, a private output tape, a public output tape, and input and output communication tapes. The random tape and the input tapes are read-only, and the output tapes are write-only. The private work tape is read-write. Suppose* **info** *is agreed common information between U and S. The public input tape of U contains pk generated by* $\mathcal{G}(1^k)$, *and* **info**. *The public input tape of S contains* **info**. *The private input tape of S contains sk, and that for U contains a message m which he knows a representation with respect to some bases in* Params. *The lengths of* **info** *and m are polynomial to k. U and S engage in the signature issuing protocol and stop in polynomial-time. When they stop, the public output of S contains either completed or not-completed. If it is completed, the private output tape of U contains either* $\perp$ *or* $(info, m, \sigma)$.
- **Signature Verification** $\mathcal{SV}$**:** *On input* $(pk, info, m, \sigma)$ *and outputs either accept or reject.*

Definition 2. *(Completeness) If S and U follow the signature issuing protocol, the signature scheme is complete if, for every constant $c > 0$, there exists a bound k_0 such that S outputs completed and* info *on its proper tapes, and U outputs* $(info, m, \sigma)$ *that satisfies*

$$\mathcal{SV}(info, m, \sigma) = accept$$

with probability at least $1 - 1/k^c$ for $k > k_0$. The probability is taken over the coin flips of $\mathcal{KG}, S$ and U.

We say a message-signature tuple $(info, m, \sigma)$ is valid with regard to pk if it leads to $\mathcal{SV}$ to accept.

Definition 3. *(Restrictiveness) Let m be a message such that the user U knows a representation $(a_1, \cdots, a_k)$ of m with respect to a generator-tuple $(g_1, \cdots, g_k)$ at the start of a blind signature issuing protocol. Let $(b_1, \cdots, b_k)$ be the representation U knows of the blinded number m' of m after the protocol finished. If there exist two function I_1 and I_2 such that*

$$I_1(a_1, \cdots, a_k) = I_2(b_1, \cdots, b_k)$$

regardless of m and the blinding transformation applied by U, then the protocol is called a restrictive blind signature protocol. The function I_1 and I_2 are called blinding-invariant functions of the protocol with respect to $(g_1, \cdots, g_k)$.

Definition 4. *(Partial Blindness) Let U_0 and U_1 be two honest users that follow the signature issuing protocol.*

1. *$(pk, sk) \leftarrow \mathcal{KG}(\mathsf{Params})$.*
2. *$(m_0, m_1, info_0, info_1) \leftarrow S^*(1^k, pk, sk)$.*
3. *Set up the input tapes of U_0 and U_1 as follows:*
   - *Select $b \in_R \{0, 1\}$ and put m_b and m_{1-b} on the private input tapes of U_0 and U_1, respectively.*
   - *Put $info_0$ and $info_1$ on the public input tapes of U_0 and U_1, respectively. Also put pk on their public input tapes.*
   - *Randomly select the contents of the private random tapes.*
4. *S^* engages in the signature issuing protocol with U_0 and U_1.*
5. *Let U_0 and U_1 output $(info_0, m_b, \sigma_b)$ and $(info_0, m_{1-b}, \sigma_{1-b})$, respectively, on their private tapes. If $info_0 \neq info_1$, then give $\perp$ to S^*. If $info_0 = info_1$, then provide S^* with the additional inputs (σ_b, σ_{1-b}) ordered according to the corresponding messages (m_b, m_{1-b}).*
6. *S^* outputs $b' \in \{0, 1\}$. We say that S^* wins if $b' = b$.*

A signature scheme is partially blind if, for every constant $c > 0$, there exists a bound k_0 such that for all probabilistic polynomial-time algorithm S^*, S^* outputs $b' = b$ with probability at most $1/2 + 1/k^c$ for $k > k_0$. The probability is taken over the flips of $\mathcal{KG}, U_0, U_1$, and S^*.

Definition 5. *(Unforgeability) Let S be an honest signer that follows the signature issuing protocol.*

1. $(pk, sk) \leftarrow \mathcal{KG}(\textit{Params})$.
2. *Put sk and **info** on proper tapes of S.*
3. *U^* engages in the signature issuing protocol with S in a concurrent and interleaving way. For each **info**, let l_{info} be the number of executions of the signature issuing protocol where S outputs completed and **info** on its output tapes. (For **info** that has never appeared on the private output tapes of S, define $l_{info} = 0$.)*
4. *U^* outputs a single piece of common information, **info**, and $l_{info} + 1$ signatures $(m_1, \sigma_1), \cdots, (m_{l_{info}+1}, \sigma_{l_{info}+1})$.*

A partially blind signature scheme is unforgeable if, for any probabilistic polynomial-time algorithm U^* that plays the above game, the probability that the output of U^* satisfies

$$\mathcal{SV}(pk, \textit{info}, m_j, \sigma_j) = accept$$

for all $j = 1, \cdots, l_{info} + 1$ is at most $1/k^c$ where $k > k_0$ and some constant $c > 0$. The probability is taken over the coin flips of $\mathcal{KG}, S,$ and U^*.

3   Restrictive Blind Signatures from Pairings

In Brand's restrictive blind signature scheme, the Chaum-Pedersen's protocol must be used to provide a proof that $\log_g y = \log_m z$, i.e., $< g, y, m, z >$ is a valid Diffie-Hellman tuple. We argue the knowledge proof can be avoided in the gap Diffie-Hellman (blind) signature scheme [6,3]. However, if we directly use the gap Diffie-Hellman blind signature scheme as a building block to design our restrictive blind signature scheme from pairings, there exists a cheating attack.[1] In this section, we first propose a variant of gap Diffie-Hellman blind signature scheme, the security of which is based on a variant of CDHP, named RCDHP, which is equivalent to CDHP. We then propose a restrictive blind signature scheme which is derived from the variant of gap Diffie-Hellman blind signature scheme and Brand's original blind signature scheme.

3.1   A Variant of Gap Diffie-Hellman Blind Signature Scheme

We firstly introduce a variant of CDHP in G which we call Reversion Computational Diffie-Hellman Problem (RCDHP).[2]

RCDHP: Given g, g^a and g^b, to compute g^c which satisfies $a \equiv bc \bmod q$.

---

[1] It is trivial to see that the user can get the signature $\tilde{\sigma} = \tilde{m}^x$ for any message $\tilde{m}$ with the signature $z = m^x$ for a message m. This will destroy the property of restrictiveness of the signature scheme. We argue that this attack can be avoidable if the form of z and $\tilde{\sigma}$ is different. For details, refer to section 3.2.

[2] We distinguish it with Inversion Computational Diffie-Hellman Problem: Given g and g^a, to compute $g^{a^{-1}}$.

Theorem 1. RCDHP *is equivalent to* CDHP *in* G.

Proof. Given (g, g^a, g^b), suppose we can solve RCDHP in G, then we can obtain $g^{b^{-1}}$ from g and g^b. Note $a = (ab)b^{-1} \bmod q$, we can compute g^{ab} from g^a and $g^{b^{-1}}$, i.e., we can solve CDHP in G.

Given (g, g^a, g^b), let $h = g^b$, so $g = h^{b^{-1}}$. Suppose we can solve CDHP in G, so with h and $h^{b^{-1}}$ we can obtain $h^{b^{-2}}$, i.e., $g^{b^{-1}}$. Then we can obtain $g^{ab^{-1}}$ from g^a and $g^{b^{-1}}$, i.e., we solve RCDHP in G.   □

In the following, we present a variant of Boneh *et al*'s signature scheme, the security of which is based on the assumption that RCDHP in G is intractable. The system parameters are the same as above.

Given the signed message m and the signer's secret key x, the signature on m is $\sigma = H(m)^{x^{-1}}$. Anyone can verify that $< g, y, \sigma, H(m) >$ is a valid Diffie-Hellman tuple.

Similarly, we can present the corresponding blind signature scheme based on the above variant of Boneh *et al*'s signature scheme.

- The user picks a random number $r \in_R Z_q^*$, and sends $\tilde{m} = H(m) \cdot y^r$ to the signer.
- The signer computes $\tilde{\sigma} = \tilde{m}^{x^{-1}}$ and sends it to the user.
- The user computes $\sigma = \tilde{\sigma} \cdot g^{-r}$.

If $< g, y, \sigma, H(m) >$ is a valid Diffie-Hellman tuple, then σ is a valid signature on message m.

3.2   The Proposed Restrictive Blind Signature Scheme

- **System Parameters Generation:** Given a security parameter k, let G_1 be a gap Diffie-Hellman group generated by g, whose order is a prime q, and G_2 be a cyclic multiplicative group of the same order q. A bilinear pairing is a map $e : G_1 \times G_1 \rightarrow G_2$. $H : G_1 \times G_1 \rightarrow G_1$ is a cryptographic hash function. The system parameters are $Params = \{G_1, G_2, e, q, g, k, H\}$.
- **Key Generation:** Let $(x, y = g^x)$ be the private and public key pair of the signer.
- **Signature Generation:** Let m be a message from the receiver.
  - The signer generates a random number $r \in_R Z_q$ and sends $z = m^{rx}$, $b = m^r$, and $a = y^r$ to the receiver.
  - The receiver checks whether $e(z, g) = e(b, y) = e(m, a)$. If not, he terminates the protocol. Else, he generates random numbers $\alpha, \lambda, u \in_R Z_q$ and computes

  $$m' = m^\alpha, z' = z^{\alpha\lambda}, b' = b^{\alpha\lambda}, a' = a^\lambda, \tilde{m} = H(m', z', b', a')y^u.$$

  The receiver then sends $\tilde{m}$ to the signer.
  - The signer responds with $\tilde{\sigma} = \tilde{m}^{x^{-1}}$ and the receiver computes $\sigma = \tilde{\sigma}g^{-u}$.

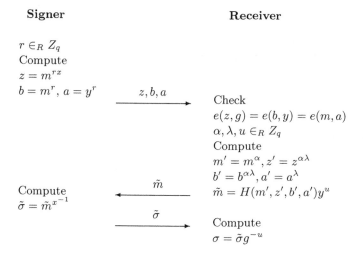

Fig. 1. Restrictive Blind Signature Scheme from Pairings

Thus, the receiver obtains a signature on the message m' where $m' = m^\alpha$ and α is chosen by the receiver.

- **Signature Verification:** (z', b', a', σ) is a valid signature on m' if the following equations hold:

$$e(\sigma, y) = e(H(m', z', b', a'), g); \quad e(z', g) = e(b', y) = e(m', a').$$

3.3 Security Analysis of the Proposed Scheme

Theorem 2. *The proposed restrictive blind signature scheme achieves the properties of Correctness, Blindness, Restrictiveness.*

Proof. We show that our scheme satisfies all the security properties.

- *Correctness*: Firstly, note that $\sigma = \tilde{\sigma} g^{-u} = H(m', z', b', a')^{x^{-1}}$, we have $e(\sigma, y) = e(H(m', z', b', a'), g)$. Secondly, since $z' = z^{\alpha\lambda} = m^{r x \alpha \lambda}$, $b' = m^{r \alpha \lambda}$, and $a' = y^{r\lambda}$, so $e(z', g) = e(b', y) = e(m', a')$.
- *Blindness*: Let $(\tilde{m}, m, z, b, a, \tilde{\sigma})$ be any of the review of the protocol as seen by the signer. Therefore, $\tilde{\sigma} = \tilde{m}^{x^{-1}}$ and $e(z, g) = e(b, y) = e(m, a)$. Let (z', b', a', σ) be a valid signature on message m' obtained by the receiver. Choose the unique blinding factor $F = \tilde{\sigma}/\sigma$ and determine three representations $m' = m^\alpha, a' = a^\lambda, F = g^u$.[3] Note that $\sigma = H(m', z', b', a')^{x^{-1}}$ and $e(z', g) = e(b', y) = e(m', a')$ have been established by the fact that the blind signature is valid, therefore we have

$$\tilde{m} = \tilde{\sigma}^x = (\sigma F)^x = H(m', z', b', a')y^u, z' = z^{\alpha\lambda}, b' = b^{\alpha\lambda}.$$

---

[3] Though it is difficult to compute (α, λ, u), we only need to exploit the existence of them.

- *Restrictiveness*: Similar to [7,15], the restrictiveness nature of the scheme can be captured by the following assumption: The recipient obtains a signature on a message that can only be the form $m' = m^\alpha$ with α randomly chosen by the receiver. In addition, if there exists a representation (μ_1, μ_2) of m with respect to bases g_1 and g_2 such that $m = g_1^{\mu_1} g_2^{\mu_2}$ and if there exists a representation (μ'_1, μ'_2) of m' with respect to g_1 and g_2 such that $m' = g_1^{\mu'_1} g_2^{\mu'_2}$, then the relation $I_1(\mu_1, \mu_2) = \mu_1/\mu_2 = \mu'_1/\mu'_2 = I_2(\mu'_1, \mu'_2)$ holds. In the applications of an electronic cash system, a user chooses a random number u as his identification information and computes $m = g_1^u g_2$. He then with the bank performs the signature issuing protocol to obtain a coin. When spending the coin at a shop, the user must provide a proof that he knows a representation of m' with respect to base g_1 and g_2. This restricts m' must be the form of m^α. For more details, refer to [7].   □

4   Restrictive Partially Blind Signatures from Pairings

In this section, we firstly propose a concrete restrictive partially blind signature scheme from pairings based on [19,20]. The proposed restrictive blind signature scheme in section 3 can be regarded as a special case of it when $H_0(c)$ equals to 0. We then discuss the security and efficiency of the scheme under the assumption of ideal randomness of hash functions H and H_0. Finally, we describe an electronic cash system using the proposed signature scheme.

4.1   The Proposed Restrictive Partially Blind Signature Scheme

- **System Parameters Generation** $\mathcal{PG}$: Given a security parameter k. Let G_1 be a gap Diffie-Hellman group generated by g, whose order is a prime q, and G_2 be a cyclic multiplicative group of the same order q. A bilinear pairing is a map $e : G_1 \times G_1 \to G_2$. Define two cryptographic hash functions $H : G_1 \times G_1 \times \{0,1\}^* \to G_1$, $H_0 : \{0,1\}^* \to Z_q$. The system parameters are $Params = \{G_1, G_2, e, q, g, k, H, H_0\}$.
- **Key Generation** $\mathcal{KG}$: On input $Params$, outputs the private and public key pair $(x, y = g^x)$ of the signer.
- **Signature Generation** $\mathcal{SG}$: Let the shared information $info = c$, and the signed message be $m' = m^\alpha$, where α is a value chosen by the receiver.
  - The signer generates a random number $r \in_R Z_q$ and sends $z = m^{rx}$, $b = m^r$, and $a = y^r$ to the receiver.
  - The receiver checks whether $e(z, g) = e(b, y) = e(m, a)$. If not, he terminates the protocol. Else, he generates random numbers $\alpha, \lambda, u \in_R Z_q$ and computes

    $$m' = m^\alpha, z' = z^{\alpha\lambda}, b' = b^{\alpha\lambda}, a' = a^\lambda, \tilde{m} = H(m', z', b', a', c)(g^{H_0(c)}y)^u.$$

    The receiver then sends $\tilde{m}$ to the signer.
  - The signer responds with $\tilde{\sigma} = \tilde{m}^{\frac{1}{H_0(c)+x}}$ and the receiver computes $\sigma = \tilde{\sigma} g^{-u}$.

The resulting signature for the shared information c and message m' is (z', b', a', σ).

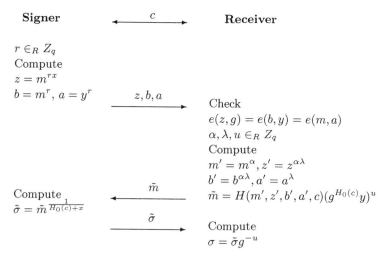

Fig. 2. Restrictive Partially Blind Signature Scheme from Pairings

- **Signature Verification** $\mathcal{SV}$: (z', b', a', σ) is a valid signature on c and m' if the following equations hold:

$$e(\sigma, g^{H_0(c)}y) = e(H(m', z', b', a', c), g); \quad e(z', g) = e(b', y) = e(m', a').$$

4.2   Security Analysis of the Proposed Scheme

Theorem 3. *The proposed scheme achieves the property of completeness.*

Proof

$$
\begin{aligned}
e(\sigma, g^{H_0(c)}y) &= e(\tilde{\sigma}g^{-u}, g^{H_0(c)}y) = e(\tilde{m}^{\frac{1}{H_0(c)+x}}g^{-u}, g^{H_0(c)}y) \\
&= e(H(m', z', b', a', c)^{\frac{1}{H_0(c)+x}}, g^{H_0(c)}y) \\
&= e(H(m', z', b', a', c), g) \\
e(z', g) &= e(m^{rx\alpha\lambda}, g) = e(b', y) = e(m^{\alpha}, g^{rx\lambda}) = e(m', a')
\end{aligned}
$$

Theorem 4. *The proposed scheme achieves the property of restrictiveness.*

Proof. It is same to Theorem 2.   □

Theorem 5. *The proposed scheme achieves partial blindness.*

Proof. Suppose S^* is given $\bot$ in step 5 of the game in definition 4, S^* determines b with a probability $1/2$ (the same probability as randomly guessing b).

Suppose that in step 5, the shared information $c_0 = c_1$. Let (z', b', a', σ, m') be one of the signatures subsequently given to S^*. Let $(z, b, a, \tilde{m}, \tilde{\sigma}, m, c)$ be data appearing in the view of S^* during one of the executions of the signature issuing protocol at step 4. Therefore, $\tilde{\sigma} = \tilde{m}^{\frac{1}{H_0(c)+x}}$ and $e(z, g) = e(b, y) = e(m, a)$.

It is sufficient to show that there exists a tuple of random blinding factors (α, λ, u) that maps $(z, b, a, \tilde{m}, \tilde{\sigma}, m)$ to (z', b', a', σ, m'). Suppose $m' = m^\alpha, a' = a^\lambda$, and $F = \tilde{\sigma}/\sigma = g^u$.[4] Note that $\sigma = H(m', z', b', a', c)^{\frac{1}{H_0(c)+x}}$ and $e(z', g) = e(b', y) = e(m', a')$ have been established by the fact the signature is valid. Therefore, we have

$$\tilde{m} = \tilde{\sigma}^{H_0(c)+x} = (\sigma F)^{H_0(c)+x} = H(m', z', b', a', c)(g^{H_0(c)}y)^u, z' = z^{\alpha\lambda}, b' = b^{\alpha\lambda}.$$

Thus, the blinding factors which lead to the same relation defined in the signature issuing protocol always exist. Therefore, even an infinitely powerful S^* succeeds in determining b with probability $1/2$.   □

Theorem 6. *The proposed scheme is unforgeable if $l_{info} < poly(\log k)$ for all info.*

Proof. The proof follows the security argument given by Abe and Okamoto [2]. We first deal with the common-part forgery where an attacker forges a signature with regard to common information c that has never appeared in the game of the definition 5, *i.e.*, $l_c = 0$. We then treat one-more forgery where $l_c \neq 0$.

Suppose a successful common-part forger $\mathcal{U}^*$ who plays the game of the definition 5 and produces a valid message-signature tuple $(z', b', a', \sigma, c, m')$ such that $l_c = 0$ with a non-negligible probability ϵ, we can construct a machine $\mathcal{M}$ to solve the q-Strong Diffie-Hellman Problem for $q = 0$ [4]: given (g, y), output a pair $(c, g^{\frac{1}{c+x}})$ where $c \in Z_q^*$.

Let q_H and q_{H_0} be the maximum number of queries asked from $\mathcal{U}^*$ to $\mathcal{H}$ and $\mathcal{H}_0$, respectively. Similarly, let q_S be the maximum number of invocation of the signer S. All those parameters are limited by a polynomial in the security parameter k. For simplicity, we assume that all queries are different. Let $(x, y = g^x)$ be the private and public key pair of the signer. Machine $\mathcal{M}$ simulates the game in definition 5 as follows:

1. Choose randomly $v_i, w_j, \omega \in Z_q$ for $i = 1, 2, \cdots, q_H + q_S, j = 1, 2, \cdots, q_{H_0} + q_S$.
2. Select $I \in_U \{1, 2, \cdots, q_H + q_S\}$ and $J \in_U \{1, 2, \cdots, q_{H_0} + q_S\}$. Run $\mathcal{U}^*$ with (g, y, q) simulating $\mathcal{H}, \mathcal{H}_0$ and S as follows.
   - For i-th query to $\mathcal{H}$, respond

$$H(m_i, z_i, b_i, a_i, c_i) = \begin{cases} g^\omega, & \text{if } i = I \\ (y \cdot g^{w_i})^{v_i}, & \text{if } i \neq I \end{cases}$$

   - For j-th query to $\mathcal{H}_0$, respond $H_0(c_j) = w_j$.

---

[4] Similarly, we only need to exploit the existence of (α, λ, u).

- For requests to $\mathcal{S}$, first negotiate the common information. Let c_k be the result of negotiation, then respond

$$\sigma_k = \begin{cases} \text{``Fail''}, & \text{if } c_k = c_I \\ g^{v_k}, & \text{if } c_k \neq c_I \end{cases}$$

3. If $\mathcal{U}^*$ eventually outputs a valid signature σ with regard to c_J and m_I, output them.

The probability that $\mathcal{U}^*$ is successful without querying $\mathcal{H}, \mathcal{H}_0$ in a proper way is negligible because of the randomness of those hash functions.

Now we use $\mathcal{M}$ to solve the q-Strong Diffie-Hellman Problem for $q{=}0$. Note that $\sigma = g^{\omega \frac{1}{H_0(c_J)+x}}$, therefore we can output a valid pair $(H_0(c_J), \sigma^{\omega^{-1}})$.

We then consider the case where the forgery is attempted against the common information such that $l_c \neq 0$. Here we only need to consider a single c in the game of the definition 5. For the case where c is not all the same in the game of the definition 5, we can follow the solution [2] to turn the game into the fixed-info version.

Since there is a unique c in the game of the definition 5, we only need to prove the security of fully blind version of our scheme. For any public information c, the signer sets up the system parameters $params = \{G_1, G_2, e, q, g, k, H, H_0\}$. Let $(X = H_0(c) + x, Y = g^{H_0(c)+x})$ be the private and public key pair of the signer, here $x \in_R Z_q^*$. Let m' be the signed message. The blind signature issuing protocol of this fully blind signature scheme is shown as follows:

- The signer generates a random number $r \in_R Z_q$ and sends $z = m^{rX}$, $b = m^r$, and $a = Y^r$ to the receiver.
- The receiver checks whether $e(z, g) = e(b, Y) = e(m, a)$. If not, he terminates the protocol. Else, he generates random numbers $\alpha, \lambda, u \in_R Z_q$ and computes

$$m' = m^\alpha, z' = z^{\alpha\lambda}, b' = b^{\alpha\lambda}, a' = a^\lambda, \tilde{m} = H(m', z', b', a')Y^u.$$

The receiver then sends $\tilde{m}$ to the signer.
- The signer responds with $\tilde{\sigma} = \tilde{m}^{\frac{1}{X}}$ and the receiver computes $\sigma = \tilde{\sigma}g^{-u}$.

(z', b', a', σ) is a valid signature on m' if the following equations hold:

$$e(\sigma, Y) = e(H(m', z', b', a'), g); \ e(z', g) = e(b', Y) = e(m', a').$$

We call above fully blind signature scheme FuBS, which is actually the restrictive blind signature scheme proposed in section 3. It is easy to see that if a message-signature pair (m, c, S) can be forged for the proposed partially blind signature scheme, then a blind signature on the message $m' = m\|c$ for the corresponding FuBS can be forged.

Next, we show that FuBS is secure against one-more forgery under chosen message attack using the similar technique in [3]. In the following we firstly introduce a variations of chosen-target CDHP, named "Chosen target RCDHP".

Definition 6. *Let G_1 be a gap Diffie-Hellman group of prime order q and g is a generator of G_1. Let x be a random element of Z_q^* and $y = g^x$. Let $H_0 : \{0,1\}^* \rightarrow G_1$ be a cryptographic hash function. The adversary $\mathcal{A}$ is given input (q, g, y, H_0) and has access to the target oracle T_{G_1} that returns a random element z_i in G_1 and the helper oracle RCDH-$x(\cdot)$, i.e., compute $(\cdot)^{x^{-1}}$. Let q_T and q_H be the number of queries $\mathcal{A}$ made to the target oracle and the helper oracle, respectively. The advantage of the adversary attacking the chosen-target RCDHP $Adv_{G_1}^{ct-rcdh}(\mathcal{A})$ is defined as the probability of $\mathcal{A}$ to output a set of l pairs $((v_1, j_1), (v_2, j_2), \ldots, (v_l, j_l))$, for all $1 \le i \le l \ni 1 \le j_i \le q_T$ such that $v_i = z_{j_i}^{x^{-1}}$ where all v_i are distinct and $q_H < q_T$.*

The chosen-target RCDH assumption states that there is no polynomial-time adversary $\mathcal{A}$ with non-negligible $Adv_{G_1}^{ct-icdh}(\mathcal{A})$.

The following lemma shows that FuBS is secure under the assumption that the chosen-target RCDHP in G_1 is intractable.

Lemma 1. *If the chosen-target RCDH assumption is true in the group G_1 then FuBS is secure against one-more forgery under the chosen message attack.*

Proof. (sketch). If there is a probabilistic polynomial time one-more forger algorithm $\mathcal{F}$ with a non-negligible probability ϵ for FuBS under a chosen message attack, then we can use $\mathcal{F}$ to construct an algorithm $\mathcal{A}$ to solve the chosen-target RCDHP with a non-negligible probability.

Suppose that a probabilistic polynomial time forger algorithm $\mathcal{F}$ is given. Suppose that $\mathcal{A}$ is given a challenge as in Definition 6. Now $\mathcal{F}$ has access to a blind signing oracle $x(\cdot)$ and the random hash oracle $H_0(\cdot)$. First, $\mathcal{A}$ provides $(G_1, G_2, e, q, g, H_0, y)$ to $\mathcal{F}$ and $\mathcal{A}$ has to simulate the random hash oracle and the blind signing oracle for $\mathcal{F}$.

Each time $\mathcal{F}$ makes a new hash oracle query which differs from previous one, $\mathcal{A}$ will forward to its target oracle and returns the reply to $\mathcal{F}$. $\mathcal{A}$ stores the pair query-reply in the list of those pairs. If $\mathcal{F}$ makes a query to blind signing oracle, $\mathcal{A}$ will forward to its helper oracle RCDH-$x(\cdot)$ and returns the answer to $\mathcal{F}$.

Eventually $\mathcal{F}$ halts and outputs a list of message-signature pairs $((m_1, S_1), (m_2, S_2), \ldots, (m_l, S_l))$. $\mathcal{A}$ can find m_i in the list stored hash oracle query-reply for $i = 1, 2, \ldots, l$. Let j_i be the index of the found pair, then $\mathcal{A}$ can output its list as $((S_1, j_1), (S_2, j_2), \ldots, (S_l, j_l))$. Then this list is a solution to the problem in Definition 6. $\square$

4.3   Efficiency

We compare our signature scheme to previous restrictive partially blind signature scheme. In the following table we denote by $|G_1|$ the bits of representing any element of G_1. Similarly, let $|p|$ and $|q|$ denote the bits of primes p and q such that $q|p-1$, respectively. Also, let P be the pairings operation, M exponentiation in G_1, E exponentiation in Z_p and R inversion in Z_q (we ignore other operations such as hash in both schemes).

Table 1. Comparison with Maitland-Boyd's signature scheme

Properties	Scheme [14]	Our Proposed Scheme
Length of signature	$\lvert p \rvert + 4\lvert q \rvert$	$4\lvert G_1 \rvert$
Communication	$4\lvert p \rvert + 5\lvert q \rvert$	$5\lvert G_1 \rvert$
Computation (for signature generation)	$20E + 2R$	$9M + 1R + 3P$
Computation (for signature verification)	$6E$	$5P$

The computation complexity of our signature scheme requires more overhead than that of Maitland-Boyd's signature scheme since the pairing computation is the operation which by far takes the most running time. However, the advantages of our scheme are the short length of the signature and low communication complexity (remember that the order of G_1 is only q). Therefore, it is more suitable for low-bandwidth communication environments.

4.4 Application for Electronic Cash System

We follow Brand's construction to describe an electronic cash system using the proposed restrictive partially blind signature scheme from pairings. We denote the bank by $\mathcal{B}$, a generic account-holder by $\mathcal{U}$, and a generic shop by $\mathcal{S}$.

The setup of the system. Let G be a gap Diffie-Hellman group with the prime order q, (g, g_1, g_2) be a random generator tuple. The key pair of $\mathcal{B}$ is $(x, y = g^x)$. Define three cryptographic secure hash functions $H : G \times G \times G \to G$, $H_0 : \{0,1\}^* \to Z_q$ and $H_1 : G \times G \times ID_S \times Date/Time \to Z_q$.

Opening an account. When $\mathcal{U}$ opens an account at $\mathcal{B}$, $\mathcal{B}$ requests $\mathcal{U}$ to identify himself. $\mathcal{U}$ then generates at random a number $u_1 \in_R Z_q$, and computes the unique account number $I = g_1^{u_1}$. If $g_1^{u_1} g_2 \neq 1$, then $\mathcal{U}$ transmits I to $\mathcal{B}$, and keeps u_1 secret. $\mathcal{B}$ stores the identifying information of $\mathcal{U}$ in the account database, together with I. The information I enables $\mathcal{B}$ to uniquely identify $\mathcal{U}$ in case he double-spends.

The withdrawal protocol. When $\mathcal{U}$ wants to withdraw a coin, he first proves ownership of his account and negotiates a common information c. To this end, the following withdrawal protocol between $\mathcal{U}$ and $\mathcal{B}$ is performed:

Step 1. $\mathcal{B}$ generates a random number $r \in_R Z_q$ and sends $z = (Ig_2)^{rx}$, $b = (Ig_2)^r$, and $a = y^r$ to $\mathcal{U}$.

Step 2. $\mathcal{U}$ checks whether $e(z, g) = e(b, y) = e(Ig_2, a)$. If the equation does not hold, he terminates the protocol. Else, he generates random numbers $\alpha, \lambda, x_1, x_2, u \in_R Z_q$ and computes $A = (Ig_2)^\alpha$, $z' = z^{\alpha\lambda}$, $b' = b^{\alpha\lambda}$, $a' = a^\lambda$, $B = g_1^{x_1} g_2^{x_2}$ and $\tilde{m} = H(A, B, z', b', a', c)(g^{H_0(c)} y)^u$. He then sends $\tilde{m}$ to $\mathcal{B}$.

Step 3. $\mathcal{B}$ responds with $\tilde{\sigma} = \tilde{m}^{\frac{1}{H_0(c)+x}}$, and $\mathcal{U}$ computes $\sigma = \tilde{\sigma} g^{-u}$.

If $e(\sigma, g^{H_0(c)}y) = e(H(A, B, z', b', a', c), g)$, then $A, B, c, (z', b', a', \sigma)$ is a valid coin of which $\mathcal{U}$ knows a representation.

The payment protocol. When $\mathcal{U}$ wants to spend his coin at $\mathcal{S}$, the following protocol is performed:

Step 1. $\mathcal{U}$ sends $A, B, c, (z', b', a', \sigma)$ to $\mathcal{S}$.
Step 2. If $A \neq 1$, $\mathcal{S}$ then sends a challenge $d = H_1(A, B, ID_{\mathcal{S}}, date/time)$ to $\mathcal{U}$, where $ID_{\mathcal{S}}$ can be the account number of $\mathcal{S}$, $date/time$ is the number representing date and time of the transaction.
Step 3. $\mathcal{U}$ computes the responses $r_1 = d(u_1\alpha) + x_1$ and $r_2 = d\alpha + x_2$ and sends them to $\mathcal{S}$.

$\mathcal{S}$ accepts the coin if and only if the equations $e(\sigma, g^{H_0(c)}y) = e(H(A, B, z', b', a', c), g)$, $e(z', g) = e(b', y) = e(A, a')$, and $g_1^{r_1} g_2^{r_2} = A^d B$ hold.

The deposit protocol. After some delay in time, $\mathcal{S}$ sends $\mathcal{B}$ the payment transcript, consisting of $A, B, c, (z', b', a', \sigma), (r_1, r_2)$ and date/time of transaction. $\mathcal{B}$ first checks the validity of the coin. If the verifications hold, he then searches its deposit database to find out whether A has been stored before. If A has not stored before, $\mathcal{B}$ stores $A, c, date/time, (r_1, r_2)$ in its database; Else, $\mathcal{B}$ can detect double-depositing (the same challenge) or double-spending (the different challenge). The number $(r_1 - r_1')/(r_2 - r_2')$ serves as a proof of double-spending.

5   Conclusions

In this paper we first propose a new restrictive blind signature scheme and a restrictive partially blind signature scheme from bilinear pairings. The former can be regarded as a special case of the latter. Compared to other schemes, our schemes have the advantages of the shorter signature length and lower communication complexity. We also provide a formal security proof for the proposed schemes in the random oracle model.

Acknowledgement

We would like to express our gratitude to Jacques Traoré for pointing out a security flaw in the first version of this paper. Also, we would like to thank Marina Blanton for the suggestions to improve this paper. Finally, we are grateful to the anonymous referees of Financial Cryptography and Data Security 2006 for their invaluable suggestions.

References

1. M. Abe and E. Fujisaki, *How to date blind signatures*, Advances in Cryptology-Asiacrypt 1996, LNCS 1163, pp. 244-251, Springer-Verlag, 1996.
2. M. Abe and T. Okamoto, *Provably secure partially blind signature*, Advances in Cryptology-Crypto 2000, LNCS 1880, pp. 271-286, Springer-Verlag, 2000.

3. A. Boldyreva, *Efficient threshold signature, multisignature and blind signature schemes based on the Gap-Diffie-Hellman-group signature scheme*, PKC 2003, LNCS 2567, pp. 31-46, Springer-Verlag, 2003.
4. D. Boneh and X. Boyen, *Short signatures without random oracles*, Advances in Cryptology-Eurocrypt 2004, LNCS 3027, pp. 56-73, pringer-Verlag, 2004.
5. D. Boneh and M. Franklin, *Identity-based encryption from the Weil pairings*, Advances in Cryptology-Crypto 2001, LNCS 2139, pp. 213-229, Springer-Verlag, 2001.
6. D. Boneh, B. Lynn, and H. Shacham, *Short signatures from the Weil pairings*, Advances in Cryptology-Asiacrypt 2001, LNCS 2248, pp. 514-532, Springer-Verlag, 2001.
7. S. Brands, *Untraceable off-line cash in wallet with observers*, Advances in Cryptology-Crypto 1993, LNCS 773, pp. 302-318, Springer-Verlag, 1993.
8. S. Brands, *An efficient off-line electronic cash system based on the representation problem*, Technical Report CS-R9323, Centrum voor Wiskunde en Informatica (CWI), 1993.
9. J. Cha and J.H. Cheon, *An identity-based signature from gap Diffie-Hellman groups*, PKC 2003, LNCS 2567, pp. 18-30, Springer-Verlag, 2003.
10. D. Chaum, *Blind signature for untraceable payments*, Advances in Cryptology-Eurocrypt 82, Plenum Press, pp. 199-203, 1982.
11. D. Chaum, A. Fiat, and M. Naor, *Untraceable electronic cash*, Advances in Cryptology-Crypto 1988, LNCS 403, pp. 319-327, Springer-Verlag, 1990.
12. D. Chaum and T.P. Pedersen, *Wallet databases with observers*, Advances in Cryptology-Crypto 1992, LNCS 740, pp. 89-105, Springer-Verlag, 1992.
13. F. Hess, *Efficient identity based signature schemes based on pairingss*, SAC 2002, LNCS 2595, Springer-Verlag, pp. 310-324, 2002.
14. A. Juels, M. Luby, and R. Ostrovsky, *Security of blind signatures*, Advances in Cryptology-Crypto 1997, LNCS 1294, pp. 150-164, Springer-Verlag, 1997.
15. G. Maitland and C. Boyd, *A provably secure restrictive partially blind signature scheme*, PKC 2002, LNCS 2274, pp. 99-114. Springer-Verlag, 2002.
16. D. Pointcheval, *Strengthened security for blind signatures*, Advances in Cryptology-Eurocrypt 1998, LNCS 1403, pp. 391-403, Springer-Verlag, 1998.
17. D. Pointcheval and J. Stern, *Provably secure blind signature schemes*, Advances in Cryptology-Asiacrypt 1996, LNCS 1163, pp. 252-265, Springer-Verlag, 1996.
18. D. Pointcheval and J. Stern, *Security arguments for digital signatures and blind signatures*, Journal of Cryptography, Vol.13, No.3, pp. 361-396, Springer-Verlag, 2000.
19. F. Zhang, R. Safavi-Naini, and W. Susilo, *Efficient verifiably encrypted signature and partially blind signature from bilinear pairings*, Indocrypt 2003, LNCS 2904, pp. 191-204, Springer-Verlag, 2003.
20. F. Zhang, R. Safavi-Naini and W. Susilo, *An efficient signature scheme from bilinear pairings and its applications*, PKC 2004, LNCS 2947, pp. 277-290, Springer-Verlag, 2004.

Privacy-Protecting Coupon System Revisited

Lan Nguyen

CSIRO ICT Centre, Australia
LanD.Nguyen@csiro.au

Abstract. At FC'05, Chen et al. introduced an elegant privacy protecting coupon (PPC) system, CESSS05 [13], in which users can purchase multi-coupons and redeem them unlinkably while being prevented from overspending or sharing the coupons. However, the costs for issuing and redeeming coupons are linear to the redeeming limit. Security of the system is not proved and only some arguments on system properties are provided. Coupons last indefinitely and can not be terminated. In this paper, we propose the first PPC system with constant costs for communication and computation. Coupons are revokable and the system is provably secure.

Keywords: coupon, transaction, anonymity and privacy.

1 Introduction

Coupons are a useful means by which businesses may attract the attention of new customers, or to increase the attractiveness of their business to existing customers. A coupon can be redeemed for value in a transaction, but only with the businesses associated with the coupon issuer, and so provides an incentive for the user to buy products from those businesses rather than from other potential suppliers [21]. A coupon may be able to be presented for more than one instance of service: e.g. a cinema may sell a booklet of prepaid vouchers at a discount that can be redeemed in the future for movie tickets. Prescriptions for medicines can also be seen as a form of coupon, where the value to users is not in price, but in access to some otherwise restricted goods, and a prescription may be valid for the supply of several courses of the medication. Such coupons are called multi-coupons. Because multi-coupons (like other coupons) can be only redeemed at outlets associated with the coupon issuer, they represent a form of loyalty scheme by giving a price incentive to use the issuer's preferred businesses over other businesses. Coupons are particularly interesting in Internet commerce, because some of the costs normally associated with changing one's business from one supplier to another, for example ease of access to their retail outlets, or familiarity with their staff, can be much lower on the Internet than in traditional retail markets.

If coupons can be associated with their users, they represent a further advantage for the business, since they allow purchases to be linked and the user's buying habits to be collected by the vendor, even for transactions otherwise paid in cash. This allows the business to target their marketing, including their

G. Di Crescenzo and A. Rubin (Eds.): FC 2006, LNCS 4107, pp. 266–280, 2006.

marketing through coupons, more closely to the individual. However, it is not attractive to the coupon user, since they may wish to maintain the privacy of the nature of their purchasing from the business, as they can by using cash payments. If unlinkability between purchases and untraceability of users of the coupon can be assured, those who might otherwise do cash business with normal retail outlets might be attracted to do Internet business using coupons. A coupon issuer who wishes to attract privacy-sensitive users may wish to forgo some of the other marketing advantages offered by linkable or traceable coupons, and provide users with a coupon system that assures them that their purchasing history cannot be captured by their use of coupons, but maintains the other desirable properties of a coupon system. PPC systems can be used in such situations.

In a PPC system, a multi-coupon presented for redemption will only reveal that it is still valid for redemption and no further information can be deduced. Redemptions cannot be linked with each other, and no information is revealed that can link the coupon with the issuing process, so even if a coupon is purchased by credit card, its use cannot be linked back to the owner of the card.

Chen et al. argue that on-selling a coupon, where the whole of the coupon's remaining value is purchased by another user, or splitting a coupon, where several users each agree to only use some fraction of the coupon, can both be discouraged if it is not possible to determine from an examination of the multi-coupon how many of the component coupons are still redeemable [13]. In the case of on-selling, the purchaser must then trust the seller as to the number of valid coupons remaining on the multi-coupon. For splitting, each of the users who split a multi-coupon must trust all the other users not to use more than their share of the multi-coupon. A PPC system should at least provide this property, which is termed all-or-nothing-sharing.

The CESSS05 system does not provide revocability, another important property. It is common practice for coupons to have a limited validity in time, and they commonly carry an expiry date. This provides an incentive for the coupon user to possibly make a purchase earlier than they would otherwise, or consume more than they would otherwise (to, say, use all the coupons in a multi-coupon to avoid loss if they have some investment in the multi-coupons).

Our construction

Taking a different approach from CESSS05, we propose a PPC system providing these properties with improved efficiency, security and functionality. This is the first multi-coupon system whose costs, both communication and computation, do not depend on the bound on the value of the multi-coupon. Our system is also the first to combine protection of the user's privacy with revocability of the multi-coupon. We present a security model for PPC systems and prove security of our system in this model.

Several coupon systems have been proposed, but none of them provides the properties offered by our system, especially in term of efficiency. Some systems, such as [12], [5] and [19], protect user privacy but allow coupon splitting. Some systems [15,23], reveal the coupon's remaining value or allow transaction linkability. And coupon redemption can not be limited in some other systems [6,20].

The k-times anonymous authentication systems proposed in [22,18] can be modified to be a PPC system of k-redeemable coupons, but its redeem protocol requires a proof of knowledge of one-out-of-k discrete logs, so its communication and computation costs for redeeming are linear to k.

The following section details some preliminary cryptographic primitives on which our system depends. Section 3 presents our PPC system and compares it in more detail with the CESSS05 system. Sections 4 presents the PPC security model and security proofs of our system are shown in section 5.

2   Preliminaries

This section reviews the bilinear mapping concept, related complexity assumptions, signature schemes with efficient protocols and the CESSS05 PPC system. The following notation, introduced in [10] for proofs of knowledge, will be used in this paper. For example,

$$PK\{(\alpha, \beta, \gamma) : y = g^\alpha h^\beta \wedge z = a^\alpha b^\gamma\}$$

denotes "a zero-knowledge Proof of Knowledge of integers α, β and γ satisfying $y = g^\alpha h^\beta$ and $z = a^\alpha b^\gamma$". By $x \in_R S$ we mean x is randomly chosen from a set S. PPT denotes probabilistic polynomial time.

2.1   Bilinear Groups

Suppose $\mathbb{G}_1$, $\mathbb{G}_2$ and $\mathbb{G}_T$ are multiplicative cyclic groups of the same prime order p, and there is an isomorphism $\psi : \mathbb{G}_2 \to \mathbb{G}_1$. Let g_1 and g_2 be generators of $\mathbb{G}_1$ and $\mathbb{G}_2$, respectively, such that $\psi(g_2) = g_1$. A bilinear map is a function $e : \mathbb{G}_1 \times \mathbb{G}_2 \to \mathbb{G}_T$ satisfying the following properties:

1. Bilinear: $e(u^a, v^b) = e(u, v)^{ab}$ for all $u \in \mathbb{G}_1$, $v \in \mathbb{G}_2$ and $a, b \in \mathbb{Z}$.
2. Non-degeneracy: $e(g_1, g_2) \neq 1$.
3. Computability: There exists an efficient algorithm for computing e.

2.2   Complexity Assumptions

Let $\mathbb{G}_1$ and $\mathbb{G}_2$ be cyclic groups of prime order p, and let g_1 and g_2 be generators of $\mathbb{G}_1$ and $\mathbb{G}_2$, respectively. The Strong Diffie-Hellman (SDH) [2] and Decisional Bilinear Diffie-Hellman Inversion (DBDHI) [3] assumptions are briefly reviewed as follows.

Strong Diffie-Hellman assumption. The q-SDH problem is defined as "computing a pair $(x, g_1^{1/(\gamma+x)})$, given a tuple $(g_1, g_2, g_2^\gamma, g_2^{(\gamma^2)}, \ldots, g_2^{(\gamma^q)})$". The q-SDH assumption states that no PPT algorithm can solve the q-SDH problem with non-negligible probability.

Decisional Bilinear Diffie-Hellman Inversion assumption. The DBDHI problem is defined as "distinguishing between $(g_1, g_2, g_2^\gamma, \ldots, g_2^{(\gamma^q)}, e(g_1, g_2)^{1/(\gamma)})$ and $(g_1, g_2, g_2^\gamma, \ldots, g_2^{(\gamma^q)}, \Lambda)$, where γ is randomly chosen from $\mathbb{Z}_p^*$ and Λ is randomly chosen from $\mathbb{G}_T^*$". The DBDHI assumption states that no PPT algorithm can solve the DBDHI problem with non-negligible probability.

2.3   BB Signature Scheme

This signature scheme [2], which is unforgeable under a weak chosen message attack, allows simple and efficient signature generation and verification. It is also efficient to prove knowledge of a BB signature without revealing anything about the signature and message.

Key Generation. Let $\mathbb{G}_1$, $\mathbb{G}_2$, p, g_1 and g_2 be bilinear mapping parameters as generated above. Generate random $\gamma \in_R \mathbb{Z}_p^*$ and compute $w \leftarrow g_2^\gamma$. The public key is (g_1, g_2, w) and the secret key is γ.

Signing. Given a message $r \in \mathbb{Z}_p \setminus \{-\gamma\}$, output the signature $a \leftarrow g_1^{1/(\gamma+r)}$.

Verification. Given a public key (g_1, g_2, w), a message $r \in \mathbb{Z}_p \setminus \{-\gamma\}$, and a signature $a \in \mathbb{G}_1$, verify that $e(a, wg_2^r) = e(g_1, g_2)$.

2.4   CL-SDH Signature Scheme

Camenisch and Lysyanskaya proposed a signature scheme (CL) [8] which possesses 3 valuable properties. It is possible to generate a single CL signature for multiple messages. A signer can produce a CL signature for many messages without learning anything about the messages. And there is an efficient zero-knowledge proof of knowledge of a CL signature and its messages.

A variant with these properties is the CL-SDH signature scheme, whose security relies on the SDH assumption. As we do not use this scheme to generate a single signature for multiple messages, the following just present signing and verifying algorithms for a single message.

Key Generation. Let $\mathbb{G}_1$, $\mathbb{G}_2$, p, g_1 and g_2 be bilinear mapping parameters. Generate random $\gamma \in_R \mathbb{Z}_p^*$ and $b, c \in_R \mathbb{G}_1$ and compute $w \leftarrow g_2^\gamma$. The public key is (b, c, g_1, g_2, w) and the secret key is γ.

Signing. On input $x \in \mathbb{Z}_p^*$, generate random $s \in_R \mathbb{Z}_p$ and $d \in_R \mathbb{Z}_p \setminus \{-\gamma\}$ and compute $v \leftarrow (g_1^x b^s c)^{1/(\gamma+d)}$. The signature is (v, d, s).

Verification. Given a public key (b, c, g_1, g_2, w), a message $x \in \mathbb{Z}_p^*$, and a signature (v, d, s), verify that $e(v, wg_2^d) = e(g_1^x b^s c, g_2)$.

Security of the CL-SDH signature scheme is stated in Theorem 1, which can be proved similarly to the proof for the CL signature scheme [8].

Theorem 1. *The CL-SDH signature scheme is unforgeable under chosen message attacks if the SDH assumption holds.*

2.5   BlindSign-SDH Protocol

In the CESSS05 system, the vendor runs a *BlindSign* protocol [8] to issue a CL signature for multiple messages to a user without learning anything about the messages. Similarly, the *BlindSign-SDH* protocol allows a user to obtain a CL-SDH signature without revealing anything about the corresponding message to the signer. Let $\mathbb{G}_1$, $\mathbb{G}_2$, p, g_1 and g_2 be bilinear mapping parameters. Suppose

$((b, c, g_1, g_2, w), \gamma)$ is a pair of CL-SDH public key and secret key, the BlindSign-SDH protocol between a user $\mathcal{U}$ and a signer $\mathcal{S}$ is executed as follows.

Common input: the CL-SDH public key (b, c, g_1, g_2, w).
User's input: a message $x \in \mathbb{Z}_p^*$.
Signer's input: the CL-SDH secret key γ.

Protocol

- $\mathcal{U}$ chooses $s' \in_R \mathbb{Z}_p$, sends $D = g_1^x b^{s'}$ to $\mathcal{S}$ with a proof $PK\{(\xi, \sigma) : D = g_1^\xi b^\sigma\}$.
- After checking that the proof is valid, $\mathcal{S}$ generates random $s'' \in_R \mathbb{Z}_p$ and $d \in_R \mathbb{Z}_p \setminus \{-\gamma\}$ and computes $v \leftarrow (Db^{s''}c)^{1/(\gamma+d)}$. $\mathcal{S}$ then sends (v, d, s'') to $\mathcal{U}$.
- $\mathcal{U}$ computes $s \leftarrow s' + s''$, checks if $e(v, wg_2^d) = e(g_1^x b^s c, g_2)$, and obtains the CL-SDH signature (v, d, s) for x.

Note that x and s are $\mathcal{U}$'s secrets and $\mathcal{S}$ does not learn anything about x from the protocol.

2.6   CESSS05 PPC System

The system consists of an *Initialisation* algorithm and 2 protocols, *Issue* and *Redeem*. There is a *vendor* and many *users*. The vendor can issue a m-redeemable coupon to a user such that the user can *unlinkably* redeem the coupon for exactly m times. The system also provides *all-or-nothing-sharing* property.

The *initialisation* algorithm generates a system public key, which is a CL public key, and a vendor secret key, which is the corresponding CL secret key. In the *issue* protocol, the user generates m random messages $X = (x_1, x_2, \ldots, x_m)$, performs the BlindSign protocol with the vendor to obtain a CL signature (v, e, s) for the m messages without revealing anything about the messages. The user's m-redeemable coupon is (X, v, e, s). In the *redeem* protocol, the user reveals a message x_i to the vendor without revealing i and the vendor checks that x_i has not been revealed previously and stores x_i. The user then runs a zero-knowledge proof of knowledge of m messages X and their CL signature (v, e, s) and also proves that $x_i \in X$ without revealing i. A component coupon of the multi-coupon is redeemed if the vendor accepts these proofs as valid. The component coupon can not be redeemed again as the vendor has stored x_i. The protocols and proofs are zero-knowledge and X is the user's secret, hence, the redeem execution is unlinkable. The user is required to know (X, v, e, s) to perform the redeem protocol, so the coupon (X, v, e, s) has all-or-nothing-sharing property.

3   A New Privacy-Protecting Coupon System

3.1   Overview

We first outline general construction of our scheme and compare it with the CESSS05 system. As in the CESSS05 system, participants include a vendor and many users, and there is an Initialisation algorithm, an Issue protocol and a Redeem protocol, but there is one more algorithm, Terminate, which allows the vendor to terminate coupons.

The Initialisation algorithm generates a system public key and a vendor secret key. The vendor secret key consists of a CL-SDH secret key and a BB secret key. The system public key includes the corresponding CL-SDH and BB public keys, m random messages $a_1, a_2, \ldots, a_m$ and their BB signatures $o_1, o_2, \ldots, o_m$. Some other signature schemes, such as CL-SDH or those proposed in [2,9], can be used in place of the BB scheme, but the BB scheme is used for the sake of efficiency and simplicity.

In the Issue protocol, the user generates a random x and runs the BlindSign-SDH with the vendor to obtain a CL-SDH signature (v, d, s) for x and the coupon is (x, v, d, s). So the issuing costs do not depend on the coupon bound m. In contrast, in the issue protocol of the CESSS05 system, the user and the vendor perform the BlindSign protocol to obtain a CL signature for m random messages, so the numbers of exponentiations and transmitted bytes are linear to m.

In the Redeem protocol, the user chooses a message a_i with a BB signature o_i and reveals $C = f_{a_i}(x)$ to the vendor without revealing a_i, where f is a one-way function. The vendor checks that C has not been revealed previously and stores C. The user then shows a zero-knowledge proof of knowledge of a BB message-signature pair (a, o) and a CL-SDH message-signature pair $(x, (v, d, s))$ such that $C = f_a(x)$. The coupon is redeemed if the vendor successfully verifies the proof. So the redeeming costs do not depend on m, whereas in previous PPC schemes these costs depend on m. One important issue is that, in order to protect privacy of the coupon system, the one-way function f must be "unlinkable". That means it is hard to distinguish between $(f_{a_i}(x), f_{a_j}(x))$ and $(f_{a_i}(x), f_{a_j}(x'))$. Fortunately, the DBDHI assumption [3] can be employed to construct such a one-way function that can be efficiently used for our scheme. The function is the same as a recent verifiable random function [14].

We use the "accumulating" approach [7,4] for coupon revocation. To terminate a coupon, the vendor recomputes the system public key and adds some information to a public revocation list (RL) such that unrevoked coupons can be efficiently updated to be valid under the new system public key but it is hard to update the terminated coupon. This approach can also be used to provide coupon revocation for the CESSS05 system.

The CESSS05 system has not been presented in details, so we can not provide a thorough efficiency comparison with this system. Even if m is small, the numbers of transmitted bytes and exponentiations in our scheme are quite smaller than those in the CESSS05 scheme. Our scheme requires a number of pairings, but most of them can be pre-computed before the protocols: $e(g_1', g_2')$, $e(g_1, g_2)$, $e(b, g_2)$, $e(b, w)$, $e(b, g_2')$, $e(b, w')$ and $e(c, g_2)$. The user $\mathcal{U}$ can compute $e(v, wg_2^d)$, $e(g_1^x b^s c, g_2)$, $e(T_1, g_2)$ and $e(T_2, g_2')$ without computing any pairing online if $e(v, w)$, $e(v, g_2)$, $e(g_1, g_2)$, $e(b, g_2)$, $e(c, g_2)$, $e(o_i, g_2')$ and $e(b, g_2')$ are pre-computed. So only four pairings are needed to be computed online by the verifier in the PKSign Proof: $e(T_1, g_2)$, $e(T_1, w)$, $e(T_2, g_2')$ and $e(T_2, w')$.

3.2 Description

The system consists of an *Initialisation* algorithm, a *Terminate* algorithm, an *Issue* protocol and a *Redeem* protocol and involves a *vendor* $\mathcal{V}$ and a number of *users*.

Initialisation
Let $\mathbb{G}_1$, $\mathbb{G}_2$, p, g_1 and g_2 be bilinear mapping parameters. Generate random $b, c, g_1' \in_R \mathbb{G}_1$, $g_2' \in_R \mathbb{G}_2$ and $\gamma, \gamma' \in_R \mathbb{Z}_p^*$ and compute $w \leftarrow g_2^{\gamma}$ and $w' \leftarrow g_2'^{\gamma'}$. Generate different $a_1, a_2, \ldots, a_m \in_R \mathbb{Z}_p \setminus \{-\gamma\}$ and their BB signatures $o_1, o_2, \ldots, o_m \in \mathbb{G}_1$ where $o_i = g_1'^{1/(\gamma' + a_i)}$, $(i = 1 \ldots m)$. The system public key is $PK = (A, R, b, c, g_1, g_2, w, g_1', g_2', w')$ and the vendor secret key is $SK = (\gamma, \gamma')$, where $A = (a_1, a_2, \ldots, a_m)$ and $R = (o_1, o_2, \ldots, o_m)$. There is a public Revocation List RL, which is empty initially.

Issue
The vendor $\mathcal{V}$ and a user $\mathcal{U}$ perform this protocol. $\mathcal{U}$ chooses a random $x \in_R \mathbb{Z}_p^*$ and runs the *BlindSign-SDH* protocol with $\mathcal{V}$ to obtain a blind CL-SDH signature (v, d, s) on x (the CL-SDH public key is (b, c, g_1, g_2, w) and the CL-SDH secret key is γ). The user's multi-coupon is $M = (x, v, d, s)$, where v and d are known by $\mathcal{V}$ and x and s are $\mathcal{U}$'s secrets.

Terminate
Suppose the current public key is $PK = (A, R, b, c, g_1, g_2, w, g_1', g_2', w')$, $\mathcal{V}$ terminates a coupon $(\cdot, \cdot, d_1, \cdot)$ by computing $\bar{g}_1 \leftarrow g_1^{1/(\gamma + d_1)}$, $\bar{g}_2 \leftarrow g_2^{1/(\gamma + d_1)}$, $\bar{b} \leftarrow b^{1/(\gamma + d_1)}$, $\bar{c} \leftarrow c^{1/(\gamma + d_1)}$ and $\bar{w} \leftarrow (\bar{g}_2)^{\gamma}$, setting the new public key $PK = (A, R, \bar{b}, \bar{c}, \bar{g}_1, \bar{g}_2, \bar{w}, g_1', g_2', w')$, and adding $(d_1, \bar{g}_2, \bar{b}, \bar{c})$ to RL.

Redeem
This is a protocol between the vendor $\mathcal{V}$ and a user $\mathcal{U}$. It consists of 2 stages, Updating and Proof of Signatures.

Updating
In this stage, $\mathcal{U}$ updates the system public key and his unrevoked coupon, as the vendor may have terminated some coupons and changed the system public key.

$\mathcal{U}$ obtains RL and suppose $(d_1, g_1^*, b_1^*, c_1^*), (d_2, g_2^*, b_2^*, c_2^*), \ldots, (d_k, g_k^*, b_k^*, c_k^*)$ are the new items on RL (in that order) since the last time $\mathcal{U}$ updated the public key and his coupon. $\mathcal{U}$ can update the current public key and his coupon by repeating the following process for each of these items.

For terminated item $(d_1, g_1^*, b_1^*, c_1^*)$, $\mathcal{U}$ (or anyone) can simply compute a new public key from the old public key $PK = (A, R, b, c, g_1, g_2, w, g_1', g_2', w')$ as $\hat{g}_1 \leftarrow \psi(g_1^*)$, $\hat{g}_2 \leftarrow g_1^*$, $\hat{b} \leftarrow b_1^*$, $\hat{c} \leftarrow c_1^*$ and $\hat{w} \leftarrow g_2(g_1^*)^{-d_1}$. Then $\hat{g}_1 = g_1^{1/(\gamma + d_1)}$ and $\hat{w} = (g_1^*)^{\gamma + d_1}(g_1^*)^{-d_1} = \hat{g}_2^{\gamma}$. The new public key is $PK = (A, R, \hat{b}, \hat{c}, \hat{g}_1, \hat{g}_2, \hat{w}, g_1', g_2', w')$.

$\mathcal{U}$ then updates his unrevoked coupon (x, v, d, s) by computing $v^* \leftarrow \psi(g_1^*)^x (b_1^*)^s c_1^*$ and $\hat{v} \leftarrow (v^*/v)^{1/(d - d_1)}$. Then $v^* = v^{(\gamma + d)/(\gamma + d_1)}$ and $\hat{v}^{\gamma + d} = (v^{(\gamma + d)/(\gamma + d_1)}/v)^{(\gamma + d)/(d - d_1)} = v^{(\gamma + d)/(\gamma + d_1)} = \psi(g_1^*)^x (b_1^*)^s c_1^*$. So the updated coupon $(x, \hat{v}, d, s)$ is valid.

By orderly repeating the process for each of the items $(d_1, g_1^*, b_1^*, c_1^*)$, $(d_2, g_2^*, b_2^*, c_2^*)$, ..., $(d_k, g_k^*, b_k^*, c_k^*)$, the user can update the current public key and his unrevoked coupon.

Proof of Signatures

Suppose the updated system public key is $PK = (A, R, b, c, g_1, g_2, w, g_1', g_2', w')$ and $\mathcal{U}$'s updated coupon is (x, v, d, s).

$\mathcal{U}$ sends $h = f_{a_i}(x)$ to the vendor $\mathcal{V}$ where $f_{a_i}(x) = e(g_1', g_2')^{1/(x+a_i)}$. $\mathcal{V}$ checks if h has been revealed before (from its storage S of these values). If it has, $\mathcal{V}$ stops the protocol and output *reject*. Otherwise, $\mathcal{V}$ stores h in S. Then $\mathcal{U}$ shows $\mathcal{V}$ the following proof

$$PKSign = PK\{(\alpha, \tau, \beta, \delta, \epsilon, \varepsilon) : e(\delta, wg_2^\epsilon) = e(g_1^\beta b^\varepsilon c, g_2)$$
$$\wedge e(\tau, w'g_2'^\alpha) = e(g_1', g_2') \wedge h^{\alpha+\beta} = e(g_1', g_2')\}$$

PKSign proves that $\mathcal{U}$ knows a CL-SDH message-signature pair $(x, (v, d, s))$ and a BB message-signature pair (a, o) such that $h = e(g_1', g_2')^{1/(x+a)}$. *PKSign* is presented in details in the next subsection.

3.3 PKSign Proof

The following PKSign proof between $\mathcal{U}$ and $\mathcal{V}$ is an honest-verifier zeroknowledge proof under the Discrete Log assumption in $\mathbb{G}_1$ (its proof is standard and so omitted).

- *Common input*: $PK = (A, R, b, c, g_1, g_2, w, g_1', g_2', w')$; $h = e(g_1', g_2')^{1/(x+a_i)}$.
- *$\mathcal{U}$'s input*: a_i, o_i, x, v, d, s.
- *Proof*: $PK\{(\alpha, \tau, \beta, \delta, \epsilon, \varepsilon) :$
  $e(\delta, wg_2^\epsilon) = e(g_1^\beta b^\varepsilon c, g_2) \wedge e(\tau, w'g_2'^\alpha) = e(g_1', g_2') \wedge h^{\alpha+\beta} = e(g_1', g_2')\}.$

Protocol

$\mathcal{U}$ generates random $t_1, t_2, u_1, u_2 \in_R \mathbb{Z}_p$ and computes
$$y_1 \leftarrow t_1 d, \ y_2 \leftarrow t_2 a_i,$$
$$T_1 \leftarrow vb^{t_1}, \ U_1 \leftarrow b^{t_1}c^{u_1}, \ T_2 \leftarrow o_i b^{t_2}, \ U_2 \leftarrow b^{t_2}c^{u_2}.$$

$\mathcal{U}$ and $\mathcal{V}$ then perform a proof of knowledge of $(t_1, t_2, u_1, u_2, y_1, y_2, a_i, x, d, s)$ satisfying
$$b^{t_1}c^{u_1} = U_1, \ b^{t_2}c^{u_2} = U_2,$$
$$e(g_1, g_2)^x e(b, g_2)^{s+y_1} e(T_1, g_2)^{-d} e(b, w)^{t_1} = e(T_1, w)e(c, g_2)^{-1},$$
$$e(T_2, g_2')^{-a_i} e(b, w')^{t_2} e(b, g_2')^{y_2} = e(T_2, w')e(g_1', g_2')^{-1},$$
$$h^{x+a_i} = e(g_1', g_2'),$$
$$U_1^d b^{-y_1} c^{-u_1 d} = 1, \ U_2^{a_i} b^{-y_2} c^{-u_2 a_i} = 1.$$

It proceeds as follows. $\mathcal{U}$ generates random
$$r_{t_1}, r_{t_2}, r_{u_1}, r_{u_2}, r_{y_1}, r_{y_2}, r_{a_i}, r_x, r_d, r_s, r_{u_1 d}, r_{u_2 a_i} \in_R \mathbb{Z}_p$$
and computes
$$R_1 \leftarrow b^{r_{t_1}} c^{r_{u_1}}, \ R_2 \leftarrow b^{r_{t_2}} c^{r_{u_2}},$$
$$R_3 \leftarrow e(g_1, g_2)^{r_x} e(b, g_2)^{r_s + r_{y_1}} e(T_1, g_2)^{-r_d} e(b, w)^{r_{t_1}},$$

$$R_4 \leftarrow e(T_2, g_2')^{-r_{a_i}} e(b, w')^{r_{t_2}} e(b, g_2')^{r_{y_2}},$$
$$R_5 \leftarrow h^{r_x + r_{a_i}},$$
$$R_6 \leftarrow U_1^{r_d} b^{-r_{y_1}} c^{-r_{u_1 d}}, \; R_7 \leftarrow U_2^{r_{a_i}} b^{-r_{y_2}} c^{-r_{u_2 a_i}}.$$

$\mathcal{U}$ sends $(T_1, T_2, U_1, U_2, R_1, \dots, R_7)$ to $\mathcal{V}$. $\mathcal{V}$ returns a challenge $\mu \in_R \mathbb{Z}_p$. $\mathcal{U}$ then responses with the following values

$$z_{t_1} \leftarrow r_{t_1} + \mu t_1, \; z_{t_2} \leftarrow r_{t_2} + \mu t_2, \; z_{u_1} \leftarrow r_{u_1} + \mu u_1, \; z_{u_2} \leftarrow r_{u_2} + \mu u_2,$$
$$z_{y_1} \leftarrow r_{y_1} + \mu y_1, \; z_{y_2} \leftarrow r_{y_2} + \mu y_2,$$
$$z_{a_i} \leftarrow r_{a_i} + \mu a_i, \; z_x \leftarrow r_x + \mu x, \; z_d \leftarrow r_d + \mu d, \; z_s \leftarrow r_s + \mu s$$
$$z_{u_1 d} \leftarrow r_{u_1 d} + \mu u_1 d, \; z_{u_2 a_i} \leftarrow r_{u_2 a_i} + \mu u_2 a_i.$$

$\mathcal{V}$ finally verifies that

$$b^{z_{t_1}} c^{z_{u_1}} = U_1^{\mu} R_1, \; b^{z_{t_2}} c^{z_{u_2}} = U_2^{\mu} R_2,$$
$$e(g_1, g_2)^{z_x} e(b, g_2)^{z_s + z_{y_1}} e(T_1, g_2)^{-z_d} e(b, w)^{z_{t_1}} = (e(T_1, w) e(c, g_2)^{-1})^{\mu} R_3,$$
$$e(T_2, g_2')^{-z_{a_i}} e(b, w')^{z_{t_2}} e(b, g_2')^{z_{y_2}} = (e(T_2, w') e(g_1', g_2')^{-1})^{\mu} R_4,$$
$$h^{z_x + z_{a_i}} = e(g_1', g_2')^{\mu} R_5,$$
$$U_1^{z_d} b^{-z_{y_1}} c^{-z_{u_1 d}} = R_6, \; U_2^{z_{a_i}} b^{-z_{y_2}} c^{-z_{u_2 a_i}} = R_7.$$

$\mathcal{V}$ *accepts* if and only if all equations hold.

3.4   Remark

- By removing the Terminate algorithm and the Updating stage of the Redeem protocol, we have a PPC system without coupon revocation that has the same functionality as the CESSS05 system.
- Both of the CESSS05 system and our system can be modified to allow the vendor to assign different redeeming bounds to different coupons, where the bounds are not greater than some value m. For instance, the vendor $\mathcal{V}$ wants to issue n-redeemable coupon to a user $\mathcal{U}$ where $n \leq m$. In the Issue protocol of the CESSS05 system, $\mathcal{U}$ also reveals $x_{n+1}, \dots, x_m$ to $\mathcal{V}$ with a zero-knowledge proof that $x_{n+1}, \dots, x_m \in X$. In the Issue protocol of our system, $\mathcal{U}$ also reveals $e(g_1', g_2')^{1/(x + a_{n+1})}, \dots, e(g_1', g_2')^{1/(x + a_m)}$ with a zero-knowledge proof of knowledge of x corresponding to (v, d, s).

4   Security Model

4.1   Syntax

A Privacy-Protecting Coupon System is a tuple of polynomial-time algorithms (*Init*, *Issue^U*, *Issue^V*, *Terminate*, *Redeem^U*, *Redeem^V*). Participants include a *vendor* and a number of *users*. There is a public *Revocation List* (RL) which consists of terminated coupons and is empty initially.

- *Init*: The *initialisation* algorithm Init on input 1^k returns a pair (PK, SK) where PK is the system public key and SK is the vendor secret key.
- (*Issue^U*, *Issue^V*): These interactive algorithms form the *issue* protocol between a user (Issue^U) and the vendor (Issue^V). The common input is PK and Issue^V also takes SK as the private input. Issue^U outputs a coupon M and Issue^V returns the coupon's public information d_M.

- *Terminate*: This *termination* algorithm takes as input PK, SK, RL and a coupon's public information d. It outputs a new pair $(\bar{PK}, \bar{SK})$ and appends (d, inf) to RL where inf is some public information about this termination. The new system public key is $\bar{PK}$ and the new vendor secret key is $\bar{SK}$. Coupon d can no longer be redeemed afterwards.
- $(Redeem^U, Redeem^V)$: These interactive algorithms form the *redeem* protocol which allows a user (Issue^U) to redeem a coupon with the vendor (Issue^V). The common input includes the current public key PK and the revocation list RL. The vendor's private input is the current secret key SK and the user's private input is its coupon M. At the end, Issue^V returns *accept* or *reject*, which indicates if the coupon is redeemed or it is invalid, respectively. Issue^U outputs $\bar{M}$ which is a coupon updated from M.

CORRECTNESS: Informally, it requires that if a coupon is obtained by correctly performing the issue protocol, has not been redeemed more than its bound and has not been terminated, then an execution of the redeem protocol for the coupon shall end successfully with the vendor outputting accept, with overwhelming probability.

4.2   Oracles

Security requirements of PPC systems are formulated in experiments between an adversary and an honest party. In each experiment, the adversary plays a vendor and the party plays a user or vice versa. The adversary's capabilities are modelled by access to the following oracles.

$\mathcal{O}_{Is}(\cdot, \cdot)$: The adversary can request this *issue* oracle to execute the Issue protocol. The oracle takes 2 inputs and the first input can be either $'user'$ or $'vendor'$. If the adversary plays a user, it does not need to call $\mathcal{O}_{Is}('user', \cdot)$, and if the adversary plays a vendor, it does not need to call $\mathcal{O}_{Is}('vendor', \cdot)$. If the first input is $'user'$, the oracle plays the honest user, takes the second input as the vendor's message of the Issue protocol and outputs a message back to the vendor. If the first input is $'vendor'$, the oracle plays the honest vendor, takes the second input as the user's message of the Issue protocol and outputs a message back to the user.

$\mathcal{O}_{Rd}(\cdot, \cdot, \cdot)$: This *redeem* oracle allows the adversary to run the Redeem protocol. It takes 3 input where the first input can be $'user'$, $'vendor'$ or $'correct'$, the second input is the public information of the coupon to be redeemed. If the adversary plays a user, it does not need to call $\mathcal{O}_{Rd}('user', \cdot, \cdot)$, and if the adversary plays a vendor, it does not need to call $\mathcal{O}_{Rd}('vendor', \cdot, \cdot)$. If the first input is $'user'$, the oracle plays the honest user, takes the third input as the vendor's message of the Redeem protocol and outputs a message back to the vendor. If the first input is $'vendor'$, the oracle plays the honest vendor, takes the third input as the user's message of the Redeem protocol and outputs a message back to the user. If the first input is $'correct'$, the oracle just correctly executes the Redeem protocol on the coupon and outputs either accept or reject to indicate whether the vendor accepts the coupon or not.

$\mathcal{O}_{Op}(\cdot)$: On input a coupon's public information, this *open* oracle returns the coupon's content.

$\mathcal{O}_{Te}(\cdot)$: This *terminate* oracle takes as input a coupon's public information and terminates the coupon.

$\mathcal{O}_{Ch}(\cdot, \cdot)$ This *challenge* oracle takes as input 2 coupons with public information d_0 and d_1. It randomly chooses a bit j, correctly runs the Redeem protocol on the coupon d_j and returns the transcript.

$\mathcal{O}_{Co}(\cdot)$ This *count* oracle takes as input either $'total'$ or a coupon's public information. If it is $'total'$, the oracle returns the total number of successful redemptions. If it is a coupon's public information d, the oracle returns the number of times d has been successfully redeemed. In case d has been terminated, the oracle outputs the number of successful redemptions by using d before it was terminated.

4.3   Security Notions

A PPC system is secure if it satisfies 3 security requirements: Unlinkability, Unforgeability and Unsplittability. Each requirement is defined by an experiment between a PPT adversary and an honest party. Suppose m is each coupon's redeemable number.

UNLINKABILITY
Loosely stated, Unlinkability requires that, given 2 coupons and a redeeming transcript generated by using one of the coupons, the adversary can not decide which coupon has been used. In the Unlinkability experiment, the adversary $\mathcal{A}$ plays a vendor $\mathcal{V}$ and the party plays an honest user $\mathcal{U}$. The adversary can access oracles $\mathcal{O}_{Is}$, $\mathcal{O}_{Rd}$, $\mathcal{O}_{Op}$, $\mathcal{O}_{Ch}$, $\mathcal{O}_{Co}$. $\mathcal{O}_{Te}$ is not needed as $\mathcal{A}$ can terminate any coupon.

The adversary first runs the Init algorithm on input 1^k to obtain a key pair $(PK, SK) \leftarrow \text{Init}(1^k)$. The adversary can then query $\mathcal{O}_{Is}$ to issue many coupons to $\mathcal{U}$, query $\mathcal{O}_{Rd}$ to redeem any coupon, query $\mathcal{O}_{Op}$ to open any coupon, query $\mathcal{O}_{Co}$ to obtain the number of successful redemptions totally or for any coupon, and terminate any coupon. At some point, the adversary query $\mathcal{O}_{Is}$ twice to issue $\mathcal{U}$ two coupons with public information d_0 and d_1. The adversary then continues the experiment as before, except that it can not query $\mathcal{O}_{Op}$ on d_0 and d_1 and can not terminate d_0 and d_1. After a while, the adversary query $\mathcal{O}_{Ch}(d_0, d_1)$ to obtain a challenge transcript, which has been generated by $\mathcal{O}_{Ch}$ using a random bit j. It then continues the experiment as before, except that it now can not query $\mathcal{O}_{Co}$ and $\mathcal{O}_{Op}$ on d_0 and d_1. The adversary finally output a bit j'. At this point, it is required that $\mathcal{O}_{Co}(d_0), \mathcal{O}_{Co}(d_1) < m$. Let

$$\mathbf{Adv}_{\mathcal{A}}^{unli}(k) = |\Pr(j' = 0 \mid j = 0) - \Pr(j' = 0 \mid j = 1)|$$

Definition 1. *A PPC system is said to be unlinkable if* $\mathbf{Adv}_{\mathcal{A}}^{unli}(k)$ *is negligible for any PPT adversary* $\mathcal{A}$.

UNFORGEABILITY

Intuitively, Unforgeability requires that the adversary can not forge any successful redemption, i.e. it can not forge a new valid coupon or successfully redeem an
overspent or terminated coupon. In the Unforgeability experiment, the adversary
$\mathcal{A}$ plays a user $\mathcal{U}$ and the party plays an honest vendor $\mathcal{V}$. The adversary can
access oracles $\mathcal{O}_{Is}$, $\mathcal{O}_{Rd}$, $\mathcal{O}_{Te}$, $\mathcal{O}_{Co}$. $\mathcal{O}_{Op}$ is not needed as $\mathcal{U}$ obtains all coupons
issued from $\mathcal{V}$ ($\mathcal{A}$ actually represents all users).

The party first runs the Init algorithm on input 1^k to obtain a key pair
$(PK, SK) \leftarrow \mathsf{Init}(1^k)$ and publish PK. The adversary can then query $\mathcal{O}_{Is}$ to
obtain many coupons from $\mathcal{V}$, query $\mathcal{O}_{Rd}$ to redeem any coupon, query $\mathcal{O}_{Te}$
to terminate any coupon and query $\mathcal{O}_{Co}$ to obtain the number of successful
redemptions totally or for any coupon. At the end, suppose $\mathcal{A}$ has obtained l
unrevoked coupons from the vendor. If $\mathcal{O}_{Co}('total') > m \times l + \sum_{d \in RL} \mathcal{O}_{Co}(d)$,
then the adversary is considered to be successful. Let $\mathbf{Adv}_{\mathcal{A}}^{unfo}(k)$ denote the
probability that the adversary is successful.

Definition 2. *A PPC system is said to be unforgeable if $\mathbf{Adv}_{\mathcal{A}}^{unfo}(k)$ is negligible for any PPT adversary $\mathcal{A}$.*

UNSPLITTABILITY

Unsplittability, i.e. all-or-nothing-sharing, intuitively means that if a user can
spend a coupon once, then he can spend it for m times. We do not model
the complete protection against splitting a coupon (Strong Unsplittability) as
neither CESSS05 nor our scheme satisfies this requirement. In the Unsplittability
experiment, the adversary $\mathcal{A}$ plays a user $\mathcal{U}$ and the party plays an honest vendor
$\mathcal{V}$. The adversary can access oracles $\mathcal{O}_{Is}$, $\mathcal{O}_{Rd}$, $\mathcal{O}_{Te}$, $\mathcal{O}_{Co}$. As for Unforgeability,
$\mathcal{O}_{Op}$ is not needed as $\mathcal{U}$ obtains all coupons issued from $\mathcal{V}$.

The party first runs the Init algorithm on input 1^k to obtain a key pair
$(PK, SK) \leftarrow \mathsf{Init}(1^k)$ and publish PK. The adversary can then query $\mathcal{O}_{Is}$ to
obtain many coupons from $\mathcal{V}$, query $\mathcal{O}_{Rd}$ to redeem any coupon, query $\mathcal{O}_{Te}$ to
terminate any coupon and query $\mathcal{O}_{Co}$ to obtain the number of successful redemptions totally or for any coupon. At some point, $\mathcal{A}$ outputs a coupon with
public information d and terminates. At that time, if $0 < \mathcal{O}_{Co}(d) < m$, d is
not in RL and $\mathsf{reject} \leftarrow \mathcal{O}_{Rd}('correct', d, \emptyset)$, then the adversary is considered
to be successful. Let $\mathbf{Adv}_{\mathcal{A}}^{unsp}(k)$ denote the probability that the adversary is
successful.

Definition 3. *A PPC system is said to be unsplittable if $\mathbf{Adv}_{\mathcal{A}}^{unsp}(k)$ is negligible for any PPT adversary $\mathcal{A}$.*

4.4   Remarks

This model can be simplified for PPC systems without coupon termination by
removing the Terminate algorithm, the revocation list RL and $\mathcal{O}_{Te}$.

The above requirements are strong enough to capture the informal requirements listed in [13]. *Minimum disclosure*, which means the vendor should not

learn from the Redeem protocol how many times more the coupon can be redeemed, follows from the *unlinkability* requirement. *Unforgeability* implies *double spending detection* and *redemption limitation*, which means an m-redeemable coupon should not be accepted more than m times. And *unsplittability* means *all-or-nothing-sharing*.

5   Security of the Privacy-Protecting Coupon System

Correctness can be easily checked and proofs of the security requirements are quite routine using approaches in [2,3,17]. Due to space limitation, we only provide sketches of the security proofs.

Theorem 2. *The PPC scheme provides unlinkability if the DBDHI assumption holds.*

Proof Sketch. We show that if a PPT adversary $\mathcal{A}$ can break the unlinkability property of the PPC system, then we can construct a PPT adversary $\mathcal{B}$ that can break the DBDHI assumption. Suppose $\mathbb{G}_1$, $\mathbb{G}_2$, p, $\tilde{g}_1$ and $\tilde{g}_2$ are bilinear mapping parameters. Suppose a tuple $\theta = (\tilde{g}_1, \tilde{g}_2, \tilde{g}_2^{\vartheta}, \ldots, \tilde{g}_2^{(\vartheta^q)}, \Theta)$ is uniformly chosen from one of the sets $S_0 = \{(\tilde{g}_1, \tilde{g}_2, \tilde{g}_2^{\nu}, \ldots, \tilde{g}_2^{(\nu^q)}, e(\tilde{g}_1, \tilde{g}_2)^{1/(\nu)})|\nu \in_R \mathbb{Z}_p^*\}$ and $S_1 = \{(\tilde{g}_1, \tilde{g}_2, \tilde{g}_2^{\nu}, \ldots, \tilde{g}_2^{(\nu^q)}, \Lambda)|\nu \in_R \mathbb{Z}_p^*, \Lambda \in_R \mathbb{G}_T^*\}$. To decide whether θ is chosen from S_0 or S_1, $\mathcal{B}$ simulates the Unlinkability experiment with $\mathcal{A}$ where $\mathcal{B}$ plays the honest party and provides oracles.

$\mathcal{B}$ selects a random bit $j \leftarrow \{0,1\}$ and let j' be the other bit. From θ, $\mathcal{B}$ can construct $H_j = \{e(g_1', g_2')^{1/(x_j+a_1)}, \ldots, e(g_1', g_2')^{1/(x_j+a_{m-1})}\}$ and $\bar{\Theta}$ for some g_1', g_2', x_j and $\{a_i\}_{i=1}^m$, where $m < q$ and x_j is $\mathcal{B}$'s only unknown value, such that $\bar{\Theta} = e(g_1', g_2')^{1/(x_j+a_m)}$ if and only if $\Theta = e(\tilde{g}_1, \tilde{g}_2)^{1/\vartheta}$. $\mathcal{B}$ then generates $x_{j'} \in_R \mathbb{Z}_p^*$ and computes $H_{j'} = \{e(g_1', g_2')^{1/(x_{j'}+a_1)}, \ldots, e(g_1', g_2')^{1/(x_{j'}+a_m)}\}$. $\mathcal{B}$ then generates random $b, c, g_1 \in_R \mathbb{G}_1$, $g_2 \in_R \mathbb{G}_2$ and $\gamma, \gamma' \in_R \mathbb{Z}_p^*$ and computes $w \leftarrow g_2^{\gamma}$ and $w' \leftarrow g_2'^{\gamma'}$. For $a_1, a_2, \ldots, a_m$, $\mathcal{B}$ computes their BB signatures $o_1, o_2, \ldots, o_m \in \mathbb{G}_1$ where $o_i = g_1'^{1/(\gamma'+a_i)}$, $(i = 1 \ldots m)$. The system public key is $PK = (A, R, b, c, g_1, g_2, w, g_1', g_2', w')$ and the vendor secret key is $SK = (\gamma, \gamma')$, where $A = (a_1, a_2, \ldots, a_m)$ and $R = (o_1, o_2, \ldots, o_m)$. As knowing γ, γ' and playing the honest user, $\mathcal{B}$ can easily simulate oracles $\mathcal{O}_{Is}$, $\mathcal{O}_{Op}$ and $\mathcal{O}_{Co}$ and a pair of challenge coupons (x_0, v_0, d_0, s_0) and (x_1, v_1, d_1, s_1) for $\mathcal{O}_{Ch}$.

For a query to $\mathcal{O}_{Rd}$ from $\mathcal{A}$ on d_0 or d_1, $\mathcal{B}$ can choose h from either H_0 or H_1, respectively and simulates the $PKSign$ proof (as $PKSign$ is zero-knowledge). For the query to $\mathcal{O}_{Ch}$, $\mathcal{B}$ uses $\bar{\Theta}$ as h to simulate $PKSign$. Finally, if $\mathcal{A}$ returns j, $\mathcal{B}$ decides that θ is chosen from S_0. Otherwise, $\mathcal{B}$ decides that θ is chosen from S_1. Therefore, if $\mathcal{A}$ can break the unlinkability property of the PPC system, then $\mathcal{B}$ can break the DBDHI assumption.

Theorem 3. *The PPC scheme provides unforgeability if the SDH assumption holds.*

Proof Sketch. We show that if a PPT adversary $\mathcal{A}$ can break the unforgeability property of the PPC system, then we can construct a PPT adversary $\mathcal{B}$ that can break the SDH assumption. As $\mathcal{A}$ breaks unforgeability, one of the 3 cases below happens. $\mathcal{B}$ will randomly play one of 3 corresponding games such that if $\mathcal{B}$ plays a game when the corresponding case happens, then $\mathcal{B}$ can break the SDH assumption.

As PKSign is zero-knowledge, if it is accepted (when a coupon is successfully redeemed), $\mathcal{A}$ knows (a, o, x, v, d, s) satisfying the equations in PKSign. Following the Unforgeability experiment, if $\mathcal{A}$ is successful $(\mathcal{O}_{Co}('total') > m \times l + \sum_{d \in RL} \mathcal{O}_{Co}(d))$, there are 3 cases.

- $\mathcal{A}$ can generate a new BB message-signature pair $(a_{m+1}, o_{m+1}) \notin \{(a_1, o_1), (a_2, o_2), \ldots, (a_m, o_m)\}$. If $\mathcal{B}$ plays a game similar to the game in the proof of BB's unforgeability under a weak chosen message attack [2], then $\mathcal{B}$ can break the SDH assumption.
- $\mathcal{A}$ can redeem a revoked coupon. If $\mathcal{B}$ plays a game constructed using the approach of proofs in [17], then $\mathcal{B}$ can break the SDH assumption.
- $\mathcal{A}$ can forge a new CL-SDH message-signature pair $x, (v, d, s)$. If $\mathcal{B}$ plays a game similar to the game in the proof of CL-SDH's unforgeability under a chosen message attack, then $\mathcal{B}$ can break the SDH assumption.

Theorem 4. *The PPC scheme provides unsplittability.*

Proof Sketch. Following the Unsplittability experiment, suppose the adversary outputs a coupon (x, v, d, s) at the end, such that it has been successfully redeemed at least once but less than m times and it has not been terminated. That means there are elements of $\{(a_1, o_1), (a_2, o_2), \ldots, (a_m, o_m)\}$ which have not been used by the coupon. So if $\mathcal{O}_{Rd}$ is queried with input $'correct'$ on the coupon, one of the unused elements can be used and $\mathcal{O}_{Rd}$ outputs accept. Therefore, the adversary is not successful and it indicates unsplittability.

Acknowledgements. Thanks go to Peter Lamb, who contributed to this paper but declined to be a co-author.

References

1. M. Bellare, H. Shi, and C. Zhang. Foundations of Group Signatures: The Case of Dynamic Groups. CT-RSA 2005, Springer-Verlag, LNCS 3376, pp. 136-153.
2. D. Boneh, and X. Boyen. Short Signatures Without Random Oracles. Eurocrypt 2004, Springer-Verlag, LNCS 3027, pp. 56-73.
3. D. Boneh and X. Boyen. Efficient Selective-ID Secure Identity-Based Encryption Without Random Oracles. Eurocrypt 2004, Springer-Verlag, LNCS 3027, pp. 223-238.
4. D. Boneh, X. Boyen, and H. Shacham. Short Group Signatures. Crypto 2004, Springer-Verlag, LNCS 3152, pp. 41-55.
5. S. Brands. An Efficient Off-line Electronic Cash System Based On The Representation Problem. Technical Report CS-R9323, Centrum voor Wiskunde en Informatica, 1993.
6. S. Brands. Rethinking Public Key Infrastructure and Digital Certificates . Building in Privacy. PhD thesis, Eindhoven Institute of Technology, The Netherlands, 1999.

7. J. Camenisch and A. Lysyanskaya. Dynamic Accumulators and Application to Efficient Revocation of Anonymous Credentials. Crypto 2002, Springer-Verlag, LNCS 2442, pp. 61-76.

8. J. Camenisch and A. Lysyanskaya. A Signature Scheme with Efficient Protocols. SCN 2002, Springer-Verlag, LNCS 2576.

9. J. Camenisch and A. Lysyanskaya. Signature Schemes and Anonymous Credentials from Bilinear Maps. CRYPTO'04, Springer-Verlag, LNCS 3152, 2004.

10. J. Camenisch and M. Stadler. Efficient group signature schemes for large groups. Crypto 1997, Springer-Verlag, LNCS 1296, pp. 410-424.

11. D. Chaum. Blind signature system. Crypto 1983, Plenum Press, pp. 153-153.

12. D. Chaum. Privacy protected payments: Unconditional payer and/or payee untraceability. Smart Card 2000, Proceedings. North Holland, 1989.

13. L. Chen, M. Enzmann, A. Sadeghi, M. Schneider, and M. Steiner. A Privacy-Protecting Coupon System. Financial Cryptography 2005, Springer-Verlag, LNCS 3570, pp. 93-109.

14. Y. Dodis and A. Yampolskiy. A Verifiable Random Function with Short Proofs and Keys. Public Key Cryptography 2005, Springer-Verlag, LNCS 3386, pp. 416-431.

15. N. Ferguson. Extensions of single term coins. Adv. in Cryptology - CRYPTO '93, LNCS 773. Springer, 1993.

16. A. Fiat and A. Shamir. How to prove yourself: practical solutions to identification and signature problems. Crypto 1986, Springer-Verlag, LNCS 263, pp. 186-194, 1986.

17. L. Nguyen. Accumulators from Bilinear Pairings and Applications. RSA Conference 2005, Cryptographers' Track (CT-RSA), Springer-Verlag, LNCS 3376, pp. 275-292, 2005.

18. L. Nguyen and R. Safavi-Naini. Dynamic k-Times Anonymous Authentication. Applied Cryptography and Network Security (ACNS) 2005, Springer-Verlag, LNCS 3531, 2005.

19. T. Okamoto and K. Ohta. Disposable zero-knowledge authentications and their applications to untraceable electronic cash. CRYPTO '89, LNCS 435. Springer, 1990.

20. P. Persiano, I. Visconti. An efficient and usable multi-show non-transferable anonymous credential system. Financial Cryptography, LNCS 3110. Springer, Feb. 2004.

21. G. Shaffer and Z. Zhang. Competitive coupon targeting. Marketing Science, 14(4), 1995.

22. I. Teranisi, J. Furukawa, and K. Sako. k-Times Anonymous Authentication. Asiacrypt 2004, Springer-Verlag, LNCS 3329, pp. 308-322.

23. E. Verheul. Self-blindable credential certificates from the weil pairing. Adv. in Cryptology - ASIACRYPT '01, LNCS 2248. Springer-Verlag, 2001.

Efficient Broadcast Encryption Scheme with Log-Key Storage[*]

Yong Ho Hwang and Pil Joong Lee

Dept. of Electronic and Electrical Eng., POSTECH, Pohang, Korea
yhhwang@oberon.postech.ac.kr, pjl@postech.ac.kr

Abstract. In this paper, we present a broadcast encryption scheme with efficient transmission cost under the *log-key* restriction. Given n users and r revoked users, our scheme has the transmission cost of $O(r)$ and requires the storage of $O(\log n)$ keys at each receiver. These are optimal complexities in broadcast encryptions using one-way hash functions (or pseudo-random generators.) To achieve these complexities, the stratified subset difference (SSD) scheme and the $\overline{B1}$ scheme were introduced by Goodrich *et al.* and Hwang *et al.* respectively. However, their schemes have the disadvantage that transmission cost increases linearly according to the number of stratifications. By assigning the related keys between stratifications, our scheme remedies the defect and achieves very efficient transmission cost even in an environment where the key storage is restricted. To the best of our knowledge, our scheme has the most efficient transmission cost in the existing schemes with *log-key* storage. In addition, our result is comparable to other schemes that allow a large key storage.

1 Introduction

Broadcast encryption is an encryption scheme that enables a center to securely distribute messages to a dynamically changing group of users over an insecure channel, where only predetermined users can obtain available information. The center should efficiently deliver information to the group of legitimate users and prevent the group of revoked users from decrypting transmitted messages. There are various practical applications such as pay-TV, multicast communication, satellite-based commerce, and distribution of copyrighted materials (CD/DVD, etc). In this area, an important requirement is for *stateless* receivers, which cannot update their original state, i.e., they are not capable of recording the past history of transmission and changing their state accordingly. Hence, each receiver must be able to decrypt the current transmission with only its initial configuration. Actually, in many practical environments most devices should be *stateless* since it is difficult to keep the receiver constantly on-line and it is very cumbersome for both the receiver and the center to keep the history of every transmission.

---

[*] This research was supported by University IT Research Center Project, the Brain Korea 21 Project.

With the advent of mobile networks and other digital support services, the need to deliver multimedia data to user's handheld devices over a wireless network becomes more important. This situation is more intricate since handheld devices such as cellular phones and PDAs have only a small storage capability and low computing power. In addition, the bandwidth of wireless networks is narrower than that of wired networks. Therefore, we need an efficient broadcast encryption scheme to overcome these obstacles.

RELATED WORKS. The notion of broadcast encryption was first discussed by Berkovits [5]. Fiat and Naor [11] formalized the basic definitions and proposed a systematic paradigm. However, their scheme is difficult to apply to a practical system because it is highly complex. After the multicast scheme based on a *logical tree hierarchy* was independently introduced by Wallner et al.[21] and Wong et al.[22], various schemes [1,2,19,15,12] based on a tree structure were suggested. There are two approaches to construct an efficient tree-based scheme. One is a scheme based on sequential one-way hash functions (or pseudo-random generators)[19,15,12] and the other is based on the RSA accumulator [1,2]. One-way hash function-based schemes have various trade-offs between $O(r)$ transmission cost and $O(\log n)$ key storage where n is the number of users and r is the number of revoked users. While RSA accumulator-based schemes can reduce key storage to $O(1)$, their transmission cost depends on n.[1] Moreover, these schemes require expensive computations such as modular exponentiation and prime number generation. We deal with one-way function based schemes in this paper.

In 2001, Naor et al.[19] introduced a *Subset-Cover* framework and designed two broadcast encryption schemes for stateless receivers under this framework. One is the CS (Complete Subtree) scheme which requires $O(r \log n/r)$ transmission cost and $O(\log n)$ key storage, and the other is the SD (Subset Difference) scheme which guarantees $2r - 1$ transmission cost and $O(\log n)$ key computation cost, while each user should store $O(\log^2 n)$ keys. The transmission cost of $O(r)$ and the key storage of $O(\log n)$ have been regarded as the optimal bounds of tree-based schemes, which use the key assignment technique of sequentially applying a one-way function (or a pseudo-random generator). Afterwards, a number of papers tried to reduce the storage size by sacrificing the transmission cost of the SD scheme. Halevy and Shamir [15] proposed the LSD (Layered Subset Difference) scheme that lowers the key storage to $O(\log^{1+\epsilon} n)$ while maintaining $O(r)$ transmission cost by labelling special layers in a binary tree. In addition, Goodrich et al. [12] presented the SSD (Stratified Subset Difference) scheme that can lower the transmission cost to $O(r)$ with $O(\log n)$ key storage by stratifying subtrees between special layers in a binary tree. The SSD scheme seems to be able to achieve the lower bounds of both the transmission cost and the key storage in

---

[1] Recently, an RSA accumulator-based scheme with transmission cost independent of n was accepted by Asiacrypt 2005[3]. However, this scheme also has the disadvantage that transmission cost linearly increases according to the number of stratifications, like the SSD scheme.

tree-based schemes using one-way functions. However, the LSD scheme and the SSD scheme linearly increase the transmission cost according to the number of layers or stratified subtrees, although key storage does approach the $O(\log n)$ bound. Other interesting improvements were introduced in [4] and [18]. In [4] the key storage of the SD scheme and the LSD scheme were slightly reduced by the sequential key derivation method while maintaining their transmission costs. In [18] the system complexity was adjusted by a hybrid structure based on the CS, SD, and LSD schemes. Moreover, other variants related to broadcast encryption have been investigated in [8,6,13,20,10,17].

Recently, new broadcast encryption schemes based on a hash-chain [16] were proposed which can reduce the transmission cost below r by exploiting the trade-off between the transmission cost and the key storage. In doing so, however, too much secure memory must be sacrificed. For example, the transmission cost of these schemes is similar to that of the SD scheme when key storage is bounded as in the SD scheme. This approach seems useful in practical applications, since the storage size of user's devices, even in the case of cellular phones or PDAs, seems to no longer be a problem because storage devices have become larger and cheaper. However, to guarantee security, user keys must be securely stored in tamper-proof storage devices, which are still small and expensive. To solve this problem, Hwang *et al.* [14] introduced a compiler that made scalable broadcast encryption schemes by transforming ones that had impractical computation costs or key storage requirements when there are huge numbers of users. They applied a given broadcast encryption scheme to a relatively small subset in a hierarchical and independent manner. Their compiler makes the computation cost and the key storage reasonable by slightly increasing the transmission cost. However, their compiler also does not achieve $O(r)$ transmission cost when users are holding strictly resource-restricted devices.

In addition, Boneh *et al.* [7] introduced a *public key* broadcast encryption scheme with $O(1)$ for both the transmission cost and the private key. Their scheme requires $O(n)$ non-secure key storage and $O(n-r)$ computation cost. To achieve reasonable storage and computation cost, they constructed a general scheme divided into a number of subsets. This scheme has $O(\sqrt{n})$ transmission cost and $O(\sqrt{n})$ key storage. Consequently, their complexity is not independent of n.

OUR CONTRIBUTION. In this paper, we focus on stateless receivers which can store at most $O(\log n)$ keys since it is actually difficult to store much data in tamper-proof storage. We refer to this as the *log-key* restriction. We propose a new broadcast encryption scheme which satisfies $O(r)$ transmission cost and $O(\log n)$ key storage at a reasonable computation cost. Our scheme has the most efficient transmission cost under the *log-key* restriction. Table 1 shows the comparison between schemes with $O(\log n)$ key storage per user.

In [14], Hwang *et al.* introduced the B1 scheme with the computation cost proportional to n and transformed it to the $\overline{B1}$ scheme, which has a practical computation cost and *log-key* storage, by their compiler. Our scheme is also based on the B1 scheme and extends it in a hierarchical manner to a scheme with at

Table 1. Complexity of BE schemes with $O(\log n)$ key storage

		Transmission cost (Bound)		Key storage	Computation cost
CS	[19]	$O(r \log n/r)$		$O(\log n)$	$O(\log \log n)$
SSD	[12]	$O(r)$	$4kr$	$O(\log n)$	$O(n^{1/k})$
$\overline{\text{B1}}$	[14]	$O(r)$	$2kr$	$O(\log n)$	$O(n^{1/k})$
Our scheme		$O(r)$	$2r$	$O(\log n)$	$O(n^{1/k})$

(k is an arbitrary system parameter.)

most $2r$ transmission cost under the *log-key* restriction. To achieve a transmission cost free of the level of stratification, our scheme additionally assigns the related keys between stratifications to the $\overline{\text{B1}}$ scheme. There is a trade-off between the key storage and the computation cost in our scheme. Consequently, while our scheme reduces an upper bound of the transmission cost to $2r$, $(d + \frac{d+1}{2} \cdot \log n)$ key storage and $(d \cdot n^{1/d})$ computation cost are required.

ORGANIZATION OF THE PAPER. The remainder of this paper is organized as follows. In Section 2, we formalize a model for a broadcast encryption scheme based on a *Subset-Cover* framework. In Section 3, we first introduce our basic scheme and propose the complete scheme based on it. Then we discuss the performance and the properties of our scheme in detail and compare it with various broadcast encryption schemes in Section 4. Finally, we give concluding remarks in Section 5.

2   Model for Broadcast Encryption

We define a model for a broadcast encryption based on the *Subset-Cover* framework introduced by Naor *et al.*[19] since our scheme is also based on it.

2.1   Generic Model

In broadcast encryption the center (or the broadcaster) assigns secret keys to all users and broadcasts a encrypted message with the subset keys. Legitimate users can derive the subset keys from the assigned secret keys and decrypt the ciphertext with them. Let $\mathcal{N}$ be the set of all users, $\mathcal{R}$ the set of revoked users, and $\mathcal{N} \backslash \mathcal{R}$ the set of remaining users. We suppose that $|\mathcal{N}| = n$ and $|\mathcal{R}| = r$. A *broadcast encryption scheme* BE consists of 3 phases (Setup, Broadcast, Decryption):

- Setup: The center generates secret keys for each user and delivers them to each user over a secure channel.
- Broadcast: In this phase, the center broadcasts a message to users. Given $\mathcal{R}$, the center divides $\mathcal{N} \backslash \mathcal{R}$ into disjoint subsets $S_1, \ldots, S_m$ so that $\mathcal{N} \backslash \mathcal{R} = \bigcup_{i=1}^{m} S_i$, and computes a subset key sk_i for each subset S_i. At this time, sk_i is generated by a pre-defined algorithm. The center chooses a session

key K at random and encrypts it m times with $sk_1, \ldots, sk_m$. In addition, an "actual" message M is encrypted with K. The center broadcasts a ciphertext $\langle \mathsf{Hdr}, \mathsf{Enc}_K(M) \rangle$ where

$$\mathsf{Hdr} = <I_1, \ldots, I_m, E_{sk_1}(K), \ldots, E_{sk_m}(K)>.$$

$E{:}\{0,1\}^l \rightarrow \{0,1\}^l$ and $\mathsf{Enc}{:}\{0,1\}^* \rightarrow \{0,1\}^*$ are symmetric encryptions where l is a security parameter and I_j is the information on the subset S_j. Generally, a fast encryption scheme such as a stream cipher is used for Enc to encrypt the *actual* message. We call Hdr a *Header* (or an *enabling block*).
- Decryption: After receiving the ciphertext, a user u first finds the subset S_i including him from I_i. A legitimate user can then generate a subset key sk_i from his secret keys. He decrypts $E_{sk_i}(K)$ with it and obtains the *actual* message M from K.

A legitimate user should be included in an arbitrary subset and be able to derive its subset key from his secret keys and the current transmission. In addition, even though all the revoked users collude with one another, it must be impossible for them to obtain any of the subset keys. The important factors for evaluating the broadcast encryption scheme are as follows.

- *Transmission cost* - the length of the Header for delivering the session key to users in $\mathcal{N} \backslash \mathcal{R}$. This depends on the number of subsets covering $\mathcal{N} \setminus \mathcal{R}$; namely, the number of partitions included in a Header.
- *Key storage* - the number of secret keys which each user should store in his secure device.
- *Computation cost* - the processing time to compute the subset key from the user's secret keys.

2.2   Adversarial Model

Our adversarial model follows the security model of Definition 10 in [19]. We briefly review their attack scenario. The attack game between the challenger and the adversary is as follows.

- **Setup:** The challenger runs the Setup algorithm and generates secret keys for all users.
- **Phase 1:** The adversary adaptively selects a set $\mathcal{R}$ of revoked users and obtains the secret keys of users in $\mathcal{R}$ from the challenger. He can get the encryption of message selected by himself when $\mathcal{R}$ is chosen. In addition, he can also create a ciphertext and see how any non-corrupted user decrypts it.
- **Challenge:** The adversary chooses a message M and a set $\mathcal{R}'$ including all the sets of revoked users selected in Phase 1. The challenger picks a random bit $b \in \{0,1\}$ and sets $C = \mathsf{Broadcast}(\mathcal{R}', M_b)$ where M_1 is M and M_0 is a random message of similar length. Then he sends it to the adversary.
- **Guess:** The adversary outputs a guess $b' \in \{0,1\}$.

We say that a broadcast encryption scheme is secure if for any polynomial time adversary, the probability that he distinguishes between M_0 and M_1 is negligible.

3   Proposed Scheme

In this section we propose an efficient broadcast encryption scheme with *log-key* storage. Our construction is based on the B1 scheme by Hwang *et al.* [14]. While the B1 scheme has at most $2r$ transmission cost and $O(\log n)$ key storage, its computation cost is proportional to n. To achieve a reasonable computation cost, in [14] the $\overline{\text{B1}}$ scheme was constructed from the B1 scheme by their compiler. However, its transmission cost increases in proportion to the number of levels in the hierarchy. While our complete scheme has a similar structure to the B1 scheme, it achieves efficient transmission cost by the related keys between each level in the hierarchy. We first introduce the modified B1 scheme and construct an efficient broadcast encryption scheme from it.

3.1   Basic Scheme

In this section, we slightly modify the B1 scheme. Actually, this scheme is identical to the B1 scheme except for technique that the information I on the subset is represented and a user searches a subset including him. In the B1 scheme, a non-revoked user first finds two adjacent revoked users and should performs a binary search in an interval of two revoked users. In our scheme, a user can directly search his subset from the indexes and the direction of a hash chain.

We define two one-way chains for users between u_i and u_j $(i \leq j)$ as $\mathcal{OC}_{i \rightarrow j}$ and $\mathcal{OC}_{i \leftarrow j}$. Let $f : \{0,1\}^l \rightarrow \{0,1\}^l$ be a one-way function. Then $\mathcal{OC}_{i \rightarrow j}$ is a one-way chain from i to j that, given a label $L_i \in_R \{0,1\}^l$ for u_i, has the value $f^{j-i}(L_i)$. On the other hand, $\mathcal{OC}_{i \leftarrow j}$ is a one-way chain from j to i that, given a label $L_j \in_R \{0,1\}^l$ for u_j, has the value is $f^{j-i}(L_j)$. Our basic scheme is as follows.

- Setup: The center imagines the number line $\mathfrak{L}$ with n nodes where each node is numbered i $(i = 1, \ldots, n)$ with level order from left to right. Each user is assigned to each node. Let a user assigned to a node i be u_i. The center randomly selects a label $L_i \in \{0,1\}^l$ for each node i $(1 \leq i \leq n)$. We denote a set of users in an interval of i and j by $\mathcal{I}_{i;j}$. The center recursively repeats the following key assignment staring from $\mathcal{I}_{1;n}$. Assume that a user u_m is included in $\mathcal{I}_{i;j}$. Then $f^{m-i}(L_i)$ and $f^{j-m}(L_j)$ are given to u_m as the secret key. After secret keys for $\mathcal{I}_{i;j}$ are assigned, $\mathcal{I}_{i;j}$ is divided into two intervals, $\mathcal{I}_{i;t}$ and $\mathcal{I}_{t+1;j}$ where $t = \lfloor \frac{i+j}{2} \rfloor$ and then u_m is assigned secret keys for $\mathcal{I}_{i;t}$ or $\mathcal{I}_{t+1;j}$ by the same method. If $m \leq t$, it assigns only $f^{t-m}(L_t)$ to u_m for $\mathcal{I}_{i;t}$ since $f^{m-i}(L_i)$ can be used for both $\mathcal{I}_{i;j}$ and $\mathcal{I}_{i;t}$. If $m > t$, only $f^{m-t}(L_t)$ is assigned for $\mathcal{I}_{t+1;j}$. Therefore, one additional key is given to a user whenever a new interval is made. This procedure starts from $\mathcal{I}_{1;n}$ and finish at $\mathcal{I}_{m;m}$. Consequently, a user should store $1 + \log n$ keys in his secure storage. For example, assume that there are 16 users in total. Then the secret keys for u_7 are $f^6(L_1)$, $f^9(L_{16})$, $f(L_8)$, $f^2(L_5)$, and L_7 as shown in Figure 1.
- Broadcast: Given $\mathcal{R}$, the center first divides the number line $\mathfrak{L}$ into the intervals where each interval include one revoked user or successively revoked

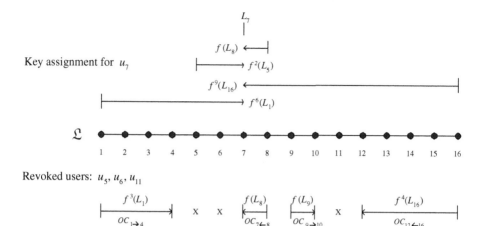

Fig. 1. An example of the basic scheme for $n=16$

users. If a user u_t in $\mathcal{I}_{i;j}$ is revoked, non-revoked users in $\mathcal{I}_{i;j}$ are covered by two hash chains $\mathcal{OC}_{i\leftarrow t-1}$ and $\mathcal{OC}_{t+1\leftarrow j}$. Then, for users in $\mathcal{I}_{i;j}$, a session key K is encrypted with the chain values of $\mathcal{OC}_{i\rightarrow t-1}$ and $\mathcal{OC}_{t+1\leftarrow j}$, namely $f^{t-1-i}(L_i)$ and $f^{j-(t+1)}(L_j)$. Here, the subset information for two hash chains $\mathcal{OC}_{i\leftarrow t-1}$ and $\mathcal{OC}_{t+1\leftarrow j}$ can be $[+;i, t-1]$ and $[-;t+1, j]$.

- Decryption: After receiving the ciphertext, a user u_m first finds the subset including him from the subset information $[\pm;i, j]$ by checking whether $i \leq m \leq j$. If the direction of his subset is $+$, then he computes $\mathcal{OC}_{i\rightarrow j}$ by $f^{j-m}(f^{m-i}(L_i))$. Otherwise, he computes $\mathcal{OC}_{i\leftarrow j}$ by $f^{m-i}(f^{j-m}(L_j))$.

In Figure 1, if u_5, u_6 and u_{11} are revoked, the session key is encrypted with $f^3(L_1)$, $f(L_8)$, $f(L_9)$, and $f^4(L_{16})$ respectively. The scheme requires at most $2r$ transmission cost because at most two ciphertexts for one revoked user are generated. Its security is provided under the pseudo-randomness of f [14].

3.2   Complete Scheme

The basic scheme is not reasonable for practical applications because it has a computation cost proportional to n, though it satisfies the *log-key* restriction and $2r$ bound of the transmission cost. We extend the basic scheme to a hierarchical structure similar to the generic transformation of [14]. Actually, in all the schemes with hierarchical structure for efficient trade-offs among the transmission cost, the key storage, and the computation cost, the transmission cost increases linearly according to the number of hierarchies (or stratifications).[2]

However, our construction can maintain the $2r$ bound of the transmission cost while satisfying the reasonable computation cost and log-key storage re-

---

[2] For example, the LSD scheme, the SSD scheme, and the $\overline{\text{B1}}$ scheme have a transmission cost proportional to the number of layers, stratifications, and the levels in the hierarchy respectively.

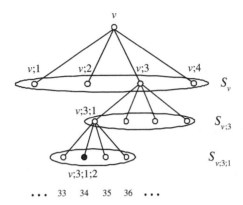

Fig. 2. An example of the complete scheme for $n=64$

quirements. Our scheme achieves it from additional keys and computation cost proportional to the number of the levels in the hierarchy. In addition, our scheme has a trade-off between the key storage and the computation cost under a reasonable bound. The complete scheme is as follows.

- Setup: We assume that n is a^d. The center imagines a-ary tree T_v with a depth d and assigns one user to each leaf. Then, each leaf in T_v is numbered i $(i = 1, \ldots, n)$ with level ordered from left to right. Let a root of T_v denote v and i-th child of a node w denote $w; i$. Note that this notation can be sequentially represented as $w; i_1; \ldots; i_l$. In addition, we call a set of children of a node w a sibling set S_w. In an example of Figure 2, a node 34 is represented as $v; 3; 1; 2$ and $S_{v;3;1}$ is $\{33, 34, 35, 36\}$.

Let T_w be a subtree rooted at a node w of T_v. The center randomly selects each label L_w for each node w in T_v. Then it generates keys for S_w by Setup of the basic scheme. Keys for $w; t$ in S_w are given to users assigned to leaves of $T_{w;t}$. In consequence, a user assigned to $v; i_1; \cdots; i_d$ has keys for $S_v, S_{v;i_1}$, $\ldots, S_{v;i_1;\cdots;i_{d-1}}$. Then, in Figure 2, a user u_{34} has secret keys, $f^2(L_{v;1})$, $f(L_{v;4})$, $L_{v;3}$ $L_{v;3;1}$, $f^3(L_{v;3;4})$, $f(L_{v;3;2})$ $f(L_{33})$, $f^2(L_{36})$, L_{34}. This assignment is actually identical to that by the compiler introduced in [14].

In our scheme, to eliminate the transmission cost of the hierarchical structure, users are assigned additional keys. Let $g : \{0, 1\}^l \rightarrow \{0, 1\}^l$ be a different one-way function with f. Let $f(f(L))$ denote $f \circ f(L)$, and $g \circ f^k(L)$ denote $g_k(L)$. Then $g \circ f^x \circ g \circ f^y(L)$ can be represented as $g_x \circ g_y(L)$ and $g_0(L)$ is equal to $g(L)$.

If a user $w; i_1; ..i_t$ is given $f^j(L_{w;m})$ for S_w where $m < i_1$, the center additionally assigns the following keys;

$$f^{i_2} \circ g_{j-1}(L_{w;m}), f^{i_3} \circ g_{i_2-1} \circ g_{j-1}(L_{w;m}),$$
$$\ldots, f^{i_t} \circ g_{i_{t-1}-1} \circ \cdots \circ g_{i_2-1} \circ g_{j-1}(L_{w;m}). \tag{1}$$

On the other hand, if $m > i_1$, the center assigns the following keys;

$$f^{a-i_2+1} \circ g_{j-1}(L_{w;m}), f^{a-i_3+1} \circ g_{a-i_2} \circ g_{j-1}(L_{w;m}),$$
$$\ldots, f^{a-i_t+1} \circ g_{a-i_{t-1}} \circ \cdots g_{a-i_2} \circ g_{j-1}(L_{w;m}). \tag{2}$$

When $i_1 = m$, the additional keys are not given. Consequently, $1 + t \cdot \log a$ keys are assigned to a user for S_w. A user $v; i_1; \ldots; i_d$ in T_v has all secret keys for $S_v, S_{v;i_1}, \ldots, S_{v;i_1;\ldots;i_{d-1}}$. Therefore, the number of secret keys for a user is $d + \frac{(d+1)}{2} \cdot \log n$ in total;

$$\sum_{t=1}^{d} 1 + t \log a = d + \log a \cdot \sum_{t=1}^{d} t = d + \frac{d^2 + d}{2} \cdot (\log a) = d + \frac{(d+1)}{2} \cdot \log n.$$

Therefore, user 34 in the example of Figure 2 is assigned his secret keys as follows.

$$
\begin{aligned}
S_v \quad &: f^2(L_{v;1}), \quad f \circ g_1(L_{v;1}), \quad f^2 \circ g \circ g_1(L_{v;1}) \\
&\quad f(L_{v;4}), \quad f^4 \circ g(L_{v;4}), \quad f^3 \circ g_3 \circ g(L_{v;4}) \\
&\quad L_{v;3} \\
S_{v;3} \quad &: f^3(L_{v;3;4}), f^3 \circ g_2(L_{v;3;4}) \\
&\quad f(L_{v;3;2}), \quad f^3 \circ g(L_{v;3;2}) \\
&\quad L_{v;3;1} \\
S_{v;3;1} &: f(L_{33}), \quad f^2(L_{36}), \quad L_{34}
\end{aligned}
$$

User 34 receives the additional keys $f \circ g_1(L_{v;1})$, $f^2 \circ g \circ g_1(L_{v;1})$ derived from $f^2(L_{v;1})$, and $f^4 \circ g(L_{v;4})$, $f^3 \circ g_3 \circ g(L_{v;4})$ from $f(L_{v;4})$ for S_v, and $f^3 \circ g_2(L_{v;3;4})$, $f^3 \circ g(L_{v;3;2})$ for $S_{v;3}$ by (1), (2). Figure 3 shows the paths generating the additional keys of the user 34 for S_v. In consequence, a user has 15 secret keys in total because $d = 3$ and $n = 2^6$.

- Broadcast: The center imagines the number line $\mathfrak{L}$ composed by leaves of T_v. Given $\mathcal{R}$, the center makes the hash chains in the form of $\mathcal{OC}_{i \to j}$ or $\mathcal{OC}_{i \leftarrow j}$ which cover $\mathfrak{L}$ as in Broadcast of the basic scheme. If a least common ancestor of nodes from i to j is w, we denote this chain by $\mathcal{OC}^w_{i \to j(\text{or } i \leftarrow j)}$. Then i and j can be represented as $w; i_1; \cdots ; i_t$ and $w; j_1; \cdots ; j_t$ $(t \le d.)$ First, we consider $\mathcal{OC}^w_{i \to j}$. The chain value of $\mathcal{OC}^w_{i \to j}$ is computed by the following process.

  1. If i and j are siblings (namely, w is a parent of i and j), then the chain value of $\mathcal{OC}^w_{i \to j}$ equals that of $\mathcal{OC}_{i \to j}$ in the basic scheme.
  2. Else if j is the rightmost leaf in a subtree $T_{w;j_1;\cdots;j_m}$ of T_w where $1 \le m < t$.
     - If $m = 1$, then the chain value of $\mathcal{OC}^w_{i \to j}$ is $f^{j_1 - i_1}(L_{w;i_1})$.
     - Otherwise, the chain value of $\mathcal{OC}^w_{i \to j}$ is $f^{j_m} \circ g_{j_{m-1}-1} \circ \cdots \circ g_{j_2-1} \circ g_{j_1 - i_1 - 1}(L_{w;i_1})$
  3. Otherwise, the chain value of $\mathcal{OC}^w_{i \to j}$ is $f^{j_t} \circ g_{j_{t-1}-1} \circ \cdots \circ g_{j_2-1} \circ g_{j_1 - i_1 - 1}(L_{w;i_1})$.

The chain value of $\mathcal{OC}^w_{i \leftarrow j}$ is generated by the opposite operation with the above process. Consequently, our scheme has the same transmission cost as the basic scheme.

In Figure 4, we assume that three users u_{19}, u_{57}, and u_{59} are revoked. Then the following one-way chains are generated:

$$\mathcal{OC}^v_{1 \to 18}, \mathcal{OC}^{v;2}_{20 \leftarrow 32}, \mathcal{OC}^v_{33 \to 56}, \mathcal{OC}_{58 \leftarrow 58}, \text{ and } \mathcal{OC}^{v;4}_{60 \leftarrow 64}.$$

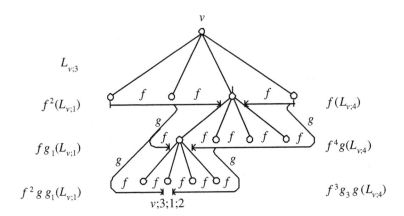

Fig. 3. Key assignment to u_{34} for S_v

For them, the chain values are $f^2 \circ g \circ g(L_{v;1})$, $f \circ g_2(L_{v;2;4})$, $f^2 \circ g(L_{v;3})$, and $f \circ g(L_{v;4;4})$ respectively. For a specific example of a chain value, consider $\mathcal{OC}^v_{33 \to 56}$. A least common ancestor of 33 and 56 is v and 56 is the rightmost leaf of $T_{v;4;2}$. Hence, this chain value $f^2 \circ g(L_{v;3})$ is computed from $f^2 \circ g_{4-3-1}(L_{v;3})$ because a node $v; 3$ is an ancestor of 33 and a child of v.

- Decryption: After receiving the ciphertext, a user u_k finds his subset from $[\pm; i, j]$. If $i \leq k \leq j$, u_k is included in the subset $[\pm; i, j]$. Suppose that k can be represented as $w; k_1; \cdots ; k_t$ and the direction is $+$.
  1. If i and j are siblings, then he computes a subset key $f^{j-i}(L_i)$ by $f^{j-k} \circ f^{k-i}(L_i)$ from his secret key $f^{k-i}(L_i)$.
  2. Else if j is the rightmost leaf in a subtree $T_{w;j_1;\cdots;j_m}$ of T_w where $1 \leq m < t$.
     - If $m = 1$, then he computes the chain value $f^{j_1-i_1}(L_{w;i_1})$ for $\mathcal{OC}^w_{i \to j}$ by iteratively operating the f function with his secret key $f^{k_1-i_1}(L_{w;i_1})$.
     - Otherwise, he finds a common ancestor $w; k_1; \cdots ; k_l$ of j and himself where $0 \leq l < m$ and computes the chain value $f^{j_m} \circ g_{j_{m-1}-1} \circ \cdots \circ g_{j_2-1} \circ g_{j_1-i_1-1}(L_{w;i_1})$ for $\mathcal{OC}^w_{i \to j}$ using g and f with his secret key $f^{j_{l+1}-k_{l+1}} \circ g_{j_l-1} \circ \cdots \circ g_{j_2-1} \circ g_{j_1-i_1-1}(L_{w;i_1})$.
  3. Otherwise, he computes the chain value $\mathcal{OC}^w_{i \to j}$ is $f^{j_t} \circ g_{j_{t-1}-1} \circ \cdots \circ g_{j_2-1} \circ g_{j_1-i_1-1}(L_{w;i_1})$ using g and f with his secret key $f^{j_{l+1}-k_{l+1}} \circ g_{j_l-1} \circ \cdots \circ g_{j_2-1} \circ g_{j_1-i_1-1}(L_{w;i_1})$.

If the direction is $-$, then it performs the above method in the opposite direction. For example, u_{34} is included in $\mathcal{OC}^v_{33 \to 56}$. A least common ancestor of nodes from 33 to 56 is v and an ancestor of 33 in the children of v is $v; 3$. Because 56 is a rightmost leaf of $T_{v;4;2}$, a chain value for $\mathcal{OC}^v_{33 \to 56}$ is $f^2 \circ g(L_{v;3})$. User u_{34} is also a descendent of $v; 3$, so he has $L_{v;3}$ as his secret key. Therefore, he can obtain the subset key by $f^2 \circ g(L_{v;3})$. Because a revoked user u_{57} has secret keys $f \circ g_2 \circ g(L_{v;3})$ generated by $L_{v;3}$, he cannot obtain the subset key without inverting $f \circ g$.

Efficiency. Transmission cost of the complete scheme is less than $2r$ because at most two ciphertexts per revoked user are generated, as in the basic scheme. To generate a subset key, a user needs at most $d \cdot a$ computation cost. In addition, a

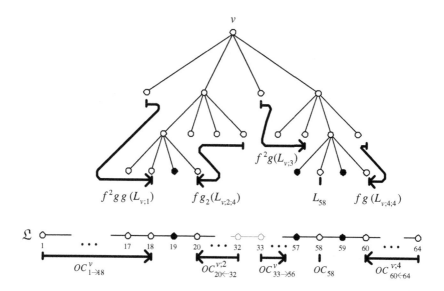

Fig. 4. Revocation in the complete scheme

user stores $d + \frac{d+1}{2} \cdot \log n$ keys as shown above. Our scheme achieve the efficient transmission cost from a trade-off with the computation cost and the key storage by the number of stratification in hierarchical structure.

Security. The security of our scheme is provided under the pseudo-randomness of f and g. Actually, because all secret keys given to users are generated by one-way chains, excluded users (i.e. revoked users) by one-way chains cannot compute any subset key without inverting the given one-way functions f and g. However, a more formal security analysis is needed. We show that our scheme is resilient to collusion of any set of revoked users.

Lemma 1. *The key assignment of the complete scheme satisfies the key indistinguishability property under the pseudo-randomness of two functions f, g.*

Proof. Let $f \circ g$ define a function $h : \{0,1\}^l \to \{0,1\}^l$. If an adversary $\mathcal{A}$ can break the key-indistinguishability property of our scheme, we show that the pseudo-randomness of f and h is also broken by simulating $\mathcal{A}$. We assume that our scheme is defined by a collection of subsets $S_1, \ldots, S_w$. For any $1 \leq i \leq w$, let $S_{i_1}, \ldots, S_{i_t}$ be all the subsets that are contained in S_i and $sk_{i_1}, \ldots, sk_{i_t}$ be their corresponding keys. An adversary $\mathcal{A}$ attempts to distinguish the keys $sk_{i_1}, \ldots, sk_{i_t}$ from the random keys $rk_{i_1}, \ldots, rk_{i_t}$. Consider a feasible adversary $\mathcal{A}$ that

1. Selects i, $1 \leq i \leq w$
2. Receives the secret keys K_u's for all $u \in \mathcal{N} \setminus S_i$

We denote the probability that $\mathcal{A}$ distinguishes the key from the random key by ε as follows.

$$|\Pr[\mathcal{A} \text{ outputs } i|sk_i] - \Pr[\mathcal{A} \text{ outputs } i|rk_i]| \leq \varepsilon.$$

If an adversary $\mathcal{A}$ can distinguish the key from the random key, we can break the pseudo-randomness of f or h, since K_u includes an output of the function f or h on the key. Hence, if the pseudo-randomness of two one-way functions f and h is guaranteed, ε is negligible.

Also, let P_{i_j} be the probability that given the subset keys contained in S_i, $\mathcal{A}$ outputs i, where the first j keys are the true keys and the remaining $t - j$ keys are the random keys. Namely,

$$P_{i_j} = \Pr[\mathcal{A} \text{ outputs } i|sk_{i_1}, \ldots, sk_{i_j}, rk_{i_{j+1}}, \ldots, rk_{i_t}].$$

Then we can obtain the following equation by the standard hybrid argument, since $|P_{i_j} - P_{i_{j+1}}| < \varepsilon$ for $1 \leq j < t$.

$$|\Pr[\mathcal{A} \text{ outputs } i|sk_{i_1}, \ldots, sk_{i_t}] - \Pr[\mathcal{A} \text{ outputs } i|rk_{i_1}, \ldots, rk_{i_t}]| \leq t \cdot \varepsilon.$$

In consequence, our scheme satisfies the key-indistinguishability property under the pseudo-random-ness of given functions f and g.   □

In addition, Naor *et al.* showed that the key-indistinguishability property is sufficient for a scheme in the subset-cover framework to be secure in the adversarial model of Section 2.2 [19]. By Lemma 1 and Theorem 11 of [19], the security of the complete scheme is provided.

4   Discussions

We analyze the complexities of various broadcast encryption schemes in this section. While the SD scheme needs at most $2r$ transmission cost, $O(\log^2 n)$ key storage is required. The LSD scheme, the SSD scheme, the π scheme, and the $\overline{\text{B1}}$ scheme have trade-offs among the transmission cost, the computation cost and the key storage. Their complexities change depending on the system parameters that define the degree of stratification. Table 2 shows the comparison between our scheme and other efficient schemes. In the transmission cost column of Table 2, '$\leq$' means an upper bound of the transmission cost.

We assume that the size of keys is 128 bits and n is 10^8 for a practical instance. While the computation cost of the SD scheme and the LSD scheme is fixed to $O(\log n)$, that of other schemes varies with the system parameters. Hence, we bound the computation cost to 100. This computation cost is reasonable even for low-power devices. If the computation cost of the SSD scheme and the $\overline{\text{B1}}$ scheme is bounded to 100, their system parameters d and k are 4. Therefore, their transmission cost is $2 \cdot (4r)$.[3] In addition, we compare other schemes to

---

[3] The upper bound of the transmission cost of the SSD scheme should be $16r$ from Table 1 when $k = 4$. However, its transmission cost is actually similar to that of the $\overline{\text{B1}}$ scheme. Hence we regard a upper bound of its transmission cost as $2kr$.

Table 2. Complexity of efficient BE schemes for $n = 10^8$

		Transmission cost	Key storage	Computation cost
SD	[19]	$\leq 2r$	368 (5.74 Kbyte)	27
Basic LSD	[15]	$\leq 4r$	143 (2.24 Kbyte)	27
SSD	[12]	$\leq 8r$	213 (3.33 Kbyte)	100
$(1,100)$-π_1	[16]	$\leq 2r + 10^6$	5274 (82.4 Kbyte)	100
$\overline{B1}$	[14]	$\leq 8r$	27 (0.432 Kbyte)	100
Our scheme		$\leq 2r$	129 (2.06 Kbyte)	80

the Basic LSD with $k = 2$ because the LSD scheme satisfies the most efficient transmission cost when having two layers.

The SSD scheme and the $\overline{B1}$ scheme have high transmission cost proportional to the parameters d and k, and the $(1,100)$-π_1 scheme does not have a good transmission cost where the revocation rate is very small (i.e less than 1%). However, our scheme maintains a low transmission cost regardless of the parameter and revocation rate. For our scheme, we consider the case of $a = 10$ and $d = 8$ to achieve a reasonable computation cost. At this time, the computation cost of our scheme is less than 80. As shown in Table 2, our scheme has the most efficient transmission cost under the reasonable computation cost and *log-key* restriction.

Because our scheme possesses low transmission cost and small storage size, it can be efficiently used where the computation and the storage are restricted as in a handheld device, or where the transmission is expensive as in a set-top box and CD/DVD. In addition, when a group of malicious users (called traitors) combines their secret keys to produce a pirate decode, the center can trace at least one of the traitors given access to this decoder by a subset tracing procedure introduced in [19] since our scheme is based on a subset-cover framework.

Our scheme is also suitable for broadcast encryption over wireless networks. In a wireless network, the target of messages is a handheld device with small memory and low computing power. Moreover, the bandwidth of wireless networks is narrower than that of wired networks. Therefore, our scheme is of great use for broadcast encryption scheme over wireless networks.

In addition, the key assignment technique used to construct our scheme can be applied to the schemes with a hierarchical structure such as the SSD scheme [12] and the $\overline{B2}$ scheme [14]. The transmission cost of the modified schemes would be independent of the number of levels in hierarchy.

5   Concluding Remarks

We have presented a communication-efficient broadcast encryption scheme under the *log-key* restriction. In many practical applications, the systems should be efficiently able to deal with a very large group of users having a wide variety of devices. Our scheme can provide an efficient transmission cost under a reasonable computation cost for a large number of users by requiring key storage proportional to the log of the number of users. It is also a good solution for systems that rely on devices with limited secure storage.

References

1. T. Asano, "A Revocationn Scheme with Minimal Storage at Receivers," *Advances in Cryptology - ASIACRYPT'02*, LNCS vol. 2501, pp. 433-450, 2002.
2. T. Asano and K. Kamio, "A Tree Based One-Key Broadcast Encryption Scheme with Low Computational Overhead," *Information Secrutiy and Privacy - ACISP'05*, LNCS vol. 3574, pp. 89-100, 2005.
3. N. Attrapadung and H. Imai, "Graph-Decomposition-Based Framework for Subset-Cover Broadcast Encryption and Efficient Instantiations," *Advances in Cryptology - ASIACRYPT'05*, LNCS vol. 3788, pp. 100-120, 2005.
4. N. Attrapadung, K. Kobara, and H. Imai, "Sequential Key Derivation Patterns for Broadcast Encryption and Key Predistribution Schemes," *Advances in Cryptology - ASIACRYPT'03*, LNCS vol. 2894, pp. 374-391, 2003.
5. S. Berkovits, "How to broadcast a secret," *Advances in Cryptology - EURO-CRYPT'91*, LNCS vol. 547, pp. 535-541, 1991.
6. C. Blundo, L. A. Frota, and D. R. Stinson, "Trade-off between Communication and Storage in Unconditionally Secure Schemes for Broadcast Encryption and Interactive Key Distribution," *Advances in Cryptology - CRYPTO'96*, LNCS vol.1109, pp. 387-400, 1996.
7. D. Boneh, C. Gentry, and B. Waters, "Collusion Resistant Broadcast Encryption with Short Ciphertexts and Private Keys," *Advances in Cryptology - CRYPTO'05*, LNCS vol.3621, pp. 258-275, 2005.
8. B. Chor, A. Fiat, and M. Naor, "Tracing traitor," *Advances in Cryptology - CRYPTO'94*, LNCS vol. 839, pp. 257-270, 1994.
9. T. H. Cormen, C. E. Leiserson, R. L. Rivest, and C. Stein, "Introduction to Algorithms," *MIT Press*, 2001.
10. Y. Dodis and N. Fazio, "Public Key Trace and Revoke Scheme Secure Against Adapitive Chosen Ciphertext Attack," *Public Key Cryptography - PKC'03*, LNCS vol. 2567, pp. 100-115, 2003.
11. A. Fiat and M. Naor, "Broadcast Encryption," *Advances in Cryptology - CRYPTO'93*, LNCS vol. 773, pp. 480-491, 1993.
12. M. T. Goodrich, J. Z. Sun, and R. Tamassia, "Efficient Tree-Based Revocation in Groups of Low-State Devices," *Advances in Cryptology - CRYPTO'04*, LNCS vol. 3152, pp. 511-527, 2004.
13. E. Gafni, J. Staddon, and Y. L. Yin, "Efficient Methods for Intergrating Traceability and Broadcast Encryption," *Advances in Cryptology - CRYPTO'99*, LNCS vol. 1666, pp. 372-387, 1999.
14. J. Y. Hwang, D. H. Lee, and J. Lim, "Generic Transformation for Scalable Broadcast Encryption Scheme," *Advances in Cryptology - CRYPTO'05*, LNCS vol. 3621, pp. 276-292, 2005.
15. D. Halevy and A. Shamir, "The LSD broadcast encryption scheme," *Advances in Cryptology - CRYPTO'02*, LNCS vol. 2442, pp. 47-60, 2002.
16. N.-S. Jho, J. Y. Hwang, J. H. Cheon, M.-H. Kim, D. H. Lee, and E. S. Yoo, "One-Way Chain Based Broadcast Encryption Schemes," *Advances in Cryptology - EUROCRYPT'05*, LNCS vol. 3494, pp. 559-574, 2005.

17. C. H. Kim, Y. H. Hwang, and P. J. Lee, "An Efficient Public Key Trace and Revoke Scheme Secure against Adaptive Chosen Ciphertext Attack," *Advances in Cryptology - ASIACRYPT'03*, LNCS vol. 2894, pp. 359-373, 2003.

18. M. Mihaljevic, "Key Management Schemes for Stateless Receivers Based on Time Varying Heterogeneous Logical Key Hierarchy," *Advances in Cryptology - ASIACRYPT'03*, LNCS vol. 2894, pp. 137-154, 2003.

19. D. Naor, M. Naor, and J. Lostpiech, "Revocation and tracing schemes for stateless receivers," *Advances in Cryptology - CRYPTO'01*, LNCS vol. 2139, pp. 41-62, 2001.

20. M. Naor and B. Pinkas, "Efficient Trace and Revoke Schemes," *Financial Cryptography'00*, LNCS vol. 1962, pp. 1-20, 2000.

21. D. M. Wallner, E. J. Harder, and R. C. Agee, "Key management for multicast: Issues and Architectures," *IETF Network Working Group*, RFC 2627, 1999.

22. C. K. Wong, M. Gouda, and S. Lam, "Secure group communications using key graphs," *ACM SIGCOMM'98*, pp. 68-79, 1998.

Efficient Correlated Action Selection*

Mikhail J. Atallah, Marina Blanton, Keith B. Frikken, and Jiangtao Li

Department of Computer Science
Purdue University
{mja, mbykova, kbf, jtli}@cs.purdue.edu

Abstract. Participants in e-commerce and other forms of online collaborations tend to be selfish and rational, and therefore game theory has been recognized as particularly relevant to this area. In many common games, the joint strategy of the players is described by a list of pairs of actions, and one of those pairs is chosen according to a specified correlated probability distribution. In traditional game theory, a trusted third party mediator carries out this random selection, and reveals to each player its recommended action. In such games that have a correlated equilibrium, each player follows the mediator's recommendation because deviating from it cannot increase a player's expected payoff. Dodis, Halevi, and Rabin [1] described a two-party protocol that eliminates, through cryptographic means, the third party mediator. That protocol was designed and works well for a uniform distribution, but can be quite inefficient if applied to non-uniform distributions. Teague [2] has subsequently built on this work and extended it to the case where the probabilistic strategy no longer assigns equal probabilities to all the pairs of moves. Our present paper improves on the work of Teague by providing, for the same problem, a protocol whose worst-case complexity is exponentially better. The protocol also uses tools that are of independent interest.

1   Introduction

Many potentially beneficial collaborations over the Internet do not take place, even when both participants stand to gain from the interaction. One of the major reasons for this is the difficulty of finding a third party that they can both trust with not revealing (to their counterpart, or to outsiders) their private data or planned future actions and business moves. This reluctance to engage in apparently win-win collaborations results in organizations making lower-quality (and sometimes far-reaching) decisions and plans. Although this reluctance to collaborate causes large potential benefits to go unrealized, there are good reasons for it: the information learned by the third party mediator could be highly proprietary, help the competition, be inadvertently (or maliciously) leaked out and

* Portions of this work were supported by Grants IIS-0325345, IIS-0219560, IIS-0312357, and IIS-0242421 from the National Science Foundation, Contract N00014-02-1-0364 from the Office of Naval Research, by sponsors of the Center for Education and Research in Information Assurance and Security, and by Purdue Discovery Park's e-enterprise Center.

G. Di Crescenzo and A. Rubin (Eds.): FC 2006, LNCS 4107, pp. 296–310, 2006.

cause embarrassment and lawsuits, be misused, etc. In addition to this, there are substantial costs to being a mediator, not only in terms of the electronic infrastructure but in other operational costs (such as liability insurance against accidental data disclosure). Cryptography has much to contribute in solving the problem, by obviating the need for a third-party mediator. This is why the recent work of Dodis, Halevi, and Rabin [1] and Teague [2], in getting rid of the need for a mediator, has such huge practical potential in addition to its intellectual content. As our work builds on these papers, we briefly review these and explain where our contribution lies.

The framework of this paper is the same as in [1,2]: two entities want to coordinate their respective actions, implementing a strategy that is described as a set of m pairs of actions, with each pair having an associated probability of being selected (the action choices are correlated). If a pair is selected, the first (second) element of the pair is the first (second) entity's recommended action; no entity should learn the recommended action of the other (although, unavoidably inferences can be made from their knowledge of the public strategy and their own recommended action). Each party is incentivized to follow the recommendation given that an equilibrium exists, i.e., deviating from the recommended action cannot increase a party's expected payoff.

1.1   Related Work

Dodis, Halevi, and Rabin [1] described a two-party protocol that eliminates, through cryptographic means, the third party mediator: The protocol assumes a uniform distribution, selects at random and reveals to each party their respective selected action only (i.e., not the other party's action). Since cryptographic solutions have to be efficient, one might ask at what computational and communication cost this is achieved. The protocol of [1] works efficiently for a uniform distribution, but not if the distribution is non-uniform (particularly if a pair can have an associated probability much smaller than the probability of another pair). Teague [2] subsequently extended the work to non-uniform distributions, and gave a better (but still worst-case exponential) protocol for the case where pairs of moves can have widely differing probabilities. Other prior work that addresses the same problem without help from a third-party mediator includes [3,4,5,6]. All of the protocols of [3,4,1,2,5] may require communication exponential in the size of the binary description of the correlated equilibrium strategies. Our present paper improves on the work of Teague by providing, for the same problem, a protocol whose worst-case complexity is exponentially better. In addition, our protocol uses tools that are of independent interest and advantageously modify protocols recently presented in areas unrelated to the game-theoretic framework, such as [7].

Our work is not comparable to the polynomial solution given in [6], which does not apply to the important two-party case we consider here, and imposes assumptions (akin to ideal envelopes) on the physical channels used: they use general results to perform the computation for three or more parties, and then extend the protocols to achieve complete fairness during output recovery. Our work is also similar to the cryptographic randomized response techniques [8]: the protocols in [8] allow a party to choose a value according to a probability distribution. The primary difference is that in [8] one party (the pollster) learns the result, but in our problem each of the two parties learns part of the result.

1.2   Notation

The rest of the paper uses the following notation. Let k denote a security parameter. The m action pairs are denoted as $\{(a_i, b_i)\}_{i=1}^m$. Each of these pairs is chosen with a certain probability q_i, such that their overall sum is equal to 1. Each q_i is given in the rational form (i.e., same form as in prior work in this area) as a pair of integers α_i, β_i such that $q_i = \alpha_i/\beta_i$. As our protocol will use a somewhat different representation, we next describe an input conversion that we thereafter assume has already taken place prior to the protocol.

Input Conversion: Our algorithms require us to convert each q_i into an l-bit integer p_i such that $q_i = p_i / \sum_{j=1}^m p_j$. If we let L denote the least common multiple of all β_j's, then we can set $p_i = L \cdot q_i = \alpha_i(L/\beta_i)$, which implies that $\sum_{j=1}^m p_j = L$ and hence $q_i = p_i/L$. This conversion can be done in polynomial time and results in the p_i integers having a length l, which is polynomial in the number of bits in the original representation. To achieve worst-case polynomial time performance, it therefore suffices for our protocols to be polynomial in l. Let ℓ denote the integer such that $2^{\ell-1} < L \leq 2^\ell$: if $L < 2^\ell$, we pad the probabilities with a "dummy" $p_{m+1} = 2^\ell - L$, so that $\sum_{i=1}^{m+1} p_i = 2^\ell$. Note that this is done only for ease of computation and the $(1+m)$th outcome is never chosen: if a protocol execution returns the $(1+m)$th outcome, the computation is restarted. The probability of restart is $p_{m+1}/(2^\ell) < 1/2$. In the rest of this paper we assume that the m tuples (a_i, b_i, p_i) contain a dummy element (whose action pair is a "restart protocol" recommendation to both parties) if necessary.

1.3   Comparison with Previous Work

Our results are the following: a protocol for the malicious (resp., honest-but-curious) model has computation and communication complexity $O(m\ell)$ (resp., $O(m + \ell \log m)$). See Table 1 for performance comparison with the prior work.

Note that secure function evaluation using generic garbled circuits constitutes a viable alternative to the solutions given in this work, especially since recent results (see, e.g., [9]) provide significant improvements over the initial results. Any solution using circuits, however, will require at least $O(m\ell)$ gates, while in this work we concentrate on finding solutions asymptotically as low as possible. In addition, any protocol that requires a majority of the players to be honest (which is the case in [9]) does not provide security against malicious behavior in the two-party case.

In the equal-probabilities case, the protocol of choice is that of [1]. Thus the following discussion is for the case of unequal probabilities. For the malicious model, our protocol is better than the previous approach of [2] in both asymptotic worst-case and in practical sense, as our protocol is polynomial *and* does

Table 1. Comparisons of *worst case* performance (computation and communication cost) of our and prior work. Here m is the number of action pairs, ℓ is the number of bits representing the probabilities, and σ is a security parameter for the cut-and-choose technique (i.e., the adversary can cheat with the probability no more than $1/\sigma$) that must be linear in the payoffs to make the expected gain from cheating negative.

	Teague [2]	SFE [10,11,9]	Our Protocols
honest-but-curious	$O(\max\{m, 2^\ell\})$	$O(m\ell)$	$O(m + \ell \log m)$
malicious	$O(\sigma \cdot \max\{m, 2^\ell\})$	$O(m\ell)$	$O(m\ell)$

not use the cut-and-choose technique as in [2]. For the honest-but-curious model, however, we can only claim an improvement in the worst-case asymptotic complexity, as there are inputs for which the approach of [2] is more practical, e.g., inputs where the number of bits (call it t) representing the smallest input probability is small enough that a complexity proportional to 2^t can compete with our $poly(\ell)$ complexity. Of course, the honest-but-curious model is of limited practical value in the kind of environments where these protocols are used, so one would almost always need to assume a stronger adversary model.

The rest of the paper is organized as follows. Section 2 gives preliminaries, our protocol, and security proofs for the semi-curious model. In section 3, we deal with malicious adversaries and provide additional cryptographic tools and our protocols for that setting.

2   A Protocol for the Honest-But-Curious Case

2.1   Security Model

Informally, we say that a two-party protocol Π *privately* computes function f if anything that can be obtained from a party's view during a semi-honest execution of Π could also be obtained from the input and the output of that party themselves. We use the standard model, and the following definition, similar to the one given in [11], formalizes our notion of security.

Definition 1. *Let $f_1(x, y)$ and $f_2(x, y)$ be the first and the second elements of $f(x, y)$, respectively. Let $\mathrm{VIEW}_1^\Pi(x, y)$ (resp., $\mathrm{VIEW}_2^\Pi(x, y)$) denote the view of the first (resp., second) party during an execution of Π on (x, y). The views are defined as $(x, r_1, m_1, \ldots, m_d)$ and $(y, r_2, m_1, \ldots, m_d)$ for the first and second parties, respectively, where r_1 (resp., r_2) is the outcome of internal coin tosses of the first (resp. second) player and $m_1, \ldots, m_d$ are the messages that it received during the protocol execution. Also let $\mathrm{OUTPUT}_1^\Pi(x, y)$ (resp, $\mathrm{OUTPUT}_2^\Pi(x, y)$) denote the first (resp., second) player's output after an execution Π on (x, y); and let $\mathrm{OUTPUT}^\Pi(x, y) = (\mathrm{OUTPUT}_1^\Pi(x, y), \mathrm{OUTPUT}_2^\Pi(x, y))$. Then Π privately computes f if there exist probabilistic polynomial-time algorithms M_1 and M_2 such that the ensembles $\{M_1(x, f_1(x, y)), f(x, y)\}_{x,y}$ and $\{\mathrm{VIEW}_1^\Pi(x, y), \mathrm{OUTPUT}^\Pi(x, y)\}_{x,y}$ and the ensembles $\{M_2(y, f_2(x, y)), f(x, y)\}_{x,y}$ and $\{\mathrm{VIEW}_2^\Pi(x, y), \mathrm{OUTPUT}^\Pi(x, y)\}_{x,y}$ are computationally indistinguishable. Machine M_1 (resp., M_2) is* called a *simulator for the interaction of the first (resp., second) player with the second (resp., first) player.*

2.2 Homomorphic Paillier Encryption

Our protocols in the honest-but-curious setting use the homomorphic Paillier encryption scheme [12,13], which was first developed by Paillier [12] and then extended by Damgård and Jurik [13]. Let $n = pq$ be an RSA modulus, with $p = 2p'+1$ and $q = 2q'+1$ where p, q, p', and q' are primes. Given a message $M \in \mathbb{Z}_n$, we use $Enc^P(M)$ to denote encryption of M under the Paillier encryption scheme. By the homomorphic property, $Enc^P(a) \cdot Enc^P(b) = E(a + b \bmod n)$. It is easy to see that $Enc^P(a)^c = Enc^P(c \cdot a \bmod n)$. A homomorphic Paillier encryption scheme is *semantically secure* under the decisional composite residuosity assumption [12].

2.3 The Element Selection Protocol

As before, the (a_i, b_i) pairs are the move pairs in the joint strategy of the game, where the a_i's (resp., b_i's) are possible moves for Alice (resp., Bob). During the protocol, one of the indices $\{1, \dots, m\}$ is selected randomly, where the probability of i being selected is $p_i/2^\ell$. The selected index (call it j) is not known to either Alice or Bob, who learn only their respective recommended moves: a_j for Alice, b_j for Bob. Note that, unavoidably, Alice's learning of her move does probabilistically reveal something about Bob's recommended move, and vice-versa (this comes from the game theoretic problem formulation and is true of any protocol, including [1,2]).

Our protocol can be thought of as a secure version of the following naive (and in this form flawed) approach: Alice and Bob compute $P_i = \sum_{k=1}^{i} p_k$ for $1 \le i \le m$, and then generate a random value $r \in [0, 2^\ell - 1]$. Since the probability that $r \in [P_{i-1}, P_i)$ equals to $p_i/2^\ell$, Alice and Bob find the index i corresponding to the chosen r and choose actions a_i and b_i, respectively. Making the above simple idea work involves many challenges. Our protocol is presented next.

Setup: Alice generates a key pair (pk, sk) for the homomorphic Paillier encryption scheme such that $|n| = k$ and $n > 2^\ell + 1$, where k is a security parameter. We separate this step from the protocol itself, because in this application the correlated element selection may be executed by two parties on a regular basis, while it is sufficient to select the keys only once.

Input: Items $\{(a_i, b_i, p_i)\}_{i=1}^{m}$ are known to both parties; public key pk is known to both and secret key sk is known only to Alice.

Output: Alice obtains the value of a_j, and Bob obtains the value of b_j, where j is the index selected according to the probability distribution.

Protocol Steps

1. Alice encrypts each item in each triplet obtaining $\{(Enc^P(a_i), Enc^P(b_i), Enc^P(p_i))\}_{i=1}^{m}$. She then picks a random permutation π_a over $[m]$ and

permutes the encrypted triplets obtaining $\{Enc^P(a_{\pi_a(i)}),\ Enc^P(b_{\pi_a(i)}),\ Enc^P(p_{\pi_a(i)})\}_{i=1}^m$ and sends them to Bob.

2. Bob picks a random permutation π_b over $[m]$ and permutes the encrypted triplets received in the previous step. Let $(Enc^P(a_i'), Enc^P(b_i'), Enc^P(p_i'))$ denote $(Enc^P(a_{\pi_b(\pi_a(i))}),\ Enc^P(b_{\pi_b(\pi_a(i))}),\ Enc^P(p_{\pi_b(\pi_a(i))}))$ for $i = 1, \ldots, m$.

3. We use P_i' to denote $\sum_{k=1}^i p_k'$. For each $i = 1, \ldots, m$, Bob computes $Enc^P(P_i')$ $= \prod_{k=1}^i Enc^P(p_k') = Enc^P(p_1' + \cdots + p_i')$.

4. For $i = 1, \ldots, m$, Bob uniformly generates a random value $y_i \overset{R}{\leftarrow} \mathbb{Z}_n$ and computes $Enc^P(P_i' - y_i) = Enc^P(P_i') \cdot Enc^P(-y_i)$. He sends $\{Enc^P(P_i' - y_i)\}_{i=1}^m$ to Alice.

5. Alice decrypts $\{Enc^P(P_i' - y_i)\}_{i=1}^m$ and obtains $\{P_i' - y_i \bmod n\}_{i=1}^m$. Let x_i denote $P_i' - y_i \bmod n$. At this point, Alice has $\{x_i\}_{i=1}^m$ and Bob has $\{y_i\}_{i=1}^m$, such that $x_i + y_i \bmod n = P_i'$.

6. Alice picks $r_a \overset{R}{\leftarrow} \{0,1\}^\ell$ and Bob picks $r_b \overset{R}{\leftarrow} \{0,1\}^\ell$. Let r denote $r_a \oplus r_b$. Clearly, r is a random ℓ-bit integer.

7. Alice and Bob jointly find the index of the value P_i' such that $r < P_i'$ and $r \geq P_{i-1}'$ (if P_{i-1}' exists) from the list $\{P_i'\}_{i=1}^m$ using the binary search protocol described in section 2.4. Let the outcome of the search be index j.

8. Bob chooses a random $\rho \overset{R}{\leftarrow} \mathbb{Z}_n$, computes $\{\gamma_1, \gamma_2\} = \{Enc^P(a_j' + 0), Enc^P (b_j' - \rho)\}$, and sends the pair to Alice[1]. Alice decrypts $\{\gamma_1, \gamma_2\}$, obtains $\{a_j', b_j' - \rho\}$, and sends $b_j' - \rho$ back to Bob. In the end, Alice learns a_j' and Bob learns b_j'.

The complexity of this protocol is $O(m + \ell \log m)$ and the round complexity is $O(\log m)$. Note that any other known solution (e.g., using general circuit simulation results) is less efficient and requires at least $O(m\ell)$ computation.

2.4   Binary Search Protocol

This section gives an efficient search protocol for step 7 of the element selection protocol for semi-honest players. We use binary search to compute which action the randomly chosen r corresponds to, i.e., the index j such that $r \in [P_{i-1}', P_i')$.

Input: Alice has $\{x_i\}_{i=1}^m$ and Bob has $\{y_i\}_{i=1}^m$ such that $P_i' = x_i + y_i \bmod n$, $0 < P_i' \leq 2^\ell$, and $P_i' < P_{i+1}'$. Alice has r_a and Bob has r_b, such that $r = r_a \oplus r_b$.

Output: The index j such that $r < P_i'$ and $r \geq P_{i-1}'$ (if P_{i-1}' exists).

Protocol Steps: Alice and Bob execute the following recursive procedure on the list $\{P_i'\}_{i=1}^m$:

1. If the size of the current working set $|\{P_i', \ldots, P_j'\}| = 1$, return i.
2. Otherwise, Alice and Bob run a scrambled circuit evaluation protocol [10,11] to compute whether $r \geq P_{\lceil \frac{j-i+1}{2} \rceil}'$ (i.e., compute whether $r_a \oplus r_b \geq x_{\lceil \frac{j-i+1}{2} \rceil} +$

---

[1] Here $Enc^P(a_j' + 0)$ is computed by $Enc^P(a_j') \cdot Enc^P(0)$. We intentionally randomize $Enc^P(a_j')$.

$y_{\lceil\frac{i-i+1}{2}\rceil}$ mod n). Let c denote the outcome of the protocol that returns 1 if the condition holds, and 0 otherwise. Note that we can use the technique from [14] to reduce the communication and computation from being a function of $k = |n|$ to a function of $\ell + 1$ (i.e., the number of bits required to represent the value $P'_{\lceil\frac{i-i+1}{2}\rceil}$).

3. If $c = 1$, recurse on list $\{P'_{\lceil\frac{i-i+1}{2}\rceil+1}, \ldots, P'_j\}$; otherwise, recurse on list $\{P'_i, \ldots, P'_{\lceil\frac{i-i+1}{2}\rceil}\}$.

Step 2 takes $O(\ell)$ communication and computation and $O(1)$ rounds, therefore the overall complexity is $O(\ell \log m)$ and the round complexity is $O(\log m)$.

Lemma 1. *The protocol for binary search is secure against honest-but-curious adversaries.*

Proof (Sketch). The basic idea behind this proof is that from a particular index, i.e., from the output of the binary search, one can easily simulate the individual zigs and zags of the binary search. It is worth noting that this is similar to the proof of [15]. □

2.5   Security Proofs

To be able to show the correctness of the element-selection protocol, we first prove that, if both Alice and Bob follow the protocol, the output pair of actions is selected according to the probability distribution.

Lemma 2. *For any $i \in \{1, \ldots, m\}$, the probability that the randomly chosen $r \in \{0, 1\}^\ell$ results in index i being returned, is equal to $p'_i/2^\ell$.*

Proof. Let us set $P'_0 = 0$. The probability that index i is returned, equals the probability that $r \in [P'_{i-1}, P'_i)$. This is equal to $(P'_i - P'_{i-1})/2^\ell = p'_i/2^\ell$. □

Recall that the binary search step of the element-selection protocol reveals the index, so we next prove that this index does not leak any information.

Lemma 3. *Let π be a random permutation over $[m]$ and let r be a random value in $\{0, 1\}^\ell$. Given any set $\{p_i\}_{i=1}^m$ such that $\sum_{i=1}^m p_i = 2^\ell$, the probability of $r \in \left[\sum_{k=1}^{i-1} p_{\pi(k)}, \sum_{k=1}^i p_{\pi(k)}\right)$ is equal to $1/m$ for $i = 1, \ldots, m$.*

Proof. Let us fix i. We have

$$\mathbf{Pr}\left[r \in \left[\sum_{k=1}^{i-1} p_{\pi(k)}, \sum_{k=1}^i p_{\pi(k)}\right)\right] = \frac{p_k \cdot \mathbf{Pr}[k = \pi(i)]}{2^\ell} = \frac{1}{2^\ell}\sum_{k=1}^m \frac{p_k}{m} = \frac{1}{2^\ell}\cdot\frac{2^\ell}{m} = \frac{1}{m}$$

In other words, if π and r are random, the output of the binary search in the element-selection protocol does not depend on $\{p_i\}_{i=1}^m$ and is uniformly distributed over $[1, m]$, i.e., it can be simulated by a random value in $[1, m]$. □

Theorem 1. *The element-selection protocol is secure against honest-but-curious adversaries.*

Proof. Correctness: Follows directly from Lemma 2.

Secrecy: To show that the element-selection protocol is secure, it is sufficient to show that there exists a simulator M_1 (resp., M_2) that, given Alice's (resp., Bob's) input and output, can simulate Alice's (resp., Bob's) interaction with Bob (resp., Alice) during the execution of the protocol, such the Alice's (resp., Bob's) view in real execution is computationally indistinguishable from the view produced by the simulator. That is, according to Definition 1:

$$\{M_1(x, f_1(x,y)), f(x,y)\}_{x,y} \overset{c}{\equiv} \{\text{VIEW}_1^{\Pi}(x,y), \text{OUTPUT}^{\Pi}(x,y)\}_{x,y}$$

$$\{M_2(y, f_2(x,y)), f(x,y)\}_{x,y} \overset{c}{\equiv} \{\text{VIEW}_2^{\Pi}(x,y), \text{OUTPUT}^{\Pi}(x,y)\}_{x,y}$$

where $\overset{c}{\equiv}$ denotes computational indistinguishability by families of polynomial-size circuits.

Consider the following simulator $M_1(\{(a_i, b_i, p_i)\}_{i=1}^m, a'_j)$:

1. On receipt of the first message from Alice, for $i = 1, \ldots, m$ randomly select $x_i \overset{R}{\leftarrow} \mathbb{Z}_n$ and send $\{Enc^P(x_i)\}_{i=1}^m$ to Alice.
2. Select $r_b \overset{R}{\leftarrow} \{0,1\}^\ell$. At random select m distinct values from $\{0,1\}^\ell$, sort them in the increasing order obtaining $\{r_1, \ldots, r_m\}$, and set $y_i = Enc^P(r_i - x_i \bmod n)$ for $i = 1, \ldots, m$. Engage in the execution of the binary search protocol with Alice using r_b and $\{y_i\}_{i=1}^m$ as input. At the end of the execution Alice receives a random index i as the outcome of the protocol.
3. Select a random $w \overset{R}{\leftarrow} \mathbb{Z}_n$, compute $\{Enc^P(a'_j), Enc^P(w)\}$, and send the pair to Alice.

According to Definition 1, Alice's view during an execution of the element-selection protocol Π is $\text{VIEW}_1^{\Pi} = (x, r_1, m_1, m_2, m_3)$. The distribution of x and r_1 remains the same for all possible input values, regardless of whether M_1 is used or a real protocol execution is performed. Next, we examine the messages that Alice receives. Let $M_1(x, f_1(x,y)) = (x', r'_1, m'_1, m'_2, m'_3)$.

Message m_1 is received in Step 4 of Π and is $m_1 = \{Enc^P(P'_i - y_i)\}_{i=1}^m$; message m'_1 is received in Step 1 of simulation and is $m'_1 = \{Enc^P(x_i)\}_{i=1}^m$. Due to the semantic security of the encryption scheme, encrypted values are uniformly distributed over the entire range resulting in identical distributions. After Alice decrypts the values, she still cannot distinguish between $P'_i - y_i$ and x_i because y_i's and x_i's are uniformly distributed over $\mathbb{Z}_n$.

Let us use Π_s to denote the binary search protocol of section 2.4. Then $m_2 = (\text{VIEW}_1^{\Pi_s}(x_s, y_s), i)$ and $m'_2 = (\text{VIEW}_1^{\Pi_s}(x'_s, y'_s), i')$, where $x_s = (\{x_i\}_{i=1}^m, r_a)$, $y_s = (\{y_i\}_{i=1}^m, r_b)$, $x'_s = (\{x'_i\}_{i=1}^m, r'_a)$, and $y'_s = (\{y'_i\}_{i=1}^m, r'_b)$, and all of $\{x_i\}_{i=1}^m$ and $\{x'_i\}_{i=1}^m$, $\{y_i\}_{i=1}^m$ and $\{y'_i\}_{i=1}^m$, r_a and r'_a, and r_b and r'_b are pair-wise identically distributed. From Lemma 1 we obtain that the execution of Π does not leak any private information, and Lemma 3 tells us that i is uniformly distributed over $[1, m]$, and so is i'. Therefore m_2 and m'_2 are also indistinguishable.

Lastly, $m_3 = \{Enc^P(a_j'), Enc^P(b_j' - \rho)\}$ and $m_3' = \{Enc^P(a_j'), Enc^P(\omega)\}$. After Alice decrypts the values, the value of $b_j' - \rho$ is identically distributed to ω, and a_j' is the same in both messages. Also, no information can be gained from the encrypted values themselves. Thus m_3 and m_3' are also indistinguishable.

Since we had $f(x, y) = \text{OUTPUT}^\Pi(x, y)$, we conclude Alice's view during an execution of Π is computationally indistinguishable from a simulation. The simulator M_2 for Bob's interaction can be constructed in a similar way and is omitted. Thus, Π privately computes the correlated action selection function.   □

3   Handling Dishonest Behavior

In the previous section, we gave an efficient element-selection protocol for the honest-but-curious model. However, it is inefficient to make the preceding protocol secure against malicious adversaries, as the zero-knowledge proofs for certain steps of the protocol are very expensive. Instead, we present a new protocol for the malicious model, which uses two-party computation based on the conditional gate and relies on the use of threshold homomorphic ElGamal encryption.

3.1   Review of Cryptographic Tools Used

Homomorphic ElGamal Encryption. Let G_q be a finite cyclic group of a prime order q, $|q| = k$, and g be the group's generator such that the Decision Diffie-Hellman (DDH) problem for G_q is assumed to be hard.[2] Given a published generator g, a public-private key pair for ElGamal encryption is generated as $(pk, sk) = (y, x)$, where $x \xleftarrow{R} \mathbb{Z}_q$ and $y = g^x$. Given a public key y and a message $M \in \mathbb{Z}_q$, encryption is performed as $Enc_y^G(M) = (\alpha, \beta) = (g^r, g^M y^r)$, where $r \xleftarrow{R} \mathbb{Z}_q$. Given the private key x, decryption of $(\alpha, \beta) = (g^r, g^M y^r)$ is performed by first computing $\beta/\alpha^x = g^M$ and then solving it for $M \in \mathbb{Z}_q$. This amounts to solving a discrete log problem and thus the message space must be small. In our protocols, the message space is $\{0, 1\}$ in most cases.

Such encryption is additively homomorphic, that is $Enc_y^G(a_1) \cdot Enc_y^G(a_2) = (g^{r_1} \cdot g^{r_2}, g^{a_1} y^{r_1} \cdot g^{a_2} y^{r_2}) = (g^{r_1+r_2}, g^{a_1+a_2} y^{r_1+r_2}) = Enc_y^G(a_1 + a_2)$. In addition, $Enc_{pk}^G(a)^b = Enc_{pk}^G(ab)$. Also, homomorphic ElGamal encryption is semantically secure assuming that the DDH problem is hard. When it is clear from the context or not essential to the discussion, we omit the encryption key from the notation and use $Enc^G(x)$ instead.

When Alice generates a ciphertext using homomorphic ElGamal encryption, she can prove that she knows the plaintext for the encryption using the techniques of [16]. She can make this a non-interactive proof of knowledge using Fiat-Shamir techniques [17]. Another proof of knowledge used in our protocols is a proof that a particular encryption is the encryption of 0 or 1. This protocol follows from the ability to prove the disjunction of two boolean values [18], and was given in [19].

---

[2] From this point on, arithmetic is assumed to be modulo q and operator $\mod q$ is implicit for each arithmetic operation.

Threshold Homomorphic ElGamal Encryption. Homomorphic ElGamal encryption scheme can be used to construct (t, n)-threshold cryptosystem, where $0 < t \leq n$. In this case, the key is generated jointly by n parties, and decryption succeeds only if at least t parties participate. Encryption is performed in the traditional way, where anyone can use the public key y to encrypt messages.

Let $A_1, \ldots, A_n$ denote n players. As before, let the public key be y and let the private key be x with $y = g^x$. Then player A_i has a share x_i of the private key, where $y_i = g^{x_i}$ is public. Such shares can be generated using a secure distributed key generation protocol such as [20,21], with communication complexity of $O(n^2 k)$ and a small hidden constant, where k is a security parameter.

To recover message M from its encryption (α, β), each player A_i computes a decryption share $d_i = \alpha^{x_i}$ and a proof that $\log_\alpha d_i = \log_g h_i$. Then having t correct decryption shares, M can be recovered from $g^M = \beta/\alpha^x$ by computing α^x from these shares using Lagrange interpolation. Decryption of private outputs is also possible in this framework, and it was shown in [7] how private output decryption used in RSA-like cryptosystem (such as Paillier's) can be modified to avoid having to decrypt an ElGamal encryption of a random messages in $\mathbb{Z}_q$. A non-interactive version of the protocol is also possible and can be found in [7].

Threshold homomorphic ElGamal cryptosystem is robust for $t < n/2$, but (non-robust) fairness can also be achieved for the two-party case using $(2, 2)$-threshold scheme. Note that neither party gains any advantage by quitting at an intermediate step of a protocol, and thus to achieve fairness, only the decryption phase of the protocols needs to be considered. This can be done using gradual release of information for a security parameter $k' < \log q$. See [7] for more detail. Note that allowing parties to prematurely quit during protocol execution will not allow us to finish the execution (and thus prove indistinguishability with the view in the ideal setting), and the protocol must be restarted.

Two-Party Computation Based on the Conditional Gate. A recent work of Schoenmakers and Tuyls [7] introduced a new type of multiplication gate called *conditional gate* that permits efficient computation of two-party multiplication. In short, conditional gates permit efficient multiplication of x and y using homomorphic threshold ElGamal, where x is from a two-valued domain and y is unrestricted. In that work, conditional gates are also used to perform other types of secure computations such as XOR and different kinds of comparisons. In particular, the authors show how to perform comparison of two bitwise encrypted values x and y. Such operation requires ℓ rounds and $2\ell - 1$ conditional gates, where $|x| = |y| = \ell$, with the total of about 12ℓ modular exponentiations.

While individual operations are rather efficient and secure against malicious adversaries, the difficulty in applying these techniques to general function evaluation is in different representation of operands in such operations. That is, some operands are encrypted integers $x \in \mathbb{Z}_q$, while others are required to be encrypted in bitwise form, and there is no conversion procedure available between the two encryption formats.

Mixes. One of the building blocks in our work is a mix, which was introduced in [22]. The parties "mix" a list of values by re-encrypting the values and permuting the order of the individual values. Furthermore, our protocols for the malicious model require that the mixing party be able to prove that the values were mixed properly. Also, we require that the protocols be able to mix vectors of values (where the vector consists of several encrypted values and the vector must be preserved). Examples of efficient mixes are [23,24], and protocols for achieving a permutation of vectors can be found in [25].

3.2   The Element Selection Protocol

As before, we assume that $\sum_{i=1}^{m} p_i = 2^\ell$. We use $[a_i]_{\ell-1} \ldots [a_i]_0$ to denote the binary representation of a_i. For the purposes of this and subsequent sections, homomorphic ElGamal $(2, 2)$-threshold encryption is used.

Setup: Alice and Bob generate a key pair (pk, sk) for a security parameter k, where public key pk is known to both, but secret key sk is shared and is not known to either party.

Input: Items $\{(a_i, b_i, p_i)\}_{i=1}^{m}$ are known to both parties; public key pk is known to both and secret key sk is not known to either.

Output: Alice learns a_j, and Bob learns b_j, where j is the index selected according to the probability distribution.

Protocol Steps

1. Alice encrypts tuples $\{(a_i, b_i, [p_i]_\ell, [p_i]_{\ell-1} \ldots [p_i]_0)\}_{i=1}^{m}$ with pk and then mixes them using a permutation π_a that she randomly generates. In the above, each of a_i and b_i are encrypted as an integer, but p_i's are encrypted bit by bit as $\ell + 1$ bit integers (i.e., the most significant bit is always 0).
   Alice proves in zero-knowledge that the output of this step was obtained using mixing π_a on the tuples $\{(a_i, b_i, p_i)\}_{i=1}^{m}$. Note that in order for Alice to prove proper mixing using known techniques, she first encrypts the list using no randomness (i.e., 0 in place of random values) and then proves that her output is a blinded permuted re-encryption of this list.
2. Bob blinds each of the items $(Enc^G(a_{\pi_a(i)}), Enc^G(b_{\pi_a(i)}), Enc^G([p_{\pi_a(i)}]_\ell),$ $\ldots, Enc^G([p_{\pi_a(i)}]_0))$ by multiplying each value with $Enc^G(0)$ and mixes the tuples using a random permutation π_b. Let $(Enc^G(a_i'), Enc^G(b_i'), Enc^G(p_i'))$ denote $(Enc^G(a_{\pi_b(\pi_a(i))}), Enc^G(b_{\pi_b(\pi_a(i))}), Enc^G(p_{\pi_b(\pi_a(i))}))$ for $i = 1, \ldots, m$. Bob proves in zero-knowledge that his output was constructed by applying a random mix π_b to his input.
3. Alice and Bob compute $(Enc^G(a_i'), Enc^G(b_i'), Enc^G([P_i']_\ell), \ldots, Enc^G([P_i']_0))$, where $P_i' = \sum_{i=1}^{m} p_i'$. The description of this step (i.e., the addition operation) is given in section 3.3.
4. Alice picks $r_a \overset{R}{\leftarrow} \{0,1\}^\ell$, computes $\{Enc^G([r_a]_{\ell-1}), \ldots, Enc^G([r_a]_0)\}$ and sends it to Bob. She also proves in zero-knowledge that each $[r_a]_i$ in the encryptions corresponds to either 0 or 1. Similarly, Bob picks $r_b \overset{R}{\leftarrow} \{0,1\}^\ell$,

sends Alice $\{Enc^G([r_b]_{\ell-1}), \ldots, Enc^G([r_b]_0)\}$, and proves in zero-knowledge that each $[r_b]_i$ corresponds to a single bit.

5. Alice and Bob compute the bitwise encrypted value of $x = r_a + r_b \mod 2^\ell$ using the addition protocol of section 3.3. They prepend bitwise encrypted x with $Enc^G(0)$ to obtain $(\ell + 1)$-bit representation of x.

6. Alice and Bob jointly find the index of the value P'_i such that $x < P'_i$ and $x \geq P'_{i-1}$ (if P'_{i-1} exists) from the list $\{Enc^G([P'_i]_\ell), \ldots, Enc^G([P'_i]_0)\}_{i=1}^m$ using the binary search algorithm described in section 3.5. Let the outcome of the search be index j.

7. Having $Enc^G(a'_j)$ and $Enc^G(b'_j)$, Alice helps Bob to decrypt b'_j and Bob helps Alice to decrypt a'_j (see section 3.1 for detail).

Note that most of the work done in step 1 can be performed in advance (if the public key is available prior to protocol execution), by generating as many encryptions of 0's and 1's as needed. At the time of protocol execution, Alice then just selects the right combination of such encryptions to match the p_i's. Similarly, values for the zero-knowledge proof in that step and encryptions of 0 in step 2 can be pre-computed, thus reducing computational cost of asymptotically least efficient parts of the protocol.

The security proof of the protocol is omitted. One interesting direction for future work is to narrow the gap in the complexities between the semi-honest and malicious models.

3.3   Addition of Bitwise Encrypted Values

Here we first present an addition protocol with computational and round complexity of $O(\ell)$. After its description we show how its round complexity can be significantly lowered using standard techniques.

Input: Common input consists of encryptions $\{Enc^G([x]_{\ell-1}), \ldots, Enc^G([x]_0)\}$ and $\{Enc^G([y]_{\ell-1}), \ldots, Enc^G([y]_0)\}$.

Output: Alice and Bob obtain $\{Enc^G([z]_{\ell-1}), \ldots, Enc^G([z]_0)\}$, where $z = x + y \mod 2^\ell$.

Protocol Steps

1. Alice and Bob compute encryptions of $[z]_0 = [x]_0$ XOR $[y]_0$ and $c = x_0$ AND y_0 as follows. Computation of $Enc^G(c) = Enc^G([x]_0 \cdot [y]_0)$ is performed using the conditional gate; then computation of $Enc^G([z]_0) = Enc^G([x]_0 + [y]_0 - 2[x]_0 \cdot [y]_0) = Enc^G([x]_0 + [y]_0 - 2c)$ is performed locally using common randomness.

2. For $i = 1, \ldots, \ell - 1$, Alice and Bob compute encryptions of $[z]_i = (([x]_i$ XOR $[y]_i)$ XOR $c)$ and $c = $ MAJ$([x]_i, [y]_i, c)$ as follows:

   (a) Using the conditional gate, Alice and Bob compute $Enc^G(a_{xy}) = Enc^G([x]_i \cdot [y]_i)$, $Enc^G(a_{xc}) = Enc([x]_i \cdot c)$, $Enc^G(a_{yc}) = Enc([y]_i \cdot c)$, and $Enc^G(a_{xyc}) = Enc^G([x]_i \cdot [y]_i \cdot c)$.

(b) Using common randomness, Alice and Bob locally compute $Enc^G([z]_i) = Enc^G(4a_{xyc} - 2a_{xy} - 2a_{xc} - 2a_{yc} + [x]_i + [y]_i + c)$ and then $Enc^G(c) = Enc^G(a_{xy} + a_{xc} + a_{yc} - 2a_{xyc})$.

Logarithmic depth addition of two integers is carried out by the textbook carry-lookahead addition circuit [26] that has logarithmic depth and linear size (number of Boolean gates). Given $p_1, \ldots, p_m$, the prefix sum problem [27] is to compute all the sums $p_1 + \ldots + p_i$, $i = 1, \ldots, m$. It can be solved by a logarithmic depth circuit with a linear number of addition nodes [27]. If each addition node of the circuit of [27] is replaced by the circuit of [26], then the resulting Boolean circuit for the prefix problem for ℓ-bit numbers has $O(m\ell)$ gates and depth $O(\log m \log \ell)$. However, the use of the Wallace tree technique [28] is known to reduce the depth to $O(\log m + \log \ell)$ (see, e.g., [29]).

3.4 Constant-Round Comparison

Although we could carry out comparison in our model using the method given in [7], this would require $O(\ell)$ number of rounds. Below we give a constant-round comparison protocol, which is of independent interest.

Input: Alice and Bob each have encryptions $\{Enc^G([x]_{\ell-1}), \ldots, Enc^G([x]_0)\}$ and $\{Enc^G([y]_{\ell-1}), \ldots, Enc^G([y]_0)\}$.

Output: Alice and Bob obtain 1 if $x \geq y$, and 0 otherwise.

Protocol Steps

1. Alice and Bob both locally compute $Enc^G(e_{\ell-1}) = Enc^G(x_{\ell-1} - y_{\ell-1})$ and then compute $Enc^G(e_i) = Enc^G(2e_{i+1} + x_i - y_i)$ for all $i \in \{\ell - 2, \ldots, 0\}$. Note that the value e_i will be 0 until the first difference between x and y.
2. Alice and Bob locally compute $Enc^G(f_{\ell-1}) = Enc^G(y_{\ell-1} - x_{\ell-1} - 1)$ and then $Enc^G(f_i) = Enc^G(3e_{i+1} + y_i - x_i - 1)$ for all $i \in \{\ell - 2, \ldots, 0\}$. Note that the value f_i will be 0 if the first $i - 1$ bits are equal and the ith bit of x is false and the ith bit of y is true. Thus if there is a single 0 entry (and there will be at most one) then $x < y$ and otherwise $x \geq y$.
3. Alice and Bob raise $Enc^G(f_i)$ to a random power (a protocol for doing this was described in [30]). Note that now the list of values will contain a 0 if $x < y$ and will be a set of random non-zero values otherwise.
4. Alice mixes the list and sends the mixed list to Bob along with a proof of proper mixing. Similarly, Bob mixes the list and sends the mixed list to Alice along with a proof of proper mixing.
5. Alice and Bob jointly decrypt the list and if a single entry is 0, then they output 0. If no entry is 0, then they output 1.

3.5 Binary Search

Here we give an efficient search protocol for step 6 of the main protocol. The overall complexity is $O(\ell \log m)$ and the round complexity is $O(\log m)$.

Input: A list of sorted bitwise encrypted m values $\{Enc^G([y_i]_{\ell-1}), \ldots, Enc^G([y_i]_0)\}_{i=1}^m$ and value x bitwise encrypted as $Enc^G([x]_{\ell-1}), \ldots, Enc^G([x]_0)$.

Output: The smallest index j such that $y_j > x$.

Protocol Steps: Alice and Bob execute the following recursive procedure on the bitwise-encrypted list $\{y_i\}_{i=1}^m$:

1. If the size of the current working set $|\{y_i, \ldots, y_j\}| = 1$, return i.
2. Otherwise, Alice and Bob execute the constant-round comparison protocol (see section 3.4) on (the encrypted values of) x and $y_{\lceil \frac{j-i+1}{2} \rceil}$ (i.e., check whether $x \geq y_{\lceil \frac{j-i+1}{2} \rceil}$). Let c denote the outcome of the protocol.
3. If $c = 1$, recurse on list $\{y_{\lceil \frac{j-i+1}{2} \rceil+1}, \ldots, y_j\}$; otherwise, recurse on list $\{y_i, \ldots, y_{\lceil \frac{j-i+1}{2} \rceil}\}$.

Acknowledgments

The authors are thankful to anonymous reviewers for their valuable feedback on this work.

References

1. Dodis, Y., Halevi, S., Rabin, T.: A cryptographic solution to a game theoretic problem. In: Advances in Cryptology – Crypto'00. (2000)
2. Teague, V.: Selecting correlated random actions. In: Financial Cryptography. Volume 3110. (2004) 181–195
3. Bárány, I.: Fair distribution protocols or how the players replace fortune. Mathematics of Operation Research **17** (1992) 327–341
4. Ben-Porath, E.: Correlation without mediation: Expanding the set of equilibria outcomes by "cheap" pre-play procedures. Journal of Economic Theory **80** (1998) 108–122
5. Gerardi, D.: Unmediated communication in games with complete and incomplete information. Journal of Economic Theory **114** (2004)
6. Lepinski, M., Micali, S., Peikert, C., Shelat, A.: Completely fair SFE and coalition-safe cheap talk. In: Symposium on Principles of Distributed Computing (PODC'04). (2004) 1–10
7. Schoenmakers, B., Tuyls, P.: Practical two-party computation based on the conditional gate. In: ASIACRYPT'04. Volume 3329. (2004) 119–136
8. Ambainis, A., Jakobsson, M., Lipmaa, H.: Cryptographic randomized response techniques. In: Workshop on Theory and Practice in Public Key Cryptography (PKC'04). Volume 2947 of LNCS. (2004) 425–438
9. Damgård, I., Ishai, Y.: Constant-round multiparty computation using a black-box pseudorandom generator. In: Advances in Cryptology – CRYPTO'05. Volume 3621 of LNCS. (2005) 378–411
10. Yao, A.: How to generate and exchange secrets. In: Proceedings of the 27th IEEE Symposium on Foundations of Computer Science, IEEE Computer Society Press (1986) 162–167

11. Goldreich, O.: The Foundations of Cryptography — Volume 2. Cambridge University Press (2004)
12. Paillier, P.: Public-key cryptosystems based on composite degree residuosity classes. In: Advances in Cryptology: EUROCRYPT '99. Volume 1592 of Lecture Notes in Computer Science., Springer (1999) 223–238
13. Damgård, I., Jurik, M.: A generalisation, a simplification and some applications of paillier's probabilistic public-key system. In: PKC '01: Proceedings of the 4th International Workshop on Practice and Theory in Public Key Cryptography, Springer (2001) 119–136
14. Frikken, K., Atallah, M.: Privacy preserving route planning. In: Proceedings of the 3rd ACM Workshop on Privacy in the Electronic Society, Washington, DC, USA (2004) 8–15
15. Aggarwal, G., Mishra, N., Pinkas, B.: Secure computation of the k th-ranked element. In: Advances in Cryptology – EUROCRYPT'04. Volume 3027 of LNCS. (2004) 40–55
16. Schnorr, C.: Efficient signature generation by smart cards. Journal of Cryptology 4 (1991) 161–174
17. Fiat, A., Shmair, A.: How to prove yourself: Practical solutions to identification and signature problems. In: Advances in Cryptology – CRYPTO'86. Volume 263 of LNCS. (1986) 186–194
18. Cramer, R., Damgård, I., Schoenmakers, B.: Proofs of partial knowledge and simplified design of witness hiding protocols. In: Advances in Cryptology – EUROCRYPT'94. Volume 839 of Lecture Notes in Computer Science., Springer (1994) 174–187
19. Jakobsson, M., Juels, A.: Mix and match: Secure function evaluation via ciphertexts. In: Advances in Cryptology – ASIASCRYPT'00. Volume 1976 of LNCS. (2000) 162–177
20. Pedersen, T.: A threshold cryptosystem without a trusted party. In: Advances in Cryptology – EUROCRYPT'91. Volume 547 of LNCS. (1991) 522–526
21. Gennaro, R., Jarecki, S., Krawzyk, H., Rabin, T.: Secure distributed key generation for discrete-log based cryptosystem. In: Advances in Cryptology – EUROCRYPT'99. Volume 1592 of LNCS. (1999) 295–310
22. Chaum, D.: Untraceable electronic mail, return addresses, and digital pseudonyms. In: Communications of the ACM. Volume 24(2). (1981) 84–88
23. Jakobsson, M.: A practical mix. In: Advances in Cryptology – EUROCRYPT '98. Volume 1403. (1998) 448–461
24. Jakobsson, M., Juels, A., , Rivest, R.: Making mix nets robust for electronic voting by randomized partial checking. In: USENIX. (2002) 339–353
25. Golle, P., Jakobsson, M.: Reusable anonymous return channels. In: ACM Workshop on Privacy in the Electronic Society (WPES'03). (2003) 94–100
26. Ofman, Y.P.: On the algorithmic complexity of discrete functions. English translation of Soviet Physics Doklady 7 (1963) 589–591
27. Ladner, R., Fischer, M.: Parallel prefix computation. Journal of the Association for Computing Machinery (27) (1980) 831–838
28. Wallace, C.: A suggestion for a fast multiplier. IEEE Transactions on Electronic Computers 13 (1964) 14–17
29. Zheng, S., Yang, M., Masetti, F.: Constructing schedulers for high-speed, high-capacity switches/routers. International Journal of Computers and Applications 26 (2003) 4–271
30. Brandt, F.: Fully private auctions in a constant number of rounds. In: Financial Cryptography Conference (FC'03). Volume 2742 of LNCS. (2003) 223–238

Efficient Cryptographic Protocols Realizing E-Markets with Price Discrimination

Aggelos Kiayias[1] and Moti Yung[2]

[1] Computer Science and Engineering,
University of Connecticut Storrs, CT, USA
`aggelos@cse.uconn.edu`
[2] RSA Laboratories, Bedford, MA, USA and Computer Science,
Columbia University, New York, NY, USA
`moti@cs.columbia.edu`

Abstract. Perfect (or "first degree") Price Discrimination is a standard economic practice that is used to increase the pricing effectiveness over a diverse population of prospective buyers. It is done by selling to different buyers at different prices based on their respective willingness to pay. While the strategy achieves Pareto efficiency, there are a number of problems in realizing and giving incentive to buyers to participate (and stay) in a market with price discrimination. This is especially true in an open process (like Internet commerce), where parties may learn about their price's individual standing (within the group of buyers) and may withdraw due to being relatively "over-charged" or may "resell" due to getting the goods at a relatively low price. We investigate the difficulties of realizing perfect price discrimination markets when full information is available to the participants even under the assumption of using standard cryptographic techniques. We then propose a "fair solution" for price discrimination in e-markets: using efficient cryptographic protocols (much more efficient than secure function evaluation protocols) we give incentives to users to stay in a market that utilizes price discrimination. Our protocols assure that the seller obtains the total revenue it expects and no buyer learns the price of other buyers. In addition, each buyer gets a "fair" discount off the surplus (the accumulated suggested payments by buyers minus the seller's expected revenue) when applicable and the seller may get part of the surplus as well. Further, the seller gets to learn the market "willingness to pay" (for potential future use), while this knowledge does not affect the pricing of the current e-market instance. Along the way we investigate the cryptographic primitive of "robust distributed summation" that may be of independent interest as a protocol construction.

1 Introduction

Economics is a field where decision making is being studied and where methods, mechanisms and procedures are developed to solve market situations under rationality and other assumptions about agents. On the other hand computer science and cryptography in particular, study manipulation and exchanges of

G. Di Crescenzo and A. Rubin (Eds.): FC 2006, LNCS 4107, pp. 311–325, 2006.
© IFCA/Springer-Verlag Berlin Heidelberg 2006

information in the electronic world, based on the computational model and computational environment constraints. In this paper we investigate the concept of using cryptographic protocols to solve problems of economics: markets, exchanges and collaboration of agents, can be assisted in various environments where exchange and combination of information is done in a setting that due to partial-information constraints cryptography can help. We demonstrate the usefulness of what may be called a "Crypto-Economics" proposal by showing how under certain operational constraints we can employ efficient cryptographic protocols to realize e-markets with first order price discrimination.

Price Discrimination is a standard economic practice that can be used to increase the market efficiency in cases where there is a diverse population of prospective buyers of a certain good or service. We deal here with first-degree price discrimination, where users express their "willingness to pay" which is accumulated and if it is above or equal the revenue the seller wants to obtain (this is called "the surplus"), then the market transaction is performed. While having "Pareto efficiency" (no party's situation can be made better off without making someone else worse off), the practice generates "consumer discomfort" since users may realize that relative to other users they have paid too much (discouraging loyalty) or too little (encouraging re-sale). We refer to the works of Varian [Va96] and Odlyzko [Od02] for more information of such issues in the setting of Internet commerce. The present work focuses on the problem of how to incentivize agents to remain in such markets not using economic means and business tricks (versioning, bundling, etc. see below) but rather through cryptographic techniques.

Suppose that a seller S advertises a good and attracts a number of prospective buyers $B_1, \ldots, B_n$. Let ρ be the total revenue that S wishes to extract out of selling the good. Suppose additionally that buyer B_i is willing to pay an amount v_i for obtaining the advertised good. In the perfect price discrimination setting the good is sold to buyer B_i at price v_i resulting in a total revenue of $\sum_{i=1}^{n} v_i$. If the summation exceeds ρ the transaction can take place.

To illustrate the benefits of price discrimination consider the following scenario: the seller wishes to sell an advertised good expecting a total revenue of $\rho = \$1500$. Three buyers express interest for the product with respective prices $v_1 = \$400$, $v_2 = \$600$ and $v_3 = \$800$. Without price discrimination the seller can set an average price of $\$1500/3 = \$500$. This will result in a revenue of $\$1000$ that is below the expectations of the seller (this is because the product would be too expensive for the first buyer). In the perfect price discrimination setting the total revenue is $\$1800$ but it is quite likely that the third buyer will not be willing to pay $\$500$ more than the first buyer for the same product (and similarly for the second).

Indeed, this setting, although ideal from a simple economical point of view (the "name your price" practice as in priceline.com and other Internet selling sites follow this strategy), it is not practical in many cases, and it is hardly possible to enforce in cases where potential buyers have concerns about fairness. Indeed, economists have noticed that there are numerous problems that arise in the employment of price-discrimination despite the fact that in most settings it is beneficial both for the buyers as well as for the seller. One of the most important problems is convincing the buyers to accept the price discrimination scheme. Possible techniques include versioning and bundling, nevertheless these do not apply to all settings and types of goods. When the same product or service is to be sold in different prices, buyers may worry about their relative price and the unfairness of the process. They may realize that they pay "too much" and hold it against the seller, or may realize that they can resell in case their price was low.

We would like a mechanism that employs price discrimination, yet assures some conditions of fairness. First we view a number of potential realizations of a market with perfect price discrimination. We explain the difficulties in these realizations. Then, a fair solution that we propose in this setting is to use cryptographic methods to enable the sale only under certain conditions and without leaking private information. In particular, the protocol allows the transaction to take place only if the seller gets the expected revenue he has expressed ρ. The solution then yields a discount to all buyers (this will be the incentive to remain in the price discriminated market). The price discrimination happens in an *oblivious manner* and is distributed among all buyers based on buyer i calling a price v_i that remains private. In this case all users will be willing to participate motivated by the potential discount. Moreover, they will be given a (cryptographic) guarantee that their price will be kept secret while computing the discount and they will not be treated unfairly, in case the seller's constraints are satisfied.

The total discount that can be applied is $\sum_{i=1}^{n} v_i - \rho$ (the slack), and in the particular example above it is $300. This slack can be divided among the buyers using some method accepted by all parties. In the simplest example we consider, all buyers should get a $300/3 = 100 discount: in particular the buyers will pay $300, $500, 700 respectively. Provided that no buyer learns the price paid by other buyers, all parties are motivated to participate in the protocol: the seller obtains the total revenue he expected; all buyers get a discounted price. In our second solution we consider weighted discounts where the slack will be divided according to the relative bids of each party; in this setting the buyers will pay $333, $500, 667 respectively (i.e., the higher bidder receives more discount).

Let us complete the section by clarifying the distributed secure computation problem that we consider:

- $n+1$ active participants: S denotes the seller, and $B_1, \ldots, B_n$ the prospective buyers.
- The private inputs of the participants $S, B_1, \ldots, B_n$ are $\rho, v_1, \ldots, v_n$.
- The goal of the the protocol is the following: provided that $\sum_{i=1}^{n} v_i \geq \rho$, each buyer B_i privately computes a value v_i' so that (i) no other participant gets to learn the value v_i; (ii) the values $\sum_{i=1}^{n} v_i' = \rho$; (iii) $v_i' \leq v_i$.
- In case of a transaction, the seller gets the revenue he declared as its desire (this is an incentive for the seller to input its "real willingness for revenue.")

- The seller gets a feedback about the "market willingness to pay as a whole" which does not influence the current transaction. On the other hand, the seller does not learn the individual price bids (v_i's).
- We consider two alternative methods for the calculation of the discounted values v'_k:
    - (a) Same discount for all buyers: $v'_k = v_k - \frac{\sum_{i=1}^{n} v_i - \rho}{n}$.
    - (b) Weighted Discount: $v'_k = v_k \frac{\rho}{\sum_{i=1}^{n} v_i}$.

The cryptographic protocol realizing this "oblivious price discrimination method" assures secrecy (no buyer or seller learns the initial price bid of another buyer), auditability (the buyers are sure the realization was calculated correctly) and robustness (the solution can be calculated distributedly with no disruptions).

We can also vary the treatment of the surplus. The parties may decide a-priori to split it between the buyers and the seller (in some chosen way that can be calibrated); this allows markets that support sellers based on global conditions. For example, in depressed markets, the buyers may be willing (or be regulated) to give half the surplus to the seller, in order to keep it in business.

1.1   Motivation: Problems with Potential Realizations

The motivation for our cryptographic protocol designs is illustrated by the following potential "solutions" to the above problem, that are not satisfactory:

1. Non-Cryptographic Solution #1: All buyers send their values v_i to the seller who, in turn, returns the values v'_i. **Problem:** This may result in over-pricing since there is no guarantee that the seller will not get for more revenue than it expects and the fairness-minded group of buyers do not like this situation. (This is the "name your price" mechanism).
2. Non-Cryptographic Solution #2: The seller publicizes the expected revenue ρ. **Problem:** It is hard to achieve price-discrimination in this setting, since the seller has "revealed its cards" and it is unreasonable to expect that buyers would be willing to pay more than ρ/n.
3. Commitment Based Setting: Seller commits to his value and buyers communicate their prices to him. **Problem:** Buyers only collectively can verify the commitment of the seller with respect to the slack. Without employing any other cryptographic techniques, this results in revealing all buyers' prices and this level of insecurity may allow buyers to learn prices of other buyers. Naturally a trusted third party may carry the checking but this would centralize too much trust on a single entity.
4. Cryptographic Setting: The seller and buyer may employ generic secure function evaluation [Ya86, GMW87] to compute the total discount $\sum_{i=1}^{n} v_i - \rho$ or the discount ratio $\rho / \sum_{i=1}^{n} v_i$. These general procedures, in fact, can solve any mechanism design problem as noted in [Ni99]. **Problem:** While these methods are "universal protocols" that solve any problem, these methods are computationally very demanding and serve only as plausibility results; instead here we seek more efficient solutions of a specific secure function evaluation problem, (cf. [G97]).

We assume that a seller and a buyer have signed a contract clarifying the rules of payments after the protocol is over and the confidentiality of payments; this can also use cryptography (digital signing). In addition, we need to assure the seller its revenue. The protocol has to be auditable by the participants assuming they are fairness-minded users who monitor the publicly available protocol transcript. Furthermore, the tool has to be robust against users who attempt to fail the system.

2   Tools

In this section we go over some basic cryptographic tools that we employ in our construction. In particular, Homomorphic Encryption Schemes, Paillier Encryption, Proofs of Knowledge, Interval Proofs, etc. Readers familiar with these tools may skim read this section and move on to section 3.

Homomorphic Encryption Schemes. An encryption scheme is a triple $\langle \mathcal{K}, \mathcal{E}, \mathcal{D} \rangle$. The key-generation $\mathcal{K}$ is a probabilistic TM which on input a parameter 1^w (which specifies the key-length) outputs a key-pair pk, sk (public-key and secret-key respectively).

The encryption function is a probabilistic TM $\mathcal{E}_{\mathsf{pk}} : \mathbb{R} \times \mathbb{P} \to \mathbb{C}$, where $\mathbb{R}$ is the randomness space, $\mathbb{P}$ is the plaintext space, and $\mathbb{C}$ the ciphertext space. When the $\mathbb{P} = \mathbb{Z}_a$ for some integer a, we will say that encryption function has "*additive capacity*" (or just capacity) a.

The basic property of the encryption scheme is that $\mathcal{D}_{\mathsf{sk}}(\mathcal{E}_{\mathsf{sk}}(\cdot, x)) = x$ for all x independently of the coin tosses of the encryption function $\mathcal{E}$. If we want to specify the coin tosses of $\mathcal{E}$ we will write $\mathcal{E}_{\mathsf{pk}}(r, x)$ to denote the ciphertext that corresponds to the plaintext x when the encryption function $\mathcal{E}_{\mathsf{pk}}$ makes the coin tosses r. Otherwise we will consider $\mathcal{E}_{\mathsf{pk}}(x)$ to be a random variable.

For homomorphic encryption, we assume additionally the operations $+, \oplus, \odot$ defined over the respective spaces $\mathbb{P}, \mathbb{R}, \mathbb{C}$, so that $\langle \mathbb{P}, + \rangle$, $\langle \mathbb{R}, \oplus \rangle$, $\langle \mathbb{C}, \odot \rangle$ are groups written additively (the first two) and multiplicatively respectively.

Definition 1. *An encryption function $\mathcal{E}$ is homomorphic if, for all $r_1, r_2 \in \mathbb{R}$ and all $x_1, x_2 \in \mathbb{P}$, it holds that $\mathcal{E}_{\mathsf{pk}}(r_1, x_1) \odot \mathcal{E}_{\mathsf{pk}}(r_2, x_2)$ equals $\mathcal{E}_{\mathsf{pk}}(r_1 \oplus r_2, x+y)$.*

Here we will employ a Homomorphic Encryption scheme due to Paillier, [Pai99], that is presented in the next section.

Paillier Encryption. We use the first encryption scheme presented in [Pai99]. It is a triple $\langle \mathcal{K}, \mathcal{E}, \mathcal{D} \rangle$, defined as follows: the key-generation $\mathcal{K}$ outputs an integer N, that is a product of two safe primes, and an element $g \in \mathbb{Z}_{N^2}^*$ of order a multiple of N. The public-key of the system pk is set to $\langle g, N \rangle$ and the secret-key sk is set to the factorization of N.

For a public-key $\langle g, N \rangle$, the encryption function $\mathcal{E}(r, x)$ equals the value $g^x r^N \pmod{N^2}$ and the domains $\mathbb{P} := \mathbb{Z}_N$, $\mathbb{R} := \mathbb{Z}_N^*$, and $\mathbb{C} := \mathbb{Z}_{N^2}^*$. The operation $+$ is defined as addition modulo N, and the operations $\oplus, \odot$ are defined as multiplication modulo N^2. The decryption function $\mathcal{D}$ for a secret-key p, q it operates as follows: first it computes $\lambda := \lambda(N)$ the Carmichael function of

N, and given a ciphertext c, it returns $L(c^\lambda (\mathrm{mod}N^2))/L(g^\lambda (\mathrm{mod}N^2))$ where $L(u) = \frac{u-1}{N}$ and L is defined over the set of integers $\{u \mid u \equiv 1(\mathrm{mod}N)\}$.

Observe that $\langle \mathbb{P}, + \rangle$, $\langle \mathbb{R}, \oplus \rangle$ and $\mathbb{C}, \odot \rangle$ are all groups, and the encryption $\mathcal{E}$ is homomorphic with respect to these operations. Finally notice that the capacity of $\mathcal{E}$ is N.

Threshold Variant. A (t, m)-threshold homomorphic encryption scheme is a triple $\langle \mathcal{K}, \mathcal{E}, \mathcal{D} \rangle$ so that $\mathcal{K}$ is a protocol between a set of participants $A_1, \ldots, A_m$, that results in the publication of the public-key pk and the sharing of the secret-key sk so that any t of them can reconstruct it. Additionally, $\mathcal{D}$ is also a protocol between the participants $A_1, \ldots, A_m$ that results in the decryption of the given ciphertext in a publicly verifiable manner (i.e. each participant writes a proof that he follows the decryption protocol according to the specifications). Paillier encryption has a threshold variant see [FPS00, DJ00].

Proofs of Knowledge. Proofs of knowledge are protocols between two players, the Prover and the Verifier. In such protocols there is a publicly known predicate Q_y with parameter y for which the prover knows some witness x, i.e. $Q_y(x) = 1$. The goal of such protocols is for the prover to convince the verifier that he indeed knows such witness. The reader may refer to [DDPY94, CDS94] for descriptions of such protocols and their composition in AND-OR circuit fashion. We note that we will employ such protocols based on a computational soundness argument: i.e., soundness on the side of the prover will be ensured only under the presumed hardness of a certain computational problem. This technique was used in a number of previous works, notably in [FO97, DF02].

Interval Proof for Paillier Encryption. An interval proof shows that a committed integer value belongs to a certain interval. Such proofs have been used in a variety of settings, e.g. in group-signatures [ACJT00], or e-cash [CFT98]. In our protocol constructions we will need the design of an interval proof for an integer that is encrypted into a Paillier ciphertext. We start by presenting in figure 1 a basic interval proof for a commitment (for related previous work see also [CFT98, Bou00, KTY04]).

For the proof, we consider security parameters k, l and further let N' be a safe RSA Modulus with unknown factorization to the prover and verifier. Also let g_0 be an element that generates the quadratic residues in $\mathbb{Z}_{N'}^*$ and h a full order element inside $\langle g_0 \rangle$ with unknown discrete logarithm base g_0. Let $0, \ldots, B$ be the interval over which the prover will show that a committed value belongs to. The commitment scheme that is used is defined as follows: $V = g_0^x h^r (\mathrm{mod}N')$ where r is selected at random from the interval $\{0, \ldots, \lceil N'/4 \rceil\}$.

A crucial tool for the soundness of interval proofs is the Strong-RSA assumption, defined below:

Strong-RSA Assumption. Given N' and $v \in \mathbb{Z}_{N'}^*$ it is computationally hard to find $b \in \mathbb{Z}_{N'}^*$ and e a prime number such that $b^e = v(\mathrm{mod}N')$.

We remark that the proof of knowledge of figure 1 has the following properties: (1) If $x \in \{0, \ldots, B\}$ the honest prover always convinces the honest

Prover	Verifier
selects $\omega \in_R \{-2^{k+l}B, \ldots, 2^{k+l}B\}$	
$\eta \in_R \{-2^{k+l}\lceil N'/4 \rceil, \ldots, 2^{k+l}\lceil N'/4 \rceil\}$	
computes $W = g_0^\omega h^\eta (\mathrm{mod}\, N')$ $\quad\xrightarrow{W}$	
$\quad\xleftarrow{c}$	$c \in_R \{0, \ldots, 2^k\}$
$d_1 = \omega - xc, d_2 = \eta - rc$ (in $\mathbb{Z}$) $\xrightarrow{d_1, d_2}$	$d_1 \in_? \{-2^{k+l}B - (2^k - 1)B, \ldots, 2^{k+l}B\}$
	$g_0^{d_1} h^{d_2} V^c \stackrel{?}{=} W (\mathrm{mod}\, N')$

Fig. 1. Interval Proof $x \in \{0, \ldots, B\}$ for the commitment $V = g_0^x h^r$

verifier. (2) Conditional Soundness. A cheating prover using an integer $x \notin \{-2^{k+l+2}B, \ldots, B + 2^{k+l+2}B\}$ can succeed with probability less than 2^{-k}, under the Strong-RSA assumption. (3) The protocol is statistical zero-knowledge for a honest verifier with statistical distance negligible in the parameter l.

We can combine the above protocol using regular AND composition with a standard proof of knowledge of a Paillier encryption (e.g. as those presented in [DJ00]) in order to obtain a proof of knowledge that shows that a Paillier Encryption hides a value in the interval $\{-2^{k+l+2}B, \ldots, B + 2^{k+l+2}B\}$. Let g, N be a public-key for the Paillier encryption function with $N > N'$. This can be done as shown in figure 2.

Prover	Verifier
selects $r \in \{0, \ldots, \lceil N'/4 \rceil\}$	
$\omega \in_R \{-2^{k+l}B, \ldots, 2^{k+l}B\}$	
$\eta \in_R \{-2^{k+l}\lceil N'/4 \rceil, \ldots, 2^{k+l}\lceil N'/4 \rceil\}$	
$u \in_R \mathbb{Z}_N^*$	
computes $W = g_0^\omega h^\eta (\mathrm{mod}\, N')$, $V = g_0^x h^r (\mathrm{mod}\, N')$,	
$U = g^\omega u^N (\mathrm{mod}\, N^2)$ $\quad\xrightarrow{W, U, V}$	
$\quad\xleftarrow{c}$	$c \in_R \{0, \ldots, 2^k\}$
$d_1 = \omega - xc$, $d_2 = \eta - rc$ (in $\mathbb{Z}$)	
$z = uv^c (\mathrm{mod}\, N^2)$ $\quad\xrightarrow{d_1, d_2, z}$	$d_1 \geq_? -2^{k+l}B - (2^k - 1)B$
	$d_1 \leq_? 2^{k+l}B$
	$g_0^{d_1} h^{d_2} V^c \stackrel{?}{=} W (\mathrm{mod}\, N')$
	$g^{d_1} z^N \stackrel{?}{=} U E^c (\mathrm{mod}\, N^2)$

Fig. 2. Interval Proof $x \in \{0, \ldots, B\}$ for the Paillier Encryption $E = g^x v^N (\mathrm{mod}\, N^2)$

Boudot, in [Bou00], improved interval proofs of the type described above so that they become tight (i.e. there does not exist a discrepancy between the interval used for completeness, and the interval used for soundness). We can combine Boudot's proof in a standard AND fashion with a proof of knowledge of a Paillier encryption as we did above in figure 2 in order to obtain a interval proof for a Paillier encryption.

Notation. In the sequel we will use the notation $Q_{\text{interval}}^{E, [0..B]}$ for the predicate that is 1 for values x, v such that $E = g^x v^N (\mathrm{mod}\, N^2)$ and $x \in \{0, 1, \ldots, B\}$. We will say that a player writes a proof for $Q_{\text{interval}}^{E,[0..B]}$ when he executes an interval proof for the Paillier encryption E.

Proving Equality of Paillier Ciphertexts with Different Bases. Let g, N be a public-key for the Paillier encryption. Let g_0 be an additional value in $\mathbb{Z}_{N^2}^*$ with order a multiple of N. In this section we will show how the prover can show that two ciphertexts C, C' encrypted under the public-keys g, N and g_0, N can be shown to encrypt the same plaintext. We will denote the corresponding predicate by $Q_{\text{equal}}^{C,C',g,g_0,N}$, i.e. $Q_{\text{equal}}^{C,C',g,g_0,N}(x) = 1$ if and only if there exist $v, v' \in \mathbb{Z}_N^*$ such that $C = g^x v^N (\text{mod} N^2)$ and $C' = g_0^x (v')^N (\text{mod} N^2)$. The proof of knowledge is presented in figure 3.

	Prover	Verifier
	select $y, y' \in_R \mathbb{Z}_N^*$ and $r \in_R \mathbb{Z}_N$	
$A := g^r y^N (\text{mod} N^2) \bmod N^2$, $A' = g_0^r (y')^N (\text{mod} N^2)$ $\xrightarrow{A,A'}$		
	$\xleftarrow{c}$	$c \leftarrow_R \{0, 1, \ldots, N-1\}$
$z = yv^c$, $z' = y'(v')^c$, $s = r + cx(\text{mod} N)$ $\xrightarrow{s}$		$g^s z^N \stackrel{?}{=} AC^c (\text{mod} N^2)$
		$g_0^s (z')^N \stackrel{?}{=} A'(C')^c (\text{mod} N^2)$

Fig. 3. Proof of knowledge for the predicate $Q_{\text{equal}}^{C,C',g,g_0,N}$ where $C = g^x v^N (\text{mod} N^2)$ and $C' = g_0^x (v')^N (\text{mod} N^2)$

3   Price Discrimination Protocols

- Active Participants: The Seller (S), the prospective buyers $(B_1, \ldots, B_n)$. All communication takes place through a "bulletin board," a model that abstracts away all lower level communication details [CF85].
- Inputs: the expected revenue $\rho \in \mathbb{Z}$ of the Seller. The maximum amount that player B_i is willing to spend $v_i < B$.
- Output: The seller computes the total contribution $\sum_{i=1}^n v_i$. Each buyer either,
  1. receives the discounted price v_i', that has the properties (i) $v_i' \leq v_i$, (ii) $\sum v_i' = \rho$.
  2. receives a notification that the expected revenue of the Seller has not been met.
- Correctness. Each active participant computes the outputs as specified above.
- Security Specifications.
  1. Privacy. The initial amount that each Buyer is willing to spend is kept secret (modulo the information that is leaked by the results of the procedure). Formally, privacy is intended to be shown by comparison to the ideal implementation of the scheme using a trusted third party: All buyers and sellers transmit privately their values to the trusted third party who announces the output as defined above.

2. Robustness. No participant can prevent the procedure from terminating.
3. Verifiability. Participants' actions can be verified to follow the protocols' specifications.

As explained above, we will consider two discount schemes: (i) absolute discount where $v_i' = v_i - \frac{\sum_{i=1}^{n} v_i}{\rho}$, and (ii) weighted discount where $v_i' = v_i \frac{\rho}{\sum_{i=1}^{n} v_i}$.

We remark that in the absolute discount case, some buyers may compute a negative value as their final price v_i'. This is not inconsistent with the specifications of price discrimination with absolute discount (i.e. in this case these buyers may end up getting some credit for participating in the procedure).

Meeting the security specifications will rely on assuming the semantic security of Paillier scheme, and on the assumptions (and idealized model, if used) needed for the proofs of knowledge (as explained above). More detailed treatment will be given in the full version of this work.

3.1   Robust Private Distributed Summation

Our protocol constructions can be seen as modifications of a basic primitive which we call Robust Private Distributed Summation. The primitive may be of independent interest and as it is quite general we present it first. As a primitive it relates to homomorphic encryption based voting schemes, e.g. [CGS97, FPS00]; the goal of the primitive is to add a sequence of distributed numbers into their sum while at the same time avoiding wraparounds (as the calculation is performed in a finite ciphertext domain).

We stress that distributed summation is very different from e-voting. To begin with, the individual summation terms are not supposed to be revealed and as a result no e-voting procedure based on blind-signatures and/or anonymous channels is suitable. Further, in case of homomorphic encryption based voting the difference is that the range of each summation term may be exponentially large and thus standard OR proofs ranging through the entire allowed domain cannot be used to validate the encrypted bid. Moreover the range of the summation register is exponentially large itself. Finally, we only need to avoid wraparounds, and thus a tight range proof may even not be required. For the above reasons a new construction is in place to solve the distributed summation problem. Below we outline the protocol problem we intend to solve.

We describe the protocol below. Let $\langle \mathcal{K}, \mathcal{E}, \mathcal{D} \rangle$ be the (t, m)-threshold variant of Paillier encryption defined in section 2.

1. **Setup.** The authorities $A_1, \ldots, A_m$ execute the protocol $\mathcal{K}$ which results in the publication in the bulletin board of the public-key pk. At the same time the secret-key sk is shared amongst the authorities $A_1, \ldots, A_m$.
2. **Value Submission.** Each eligible player gets authorized to the bulletin board and reads the public-key pk of the system. The player P_i publishes the encryption $C[i] := \mathcal{E}_{\mathsf{pk}}(s_i)$, where $s_i \in \{0, \ldots, B\}$.
   At the same time the player must publish an interval proof to show that he is not exceeding the boundary B. So he writes a proof of knowledge for the predicate $Q_{\mathsf{interval}}^{C[i],[0..B]}$.

Parameters $t, m, B \in \mathbb{Z}$. Number of players is n.

Tools Paillier Encryption $\langle \mathcal{K}, \mathcal{E}, \mathcal{D} \rangle$ with capacity N such that $N > nB$.

Participants A set of players $P_1, \dots, P_n$. We also assume a set of authorities $A_1, \dots, A_m$ (which may coincide or overlap with the set of players).

Input Each player has a private input, an integer $s_i \in \{0, 1, \dots, B\}$.

Output The sum $\sum_{i=1}^{n} s_i$.

Properties

Security Any adversary that controls a number of participants so that less than t Authorities are controlled by the adversary is incapable of computing the private input of any of the participants, prior to the announcement of the sum, the output of the protocol.

Robustness Any adversary that controls a number of participants so that less than $m-t$ Authorities are controlled by the adversary is incapable of preventing the publication of the output sum of the protocol.

Verifiability Any third party can verify that the participants are following the protocol according to the specifications.

Fig. 4. Specifications of the Secure Distributed Summation Protocol

3. **Aggregation.** The bulletin board authority terminates the value submission phase, and it collects the encrypted ballots $C[1], \dots, C[n]$ to compute the "summation ciphertext" $C_{\mathsf{sum}} = C[1] \odot \dots \odot C[n]$. Observe that due to the homomorphic property of the Paillier encryption scheme it holds that C_{sum} is indistinguishable from encryptions of the value $T := \sum_{i=1}^{n} s_i$.

4. **Decryption and Announcement of the Sum.** The authorities $A_1, \dots, A_m$ execute the protocol $\mathcal{D}$ to reveal the the value T. Note that due to the capacity assumption there will be no wrap-arounds during the computation of the summation ciphertext C_{sum}.

Based on the properties of the cryptographic tools that are employed in our scheme, one can formulate and prove a theorem as follows:

Theorem 1. *The Distributed Summation Protocol defined above satisfies Security, Robustness, and Verifiability, under the assumptions (i) Semantic Security of Paillier encryption (ii) the strong-RSA assumption to show the soundness of the necessary interval proofs.*

Remark 1. A summation protocol for encrypted values appeared as part of a different application scenario in [C01]; the approach taken there was based on cut and choose techniques for ensuring proper value selection and thus compared to the solution presented here is much less efficient.

Remark 2. By calibrating the capacity of the encryption function to be $N > nB2^t$ where t is an appropriately chosen security parameter one can use more efficient proofs of knowledge compared to the ones of Boutot [Bou00] as the one in figure 2. We omit further details for the full version.

3.2 The Absolute Discount Protocol

Let $\langle \mathcal{K}, \mathcal{E}, \mathcal{D} \rangle$ be the (t, m)-threshold version of the Paillier homomorphic encryption as defined in section 2. We assume a set of "authorities" $A_1, \ldots, A_m$ that may either overlap with some of the active participants $S, B_1, \ldots, B_n$ or they may be third parties that participate in the procedure. We will denote by B an upper bound on the maximum price that a certain buyer is willing to pay to the seller.

Initialization. The Authorities $A_1, \ldots, A_m$ execute the key-generation protocol $\mathcal{K}$. This results in writing the public-key g, N in the bulletin board of the system. We assume that $N > 2Bn$ where B is the bound to the input of each buyer[1].

Depositing the Price-bids. Each buyer B_i selects his maximum price bid v_i and publishes $C[i] = \mathcal{E}(v_i) = g^{v_i} x_i^N (\mathrm{mod} N^2)$ where $v_i \in \{0, \ldots, B\}$ and $x_i \in_R \mathbb{Z}_N^*$.

In addition B_i writes a proof for the predicate $Q_{\mathrm{interval}}^{C[i],[0..B]}$, to ensure that the bid v_i is in the range $\{0, \ldots, B\}$.

The seller writes the encryption $C = \mathcal{E}(\rho) = g^\rho x^N (\mathrm{mod} N^2)$, together with an interval proof for the predicate $Q_{\mathrm{interval}}^{C,[0..\frac{N}{2}]}$.

Closing the Deposition Phase. The bulletin board server closes the deposition phase by signing and time-stamping the contents of the bulletin board. All proofs of knowledge are checked to ensure that all buyers have conformed to the interval requirement.

Computation of the Total Discount. The bulletin board server computes $C_{\mathrm{t-disc}} = \prod_{i=1}^n C[i]/C$. Observe that due to the capacity of the encryption function $\mathcal{E}$ and the homomorphic properties of the Paillier encryption function it follows that $C_{\mathrm{t-disc}}$ is a valid Paillier ciphertext that hides the integer $D = \sum_{i=1}^n v_i - \rho \in \{-\lfloor \frac{N}{2} \rfloor, \ldots, 0, \ldots, \lfloor \frac{N}{2} \rfloor\}$.

The authorities $A_1, \ldots, A_m$ execute the decryption protocol on the ciphertext $C_{\mathrm{t-disc}}$ to reveal the value D. Note that if $D < 0$ all parties conclude that the market cannot be realized (too high revenue expected / too little market interest).

Computation of Individual Prices. Provided that $D \geq 0$ each buyer B_i computes his discounted value as follows: $v_i' := v_i - \frac{D}{n}$. The Seller can also compute the gross value that its offer raised by calculating the sum $\sum_{i=1}^n v_i = D + \rho$.

Observe that the publication of the total discount $D = \sum_{i=1}^n v_i - \rho$ is not inconsistent with the security properties dictated by an ideal implementation of the absolute discount protocol since the value D is accessible also in the ideal implementation by each one of the buyers: indeed given v_i, v_i' in the ideal implementation one can compute D as follows: $D = n(v_i - v_i')$ (recall that we assume that the total number of buyers n is common knowledge).

---

[1] Note that the bound B will be chosen to be substantially larger from the actual bid and will be the same for all buyers. The only purpose of the bound is to ensure that no wraparound occurs during the modular addition of the buyers' bids. It will be easy to select B high enough so that no information about the buyers' prices leaks from the disclosure of B.

Under our cryptographic assumptions, one can argue that the absolute discount protocol above satisfies privacy, robustness and verifiability.

3.3   The Weighted Discount Protocol

The main technical issue for the weighted discount protocol compared to the absolute discount protocol is that the computation of the summation of the bid-prices appears in the denominator of the discounted final price values.

As in the case of the absolute discount protocol, let $\langle \mathcal{K}, \mathcal{E}, \mathcal{D} \rangle$ be the (t, m)-threshold version of the Paillier homomorphic encryption as defined in section 2. As before, we also assume a set of "authorities" $A_1, \ldots, A_m$ that may either overlap with some of the active participants $S, B_1, \ldots, B_n$ or they may be third parties that participate in the procedure.

Initialization. The Authorities $A_1, \ldots, A_m$ execute the key-generation protocol $\mathcal{K}$. This results in writing the public-key g, N in the bulletin board of the system. We assume that the capacity of the encryption N satisfies $N > ABn$ where B is the bound to the input of each buyer, and A is an integer parameter.

Seller-Initialization. The seller computes $\rho' := \lceil 10^e \frac{1}{\rho} \rceil$ where e is a public parameter so that $\rho' < A$. The seller publishes the encryption $C = \mathcal{E}(\rho') = g^{\rho'} x^N (\mathrm{mod}\, N^2)$. together with an interval proof for the predicate $Q_{\mathrm{interval}}^{C,[0..A]}$.

Depositing the Price-bids. Each buyer B_i selects his maximum price bid v_i and publishes $C[i] = C^{v_i} x_i^N (\mathrm{mod}\, N^2)$ and $C'[i] = g^{v_i}(x_i')^N (\mathrm{mod}\, N)$ where $v_i \in \{0, \ldots, B\}$ and $x_i \in_R \mathbb{Z}_{N^2}^*$.

In addition B_i writes a proof for the predicate $Q_{\mathrm{interval}}^{C'[i],[0..B]}$, to ensure that the bid v_i is in the range $\{0, \ldots, B\}$, and additionally it writes a proof for the predicate $Q_{\mathrm{equal}}^{C'[i],C[i],g,C,N}$ to ensure that the two Paillier ciphertexts $C[i], C'[i]$ that have different bases hide the same value v_i.

Closing the Deposition Phase. The bulletin board server closes the deposition phase by signing and time-stamping the contents of the bulletin board. All proofs of knowledge are checked to ensure that all participants have conformed to the interval requirements.

Computation of the Discounts. The bulletin board server (or any observer) computes $C_{\mathrm{factor}} = \prod_{i=1}^{n} C[i]$. Observe that due to the capacity of the encryption function $\mathcal{E}$ and the homomorphic properties of the Paillier encryption function it follows that C_{factor} is a valid Paillier ciphertext that hides the integer $F = \rho' \sum_{i=1}^{n} v_i$.

The authorities $A_1, \ldots, A_m$ execute the decryption protocol on the ciphertext C_{factor} to reveal the value F. Note that if $F < 10^e$ all parties conclude that the market cannot be realized (too high revenue expected / too little market interest). Otherwise, each buyer B_i computes his discounted price bid by as follows

$$v_i' := v_i \frac{10^e}{F} = v_i \frac{10^e}{\lceil \frac{10^e}{\rho} \rceil \sum_{i=1}^{n} v_i} \approx v_i \frac{\rho}{\sum_{i=1}^{n} v_i}$$

The Seller can also compute the total contribution $\sum_{i=1}^{n} v_i = F/\rho'$.

As an example of the above computation consider the case where $\rho = 500$ and there are three prospective buyers with initial price bids $v_1 = 60, v_2 = 300, v_3 = 400$. Let $e = 4$. In this case $\rho' = 20$ and $F = \rho' \sum_{i=1}^{n} v_i = 15200$. It follows that $\frac{10^e}{F} = 0.657$ i.e. the discounted prices will be $v_1' = 39.5, v_2' = 197.2, v_3' = 262.9$ (note that round-up can be used to ensure that the discounted values are not below the expected revenue).

Observe that the publication of the factor F, as it was the case with the total discount D for the absolute discount protocol, is not inconsistent with the security properties dictated by an ideal implementation of the weighted discount protocol since the value F is accessible also in the ideal implementation by each one of the buyers: indeed given v_i, v_i' in the ideal implementation one can compute F as follows: $F \approx v_i/v_i'$.

Under our cryptographic assumptions, one can prove that the absolute discount protocol above satisfies privacy, robustness and verifiability.

3.4 Variations on Dealing with the Surplus

In our two price-discrimination protocols, the surplus was divided among the buyers so that they could obtain a discount on their initial price bid. The seller on the other hand obtained exactly the price he named.

This is not satisfactory in some settings and for the purpose to increase the incentive of the seller, one can have some of this surplus actually be returned to the seller. We examine how this simple modification can be implemented in both of our protocols to give half the slack to the seller (other fractions are also easily implementable):

1. For the Absolute Discount Protocol: in the computation of the final prices v_i' each buyer divides the total discount D by 2, and computes he discounted price as $v_i' = v_i - \frac{\sum_{i=1}^{n} v_i - \rho}{2n}$. This will give half of the "slack" $\sum_{i=1}^{n} v_i - \rho$ back to the seller.

2. For the Weighted Discount Protocol: the multiplier $mult = \frac{10^e}{F}$ that satisfies $0 < mult < 1$ that is computed at the end of the protocol is modified to multiplier $mult' := mult + \frac{1 - mult}{2}$. Subsequently all buyers are using $mult'$ in order to compute their final discounted value.

4 Cryptographic Infrastructure for Transaction Support

A major advantage of the procedure of computing the discounted prices and the market be means of cryptographic protocol is that it is possible to use further Cryptographic tools to assist in the continuation of the transaction, after prices have been determined. The additional support can help maintaining certain privacy and enforcement properties that markets need. We will only briefly survey the methods; a more detailed description will be given in the next version.

4.1 Payment Services

To actually complete the transaction, the buyers should present a proof that they actually were assigned a certain price discount. While the total discount is publicly available on the bulletin board, this does not indicate the exact amount that a certain buyer is supposed to pay. In fact, it may be the case that an agent cheats and claims that he was actually awarded a larger discount than the one that was actually assigned by the protocol. The discrepancy would only be revealed after the last participating buyer submits his payment. As a result it is crucial during payment to produce some *proof* that a certain price bid was made. This is possible in our setting since the bid of the user appears encrypted on the bulletin-board, and acts as a public commitment to his original bid. As a result after the termination of the protocol the buyer can open the random pad that he used in the encryption of his bid and thus convince a third party (e.g. a payment server) of the real value of his discount; note that the total discount is publicly available information, and thus once the payment server is convinced that the original price bid of the user is v_i, he can verify whether the claimed discounted price by re-computing v_i' (depending on the protocol used weighted or absolute discount). Convincing can also be done in a zero-knowledge fashion. The payment server can serve as a trusted interface providing anonymity to users or a combination of anonymity and affinity programs based on user accounts.

4.2 Reducing Reselling Potential Using "Receipt-Freeness"

The ability of the buyers to present proofs of the original bids is useful on the one hand for the implementation of the final monetary transaction part, however it also raises some concerns. In particular, buyers are capable of proving to other potential buyers their price which will encourage "resell market." To prevent this we can have a private re-randomizing server (which is used in "voting protocols" to provide receipt-freeness, [Poi00]), and this server makes sure that the buyer cannot convince a third party what his price is.

Further, the same server can be the payment server above, thus it is possible for a user to be able to convince the server and only the server itself of his/her price.

References

[ACJT00]   Giuseppe Ateniese, Jan Camenisch, Marc Joye and Gene Tsudik, *A Practical and Provably Secure Coalition-Resistant Group Signature Scheme*, CRYPTO 2000.

[Ben87]   Josh Benaloh, *Verifiable Secret-Ballot Elections*, PhD Thesis, Yale University, 1987.

[Bou00]   Fabrice Boudot, *Efficient Proofs that a Committed Number Lies in an Interval*, Eurocrypt 2000.

[CFT98]   Agnes Hui Chan, Yair Frankel, Yiannis Tsiounis, *Easy Come - Easy Go Divisible Cash*, EUROCRYPT 1998.

[CF85]   Josh D. Cohen (Benaloh) and Michael J. Fischer, *A Robust and Verifiable Cryptographically Secure Election Scheme*, FOCS 1985.

[CGS97]   Ronald Cramer, Rosario Gennaro and Berry Schoenmakers, *A Secure and Optimally Efficient Multi-Authority Election Scheme*, EUROCRYPT 1997.

[CDS94]   Ronald Cramer, Ivan Damgård and Berry Schoenmakers, *Proofs of Partial Knowledge and Simplified Design of Witness Hiding Protocols*, CRYPTO 1994.(a personal generator for G).

[DF02]   Ivan Damgård and Eiichiro Fujisaki, *A Statistically-Hiding Integer Commitment Scheme Based on Groups with Hidden Order* ASIACRYPT 2002, pp. 125-142

[C01]   Giovanni Di Crescenzo, *Privacy for the Stock Market*, Financial Cryptography 2001, pp. 269-288

[DJ00]   Ivan Damgård and Mats Jurik, *A Generalisation, a Simplification and Some Applications of Paillier's Probabilistic Public-Key System*, Public Key Cryptography 2001, pp. 119-136.

[DDPY94]   Alfredo De Santis, Giovanni Di Crescenzo, Giuseppe Persiano, Moti Yung, *On Monotone Formula Closure of SZK*, FOCS 1994.

[FS87]   Amos Fiat and Adi Shamir, *How to Prove Yourself: Practical Solutions to Identification and Signature Problems*, CRYPTO 1986.

[FPS00]   Pierre-Alain Fouque, Guillaume Poupard and Jacques Stern, *Sharing Decryption in the Context of Voting or Lotteries*, In the Proceedings of Financial Cryptography 2000.

[FO97]   E. Fujisaki, T. Okamoto, Statistical Zero Knowledge Protocols to Prove Modular Polynomial Relations, Crypto 97, LNCS 1294, pp. 16-30, 1997.

[G97]   S. Goldwasser. *Multi-party computations: Past and present.* (invited talk), PODC'97, pages 1–6.

[GMW87]   O. Goldreich, S. Micali, and A. Wigderson, *How to play any mental game*, Proceedings of the Nineteenth annual ACM Symp. Theory of Computing, 1987.

[KTY04]   Aggelos Kiayias, Yiannis Tsiounis, Moti Yung, *Traceable Signatures*, EUROCRYPT 2004, pp. 571-589.

[Ni99]   N. Nisan, *Algorithms for Selfish Agents: mechanism design for distributed computation*, STACS 99.

[Od02]   A. Odlyzko, *Privacy, Economics, and Price Discrimination on the Internet*, First Workshop on Economics and Information Security, Berkeley, 2002.

[Pai99]   Pascal Paillier, *Public-Key Cryptosystems Based on Composite Degree Residuosity Classes*, EUROCRYPT 1999.

[Poi00]   David Pointcheval, *Self-Scrambling Anonymizers*, Financial Cryptography 2000, pp. 259-275.

[Rab83]   Michael Rabin, *Transactions protected by beacons*, Journal of Computer and System Sciences, Vol. 27, pp 256-267, 1983.

[Va96]   Hal R. Varian, *Differential Pricing and Efficiency*, First Monday, peer-reviewed journal on the Internet. 1996. http://www.firstmonday.dk/issues/issue2/different/

[Ya86]   A. Yao, *How to generate and exchange secrets*, IEEE FOCS, pages 162–167, 1986.

Author Index

Lecture Notes in Computer Science

For information about Vols. 1–4133

please contact your bookseller or Springer

Vol. 4185: R. Mizoguchi, Z. Shi, F. Giunchiglia (Eds.), The Semantic Web – ASWC 2006. XX, 778 pages. 2006.

Vol. 4184: M. Bravetti, M. Núñez, G. Zavattaro (Eds.), Web Services and Formal Methods. X, 289 pages. 2006.

Vol. 4183: J. Euzenat, J. Domingue (Eds.), Artificial Intelligence: Methodology, Systems, and Applications. XIII, 291 pages. 2006. (Sublibrary LNAI).

Vol. 4182: H.T. Ng, M.-K. Leong, M.-Y. Kan, D. Ji (Eds.), Information Retrieval Technology. XVI, 684 pages. 2006.

Vol. 4180: M. Kohlhase, OMDoc – An Open Markup Format for Mathematical Documents [version 1.2]. XIX, 428 pages. 2006. (Sublibrary LNAI).

Vol. 4179: J. Blanc-Talon, W. Philips, D. Popescu, P. Scheunders (Eds.), Advanced Concepts for Intelligent Vision Systems. XXIV, 1224 pages. 2006.

Vol. 4178: A. Corradini, H. Ehrig, U. Montanari, L. Ribeiro, G. Rozenberg (Eds.), Graph Transformations. XII, 473 pages. 2006.

Vol. 4176: S.K. Katsikas, J. Lopez, M. Backes, S. Gritzalis, B. Preneel (Eds.), Information Security. XIV, 548 pages. 2006.

Vol. 4175: P. Bücher, B.M.E. Moret (Eds.), Algorithms in Bioinformatics. XII, 402 pages. 2006. (Sublibrary LNBI).

Vol. 4174: K. Franke, K.-R. Müller, B. Nickolay, R. Schäfer (Eds.), Pattern Recognition. XX, 773 pages. 2006.

Vol. 4173: S. El Yacoubi, B. Chopard, S. Bandini (Eds.), Cellular Automata. XV, 734 pages. 2006.

Vol. 4172: J. Gonzalo, C. Thanos, M. F. Verdejo, R.C. Carrasco (Eds.), Research and Advanced Technology for Digital Libraries. XVII, 569 pages. 2006.

Vol. 4169: H.L. Bodlaender, M.A. Langston (Eds.), Parameterized and Exact Computation. XI, 279 pages. 2006.

Vol. 4168: Y. Azar, T. Erlebach (Eds.), Algorithms – ESA 2006. XVIII, 843 pages. 2006.

Vol. 4167: S. Dolev (Ed.), Distributed Computing. XV, 576 pages. 2006.

Vol. 4166: J. Górski (Ed.), Computer Safety, Reliability, and Security. XIV, 440 pages. 2006.

Vol. 4165: W. Jonker, M. Petković (Eds.), Secure, Data Management. X, 185 pages. 2006.

Vol. 4163: H. Bersini, J. Carneiro (Eds.), Artificial Immune Systems. XII, 460 pages. 2006.

Vol. 4162: R. Královič, P. Urzyczyn (Eds.), Mathematical Foundations of Computer Science 2006. XV, 814 pages. 2006.

Vol. 4161: R. Harper, M. Rauterberg, M. Combetto (Eds.), Entertainment Computing - ICEC 2006. XXVII, 417 pages. 2006.

Vol. 4160: M. Fisher, W.v.d. Hoek, B. Konev, A. Lisitsa (Eds.), Logics in Artificial Intelligence. XII, 516 pages. 2006. (Sublibrary LNAI).

Vol. 4159: J. Ma, H. Jin, L.T. Yang, J.J.-P. Tsai (Eds.), Ubiquitous Intelligence and Computing. XXII, 1190 pages. 2006.

Vol. 4158: L.T. Yang, H. Jin, J. Ma, T. Ungerer (Eds.), Autonomic and Trusted Computing. XIV, 613 pages. 2006.

Vol. 4156: S. Amer-Yahia, Z. Bellahsène, E. Hunt, R. Unland, J.X. Yu (Eds.), Database and XML Technologies. IX, 123 pages. 2006.

Vol. 4155: O. Stock, M. Schaerf (Eds.), Reasoning, Action and Interaction in AI Theories and Systems. XVIII, 343 pages. 2006. (Sublibrary LNAI).

Vol. 4154: Y.A. Dimitriadis, I. Zigurs, E. Gómez-Sánchez (Eds.), Groupware: Design, Implementation, and Use. XIV, 438 pages. 2006.

Vol. 4153: N. Zheng, X. Jiang, X. Lan (Eds.), Advances in Machine Vision, Image Processing, and Pattern Analysis. XIII, 506 pages. 2006.

Vol. 4152: Y. Manolopoulos, J. Pokorný, T. Sellis (Eds.), Advances in Databases and Information Systems. XV, 448 pages. 2006.

Vol. 4151: A. Iglesias, N. Takayama (Eds.), Mathematical Software - ICMS 2006. XVII, 452 pages. 2006.

Vol. 4150: M. Dorigo, L.M. Gambardella, M. Birattari, A. Martinoli, R. Poli, T. Stützle (Eds.), Ant Colony Optimization and Swarm Intelligence. XVI, 526 pages. 2006.

Vol. 4149: M. Klusch, M. Rovatsos, T.R. Payne (Eds.), Cooperative Information Agents X. XII, 477 pages. 2006. (Sublibrary LNAI).

Vol. 4148: J. Vounckx, N. Azemard, P. Maurine (Eds.), Integrated Circuit and System Design. XVI, 677 pages. 2006.

Vol. 4147: M. Broy, I.H. Krüger, M. Meisinger (Eds.), Automotive Software – Connected Services in Mobile Networks. XIV, 155 pages. 2006.

Vol. 4146: J.C. Rajapakse, L. Wong, R. Acharya (Eds.), Pattern Recognition in Bioinformatics. XIV, 186 pages. 2006. (Sublibrary LNBI).

Vol. 4144: T. Ball, R.B. Jones (Eds.), Computer Aided Verification. XV, 564 pages. 2006.

Vol. 4143: R. Lämmel, J. Saraiva, J. Visser (Eds.), Generative and Transformational Techniques in Software Engineering. X, 471 pages. 2006.

Vol. 4142: A. Campilho, M. Kamel (Eds.), Image Analysis and Recognition, Part II. XXVII, 923 pages. 2006.

Vol. 4141: A. Campilho, M. Kamel (Eds.), Image Analysis and Recognition, Part I. XXVIII, 939 pages. 2006.

Vol. 4139: T. Salakoski, F. Ginter, S. Pyysalo, T. Pahikkala, Advances in Natural Language Processing. XVI, 771 pages. 2006. (Sublibrary LNAI).

Vol. 4138: X. Cheng, W. Li, T. Znati (Eds.), Wireless Algorithms, Systems, and Applications. XVI, 709 pages. 2006.

Vol. 4137: C. Baier, H. Hermanns (Eds.), CONCUR 2006 – Concurrency Theory. XIII, 525 pages. 2006.

Vol. 4136: R.A. Schmidt (Ed.), Relations and Kleene Algebra in Computer Science. XI, 433 pages. 2006.

Vol. 4135: C.S. Calude, M.J. Dinneen, G. Păun, G. Rozenberg, S. Stepney (Eds.), Unconventional Computation. X, 267 pages. 2006.

Vol. 4134: K. Yi (Ed.), Static Analysis. XIII, 443 pages. 2006.